CONTENTS

THE THEORY OF HOSPITALITY & CATERING

13TH EDITION

David Foskett • Patricia Paskins • Andrew Pennington
CONSULTANT EDITOR: Neil Rippington

HODDER EDUCATION
AN HACHETTE UK COMPANY

Orders: please contact Bookpoint Ltd, 130 Park Drive, Milton Park, Abingdon, Oxon OX14 4SE. Telephone: (44) 01235 827720. Fax: (44) 01235 400454. Email education@bookpoint.co.uk Lines are open from 9 a.m. to 5 p.m., Monday to Saturday, with a 24-hour message answering service. You can also order through our website: www.hoddereducation.com

ISBN: 978 1 4718 6523 7

Editions before 2011 were published as *The Theory of Catering*

First published in 1964
Second edition published in 1970
Third edition published in 1974
Fourth edition published in 1978
Fifth edition published in 1984
Sixth edition published in 1989
Seventh edition published in 1992
Eighth edition published in 1995
Ninth edition published in 1999
Tenth edition published in 2003
Eleventh edition published in 2007
Twelfth edition published in 2011
This edition published in 2016 by

Hodder Education,
An Hachette UK Company
Carmelite House
50 Victoria Embankment
London EC4Y 0DZ

www.hoddereducation.com

Impression number 10 9 8 7 6 5 4 3 2 1

Year 2020 2019 2018 2017 2016

Illustrations by Aptara Inc and Barking Dog.

Typeset in AvenirLTStd, 9/11 pts. by Aptara Inc.

Printed in Italy

A catalogue record for this title is available from the British Library.

ACKNOWLEDGEMENTS

The authors thank Whitco Catering & Bakery Equipment Ltd for their assistance. Whitco design, deliver and install food service solutions and have successfully completed hundreds of projects, from coffee shops to hospitals, over the last 20 years. After installation, they provide operator training and equipment maintenance.

whitco
CATERING AND BAKERY EQUIPMENT

The authors and publishers are also grateful to the following people and organisations for their helpful advice and contributions to this edition:

- John Cousins and Dennis Lillicrap
- Joshua Ding, Training Manager, Renaissance Kuala Lumpur Hotel
- Sharani Shanmugam, Public Relations Manager, Grand Hyatt Kuala Lumpur
- Tricia Rosentreter, Regional Director PR, Peninsula Hotels
- Jonathan Crook, General Manager, The Peninsula New York
- Jennifer Lim, HR Director, Accor Hotels Singapore, India and Malaysia
- Steve Allan, Delicious Group Sdn Bhd
- Russums Catering Clothing and Equipment
- Anthony Pennington, June Pennington, Clare Bertolotti, Jane Addyman and Carole Meyer
- Joanna Kong.

We would also reiterate our thanks to the many colleagues who have contributed to this and the previous editions.

➜ Picture credits

Every effort has been made to trace and acknowledge ownership of copyright. The publishers will be glad to make suitable arrangements with any copyright holders whom it has not been possible to contact. The authors and publishers would like to thank the following for permission to reproduce copyright illustrative material:

Fig 3.3 Russums; fig 3.4 Allergen Saf-T-Zone™ System courtesy of San Jamar; fig 3.6 © Photo by Eric Erbe; digital colorization by Christopher Pooley/Material produced by ARS; fig 3.9 © Martin Lee/REX/Shutterstock; fig 3.12 © Crown copyright 2007 283373 1p 1k Sep07/http://www.nationalarchives.gov.uk/doc/open-government-licence/version/2/; fig 3.14 © Stephan Zabel/E+/Getty Images; fig 3.15 © somchaisom/iStock/Thinkstock; fig 3.16 © ElecImagery/Alamy Stock Photo; fig 4.7 Russums; fig 4.9 Compass; fig 5.6 © sickysick/iStock/Thinkstock; fig 5.8 Russums; fig 5.13 © Stefan Kiefer/imageBROKER/Alamy Stock Photo; figs 5.14, 5.16 and 5.26 Compass; fig 5.23 © ra3rn/iStock/Thinkstock; fig 5.24 © Birgit Reitz-hofmann/Hemera/Thinkstock; fig 5.25 © kev303/iStock/Thinkstock; fig 5.27 © mario beauregard/Fotolia; fig 5.28 © Andrew Callaghan/Hodder Education; fig 5.29 Lloyds; figures 7.2–7 and 7.9 © EBLEX; figs 7.11–14 and 7.16 © BPEX; figs 7.18–28 © EBLEX; fig 7.74 © Kondor83/Fotolia; figs 7.86 and 7.87 © Andrew Callaghan/Hodder Education; fig 7.99 © karam miri/Fotolia; fig 7.102 © George Dolgikh/Fotolia; fig 7.107 © Andrew Callaghan/Hodder Education; fig 8.9 © Crown copyright. Public Health England in association with the Welsh Government, the Scottish Government and the Food Standards Agency in Northern Ireland; fig 9.6 © kevin nicholson/Alamy Stock Photo; fig 10.4 © courtesy of WRAP; fig 11.1 © Antonio_Diaz/iStock/Thinkstock; fig 11.2 © KonovalikovAndrey/iStock/Thinkstock; fig 11.3 © Pyrosky/iStock/Thinkstock; fig 11.4 © Michael Blann/Photodisc/Thinkstock; fig 11.5 © Jupiterimages/Pixland/Thinkstock; fig 11.6 © é ç§ s/123RF; fig 11.7 © Courtesy of NHS Choices; fig 11.9 © Archimage/Alamy Stock Photo; fig 12.1 © Peninsula Hotels; fig 12.2 © KARIM SAHIB/AFP/Getty Images; fig 12.6 © Renaissance Hotels; fig 12.9 © omicron/Fotolia; fig 12.14 © Goodshoot RF/Thinkstock; fig 12.16 © targovcom/iStock/Thinkstock; fig 12.17 © Peninsula Hotels; fig 13.7 Delicious Group Sdn Bhd; figs 15.4–6 © Accor Hotels.

Except where stated above, photographs are by Sam Bailey.

FOREWORD

The Theory of Hospitality and Catering is a must-read. I remember in my university days reading textbooks by the authorities in their field – but that's all they are, memories. They, too, were must-reads at the time, but invariably grew dusty on the shelves after graduation.

The Theory of Hospitality and Catering, however, is a true necessity for any student of catering and hospitality anywhere in the world. It is a book you will keep with you throughout your career. Most importantly, it not only covers the theory of hospitality and catering, but also the practice. It is a comprehensive, authoritative book for everyone in the field. Whether back-of-house or front-of-house, this book is essential.

I know, having started a business from scratch, that ideas are useless on their own. It is ideas combined with action that make things happen. *The Theory of Hospitality and Catering* bridges the gap between idea and application, between theory and practice.

It was a privilege to work with Professor David Foskett MBE CMA when I was Chancellor of Thames Valley University (TVU, now the University of West London). David is truly one of the titans of the hospitality industry, and as Head of the London School of Hospitality and Tourism he helped create a beacon of excellence, renowned not just across the UK but worldwide.

And with *The Theory of Hospitality and Catering*, David and his colleagues have produced a book that is itself a beacon of the industry – a work that is clear, and clearly useful, to people at all levels. Whether a student or a practitioner, this book is indispensable.

Lord Bilimoria CBE DL

Founder and Chief Executive, Cobra Beer

LIST OF ABBREVIATIONS

ACAS	Advisory Conciliation and Arbitration Service
ASC	Assured Safe Catering
BEd	Bachelor of Education – (Hons) = Honours
BEPA	British Egg Producers Association
BHA	British Hospitality Association
BHT	butylated hydroxytoluene
BSc	Bachelor of Science
BSE	bovine spongiform encephalopathy
CAD	computer-aided design
CAP	Common Agricultural Policy
CCP	critical control points
CCTV	closed-circuit television
CEMA	Catering Equipment Manufacturers Association
CJD	Creutzfeldt-Jakob disease
CO2	carbon dioxide
COSHH	Control of Substances Hazardous to Health
CPA	Chevalier Dans L'ordre des Palmes Académique
DEFRA	Department for Environment, Food and Rural Affairs
DfES	Department for Education and Skills
DMS	Diploma in Management Studies
DNA	deoxyribonucleic acid
DSO	direct service organisation
ECA	European Catering Association
EFTA	European Free Trade Association
EHO	Environmental Health officer
EPOS	electronic point of sale
ETSU	energy technology support unit
EU	European Union
F&B	food and beverage
GDS	global distribution system
GMO	genetically modified organisms
GMS	glycerol monostearate
GNP	gross national product
HACCP	hazard analysis and critical control point
HCIMA	Hotel and Catering International Management Association
HMSO	Her Majesty's Stationery Office
HSE	Health & Safety Executive
HSEO	Health and Safety Enforcement Officer
HTF	Hospitality Training Foundation
ICT	information and communication technology
IT	information technology
JIT	just-in-time
KFC	Kentucky Fried Chicken
MAP	modified atmosphere packaging
MBA	Master of Business Administration
MBE	Member of the Order of the British Empire
NHS	National Health Service
P&O	Peninsular and Orient
PC (i)	personal computer
PC (ii)	practical cookery
PDA	personal digital assistant
pH	a measurement of acidity, alkalinity (potenz Hydrogen)
PMS	property management systems
PPE	personal protective equipment
QUID	Quantitative Ingredients Declaration
RAM	random access memory
RIDDOR	Reporting Injuries, Diseases & Dangerous Occurrences
SWOT	strengths, weaknesses, opportunities, threats
TVP	textured vegetable protein
UK	United Kingdom
VAT	value added tax
VDU	visual display unit
WTTC	World Travel and Tourism Council
YM	yield management

INTRODUCTION TO THE 13TH EDITION

As travel, tourism, recreation and hospitality become increasingly important in the economic life of the vast majority of countries, so the need for well-trained operatives and managers continues to grow.

This book is designed to meet the needs of those training for, or involved in, the hospitality and catering industry.

This 13th edition has been revised and updated to keep in line with the continuing changes both in industry and catering education. As in previous editions, we have not attempted to write a completely comprehensive book, but rather have set out an outline as a basis for further study. In this way, we hope to assist students at all levels and, for those who wish to study in greater depth, further references and websites are suggested where appropriate. This book will be relevant to those studying Professional Cookery, Food and Beverage Service and Hospitality courses at Levels 2 and 3. It also covers units/modules of Foundation degrees and BA (Hons) degrees in Hospitality Management, Event Management and Culinary Arts.

About the authors

Professor David Foskett MBE CMA FIH BEd HONS is former Dean and Head of the London School of Hospitality and Tourism at the University of West London, and now runs David Foskett Associates. He is a member of The Royal Academy of Culinary Arts, Craft Guild of Chefs, a Fellow of the Institute of Hospitality, and sits on various committees advising on hospitality education and training. He is an experienced hospitality and catering author.

Patricia Paskins MIH BEd HONS is an experienced teacher and education and training consultant, having worked with a range of high profile hospitality establishments, agencies and quality food suppliers. She previously held the role of Work-Based Learning Co-ordinator at the London School of Hospitality at the University of West London. She is an experienced hospitality author and has also written qualifications for well-known awarding organisations.

Andrew Pennington is Director of China Campus, Blue Mountains International Hotel Management School, Suzhou Tourism and Finance Institute.

Neil Rippington is Dean of the College of Food at University College Birmingham. He is an experienced hospitality and catering author.

1 What do we mean by the hospitality industry?

The defining activities of the hospitality economy are the provision of accommodation, meals and drinks in venues that are outside of the home. Hospitality consumption occurs 'on-site' in the venue. The creation of the context of consumption and management of consumption are activities that differentiate the hospitality industry from other businesses that provide accommodation, food and drink.

The British Hospitality Association (BHA) defines the UK hospitality economy as comprising the following four elements:

1 hotel and related services (including camping grounds and other accommodation)
2 restaurants and related services (including pubs, takeaway food shops, licensed clubs and motorway service areas, where hospitality services are the main activity for the latter)
3 catering (including corporate hospitality/contract catering to both private clients – for example, airlines – and public-sector clients, and in-house catering across non-hospitality direct sectors such as health and education)
4 event management (including conference and exhibition organisers).

Product and service

The hospitality product consists of the elements of food, drink and accommodation, together with the service, atmosphere and image that surround and contribute to the product. The hospitality industry contains many of the characteristics of service industries, with the added complications of the production process. It is the production process that is the complicated element as it focuses on production and delivery, often within a set period of time.

Appropriate environment

The need to provide the appropriate environment within which hospitality can be delivered means that most hospitality businesses need a substantial amount of investment in plant and premises. This creates a high fixed cost/low variable cost structure. The variable costs in servicing a room are minimal, although the hotel itself, particularly in the luxury hotel market, has a high fixed cost. In general, the financial break-even point for hospitality businesses is often fairly high. Exceeding this level will result in high profits, but low volumes will result in substantial losses.

The importance of forecasting

Hospitality services suffer from fluctuations in demand: demand fluctuates over time and by type of customer. For this reason, forecasting business is often difficult because of the mixture of patterns and variables that can affect demand, making planning, resourcing and scheduling difficult. Hospitality cannot be delivered without customers, who are involved in many aspects of the delivery of the hospitality service. Achieving a satisfactory balance between demand patterns, resource scheduling and operational capacity is a difficult task for managers in hospitality. Managing customer demand to achieve optimum volume at maximum value is extremely complex. Too few customers could spell financial ruin; too many customers without the required capacity or resources often means that the customers' experience suffers, leading to dissatisfaction. Scheduling of resources is also difficult; if too many staff are on duty to cover the forecast demand, then profitability suffers. Insufficient staffing creates problems – with servicing and staff morale. Forecasting is therefore a crucial function, which contributes to the successful operation of the hospitality business.

Consistency

The ability to deliver a consistent product to every customer is also an important consideration. Staff must be trained in teams to deliver a consistent standard of product and service. This means being able to cater not just for individual customers but to the needs of many different groups of customers, all with slightly different requirements. The success of any customer experience will be determined at the interaction point between the customer and the service provider.

Service staff

The service staff have an additional part to play in serving the customer: they are important in the future selling process, and therefore should be trained to use the opportunity to generate additional revenue.

The above description demonstrates the four characteristics of the hospitality industry that make it a unique operation.

The overlap between hospitality and tourism

The hospitality and tourism industry should be viewed as being made up of two separate sectors with a large degree of overlap (see Figure 1.1).

1 The hospitality industry covers the provision of food, drink and accommodation in venues outside of their home. These services are provided to both a country's residents and non-residents, and include everyday purposes as well as services to tourists.
2 The tourism industry can be defined as the activities of persons travelling to and staying in places outside their usual environment for more than one consecutive day, for leisure, business and purposes other than being employed in the place visited.

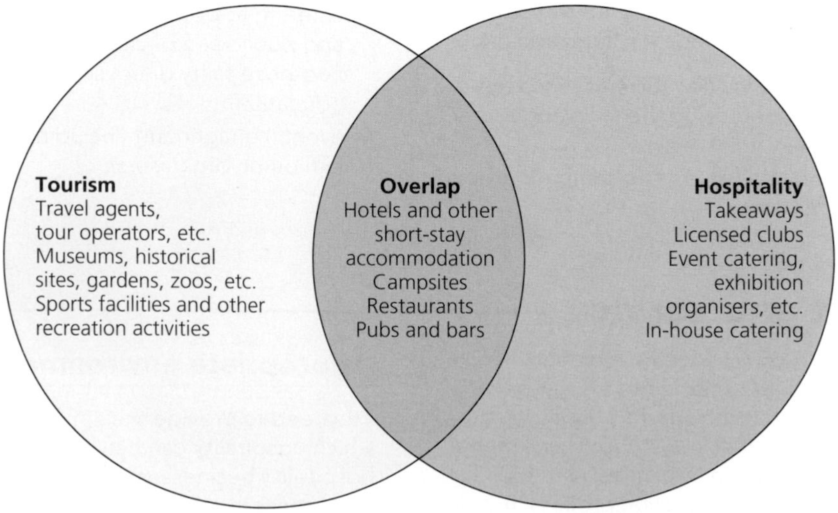

Figure 1.1 The overlap between the hospitality and tourism industries

➔ The UK hospitality industry

The largest sectors in the UK hospitality industry, in terms of number of outlets, are hotels and pubs, but the industry comprises a wide variety of outlets, from sports clubs and stadia to theme parks, historic properties and cinemas. Indeed, many researchers are unsure whether to include the leisure sector within the catering market, since it consists of so many outlets, each of which serves only small quantities of food.

Like hospitality and tourism, all leisure markets benefit from improving economic conditions. For many people, real disposable income has grown and forecasts predict that it will continue to do so. In wealthy markets, the leisure and pleasure sectors outperform the economy in general. It is usually the case that, as people become wealthier, their incremental income is not spent on upgrading the essentials but on pleasure and luxury items. However, whenever there is a downturn in the economy, the leisure sectors suffer disproportionately.

The leisure industry has been described as the biggest, fastest-growing industry in the UK. Within the leisure sector, some areas have slowed down, while others are consolidating and concentrating on core businesses. One of the most useful ways of categorising the leisure sector is to separate it into popular leisure activities – for example, theatre, ten-pin bowling and cue sports, casinos, bingo, and health and fitness.

Traditionally, catering activity has been divided into either profit- or cost-sector markets. The profit sector includes such establishments as restaurants, fast-food outlets, cafés, takeaways, pubs, and leisure and travel catering outlets; the cost sector refers to catering outlets for business and industry, education and health care. Recent developments have blurred the division between profit- and cost-orientated establishments.

The three main types of business

The industry can be divided into three main types of business: SMEs, public limited companies and private companies.

- **Small to medium-sized business enterprises (SMEs):** SMEs have up to 250 employees. In the UK as a whole, SMEs account for approximately 60 per cent of all employment. These are usually private companies that may become public limited companies if they get very large.
- **Public limited companies and private companies:** the key difference between public and private companies is that a public company can sell its shares to the public, while private companies cannot. A share is a certificate representing one unit of ownership in a company, so the more shares a person has, the more of the company they own.

Other types of business

The types of business in operation in the catering and hospitality industry can be further divided into sole traders, self-employed, partnership and limited liability companies. These are usually private companies.

- **Sole trader:** a sole trader is the simplest form of setting up and running a business. It is suited to the smallest of businesses. The sole trader owns the business, takes all the risks, is liable for any losses and keeps any profits. The only official records required are those for HM Revenue & Customs (HMRC), National Insurance and VAT. The accounts are not available to the public.
- **Self-employed:** there is no precise definition of self-employment, although guidance is offered by HMRC. In order to determine whether an individual is truly self-employed, the whole circumstances of his or her work need to be considered. This may include whether he or she:
  - is in control of their own time, the amount of work they take on and the decision making
  - has no guarantee of regular work
  - receives no pay for periods of holiday or sickness
  - is responsible for all the risks of the business
  - attends the premises of the person giving him or her the work
  - generally uses her or his own equipment and materials
  - has the right to send someone else to do the work.
- **Partnership:** a partnership consists of two or more people working together as the proprietors of a business. There are no legal requirements in setting up as a partnership. A partnership can be set up without the partners necessarily being fully aware that they have done so. The partnership is similar to a sole trader in law, in that the partners own the business, take all the risks, stand any losses and keep any profits. Each partner individually is responsible for all the debts of the partnership. So, if the business fails, each partner's personal assets are fully at risk. The advantages of operating a business as a partnership can be very similar to those of the sole trader. The main official records that are required are those for HMRC, National Insurance and VAT. The accounts are not available to the public.
- **Limited liability companies:** these are companies that are incorporated under the Companies Acts. This means that the liability of their owners (the amount they will have to pay to cover the business's debts if it fails or if it is sued) is limited to the value of the shares each shareholder (owner) owns. Limited liability companies are much more complex than sole traders and partnerships. This is because the owners can limit their liability. As a consequence people either investing in them or doing business with them need to know the financial standing of the company. Company documents are open to inspection by the public.

The UK hospitality economy

The industry covers more than 170,000 commercial businesses throughout the UK, with a further 90,000 outlets in such areas as health care and education catering. The core hospitality economy has been estimated to turn over in excess of £90 billion and to contribute £46 billion to the UK economy in terms of gross value added. (Gross value added (GVA) is the sum of the wages and profits in hospitality; it measures the net contribution of the sector of the economy since it is the difference between the goods and services offered by the sector minus the value of inputs used to produce them.) It contributes directly to approximately 2.5 million jobs (about 1 in 13, or 8 per cent, of all UK employment), making it the fifth biggest industry in employment terms, ahead of financial services, transport and communication, and construction, and comparable in scale to the education sector. This figure includes an estimate of employment in in-house catering across non-hospitality sectors and temporary agency employment in hospitality.

Additionally, it contributes to more than 1.2 million jobs through the multiple effects of the indirect supply chain and the employment included (direct and indirect employee spend related). Approximately 675,000 of these jobs are accounted for by supply chain purchases, with two-thirds of these in three sectors:

1. food manufacture, food and beverages
2. agriculture
3. business services.

The core hospitality economy is estimated to directly contribute approximately £34 billion in tax revenue to the UK Treasury, which includes VAT on sales, excise duty on on-site alcohol consumption, corporation tax, income tax and National Insurance contributions. Estimates of exports or attributable in-brand spending from core hospitality indicate that the industry accounts for approximately £7.4 billion of foreign exchange export earnings, which represents 1.8 per cent of total export earnings.

On average, 4.2 per cent of total investment in the economy is made by the hospitality economy, helping to sustain approximately 61,000 jobs, with 39,000 of these in construction and related activities.

The hospitality and tourism economy is forecast to grow 3.8 per cent per annum (faster than manufacturing, construction and retail), to around £257 billion by 2025 (10 per cent of UK GDP). It is forecast that it will provide 175,000 additional jobs – growing to 3.7 million jobs – by 2025. A key strength of the industry in the UK is that its wealth and job-creating potential is spread throughout the country, with towns, cities and rural areas all benefiting from the activities of hotels, restaurant, pubs, or other catering businesses and events. Not only is hospitality important to the economic success of local economies, it also plays a significant role in the social and cultural life of communities.

The UK hotel industry

The definition of a hotel varies according to the source consulted. Basically, any establishment that calls itself a hotel is classified as a hotel.

Table 1.1 highlights the fragmented nature of the hotel industry. The number of hotels and guest houses in the UK (which includes budget properties, private hotels and guest houses) is 46,000, the average size of a hotel in the UK is approximately 11.5 rooms, with the average-sized budget hotel having 77 rooms.

Table 1.1 The UK's ten largest hotel groups

Hotel group	Property types	Establishments
Whitbread	Budget hotel and branded restaurant	600 Premier Inns (40,000 rooms) Beefeater, Brewers Fayre and Taybarns restaurants 900 Costa Coffee outlets in the UK; 400 internationally in 25 countries (second to Starbucks)
InterContinental Hotels Group (IHG)		More than 4,300 hotels (620,000 rooms) in 100 companies, including: ● InterContinental ● Hotel Indigo ● Crowne Plaza ● Holiday Inn ● Holiday Inn Express ● Staybridge Suites
Travelodge (Dubai International Capital)	Budget hotel (the first budget hotel brand to launch in the UK)	3,801 hotels (more than 26,000 rooms) in the UK, Ireland and Spain

Hotel group	Property types	Establishments
Accor Hotels	Fifth largest hotel group by room number	4,000 hotels (500,000 rooms) in 90 countries 15 brands with 138 hotels (20,000 rooms), including: ● Sofitel ● Novotel ● Mercure ● Ibis ● Etap ● Formule 1
Hilton Hotels Corporation		3,300 hotels (550,000 rooms) in more than 77 countries Employs 135,000 people 10 brands
Best Western	Best Western International is the world's largest hotel chain of independent operators	Best Western UK: 2,801 independently owned hotels (15,000 rooms) Best Western International: 4,000 hotels (more than 300,000 rooms) in 80 countries
Wyndham Worldwide	Second-largest hospitality company in the world	7,000 hotels (588,000 rooms) in 66 countries Four major brands: ● Wyndham Grand ● Ramada ● Ramada Encore ● Jurys Inn
Marriott Hotels	The world's third-largest hotel company	3,200 hotels (577,000 rooms) in 67 countries Ten hotel brands Extended-stay apartments Vacation ownership resorts 60 UK hotels across five brands: ● JW Marriott ● Renaissance ● Marriott ● Grand Residences ● Courtyard
Carlson Hotels	The largest privately held company in the USA	Tour hospitality businesses Five brands More than 1,000 hotels in 72 countries (7,750 rooms) Three brands operating in the UK: ● Park Inn ● Park Plaza ● Radisson Hotels and Resorts (42 hotels)
The Rezidor Hotel Group	Based in Brussels	More than 380 hotels (approximately 81,000 rooms) in 59 countries under five brands 50 hotels in the UK, operating Radisson and Park Inn Hotels

Structure of the UK hotel industry

Whitbread, with its Premier Inn brand, is the largest hotel operator in the UK (in terms of number of hotel rooms), followed by InterContinental and Travelodge. Except for Premier Inn and InterContinental, all the leading hotel companies in the UK are non-UK owned. And, with the exception of Premier Inn, Travelodge and Accor, expansion now takes place mainly by franchising.

By 2030 it is expected that two-thirds of UK hotel rooms are likely to be branded as part of a corporate chain or consortia. However, approximately 300,000 hotel/bed and breakfast rooms in the UK will be unbranded.

The presence of international chains is high in the five-star accommodation market. In the UK there are more hotel bedrooms in the mid-market, three-star, category than in any other category; the independent hotelier traditionally dominates this market.

Franchising in the hotel industry

Franchising is not a new concept in the UK hotel industry, although it has undergone rapid growth in recent years.

Five of the world's top six largest hotel companies (Intercontinental Hotel Group (IHG), Wyndham, Hilton Hotels, Accor and Choice Hotels International) are active in the UK market through franchising. The exception is Marriott International. Wyndham and Choice Hotels are active only through franchising, whereas the others are also active through other business models, including management agreements, leases, and through development and ownership.

- Intercontinental Hotel group franchises almost 3,900 of its hotels worldwide; it manages 646 and owns just 10. Intercontinental franchises 94.2 per cent of its hotels in the Americas but approximately 85.5 per cent globally, including 83.6 per cent in the European region. Indigo, IHG's new lifestyle brand, and Staybridge Suites, an extended-stay brand, were launched almost exclusively as franchised properties.
- Wyndham has more than 3,000 rooms under the Ramada brand, 4,500 with Days Inn and 2,277 Ramada Encore rooms.
- Choice's UK portfolio comprises 39 hotels (3,000 rooms) mainly under the Quality and Comfort brands. Hilton's UK portfolio consists predominantly of managed hotels, with an increasing proportion of its estate operating under franchise agreements, half of its full-service DoubleTree by Hilton brand. The more standardised brands, Hampton by Hilton and Hilton Garden Inn, are growing their presence in the UK as well as across Europe, with many properties opening under franchise agreements; both brands have European pipelines of 40-plus hotels through a combination of management and franchising agreements.
- Accor, Europe's largest hotel company and a franchisor of choice in France, has also successfully deployed the franchise model in the UK.

The big companies are attracted by the limited capital investment required in franchising. This, as well as the ability to work through a broad-based franchise network, enables more rapid network growth and better local knowledge. Return on capital for the franchisor (the franchise provider) is typically strong, as capital expenditure is low and a steady stream of free income from an expanding network is an attractive proposition. The franchisor does not own the buildings or the asset, only the brand that they operate or franchise. The brand becomes a powerful asset; it generates the business, and allows the business to growth and develop through marketing and brand management.

One of the key factors in franchising is for the customer service experience to be consistent. A franchisee (franchise user) operating a franchise of a poor standard damages the whole brand. In hotels the model lends itself most easily to the mid and budget markets. Not that the upmarket hotel is unable to deliver excellent customer service, but it is more individualistic in style and that makes for a more difficult definition of standards and consistency of delivery.

We take a look at the use of the franchising model in the hospitality sector in general later in this chapter, on page 15.

Select-service hotels

Many travellers continue to show a recession-era preference for select-service hot tion – the so-called 'Y' population (anyone born between 1980 and 2000).

Select-service hotels are comparable to limited-service properties, but offer some amenities traditionally associated with full-service hotels, such as meeting space or casual dining outlets. They are increasingly favoured by hotel investors and developers due to the lower upfront cost of capital and increased operating margins. They are also more efficient to operate than full-service properties due to their limited food and beverage offerings, and the associated space required for these, as well as the absence of concierge and other services. By limiting service offerings, select-service properties are able to reduce their overhead costs, especially payroll. These higher operational efficiencies typically achieve significantly higher margins as a percentage of gross operating profits than those commanded by full-service hotels.

Budget hotels

The UK budget hotel sector continues to be dominated by two companies: Whitbread, with its Premier Inn brand, and Travelodge. Both are continuing to expand.

A budget hotel is a property without an extensive food and beverage operation, with limited en-suite and in-room facilities (limited availability of such items as hair dryers, toiletries, etc.), low staffing and service levels, and a price markedly below that of a full-service, three-star hotel.

In-house catering development

With increased consumer interest in food and eating out, hotels are becoming more focused on developing attractive food and beverage facilities in-house. Unlike in the past, when hotels typically operated food and beverage facilities merely to satisfy the demands of their guests, today's hoteliers are increasingly adopting a more proactive approach by using their food and beverage outlets as a means to generate not only profitability but also publicity, as well as to cultivate a loyal following. Traditionally, hotel restaurants have not been profitable enterprises for hotels, given that they were often considered to be only an essential value-added service for guests.

The success of in-house catering development will depend on the willingness of hotels to deliver a product that will be attractive to the outside market, and to maintain this product so that it evolves with changing consumer tastes and trends. According to human resource specialists within the hotel sector, key factors holding back further development are that food and beverage managers in hotels tend to be hoteliers rather than restaurateurs, as well as the shortage of experienced culinary and service staff.

Mintel has identified four hotel catering formats, as follows.

1 **General:** hotels featuring restaurants that cater primarily for residents of the hotel and, second, for walk-in guests who are not residents. These often take the form of casual, all-day dining facilities. The most enterprising of these are attempting to attract different consumers at different times of the day.
2 **Signature:** hotels that have developed a restaurant as a brand that stands alone from the hotel, and is therefore aimed primarily at walk-in customers. Most of these restaurants are located in luxury or upscale establishments, a number of which are managed by celebrity chefs such as Giorgio Locatelli, Gary Rhodes, Gordon Ramsay, Brian Turner, Heston Blumenthal, Marcus Wareing and Alain Ducasse. Signature restaurants tend to operate independently of the hotel they are attached to. Establishments that fall into this category include Nobu (Metropolitan Hotel, London), Chino Latino (Park Plaza, Leeds and Nottingham), Locanda Locatelli (Hyatt Churchill, London) and Dinner (Mandarin Oriental, Hyde Park, London – Heston Blumenthal).
3 **Outsourced:** hotels that outsource the management and operation of their catering provision to a third party. The outsourcing of a hotel's food and beverage operations can take several forms: a lease contract, management contract or an agreement with a contracted caterer. An example of an outsourced food and beverage hotel operation was when the Cumberland Hotel, London contracted Restaurant Associates, a division of the contract catering giant Compass plc, to operate all its bars and restaurants.
4 **Budget:** hotels that provide only a limited catering service, and sometimes no catering at all other than food from vending machines. The budget hotel sector in the UK is still expanding, and consequently the vast majority of new hotels have very limited food and beverage facilities or none at all – in part this is due to lenders providing limited capital to developers in the accommodation sector.

Many hotel chains that have come to rely upon the strength of their brand names have resorted to developing sub-brands designed to appeal to both guests and non-residents.

The contracting out of food and beverage services to third parties will continue to be a major trend in the hotel catering sector over the next few years, although this will be much stronger in London than in the provinces. As many hotels continue to remain sluggish owing to evolving consumer demand for food and beverages and intense competition from the high street, the idea of outsourcing food and beverage services will become increasingly appealing.

Vertical integration between many hotel and restaurant groups has meant that the outsourcing decision is often not such a radical step to take for many hoteliers, as costs and revenues remain within the group.

Outsourcing is not always a straightforward option for hotels, however. To attract walk-in customers, a hotel ideally needs to be located where there is easy access to the restaurant, and the location of the hotel itself (city centre, countryside, etc.) needs to fit with the clientele that are being targeted – that is, the product must be attractive to the passing trade. Despite these constraints, the number of outsourced restaurants is expected to increase considerably over the years to come.

The UK restaurant industry

For the majority of the population, pubs, restaurants and gastropubs remain the most popular places to eat out.

The UK restaurant industry is worth more than £40 billion, and this figure is expected to reach £52 billion by 2017, capitalising on customers' ever-growing interest in food. The average spend on a meal with wine is between £30 and £50 per head, with the consumers most active in the restaurant sector aged 18–24.

Table 1.2 Consumer expenditure on food, drink and catering in the UK

Total consumer expenditure on food, drink and catering (64 million people) Total £196.6 bn of which:	
Consumer expenditure on catering services Total £83.9 bn	**Household expenditure** on food and drink Total £112.7 bn
Consumers purchase from caterers (restaurants, cafés, canteens) Gross value added £26.9 bn Enterprises 115,951 Employees 1,623,000 Sites 448,958	**Households purchase from food and drink retailers** Gross value added £29.1 bn Enterprises 53,112 Employees 1,129,000 Sites 86,239
Caterers and retailers are supplied by food and drink wholesalers Gross value added £10.7 bn Enterprises 15,525 Employees 217,000	
Food and drink manufacturing Includes everything from primary processing (milling, malting, slaughtering) to complex prepared foods; many products will go through several stages Gross value added £26.5 bn Enterprises 8,228 Employees 402,000 Sites 9,625	
Exports from UK food and drink manufacturers Total £18.8 bn Of which: • highly processed £10.8 bn • lightly processed £6.5 bn • unprocessed £15 bn	**Imports to UK manufacturers, wholesalers and retailers** Total £39.5 bn Of which: • highly processed £14.6 bn • lightly processed £17.5 bn • unprocessed £7.4 bn

Based on Defra (2015), *Food Statistics Pocketbook 2015*

Table 1.3 Quick-service restaurants/takeaways in the UK

Owner	Selected brands
Gregg's	Gregg's
Subway	Subway
McDonald's	McDonald's
Yum	KFC
Domino's	Domino's
Burger King	Burger King
SSP	Upper Crust, Millie's Cookies
Unilever	Ben & Jerry's
Bridgepoint	Pret A Manger
Papa John's	Papa John's
Chicken Cottage	Chicken Cottage
Dixy Chicken	Dixy Chicken
EAT	EAT
Dunkin' Brands	Baskin Robbins
Pizza GoGo	Pizza A GoGo
Favourite Fried Chicken	Favourite
Jatinder Wasu	Perfect Pizza
West Cornwall Pasty Company	West Cornwall Pasty Company
Baguette Express	Baguette Express
Shakeaway	Shakeaway

Source: Horizons/Wordsmith and Company

While the industry remains relatively unpenetrated by chains, branded casual dining and food-to-go is well established in the high street (Table 1.3). New and traditional fast food is forecast to be the strongest-growing branded segment (Figure 1.2).

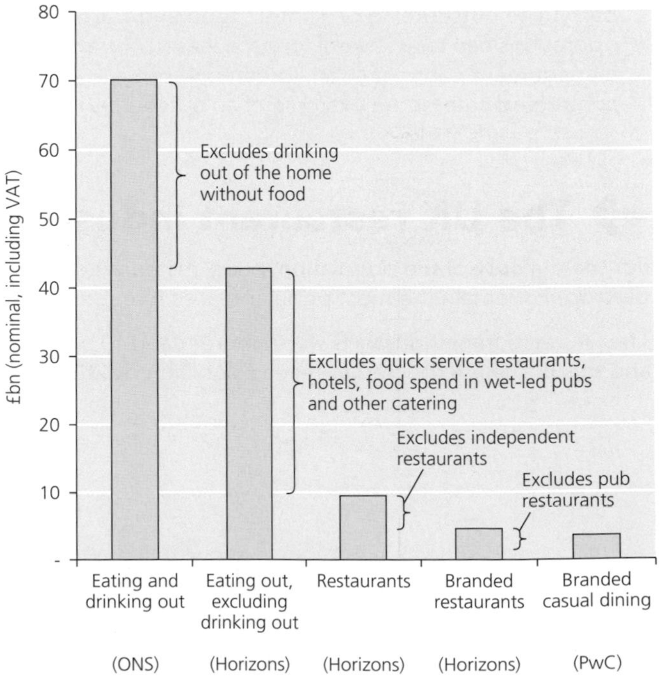

Figure 1.2 UK eating out market sizing and segmentation 2011 (£bn nominal, including VAT)

Table 1.4 Branded casual dining market

Demand			Supply	
Macro-economic trends	**Consumer/lifestyle**	**Sociodemographic**	**Number of outlets**	**Improved proposition**
Eating out is influenced by the overall economic environment	Eating out has become embedded in UK consumer behaviour. This has been a structural shift over the past 20 years or so	A greater number and proportion of more affluent and cash-rich, time-poor ABC1s who are more likely to eat out	The number of restaurants in the UK has been growing at around 1% per annum	The growth in casual dining chains has driven an improvement in:
The economic outlook remains challenging, which was forecast to limit growth in eating out in 2013–2014	Competition for leisure spending is strong, but eating out remains popular and this is likely to continue	Greater proportion of women in work and single-person households may drive future growth	Within this, casual branded chains have seen the highest growth of around 7% per annum; this is forecast to continue at the expense of independent restaurants	• variety of cuisine available • consistency and quality of offerings • the nature of informal propositions that cater to a wide range of eating out occasions

Source: Horizons ONS PwC analysis, December 2013

The long-term prospects for the eating out and casual dining markets are positive, with robust underlying demand and supply-side drivers (as shown in Table 1.4), despite difficulties experienced with fluctuations in the economy. There is a trend towards further growth in the eating out market.

However, there remains big competition from supermarkets with their speciality meals. Many restaurateurs have had to make their offer more attractive and represent better value for money. In times of difficulty, restaurateurs, pub operators and hoteliers have been forced to look at costs, and have 're-engineered' their menus using cheaper cuts of meat and smaller portions.

Leading operators use a number of levers to drive like-for-like sales, through increasing cover turn and spend per head (Table 1.5).

Comparing the UK and US eating out markets suggests that there is significant opportunity for the development of differential offerings at a number of different price points. For example, major eating out chains in the United States span a wide range of price architectures, whereas in the UK most casual dining chains are clustered around a median price point.

Table 1.5 Drivers of like-for-like revenue growth

Number of covers						Spend per head		
Capacity	**Capacity utilisation**		**Attractiveness of proposition**			**Mix**		**Pricing**
Use of space	Table turn	Marketing	Ambience/ fascia	Menu/food	Service standards	Menu architecture	Type of trade	LFL price growth
	Opening hours Day part analysis Menu offering	Special events Special menus for specific occasions Meal deals for specific occasions	Site refurbs Events to drive ambience Use of bars	Cuisine type Broadened menu to cover additional meals	Staff incentives, e.g. bonus scheme, training, mystery shopping linked to bonus scheme	Premium section Chef collaborations	Fixed-price menus Extended opening hours to include breakfast	

The EU hospitality industry

The EU restaurant industry currently employs approximately 9.5 million workers in 1.7 million enterprises in the market-orientated economy. This represents, respectively, 4.4 per cent of total employment in Europe and 8 per cent of all enterprises. It is one of the fastest-growing sectors in Europe in terms of employment.

Hotels and restaurants are major employers of young people: about half the workforce is below 35 years of age. Hospitality enterprises are predominantly of small and medium size: 99 per cent have fewer than 50 employees and as many as 92 per cent have fewer than 10 people on the payroll.

Other types of catering establishment in the hospitality industry

Catering activity can traditionally be divided into either profit (commercial) or cost (public) sector markets.

Commercial catering

The profit sector includes such establishments as restaurants, fast-food outlets, cafés, takeaways, pubs, and leisure and travel catering outlets.

Hotels and restaurants

These establishments are covered in detail earlier in this chapter.

Wine bars, fast-food outlets, takeaways: quick service

Customer demand has resulted in the rapid growth of a variety of establishments offering a limited choice of popular foods at a reasonable price, with little or no waiting time, either to be consumed on the premises or taken away.

Delicatessens and salad bars

These offer a service (usually lunch) based on a wide variety of bread and rolls (e.g. panini, focaccia, pitta, baguettes and tortilla wraps). Fresh salads, home-made soups and one hot 'chef's dish of the day' may be available.

A chilled food selection, from which customers can pick and mix, can provide the basis for a day-long service, including breakfast. A 'made to order' sandwich counter and a baked jacket potato bar with a good variety of fillings are very popular components of some of these establishments.

Private clubs

These are usually administered by a manager appointed by a management committee formed from club members. Good food and drink, often with an informal service in the 'old English' style, are required in most clubs, particularly in the St James's area of London. However, there is an increasing demand for more modern dishes and service, and members of these clubs also frequent the most prestigious hotels and restaurants.

Nightclubs and casinos usually offer the type of service associated with the restaurant trade. This provides another source of income to the business.

Chain catering organisations

These are the well-known hotel companies and restaurant chains, the popular type of restaurants, chain stores and shops with restaurants that often serve lunches, teas and morning coffee, and have snack bars and cafeterias. There are many establishments with chains spread over wide areas and in some cases overseas. Prospects for employment and promotion opportunities are often considerable.

Speciality restaurants

Moderately priced speciality eating houses are in great demand and have seen tremendous growth in recent years. In order to ensure a successful operation it is essential to assess customers' requirements accurately and plan a menu that will attract sufficient numbers of customers to generate adequate profit. A successful caterer is one that gives customers what they want and not what she or he thinks the customers want.

Pop-up restaurants

Occasionally, a restaurant may be in operation for just a short time; this is referred to as a pop-up restaurant. Such venues may operate to cover a specific time of year or theme, such as Christmas or a summer festival. They may also appear because a short-let arrangement is available on a suitable building, or because a chef or other professionals want to try out a market before committing fully to a business. These restaurants will vary in terms of style and method of service.

Street food vending

With today's busy lifestyles, transient working days and people on the move, street food, food trucks and fast-food vendors have become much more popular in recent years. They offer a variety of provision, from coffee and other drinks to sandwiches, pizza and a variety of food cooked to order. Many offer food of a particular style – for example, Thai food, which reflects the popular street food available in Thailand. Customers are served their food and drinks from the unit and pay on ordering. Some vendors may have temporary, limited seating available. These units are usually positioned on specific sites, and are licensed and managed by the local authority. Indeed, any premises or unit wishing to operate as a food business must register with the relevant local authority and comply fully with food safety legislation (for further information, see Chapter 3).

Country hotels

Country house hotels have been and are being developed in many tourist areas. Many are listed buildings, stately homes or manor houses. They normally have a reputation for good food, wine and service, reflecting the ambience of the business and surroundings.

Consortia

A consortium is a group of independent hotels that purchase products and services such as marketing from specialist companies providing members of the consortium with access to international reservation systems. This enables the group to compete against the larger chains.

Motels/travel lodges

These establishments are sited near motorways and arterial routes. They focus on the business person who requires an overnight stop or the tourist who is on a driving holiday. These properties are reasonably priced; they consist of a room only, with tea- and coffee-making facilities. Staffing is minimal and there is no restaurant. However, there will be other services close by, often managed by the same company or group.

Timeshare villas/apartments

A timeshare owner purchases the right to occupy a self-catering apartment, a room, or a suite in a hotel or leisure club for a specified number of weeks per year over a set period of years, or indefinitely. These may be exchanged with the owners of timeshares in other locations.

Other accommodation providers

Guest houses are to be found all over the UK. The owners usually live on the premises and let their bedrooms to passing customers. Many have regular clients. Guest houses usually offer bed, breakfast and evening meal, and are small, privately owned operations.

Farmers, wishing to diversify and recognising the importance of the tourism industry in the countryside, formed a national organisation called the Farm Holiday Bureau. Most members have invested to transform basic bedrooms to meet the required standards. The National Tourist Board inspects every member property to ensure good value and quality accommodation. In most cases the accommodation is on or close to working farms.

The Youth Hostels Association (YHA) runs hostels in various locations in England and Wales. These establishments cater mainly for single people and for those groups travelling on a tight budget. In some locations they also offer a number of sports facilities.

Coffee shops

Coffee shops (both chain and independent outlets) form one of the most rapidly growing parts of the hospitality and leisure industries (Table 1.6). The coffee shop sector is expected to reach £16.5 billion in turnover and 27,000 outlets by 2020 according to a report by the Allegra World Coffee Portal.

Coffee shops provide a variety of good coffee based on the espresso, as well as a range of other drinks and snacks. Both comfortable seating and a takeaway service are available.

Coffee shops may also be found within other establishments, such as airports, department stores and hospitals.

Table 1.6 Leading coffee shop groups in the UK

Owner	2012	Selected brands
Whitbread	1,390	Costa
Starbucks Corp.	743	Starbucks
Rome Bidco	450	Caffe Nero
Marks & Spencer	106	Café Revive
Arab Investments	110	Coffee Republic
SSP	109	Café Ritazza
Risk Capital Partners	70	Patisserie Valerie, Druckers Vienna Patisserie, Baker & Spice
AMT Coffee	59	AMT Coffee
Muffin Break	50	Muffin Break
Paul	39	Paul
Thornton's	37	Café Thornton's
Esquires Coffee	35	Esquires Coffee Houses
Hilton	32	Caffe Cino
BB's	29	BB's
WSH	28	Benugo
S.A. Brain	24	Coffee #1
Apostrophe	21	Apostrophe
Caffe Fratelli	14	Caffe Fratelli
Boston Tea Party	11	Boston Tea Party

Source: Horizons/Wordsmith and Company

Airports

Airports offer a range of hospitality services catering for millions of people every year. They operate 24 hours a day, every day of the year. Services include themed restaurants, speciality restaurants, coffee and seafood bars, as well as food courts. These are often supplemented with a general shopping arcade.

Spas

A spa often forms part of a luxury hotel or country house hotel. The client can access a range of health and beauty treatments to promote health and well-being. Spa treatments are also an increasingly popular leisure activity.

Pubs

Public houses (pubs) are premises licensed to sell alcohol. Around 19,000 of Britain's 48,000 pubs are run by so-called 'pubcos' (pub companies) such as Enterprise Inns and Punch Taverns. The industry is struggling: a UK Institute of Economic Affairs report calculates that, between December 2005 and March 2013, net closures represented 16.5 per cent of the pubco sector and 14.6 per cent of the independent sector. There has been a decline in alcohol consumption in the UK, with per capita consumption declining by 18 per cent since 2014. This has been driven primarily by a slump in beer sales. In 2003 the average adult drank 218 pints annually; by 2011 they were consuming just 152.

The effect of this collapse has been more significant for licensed trade premises, than for the 'off trade' (primarily supermarkets and off licences). Over the ten years to 2013, per capita sales in the latter were down 16 per cent, but by 54 per cent in the licensed trade. As people are not drinking as much in pubs, pubs that sell only drinks (known as wet pubs) are now almost extinct. Many pubs have increased their food offer, offering a meal experience, bar snacks, different types of menu and themed nights. They have introduced live music and large TV screens to show sporting events. Coffee machines have been introduced, with a barista being employed to make and serve different types of coffee. Other drinks have also been introduced, such as cocktails (including non-alcoholic cocktails). The whole pub experience continues to evolve, with some gaining Michelin stars for their food.

Gaming

Those premises that have a licence to serve alcohol without having to do so as part of a meal may provide gaming. No licence or permit is required for pubs or other eligible premises to provide gaming under the exempt gaming provisions (see below).

The UK Gaming Act allows pubs and other eligible premises to provide what it calls 'exempt gaming'. This must be 'equal choice' gaming (examples would be bingo, bridge and certain poker games). Stakes and prizes must comply with the limits prescribed in the regulations. No amount may be deducted or levied from amounts staked or won. No participation fees may be charged. The games played may take place only on one set of premises, i.e. there may not be any linking of games between premises. Children and young people must be excluded from participating.

Public-sector catering (cost sector)

This sector covers hospitals, universities, colleges, schools, prisons, the armed forces, police and ambulance services, local authority buildings, 'meals on wheels' (food delivery to the housebound or elderly in their own homes), and the like. It has been known for many years as 'welfare catering' and is characterised by its non-profit-making focus, minimising cost by achieving maximum efficiency. However, with the introduction of competitive tendering, many public-sector operations have been won by contract (and are operated by contract food service providers) and this has introduced new concepts and commercialism to the public sector. This sector is more commonly known as the cost sector.

Prisons

Prison catering may be run by contract caterers or by the Prison Service in the UK. The food is usually prepared by prison caterers and inmates. A new initiative introduced into UK prisons is the concept of 'training' restaurants and kitchens to train inmates with a few months left to serve so that they are able to gain the qualifications that will enable them to secure related employment in the hospitality industry on release. This has reduced the reoffending rate significantly (for more information, visit http://theclinkcharity.org). In addition, there are also usually staff food service facilities in prisons for all the personnel who work there, such as administrative staff, prison officers and management.

The armed forces

Services here include feeding armed service staff in barracks, in the mess, and in the field or on ships. Much of the work involved is specialist, especially field cookery. However, the forces – like every other section of the public sector – are looking to reduce costs and increase efficiency. Consequently, they too have initiated market testing and competitive tendering through the Ministry of Defence, resulting in contract caterers taking over many service operations at the aforementioned locations.

Catering for the armed services is specialised and has a dedicated training centre; details of catering facilities and career opportunities can be obtained from career information offices, although (as mentioned above) contract caterers (contract food service management operators) are increasingly being used throughout the armed services.

Hospital catering

Hospital food is an essential part of patient care; good food can encourage patients to eat well, giving them the nutrients they need to recover from surgery or illness. In the UK, approximately 145 million meals are served each year in 700 NHS and privately owned hospitals and care homes.

In many hospitals a qualified dietician is responsible for:

- collaborating with the catering manager on the planning of meals
- drawing up and supervising special diets
- instructing diet cooks on the preparation of special dishes
- advising the catering manager and assisting in the training of cooks with regard to nutritional aspects
- advising patients.

In some hospitals the food for special diets will be prepared in a diet bay by diet cooks.

Information about the type of meal or diet to be given to each patient is supplied daily to the kitchen. This information will give the number of full, light, fluid and special diets, and each special diet will be accompanied by the name of the patient and the type of diet required.

WEBLINKS

The Hospital Caterers Association aims to promote better hospital food and improve the standards of catering in hospitals and health care in Great Britain and Northern Ireland. Its Better Hospital Food programme was introduced to ensure the consistent delivery of high-quality food and food services to patients. For more information, see:

www.hospitalcaterers.org

For further information on NHS and hospital catering, visit the following websites.

NHS Estates Information Centre:

www.nhsestates.gov.uk

British Dietetic Association:

www.bda.uk.com

Catering for the education sector (school and college food)

More than 350 million meals are served to students, lecturers and teachers in nearly 4,500 establishments across the UK, including state schools, private independent schools and public schools.

WEBLINK

In England, the School Food Plan was published in July 2013. It provides a set of mandatory standards that all maintained schools, academies and free schools in England must follow. These are designed to make it easier for school cooks to create tasty, nutritious menus at school. To see the full standards visit:

www.schoolfoodplan.com/standards

Residential establishments

These include schools, colleges, universities, halls of residence, nursing homes, homes for the elderly and hostels, where all meals are provided. It is essential in these establishments that the nutritional balance of food is considered, and it should wholly satisfy residents' nutritional needs, as it is likely that the people eating in such places will have no other food provision.

Catering for business and industry

The provision of staff dining rooms in industrial or business settings has granted many catering workers employment in first-class conditions. Apart from the main meal services, beverage services, retail shops, franchise outlets and/or vending machines may form part of the service. In some cases a 24-hour, seven-days-a-week service is necessary, but generally the hours are more streamlined than in other sectors of the hospitality industry. Food and drink are provided for all employees, sometimes separately but increasingly together in high-quality restaurants and dining rooms. Many industries have realised that output is related to the welfare of employees. Satisfied workers produce more and better work and, for this reason, a great deal of money is spent on providing first-class kitchens and dining rooms, and improving the dining experience. This can also mean that the workers receive their food at a price lower than its actual cost, the remainder of the cost being borne by the company. This is called a subsidy and contributes to the overall employment benefits of an employee.

However, many companies are increasingly competing within a global economy. Competition is fierce, and this has led them to cut costs, meaning that many organisations are moving towards a nil subsidy for meals consumed at the place of work.

A company is not committed to providing any catering facility if:

- there are suitable facilities available within easy access of the employee's place of work
- these facilities offer a reasonable choice of food
- the times of opening are suitable to employer and employees.

Often, employers will provide a facility even if the above criteria exist, in order to provide better welfare and amenities for their people, hoping to retain them as employees for longer.

WEBLINK

Information on catering for business and industry can be obtained from the Association of Catering Excellence's website:

www.acegb.org

Holiday centres

Holiday centres around the UK provide leisure and hospitality facilities for families, single people and groups. Many companies have invested large sums of money in an effort to increase the quality of the holiday experience. Center Parcs, for example, has developed sub-tropical pools and also offers other sporting facilities. Included in its complexes are a range of different restaurant experiences and food courts, bars and coffee shops. These centres are examples of year-round holiday centres, encouraging people to take breaks from home, at weekends or midweek, throughout the year.

Motoring services

Many motoring services areas provide food court-type facilities for travellers, offering a comprehensive range of meals on a 24-hour, seven-day-a-week basis. These are becoming increasingly sophisticated, with baby-changing, infant and pet-feeding facilities, bathrooms and showers, extensive ranges of branded food outlets and often accommodation, fuel, convenience shops, and car washing and maintenance facilities. MOTO and Welcome Break are examples; they operate across the UK and make most of the provisions above available in all of their outlets.

Drive-thru restaurants

Drive-thru restaurants are a relatively new concept in the UK. They are an American import – the most notable of these being the McDonald's Drive-thrus located in many parts of the UK. Customers stay in their vehicles and drive up to a microphone in order to place a request. This is then relayed to a fast-food service point and, as the car moves forward in the queue, the order is prepared and then presented to the driver at the service window. This type of facility often forms part of the provision made in centres such as the motoring services described above.

Transport catering

Rail

Meals on trains may be served in restaurant cars and snacks from buffet cars. The space in a train's restaurant car kitchen is very limited and there is considerable movement, which causes difficulties for staff.

Two train services run through the Channel Tunnel:

1. Euro Tunnel's Le Shuttle train, which transports drivers and their vehicles between Folkestone and Calais; here food and drink is limited to that bought before the train departs
2. foot passengers may travel on Eurostar trains; Eurostar sees the airlines as its direct competition, therefore it provides airline catering standards on board the train for first- and premier-class passengers; this is included in the ticket price; provision for economy travellers is usually via buffet carriages or trolley services along the aisles of the train, and is another area into which contract food service providers have expanded.

Airline services

Airline catering is a specialist operation. Some airlines, such as Aer Lingus, have only one class on all UK and European services. Food and drink has to be purchased on these flights as the carrier is trying to minimise its low-cost formula. Other airlines offer food and drink as part of their ticket price. Tier systems are used by airlines, based on their frequent flyer programmes, to describe the prestige of a passenger. A first-, platinum- or premium-tier traveller will normally have travelled hundreds of thousands of miles with the carrier, and will have access to its lounges and many other extras, including a premium food and beverage offer.

Marine

The large liner's catering is of a similar standard to that of the big first-class hotels, and many shipping companies are noted for the excellence of their cuisine. The kitchens on board ship are usually oil fired, and extra precautions have to be taken in the kitchen in rough weather. Catering at sea includes the smaller ship, which has both cargo and passengers, and cargo vessels, which include giant tankers of up to 100,000 tonnes. Ferries serve routes such as the English Channel and the Irish Sea. The English Channel ferries are in direct competition with the Channel Tunnel's Eurostar and Le Shuttle services; in response to this, ferry operators have invested in leisure facilities and modern branded food outlets, sometimes in a food court arrangement, or in other cases in a buffet or carvery style.

Cruises

Cruise companies are rapidly increasing their number of cruise liners and the size of their ships. Cruise ships are floating luxury hotels, and more and more people are becoming interested in cruising as a leisure pursuit. This means that job opportunities and promotion prospects are excellent, and training is also provided. The benefits of travel all over the world, producing food and serving customers at the very highest standards make it a most interesting and worthwhile career. As an example of working conditions, staff may work for three months and then have, say, two months off. On-board hours of work could be ten hours a day, seven days a week.

On cruises where the quality of the food is of paramount importance other factors such as the dining room's ambience of refinement and elegance are also of great significance. The success of the dining operation is tied to the design of the ship. Ship architects design cruise liners to provide quick and easy access to the kitchen areas, where food is prepared, and to the galley, so waiters are able to get food quickly and with as little traffic as possible. The food on most cruises can be described as excellent, high-quality banquet-style cuisine. A distinction can be made between traditional and modern eating on cruises, as shown in Table 1.7.

Table 1.7 The differences between traditional and modern eating on cruises

Traditional	Modern
Formal dining room	Choice of restaurants
Set times	Dine any time
Assigned tables	Choice of seating
Elaborate table settings	Self-serve, buffet or waiter service
Printed menu	Frequently changing menus
Social interaction	Wide variety of culinary styles

This does not apply as much to the new giant ships that have many different dining rooms. On such ships passengers can eat in the dining room of their choice, more or less whenever they want, at tables of various sizes.

Dining is one of the most important – and selling – points for cruise lines. People who take cruises want to dine well and generally they do, though cooking dinner for 800 people per sitting and giving people what they want takes considerable skill and management.

Outside and event catering

When functions are held where there is no catering or where the function is not within the scope of the normal catering routine, then certain firms will take over completely. Considerable variety is offered to people employed on these undertakings and often the standard will be of the very highest order. A certain amount of adaptability, ingenuity and specialist equipment is required, especially for some outdoor jobs, but there is less chance of repetitive work. Greater flexibility is necessary on behalf of the personnel, often involving considerable travel, remote locations and outdoor venues. The types of function will include garden parties, agricultural and horticultural shows, the opening of new buildings, banquets, parties in private houses, military pageants and tattoos.

Franchising

Franchising is an agreement whereby one pays a fee and some set-up costs in exchange for the use of an established name or brand that is well known by potential customers. An example of this would be where the contract caterer Compass Group franchises the Burger King brand from its owner in exchange for a fee and a proportion of the turnover. There are normally strict guidelines, or 'brand standards', laid down for the franchisee (franchise user) to perform to, and these will govern the ingredients and raw materials used, and where they come from, together with portion sizes and the general product and service 'offer'. The franchisor (the franchise provider) will 'mystery shop' or check on the brand standards and operational standards regularly to ensure that the brand's reputation is not being jeopardised. The franchisor will normally also provide advertising and marketing support, accounting processes, help with staff training and development, and design provision for merchandising and display materials.

Franchising has several advantages.

- First, it allows for many outlets to be set up nationally and, in so doing, maximises on economies of scale in purchasing promotional material in the development of the brand image.
- The franchisee gains because the opportunity is shared to invest in a pre-tested catering concept, backed by advertising, research and development, training and other resources that might otherwise be beyond their financial parameters.
- The banks also show an interest in franchising – in many ways they see it as a reasonably safe investment because of its established, tried-and-tested nature.

Many of the most active franchise schemes are based on a fast-food style of menu and operating system. Today there is a growing market involving wider menus and medium-spend restaurants, mainly licensed. Examples include Pizza Hut, Delice de France, Subway, Burger King, Krispy Kreme, TGI Friday's and many others.

Corporate hospitality

The purpose of corporate hospitality is to build business relationships and to raise corporate awareness. Corporate entertaining is also used as a means of thanking or rewarding loyal customers.

Companies are increasingly recognising the growing importance of relationship marketing and corporate reputation. Reasons for spending money on corporate hospitality include:

- building relationships with potential customers
- to reward customers/thank them for their loyalty
- as a marketing tool/raise company or product profile
- increase business/sales
- to achieve closer informal contact in a relaxed environment
- to stay ahead of competitors
- to raise and keep up the company's profile/public relations
- repeat business/retention of clients or customers
- keep the customers happy/entertain them, act as a sweetener
- to talk about business/networking
- to achieve better communication interaction/improved understanding
- to meet customer expectations
- to reward/boost staff or team morale
- social benefits/opportunity to relax.

Eventia is the professional association for the corporate and events industry. The events industry is worth £40 billion to the UK economy and accounts for 35% of the visitor economy (source: R&B Group).

The main reasons for the growth of this sector are company expansion and increased budgets for corporate hospitality. Those companies with increased budgets are committing to bigger or more superior events and increased spending per head, or holding events more frequently.

Food and service management (contract catering)

The food and services management (FSM) sector covers feeding people at work in business and industry; catering in schools, colleges and universities; hospitals and health care; welfare and local authority catering and other non-profit-making outlets. It is an important component of the UK hospitality industry, generating in excess of £4.25 billion in turnover and employing approximately 140,000 people.

Food and services remain the main focus in this sector, but it is evolving to become a multiple-services sector where catering is one of several services provided. Today contract catering also covers leisure centres, department stores, public events and places of entertainment. Other services might include reception, cleaning, portering, maintenance, security and engineering.

Outsourcing is now a key focus of many businesses as they look to cut costs, giving operators additional business from contractors that were previously in-house. There has also been an expansion of facilities management contracts, which have prospered on the back of the growing need to outsource.

Contract caterers are used by nearly every type of organisation, including the armed forces, business and industry in general, supermarkets, department stores and DIY chains, leisure centres, museums and galleries, and at sporting fixtures and events. With more than 60 companies registered in the UK, contract catering is one of the biggest and most diverse sectors in the industry. Compass and Sodexho are two of the largest food organisations in the UK, with 8,400 locations. These include Little Chef, Travelodge and motorway service stations. Other contract caterers include Harbour & Jones, Elior, Lexington and Initial Catering.

Types of contract

No two services or clients' requirements are the same. For this reason, contracts differ from company to company. Some examples of the types of contract available are as follows.

- **Executive lease:** the contractor provides a senior executive who will direct the client's catering operation. Normally the whole operation remains the responsibility of the client and the staff are employed by the client. The aim is for the contractor and the executive to bring a level of expertise, which the client is unable to provide. The senior executive will be involved in implementing the systems managers and in the policy making. The contractor will provide a manager for the unit; all staff are employed by the client on its terms and conditions.
- **Management:** the client employs the contractor to supply a total catering service using the contractor's own on-site management and staff. The client also provides all the facilities and equipment. The contractor submits a monthly account to the client, which identifies all the expenditure and income associated with the operation. The difference between the expenditure and income, including the contractor's fee, will be payable to or from the contractor.
- **Fixed price:** the contractor works to an annual budget fixed with the client. If the contractor overspends, he or she pays. However, if he or she underspends then he or she retains the difference.
- **Concession:** the contractor undertakes to manage an operation and rely for profit on his or her ability to maintain income levels over expenditure levels.

Contractor's charges

Contractors generally offset their administration costs, and gain their profits from the following three sources:

1. fees charged
2. cash spent by customers
3. discounts from food and materials supplied to the client's operation.

The fees can be made up in a number of ways:

- a set annual figure charged on a weekly or monthly basis
- a percentage of takings or costs
- a combination of the above, with different percentages applying to various sections of costs
- a per capita or per meal charge.

Key issues affecting contract food service management

- **Sustainability:** the sourcing of fish and food in general is very much at the top of the sustainability agenda for all contract food service management caterers. Locally sourced food has also become a marketing and selling point.
- **Compliance:** working towards compliance with ISO 14001, the internationally recognised standard for the environmental management of businesses, is another major focus. Companies are looking at reducing waste, addressing carbon emissions and reducing energy consumption.
- **Healthier menus:** contractors in the food and management sector have also had to respond to the demand for healthier menus. There is pressure from the Food Standards Agency to include calorie counts on menus so that consumers know how many calories they are eating. Some contract caterers have started to implement nutritional content information. However, this is not easy to achieve as food is cooked on-site for individual contracts; chefs are employed to use their skills and to be creative, so asking them to provide nutritional information is difficult. Providing this information may eventually become a legal requirement.
- **Maximising efficiencies and keeping costs to a minimum:** this has seen a growth in opportunities for 'bundled services', which is the packaging of multiple services under one contract – for example, staff, food service management hospitality services, vending, reception services, conference services, marketing services, clearing and portering all under one contract.

Case study

Vacherin

Vacherin has expanded its services beyond food and services management (FSM).

Table 1.8 Vacherin's services

Client and locations	CBRE, two sites in central London
Year contract awarded	2007; re-awarded twice since
Initial services provided in 2007	Staff FSM, private dining and hospitality, vending and refreshment points
Additional services added since 2007	Long-distance FSM for an annual event in the South of France Conference room bookings Portering Reception services for both buildings, plus a new stand-alone reception service for a group subsidiary
Key service milestones	The relocation of CBRE's West End office in 2011 and the changes this involved; this move was also a catalyst for Vacherin taking on many of these additional services and the setting up of its new reception services division, Entrée

Source: FSM driving dynamic and responsible growth, *British Hospitality Industry Report*, 2014

Case study

Allergens

Table 1.9 BaxterStorey and Elior: meeting the allergens challenge

BaxterStorey	Elior
Challenge To ensure all 670 of its premises are compliant with the Food Information Regulations and proactively manage the benefits of this extra customer communication **Actions** BaxterStorey developed a tailor-made training programme to ensure that its 7,500 employees are up to speed on the new legislation. An initial group of 1,500 Allergy Champions were trained, more or less two staff from every site, and their role was to cascade this training to their colleagues via short weekly briefing sessions, no later than three months before the legislation was due to take effect. They are also responsible for communicating allergy information to customers. The specialised training teaches staff what allergens are, how allergens make people ill, how they can treat an allergic reaction and how to avoid causing one in the first place	**Challenge** To ensure that its 10,000 employees spread over 650 outlets are fully aware of their obligations under the new allergens legislation and have the systems ready to manage it **Actions** Elior has introduced a menu and recipe management system to all sites and all managers were trained months before the legislation was due to come into effect. They developed an allergen e-learning module for training 10,000 staff and recording this training. To support its system, Elior has collected allergen information from every supplier, covering thousands of product lines, which has been uploaded onto its new menu and recipe management system. All sites have been provided with the communication materials with which to alert customers to products containing allergens; this has been supported with a new website for its You & Life programme, which provides allergen information and guidance

Source: FSM driving dynamic and responsible growth, *British Hospitality Industry Report*, 2014

The globalisation of the hospitality and tourism industries

Travel, tourism and hospitality together make up the world's largest industry. According to the World Travel and Tourism Council (WTTC), the annual gross output of the industry is greater than the gross national product (GNP) of all countries except the United States and Japan. Worldwide, the industry employs more than 112 million people. In many countries, especially in emerging tourism destinations, the hospitality and tourism industry plays a very important role in the national economy, being the major foreign currency earner. For many destinations, tourism is at the core of the region's economy, essential for job creation and economic growth. Across the world, tourism enterprises including economic development corporations, destination marketing organisations, convention centres and visitors' bureaus, tourism authorities and direct marketing organisations, are deploying tourism strategies to increase global awareness of their destinations.

Businesses today find themselves competing in a world economy for survival, growth and profitability. An international hospitality company must perform successfully in the *world's* business environment.

As the economies of countries across the world continue to become more interdependent, this will give rise to increasing amounts of business travel. With this in mind, it is clear that the global economic environment plays a significant role in the internationalisation opportunities available to hospitality and tourism companies, and that global economic policies and developments play a critical role in the hospitality and tourism industry.

The globalisation of the hospitality and tourism industries has advanced under the pressures of increased technology, communication, transportation, deregulation, elimination of political barriers, sociocultural changes and global economic development, together with growing competition in a global economy. There are a vast number of influences in the external international environment that greatly affect the multinational organisation. Some of these are as follows.

- Monetary and fiscal policies and exchange controls: some countries may limit the amount of money that can be withdrawn from them, as well as impose large payments for international transactions (e.g. joint ventures, entry to the country).
- Financial and investment markets, individual consumer and corporate interest rates, the availability of credit, exchanges, and so on.
- Taxation and tariffs: taxes on individuals, corporations and imported goods, imposed by the host country/ government.

- Trade/industrial factors: import/export measures of activity in commerce, and so on. These can serve as indices in determining the state of the economy (e.g. prosperity, depression, recession, recovery).
- Labour markets: the level of unemployment, welfare spending, and so on.

Investment in infrastructure

An additional element of effective tourism implementation lies in public infrastructure investments. Infrastructure should be recognised as an important aspect of tourism development, including investments in airports to improve air access, which can spur tourism and economic growth. Destinations around the world – for example, London, Miami and Atlanta – have committed investment to airport and rail projects to improve traveller connections and tourist zones.

Maintaining and improving the UK's international and domestic transport infrastructure will be critical to sustaining the strength of its tourism economy.

Conferences and business travel in the UK tourism industry

Business travel is an important sector of the UK tourism industry. This sector is defined by the British Association of Conference Destinations (BACD), and includes tourists who attend conferences, trade fairs and exhibitions, as well as incentive travel, corporate hospitality and business travel.

The UK is an important market for the global conference industry. As the international market continues to grow, the UK has to become increasingly competitive in order to win lucrative conference business. London attracts international conventions, international exhibitions and conferences; its major exhibition centres are ExCel and Olympia. London also attracts more meetings than most other capital centres. The reasons why it is able to attract such international business include:

- it is easily accessible by mainland Europe and the rest of the world via the five international airports and the Channel Tunnel
- it has a large number of modern landmarks – the O2, the London Eye, the Millennium Bridge, Shakespeare's Globe, and the Tate Britain and Tate Modern art galleries, as well as the traditional landmarks like the Tower of London, Buckingham Palace, Palace of Westminster, and so on
- its superior facilities – e.g. purpose-built convention and exhibition centres, museums, theatres, livery halls, stately homes, hotels with meeting facilities.

However, there is competition from mainland Europe. Some conventions require larger conference facilities than London can offer. Larger exhibition space can be found in other European cities such as Milan, Frankfurt, Paris, Hanover and Düsseldorf.

Opportunities from emerging markets

The overall contribution of emerging markets such as Brazil, Russia, India and China in terms of value will be relatively small up to 2020 compared with the traditional, established European and North American markets. However, it is recognised that there is significant opportunity for long-term growth in emerging markets over the next 30 years.

Africa

Investment in Africa continues to capture the attention of hotel investors. Approximately 30 hotel groups operate in Africa, representing around 60 brands. The established tourism destinations on Africa's northern coast, most notably Morocco and Egypt, are well established destinations for Europeans.

Increased investor attention in this region has resulted in some improvements in policy making and access to financing. However, longstanding risks and barriers to entry continue to pervade in the market. Most notably, poor transportation infrastructure has historically restricted the connectivity of the sub-Saharan region. Air travel remains limited despite investments from nations in airports and on local airlines, as seen in Kenya and South Africa.

However, despite certain challenges, sub-Saharan Africa offers significant opportunities for hotel development. Approximately 47 per cent of existing hotel rooms are in sub-Saharan Africa. From an economic standpoint the region is well positioned for growth, due to an abundance of natural resources such as oil. Sub-Saharan Africa's growing economy and internal focus on tourism, complete with the under-supply of hotel rooms, have gained the attention of investors around the world. Some countries are better positioned than others, as noted below.

- Ghana's economy has been boosted by an increase in oil production and foreign investment. Travel to Ghana has been increased due to extensive public investment in the country's infrastructure, like the Kotoka International Airport.
- In Nigeria, an equally strong economy also driven by oil production has helped hotel investment. Lagos, Nigeria's capital city, currently boasts one of the highest hotel rates in Africa.
- Tanzania relies on leisure tourists, offering guests pristine beach resorts and extensive nature reserves for safaris, and has targeted travellers from emerging markets such as China, India and Russia.

Asian investment

Asian investors have been a leading force in the hospitality industry. They have invested most heavily in international gateway cities (for example, London, Manhattan and Sydney) with a heavy population of Asian nationals and in large mixed-use projects, leveraging their development experience and significant customer base in their home countries. Cities such as Seattle and Houston have gained an increasing interest, with Chinese investors given strong job growth in the technology and energy sectors, completed with the rise in the local Chinese population.

It is anticipated the Asian investors will continue to be active buyers in hotels and commercial real estate developments as limited investment opportunities in their home countries, abundant liquidity and local currency appreciation are expected. The outlook for the international hotel industry is strong, as is interest in trophy assets in gateway cities.

China's outbound tourism industry has grown in recent years, as income levels in China's middle class have increased and a proliferation of information on outbound travel has heightened the desire to travel abroad. Several countries around the world have eased restrictions on visas to attract the Chinese market.

Food tourism

The experience of food and taste is an important element in tourism. In defining food tourism there is a need to differentiate between those tourists who consume food as a part of the travel experience and those whose activities, behaviours and even choice of destination are influenced by their interest in the food. Similar to these people are those who are interested in wine and visit the noted wine-producing areas of the world. For such people, vineyards, wineries, wine festivals, wine shows, wine tasting and/or experiencing the attributes of a wine region are the prime motivating factors. Similarly, food tourism refers to visits to food producers, food festivals, restaurants and specific locations renowned for a particular food, as well as food tasting and/or experiencing the attributes of specialist food production regions, or even visiting a restaurant to taste the dishes of a well-known chef; for food tourists, such factors provide the motivation for them to travel to a certain area. (Some people, for example, travel to Perigord in France to taste the foie gras and truffles, and sample the local Bergerac wine for which the area is renowned.)

→ The digital world

One of the principal challenges confronting the industry of the future will result from the ongoing transition to the 'information age'. The convergence of computing, telecommunications and content will shape the way and pace at which people live and work. Advances in digital capabilities will drive more activity at a global scale as geographical boundaries are broken. Above all, this will change the nature of the exchange process between providers and their customers – the latter will have more choice. To be successful, tourism organisations must invest in technology as well as have the right products and prices.

As in all areas of business, the internet is playing an increasingly important role in hospitality. It is used as a source of information, and bookings can be made online. The internet offers numerous ways to find out whether a hospitality company or restaurant, say, delivers on its promises. Dissatisfied clients are able to vent their feelings to an internet-connected community of millions.

Companies are in turn expected to systematically accumulate information about their customers, to help them to segment and understand consumers, and offer them more relevant choices. Continued support for businesses to leverage opportunities such as the use of digital technologies to understand and exploit target markets will be significant.

Along with the internet and mobile technology, social media has changed how we communicate. It has also changed how we behave and it is changing the world of business. Every business organisation has to make social media part of its strategy. Social media is able to sell products, promote services and build a company's brand. It can help engage an audience, define a hospitality and tourism message, and broadcast it far and wide. (For more on the use of social media in a catering and hospitality business, see Chapter 13.)

Further reading

British Hospitality Association (2013–2014) *Trends and Statistics*.

Deloitte/NYU (2006) *Hospitality 2010*. New York, NY: Deloitte Services/New York University (downloadable at www.nyu.edu/public.affairs/releases/detail/1116).

Mancini, M. (2004) *Cruising: A Guide to the Cruise Industry*, 2nd edition. Florence, KY: Thomson Delmar Learning.

British Hospitality Association (2010) *Creating Jobs in Britain: A Hospitality Economy Proposition 2010*.

British Hospitality Association (2011) *Hospitality Driving Local Economies 2011*.

British Hospitality Association (2012) *Trends and Developments*.

Deloitte Oxford Economics (2013) *The Economic Contribution of the Tourism Economy in the UK 2013*.

Dimbleby and Vincent (2013) *The School Food Plan 2013*.

Global Hospitality Insights (2013) *Top Thoughts for 2014*.

Harvard University (2001) *The Role of the Tourism Sector in Expanding Economic Opportunity*.

World Travel and Tourism Council (2014) *Travel and Tourism Economic Impact 2014*.

Topics for discussion

1 Give your impressions of the food that was served at your previous schools, with suggestions for improvement.
2 Explain the importance of food for the hospital patient, with suggestions for the types of food to be offered.
3 Discuss what you think passengers travelling on aircraft would like to eat, and explain how it may, or may not, be feasible to provide it.
4 How do you think changes in the industry will occur over the next ten years? Explain why you think they will happen.
5 Each student in the group should obtain a number of menus from each type of catering organisation referred to in this chapter; the information should then be pooled for group discussion.
6 What essential differences attract staff to the various aspects of the industry (consider, for example, pay, conditions of work, career prospects)?
7 Establishments such as motorway facilities should meet special needs; explain what they are and how they are met, then select another area of catering and state what those needs are and how they are achieved.
8 Discuss the advantages for a hotel in outsourcing its food and beverage provision.
9 Discuss ways to reduce food waste in the hospitality industry.
10 Discuss the future of the British pub industry. What must it do to sustain and grow?

2

Employment law in the hospitality and catering industry

For those employed in the hospitality industry it is important to understand that there is a considerable amount of legislation that regulates both the industry itself and employment in the industry. Employers who contravene the law or attempt to undermine the statutory rights of their workers (for example, paying less than the national minimum wage or by denying them their right to paid annual holidays) are not only liable to prosecution and fines but could be ordered by tribunals and courts to pay substantial amounts of compensation.

This chapter outlines the main principles of employment legislation that a hospitality professional should be aware of in the UK. When working in other jurisdictions internationally, it is important to understand other legislation that may apply.

Workers and employees

An employee is a person who is employed under a contract of employment or service. An essential feature of a contract of employment is the 'mutuality of obligation'. The employer undertakes to provide the employee with work on specified days of the week for specified hours, and, if employed under a limited-term contract (e.g. 12 months), while the employee undertakes to carry out the work in turn for an agreed wage or salary.

The only workers who can be characterised as not being employees are those engaged on an 'as and when required' basis, referred to as 'zero hours' contracts (for example, from a list of casual workers who help out in banqueting, restaurant and bar when a member of the regular staff is ill or when extra staff are needed for a function). They are not 'employees' in the accepted sense of the word as there is no 'mutuality of obligation' between them and the employers who engage their services. These workers are free to reject work offered to them. Unfair dismissal is exclusive to employees who have a contract of employment.

Workers who are not necessarily employees still have certain levels of protection; in the UK they are protected by:

- health and safety legislation
- anti-discriminatory laws
- National Minimum Wage Act 1998
- Part-time Workers (Prevention of Less Favourable Treatment) Regulations
- Working Time Regulations 1998
- Public Interest Disclosure Act 1998
- Equality Act 2010
- Data Protection Act 1998.

Legislation protecting workers in the UK

The Equality Act 2010

Since the first Race Relations Act was introduced in the UK in 1965, many other personal characteristics besides race have been protected from discrimination as a result of both domestic initiatives and European Directives.

UK law relating to discrimination is mainly contained in the following legislation:

- Equal Pay Act 1970
- Sex Discrimination Act 1975
- Race Relations Act 1976
- Disability Discrimination Act 1995
- Employment Equality (Religion or Belief) Regulations 2003
- Employment Equality (Sexual Orientation) Regulations 2003
- Employment Equality (Age) Regulations 2006
- Equality Act 2006 Part 2
- Equality Act (Sexual Orientation) Regulations 2007.

In 2010, the government introduced new equality laws to speed up issues of equality: the Equality Act 2010.

The Equality Act 2010 requires:

- *some* public bodies to consider how they can help to stop people doing less well than other people because of their family background or where they were born; they have to think about what they can do to make their services more helpful to poorer people
- *all* public bodies to think about treating people from different groups fairly and equally (this is called the Equality Duty); all public bodies must make sure their work supports equality and treats people from different groups fairly and equally – for example, in their services, through their jobs and through the money they spend.

Public bodies already need to think about treating people of different races, disabled people and men and women fairly and equally. The Act adds extra groups of people to the Equality Duty:

- people of different ages – younger and older people
- lesbian, gay and bisexual people
- people who have changed their sex or are in the process of doing so
- people with a religion or belief, or people without a religion or belief
- women having a baby and women just after they have had a baby.

The Act also allows civil partnerships for gay and lesbian couples to be held in religious buildings.

The Act makes it easier for employers to use positive action, and it lets them choose a person who will make their workers more diverse when choosing between people who are right for the job.

Equal pay

If a UK company has 250 or more workers it may have to publish information about any differences in men and women's pay. The Equality Act also enables the government to tell public bodies to publish information about equal pay and how many workers it has who are disabled or people of different races. The government plans to do this for public bodies with 150 or more workers. The Act also stops employers telling workers they must not talk to one another about how much they are paid.

Extra powers for employment tribunals

Employment tribunals can suggest how an employer can put things right for a worker if they were treated unfairly. However, this does not help the employer's other workers because most people who complain to employment tribunals have stopped working for the employer. The Equality Act allows the employment tribunal to tell the employer their advice should apply to all their workers.

Reasonable adjustments

In the UK, the Equality Act has introduced several new rules to better protect people with disabilities. It makes the law on 'reasonable adjustments' clearer. These are changes an employer or someone providing a service has to make so that people with disabilities can do something like getting into a shop, restaurant or bank. Sometimes making a reasonable adjustment will cost extra money: the Equality Act says that most of the time the service provider or employer can't expect the person with a disability to pay them back that extra money.

The Equality Act will make it harder for an employer to be unfair because it says they can only sometimes ask if a person is disabled. For example, an employer might need to know if a person is disabled so they can make changes to a test or a job interview.

Dual discrimination

The Act makes dual discrimination against the law. This is when someone is treated worse than other people because of a combination of two things:

- if they are a woman or a man
- if they are transsexual
- if they have a disability
- if they are heterosexual, lesbian, gay or bisexual
- their age
- their race
- their religion or belief.

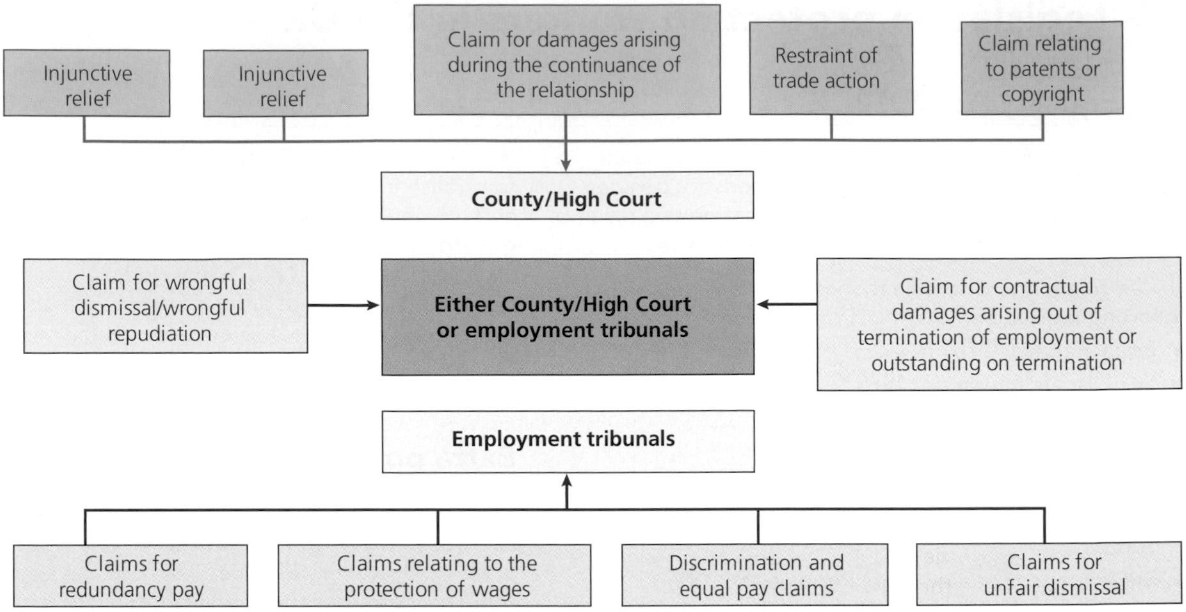

Figure 2.1 **Jurisdiction of the courts and employment tribunals**

WEBLINK

Details of the Equality Act 2010 can be found at:
www.legislation.gov.uk/ukpga/2010/15/contents

Recruitment and selection

When advertising for and recruiting new or replacement staff, employers in the UK hospitality industry need to be mindful of the following legislation:

- Children and Young Persons Act 1933
- Licensing Act 1964
- Rehabilitation of Offenders Act 1974
- Data Protection Act 1988
- Immigration, Asylum and Nationality Act 2006
- National Minimum Wage Act 1998
- Working Time Regulations 1998
- Sex Discrimination Act 1975
- Race Relations Act 1976
- Disability Discrimination Act 1995
- Human Rights Act 1998
- Equality Act 2010.

Job advertisements

When placing adverts, British employers must be conscious of their duty under the Equality Act 2010 not to discriminate against job applicants and existing members of staff because of a protected characteristic on the grounds of:

- age (although see 'Legislation affecting the employment of children and young persons', below)
- disability
- gender reassignment
- marriage and civil partnerships
- pregnancy and maternity
- race
- religion or belief
- sex
- sexual orientation
- trades union membership (or non-membership) or activities.

Job applications

Job application forms should be designed to gain relevant information about a job applicant's schooling, qualifications, training and previous work experience. Requests for personal information such as age, sex, marital status, ages of children, address, telephone numbers, details of next of kin, and so on, can be justified on a variety of grounds, as can requests for information on any recent illness or injury, allergies or disability. The application form must state the need for this sensitive data, and reassure candidates that this information will be treated and held in strictest confidence, in keeping with the provisions of the Data Protection Act 1998.

Providing advance information to job applicants

Under the Human Rights Act 1998, job application forms, job descriptions and offers of employment should, where applicable, forewarn applicants that offers of employment will be conditional on their wearing of uniforms while on duty and/or complying with employers' rules regarding dress or appearance, including restrictions on unsightly tattoos, facial piercings and the wearing of protective clothing. It should also be made known if the place of work is monitored by CCTV surveillance equipment, and if workers' telephone calls, emails and use or abuse of the internet are routinely monitored, together with the reasons for such surveillance or monitoring. These requirements should also be addressed during the job interview.

UK contracts of employment

A contract of employment must be provided within two months of beginning the employment. The terms of an employment contract set out what an employee and employer have agreed and what they can expect of each other, as well as both the employer's and employee's rights and duties.

A contract of employment should cover the following information:

- job title and location
- head office address of employer
- employment start date
- rate of pay and method of payment
- details of any other payments
- working days and hours
- meal breaks and other break entitlements
- whether overtime is expected and, if so, at what rate
- any shift work or night work
- holiday entitlements
- information on collective agreements
- details of sickness pay
- pension arrangements
- notice period
- disciplinary rules and procedures
- grievance procedures.

Right to live or work in the UK

An employer who negligently employs a person subject to immigration control, who does not have the legal right to live or work in the UK, is liable for a substantial fine. An employer who knowingly employs such a person is guilty of an offence under the Immigration, Asylum and Nationality Act 2006, and is liable to be convicted or be given an unlimited fine and/or imprisonment not exceeding two years. To avoid any unwitting breach of the 2006 Act, job application forms should caution applicants that, if they are shortlisted, they will be required to produce documents confirming their right to be in and take up employment while in the UK. Employers must demand to see and take copies of one or more specified document(s) (see 'Weblink') before offering employment to a job applicant.

Employers wishing to employ a non-EU or Swiss national must submit their applicants under tier 2 of the UK Border Agency points-based system.

WEBLINK

For a list of acceptable documents, refer to the Home Office website (Home Office guidance on employers' right-to-work checks):

www.gov.uk/government/publications/right-to-work-checks-employers-guide

Health questionnaires

Although the UK's Equality Act 2010 does not outlaw pre-employment health questionnaires, it does caution employers and those responsible for screening and interviewing job applicants that they must not enquire about the health of any applicant before offering employment or when preparing a shortlist of applicants. If pre-employment questionnaires are incorporated in or accompany job application forms, they must be detached and set aside before these application forms are relayed to the person or persons involved in the screening, interviewing and selection process. However, a health-related question can be asked if its purpose is to establish whether the candidate would be able to carry out a function that is intrinsic to the work concerned – for example, heavy manual handling, working at heights, or exposure to hot or humid working conditions.

Job offers

An offer of employment should be made or confirmed in writing, and is often conditional on the receipt of satisfactory references from former employers. Withdrawing an offer of employment once it has been accepted could result in a civil action for damages.

Blacklists

Under the Employment Relations Act 1999 (Blacklists) Regulations 2010, it is unlawful to refuse to interview or employ someone whose name appears on a blacklist. A blacklist is a list of names of prohibited people who will be denied employment. The law applies whether recruiting new members of staff direct or through an employment agency.

Written statement of employment particulars

According to UK law, every employee, whether full-time, part-time, casual, seasonal or temporary, has a legal right to be provided with a written statement outlining the principal terms and conditions of his or her employment. This must be issued within two months of the date on which the employee first starts work, but ideally on the employee's first day at work.

Any employee who is not provided with a written statement of employment particulars may refer the matter to an employment tribunal. If the employee's complaint is upheld the employer will be ordered either to provide the statement or accept a statement written by the tribunal. An employer who presumes to discipline, dismiss or otherwise punish an employee for asserting his or her statutory rights, before an employment tribunal, may be ordered to pay that employee compensation. Any change in the particulars included in the written statement must be notified in writing to each affected employee at the earliest opportunity, but no later than one month after the change in question.

Legislation affecting the employment of children and young persons in the UK

Employers, before recruiting staff, must be aware of the legislation that imposes restrictions on the employment of school-age children and young persons under the age of 18.

Employment of young persons under the age of 18

As a rule, young persons under the age of 18 must not be employed for more than 40 hours in any week including overtime, nor for more than eight hours a day, nor other than in exceptional circumstances after 10 o'clock at night. They must also be allowed two consecutive rest days in every week. If they are required to work a shift lasting more than four and a half hours they must be permitted a minimum 30-minute meal break in the course of that shift. This also applies to apprentices under the age of 18.

The Licensing Act 2003 also prohibits the employment of persons under the age of 18 working in bars and public houses.

If an employee is under the age of 18, any other employee who works closely with the young person must be checked with the Criminal Records Bureau (CRB).

Employment of school-age children

The employment of school-age children in hotels, restaurants and public houses at weekends and during the school holidays is regulated by the Children and Young Persons Act 1933 and by local authority by-laws. As a rule no child may be employed:

- if under the age of 14
- during school hours
- before 7.00 a.m. or after 7.00 p.m. on any day
- for more than two hours in a school day or on a Sunday
- for more than eight hours (or, if under 15, for more than five hours) on any one day (other than a Sunday) that is not a school day
- for more than 12 hours in any week that is a normal school week
- for more than 35 hours (or, if under 15, for more than 25 hours) in any week in which the child is not required to be at school
- for more than four hours on any day without a rest break of at least one hour
- at any time in a year unless, at that time, he or she has had, or could still have, during school holidays, at least two consecutive weeks without employment
- to do any work other than light work (i.e. work of a kind that is unlikely to affect the safety, health or development of a school-age child or to interfere with the child's education, or regular and punctual attendance at school).

Before employing a school-age child (or within seven days of doing so) an employer must apply to the relevant local education authority for an employment certificate. Most local authority by-laws prohibit the employment of school-age children in:

- hotel kitchens
- cook shops
- fish and chip shops
- restaurants
- snack bars and cafeterias
- any premises in connection with the sale of alcohol, except where alcohol is sold exclusively in sealed containers.

Legislation affecting the employment of convicted persons

Under the Rehabilitation of Offenders Act 1974, a person applying for work in the hospitality industry need not admit or disclose any criminal conviction that has been 'spent' either when completing a job application form or when answering questions at an interview.

Employment of women

UK employers who employ women of child-bearing age must, when carrying out the risk assessments prescribed by the management of Health and Safety at Work Regulations 1999, identify any workplace hazards that could pose a risk to pregnant employees, breast-feeding mothers or to women who have given birth within the previous six months, and take appropriate steps to minimise these risks.

Employment of door supervisors

Door supervisors, whose job it is to deal with unruly behaviour and to screen the suitability of people entering pubs, clubs and other licensed premises open to the public, will be liable to criminal prosecution if they carry on working without the benefit of a Security Industry Authority (SIA) licence. Pub landlords and club owners in England and Wales will themselves be guilty of an offence under the Private Security Industry Act 2001 if they use or engage the services of unlicensed door staff.

Employment legislation

The meaning of 'pay'

Pay means any sums payable to a worker in connection with his or her employment, including any fee, bonus, commission, holiday pay or other emolument. It also includes statutory sick pay, statutory maternity pay, statutory adoption pay, statutory paternity pay, guaranteed payments, payments in respect of time off work, remuneration on suspension on medical or maternity grounds or under a protective award, and any sum payable in pursuance of a tribunal order for the worker's reinstatement or re-engagement.

Pay does not include any loan or advance on wages, payments in respect of expenses incurred by a worker in the carrying out of his or her employment, pension payments, or redundancy and severance payments.

Equal Pay Act 1970

Under the UK's Equal Pay Act 1970, a woman engaged in like work, or work of a basically similar nature, or in work rated as equivalent, or in work of equal value to that undertaken by a man in the same employment, is entitled to be paid the same as that man, and to enjoy equivalent terms and conditions of employment. The same rule applies if a woman is appointed or promoted to a job previously occupied by a man. In the absence of any express term, every contract of employment (and every collective agreement imported with an employee's contract) will be treated in law as containing an implied equality clause.

The national minimum/living wage

In the UK there is a national minimum wage for adult workers (workers aged 21 and over) and a separate low minimum wage for employees aged 18–20. Following the July 2015 budget this is now known as the **National Living Wage**. These rates are reviewed periodically by government and apply to all workers, whether full- or part time, temporary, permanent, seasonal or casual, regardless of the nature of the contractual relationship between them and the people or organisations that employ them.

An employer's refusal or failure to pay the appropriate national minimum wage could lead to a criminal prosecution and an appearance before an employment tribunal. Employers who fail to pay the current national minimum wage to former workers (for example, workers who have since left their employment) are liable to be ordered by Her Majesty's Revenue and Customs (HMRC) Enforcement Agency to reimburse up to six years' arrears of pay to each of those workers.

Statutory Sick Pay

Employers in the UK are liable to pay up to 28 weeks' Statutory Sick Pay (SSP) to any qualified employee who is incapable of work because of illness or injury. The relevant legislation is to be found in the Social Security Contributions and Benefits Act 1992 and the Statutory Sick Pay (General) Regulations 1992.

Employers who operate their own occupational sick pay schemes may opt out of the Statutory Sick Pay scheme, so long as the payments available to their employees under such schemes are equal to or greater than payments to which they would otherwise be entitled under the terms of Statutory Sick Pay, and so long as these employees are not required to contribute towards the cost of funding such a scheme. Payments made under Statutory Sick Pay may be offset against contractual sick pay, and vice versa.

Meaning of 'incapacity for work'

An employee is incapacitated for work if he or she is incapable, because of disease or bodily or mental disablement, of doing work that he or she can reasonably be expected to do under the contract of employment. Under the Food Safety (General Food Hygiene) Regulations 1995, food handlers suffering from (or carriers of) a disease likely to be transmitted through food, or while afflicted with infected wounds, skin infections, sores or diarrhoea, must not be allowed to work in any food handling, even in any capacity in which there is a likelihood of directly or indirectly contaminating food with pathogenic micro-organisms. In these circumstances, the worker is deemed to be incapacitated for work and, subject to the usual qualifying conditions, entitled to be paid Statutory Sick Pay until such time as the risk has passed.

Working Time Regulations

The Working Time Regulations apply to all employees and workers who undertake to do or perform work or service for an employer. The 1998 Regulations are policed and enforced by employment tribunals (in relation to a worker's statutory rights to rest breaks, rest periods and paid annual holidays) and by local authority environmental health officers.

The 1998 Regulations (as amended from 6 April 2003) impose a number of restrictions on working hours and periods of employment for workers aged 18 and over, as follows.

- Adult workers have the right not to be employed for more than an average of 48 hours a week.
- Adolescent workers may not lawfully be employed for more than 8 hours a day or for more than 40 hours a week.

- Adult workers may not lawfully be employed at night for more than an average 8 hours in any 24-hour period.
- Adolescent workers may not lawfully be employed at night between the hours of 10 p.m. and 6 a.m. (or between 11 p.m. and 7 a.m. if their contracts require them to work after 10 p.m.).
- Every worker is entitled to a minimum weekly rest period of 24 hours (or 48 hours in every fortnight); or, if under the age of 18, a minimum weekly rest period of 48 consecutive hours.
- Every worker is entitled to a daily rest period of a minimum of 11 consecutive hours or, if under the age of 18, a daily rest period of a minimum of 12 consecutive hours.
- Every worker is entitled to a minimum 20-minute rest break during the course of any working day or shift lasting or expected to last for more than 6 hours or, if under the age of 18, a minimum 30-minute break during the course of any working day or shift lasting, or expected to last, for more than 4.5 hours.
- If an adult worker is content to work more than an average 48 hours a week, he or she must sign an agreement to that effect.
- Night workers are entitled to free initial and follow-up health assessments (or, if under the age of 18, free initial follow-up health and capability assessments).
- The upper limits on the working hours and periods of employment of adolescent workers aged 16 and 17 are fixed, and they have no legal right to opt out of these limits whether they wish to or not.

Holidays and holiday pay

From April 2009, every worker in the UK, whether full-time, part-time, temporary, permanent, seasonal or casual, is entitled to 5.6 weeks' paid holiday in every holiday year. For example, for a person who works a standard five-day week, 5.6 weeks translates to 28 working days' paid annual holiday.

WEBLINK

To calculate the holiday entitlement of workers pro rata, visit:

www.gov.uk/holiday-entitlement-rights/entitlement

Part-time workers

Under the Part-time Workers (Prevention of Less Favourable Treatment) Regulations 2000, part-time workers, regardless of the number of hours they work, must not be treated less favourably than comparable full-time workers employed or engaged under the same type of contract and doing the same or similar work.

Fixed-term contracts

'Fixed-term employee' means an employee who is employed under a fixed-term contract, which is a contract that terminates (ends) after a certain date, or at the end of a set project or task.

Under the Fixed-term Employees (Prevention of Less Favourable Treatment) Regulations 2002, employers who use the services of temporary employees, for short or long periods (for example, relief managers, to cover long-term sickness or maternity leave, or during busy operation periods such as summer or Christmas), must treat these employees in the same way as permanent employees.

The rights of fixed-term employees include:

- to be paid the same (albeit on a pro rata basis) as comparable permanent employees working in the same establishment
- to be employed under the same terms and conditions as permanent employees unless there are objective reasons for any less favourable treatment
- to be given equal access to opportunities for promotion, transfer, training or permanent employment
- to be informed of any suitable permanent vacancies that may arise
- to request a written statement from their employers explaining the reasons for what appears to be less favourable treatment (the statement to be provided within 21 days)
- not to be victimised, dismissed, selected for redundancy or subjected to any other detriment for asserting their rights, for questioning or challenging their employers' refusal or failure to comply with the 2002 Regulations, for demanding a written explanation for any such failure, for refusing to forego a right conferred by the 2002 Regulations, for pursuing their rights before an employment tribunal, or for giving evidence or information in connection with such proceedings on behalf of another employee
- to be paid Statutory Sick Pay when incapacitated for work
- to be paid guarantee payments in respect of workless days
- to receive redundancy payments on completion of two years' continuous service
- to payment of their normal wages or salary if suspended from work on medical grounds
- to receive written reasons for dismissal
- to give and receive statutory minimum notice to terminate their contract of employment and to automatic permanent status if their service under one or more fixed-term contracts extends beyond four years (unless there are objective reasons for continuing to engage them under fixed-term contracts).

The Employment Appeal Tribunal in the case of *Department for Work and Pensions v. Sutcliffe* held that an employee who fell ill during her ordinary maternity leave is not entitled to be paid contractual sick pay during that period. Since October 2008 that rule applies to women taken ill during additional maternity leave.

Equal treatment of agency workers

The Agency Workers Regulations 2010 state that workers coming from employment agencies to work in hotels, restaurants, pubs, contract catering, and so on, are entitled to equal treatment in relation to working hours, rest breaks, holidays, etc., as if they had been directly recruited by the establishment that hires their services. This covers waiters, food service staff, chefs, bar staff and housekeepers. They must not only be paid the same as any regular member of staff doing the same job, but cannot lawfully be required to work longer hours or take shorter breaks for meals and rest. However, an agency worker's right to equal treatment under the 2010 regulations does not arise until and unless he or she has worked continuously with the same hirer in the same job for 12 continuous weeks. Intervals of up to six weeks between assignments in the same type of work with the same hirer do not break continuity for these purposes.

WEBLINK

To find information on the entitlements of agency workers, visit:
www.nidirect.gov.uk

The self-employed (freelancers and contractors)

The self-employed are not entitled to:

- their client company's sick leave, company maternity pay or company pension provisions
- legal rights to protection under their clients company's internal disciplinary and grievance schemes
- the legal right not to be dismissed (always, however, read the contract of service agreed as this may contain clauses relating to termination of agreement and time periods).

There is, however, some legal protection for self-employed people. They:

- should not be discriminated against in the workplace in most cases, and if they are could make a claim to an Employment Tribunal; this protection applies only to freelancers who fall under Part 5 of the Equality Act 2010 – that is, those who are described as 'contract workers' and are contracted personally to do the work, i.e. they cannot claim discrimination against their employer if they are contracted for the provision of services and hire someone else or sub-contract someone else to do the work, they must personally do the work themselves
- should be paid for the work they have done.

Contractors working through employment agencies also have rights under the Conduct of Employment Agencies and Employment Business Regulations 2003 Statutory Maternity Allowance if they are pregnant and have recently left an engagement.

Statutory Maternity Pay

A pregnant employee who has worked for her employer for a minimum period of 26 weeks, up to and into the 15th week before her expected week of childbirth, and who has average weekly earnings equal to or greater than the current 'lower' earnings limit for these and other purposes, is entitled to be paid up to 39 weeks' Statutory Maternity Pay (SMP) during her absence from work on maternity leave.

Providing an employee informs her employer, the pregnant woman may begin her ordinary maternity leave at any time on or after the beginning of the 11th week before her expected week of childbirth unless she gives birth prematurely. Then the leave starts the day after the birth occurs.

Unless the employee's contract states otherwise, an employee absent on maternity leave does not have the right to be paid her normal wages or salary during her period of leave. Her other terms and conditions remain the same, such as holiday entitlement, sickness benefits, seniority, pension rights, company car, mobile phone, etc.

A woman returning to work at the end of her ordinary maternity leave has the right to return to the job she had before the period of leave. She can return to work before the end of the 26 weeks if she so wishes.

Additional maternity leave

Every pregnant employee, regardless of her length of service, is entitled to a total of 52 weeks' maternity leave, comprising 26 weeks' ordinary maternity leave (OML) and 26 weeks' additional maternity leave (AML). An employee has no need to forewarn her employer of her intentions so far as her entitlement to AML is concerned, nor is she under any legal obligation to give her employer advance notice of her intentions when that additional period of leave comes to an end.

An employee who takes AML is entitled to return to work in the job in which she was employed before her OML began or, if that is not reasonably practicable, to another job that is both suitable for her and appropriate for her to do in the circumstances, and on terms and conditions no less favourable to her than those that would have applied to her but for her absence on maternity leave.

Paternity leave or pay

Under the Paternity and Adoption Leave Regulations 2002, complemented by the Paternity and Adoption Leave Regulations 2003, an employee has the right to one or two weeks' paid paternity leave to enable him or her to care for a child or to support the child's mother. That right applies if he is the child's biological father or the current spouse or partner of the child's mother. That same qualified right extends to an employee who has adopted a child or who is one of the couple who has jointly adopted a child. Paternity leave must be taken within 56 days of a child's birth or placement for adoption.

Parental leave

Under the Maternity and Parental Leave etc. Regulations 1999, the employed parents of a child who is under the age of five (or under the age of 18 if adopted) have the legal right to take up to 13 weeks' unpaid parental leave during the first five years of the child's life or, if the child is adopted, until the fifth anniversary of adoption or until the child's 18th birthday, whichever occurs sooner.

To establish eligibility for shared parental leave, the child's mother or adoptive parent must be eligible for either:

- maternity leave or pay
- state maternity allowance
- adoption leave or pay.

The statutory right of eligible employees to take additional paternity leave ended on 5 April 2015.

Adoption leave and pay

From 5 April 2015 an eligible employee with whom a child is to be placed for adoption is entitled (regardless of his or her length of service when the placement occurs) to take up to 52 weeks' adoption leave comprising 26 weeks' ordinary adoption leave followed immediately by up to 26 weeks' additional adoption leave.

Stakeholder pensions

When starting a new job or returning to one, an employer does not have to offer the employee access to a stakeholder pension scheme. If an employee is in a stakeholder pension scheme that was arranged by the employer before 1 October 2012 they must continue to take and pay contributions from the wages. This arrangement is in place until the employee asks them to stop; the employee stops paying contributions at regular intervals or leaves the job.

WEBLINK

For more on pensions see:
www.gov.uk/personal-pensions-your-rights

Flexible working

From June 2014, under the Flexible Working Regulations and the Revocation of Flexible Working (Eligibility Complaints and Remedies) Regulations 2002, the right to request flexible working is now available to any employee who has been continuously employed for 26 weeks or more. In short, that right is no longer limited to carers or parents of children under the age of 17 (or, if disabled children, under the age of 18).

Time off work

Employees have the legal right to be permitted a reasonable amount of paid or unpaid time off work to enable them to carry out their functions as public officials, shop stewards, members of recognised independent trades unions, safety representatives, pension schemes, trustees, and so on.

The legislation does not specify what constitutes a 'reasonable' amount of time off. A great deal will depend on the particular circumstances and a degree of common sense.

In summary, employees have the right to paid or unpaid time off work in the following circumstances:

- having responsibilities for dependents – unpaid
- having children under the age of 5 or adopted children under the age of 18 – unpaid
- for antenatal care during pregnancy – paid
- acting as a justice of the peace or official of a public body – paid/unpaid
- accompanying another worker at a disciplinary or grievance hearing – paid
- acting as a pension scheme trustee – paid
- redundant employees – paid
- acting as an employee representative – paid
- young employees in education or training – paid
- acting as a safety representative – paid
- acting as a trades union official (shop steward) – paid
- trades union members – unpaid
- members of European Works council (EWCs) or negotiating bodies – paid.

Trades union officials

Employees who are officials of an independent trade union that is recognised by their employer as having collective bargaining rights for the entire workforce (or for one or more groups within the workforce; this includes shop stewards or work convenors) have the right to be permitted a reasonable amount of paid time off work to enable them to carry out such of their duties as are concerned with pay and other terms and conditions of employment, working conditions, grievances, disciplinary matters affecting their members, etc. This will also include time off for training in industrial relations.

Jury service

Section 1 of the Juries Act 1974 states that every UK resident aged 18 and over who is not otherwise ineligible or disqualified is liable to be summoned for jury service in the Crown Court, High Court and the County Courts.

Unlawful discrimination

The Equality Act 2010 reminds employers and employer agencies that it is unlawful to discriminate against job applicants and existing members of staff because of a 'protected characteristic' or because they associate with or are perceived, rightly or wrongly, to possess a protected characteristic.

The following are protected characteristics:

- age
- disability
- gender reassignment
- marriage and civil partnership
- pregnancy and/or maternity
- race
- religion or belief
- sex
- sexual orientation.

The 2010 Act identifies several types of unlawful discrimination, as follows.

- **Direct discrimination:** when a job applicant or existing worker is refused employment or opportunities for promotion, transfer or training because of a protected characteristic (see above).
- **Associative discrimination:** this is another form of direct discrimination. It arises when a job applicant or existing member of staff is treated less favourably because he or she is known to associate with another person who has a protected characteristic.
- **Perceptive discrimination:** this is when an employer rejects an otherwise suitable job applicant, or refuses to promote or transfer an existing member of staff, because he or she is rumoured or perceived to be gay or about to start a family, or to be a person whose religious beliefs could interfere with his or her timekeeping or ability to carry out an efficient job of work.
- **Indirect discrimination:** one form of indirect discrimination is imposing a requirement or condition, which although applied equally to all job applicants and existing members of staff, disadvantages people who share a particular protected characteristic.

Harassment and victimisation

Harassment is unwanted conduct relating to a relevant protected characteristic, which has the purpose or effect of violating an individual's dignity or creating an intimidating, hostile, degrading, humiliating or offensive environment for that individual.

Victimisation occurs when a member of staff is disciplined or subjected to some other detriment. For example:

- the withholding of an expected promotion, transfer or pay rise for having alleged that he or she has been unlawfully discriminated against
- having complained to an employment tribunal
- having given evidence or information in connection with proceedings before an employment tribunal, or
- having supported other members of staff who have lodged similar complaints.

Positive discrimination

It is unlawful for an employer to recruit or promote a candidate who is of equal merit to another candidate if the employer reasonably thinks the candidate has a protected characteristic that is under-represented in the workplace or that people with that characteristic suffer a disadvantage connected to that characteristic.

Age discrimination and retirement

It is no longer lawful for an employer to prescribe a compulsory retirement age for any member of staff, unless the employer can justify doing so on the grounds that it is a proportionate means of achieving a legitimate aim.

Disability discrimination

The Equality Act 2010, supplemented by the Equality Act 2010 (Disability) Regulations 2010, states that a person has a disability if he or she has a physical or mental impairment and the impairment has a substantial and long-term adverse effect on that person's ability to carry out normal day-to-day activities. The effect of the impairment is 'long term' if it has lasted for 12 months, is likely to last for 12 months or is likely to last for the rest of the life of the person affected. An impairment is to be treated as having a substantial adverse effect on the ability of the person concerned to carry out normal day-to-day activities even if he or she is receiving medical treatment or has been equipped with a prosthesis or other aid. Each of cancer, HIV infection and multiple sclerosis is a disability, as is severe disfigurement (other than deliberately acquired disfigurements such as tattoos and decorative body piercings).

Any job advertisement that indicates, or might reasonably be understood to indicate, an intention to discriminate against those job applicants with a disability, or that suggests a reluctance or inability on the employer's part to make appropriate adjustments to the workplace to accommodate the needs of people with particular disabilities, is admissible as evidence in any subsequent tribunal.

The employer's duty to make adjustments

Employers must take appropriate steps to accommodate a disabled person who might otherwise be at a disadvantage relative to able-bodied persons doing (or applying for) the same or similar work. These would include making adjustments to the premises, allocating some of the disabled person's duties to another person, altering his or her working hours, requiring or modifying equipment, providing supervision, and so on.

An employer's refusal to appoint a person with a disability to a particular job may be justifiable on health and safety grounds, or because it is self-evident that the applicant would be incapable of doing that job, given the nature and extent of the applicant's disability, the type of work to be done and the conditions in which that work is to be carried out.

Chronically sick and disabled persons

The Chronically Sick and Disabled Persons Act 1970 (amended by the Chronically Sick and Disabled Persons (Amendment) Act 1976) imposes a duty on the owners and developers of new commercial premises (hotels, pubs, restaurants) to consider the needs of disabled persons when designing the means of access to (and within) these premises, including the means of access to parking facilities, toilets, cloakrooms and washing facilities.

Discrimination on grounds of religion or belief

The Employment Equality (Religion or Belief) Regulations 2003 state that it is unlawful for any employer to discriminate against a job applicant or existing employee because of that applicant's or employee's religion or beliefs. The regulations prohibit discrimination, victimisation or harassment occurring after an employment relationship has come to an end.

The term 'religion or belief' means any religion, religious belief or similar philosophical belief.

Employers are not obliged to allow members of staff, whose religions require them to pray at certain intervals during the day, to take time off in order to comply with their religion's obligations.

Exceptions for genuine occupational requirements

The regulations allow that it is permissible in certain circumstances for an employer to discriminate against a job applicant (or a candidate for promotion or transfer) on the grounds of his or her religion or belief if being of a particular religion or having certain beliefs is a genuine and determining occupation or requirement for the vacancy in question.

A restaurant serving kosher or halal foods, for example, may be justified in its refusal to engage the services of cooks or waiting staff that are not of the Jewish or Islamic faiths, if certain foods have to be treated and prepared in a particular way before being served to customers.

Disciplinary and grievance procedures

When issuing written statements (or contracts) to members of staff, employers have a duty in law to ensure that these statements incorporate, or are accompanied by, a note explaining their disciplinary rules and the procedures to be followed should any employee fail to follow these rules. Alternatively the note must refer employees to the existence and ready accessibility of some other documents that explain these rules and procedures in detail – for example, the staff handbook. Employees should be left in no doubt as to the standards of conduct expected of them while carrying out their workday activities, a breach of which could well result in their being disciplined or dismissed. The written statement must also explain the employer's procedures for dealing with and resolving workplace grievances.

ACAS Code of Practice

The Advisory Conciliation and Arbitration Service (ACAS) provides free and impartial information and advice to employers and employees on all aspects of workplace relations and employment law. The ACAS Code of Practice for grievance and disciplinary procedures sets out principles for handling disciplinary and grievance situations in the workplace.

Problems associated with minor cases of misconduct and most cases of poor performance, says the Code, may best be dealt with by informal advice, training, coaching and counselling before a more formal approach is adopted. Should that informal approach not have the desired effect, a more formal approach may be necessary. This may well comprise a formal verbal warning, followed by a first written warning, a final written warning and, if at the end of that sequence of warnings there is still not improvement in the worker's conduct or performance within specified time limits, dismissal or demotion.

WEBLINK

Full details of the ACAS Code of Practice can be found at: **www.acas.org.uk**

Records of formal warnings

Employers should keep a record of all formal verbal and written warnings served on employees, as well as copies of any associated documents detailing the nature of any breach of disciplinary rules or unsatisfactory performance. The worker's defence or mitigation, the action taken and the reasons for it, whether an appeal was lodged, its outcomes and any subsequent developments. These records, which may need to be produced in evidence before an employment tribunal, should be kept under lock and key and made available on demand to employees and other workers, in keeping with their rights under the Data Protection Act 1998.

Disputes

If an employee has a dispute or grievance with their employer, the organisation's grievance procedure should be followed. All employees should have access to this procedure. It is likely to recommend that employees, in the first instance, talk to their manager or personnel/HR department.

Other sources of advice and support for dealing with disputes include:

- talking to a trades union or employee representative
- the local Citizens Advice Bureau (CAB), which offers free and impartial advice on employment matters
- ACAS (the Advisory Conciliation and Arbitration Service), which offers free confidential advice on all employment rights issues.

WEBLINKS

Citizens Advice Bureau:
www.citizensadvice.org.uk
ACAS:
www.acas.org.uk
The Employment Tribunal Service:
www.employmenttribunals.gov.uk

Termination of employment

Under the Employment Rights Act 1996 (as amended by the Fixed Term Employees (Prevention of Less Favourable Treatment) Regulations 2002) a dismissal in law occurs:

- when an employer terminates an employee's contract of employment (with or without notice)
- when an employee resigns (with or without notice) in circumstances in which he or she is entitled to do so, without notice, because of the employer's unreasonable conduct
- when a limited-term contract comes to an end without being renewed under the same contract.

Notice periods

Notice periods are the written statement of initial employment particulars necessarily issued to every employee, in compliance with the Employment Rights Act 1996.

Notice to be given by employees

Unless the contract of employment specifies a longer period of notice, an employee who has worked for his or her employer for one month or more is required to give his employer at least one week's notice to terminate his or her employment. If an employee's contract specifies longer periods of notice than those prescribed by the 1996 Act, those longer notice periods take precedence. If the contract specifies a shorter period of notice, the statutory minimum periods of notice take precedence.

Notice to be given by employers

Under the 1996 Act, the statutory notice to be given by an employer to terminate an employee's contract of employment is determined by the employee's length of continuous service at the material time, as shown in Table 2.1.

Table 2.1 **Statutory notice periods**

Length of service	Minimum notice
Less than 1 month	Nil
1 month but less than 2 years	1 week
2 years or more	1 week for each year of service
12 years or more	Maximum 12 weeks

If an employee's contract states that he or she is entitled to longer periods of notice to terminate his or her employment (based on length of service, or for whatever reason), those longer periods prevail. If the contract states that the employee is entitled to shorter periods of notice, the statutory minimum entitlement prevails.

Dismissal

The question as to whether the dismissal of an employee was fair or unfair will depend on whether in the circumstances (including the size and administrative resources of the employers undertaking) the employer had acted reasonably or unreasonably in treating that reason as sufficient for dismissing the employee and 'shall be determined in accordance with equity and the substantial merits of the case'.

A complaint of unfair or unlawful dismissal must be lodged with the nearest Regional Office of the Employment Tribunal Service.

Permitted and unlawful reasons for dismissal

The Employment Rights Act 1996 allows that it is acceptable to dismiss an employee in the UK for one or other of the following reasons:

- incompetence, associated with a lack of qualifications, or of the skills or aptitude needed to do an efficient or satisfactory job of work
- sickness or a debilitating injury (often associated with a poor timekeeping record, or persistent or prolonged absenteeism)
- misconduct (including gross misconduct)
- redundancy
- illegality of continued employment (for example, being under the age of 18 if employed as a barman or barmaid), or
- for 'some other substantial reason' of a kind such as to justify the dismissal of an employee holding the position which that employee held (for example, unreasonably refusing to accept a change in working methods, the introduction of new technology and similar changes prompted by the need to improve business efficiency or profitability).

When responding to a complaint of unfair dismissal, it is the employer's responsibility to explain to an employment tribunal only if the employee was dismissed, and to convince the tribunal that the employee had been dismissed for a permitted or legitimate reason.

An employee who is dismissed for an inadmissible or unlawful reason may present a complaint of unfair dismissal to an employment tribunal regardless of his or her age or length of service at the material time. The term 'inadmissible and unlawful' applies to a dismissal on grounds of an employee's age, sex, marital status, race, colour, nationality, national or ethnic origins, sexual orientation, religion or beliefs, disability, or trade union membership or non-membership. It is also unlawful and automatically unfair to dismiss employees (regardless of age or length of service when dismissed):

- for asserting their statutory employment rights, or for challenging or questioning their employer's refusal to acknowledge those rights (including the right to be paid the appropriate national minimum wage, the right to 5.6 weeks' paid annual holiday, the right not to be required to work more than an average 48 hours a week, the right to be provided with a written statement of employment particulars, and so on)
- for exercising or presuming to exercise their rights to maternity leave and pay, adoption leave and pay, parental leave, paternity leave, time off for dependants, time off for antenatal care, and other family-friendly rights
- for carrying out or proposing to carry out their functions as elected or appointed safety representatives, members of safety committees, or trustees of occupational pension schemes
- for performing or proposing to perform his or her functions as an employees' representative, a negotiating representative, an information and consultation representative, or a candidate in an election in which any person elected will, on being elected, be such a representative
- for leaving the workplace in circumstances of danger, which they reasonably believed to be serious and imminent (for example, the possibility of a gas explosion) and which they could not reasonably have been expected to avert; or for refusing to return to the workplace until reassured that it was safe for them to do so
- for having made a 'protected disclosure' (such as for having disclosed information to the relevant enforcing authority, such as the Inland Revenue, HM Customs & Excise, the Environmental Health Department) concerning alleged breaches by their employer of legislation such as the Licensing Act 1964, the Food Safety Act 1990, the Environment Protection Act 1990, the Working Time Regulations 1998, the National Minimum Wage Regulations 1999, health and safety legislation, and so on.

Constructive dismissal

An employee will be treated in law as having been constructively dismissed if he or she is bullied, harassed, ridiculed or intimidated to the point where he or she is left with little choice but to resign, with or without notice. The same rule applies if an employer, without reasonable and proper cause, conducts himself or herself in a manner calculated or likely to destroy or seriously damage the relationship of confidence and trust that should exist between employer and employee.

Redundancy payments

Under the Employment Rights Act 1996 any redundant employee with two or more years' service is entitled to be paid a statutory redundancy payment on the termination of his or her employment. When calculating an employee's entitlement to a redundancy payment, service before the age of 18 and beyond the age of 65 must now be taken into account. A statutory redundancy payment, otherwise payable to an employee aged 64 or over, may no longer lawfully be reduced by one-twelfth for each complete month of service beyond the employee's 64th birthday.

Dress codes

People applying for work in establishments with particular dress codes should be given to understand that their employment would be dependent on their adhering to these codes. The Equal Opportunities Commission (EOC) is unhappy about dress codes that require female workers to wear short or revealing skirts or low-cut blouses while at work. However, its view is that there is no breach of the Sex Discrimination Act 1975 or the Human Rights Act 1998 so long as the employer's policy on dress and appearance is made known to job applicants at employment interviews, and employees are willing to accept it as part of their terms and conditions of employment.

The Data Protection Act

Most employers keep files containing information (or personal data) about the people they employ. 'Personal data' means information about an employee or worker who can readily be identified from that data, or from any other information or document held by a worker's employer in a computerised or paper-based filing system. The sort of information held is likely to include age, qualifications, marital status, health, attendance record, conduct and capabilities.

Under the Data Protection Act 1998, workers have the right not only to see their personal files but also to be provided with hard copies or photocopies of most, and in some cases all, of the documents held in these files. They also have the right to know who within the organisation has access to these files.

The 1998 Act lists eight data protection principles relating to the 'processing' of personal data held on manual or computerised filing systems. Thus, personal data held in an employee's or other worker's personnel file or in a computerised filing system:

- must have been obtained fairly and lawfully (see above)
- must not be held on file other than for a legitimate purpose (nor be used or made use of for any other purpose)
- must be adequate, relevant and not excessive in relation to the purpose or purposes for which it is kept
- must be accurate and, where necessary, kept up to date
- must not be kept for longer than is absolutely necessary
- must be held in compliance with a worker's rights of access to personal data; must not be processed in a way calculated (or likely) to cause damage or distress to a worker, and must be corrected, erased or destroyed if inaccurate or no longer relevant

- must be protected, by the best available means, against unauthorised access or disclosure, and against accidental loss, damage or destruction, and must be treated as confidential by the staff to whom they are entrusted
- must not be transferred to any country or territory (e.g. to a parent or controlling company) outside the European Economic Area (EEA) whose data protection laws or codes are non-existent or less than adequate
- unless the worker agrees otherwise or the transfer is necessary for employment purposes (e.g. a proposed transfer or secondment overseas).

'Sensitive personal data' consists of information about employees' racial or ethnic origins, political opinions, religious beliefs, trade union membership (or non-membership), physical or mental health conditions, sexual orientation, criminal (or alleged criminal) activities, and criminal proceedings or criminal convictions (or any sentences imposed by the courts). Sensitive personal data must not be held on a worker's personal file without his or her explicit consent, unless held in compliance with the employer's legal obligations (e.g. under health and safety legislation) or to protect the employee's vital interests (e.g. under the Disability Discrimination Act 1995).

Further reading

Croners Catering

Home Office guidance on employers' right-to-work checks: www.gov.uk/government/publications/right-to-work-checks-employers-guide

Topics for discussion

1. What are the functions of an employment tribunal?
2. Discuss the reasons why the hospitality industry is poorly represented by trades unions.
3. Discuss some of the legislation that protects people from employment discrimination.
4. Why is it important to any organisation to develop good industrial relations?
5. Do you believe that the current employment legislation is adequate, inadequate or prohibits the development of the hospitality industry?
6. Why did the government introduce the Equality Act 2010 when there was already so much legislation governing equality?
7. What are the restrictions on the working time limits when employing young people aged 16–17?
8. Discuss what is meant by flexible working.
9. Discuss the different forms of unlawful discrimination covered by the Equality Act 2010.
10. As a group, list examples of sensitive data referred to by the Data Protection Act 1998.

3 Food safety

Why is food safety important?

Food safety is of paramount importance to any food business, and the standards applied to each food business are protected by law. Effective, professional food safety means managing all of the processes to ensure that food is safe for the consumer to eat. It involves:

- designing and equipping premises to comply with food safety requirements
- employing and training staff effectively
- selecting suppliers to provide food of the required quality
- ensuring hygienic delivery and safe storage of food
- preparing and cooking food safely and effectively
- hot holding, cooling and reheating food correctly and safely
- serving the food to the customer safely and hygienically.

A recorded food safety management system based on the principles of Hazard Analysis and Critical Control Points (HACCP) is now a legal requirement for *all* food businesses in the UK. HACCP identifies the stages where contamination and other hazards could occur. These are the critical control points, or CCPs. Hazards at each CCP are then managed, monitored and recorded to ensure the process is under control and safe food is being produced.

As well as complying with the law, good standards of food safety will enable a business to:

- avoid the possibility of food poisoning
- build a good reputation locally, resulting in personal recommendations
- receive favourable press/social media reviews
- give customers and staff confidence in the food provided
- incur less food wastage, meaning that running costs will be lower
- provide pleasant working conditions, leading to staff retention and greater job security.

Failure to manage food safety effectively can be extremely damaging to a business and can lead to: bad publicity, poor reputation, the serving of notices by enforcement officers, legal action, fines, and even closure and prison sentences.

➔ What is required under UK food safety legislation?

Food safety legislation covers a wide range of topics, including:

- controlling and reducing outbreaks of food poisoning
- training of all food handlers
- preventing contamination of food, equipment and premises
- provision of clean water, sanitary facilities and washing facilities
- registration of premises and vehicles
- content and labelling of food, including allergen information
- preventing the manufacture and sale of any food that could cause illness or injury
- monitoring of food imports.

Food Hygiene Regulations 2006 and Food Safety Act 1990

The most important and relevant regulations for all food businesses in the United Kingdom are the Food Hygiene (England/Wales/Scotland/Northern Ireland, as applicable) Regulations 2006. This legislation strengthened the existing 1990 Food Safety Act and related regulations, although most of the requirements remain the same.

The laws provide a framework for EU Regulation (EC) No. 852/2004 to be enforced in the UK. Regulation (EC) No. 852/2004 governs the general hygiene requirements for all member countries of the EU.

Under this legislation it is a *legal requirement* for food businesses to have a system based on the seven principles of HACCP, which will identify, assess and monitor the critical control points in food production procedures, and ensure that corrective actions are put in place and the systems verified frequently, with accurate documentation available for inspection and review.

Those responsible for food businesses must ensure that:

- where a HACCP system is established, at least one person who has been trained in the principles of HACCP must be involved in setting up the system
- the premises (and food vehicles) are fully registered with the local authority
- they can supply records of staff training commensurate with the different job roles
- policies are in place for planning and monitoring staff training
- appropriate levels of supervision are in place
- they provide adequate hygiene and welfare facilities for staff
- there is an adequate supply of materials and equipment for staff
- there is sufficient ventilation, potable water supplies and adequate drainage
- there are separate washing/cleaning facilities for premises, equipment and food, as well as hand-washing facilities
- there are records of all food suppliers used
- there are systems for accident and incident reporting.

Employees also have food safety responsibilities. They must:

- not do anything or work in such a way that would endanger or contaminate food
- cooperate with their employers and the measures they have put in place to keep food safe
- partake in planned training and instruction
- maintain high standards of personal hygiene
- report illnesses to supervisors/managers before entering the food preparation area
- report any faulty equipment, shortages or defects that could affect food safety.

Food safety records are mandatory and will always include written records of:

- supplier contacts, and that suppliers are reputable
- equipment and premises maintenance temperature controls
- staff sickness
- cleaning schedules
- pest audits
- equipment replacement and maintenance
- recruitment and supervision of staff
- initial and ongoing staff training
- working practices and reporting procedures.

WEBLINKS

Further information is available on the Food Standards Agency (FSA) website:

www.food.gov.uk

See *Food Hygiene – A Guide for Business*, *Food Law, Inspections and Your Business*, *Food Hygiene Legislation*.

NHS Choices, food safety information:

www.nhs.uk/Livewell/homehygiene

Chartered Institute of Environmental Health, food safety training:

www.cieh.org/training/food_safety.html

Highfield International, food safety training materials:

www.highfield.co.uk/products/sector/food-safety

All local authority websites

Allergen legislation

In December 2014, regulations (EU FIC) were introduced relating to allergens used as ingredients in food. Although there are others, 14 major allergens are identified in the legislation, and information about these must be given to the consumer, however food is sold. This could be done verbally or on menus, in a restaurant, or over the phone in a takeaway, for non-pre-packed foods, and must be on the labels of pre-packaged foods (usually emphasised in bold in the ingredients list). The information must be accurate and verifiable. Authorised food officers have powers to take action against breaches in this legislation.

14 allergens

There are 14 major allergens which need to be mentioned (either on a label or through provided information such as menus) when they are used as ingredients in a food. Here are the allergens, and some examples of where they can be found.

1 Celery
This includes celery stalks, leaves, seeds and the root called celeriac. You can find celery in celery salt, salads, some meat products, soups and stock cubes.

2 Cereals containing gluten
Wheat (such as spelt and Khorasan wheat/Kamut), rye, barley and oats is often found in foods containing flour, such as some types of baking powder, batter, breadcrumbs, bread, cakes, couscous, meat products, pasta, pastry, sauces, soups and fried foods which are dusted with flour.

3 Crustaceans
Crabs, lobster, prawns and scampi are crustaceans. Shrimp paste, often used in Thai and south-east Asian curries or salads, is an ingredient to look out for.

4 Eggs
Eggs are often found in cakes, some meat products, mayonnaise, mousses, pasta, quiche, sauces and pastries or foods brushed or glazed with egg.

5 Fish
You will find this in some fish sauces, pizzas, relishes, salad dressings, stock cubes and Worcestershire sauce.

6 Lupin
Yes, lupin is a flower, but it's also found in flour! Lupin flour and seeds can be used in some types of bread, pastries and even in pasta.

7 Milk
Milk is a common ingredient in butter, cheese, cream, milk powders and yoghurt. It can also be found in foods brushed or glazed with milk, and in powdered soups and sauces.

8 Molluscs
These include mussels, land snails, squid and whelks, but can also be commonly found in oyster sauce or as an ingredient in fish stews.

9 Mustard
Liquid mustard, mustard powder and mustard seeds fall into this category. This ingredient can also be found in breads, curries, marinades, meat products, salad dressings, sauces and soups.

10 Nuts
Not to be mistaken with peanuts (which are actually a legume and grow underground), this ingredient refers to nuts which grow on trees, like cashew nuts, almonds and hazelnuts. You can find nuts in breads, biscuits, crackers, desserts, nut powders (often used in Asian curries), stir-fried dishes, ice cream, marzipan (almond paste), nut oils and sauces.

11 Peanuts
Peanuts are actually a legume and grow underground, which is why it's sometimes called a groundnut. Peanuts are often used as an ingredient in biscuits, cakes, curries, desserts, sauces (such as satay sauce) as well as in groundnut oil and peanut flour.

12 Sesame seeds
These seeds can often be found in bread (sprinkled on hamburger buns for example), breadsticks, houmous, sesame oil and tahini. They are sometimes toasted and used in salads.

13 Soya
Often found in beancurd, edamame beans, miso paste, textured soya protein, soya flour or tofu, soya is a staple ingredient in oriental food. It can also be found in desserts, ice cream, meat products, sauces and vegetarian products.

14 Sulphur dioxide (sometimes known as sulphites)
This is an ingredient often used in dried fruit such as raisins, dried apricots and prunes. You might also find it in meat products, soft drinks, vegetables as well as in wine and beer. If you have asthma, you have a higher risk of developing a reaction to sulphur dioxide.

For more information, visit food.gov.uk/allergy or nhs.uk/conditions/allergies

Figure 3.1 The 14 major allergens (source: Food Standards Agency)

The 14 identified allergens can be seen in Figure 3.1.

Practical measures to ensure good practice and legal compliance are described on page 40.

WEBLINKS

A colourful allergens chart from the Food Standards Agency:

www.food.gov.uk/allergy

The following may also provide useful information:

www.food.gov.uk/allergen-resources

Environmental Health Officers (Environmental Health Practitioners)

Compliance with food safety legislation is enforced by local authorities through inspection by Environmental Health Officers (EHOs) (Environmental Health Practitioners – EHPs).

Enforcement officers may visit food premises as a matter of routine, as a follow-up when problems have been identified, or after a complaint. The frequency of visits depends on the type of business and food being handled, possible hazards within the business, the risk rating, and any previous problems or convictions. Generally, businesses posing a higher risk will be visited more frequently.

EHOs (EHPs) can enter a food business at any reasonable time without previous notice or appointment – usually, but not always, when the business is open. The main purpose of these inspections is to identify any possible risks, to assess the effectiveness of the business's own hazard controls, and to identify any non-compliance with regulations so that this can be monitored and corrected.

A **Hygiene Improvement Notice** will be served if the EHO (EHP) believes that a food business does not comply with regulations. The notice is served in writing and states what is wrong, why it is wrong, what needs to be done to put it right and the time-frame in which this must be completed (usually not less than 14 days and does not apply to cleaning). It is an offence if the identified work is not carried out in the specified time without prior agreement.

A **Hygiene Emergency Prohibition Notice** is served if the EHO (EHP) believes that there is an imminent risk to health from the business. Such risks would include serious issues such as sewage contamination, lack of water supply or rodent infestation. Serving this notice would mean immediate closure of the business or part of the business for three days, during which time the EHO (EHP) must apply to magistrates for a **Hygiene Emergency Prohibition Order** to keep the premises closed. Notices/orders must be displayed in a visible place on the premises. The owner of the business must apply for a certificate of satisfaction before they can reopen.

A **Hygiene Prohibition Order** prohibits a person such as the owner/manager from working in a food business.

Fines and penalties for non-compliance

Magistrates courts can impose fines of up to £5,000 per offence, a six-month prison sentence, or both.

For serious offences, such as knowingly selling food dangerous to health, magistrates could impose fines of up to £20,000. In a Crown Court unlimited fines can be imposed and/or two years' imprisonment.

WEBLINK

The *Industry Guide to Good Hygiene Practice* gives advice (in plain, easy-to-understand English) on how to comply with food safety law. While the guide has no legal force, food authorities must give the information contained therein due consideration when they enforce regulations. Printed copies are available from HMSO Publications Offices or guides can be downloaded at:

www.archive.food.gov.uk

➜ Food poisoning and its prevention

The main reason for food businesses adopting high standards of food safety is to prevent food poisoning and food-borne illness.

- **Food poisoning** is an acute intestinal illness that is the result of eating foods contaminated with pathogenic bacteria and/or their toxins. Food poisoning may also be caused by eating poisonous fish or plants, chemicals or metals. Symptoms of food poisoning may include diarrhoea, vomiting, nausea, fever, headache, dehydration and abdominal pain.
- **Food-borne illness** is a range of illnesses caused by pathogenic bacteria and/or their toxins, and also viruses, but in this case pathogens do not need to multiply in the food, they just need to get into the intestine where they invade cells and start to multiply. Only tiny amounts are needed and may be transmitted from person to person, in water or air, as well as through food. Poisonous mushrooms or fish may also be the cause. Symptoms are varied, and include severe abdominal pain, diarrhoea, vomiting, headaches, blurred vision, flu-like symptoms, septicaemia and miscarriage.

At-risk groups

Food poisoning/food-borne illness can be unpleasant for anyone, but for some the illnesses can be very serious or even fatal. Extra care with food safety must be observed when providing food for the following groups:

- babies and the very young
- elderly people
- pregnant women
- those with an impaired or reduced immune system
- those who are already unwell.

Contamination

Contamination of food can be a major hazard. A contaminant is anything that is present in food that should not be there. Food contaminants can range from the inconvenient or slightly unpleasant through to the dangerous and even fatal. It is essential to protect food from contamination and remove or destroy contaminants already present (e.g. possible pathogens in raw poultry).

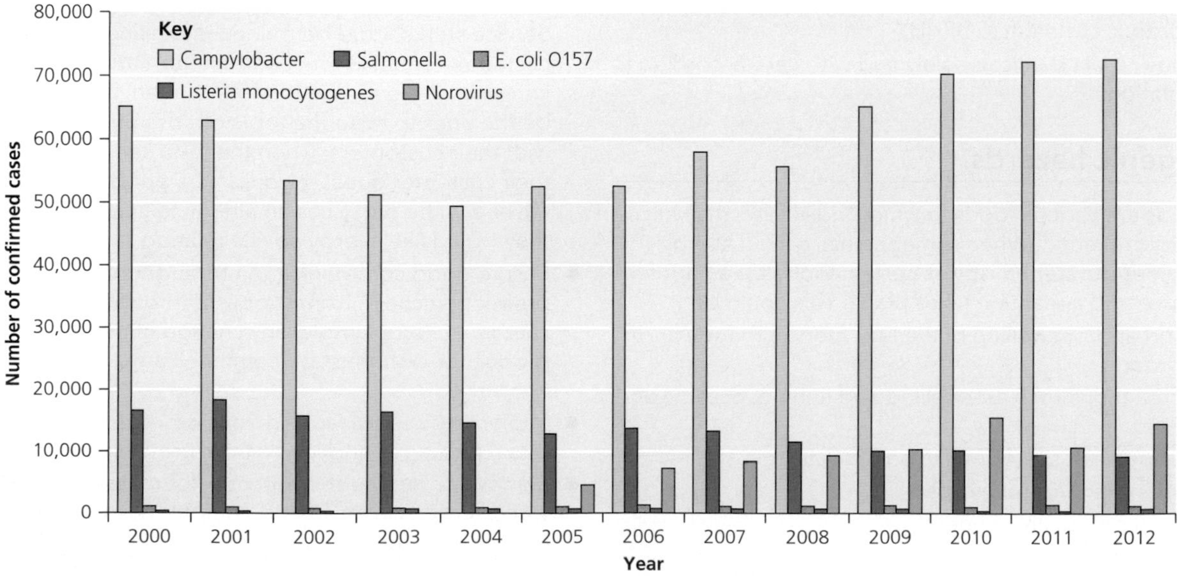

Figure 3.2 Confirmed cases of infectious intestinal disease in the UK, 2000–12 (with norovirus data from 2005)
Source: Food Standards Agency

Physical hazards

This includes physical objects such as glass, machine parts, paperclips, hair, fingernails, insects, packaging materials, coins, buttons, blue plasters and other physical items that can get into food. Some of these could well be harmful if eaten, but they are mostly objectionable and cause for customer complaint. Good staff training, including 'clean as you go', good storage procedures and general 'housekeeping', as well as the food safety management system, should help to prevent physical contamination.

Chemical hazards

Chemical hazards arise from chemicals such as disinfectants, pesticides, degreasers, agricultural chemicals and beer line cleaners. Residues of drugs, pesticides and fertilisers may be present in raw food. Pesticides sprayed on to fruit and vegetables just prior to harvesting may result in a toxic build-up. Chemicals can get into food by leakage, spillage, or other accidents during food processing or preparation.

Acid foods such as vinegar and acidic fruits should not be cooked or stored in equipment containing metals such as antimony, cadmium, lead, tin, zinc, aluminium or copper, unless the metal is intended for that specific purpose.

Chemical food poisoning can be prevented by:

- purchasing food from reliable sources, with good farming practices and suppliers with proper storage procedures
- using containers (especially metal containers) only for their intended use
- safe storage of kitchen chemicals well away from food
- accurate dilution of chemicals used in the kitchen
- not spraying chemicals such as sanitiser or fly spray around open food
- up-to-date, recorded training in the use of substances hazardous to health (COSHH)
- disposing of chemicals safely and with care according to regulations.

Allergenic hazards

Allergens are various foods to which individuals may have an allergic reaction. When someone has a food allergy, their immune system mistakes certain foods for a harmful substance and a reaction takes place. This could be:

- itching and/or swelling of the lips, mouth, tongue and/or throat
- skin reactions such as, swelling and itching, eczema and flushing
- diarrhoea, nausea, vomiting and bloating
- coughing and/or runny nose
- breathlessness and wheezing
- sore, itchy eyes.

There may also be symptoms such as extreme fatigue or arthritis symptoms.

Some food allergies result in an immediate, severe allergic reaction called **anaphylactic shock**, which is potentially fatal. This is often linked to peanuts and other nut or seed products. Symptoms can include dizziness, rapid pulse, a drop in blood pressure, and swelling of the airways and throat, making it difficult to breathe. This could result in loss of consciousness and can be fatal if left untreated.

Other food reactions cause symptoms that may take longer to develop – for example, gluten intolerance (coeliac disease).

Food intolerance is different from an allergy and does not involve the immune system, though people suffering from a food intolerance may still suffer illness or discomfort after eating certain foods.

Some establishments that provide foods for vulnerable groups such as young children completely remove certain allergenic foods like nuts from their menus.

It is important to provide completely accurate information to customers about ingredients and allergens in food (see above).

Allergenic food poisoning can be avoided by the following means.

- Provide full, useful menu and verbal information, as required by law.
- Ensure that everyone involved in producing and serving the food is well informed of the allergens there may be in each product/menu item (including in frying oils, sauces and garnishes). Records of this must be kept up to date. Can service staff easily check if a menu item contains specific allergens? A chart such as the one shown in Table 3.1 would enable staff to provide the correct information to customers.
- Provide good 'allergy training' for all staff. Kitchen staff must understand the importance of thorough hand washing before preparing food for an allergic customer. Service staff should be trained in dealing with specific customer requests for allergen information and in knowing where to find this information. They may also be the ones to raise the topic of possible allergies with their customers: when the food server greets their customer/guest it would be a good time to ask if anyone in the party has an allergy to certain items and if they would like allergy advice relating to the menu.
- Ensure good communication throughout the food production chain, from suppliers through to the customer. For example, any change of ingredient in a product or dish must be communicated to everyone concerned.
- Implement careful labelling and storage of foods, and retain packages and labels from pre-prepared items.
- Remove or reduce the potential for cross-contamination with allergens from shared equipment such as chopping boards, serving equipment or work surfaces. This includes having separate preparation areas for dealing with food for an allergic customer or use of special colour-coded equipment (see page 42).

Table 3.1 Example of an allergen information chart

	Egg	Fish	Lupin	Milk	Celery/ celeriac	Molluscs	Mustard	Peanuts	Sesame	Soya	Sulphite	Tree nuts	Wheat	Crustacean
Minestrone with Parmesan	✓			✓	✓		✓						✓	
Soupe de poisson with rouille and croutes	✓	✓			✓	✓	✓				✓		✓	✓
Celery and walnut soup with edamame beans				✓						✓		✓		

- Use alternative ingredients, such as vegetable oil instead of nut oil, at all times.
- Remove ingredients such as nuts from the menu completely.
- Have measures in place to deal with language barriers (between kitchen/service staff/customers) when providing allergen information.

Microbiological hazards

Contamination from micro-organisms includes pathogenic bacteria and the toxins they may produce, moulds, viruses or parasites. Microbiological contamination is of particular concern because the organisms are often not visible on the food. In the case of pathogenic bacteria, very large numbers can be present in food, certainly enough to cause food poisoning, but the food will smell, taste and look fine. High standards of food safety practices and awareness are needed by all food handlers to avoid contamination by micro-organisms, especially pathogens.

Contamination with pathogens can occur in many ways and particularly by:

- humans – from hands, poor personal hygiene or by coughing or sneezing on food
- people with illnesses or infections, or those who are 'carriers' of organisms
- inadequate or contaminated clothing worn by food handlers
- animals, insects, birds getting into the kitchen and spreading pathogens from droppings, hair, saliva or urine
- kitchen equipment – tea towels, dishcloths, knives, boards, bowls, etc.

The approaches below will help to avoid contamination:

- training for food handlers
- the highest standards of personal hygiene
- planned processes for dealing with raw foods
- planned and monitored storage, preparation, cooking and hot holding of all foods
- temperature control of food
- pest control
- effective cleaning and disinfection procedures.

All these measures are described in more detail later in this chapter.

Cross-contamination

Cross-contamination occurs when pathogenic bacteria or other contaminants are transferred from one place to another – for example, from contaminated food (usually raw food), surfaces or food handlers to ready-to-eat food. It is the cause of significant amounts of food poisoning and care must be taken to avoid it. Cross-contamination could be caused by:

- certain foods touching each other, such as raw and cooked meat
- raw meat or poultry dripping on to cooked ready-to-eat foods (for example, when frozen raw items are defrosting)
- soil from dirty vegetables coming into contact with high-risk foods
- dirty cloths, staff uniforms or equipment
- equipment such as chopping boards and knives used for raw then cooked food
- hands – touching raw then cooked food, not washing hands between different tasks
- pests spreading bacteria from their own bodies
- different people touching hand-contact surfaces such as refrigerator or cupboard doors.

To prevent the transfer of bacteria by cross-contamination, the following points should be observed:

- ensure food is obtained from reliable sources (traceability)
- handle foods as little as possible; when practicable, use tongs, ladles, palette knives, disposable plastic gloves, etc.

- ensure utensils and work surfaces are clean and sanitised
- use disposable cloths or kitchen paper, or use different colour-coded cloths for raw and cooked food areas
- take care to avoid any contamination when handling raw poultry, meat and fish
- wash raw fruits, salads and vegetables thoroughly
- clean methodically and frequently, in line with the cleaning schedule; 'clean as you go'
- unpack food delivery boxes away from open food
- protect food from contamination while it is cooling in the kitchen
- keep food covered and refrigerated as much as possible
- use colour-coded kitchen equipment (see below).

Colour-coded equipment

A variety of equipment is now available to help avoid cross-contamination, and can be identified by colour. The equipment used may include chopping boards, knife handles, food storage trays and bowls, food wrapping/packaging, cleaning equipment, cloths and staff uniforms. The most widely used of these are chopping boards; the *usual* colour coding of these is shown in Figure 3.3.

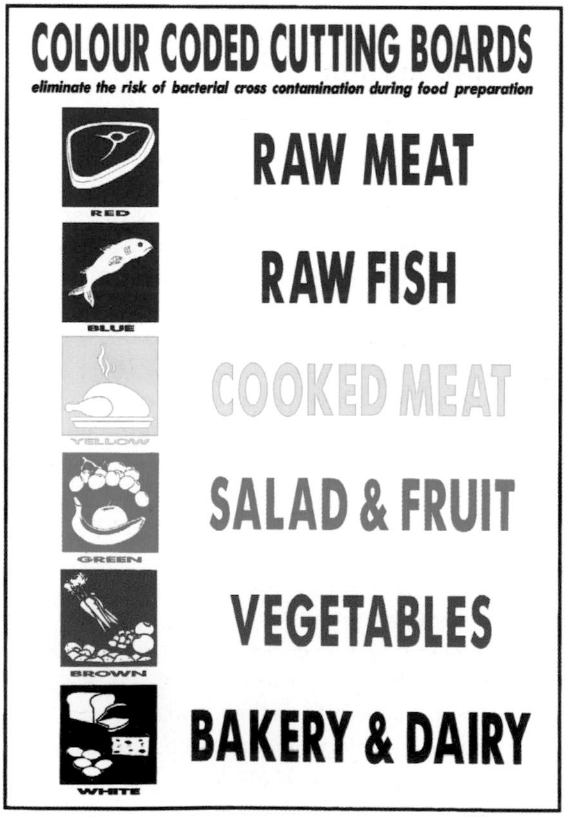

Figure 3.3 Chopping board colours (the board for bakery and dairy is actually white)

Further colour-coded equipment (usually purple; see Figure 3.4) is now available for use when preparing food for a customer with allergies. These must be thoroughly cleaned and disinfected before and after use, and preferably used in a separate area away from possible cross-contamination.

Figure 3.4 Purple board to use with allergen-free food

Pathogenic bacteria and poisonous foods

Bacteria are minute, single-celled organisms that can be seen only under a microscope. They are the most common cause of food poisoning and food-borne illness. Not all bacteria are harmful; some are essential to maintain good health (for example, in the digestive system), some are used in the manufacture of medicines and others in food production, as in the making of cheese and yoghurt. Others simply cause food to spoil, as in the souring of milk.

The harmful bacteria that cause food poisoning are referred to as pathogenic bacteria. These are dangerous once they get into food because they are not visible and the food may remain unchanged. It is not possible to completely eliminate pathogenic bacteria from food premises as they are found widely in the environment, including in raw foods, dirty vegetables, animal pests and humans. They can very easily be transferred on to hands, surfaces, cooked foods, equipment and cloths; this is called cross-contamination (see above). Bacteria may be carried from one place to another in the kitchen by 'vehicles of contamination' – for example, on hands or equipment.

The ways pathogens act

Some bacteria cause food poisoning by virtue of very large numbers of them multiplying in food then being eaten, entering the digestive system and infecting the body. Others can form spores; these are often referred to as 'a resistant resting phase of bacteria'. Spores can withstand high temperatures for long periods of time, and can also withstand disinfection and dehydration. Then, on return to favourable conditions, they germinate into normal bacteria again, which can then multiply.

Other bacteria produce toxins (poisons) outside their cells as they multiply in food or at the end of their life. These toxins make the food poisonous. Toxins in food are resistant to heat and can still cause illness, even if the food is heated to boiling point. Different toxins can be released by some pathogens as they multiply in the human body.

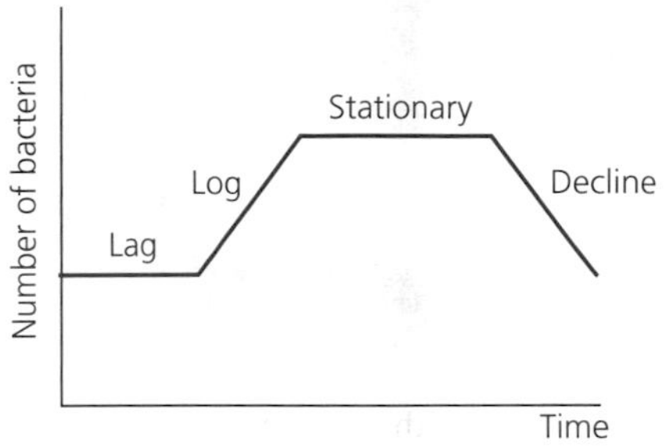

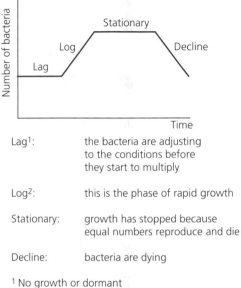

Lag[1]:	the bacteria are adjusting to the conditions before they start to multiply
Log[2]:	this is the phase of rapid growth
Stationary:	growth has stopped because equal numbers reproduce and die
Decline:	bacteria are dying

[1] No growth or dormant
[2] Abbreviation for logarithm, which is the means of using tables to calculate growth

Figure 3.5 How pathogens multiply

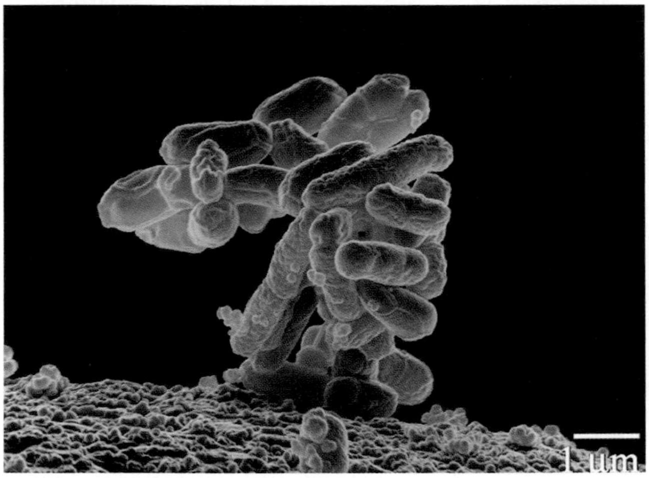

Figure 3.6 Bacteria multiplying

In the right conditions, bacteria multiply by dividing in two once every 10–20 minutes. This is called 'binary fission'. Therefore a few bacteria could multiply to 1,000 million in 10–12 hours – enough to cause illness.

For bacteria to multiply, they need the correct food (nutrients), moisture (water), temperature and time, as described below.

Food

Most foods can be easily contaminated by bacteria; those less likely to cause food poisoning are dry or have a high concentration of vinegar, sugar or salt, or are preserved in some way. Some foods support the multiplication of bacteria more than others when given the right conditions; these are referred to as *high-risk foods*. They are usually foods that are ready to eat, have a protein and moisture content, and will not always go through a cooking process that will destroy bacteria. High-risk foods include:

- stock, sauces, gravies, soups
- eggs and egg products
- meat and meat products (sausages, pâté/parfait, pies, cold meats, sandwiches)
- milk and milk products
- cooked rice
- all foods that are handled then have no further cooking
- all foods that are reheated.

Extra care must be taken to prevent these foods from being contaminated and being left in conditions where bacteria can multiply.

Moisture

Bacteria need water to support their life cycle and processes. The amount of water in food is referred to as 'a_w' (water activity). Most food contains some moisture, and a wide variety of foods contain enough water to support bacterial multiplication. Even dry foods such as dried pasta or rice will have water added to them in the cooking process, so once again will become vulnerable to bacterial growth. Some food preservation methods remove enough moisture to make the food safe for long periods, e.g. sundried tomatoes or food preserved with salt or sugar (osmosis).

Temperature

Food poisoning bacteria multiply most rapidly at human body temperature (37°C), but can multiply anywhere between temperatures of 5°C and 63°C. This is referred to as the danger zone. Warm kitchen temperatures provide ideal conditions for bacterial growth and food should be kept refrigerated wherever possible. Chilled and frozen food deliveries should be put into temperature-controlled storage within 15 minutes of delivery. Cold foods need to be stored at temperatures below 5°C.

Bacteria are not killed by cold, although they multiply only slowly at very low temperatures; at freezer temperatures they will lie dormant for long periods. Once food is removed from cold storage, bacteria will start to multiply again as the temperature rises.

Foods that have been taken out of the refrigerator, kept in a warm kitchen and returned to the refrigerator for later use could be contaminated with a higher level of pathogenic bacteria. Food that has been taken from the freezer and defrosted will be susceptible to bacterial growth as the temperature rises, so food should never be re-frozen once it has defrosted.

Remember that, when cooking, food must be heated to a sufficiently high temperature and for the required amount of time, to be sure of safe food; any reheating of food must be done very thoroughly, to a minimum of 75°C. Water that is just warm is not suitable for washing crockery, cutlery or equipment as bacteria will not be destroyed. Hot water must be used for dish-washing or cleaning equipment and, where possible, use a dishwasher that will clean items thoroughly and disinfect them.

Boiling water will kill bacteria in a few seconds, but to destroy toxins prolonged boiling is needed. Spores are almost impossible to kill with normal cooking temperatures: long cooking times and/or very high temperatures are needed. Food canning processes use 'botulinum cook', which is high-heat cooking at 121°C for three minutes, or a tested alternative time/temperature combination, to kill any spores that may be present.

Different organisms prefer slightly different temperature ranges for growth (multiplication) – for example, *Clostridium perfringens* grows best at 45°C, while *Listeria monocytogenes* grows most efficiently at 30°C, but can still multiply right down at refrigerator temperatures.

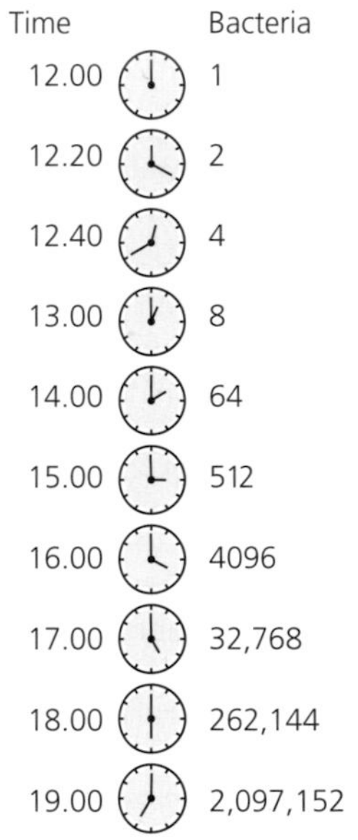
Time
Bacteria
12.00
1
12.20
2
12.40
4
13.00
8
14.00
64
15.00
512
16.00
4096
17.00
32,768
18.00
262,144
19.00
2,097,152

Figure 3.7 Under ideal conditions, bacteria can multiply by dividing into two every 20 minutes; in this way, a single bacterium could increase to 2,097,152 within 7 hours

Time

As explained above, given the conditions they need, bacteria can divide by binary fission every 10–20 minutes. Therefore foods left at ambient temperatures could contain large numbers of harmful bacteria within a few hours. Time is the element of bacterial growth that the food handler is most able to control. Make sure that food spends as little time as possible at kitchen temperatures, keep it cold in a refrigerator or hot, not in between. When heating or cooking food, take it through 'danger zone temperatures' as quickly as possible (see Figure 3.8); this may mean cooking in smaller pans or in smaller batches. Do not hold food on display for long periods without proper temperature control.

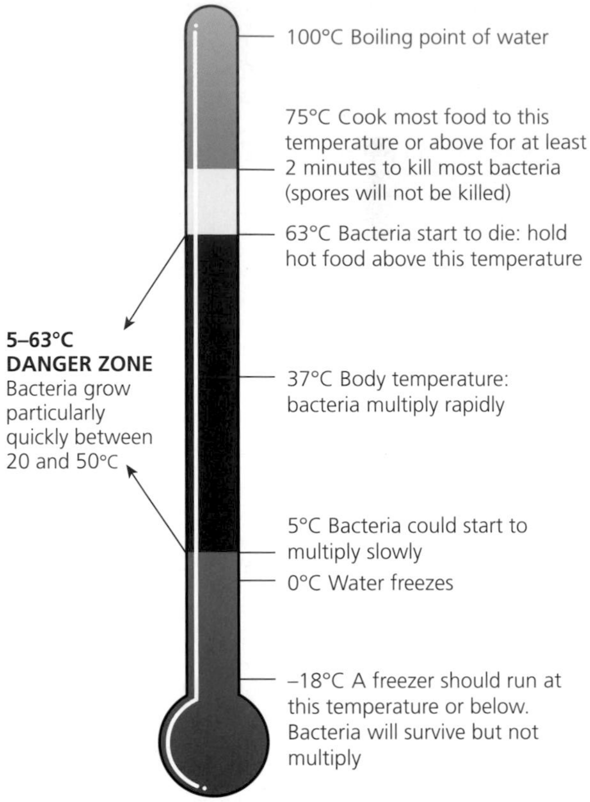

Figure 3.8 'Danger zone' thermometer

In addition to the four requirements described above, two further conditions are needed for bacteria to multiply.

- **Oxygen requirement:** some bacteria need oxygen in order to multiply; this group of bacteria are referred to as aerobes. Some can multiply only where there is no oxygen; these are called anaerobes. (Most bacteria can multiply with or without oxygen; these are called facultative anaerobes.)
- **pH:** this is a measure of how acid or alkaline a food or liquid may be. The scale runs from 1.0 to 14.0. Acid foods are below 7.0 on the scale, 7.0 is neutral and above 7.0 up to 14.0 is alkaline. Bacteria multiply best around a neutral pH and most bacteria cannot multiply at a pH below 4.0 or above 8.0, so foods such as citrus fruits would not support bacterial multiplication.

A closer look at some of the main organisms causing illness

The major food poisoning bacteria are listed and described in Table 3.2.

Different organisms from those described above cause food-borne illness. These do not multiply in food, but use food to get into the human gut, where they then multiply and cause a range of illnesses, some of them very serious. They include those described in more detail in Table 3.2.

Some of these are viruses. Viruses are even smaller than bacteria and can be seen only with a powerful microscope.

They multiply on living cells, not on food, though they may be transferred into the body on food or drinks, and may live for a short time on hard surfaces such as kitchen equipment. Viruses can be air- and water-borne, and are easily passed from person to person. Viruses are sometimes associated with shellfish that come from contaminated water.

Table 3.2 Major food poisoning bacteria

Major food poisoning pathogens	Sources of bacteria	Preferred temperature for growth	Illness onset time	Symptoms	Can it form spores?
Salmonella This used to be the main cause of food poisoning in the UK (now *campylobacter*). There are many different types, but most problems are caused by *Salmonella typhyimurium* and *Salmonella enteriditis*. These release toxins in intestines as they expire. Problems with food poisoning were reduced by measures taken to control salmonella in chickens and in eggs. Salmonella poisoning can also be passed on through human carriers (someone carrying salmonella but not showing any signs of illness).	Raw meat/poultry, raw egg, untreated milk and shellfish Intestines and excreta of humans and animals Sewage/untreated water Pests (e.g. rodents, terrapins, insects and birds) as well as domestic pets	7–45°C	12–36 hours	Stomach pain, diarrhoea, vomiting, fever (1–7 days)	No
Clostridium perfringens Food poisoning incidents from this organism have occurred when large amounts of meat have been brought up to cooking temperatures slowly then allowed to cool slowly for later use, or if meat does not get hot in the centre. Poultry, where the cavity has been stuffed, has also caused problems because the middle does not get hot enough to kill the bacteria. All these examples can lead to the formation of spores (see above).	Animal and human intestines and excreta Soil and sewage Insects Raw meat and poultry Unwashed vegetables and salads	15–50°C	12–18 hours	Stomach pain and diarrhoea (12–48 hours) Vomiting is rare	Yes
Staphylococcus aureus Produces a toxin in food; is heat-resistant and very difficult to destroy. To avoid food poisoning from this organism, food handlers need to maintain very high standards of personal hygiene.	Humans – mouth, nose, throat, hair, scalp, skin, boils, spots, cuts, burns, etc.	7–45°C	1–7 hours	Stomach pain and vomiting, flu-like symptoms, maybe some diarrhoea, lowered body temperatures (6–24 hours)	No
Clostridium botulinum A spore-forming organism, also producing toxins, but fortunately fairly rare in the UK. Symptoms can be very serious, even fatal. It is an anaerobe, so is of concern to canning industries and where food is vacuum packed.	Soil, fish intestines, dirty vegetables and some animals	7–48°C	2 hours–8 days (usually 12–36 hours)	Difficulty with speech, breathing and swallowing Double vision Nerve paralysis Death	Yes
Bacillus cereus Produces spores and two different types of toxin. One toxin is produced in food as the organisms multiply or expire, and the other in the human intestine as the organisms expire. *Bacillus cereus* is a facultative anaerobe and is more difficult to destroy when fats and oils are present. It is often associated with cooking rice in large quantities, cooling it too slowly and then reheating. The spores are not destroyed and further bacterial multiplication can then take place.	Cereal crops, especially rice, spices, dust and soil (from unwashed vegetables)	3–40°C	1–5 hours 8–16 hours	Vomiting, abdominal pain, maybe some diarrhoea (12–24 hours) Stomach pain, diarrhoea, some vomiting (1–2 days)	Yes

Table 3.3 Micro-organisms that cause food-borne illness

Bacteria or virus	Sources	Preferred temperature for growth	Illness onset time	Symptoms	Can it form spores?
Campylobacter jujuni This now causes more food-related illness than any other organism. One of the reasons is the increase in consumption of fresh chicken, which is a significant source of this organism.	Raw poultry/meat, untreated milk or water, sewage, pets and pests, birds and insects	28–46°C	2–5 days	Headache, fever, bloody diarrhoea, abdominal pain (mimics appendicitis)	No
E. coli 0157VTEC There are many strains of E. coli, but significant problems are caused by *E. coli 0157VTEC*. Symptoms can be very serious; it can even be fatal.	Intestines and excreta of cattle and humans Untreated water and sewage Untreated milk Raw meat, under-cooked mince Unwashed salad items and dirty vegetables	4–45°C	1–8 days (usually 3–4 days)	Stomach pain, fever, bloody diarrhoea, nausea Has caused kidney failure and death	No
Listeria monocytogenes This organism is of concern because it can multiply (very slowly) at fridge temperatures, i.e. below 5°C. Poisoning from this organism can be extremely serious.	Pâté, soft cheeses made from unpasteurised milk, raw vegetables and prepared salads Cook-chill meals	0–45°C	1 day–3 months	Meningitis, septicaemia, flu-like symptoms, stillbirths	No
Norovirus An air-borne virus, widely present in the environment and highly contagious. Does not grow in food – viruses grow only in living cells.	Passed from person to person Can survive on surfaces, equipment and cloths for several hours	N/A	24–48 hours	Severe vomiting and diarrhoea	No
Typhoid/paratyphoid People who have suffered from this can become long-term carriers, which means they could pass the organism on to others through food (food handlers need six negative faecal samples before returning to work after illness).	Sewage, untreated water Also dirty fruit/vegetables	N/A	8–14 days	Fever, nausea, enlarged spleen, red spots on abdomen Severe diarrhoea Some fatalities	No
Shigella sonni *Shigella flexneri* Cause dysentery	Infected carriers, sewage, water supplies, contaminated food, shellfish (faecal/oral routes)	N/A	12 hours–7 days (usually 1–3 days)	Bloody diarrhoea with mucus Fever, abdominal pain, nausea, vomiting	No
Hepatitis A This is a viral liver illness often contracted due to contamination by a food handler with the virus.	Carriers, blood, urine, faeces Sewage, untreated water Shellfish Contaminated salads, dirty vegetables	N/A	15–50 days	Nausea, vomiting, abdominal pain Jaundice	No

As shown in Tables 3.2 and 3.3, food-poisoning bacteria live in:

- the soil
- humans – intestines, nose, throat, saliva, skin, cuts, burns, hair, scalp, spots, cuts and burns
- animals, rodents, domestic pets, insects and birds – intestines, skin, fur, and so on
- kitchen refuse.

To prevent food poisoning, everyone concerned with food must:

- prevent bacteria from multiplying
- prevent bacteria from contaminating other areas
- destroy harmful bacteria.

This means that harmful bacteria must be isolated, the chain of infection broken and conditions favourable to their growth eliminated. It is also necessary to control the harmful bacteria being brought in to premises or getting on to food. This is achieved by high standards of hygiene of personnel, premises, equipment and food handling (see later in this chapter).

Poisoning from fish, vegetable and plant items

- **Scombrotoxic fish poisoning (SFP):** caused by contaminated fish of the *Scombroid* family (including tuna, mackerel, herring, marlin and sardines). The poison builds in the fish, especially in storage above 4°C. It is a chemical intoxication and symptoms occur within ten minutes to three hours after eating. Symptoms include, rash on the face/neck/chest, flushing, sweating, nausea, vomiting, diarrhoea, abdominal cramps, headache, dizziness, palpitations and a sensation of burning in the mouth. Symptoms usually disappear within 12 hours. Although most cases are not serious enough for hospital attention, some are very severe, and urgent medical attention would then be necessary and antihistamine drugs may be used. These toxins are very heat resistant and not affected by normal cooking. Scombrotoxins are thought to be responsible for up to 70 per cent of food poisoning from fish in the UK.
- **Paralytic fish poisoning:** this very dangerous form of fish poisoning occurs when some bivalve shellfish (e.g. mussels) feed on poisonous plankton and the poison can survive normal cooking temperatures. Symptoms may be nausea, vomiting, lowered temperature, diarrhoea, and also a numbness of the mouth, neck and arms, which can lead to paralysis and possibly death within 2–12 hours.
- Certain **plants** are poisonous, such as some fungi, rhubarb leaves, daffodil bulbs and the parts of potatoes that are exposed to the sun above the surface of the soil.
- **Red kidney beans (black kidney beans):** every year there are reported cases of mild poisoning from the toxin in red kidney beans (*haemagglutin*). To prevent poisoning, the beans need to be boiled rapidly for ten minutes or more, to kill the toxin; then the heat can be reduced to finish the cooking process. The symptoms of this poisoning include nausea, vomiting, pain and diarrhoea, but these usually disappear within a few hours. Canned beans are safe to use without further cooking because they have already been heated to high temperatures.
- **Mycotoxins:** as they grow, some moulds can produce toxins – these are called mycotoxins and can cause serious illness as well as having been linked with cancers. They are invisibly present in mouldy food over a much wider area than the visible mould. Mycotoxin-producing moulds can tolerate a wide range of acid/alkaline conditions, low water activity and temperature ranges from -6 to 35°C. They can withstand very high temperatures. The foods most frequently affected are cereal crops and products, nuts, and fruit products such as juices, dried fruit and jams.
- **Food parasites:** a variety of parasites such as worms, eggs, lice and grubs can live on plants or animals, from where they get their food. They can usually be destroyed by thorough cooking or very high-temperature food preservation methods. In most cases they will also be killed by freezing.

➜ Food spoilage and food preservation

From the time of slaughter, harvest, manufacture or packaging, items intended for consumption will start to deteriorate so many need to be preserved in some way to keep them in an edible condition. Spoilage is caused in a number of ways, and especially by micro-organisms such as moulds, yeasts and bacteria occurring naturally in the atmosphere.

There are two main types of spoilage:

1. **microbial:** micro-organisms attack the food leading to spoilage and, in some cases, food poisoning
2. **chemical:** over-ripening, breakdown of protein in meat leading to oxidation and rancidity.

Microbial spoilage

Moulds

These are simple plants that appear like whiskers or fur on foods, particularly sweet foods, meat and cheese. To grow, they require warmth, air, moisture, darkness and food; they are killed by heat and sunlight. Moulds can grow where there is too little moisture for yeasts and bacteria to grow, and will be found on jams, fruit, vegetables and pickles.

There are some types of moulds that are dangerous to health (such as mycotoxins) so unless the mould is meant to be there, such as in blue cheese, it is best not to use them.

Correct storage in a dry cold store prevents moulds from forming, although some moulds can still grow even at fridge temperatures.

Not all moulds are destructive. Some are used to flavour cheese (e.g. Stilton, Roquefort) or to produce antibiotics (penicillin, streptomycin).

Yeasts

These are single-cell plants or organisms, larger than bacteria, that grow on foods containing moisture and sugar. Foods containing only a small percentage of sugar and a large percentage of liquid, such as fruit juices and syrups, are liable to ferment because of yeasts. Although they seldom cause disease, yeasts do increase food spoilage; food should be kept under refrigeration to avoid spoilage by yeasts. Yeasts are also destroyed by heat.

Bacteria

As well as the pathogenic bacteria already discussed, bacteria can spoil food by attacking it, leaving waste products, or by producing toxins in the food. Their growth is checked by refrigeration and they are killed by heat.

Chemical spoilage (enzymes)

Food spoilage can occur due to chemical substances called enzymes, produced by living cells. Fruits are ripened by the action of enzymes; they do not remain edible indefinitely because other enzymes cause the fruit to become over-ripe and spoil.

When meat and game are hung they become tender; this is caused by enzymes present in the meat or by further injected hormones. To prevent enzyme activity going too far, foods must be refrigerated or heated to a temperature high enough to destroy the enzymes. Acid also retards the enzyme action.

Methods of preservation

In order to preserve food, it is important to kill the micro-organisms that cause the spoilage and then store the food in an environment where it cannot be re-contaminated, or where deterioration is slowed down or stopped.

Foods may be preserved by the methods described below.

Drying or dehydration

Water is needed by micro-organisms to survive and reproduce. Therefore, by removing the water in foods below a critical value, spoilage is reduced. In the past this was done by drying foods in the sun, but today dehydration equipment and kilns are used.

If dried and kept dry, food keeps indefinitely. Food preserved by this method occupies less space than food preserved by other methods. Dried foods are lighter so are easily transported and stored.

Milk is dried either by the roller or spray process. With the spray process the milk is sent through a fine jet as a spray into hot air, the water evaporates and the powder drops down, giving a very acceptable dried product. As the roller method produces an inferior product it has fallen from use.

Eggs are dried in similar ways to milk, and used mainly in the bakery trade. The nutritional value is mostly unchanged but they no longer have the same aerating properties. However, dried egg white does aerate well after reconstitution and is frequently used for meringue. Although pasteurised before drying, dried egg must be refrigerated once reconstituted and used quickly.

Other foods that are preserved by drying include:

- potatoes (cooked, mashed and then dried)
- tomatoes (often sundried or semi-dried and stored in olive oil)
- pulses (beans, peas and lentils) and many other vegetables
- grapes (dried grapes become sultanas, currants or raisins)
- apples (peeled and cut into rings or diced)
- many other fruits, including mango, apricots, figs and plums
- herbs and spices, ground, powdered or whole
- coffee
- meat and fish.

Freeze drying

This is a process of dehydration whereby food can be stored at ambient temperatures yet, when soaked in water, regains its original size, flavour and aroma. It can be applied to every kind of food. The food is frozen in a cabinet, the air is pumped out and the ice vaporised.

When processed in this way, food does not lose a great deal of its bulk, but is very much lighter in weight. Freeze-dried herbs and spices retain better colour and flavour.

Chilling and freezing

At low temperatures micro-organism growth is much slower. Therefore, refrigeration is used not to kill micro-organisms but to slow down or stop their multiplication and their enzyme action, prolonging the life of food. Microbial and biochemical changes that affect the flavour, texture, colour and nutritional value of foods still take place, and, eventually, the food will deteriorate.

Refrigerators are kept at a temperature of 1–4°C. The lower the temperature within the range 1°C to 5°C, the slower the growth of micro-organisms and the biochemical changes that create food poisoning hazards.

It is important to remember that the food must not be contaminated before chilling.

Meat that is chilled is kept at a temperature just above freezing point and will keep for up to one month; if the atmosphere is controlled with carbon dioxide the time can be extended to ten weeks.

Freezers should run at -18°C or slightly below.

If food is frozen slowly, large uneven crystals are formed in the cells, which damage the texture of food and cause excessive water loss. Quick freezing is more satisfactory because small ice crystals are formed in the cells of food; so, on thawing, the goodness and flavour are retained in the cells.

A very wide variety of foods are frozen, either cooked or in an uncooked state. Some examples are listed below.

- **Cooked foods:** whole cooked meals, braised meat, pastry and pastry goods, cakes and sponges, bread, ice cream and desserts, sauces, soups.
- **Raw foods:** fish, poultry, peas, French beans, broad beans, spinach, sprouts, broccoli, soft fruit, dough for bread/pizza.
- **Raw meat:** a wide range of meat joints and meat products can be frozen successfully, or purchased frozen and stored. Imported lamb carcasses are frozen; beef carcasses are not usually frozen because, owing to their size, and the time they take to freeze, large ice crystals form, which, when thawed, affect the texture of the meat. Frozen meat must be thawed before it is cooked unless it is a very small, thin item such as a thin burger.

Preservation by heating

Cooking is the most common 'heat treatment' for food. Cooking until the core of the food reaches 75°C for 2 minutes will kill most pathogens, but not spores and toxins. Cooked food does generally keep for longer than its raw equivalents. However, treat cooked items with care as, once cooked, foods may then be in the high-risk category.

The following methods use heat to preserve food for longer.

Canning and bottling

Foods are sealed in airtight bottles or cans, often with a liquid or sauce, and heated at a high enough temperature for a sufficient time to destroy harmful organisms, toxins and spores, typically 121°C for 3 minutes. This is referred to as botulinum cook and, without it, anaerobic bacteria, especially *Clostridium botulinum*, could thrive inside a can.

Spoilage does not occur because micro-organisms are killed in the heating process and no further organisms can gain access to the sealed food.

Almost any type of food can be canned or bottled, but texture and flavour may be altered.

Slightly dented cans that do not leak are safe to use, but blown cans – that is, those with bulges at either end – must not be used.

A disadvantage of canning is that, due to the heat processing, a proportion of the vitamin C and B1 (thiamin) may be lost. The quality and texture of the food may also be impaired.

Pasteurisation

Pasteurisation is a mild heat treatment, using temperatures similar to cooking temperatures, but for a very short time. It is mainly used with milk, cream and fruit juices, as well as liquid egg and wine.

The product is heated to at least 72°C for a minimum of 15 seconds and then cooled rapidly. These temperatures will kill most pathogens, bringing them to a 'safe level'. Toxins and spores will not be killed. In milk, more than 99 per cent of the micro-organisms are killed and the rest are inactivated due to the rapid cooling and refrigerated conditions the produce is held in.

The taste of the product remains mostly unchanged, because the temperatures reached are not very high and are maintained for only a short period of time. However, vitamin content is reduced by about 25 per cent.

Because relatively low temperatures are used, milk that has been pasteurised will spoil more quickly than milk preserved by some other methods and must be kept at refrigerator temperatures.

Unpasteurised milk products can legally be sold in the UK as long as they are clearly labelled as such.

Sterilisation

Sterilisation destroys all micro-organisms. The process involves heating to 100°C for 15–30 minutes by applying steam and pressure. The product is then packed in sterile containers or bottles. Sterilisation employs much higher temperatures than pasteurisation, for a longer period of time. As a result, the product has a longer shelf life than its pasteurised counterpart and the containers can be stored at ambient temperatures rather than chilled until opened.

Because very high temperatures are used over a relatively long time, some caramelisation occurs, taste is altered and vitamin content is significantly reduced.

Sterilisation is used for milk, and liquid or semi-liquid food such as soup, stock and sauces sold in pouches.

UHT

UHT (ultra heat treated) milk and cream is heated rapidly under pressure to around 135°C for one or two seconds, then chilled rapidly before storing in sterile airtight cartons. There is a change in flavour but not as much as with sterilisation. UHT milk and other items do not need refrigerated storage until they have been opened and have a long shelf life.

Salting and smoking

Salting

Micro-organisms cannot grow in high concentrations of salt. The salting process removes water from the food by osmosis, making a hostile environment for micro-organisms. This method is used mainly to preserve meat and fish.

Meats that are salted or 'pickled' in a salt solution (brine) include brisket, ox tongues and legs of pork. Salted meat lasts longer than unsalted meat but still needs refrigeration.

Fish are usually smoked and sometimes coloured as well as being salted. This includes salmon, trout, haddock and herring. The amount of salting varies for different fish.

Smoking

Smoking is mainly used to provide a popular product with an enhanced flavour and colour. Smoking has only limited preservation effects, mainly affecting the surface of the product. Smoking does not provide for long-term storage.

There are two types: hot smoking and cold smoking. Cold smoking flavours but does not cook the product. It is usually carried out at a temperature of between 10°C and 29°C. Some cold smoked products are eaten without further cooking; these include salmon, trout, beef fillet, halibut, eel and cod roe. Others, such as haddock, herring (kippers) and cod fillets, require further cooking.

Hot smoked products, after salting or brining, are first cold smoked to partially dry them out and to impart a smoked flavour. In the case of fish the temperature is then raised to 93–104°C and the fish are then cooked. Care must be taken during the initial cold smoking to see that the temperature does not exceed 26°C as this will harden the outside and stop further smoke penetration.

Preservation by sugar

A high concentration of sugar inhibits the growth of moulds, yeasts and bacteria. This method of preservation is applied to fruits in a variety of forms, with varying concentrations of sugar: jams, marmalades, jellies, candied, glacé and crystallised.

Preservation by acids

The level of acidity or alkalinity of a food is measured by its pH value. The pH can range from 1 to 14, with pH7 denoting neutral (neither acid nor alkaline).

Most micro-organisms grow best at near neutral pH. Bacteria (particularly harmful ones) are less acid-tolerant than fungi, and no bacteria will grow at a pH of less than 3.5. Spoilage of high-acid foods, such as fruit, is usually caused by yeasts and moulds. Meat and fish are more susceptible to bacterial spoilage since their pH is closer to neutral.

The pH may be lowered so that the food becomes too acidic (less than pH1.5) for any micro-organisms to grow, for example by pickling in vinegar. Pickled foods include gherkins, capers, onions, walnuts, red cabbage and chutneys.

Preservation by chemicals

A number of preservation chemicals in certain foods, such as sausages, meats and jams, are permitted by law, but their use is strictly controlled. (Campden preserving tablets can be used for domestic fruit bottling.)

Some of the more popular ones are:

- **sulphur dioxide and sulphites** – dried fruit and vegetables, sausages, fruit-based dairy products, cider, beer and wine, juices and vinegars
- **sorbic acid** – soft drinks, fruit yoghurt, processed cheese
- **sodium and potassium nitrite/nitrate** – bacon, ham, cured meats, corned beef and some cheeses.

Be aware of their presence so you can give required information to customers. For example, sulphites are now named on the EU list of allergens.

Irradiation

Foods are exposed to ionising radiation, which transfers some of its energy as it passes through the food, killing the pathogenic bacteria, or, at lower doses the spoilage bacteria, which cause food to rot. Ionising radiation is electromagnetic, like radio waves. It is similar to ultraviolet radiation but has a higher frequency and much greater energy. This is sufficient to protect food effectively, but not enough to make it radioactive. This method is popular in some areas of the world such as for meat products in the USA.

Only a limited number of countries allow irradiation of food or the import of irradiated food. Across the EU countries, irradiation of food and the importing of irradiated food are *very* strictly limited and any food that has been irradiated must be labelled as 'irradiated' or 'treated with ionising radiation'.

Preservation by gas storage

Gas storage is used in conjunction with refrigeration to preserve meat, eggs and fruit. Varying the gas composition surrounding the food increases the length of time for which it can be stored.

Vacuum packaging

Vacuum packaging of food will preserve it a little longer but most fresh foods will still need to be refrigerated or frozen. However, provided that the vacuum packing has been completed in hygienic conditions, especially keeping raw and cooked foods apart, this will protect food from cross-contamination.

Modified atmosphere packaging

Modified atmosphere packaging (MAP) can extend the shelf life of many fresh foods up to three times the normal levels. The method involves replacing the normal atmosphere within food packages with specific gases or mixtures of gases. This inhibits the growth of pathogenic bacteria and moulds, and extends the shelf life of chilled and certain ambient food products, while maintaining their appearance.

It is widely used for meats, salad items and prepared fruit. MAP is particularly successful with bakery products, where elevated CO_2 content permits high relative humidity with negligible mould growth.

The gas mixtures used vary according to the product being packaged.

Chefs employed in large food production operations and those employed as development chefs use MAP to aid food preparation and quality. There are frequent new developments as the food industries become more involved in using gases to aid preservation.

WEBLINKS

Nutritional requirements:

www.nutrition.org.uk/nutritionscience

Nutrition Society:

www.nutritionsociety.org

Education Department, Unilever Ltd:

www.unilever.co.uk

For further information on methods of preservation refer to the following sources.

Diet and Nutrition: A Guide for Students and Practitioners (HMSO).

Food (Control of Irradiation) Regulations 1990 (HMSO).

Gaman, P.M. and Sherrington, K.B. (1996) *The Science of Food*. Pergamon.

Guidelines on Pre-cooked Chilled Foods (HMSO).

Kilgour, O.F.G. (1976) *An Introduction to Science for Catering and Homecraft Students*. Heinemann.

Manual of Nutrition (HMSO).

McCance and Widdowson's The Composition of Foods (HMSO).

→ Keeping food safe

Methods and procedures for controlling food safety

Food delivered to food businesses will be taken through a number of stages before it reaches the customer. Careful control at each stage – known as critical control points (see page 65) – is essential to keep food safe and wholesome.

Food deliveries and storage

It is essential that correct storage is in place and procedures fully understood by kitchen staff. Full documentation needs to be completed for all deliveries, in line with the food safety management system. This will ensure that food is stored correctly and will be available for inspection by EHOs (EHPs) and, if necessary, as part of 'due diligence' (see page 68). Only approved suppliers should be used, who can assure that food is delivered in suitable packaging, properly date coded and at the correct temperature.

- All deliveries should be checked then moved to the appropriate storage area as soon as possible, and chilled/frozen food within 15 minutes of delivery.
- Use a food probe to check the temperature of food deliveries – chilled food should be below 5°C (reject it if above 8°C), frozen foods should be at or below -18°C (reject if above -15°C).
- Many suppliers will supply a printout of temperatures at which food was delivered (save these printouts in kitchen records, they could form an important part of due diligence).
- Dry goods should be in undamaged packaging, well within best before dates, completely dry and in perfect condition on delivery.
- Remove food items from outer boxes before putting into the refrigerator, freezer or dry store. Remove outer packaging carefully, checking for any pests that may have found their way into it. Avoid any possibility of physical contamination, such as staples or string getting into food.
- Segregate any unfit food from other food until it is thrown away or collected by the supplier. This is to avoid any possible contamination of other foods.

Table 3.4 Food storage guidelines

Food	Where to store and at what temperature	How to store	Other storage points to consider
Raw meat and poultry	In refrigerators just for meat and poultry storage, running at temperatures between 1°C and 4°C (butchers' fridges –1 to 1°C) If necessary, store in a multi-use refrigerator, running at 1–4°C	Place meat on trays, cover well with clingfilm/plastic wrap, and label If multi-use, place at the bottom of the refrigerator well away from other items that could be contaminated	
Fish	A specific fish refrigerator is preferable (running at 1°C) If necessary store fish in a multi-use refrigerator at 1–4°C	Remove fresh fish from ice containers or boxes and place on trays, cover well with clingfilm and label If multi-use place at the bottom of the refrigerator well away from other items	Odours from fish can permeate other items, such as milk or eggs

Food	Where to store and at what temperature	How to store	Other storage points to consider
Pasteurised milk and cream, eggs and cheese	In a refrigerator running at 1 to 4°C	Store in their original containers	Eggs should be stored at a constant temperature and a refrigerator is the best place to store them Prevent eggs from touching other items in the refrigerator and avoid using cracked or broken eggs
Sterilised or UHT milk	Dry store	Follow the storage instructions on the label, but once open treat as fresh milk	
Frozen foods	Freezer running at -18°C or below	Make sure that food is wrapped or packaged Separate raw foods from ready-to-eat foods in the freezer and never allow food to be re-frozen once it has defrosted	In a specific ice cream freezer, ice cream can be kept at -12°C or below for up to one week before use See below for instructions on defrosting
Fruit, vegetables and salad items	A cool, well-ventilated storeroom for sacks of potatoes, root vegetables and some fruit A specific refrigerator running at 8–10°C for salad items, green vegetables, soft fruit and tropical fruit, however, other foods such as dairy products, would not be suitable for storage at this temperature and would have to be stored separately	Storage conditions will vary according to type	
Canned products	Dry store area	Once opened, transfer any unused canned food to a clean bowl, cover and label it with the content description and the date, and store in the refrigerator for up to two days	Rotation of stock is essential Canned food will carry best before dates and it is not advisable to use after this 'Blown' swollen cans must never be used, and do not use badly dented or rusty cans
Cooked foods (ready-to-eat foods such as pies, pâté, cream cakes, desserts and savoury flans)	Refrigerate at 1–4°C, where possible in a refrigerator used only for high-risk items	For specific storage instructions see the labelling on the individual items, but generally store foods carefully, wrapped and labelled Use within the use-by date If a multi-use refrigerator needs to be used, store well away from and above raw foods to avoid any cross-contamination	Cooked foods are usually high-risk foods, so correct storage is essential

Multi-use refrigerators

If food needs to be stored in multi-use refrigerators or cold-rooms it is absolutely essential that all staff know the correct procedures to store the food and this should become part of ongoing training. Posters and charts near the refrigerator may help. Ensure that the refrigerator is running at 1 to 4°C (check/monitor and record at least once each day).

- Store raw foods such as meat, poultry and fish at the bottom of the fridge in suitable deep containers to catch any spillage; cover with clingfilm and label with the commodity name and the date; do not allow any other foods to touch these raw foods.
- Store other items above raw foods – again they should be covered and labelled; keep high-risk foods well away from raw foods.
- Never overload the refrigerator – to operate properly, cold air must be able to circulate between items.
- Wrap strong-smelling foods very well as the smell (and taste) can transfer to other foods, such as eggs and milk.
- Check date labels and use strict stock-rotation procedures.

Figure 3.9 Food in a refrigerator

Make sure that refrigerators are cleaned regularly. This needs to be part of the cleaning schedule. The procedure should be:

1. move food to another refrigerator
2. clean using a recommended sanitiser (a solution of bicarbonate of soda and water is also good for cleaning refrigerators)
3. empty and clean any drip trays, and clean door seals thoroughly
4. rinse, then dry with kitchen paper
5. clean and disinfect the refrigerator front and handle to avoid cross-contamination
6. check that the refrigerator is down to temperature (1 to 4°C), before replacing the food in the proper positions
7. check the dates and condition of all food before replacing with the newest items at the back.

Defrosting

If you need to defrost frozen food, a defrosting cabinet is the best place to do it. If no defrosting cabinet is available, place the food in a deep tray, cover with film and label with what the item is and the date when defrosting was started. Place at the bottom of the refrigerator where thawing liquid can't drip on to anything else. Defrost food completely (there should be no ice crystals on any part), then cook thoroughly within 12 hours. Make sure that you allow enough time for defrosting – it may take longer than you think. (A 2 kg chicken will take about 24 hours to defrost at 3°C.)

Some foods can be cooked directly from frozen but these tend to be very thin foods such as pizza, flat breadcrumbed fish fillet or frozen vegetables. Remember that cooking from frozen will significantly cool down cooking water or oil so allow time for this to recover.

Dry (ambient) food stores

A dry or ambient food store is an area to store foods that generally have a longer shelf life than those needing refrigerated or frozen storage. Items kept in the dry stores may include dry goods and cereal products, spices and dried herbs, packaged goods such as biscuits, canned goods, bottled items, chocolate/cocoa, tea and coffee. Fruit and vegetables not requiring refrigeration (e.g. sacks of potatoes and onions) may also be stored here. The room should be large enough to allow for the correct storage of stock. It needs to be cool (10–15°C is ideal), well ventilated, a light colour, well lit, protected to prevent entry of pests, and easy to clean/disinfect efficiently.

When fitting out the room:

- the surfaces of walls, ceilings and floors need to be smooth, impervious and easy to clean; edges where walls join the floor or ceiling should be coved if possible to prevent the build-up of debris in corners
- doors should be protected by metal kick-plates and a plastic or chain curtain to prevent pests from gaining entry (but also check the packaging on deliveries for possible pests)

- windows that open should be well protected with wire gauze or netting to prevent pests from entering, and food items should not be stored in direct sunlight from windows
- shelves/racking must be made of a non-corrosive, easy-to-clean material; tubular stainless steel is popular. Shelving must be deep enough to hold the items requiring storage and the bottom shelf should be well raised from the floor to allow cleaning underneath. Never store items directly on the floor as this prevents effective cleaning, and packaging can get wet when the floor is cleaned, causing contamination and deterioration of the contents.

Where possible, store dry goods in covered containers or wheeled bins but make sure the stock is rotated effectively – that is, 'first in, first out' (see below); this will ensure that existing stock is always used first. When new packages of dry stock are delivered do not empty them into the container on top of what is already being stored.

To avoid any possible cross-contamination, store high-risk (ready-to-eat) foods well away from any raw foods such as dirty vegetables, and make sure all items remain covered.

Using clingfilm/plastic wrap

Clingfilm is a very useful product for storing food hygienically, protecting from cross-contamination and preventing food from drying out. However, because clingfilm seals in moisture it can encourage growth of moulds on food. Do not leave clingfilm-wrapped or covered foods in direct light as this can increase the temperature of the food inside. Because of concerns about the migration of chemicals into food it is recommended that foods are never cooked or reheated when wrapped in clingfilm unless a film specifically recommended for this is used.

'First in, first out' and stock control

'First in, first out' describes stock rotation and is applied to all categories of food. It simply means that foods already in storage are used before new deliveries (provided that stock is still within recommended dates and in sound condition). Food deliveries should be labelled with delivery date and preferably the date by which the food should be used (Figure 3.10). Written stock records should form part of a food safety management system.

Figure 3.10 Date labelling stickers

Food labelling codes

The main UK food labelling codes are as follows.

- **Use-by dates:** these appear on perishable foods with a short life that usually need refrigerated storage. Legally, the food must be used by this date and not stored or used after it, or it could be a danger to health. The date will appear as 'use by', plus day, month and year. It is an offence to change this date.
- **Best before dates:** these apply to foods that are expected to have a longer life, e.g. dry products or canned food. A best before date advises that food is at its best before this date and to use it after the date is still legal but not advised. Dates will appear as follows:
  - 3 months or less – 'best before' day and month only
  - 3 to 18 months – 'best before' day, month and year, or 'best before end' month and year
  - more than 18 months – 'best before' month and year, or 'best before end' and year only.

Some foods are exempt from date marking. These include uncut fresh vegetables, sugar or high-alcohol drinks.

With both use-by and best before dates (Figure 3.11) it is essential to follow the food storage advice and guidance on the packaging.

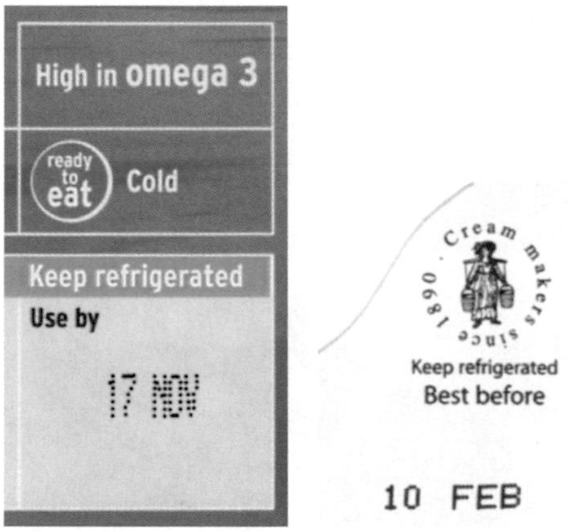

Figure 3.11 Use-by and best before dates

Food preparation

Food should not be prepared too far in advance of cooking. If it is prepared a significant time before it is to be cooked control measures must be in place to ensure that this is safe.

Preparation areas for raw and cooked food should be well separated, as should dirty and clean processes. Food being prepared should only be out of temperature control (refrigeration or cooking processes) for the shortest time possible. Avoid handling food unnecessarily; use disposable gloves, tongs, slices, spoons, etc., where possible.

High standards of personal hygiene are essential for those handling food; approved kitchen clothing must be worn, and changed if it becomes dirty or badly stained as this could contaminate food and equipment. It is essential to develop and monitor 'clean as you go' methods of work to help avoid microbial and physical contamination of food.

Use of temperature

Cooking temperatures

Cooking is one of the best measures available to destroy and control bacteria in food. The usual recommendation is to cook to a core temperature (the temperature in the centre or thickest part of the food) of 75°C for at least two minutes, but cooking at a slightly lower temperature for a longer time can be as effective. In addition, dish specifications or personal preference may require lower temperatures than this, as in rare beef and some fish dishes. However, avoid undercooked dishes when dealing with groups vulnerable to the effects of food poisoning (see page 39). The usual way to check if the required core temperature has been achieved is with a temperature probe (see below), but visual checks can also be used – for example, in a cooked chicken, no part should be pink and the juices running off should be clear. A calibrated probe is the most accurate method and provides a temperature measurement that can be recorded as part of good food safety practice.

Staff should be aware of the danger zone temperatures (5–63°C) and the need to heat food through this temperature range quickly to avoid the formation of spores (see pages 42–3). It is also good practice to use lids on cooking pans to prevent heat escaping, and to stir food frequently to keep temperatures even. Hot food can be kept out of temperature control for up to two hours under controlled conditions (see below) on any single occasion, such as a hot buffet. Food must be disposed of at the end of the two hours.

High temperatures

Normal cooking temperatures of 75°C will kill most pathogens (but not toxins and spores). Use of heat to make food safe and to preserve it, for example through pasteurisation or canning, is one of the most useful procedures available in food production and manufacture. See the earlier section on food preservation methods (page 48) for more information.

Storage temperatures

As bacteria can multiply only very slowly at low temperatures (see Figure 3.7), good practice is to keep refrigerators running at 1–4°C. The legal requirement is at or below 8°C.

Refrigerator and freezer temperatures should be checked and recorded at least once daily, and the records retained.

Holding temperatures

Hot cooked food being held for service must not fall below 63°C. Make sure that there is adequate equipment to keep food above this temperature; check the temperature frequently and record it. Make sure that equipment for keeping food hot, such as bains-marie or hot cabinets, are pre-heated and cleaned/disinfected; do not overfill food containers and allow all of the food to be used from them before topping up. Place lids on open containers to keep the heat in.

Cold food being held for service or displayed should not be above 5°C (legal requirement 8°C). Make sure that refrigeration/display cabinets run at the correct temperature, check the temperature and keep a record. Cold food held above 8°C for two hours on one occasion must be thrown away (this includes preparation time).

Cooling cooked food

When food is cooled, either to be served cold or to be reheated, this must be done carefully and quickly, to avoid the formation/germination of spores, and to reduce the risk of cross-contamination as food is cooling. It is recommended that food is cooled to 8°C within 90 minutes; this is best done in a blast-chiller. If this is not available, food in containers can be plunged into ice water baths or placed on trays and surrounded with ice or ice packs. Place cooling food in the coolest place available; fans can also be useful to speed up cooling time.

To allow food to cool more quickly it is recommended that:

- items such as soups, stews and sauces are placed in small containers; also use shallow containers – the increased surface area allows food to cool more quickly
- cook smaller joints of meat, where possible, because these will cool more quickly; a maximum weight of 2.5 kg is recommended.

Reheating

Reheating should be done thoroughly and quickly to a core temperature of at least 75°C (Scottish law requires 82°C). Reheated food should also be served quickly and never reheated more than once.

Serving food

Food must also be protected when it is being served. Do not keep food unprotected and out of temperature control in service areas longer than necessary. Make sure that all service equipment and surfaces are suitable for food service and are clean. Staff training in food safety is essential for food service staff as well as for those preparing food.

Temperature probes

Electronic temperature probes are extremely useful in food production to measure the temperature in the centre of both hot and cold food and for recording the temperature of deliveries and checking the uniformity of food temperatures in fridges. Make sure the probe is clean and disinfected before use (disposable disinfectant wipes are useful for this). Place the probe into the centre of the food, making sure it is not touching bone or the cooking container. Allow the temperature to 'settle' before reading.

Check regularly that probes are working correctly (this is called **calibration**). This can be done electronically, but a simple and low-cost check is to place the probe in icy water; the reading should be within the range -1 to 1°C. To check accuracy at high levels place the probe in boiling water and the temperature reading should be in the range of 99 to 101°C. If probes read outside of these temperatures they need to be repaired or replaced. Record when temperature probes have been checked for accuracy and store this information with food safety records.

Infrared thermometers

These are also very useful in kitchen area and give instant readings as they work by measuring radiant energy. They are very hygienic to use as they do not actually touch the food, so there is no chance of cross-contamination or damaging the food.

Data loggers

These will record information about the temperatures of refrigeration over a set period. They record highs and lows of temperature in fridges/freezers, and can provide a graph or chart of trends. Systems are available that record all refrigerator, chill units and freezer temperatures in a business and send the information to a central computer. These records can then be printed or stored electronically as part of the food safety management system.

Surplus prepared food

Some food businesses, as a matter of policy and in the interests of food safety, dispose of all unused prepared foods after set times, and always at the end of service. This is especially important when serving food to high-risk, vulnerable groups of people. Policy and procedures for using surplus food need to be planned and recorded as part of the food safety management system. Staff must be fully trained in these procedures and made aware of the potential hazards involved.

➜ Personal hygiene

As noted above, all humans are a potential source of food poisoning bacteria, and everyone working with food must be aware of the importance of personal hygiene when handling food. *Staphylococcus aureus* may be present in the nose, mouth, throat, on skin and hair, and could easily be transferred to food where it could then multiply and cause illness. It is very important that hair, nose ears mouth, etc., are not touched while preparing food. Cuts, burns and boils are also likely to be a source of bacteria so must be covered.

Anyone suffering from or who is a carrier of any disease that could be transmitted through food must not handle food. This includes diarrhoea and/or vomiting, or any food poisoning symptom, infected cuts, burns or spots, bad cold or flu symptoms. Food handlers with any such illness, infection or wound must report this to their supervisor before starting work. They should also report any illness that has occurred on a recent holiday overseas, and illnesses suffered by other members of their family. It is a legal requirement to report these.

All supervisors must be aware that food handlers can be *carriers* of dangerous pathogens that could get into the food they prepare. All known carriers must not handle food. *Convalescent carriers* are those recovering from an illness, but they still carry the bacteria and can pass it on to the food they handle. *Healthy carriers* show no signs of illness but can still contaminate the food as above; these people can remain carriers for long periods, or even all of their lives, and should not do work that involves handling food.

Before starting a job that involves food handling, managers and supervisors/head chefs must make all staff aware that they must practise high standards of personal hygiene: they must always arrive at work clean (daily bath or shower) and with clean hair. They must also be aware of the following factors.

Hands

Hands can be a major cause of contamination; if not kept clean they can very easily transfer harmful bacteria to food and equipment. Hands must be washed thoroughly and frequently (Figure 3.12). New staff need to be instructed in the correct procedure for washing hands, and existing staff will need periodic update training.

Staff involved in food handling must know that thorough hand washing should take place:

- when they enter the kitchen, before starting work and handling any food
- after a break (using the toilet, in contact with faeces)
- between different tasks, but especially between handling raw and cooked food
- after touching hair, nose, mouth, or using a tissue for a sneeze or cough
- after application of or changing a dressing on a cut or burn
- after cleaning preparation areas, equipment or contaminated surfaces
- after handling kitchen waste, external food packaging, money or flowers.

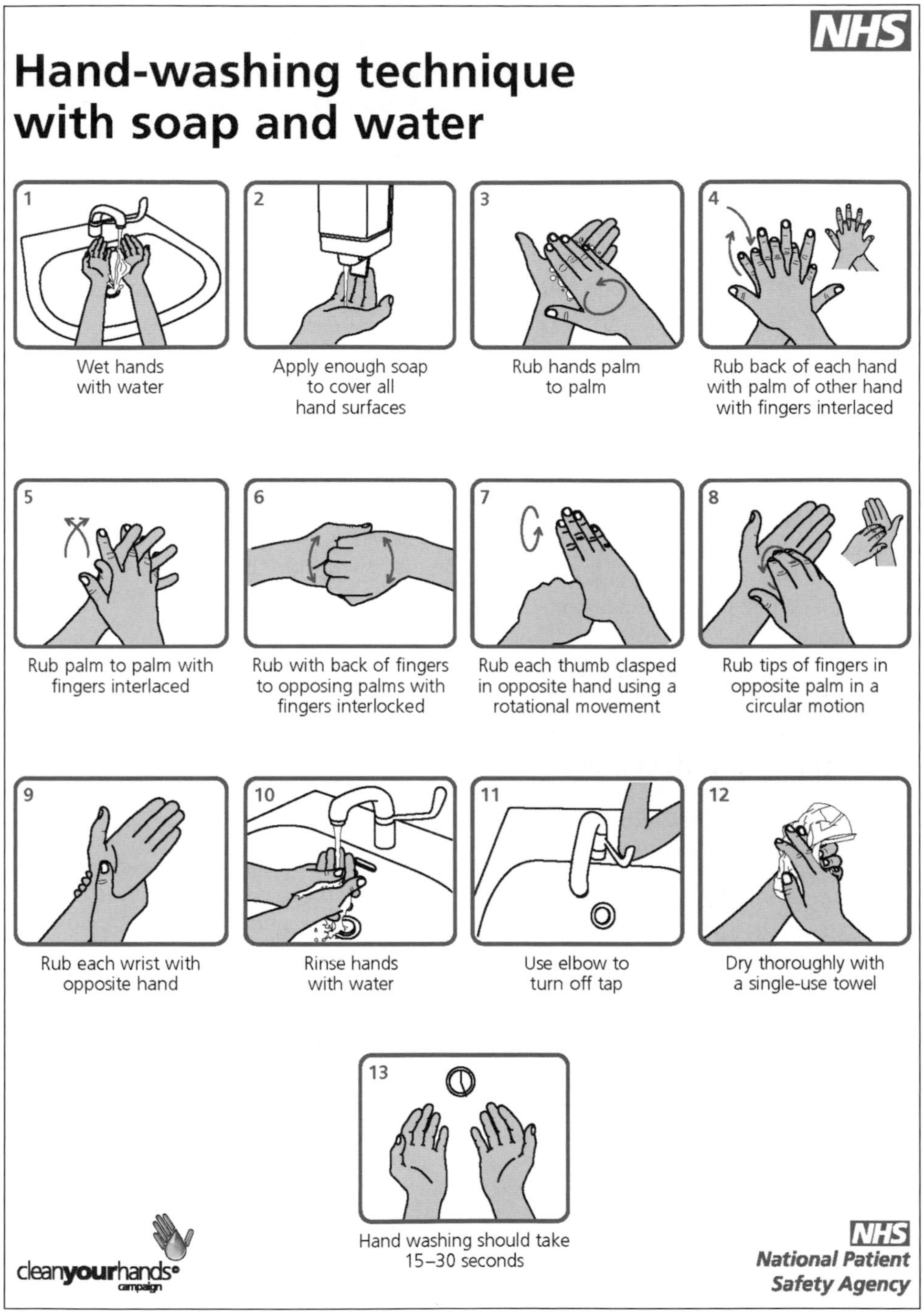

Figure 3.12

Jewellery/rings/watches

The wearing of jewellery is not acceptable when handling food. It can trap particles of food and provide a warm, damp environment for bacteria to grow; bacteria can then be transferred to food being prepared. This is particularly relevant to items worn on or near the hands, such as rings and watches. Generally a plain wedding band is permissible, but be aware that this too can be a breeding ground for bacteria. Jewellery or parts of jewellery can fall into food, especially as in some food preparation hands need to be plunged into water.

Fingernails

These should always be kept clean and short as dirt can easily lodge under the nails and be transferred to food, introducing bacteria. Nails should kept neatly trimmed and false nails or nail varnish should never be worn in food areas.

The head

Hair must be washed regularly and kept covered with a suitable hat and/or net to prevent loose hair falling into food. The head/hair should never be scratched, combed or touched in the kitchen, as bacteria and loose hair could be transferred via the hands to the food, and loose hair could also fall into food.

The **nose** should not be touched when food is being handled. If a handkerchief/tissue is used, the hands should be washed thoroughly afterwards. The nose is an area where there are vast numbers of harmful bacteria; it is therefore very important not to sneeze on food, other people or working surfaces. If a sneeze or cough is unavoidable, turn away and sneeze into your own shoulder area.

The **mouth** also harbours large numbers of bacteria, therefore the mouth or lips should not be touched when working with food. Do not use cooking utensils such as wooden spoons for tasting food, nor should fingers be used for this purpose as bacteria may be transferred to food. A clean teaspoon (or disposable plastic spoon) should be used for tasting.

Ears, too, are a source of bacteria and should not be touched when handling food.

Cuts, burns and other skin abrasions

It is particularly important to keep all cuts, burns, scratches and similar abrasions covered with a waterproof dressing. Use a blue plaster that will be visible if it falls into food. Where the wound has become infected there are vast numbers of harmful bacteria that must not be permitted to get on to food so those with infected wounds should not handle food. Report this to a supervisor or manager who will advise.

Cosmetics

Cosmetics should be used sparingly by food handlers, but ideally their use should be discouraged altogether. Cosmetics must never be applied in the kitchen and the hands should be washed thoroughly after applying them.

Smoking

Smoking is now illegal in most buildings and certainly where there is food. If food handlers smoke at break times, their hands must be washed thoroughly afterwards because when a cigarette is taken from the mouth, bacteria from the mouth can be transferred via the fingers on to food.

Use of kitchen cloths

Cloths used for holding hot dishes or removing hot items from the oven should be kept clean and dry, and should not be used for other purposes. Tea towels and dishcloths are sometimes used for wiping surfaces or knives, wiping plate edges and pans. All such uses could transfer bacteria on to food and be the cause of cross-contamination. Where cloths are used, they must be clean and changed frequently; use different cloths for raw and cooked food areas (colour-coded cloths are useful for this). Do not place cloths over the shoulder because they will transfer bacteria from the neck and hair to food and equipment. The best practice is to use disposable cloths or kitchen paper.

Protective clothing

Clean protective clothing should be worn at all times, should completely cover any other clothing and should be worn only in the kitchen area. Dirty protective clothing can cause cross-contamination and enable multiplication of bacteria, which could then get on to food or food equipment.

Outdoor clothing, and other clothing that has been taken off before wearing kitchen clothing, should be kept in a locker, away from the kitchen. Kitchen protective clothing needs to provide a barrier between the wearer and the food, and should protect the body from excessive heat.

If a food handler need to leave the kitchen it is not usually practical to remove all kitchen clothing. However good practice is to remove the hat and apron and cover everything else with a white coat. These are now provided in many kitchens and low-cost disposable white coats have become widely available.

- **Chefs' jackets** are usually made of cotton or a cotton mixture, are double-breasted and mostly have long sleeves; these protect the chest and arms from the heat of the stove, and prevent hot foods or liquids burning or scalding the body.
- **Aprons** are designed to protect the body from being scalded or burned, and particularly to protect the legs from any liquids that may be spilled; for this reason the apron should be of sufficient length to protect the legs.
- The main purpose of the **chef's hat** is to prevent loose hairs from falling into food. As well as the traditional chef's toque (tall white hat), a variety of designs are now available, some with a net incorporated to contain the hair fully. Skull caps and lightweight disposable hats are now used in many establishments.

Kitchen clothing needs to be:

- **washable** – the clothing should be of an easily washable material because many frequent changes of clothing may be needed. Kitchen clothing must be easy to wash at high temperatures, and cotton or a cotton mixture is most suitable to enable frequent changing and laundering
- **light and comfortable** – clothing must be light in weight, comfortable and should fit well (not too tight or too long)
- **strong and absorbent** – clothes worn in the kitchen must be strong enough to make them 'protective', and able to withstand the hard wear and frequent washing needed; they also need to be absorbent, to deal with perspiration caused by working in a hot kitchen.

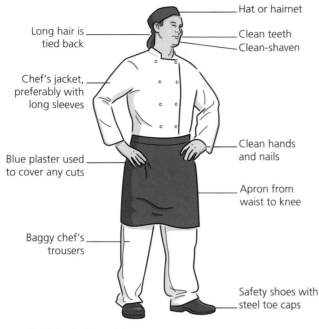

Figure 3.13 A chef in whites

Footwear

This should be strong and kept in good repair so as to protect and support the feet. As kitchen staff are on their feet for many hours, suitable, clean, comfortable kitchen footwear is essential. Kitchen staff should not wear any open-topped shoes or sandals, and 'trainers' are also unsuitable as they offer no protection from the spillage of hot liquids, falling knives or heavy items that could be dropped on the feet.

➔ A clean and hygienic food environment

Cleaning and disinfection

Clean food areas play an essential part in the production of safe food. Clean premises, work areas and equipment are essential to:

- control the organisms that cause food poisoning
- reduce the possibility of physical and chemical contamination
- make accidents less likely, such as slips on a greasy floor
- create a positive image for customers, visitors and employees
- comply with the law
- avoid attracting pests
- create a pleasant, safe and hygienic working environment, allowing for efficient and effective working methods
- assist in reducing maintenance costs and damage to equipment.

Effective cleaning uses one or more of the following:

- **physical energy**/human effort of the cleaner carrying out the task (e.g. the motion of scrubbing) or the energy generated by a cleaning machine
- **chemicals**, such as detergents
- **turbulence** – movement of liquids
- **thermal energy** – hot water and steam
- **CIP** (clean in place) – used for very large equipment.

When done properly, cleaning is effective in removing dirt, grease, debris and food particles. However, cleaning alone is not effective in the removal of micro-organisms; this will require **disinfection**. Disinfection is often carried out after the cleaning process, but sometimes the two are done together with the use of sanitiser. It is unlikely that disinfection will be guaranteed to kill all micro-organisms, but it will bring them to a safe level.

Disinfection must be done carefully to be effective. It may be completed with:

- **chemicals** – use only those recommended for kitchen use
- **hot water** – at 82°C for 30 seconds, as occurs in a dishwasher
- **steam** – use of steam disinfection is good for equipment and surfaces that are difficult to dismantle or reach, such as when cleaning in place (CIP).

There are different products designed to complete different tasks, as follows.

- **Detergent** is designed to remove grease and dirt and hold them in suspension in water. Detergents may be in the form of liquid, powder, gel or foam, and usually need to be added to water to use. Detergent will not kill pathogens (although the hot water it is mixed with may help to do this), however it will clean and degrease so disinfectant can work properly. Detergents work best in hot water.
- **Disinfectant** is intended to destroy bacteria, when used properly. Disinfectants must be left on a cleaned, grease-free surface for the required amount of 'contact time' to be effective, and usually work best in cool water.
- **Sanitiser** cleans and disinfects, and usually comes in spray form; it is very useful for work surfaces and equipment, especially between tasks.
- **Sterilisers** can be chemicals (or the action of extreme heat) and will kill all living micro-organisms.

Some areas and items may need thorough cleaning but not disinfection; this would apply to floors and walls. Other surfaces and items need to be both cleaned and disinfected regularly according to the cleaning schedule. These are:

- **direct food contact surfaces**, such as chopping boards, knives, work surfaces, mixing bowls, serving dishes, display counter inserts and slicing machines
- **hand-contact surfaces**, such as taps, door handles, drawer handles, oven doors, refrigerator doors, light switches, telephones
- **hands** – disinfection achieved by bactericidal soap, alcohol-based disinfectant
- **cleaning materials and equipment**, such as mops, cleaning cloths, scrapers, brushes.

All cleaning chemicals in kitchens and food premises must be 'food safe'. Careless use of chemicals can be dangerous, and can cause skin irritation, respiratory problems and burns. A number of cleaning substances are regarded as hazardous to health. Therefore, several precautions have to be taken to control their use:

- read the label and identify the substance and its potential hazards
- follow the manufacturer's dilution instructions carefully
- use only the appropriate substance for the job
- use the necessary and recommended protective clothing
- do not mix different chemicals
- always store chemicals in their original containers.

Always use a fresh solution of disinfectant every time a new cleaning task is carried out. Do not top up existing solutions. Mops and cloths should not be soaked in disinfectant solutions for long periods, as the solution will weaken and can allow bacteria to grow. Always rinse away disinfectant thoroughly, unless the manufacturer's instructions state that rinsing is unnecessary.

It is essential for all staff to be aware of the possible dangers and hazards from cleaning chemicals. See Chapter 4 for information about COSHH (control of substances hazardous to health).

It is important to train all staff to 'clean as you go', and not to allow waste to accumulate in the area where food preparation and cooking are being carried out. Staff need to understand that it is very difficult to keep untidy areas clean and hygienic, and it is more likely that cross-contamination will occur in untidy areas.

The cleaning of areas and equipment needs to be planned and recorded on a cleaning schedule. The cleaning schedule needs to include the following information.

- **What** is to be cleaned.
- **Who** should do it (name if possible).
- **How** it is to be done, and how long it should take.
- **When** – time of day or at what point in the shift.
- **Materials** to be used, including chemicals, dilution, cleaning equipment, protective clothing to be worn.
- **Safety precautions** necessary to complete the task safely.
- **Signatures** of cleaner and supervisor checking the work; also date and time.

The cleaning process must be monitored regularly and inspected to ensure that the schedule is being followed, in order to maintain standards. Checking can include the use of rapid bacterial tests or swabbing.

Cleaning schedules need to include information on what is to be cleaned, who is going to do it, how, when and with what, as well as the names of the person completing the work and the person who checked it. Cleaning schedules, like the one shown in Table 3.5, should form part of the food safety management system and be kept for inspection.

Table 3.5 Example of a cleaning schedule

Surface/ item	When cleaned	Cleaned by	Equipment/ chemicals	PPE	Safety measures	Method of cleaning	Checked by	Date/ time
Work surface next to salad bar	After salad preparation	Kitchen assistant 1	Hot water, bowl, detergent, sanitiser, single-use cloth	Uniform, apron, rubber gloves	'Wet floor' sign, if necessary	Remove debris, clean surface, splashback and under shelf using hot water, detergent, disposable cloth. Hot-water rinse. Spray with sanitiser, leave 30 seconds, dry with blue kitchen paper		

Kitchen waste

Kitchen waste should be placed in suitable waste bins with lids (preferably foot operated). Waste bins should be made of a strong material, be easy to clean, pest-proof and lined with a suitable bin liner. They should be emptied regularly to avoid waste build-up as this could cause problems with multiplication of bacteria and attract pests. An over-full heavy bin is also much more difficult to handle than a regularly emptied bin. Waste should never be left in kitchen bins overnight (this needs to be part of *closing checks*).

Outside waste bins also need to be strong, pest-proof and impervious, with a close-fitting lid. Bins should stand on hard surfaces that can be hosed down and kept clean easily. Planned regular emptying of the bins and cleaning of the area should be recorded in the cleaning schedule/management system.

Dishwashing

The most efficient and hygienic method of cleaning dishes and crockery is the use of a dishwasher, as this will clean and disinfect items, which will then air-dry, removing the need for cloths. See Chapter 5 for details of how a dishwasher works.

Dishwashing by hand

If items need to be washed by hand the recommended way to do this is:

- scrape/rinse/spray off food residues
- wash items in a sink of hot water; the temperature should be 50–60°C, which means rubber gloves need to be worn; use a dishwashing brush rather than a cloth (the brush will help to loosen food particles and is not such a good breeding ground for bacteria)
- rinse in very hot water; if rinsing can be done at 82°C for 30 seconds this will disinfect the dishes
- allow to air-dry; do not use tea towels.

Note that the old double-sink method, with a very hot rinsing sink, is not recommended.

Figure 3.14 Loading a commercial dishwasher

Cleaning surfaces

Two methods for cleaning kitchen surfaces are shown in Table 3.6.

Avoiding hazards

Cleaning is essential to prevent food safety hazards, but if not managed properly can become a hazard in itself. Do not store cleaning chemicals in food preparation and cooking areas, and take care with their use to avoid any possibility of *chemical contamination*. Make sure that items such as cloths and paper towels, and fibres from mops, do not get into open food (*physical contamination*). *Bacterial contamination* can occur by using the same cleaning cloths and equipment in raw food areas then in high-risk food areas, or not cleaning/disinfecting cleaning equipment properly.

Table 3.6 Recommended methods for cleaning a kitchen surface

Six-stage	Four-stage
Remove debris and loose particles Main clean using hot water and detergent to remove soiling and grease Rinse using clean hot water and cloth to remove detergent Apply disinfectant, leave for contact time recommended on container Rinse off disinfectant if recommended Allow to air-dry or use kitchen paper	Remove debris and loose particles Main clean using hot water and sanitiser Rinse using clean hot water and cloth if recommended on instructions Allow to air-dry or use kitchen paper to dry

Pests

When food premises are closed down or there are prosecutions, an infestation of pests is often the reason. Pests must be eliminated from food premises for food safety reasons and to comply with the law (Regulation (EC) 852/2004 states that 'effective pest control procedures must be implemented' and 'foods must be protected from contamination').

Pests can carry food poisoning bacteria into food premises on their fur/feathers or feet/paws, or in saliva, urine and droppings (see Table 3.2). They can cause damage to food stock and packaging, buildings, equipment and wiring, as well as blockages in equipment and piping.

Figure 3.15 Cockroaches are a common kitchen pest

Common pests in food areas are rats, mice, cockroaches, wasps, flies and ants (tiny pharaoh's ants can cause particular problems). Birds and domestic pets must be considered as pests too.

Pests can be attracted to kitchens and food stores because food, warmth, shelter, water and possible nesting materials can be found there. All reasonable measures must be put in place to keep them out. Staff must be made aware of possible signs that pests may be present, and any sightings must be reported to the supervisor or manager immediately.

Pest control

Pest management needs to be planned as part of the food safety management system. Regular visits from a recognised pest control company are highly recommended because they will offer advice, deal with any problems and provide a pest audit report, which should be kept and could be used as part of due diligence (see page 68). Any measures put in place by pest control contractors, such as bait boxes, should be left where they are placed and not handled as they will have strong poisons in them.

The role of employees in pest control is mainly about good practice, good housekeeping and working with pest control contractors. It includes:

- reporting any damage to buildings and fittings, and organising prompt repair
- keeping entrances to the building clean and clear, with undergrowth kept well cut back
- keeping food areas clean (especially under/behind equipment and in corners), and not leaving out any traces of food or liquids overnight (closing checks)
- regularly checking and cleaning refuse areas, keeping bins tightly closed and emptying them regularly
- effective stock control and regular cleaning of storage areas
- checking deliveries for any possible signs of pests
- discouraging and preventing suppliers from delivering items very early in the morning and leaving them outside where pests could get into them.

Note that pest control measures can themselves introduce food safety hazards: the bodies of dead insects or even rodents may remain in the kitchen (physical and bacterial contamination), and pesticides, insecticides and baits could cause chemical contamination if not managed properly.

Figure 3.16 Bait box

Table 3.7 Signs of pest presence and how to keep them out

Pest	Signs that they are present	How they cause food contamination	How to keep them out
Rats and mice	Sightings of rodent or its droppings, unpleasant smell, fur, gnawed wires, etc. Greasy marks on lower walls, damaged food stock and packaging, paw prints and tail marks	They carry harmful bacteria on their bodies and in their droppings Rats infest sewers and drains, and since excreta is a main source of food-poisoning bacteria, it is possible for any surface touched by rats to be contaminated Rats and mice like warm, dark corners and can be found in lift shafts, meter cupboards, lofts, pipe lagging, openings in walls where pipes enter, under low shelves and on high shelves; they enter premises through any holes, defective drains, open doorways and in sacks of food	Rats spoil ten times as much food as they eat, they are very prolific, averaging ten offspring per litter and six litters per year If any problem with rats or mice is suspected it is essential to contact a pest control contractor immediately
Flies and wasps	Sighting of flies and wasps, hearing them, dead insects Maggots	Common house flies probably spread more infection than any other insect; flies land on animal excreta, refuse and decaying matter, and contaminate their legs, wings and bodies with harmful bacteria, which could be deposited on food; they also contaminate food with their excreta and saliva Wasps can also frequent dirty and decaying objects before they land on food	An electronic fly killer (EFK) is an effective way to deal with flying insects: the blue light attracts the insects, which are then killed by an electrical charge; they fall into a collecting tray, which must be emptied regularly Windows that open and other openings to the outside environment should be fitted with insect-proof screens
Silverfish (small silver-coloured insects that feed on starchy foods, among other things)	Sightings	Found on moist surfaces	They thrive in badly ventilated areas, so improving ventilation will help to control them
Beetles	Sightings, dead or alive	Beetles are found in warm places and can also carry harmful bacteria from place to place	They tend to hide away during the day and come out at night, so it is essential that no food is left out to attract them
Cockroaches	Sightings, dead or alive, also nymphs, eggs, larvae, pupae, egg cases Live cockroaches are often seen at night Unpleasant smell	Cockroaches like warm, moist, dark places They can carry harmful bacteria on their bodies and deposit them on anything with which they come into contact	They tend to hide away during the day and come out at night, so it is essential that no food is left out to attract them
Ants	Sightings and present in food and food stores The tiny, pale-coloured pharaoh's ants are difficult to spot but can still be the source of a variety of pathogens	They transfer bacteria from one place to another. They can get under the seals of containers and jars	Insects are destroyed using an insecticide, and it is usual to employ pest controllers who are familiar with this work
Weevils	Sightings of weevils in stored products, e.g. flour/cornflour Very difficult to see: tiny black insects moving in flour, etc.		
Birds	Sightings, droppings, in outside storage areas and around refuse	Areas can be contaminated by droppings and pathogenic bacteria carried by birds	Netted windows; windows and doors closed
Domestic pets	These must be kept out of food areas as they carry pathogens on fur, whiskers, saliva, urine, etc.	They carry harmful bacteria and may also introduce fleas	Do not allow pets in kitchens or food premises

WEBLINK

The British Pest Control Association has a list of member companies:

www.bpca.org.uk

Kitchen premises and food safety

Well-planned and well-fitted kitchen premises with sufficient refrigerated storage for food are essential to food safety. Planning should consider work flow so that processes generally move in one direction without unnecessary crossing over or backtracking that could lead to cross-contamination. Raw and high-risk food processes should be well separated.

Ventilation

Adequate ventilation must be provided so that fumes from stoves are taken out of kitchen areas. This is usually achieved by use of extractor fans and hoods over stoves. Hoods and fans must be kept clean; grease and dirt are drawn up by the fan and, if they accumulate, can block vents and the grease and dirt can drop on to food.

Lighting

Good lighting is essential so that kitchen staff can work efficiently; it will also help to prevent accidents. Good lighting also enables staff to see into all areas so that the kitchen can be cleaned properly.

Plumbing

Hot water is essential for cleaning so the means of heating water must be capable of meeting cleaning requirements. Hand-washing facilities (separate from food preparation sinks) must also be available in the kitchen, with a suitable means of drying the hands – preferably paper towels.

Floors, walls and ceilings

Kitchen floors have to withstand a considerable amount of wear and tear, therefore they must be:

- capable of being cleaned easily
- even, smooth and non-slip
- without cracks or open joints
- impervious (non-absorbent).

Where possible, the join between the floor and wall should be coved, making cleaning easier and more efficient. Quarry tiles are now less popular than they were for kitchens because dirt can become trapped in the grouting between tiles. Industrial-grade vinyl or epoxy resin floors fulfil all the requirements.

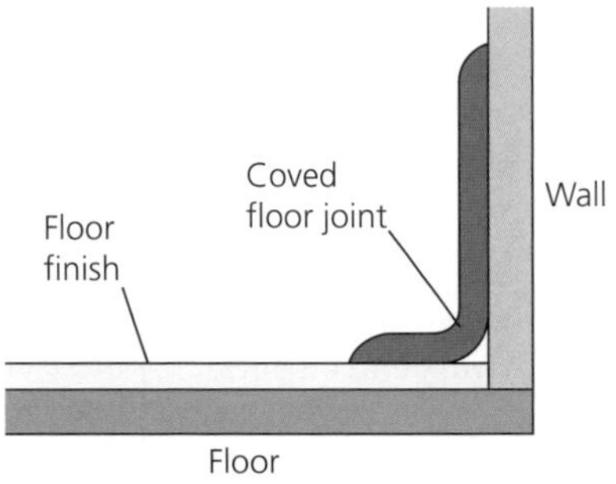

Figure 3.17 Coved floor joint

Walls should be strong, smooth, impervious, washable and light in colour. Suitable wall surfaces include heat-resistant plastic sheeting, stainless-steel sheeting and resin-bonded fibreglass. Tiles have become less popular because they can crack and loose grouting can fall into food.

Clean wall coverings with hot detergent water and then dry. Food surface 'splashbacks' need to be cleaned/sanitised frequently; this could be done at the same time as the work surface.

Ceilings must be free from cracks and flaking. They should not be able to harbour dirt, condensation or grease that could fall on to food. Good ventilation will help with this.

Doors and windows

Doors and windows should fit correctly into their frames and doors should have metal kick plates that help to prevent rodents gnawing through the door to gain entry. Include the cleaning and disinfection of door handles on the cleaning schedule as these are hand-contact surfaces so could cause cross-contamination.

Hygiene of kitchen equipment

Kitchen equipment must allow ease of cleaning and ease of inspection, to ensure it is clean and in good repair. Material used in the construction of equipment must be:

- hard and impervious, so that it does not absorb food particles and moisture
- smooth, so cleaning can take place easily
- resistant to rust, chipping or cracking.

Food must always be protected from machine lubricants.

Control and disposal of waste

Waste material is a potential source of contamination that can provide food for a variety of pests. There is a 'duty of care' under the Environmental Protection Act 1990 that makes the catering organisation responsible for its waste. It is a legal requirement to use licensed waste contractors, which must issue a *waste transfer notice*. Any special waste (e.g. chemicals or potentially infectious material) might need dealing with separately.

There is also a legal requirement to reduce packaging waste. Large businesses must register with the Environmental Protection Agency and make efforts to reduce the amount of packaging they generate as waste.

In most businesses there will be a significant amount of waste suitable for recycling, provided that the recycling meets health and safety and hygiene requirements. Separation of different items is necessary depending on local authority/contractors' policies, and regular collections are essential. Local authorities can advise on their policies and systems for recycling.

WEBLINK

WRAP (Waste Resource Action Programme), an organisation tasked to work with governments, businesses and communities to reduce waste utilise resources efficiently and effectively:

www.wrap.org.uk

HACCP and food safety management systems

It is a legal requirement for all food businesses to have a food safety management system in place. Article 5 of the Food Hygiene (England) Regulations 2006 gave effect to the EU Regulations and states that, 'Food business operators shall put into place, implement and maintain a permanent procedure based on the principles of hazard analysis critical control points (HACCP).'

This is an internationally recognised food safety management system that identifies the critical points, or stages, in any process and recognises the hazards that could occur, considering what could go wrong, when, where and how. It is a means to ensure food safety.

Controls are then put in place to deal with the risks, making the possible risks safe. Checks must be in place, as well as procedures to put any faults right, and it should be confirmed that procedures are still working. Records are kept to show the system is working and is reviewed regularly. A wide range of documents are used to support the HACCP system.

Food handlers must receive adequate instruction and/or training in food hygiene to enable them to handle food safely. Those responsible for HACCP-based procedures in the business must have enough relevant knowledge and understanding to ensure the procedures are operated effectively.

Ensuring that a suitable food safety management system is in place is an owner's or management responsibility.

Hazard analysis identifies all the factors that could lead to harm to the consumer: all ingredients, stages in the processing of foods, environmental features and human factors that could lead to unsafe food being served.

Critical control points (CCPs) are the points at which control is essential to reduce the risk of potential hazards and prevent them from causing harm.

The CCPs that would typically apply to a food business might be:

- selecting suppliers and delivery
- various methods of food storage
- preparation
- chilled storage
- cooking
- serving, hot holding, cooling
- freezing and defrosting.

Prerequisites

Before setting up a new HACCP system, certain prerequisites need to be considered. These are the processes that need to be in place first.

- **Suppliers:** these should be approved suppliers and, where possible, should provide written specifications.
- **Traceability:** systems in place to trace the source of all foods.
- **Premises, structure and equipment:** records that premises are properly maintained; a flow diagram showing the process from delivery to service, avoiding any cross-over of procedures that could result in cross-contamination.
- **Storage and stock control:** effective stock control, stock rotation and temperature-controlled storage must be in place.

- **Staff hygiene:** protective clothing, hand-washing facilities, toilets and changing facilities need to be provided; policies for personal hygiene and illness reporting need to be established, with appropriate training.
- **Pest control:** a written policy, ideally as part of a pest management system and involving a recognised contractor.
- **Cleaning/disinfection/waste:** a documented system that includes cleaning schedules and how waste removal will be managed.
- **Staff training:** records of all staff training, with dates, levels completed and topics covered.

Setting up HACCP

A team suitably trained in HACCP procedures will be established to set up the system. If the business is small, just one person may be responsible. There are also a number of specialist HACCP consultancy companies that can complete and monitor the procedure.

The hazards identified and the controls put in place will be essential to food safety – for example, core cooking temperatures, possible multiplication and survival of bacteria, time food spends in the danger zone (see page 43), cooling food, storing food. Physical and chemical hazards could occur at any stage in the process and controls must include these.

Food handlers must receive food safety training and effective supervision commensurate with the tasks being completed. Staff training records must be kept.

The stages of the HACCP system

The HACCP system involves seven stages (Figure 3.18). It needs to provide a documented record of the stages *all* food will go through, right up to the time it is eaten. Once the hazards have been identified, corrective measures can be put in place to control the hazards and keep the food safe.

The system must be updated regularly, especially when new items are introduced to the menu or systems change, such as the introduction of a new piece of cooking equipment; specific new controls must be put in place to include them. A flow chart will need to be produced for each dish or procedure showing each of the stages (CCPs) that need to be considered for possible hazards (Figure 3.19).

As an example, when dealing with fresh chicken, it is necessary to recognise the possible hazards at all the identified stages (CCPs).

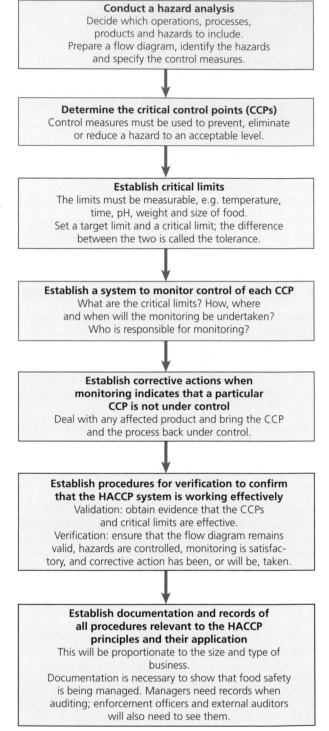

Conduct a hazard analysis
Decide which operations, processes, products and hazards to include.
Prepare a flow diagram, identify the hazards and specify the control measures.

↓

Determine the critical control points (CCPs)
Control measures must be used to prevent, eliminate or reduce a hazard to an acceptable level.

↓

Establish critical limits
The limits must be measurable, e.g. temperature, time, pH, weight and size of food.
Set a target limit and a critical limit; the difference between the two is called the tolerance.

↓

Establish a system to monitor control of each CCP
What are the critical limits? How, where and when will the monitoring be undertaken?
Who is responsible for monitoring?

↓

Establish corrective actions when monitoring indicates that a particular CCP is not under control
Deal with any affected product and bring the CCP and the process back under control.

↓

Establish procedures for verification to confirm that the HACCP system is working effectively
Validation: obtain evidence that the CCPs and critical limits are effective.
Verification: ensure that the flow diagram remains valid, hazards are controlled, monitoring is satisfactory, and corrective action has been, or will be, taken.

↓

Establish documentation and records of all procedures relevant to the HACCP principles and their application
This will be proportionate to the size and type of business.
Documentation is necessary to show that food safety is being managed. Managers need records when auditing; enforcement officers and external auditors will also need to see them.

Figure 3.18 The seven principles of HACCP

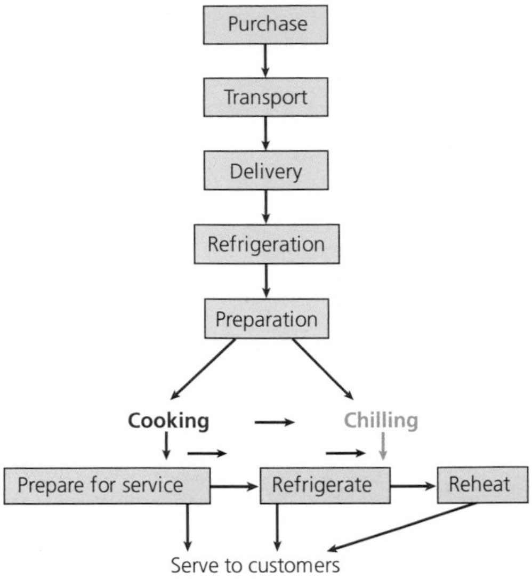

Figure 3.19 Example of a HACCP flow chart

Table 3.8 Example of a HACCP control chart for fresh food delivery

Process steps	Hazards	Controls	Critical limit	Monitoring	Corrective action
Purchase	Contamination, pathogens, mould or other contaminants present	Approved supplier	Meets business requirements	Remains consistent with initial agreements	Change supplier
Transport and delivery	Multiplication of harmful bacteria	Refrigerated vehicles, temperature printout from delivery van	Food below 5°C	Check delivery vehicles, date codes, temperatures and van printout	Reject if >5°C or out of date
Refrigerate	Bacterial growth Further contamination with bacteria, chemicals, physical items	Store below 5°C Separate raw and cooked foods Stock rotation	Food below 5°C	Check and record temperature twice a day Check date marks	Discard if signs of spoilage or past date mark
Prepare	Bacterial growth Further contamination Too long at kitchen temperatures	30 minutes maximum in 'danger zone' Good personal hygiene Clean equipment, hygienic premises	No more than 30 minutes at kitchen temperatures	Supervisor to audit at regular intervals Visual checks Cleaning schedules	Discard if >5°C for 2 hours or more
Cook	Survival of harmful bacteria Formation of spores	Thorough cooking Take through 'danger zone' quickly	>75°C	Check and record temperature/time	Continue cooking to 75°C
Prepare for service	Multiplication of bacteria Contamination	No more than 20 minutes in 'danger zone'	2 hours then throw away	Supervisor to audit at regular intervals	Discard if >5°C for 2 hours
Chill	Multiplication of bacteria Contamination	Blast-chiller	90 minutes to below 8°C	Supervisor to audit at regular intervals	Discard if above 8°C for 2 hours
Refrigerate	Multiplication of bacteria Contamination	Store below 5°C Separate raw and ready-to-eat foods	<5°C for all refrigerators and chill cabinets	Check and record temperature twice a day	Discard if >8°C for 2 hours
Reheat	Survival of bacteria	Reheat to >75°C in centre	75°C (82°C in Scotland)	Check and record temperature of each batch	Continue reheating to 75°C

Due diligence

Due diligence is the main legal defence. It means that a business took all reasonable care and precautions, and did everything reasonably practicable to prevent an offence or food poisoning outbreak – that is, it exercised all due diligence.

Every food business has a responsibility to make sure that food is safe to eat. If the food is found to be unfit to eat, prosecution can take place unless it can be proved that all reasonable precautions were taken. Therefore written records that are part of the food safety management system will be essential to prove due diligence.

The written documents could include:

- staff training records, including dates completed, level of study and topics covered
- temperature records (delivery, cooking and cold storage)
- details of suppliers and contractors, and the traceability of the food they supply
- pest control policy and audits
- cleaning schedules and deep-clean reports
- new equipment, modifications to equipment or records of repairs
- CCP monitoring activities (only CCPs, to avoid excessive paperwork)
- pest audit reports
- EHO (EHP) visit reports, including action points
- deviations, corrective actions and recalls
- modifications to the HACCP system
- customer complaints/investigation results
- calibration of instruments.

'Safer Food Better Business' and other systems

The HACCP system may seem complicated and difficult to set up for a small business. With this in mind, the Food Standards Agency launched its '**Safer Food Better Business**' system for England and Wales. This is based on the principles of HACCP but in an easy-to-understand format with no complicated jargon. It has pre-printed pages and charts to enter the relevant information, such as temperatures of individual dishes. There are two main parts: the first is about safe methods, such as avoiding cross-contamination, personal hygiene, cleaning, chilling and cooking; the second covers opening and closing checks (decided by the manager or supervisor), proving methods are safe, recording safe methods, training records, supervision, stock control, and the selection of suppliers.

Once the basic information has been recorded, the actual diary pages are very easy to complete and just need confirmation that the pre-set opening and closing checks have been completed. The only other entries in the diary are the recording of any problems occurring and what will be done about them. If no problems have occurred that day, nothing needs to be entered. This is called 'management by exception' or 'exception reporting'. Similar systems operate in Scotland (CookSafe) and Northern Ireland (Safe Catering).

Scores on the Doors is another strategy to raise food safety standards and reduce the incidence of food poisoning. After a routine EHO (EHP) inspection, a star rating for food safety compliance is awarded. It is intended that the given star rating be placed in a prominent position on the door or window of premises, but this is not mandatory.

The Scores on the Doors scheme is having a positive impact on food safety standards. No matter how good the food in a particular establishment, few people will want to eat there if the food safety score is low.

WEBLINKS

Safer Food Better Business:
www.food.gov.uk/business-industry/sfbb
CookSafe (Food Standards Agency Scotland):
www.foodstandards.gov.scot/cooksafe
Safe Catering (Northern Ireland):
www.food.gov.uk/northern-ireland/safetyhygieneni/safecateringni
Scores on the Doors:
www.scoresonthedoors.org.uk

Food safety training

Food safety training for staff, 'commensurate' to their job roles, is essential and a legal requirement. Training needs to be planned, monitored and managed for staff, making sure that training records are accurate and up to date.

Before any new member of staff handles food, initial training must cover the most important food safety issues in the job role. The food handler will also need to be supervised until formal training takes place (within one month).

Planned retraining/refresher sessions are also essential at all levels and staff must keep up to date with any developments or related issues.

The training methods chosen will depend on the type of business, and any previous training staff have been given. Training could take place by:

- supervisors or managers delivering formal or informal training
- using food safety management companies, which undertake part or all of the food safety requirements for a business, including training
- partaking in food safety qualifications accredited by CIEH, RSPH, City & Guilds, BII, Highfield and others; courses are available at colleges and universities,

through independent training providers, local authorities and adult education centres; training and testing for these can also take place in the workplace
- online or computer package training, with end tests and certification
- food safety training packs, which could include books, workbooks, DVDs and activities, etc.
- as part of another qualification
- training delivered by the EHO (EHP).

Just one or a selection of the above methods could be used, and some training materials are now available in a number of different languages with visual explanations.

Food safety training will cover all or most of the following topics with different degrees of complexity, depending on the level of the training taking place:
- food-poisoning micro-organisms – sources and types, together with simple microbiology
- common food hazards – physical, chemical and microbiological
- prevention of food contamination and cross-contamination
- personal hygiene – responsibilities
- pest prevention and control
- cleaning and disinfection
- design of premises
- food storage and preparation, including temperature control
- food safety management systems
- supervision/management
- legal requirements.

The different levels for formal food safety qualifications are usually as follows.
- **Level 1:** for those new to food handling tasks or employed on non-complex or limited tasks; often completed in the workplace.
- **Level 2:** for those handling a wide variety of foods, including 'open' and high-risk foods.
- **Level 3:** a qualification for supervisors of food premises (food operations), and for those completing more complex tasks and requiring a greater depth of knowledge.
- **Level 4:** a management-level qualification that may also be completed by more senior supervisors and anyone with specific responsibilities for the management of food safety.

The role of management in food safety

Effective planning and management of food safety is essential to ensure that high standards are achieved and maintained. There must be compliance with the law. Management need to work closely with food handlers, taking preventative measures to protect against possible occurrences of food poisoning.

Managers and supervisors are crucial in implementing and managing effective food safety procedures, and provide an important link between business owners/directors and the actual food operation. In a large business, managers and supervisors may not be the actual policy makers but it is likely that they will be involved in devising, setting and running the day-to-day food safety procedures. This will involve implementing the food safety management system (HACCP), including:
- overseeing formal and informal staff training
- managing the various temperature controls, and recording
- putting measures in place to avoid contamination of food and cross-contamination
- setting required standards for personal hygiene and requirements for protective clothing
- monitoring standards for premises and equipment, and safe disposal of waste
- monitoring and managing the correct storage of food and rotation of stock
- managing cleaning and disinfection, and the proactive control of pests.

Communication

Effective communication of food safety matters to staff is of great importance and can be achieved through: induction procedures, ongoing staff training, supervision, mentoring, information posters, leaflets, films, and a range of training materials and information from the EHO (EHP). Food safety matters and developments should form a part of staff meetings, briefings and handover sessions. Effective communication to staff of food safety standards and requirements must be ongoing and consistent.

Those managing or supervising the day-to-day food operations are in the ideal position to communicate food safety matters to business owners, senior managers, other department heads, suppliers, contractors and enforcement officers. Keeping up-to-date and accurate records is essential for effective communication as well as being a legal requirement.

Monitoring, control and auditing

Because food safety must be organised and planned, it is necessary to complete monitoring, control and auditing procedures.
- **Control** involves making sure that the food safety policies are taking place in the day-to-day operations of the kitchen. This could be implemented by making spot checks, or reminding staff of policies by various means.
- **Monitoring** involves the manager/supervisor and others checking (and recording, where appropriate) that controls are being adhered to and are working properly. Many monitoring procedures will be part of the food safety management system, such as monitoring fridge temperatures. Other methods of monitoring may include visual inspections, *organoleptic* checks (sight, smell, touch, etc.) of food

stocks, checklists, walk-through checking procedures and checking that required tasks are completed. In some establishments bacterial monitoring is completed by swabbing surfaces, equipment or processes at regular intervals to test for specific pathogens. This is referred to as total viable counts (TVCs) and swabbing kits are available from food safety management/equipment companies. The findings may be used to improve cleaning and disinfection, and also provide a good tool for staff training and meetings.

- **Auditing** is a more formal procedure, taking the form of an inspection. This could be done by an internal auditor (someone who is part of the organisation), or an external auditor or consultant, but it should be someone who is not involved in the day-to-day systems. Auditing is often used to verify that the HACCP or similar system is working properly.

E. coli puts ten in hospital

TEN people were in hospital last night after an E. coli outbreak.Two cases have been confirmed and up to 16 are suspected.

One of these involves a boy of ten. Health authorities are investigating a link with a supermarket. Yesterday the store closed its delicatessen counter and fresh fruit and vegetable stand.

Customers have been asked to return all meat, dairy and fresh produce bought there since 1 November. E. coli is a potentially fatal gastro-intestinal infection passed on from contaminated food.

Last night an NHS spokesman said none of those in hospital was dangerously ill.

Figure 3.20 Sample newspaper report on food poisoning

WEBLINKS

A wide variety of food safety information and details of food safety qualifications can be found on the Food Standards Agency (FSA) website:

www.food.gov.uk

The FSA is responsible for UK food safety and food quality. Its role is 'to protect public health from risks which may arise in connection with the consumption of food and otherwise to protect the interest of customers in relation to food'.

Chartered Institute of Environmental Health:
www.CIEH.org

Highfield Food Safety Awarding Body:
www.highfield.co.uk

BiiAB:
http://biiab.bii.org/qualifications

NHS food safety advice:
www.nhs.uk/Livewell/homehygiene

ABC Food Law:
www.abcfoodlaw.co.uk

Case study

Outbreak at wedding reception

More than 40 guests at a wedding reception suffered food poisoning after eating a chicken liver parfait. Two children and ten adults (four of them elderly) became seriously ill and needed hospital treatment.

The parfait was served chilled but pink in the centre. The chefs claimed that slight undercooking kept the parfait moist and stopped it from going 'grainy'.

1. What were the possible organisms that caused the food poisoning?
2. How could the parfait be prepared/cooked differently to stop this happening again?
3. What important temperatures should be applied to the preparation, cooking and serving of the parfait?
4. Why are the ages of the sufferers important?
5. What personal hygiene rules should be applied when handling raw chicken livers?

Case study

The hotel buffet

Buffet food is popular at a resort hotel. Hot and cold dishes, and cold desserts, are on the menu. Over a number of weeks, some of the guests started to complain of vomiting only 1–5 hours after eating and the hotel wishes to solve any problems quickly.

1 Suggest the organisms likely to cause these problems, and where it is likely these organisms came from.
2 How could these organisms get into and contaminate the food?
3 How long should the food items be left out on the buffet without temperature control? What should happen to it after this time?
4 How could contamination be avoided from guests touching or sneezing on the food displayed on the buffet?
5 Consider eight important staff rules when producing and serving buffets.

Further reading

Food Safety Direct: visit www.foodsafetydirect.co.uk for a wide variety of food safety books

Food Safety Handbook: Highfield.co.uk

Hygiene for Management: www.highfield.co.uk

Managing Food Safety in Catering: www.cieh.org

Safer Food Better Business: Food Standards Agency

Topics for discussion

1 What are the implications for food businesses of the Allergen Information Regulations (EU FIC) that came into force in December 2014?
2 Who can set up a HACCP system and what needs to be considered before setting up the system? How has of 'Safer Food Better Business' assisted smaller food businesses to comply with the Law?
3 Apart from formal food safety training courses, how can management ensure the ongoing and up-to-date training of staff?
4 What are the various pieces of refrigeration/freezer equipment that would be needed for a large hospital kitchen, also serving a staff dining area?
5 Discuss the implications an outbreak of food poisoning would have on: (a) a five-star hotel; (b) a cruise ship; (c) a home for the elderly.
6 In food businesses, why should waste be recycled wherever possible? Are there any disadvantages to recycling?
7 Why are high standards of personal hygiene and thorough hand washing so important to food safety? How could you effectively convey this message to food handlers?
8 What could be the implications for a food business if there was infestation of the premises by mice? What action should be taken: (a) short term; (b) long term?
9 Look at Table 3.1, a chart for recording allergens in soups. Use the same format for a salad bar with eight different salad items or use some menu items of your own.
10 Illnesses caused by the organism *Campylobacter jejuni* have now overtaken *Salmonella* as the major cause of food poisoning worldwide. What could be the reasons for increased food poisoning from *Campylobacter jejuni* and how could it be avoided?

4 Health, safety and security

→ Introduction

The hospitality and catering industry is substantially affected by accidents at work, and suffers a significant number of recorded days of absence due to injury and sickness.

Kitchens and hospitality premises are potentially dangerous places. It is a legal requirement for every establishment to identify risks, introduce the necessary measures to minimise possible harm and to ensure that the workplace is as safe as possible.

It is a necessary and a legal requirement to be aware of the health and safety policy and procedures of the organisation. Every employee as well as their employers needs to be alert to potentially hazardous situations so accidents and injury can be minimised.

→ Causes of accidents and injuries in the workplace

Some risks and hazards are specific to the hospitality and catering industry. Table 4.1 shows the most significant causes of accident and injury.

Table 4.1 Significant factors for the catering industry

Cause	Significant factors in hospitality and catering
Slips, trips and falls	The single most common cause of major injury in hospitality workplaces ● Wet, slippery floors due to spillages not immediately cleaned and signage not used ● Hazards left in walkways such as boxes and buckets; if carrying a tray it is not always possible to see these hazards ● Uneven floors, unexpected steps and gradients These accidents can cause further injury if a person is carrying hot liquids or sharp knives
Lifting, manual handling and upper limb disorders	Lifting heavy, awkwardly shaped items or moving items from an awkward position, such as heavy trays from low or high oven shelves; food deliveries may be heavy, large and difficult to move Especially hazardous in kitchens, where hot liquids and oils may be involved, items may be awkward shapes or could be frozen or wet Machinery and sharp objects may also cause injury if not handled properly
Exposure to hazardous substances, hot surfaces, steam	Heat and steam will always be present, in the form of: ● liquid or oil splashes ● hot objects or equipment ● steam from ovens/steamers ● using or cleaning deep-fat fryers or placing hands in very hot liquid Injuries from substances, chemicals and cleaning materials tend to be from splashing, misuse, wrong dilution and inhaling fumes
Work-related contact dermatitis (eczema)	A skin disease caused by work, where the skin's barrier layer is damaged causing symptoms like, itching, swelling, redness, blistering, flaking and cracking Most likely to happen to the hands, so barriers such as gloves may be needed
Cuts from knives and other cutting equipment	Most injury will occur from misuse or carelessness, but some will happen because the item was faulty, for example a knife with a loose handle
Injury from machinery	Injury has been recorded from the use of slicers, mixers, processors and other machinery used for vegetable cutting/slicing, mincing and grating, as well as pie and tart-forming machines, dough mixers/moulders and dishwashers
Falls from height/ walking into objects	Falls are usually from a fairly low height or stepladder, but falls down stairs are fairly frequent Injury caused by walking into objects may be because something was wrongly placed, vision was obscured or through carelessness
Fire and explosion	The most likely cause is from manually igniting gas appliances, mainly ovens Lighting them wrongly or faulty equipment can also be a cause
Electric shock	This could be due to poor maintenance, or unsafe switching and unplugging (wet conditions); another cause is equipment misuse
Being hit by transporters and trucks	Fairly rare in hospitality but accidents that do happen usually involve fork-lift trucks

Accidents may be caused by:

- excessive haste – working in hospitality areas can be pressured and with tight time constraints; this may lead to rushing and even running to complete tasks quickly; this can be very dangerous, especially in high-risk areas
- distraction – not concentrating on the job in hand, through lack of interest, personal worry or distraction by someone else
- procedures not followed, such as dealing with a wet floor or safety equipment not used
- excessive noise in the workplace so instructions and warnings cannot be heard
- poorly maintained, faulty or damaged equipment and systems
- incorrect use of equipment, the wrong piece of equipment used for a specific task
- procedures that lead to sprains, strains and pain.

Full name of injured person:			
Occupation:		Supervisor:	
Time of accident:	Date of accident:	Time of report:	Date of report:
Nature of injury or condition:			
Details of hospitalisation:			
Extent of injury (after medical attention):			
Place of accident or dangerous occurrence:			
Injured person's evidence of what happened (include equipment/items/or other persons): Use separate sheets if necessary			
Witness evidence (1):		Witness evidence (2):	
Supervisor's recommendations:			
Date:	Supervisor's signature: This form must be sent to the company health and safety officer		

Figure 4.1 Sample in-house record of accidents and dangerous occurrences

If a hospitality employee regularly works on a computer, they could be at risk of:

- eye strain and eyesight problems
- epilepsy
- upper limb pain and discomfort
- spinal problems
- fatigue and stress.

➔ Accident prevention

Everyone needs to know the potential risks and remain aware of potentially dangerous conditions that may affect health. Employees need to report any unsafe or suspicious conditions to their line manager.

Everyone is responsible for following the Health and Safety Policy and workplace procedures, to avoid injury, illness, discomfort/pain and loss of time at work.

Employees must receive appropriate training and be capable of using tools and equipment correctly and in a manner that will not harm themselves or anyone else.

Safe premises are those that are well lit and well ventilated.

Self-protection

Employees should be encouraged to keep their own health and well-being in mind. Frequent retraining and reminders to create awareness of possible hazards will have a positive impact on employee health. Employees need to treat hazardous substances and working conditions with respect, using correct procedures and never 'cutting corners' to get work done faster. All employees must be aware of the importance of following the company's health and safety policies regarding such areas as:

- exposure limits – for example, to oven-cleaning chemicals
- use of protective equipment
- correct use of guards on machinery such as slicing and mixing machines.

Preventing slips, trips and falls

Floor surfaces must be of suitable construction and in good repair. A major reason for the high incidence of this kind of accident is water and grease spilt on to floors; the combination of these makes the surface extremely slippery. Any spillage must be cleaned immediately and warning notices put in place where appropriate. Ideally a member of staff should stand guard until the hazard is cleared.

Another cause of falls is placing articles on the floor in passageways or between stoves and tables. When carrying trays and containers, vision is obstructed and items on the floor may not be visible; the fall may occur on to a hot stove or fryer and the item being carried may also be hot. These falls can have very serious consequences. The solution is to ensure that nothing is left on the floor that may cause a hazard. If it is necessary to have articles temporarily on the floor, then they should be guarded to prevent accidents.

Kitchen personnel should be trained to think and act in a safe manner so as to avoid this kind of accident.

Using personal protective equipment (PPE)

PPE is equipment and/or clothing that will protect the user against risks at work and it is the duty of an employer to provide these items where necessary. Items such as oven cloths, aprons and heatproof gloves need to be provided and maintained, or replaced so that they are safe to use.

Suitable instruction and training, including where appropriate demonstrations in the proper use of PPE, must be provided to employees. This would include how to correctly fit and wear it, its limitations, care and replacement. Managers, supervisors and other employees must also be aware of why PPE is being used and how it should be used.

Using kitchen equipment

All kitchen equipment and fittings must be safe, used correctly and properly maintained.

Blades and other sharps

Knives are essential tools in hospitality workplaces, particularly kitchens, and should never be misused; the following rules should always be observed.

- The correct knife should be used for the job.
- Knives must always be sharp and clean; a blunt knife is more likely to cause a cut because excessive pressure has to be used.
- Handles should be dry and free from grease.
- The points must be held downwards.
- Knives should be placed flat on the table with the blade pointing inwards so that the blade is not pointing upwards and the handle does not protrude over the edge of the table.
- Never carry a knife on top of a chopping board.
- Knives should be wiped clean, holding the edge away from the hands.
- Do not put knives in washing-up water.
- If a knife needs to be carried it should be done so with great care, directly by the carrier's side with the blade to the back.
- Frozen meat should not be cut or boned out until it is completely thawed because it is difficult to handle: the hands become very cold, the knife slips easily and excessive amounts of pressure need to be applied.

Like knives, choppers should be kept sharp and clean. Care should be taken that no other knives or cutting items can be struck by the chopper, which could cause them to splinter or fly into the air. This also applies when using a large knife for chopping.

Cuts from meat and fish bones

Jagged bones, particularly fish bones and sharp splintered ends of meat bones, can cause cuts. Cuts of this nature, however slight, should never be neglected. They may turn septic.

Cuts from fittings and equipment

Worn or jagged equipment and fittings can cause cuts. Keep fittings and equipment in good repair and remove from use anything sharp and potentially dangerous.

Machinery

Electrical equipment must be given special attention, particularly those listed under the Dangerous Machines Order 1964; examples are electrical mincers, choppers and mixers. Only trained people over the age of 18 are permitted to use and clean such machines, and warning signs and instructions about their use must be sited adjacent to the machine.

Gas equipment must have instructions for igniting the equipment; these must always be followed and staff trained appropriately. In the event of a gas leak or problems with pilot lights, maintenance personnel or the gas equipment suppliers should be contacted immediately.

Maintenance should be regular to ensure the correct functioning and safety of all gas and electrical equipment. This includes checking the seals on microwave equipment.

Accidents are easily caused by the misuse of machines. The following rules should always be put into practice.

- The machine should be in full and correct working order.

- Machine attachments should be correctly assembled and only the correct tools used.
- Guards must always be in place when cutting machines are used; they should not be tampered with nor should hands or fingers be inserted past the guards.
- The controls of any machine should be managed by the operative. If more than one person is involved there is the danger of a misunderstanding and the machine could be switched on when the other person does not expect it.
- Hands should not be placed inside the bowl of the mixing machine until the blades, whisk or hook have stopped revolving. Failure to observe this rule may result in a broken arm or severe cut.

Most modern machinery will not work unless the guards and shields are correctly in place.

The following guidance should be adhered to when cleaning machines.

- Before safety guards are removed for cleaning, the blade or blades must have stopped revolving.
- Electrical plugs should be removed from sockets when machines are being cleaned so the machines cannot be switched on accidentally.
- When a guard is removed for cleaning, the blade should not be left unattended in case someone puts a hand on it by accident, and it should never be placed in washing-up water.

Fryers

- Frying, especially deep frying, needs careful attention.
- Always use a thermostatically controlled fryer, and if this is portable do not move it after use until cool.
- Place foods into hot oil with great care. Wet foods should be drained and dried before being placed in the oil.
- When foods are taken out of the oil this should be done carefully with a frying basket or a 'spider', and with a tray ready at hand.

Lack of care during the emptying and cleaning of fryers is a major cause of accidents. Hazards include:

- fire from overheating or oil getting on to other cooking equipment
- burns from hot oil
- contact with hot surfaces
- fumes from hot cleaning chemicals
- danger of chemicals overflowing
- strains and sprains while lifting and moving containers of oil.

The procedure for draining is as follows.

1. Switch off the fryer.
2. Drain only when oil is cool – do not drain until oil is below 40°C.
3. Make sure you have suitable containers to drain oil into.
4. Remove debris from the bottom and sides of the fryer.
5. Clean according to the manufacturer's instructions and using the correct cleaning chemical. Dry thoroughly inside and out.
6. Ensure that the drain-off tap is turned off and cannot be turned on accidentally.
7. Refill with clean oil; get help with lifting and manoeuvring heavy oil drums.
8. Consider additional PPE, such as eye goggles, long rubber gloves and a thick apron.

Other kitchen equipment

- Tables, benching and other work surfaces must be made of a strong, impervious material such as stainless steel, which can be cleaned easily.
- It should not be possible to accidentally tilt equipment such as bratt pans.
- Extraction systems should function correctly, and particular care is needed to see that they are cleaned regularly as debris is liable to accumulate on filters, preventing the extractor from working properly.
- Walk-in refrigerators and freezers must have a door that is operable from the inside.
- Records of staff trained in the use of equipment and records of maintenance must be kept.

Hot surfaces and substances

A burn is caused by dry heat and a scald by wet heat, both can be very painful and have serious effects. Precautions should be taken to prevent burns, as follows.

- Sleeves of protective jackets should be long and kept rolled down. Protective aprons should be long enough to give adequate protection.
- A good, thick dry cloth or gloves are most important for handling hot utensils. A cloth should never be used wet on hot objects and is best folded to give greater protection. It should not be used if thin, torn or with holes.
- A hot pan brought out of the oven should have something white, such as a little flour, placed on the handle and lid or, better still, an oven cloth wrapped around the handle, as a warning that it is hot. This should be done as soon as the pan is taken out of the oven.
- Handles of pans should not protrude over the edge of the stove as a pan may be knocked off the stove. However, handles placed inwards over the stove will become hot so will need to be handled with a thick cloth.
- Large, full pans should be carried correctly: when there is only one handle the forearm should run along the full length of the handle and the other hand should be used to balance the pan where the handle joins the pan. This should prevent the contents from spilling and causing burns.
- Trays containing hot liquid should be handled carefully, one hand on the side and the other on the end of the tray, to balance it.

- Certain foods require extra care when heat is applied to them – for example, when a cold liquid is added to a hot roux or when adding cold water to boiling sugar for making caramel. (Boiling sugar is hotter than boiling water.) The hot contents of the pan will bubble and spit.
- Steam causes scalds just as hot liquids do and, as steam is hotter than boiling water, injuries can be serious. Turn off the steam before opening the steamer door. The door should be opened just a little to allow excess steam to escape, then stand well back when opening the door fully. The steamer should be maintained regularly, in proper working condition with the drainage holes clear.
- Scalds can also be caused by splashing when passing very hot liquids through strainers; keep the face well back and keep hands away from the liquid too. This also applies when hot liquids are poured into containers.

Gas explosions

To avoid explosions, ensure that the gas appliance is properly lit. On ranges with a pilot light for the oven it is important to see that the main jet has ignited from the pilot. If the pressure is low, sometimes the gas does not light at once and there is a chance that an explosion can occur. When lighting the tops of solid-top ranges it is wise not to place the centre ring back immediately after the stove is lit because the gas may go out, which could cause an explosion on older appliances. Most modern equipment now has cut-out devices that would stop such problems occurring.

Manual handling

Manual handling needs to be part of risk assessment/health and safety policy, and training in correct lifting and carrying techniques is essential.

Figure 4.2 shows how to lift heavy items in the correct way.

Handling checklist

- When goods are moved on trolleys, trucks or any wheeled vehicles, they should be loaded carefully and not overloaded so the load does not fall when moved and the handler can see the way ahead.
- When storing boxes of goods, it is essential that heavy items are stacked at the bottom and that steps are used with care.
- Particular care is needed when large containers of liquid are moved, especially hot liquid. They should not be filled to the top.

Chemicals

Chemicals used in hospitality and catering range from cleaning products to insecticides.

Staff must be trained in the safe handling and use of chemicals, and proper dilution procedures where appropriate, and must wear protective equipment: eye goggles should be worn when using oven cleaners, gloves when hands may come into contact with any chemical cleaner, and face masks when using degreasers and oven cleaners. Extra protective aprons or overalls may be needed.

Everyone should be familiar with the generic name or number of all chemicals used and information about them (data sheets) should be easily available.

Rules for using chemicals

- Always follow the manufacturer's instructions.
- Always store in the original containers. Decanting a chemical means you may lose its name and classification, and it could be misused. There could also be chemical reaction with the new container.
- Keep lids and screw tops tightly closed.
- Do not store in direct sunlight, near heat or naked flames.
- Read the labels (data sheets) and know the possible risks from the product.
- Never mix different chemicals.
- When dilution of a chemical is necessary make sure that this is done accurately. It is best to add the product to water rather than the water to product and do not top up solutions, use a new batch.
- Dispose of empty containers immediately.
- Dispose of waste chemical solutions safely to comply with legal requirements.

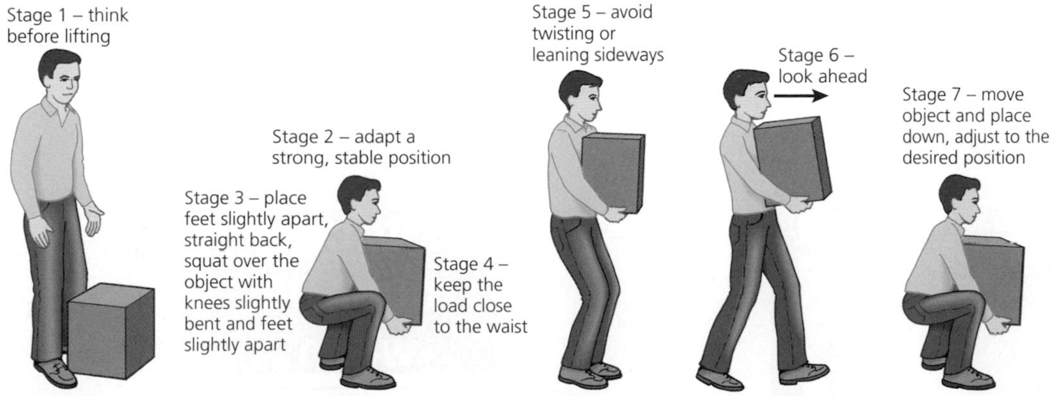
Stage 1 – think before lifting
Stage 2 – adapt a strong, stable position
Stage 3 – place feet slightly apart, straight back, squat over the object with knees slightly bent and feet slightly apart
Stage 4 – keep the load close to the waist
Stage 5 – avoid twisting or leaning sideways
Stage 6 – look ahead
Stage 7 – move object and place down, adjust to the desired position

Figure 4.2 How to lift correctly

WEBLINKS

Further information can be obtained from the Royal Society for the Prevention of Accidents (RoSPA):

www.rospa.org.uk

or the Health & Safety Executive:

www.hse.gov.uk

Using safety signage

There are two main types of signage:

1. **permanent signs**, used for prohibitions, warnings and mandatory requirements, and identifying emergency escape routes and equipment
2. **occasional signs**, including acoustic signals like fire alarms, and illuminated signs (such as fire escape signs) that operate with emergency lighting systems.

The signs should provide enough visual information to be understood by all employees whether or not English is their first language.

The correct and safe use of signs is covered in the Safety Signs and Signals Regulations 1996.

Prohibition signs

Such signs prohibit behaviour that is likely to increase or cause danger i.e. 'YOU MUST NOT'. The information is presented on a round sign with a red circular band and crossbar, featuring a black pictogram on a white background. Red should form at least 35 per cent of the area of the sign. Examples include 'No Entry' and 'No Exit' signs.

Figure 4.3 A prohibition sign

Safety signs

These are to inform of hazards, escape routes and emergency help such as first aid equipment. They are rectangular or square in shape with a white pictogram on a green background. The green part must form at least 50 per cent of the area of the sign.

Figure 4.4 A safety sign

Warning signs

These warn of a hazard or danger, and a need for extra care or precautionary measures. They are a triangular shape, with a black pictogram on a yellow background and black edging. The yellow part must form at least 50 per cent of the area of the sign. Probably the most frequently used of these signs in hospitality areas is the yellow 'wet or slippery floor' sign.

Figure 4.5 A warning sign

Mandatory signs

These warn of a hazard or danger, and the behaviour to be observed, i.e. 'YOU MUST'. They take the form of a blue circle with a white pictogram. Blue should take up at least 50 per cent of the area of the sign. Examples include 'Fire door – keep closed' and 'Guards must be in position before using'.

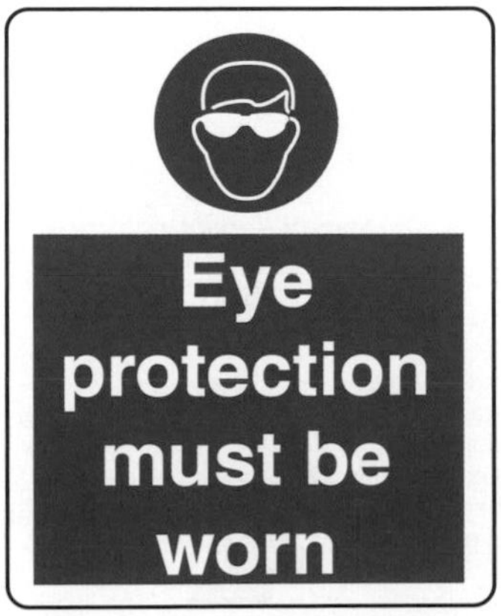

Figure 4.6 A mandatory sign

First aid

With care, attention and good training, accidents and injuries are avoidable. When accidents do happen, however, it is necessary to be trained in first aid.

The arrangements for providing first aid in the workplace are set out in the Health and Safety (First Aid) Regulations 1981. Adequate first-aid equipment, facilities and personnel must be provided at work.

First-aiders and facilities should be available to give immediate assistance to casualties with common and more serious injuries or illness. If the injury is serious the injured person should be treated by a medical professional as soon as possible. One person can stay with the injured person while the other seeks help.

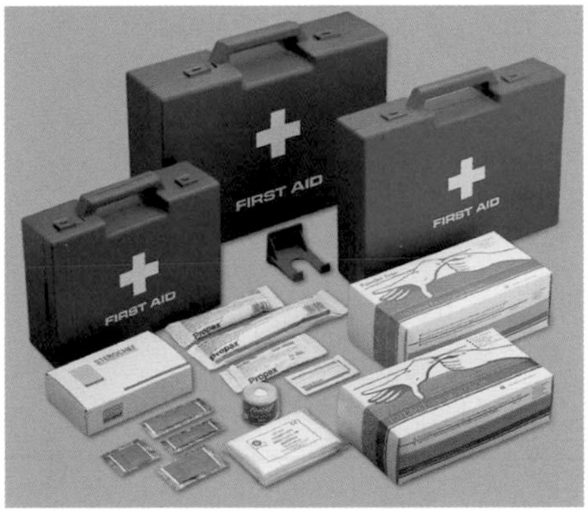

Figure 4.7 First-aid kit

First-aid equipment should be easily identifiable and accessible in the work area. A first-aid box, as a minimum, should contain:

- a card giving general first-aid guidance and information on who to contact in an emergency
- individually wrapped, sterile, adhesive, waterproof dressings of various sizes – preferably blue
- individually wrapped cotton wool packs
- safety pins
- two triangular bandages
- two sterile eye pads, with attachment
- four medium-sized sterile dressings/bandages
- two large sterile dressings/bandages
- two extra-large sterile dressings/bandages
- tweezers
- scissors
- plastic gloves.

The kit needs to be the responsibility of a named person, and should be checked regularly and refilled when necessary.

It is desirable for all establishments to have trained first-aid staff. Suitable qualifications are run by St John Ambulance, St Andrew's Ambulance Association or the British Red Cross Society. After a period of three years, trained first-aid staff must update their training to remain certificated.

Larger establishments must provide at least one person trained in first aid per 50 employees. Smaller companies may have instead an appointed person, who is a point of contact for first aid, keeps the first-aid equipment topped up and contacts the emergency services if needed. It is highly recommended that there is at least one, and preferably more than one, trained first-aider on every work shift.

Large establishments usually have medical staff, such as a nurse, and a first-aid room. The room should include a bed or couch, blankets, chairs, a table, sink with hot and cold water, towels, tissues, hooks for clothing and a first-aid box.

First-aid treatment

It is stressed that we would recommend all hospitality personnel and students complete first-aid training.

Shock

The signs of shock are faintness, sickness, clammy skin and a pale face. Treat by keeping the person comfortable, lying down and warm. Cover them with a blanket or clothing, but do not apply hot-water bottles.

Fainting

Fainting may occur after a long period of standing in a hot, badly ventilated kitchen. Some of the signs of an impending faint are paling of the skin, giddiness and sweating. Treat by raising the legs slightly above the level of the head. When the person recovers consciousness, put them in the fresh air for a while. Make sure that they have not incurred any injury in fainting.

Cuts

Wash the skin around the cut and cover immediately with a waterproof dressing. When there is considerable bleeding, stop it as soon as possible: bleeding may be controlled by direct pressure, by bandaging firmly on the cut. It may be possible to stop bleeding from a cut artery by pressing the artery with the thumb against the underlying bone; such pressure may be applied while a dressing or bandage is being prepared for application, but not for more than 15 minutes.

When assisting someone with a cut, wear disposable gloves.

Nose bleeds

Sit the person down with their head forward, and loosen their clothing around the neck and chest. Ask them to breathe through their mouth and to pinch the soft part of their nose; after 10 minutes release the pressure. Warn the person not to blow their nose for several hours. If the bleeding has not stopped, continue for a further 10 minutes. If the bleeding has still not stopped after that, or recurs in 30 minutes, obtain medical assistance. When assisting with this, wear disposable gloves.

Fractures

A person with broken bones should not be moved until the injured part has been secured so that it cannot move. Obtain medical assistance immediately.

Burns and scalds

Place the injured part gently under slowly running cool or tepid water or immerse in cool water, keeping it there for at least 10 minutes or until the pain ceases. If serious, the burn or scald should then be covered with a clean cloth or dressing (preferably sterile) and the person sent immediately to hospital.

Do not use adhesive dressings, apply lotions or ointments, or break blisters.

Electric shock

Switch off the current. Free the person using a dry insulating material such as cloth, wood or rubber, taking care not to use the bare hands as the electric shock may be transmitted. If breathing has stopped, give artificial respiration and send for a doctor. Treat any burns as above.

Gassing

Do not let the gassed person walk, but transport them into the fresh air if possible. If breathing has stopped, apply artificial respiration and send for medical help.

Artificial respiration

There are several methods of artificial respiration for someone who has stopped breathing. The most effective is mouth to mouth (or mouth to nose); this method can be used by almost all age groups and in almost all circumstances. Seek a trained person to apply this.

WEBLINK

Further information on first aid and emergency treatments can be obtained from the St John Ambulance Association:

www.sja.org.uk

Fire prevention and preparedness

The fire triangle

For a fire to start, three things are needed:

1 a source of ignition (heat)
2 fuel
3 oxygen.

If any one of these is missing, a fire cannot start. Taking steps to avoid the three coming together will therefore reduce the risk of fire.

Once a fire starts it can spread very quickly from one source of fuel to another. As it grows, the amount of heat it gives off will increase and this can cause other fuels to self-ignite.

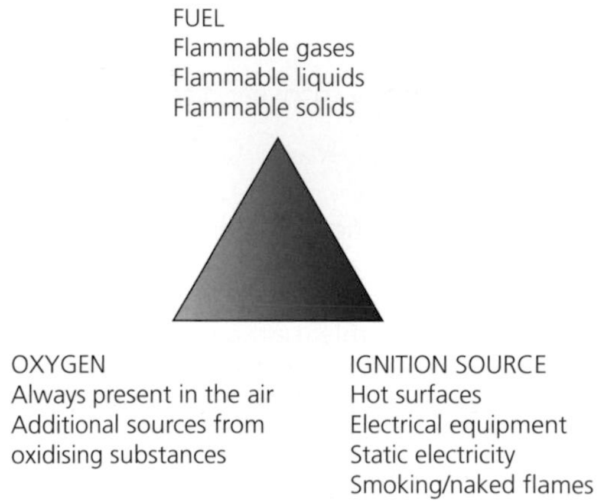

Figure 4.8 The fire triangle

Fire detection and fire warning

All premises need an effective means of detecting any fire and warning people quickly enough that they can escape before the fire makes escape routes unusable.

In very small workplaces where a fire is unlikely to cut off the means of escape (open-air areas and single-storey buildings where all exits are visible and the distances to escapes are small), it is likely that any fire will quickly be detected by the people present and a shout of 'Fire!' may be all that is needed.

In larger workplaces, particularly multi-storey premises, an electrical fire warning system with manually operated call points is likely to be needed. In unoccupied areas, where a fire could start and develop to the extent that escape routes are affected before it is discovered, it is likely that automatic fire detection will also be necessary.

Escape routes

All escape routes, including external ones, must have sufficient lighting for people to see their way out safely. Emergency escape lighting may be needed if some areas do not have natural daylight or are used at night.

Means of fighting fire

A fire requires heat, fuel and oxygen ('the fire triangle', as described above). Methods of extinguishing fires concentrate on cooling (as in a water extinguisher or fire hose) or depriving the fire of oxygen (as in an extinguisher that uses foam or powder to smother it).

There needs to be enough fire-fighting equipment in place for employees to use to extinguish a fire in its early stages, if safe to do so. Fire blankets and wet chemical fire extinguishers should be provided in every kitchen, conveniently sited, and staff should be trained in their correct use.

In small premises, one or two portable extinguishers in an obvious location may be all that is required. In larger or more complex premises, a greater number of portable extinguishers, strategically sited throughout the premises, are likely to be required.

Figure 4.9 Fire blanket

Portable fire extinguishers

Portable fire extinguishers enable trained people to tackle a fire in its early stages, if they can do so without putting themselves or others in danger.

When deciding on the types of extinguisher to provide, consider the nature of the materials likely to be found in the workplace. In the UK, fires are classified in accordance with British Standard EN 2 as Class A, B, C, D, E or F (see below).

In line with EU regulations, all fire extinguishers are red. Generally, portable fire extinguishers are categorised according to the extinguishing medium they contain, identified by a clearly visible coloured rectangle:

- water (red)
- foam (cream)
- powder (blue)
- carbon dioxide (black)
- wet chemical (yellow).

Previously, the entire body of the extinguisher was colour coded, but since 1997 British Standard EN 3: Part 5 has required that all new fire extinguisher bodies should be red.

Class A and B fires

Class A fires involve solid materials, usually organic matter such as wood, paper and fabric. Combustion normally takes place with the formation of glowing embers. The fire can be dealt with using water, foam or multi-purpose powder extinguishers, with water and foam the most suitable.

Class B fires involve liquids or liquefiable solids such as paints or oils. Use extinguishers containing foam, including multi-purpose aqueous film-forming foam (AFFF) carbon dioxide, halon or dry-powder types.

The fire extinguishers currently available for dealing with Class A or Class B fires should not be used on cooking oil or fat/oil fires (Class F).

Class C fires

Class C fires involve gas. Dry-powder extinguishers may be used. However, combine this with action such as stopping a leak to remove the risk of a subsequent explosion from the build-up of unburned gas.

Class D, E and F fires

- **Class D** fires involve combustible metals. Use a dry-powder extinguisher (blue).
- **Class E** fires involve electrically energised equipment. Use a CO_2 extinguisher (black).
- **Class F** fires involve cooking oils and fats. Use a wet chemical fire extinguisher (yellow).

Some fire extinguishers can be used on more than one type of fire. For instance, AFFF (foam) extinguishers can be used on both Class A fires and Class B fires. The local authority or equipment suppliers will be able to advise.

Figure 4.10 Types of fire extinguisher

In the UK, fire extinguishers should conform to a recognised standard such as British Standard EN 3 for new ones and British Standard 5423 for existing ones. For extra assurance, you should look for the British Standard Kitemark, the British Approvals for Fire Equipment (BAFE) mark or the Loss Prevention Council Certification Board (LPCB) mark.

Other fire-fighting equipment

The most useful fire-fighting equipment for general fire risks is the water-type extinguisher or hose reel. One should be provided for approximately each 200 square metres of floor space, with a minimum of one per floor. If each floor has a hose reel, in working order and of sufficient length for the floor it serves, there may be no need for water-type extinguishers to be provided.

Areas of special risk involving oil, fats or electrical equipment must not be sprayed with water and may need carbon dioxide, dry-powder or other types of extinguisher (see above).

Where hose reels are provided, they should be conspicuous and always accessible, such as in corridors. They should never be obstructed by placing items in front of them.

Fire-extinguishing systems

In more complex buildings, or where it is necessary to protect the means of escape and/or the property or contents of the building, it may be necessary to consider a sprinkler system as well.

Sprinkler systems are an efficient means of protecting buildings against extensive damage from fire. They are also now acknowledged as an effective means of reducing the risk to life from fire.

→ Health and safety legislation

It is important that employers and employees are well aware of the health and safety legislation that applies to their industry and workplace, and the people working within it. Legislation is updated occasionally to deal with modern working procedure and equipment, but the main acts are outlined below.

Health and Safety at Work Act (1974), updated 1994

This act imposes a general duty on an employer 'to ensure so far as is reasonably practicable, the health, safety and welfare at work of all employees'. It is largely about good health and safety practice in the workplace. Employers must comply with all parts of the act, including completing risk assessments and introducing safe ways of working. Employers will need:

- a health and safety policy that include risk assessments (unless there are fewer than five employees)
- to keep premises and equipment in safe working order and provide/maintain personal protective equipment for employees.

Employees must:

- take reasonable care for the health and safety of themselves and of other persons who may be affected by their actions or omissions at work
- co-operate with the employer so far as is necessary to meet or comply with any requirement concerning health and safety
- not interfere with, or misuse, anything provided in the interests of health, safety or welfare.

The act is particularly relevant to the hospitality and catering industries, where many hazards occur naturally. Staff must partake in regular safety training, and risk assessments must address any dangers and regularly update the controls in place.

WEBLINK

The Health and Safety Executive (HSE):

www.hse.gov.uk

The HSE produces training packs, leaflets, posters, DVDs and stickers to provide health and safety information.

Other health and safety at work legislation

The Workplace (Health, Safety and Welfare) Regulations 1992 ensure the safety and well-being of employees within their working environment, covering matters including suitable working premises, staff hygiene facilities, heating, ventilation and lighting.

The Management of Health and Safety at Work Regulations 1999 state that health and safety information must be provided for all employees. Where an employer has five or more employees, there must be a written health and safety policy issued to every member of staff, outlining the responsibilities of the employer and employees.

Provision and Use of Work Equipment Regulations 1998 (PUWER)

'Work equipment' covers machinery such as food processors, slicers, ovens, knives, and a range of other equipment specific to the hospitality and catering industry. These regulations place duties on employers to ensure that work equipment is suitable for its intended use, is maintained in working order and in good repair, and that adequate information, instruction and training on the use and maintenance of the equipment and any associated hazards is given to employees.

Control of Substances Hazardous to Health (COSHH) 2002

Under COSHH, risk assessments must be completed by employers of all hazardous chemicals and substances that employees may be exposed to at work, their safe use and proper disposal.

A range of chemicals are used in hospitality establishments. Each must be given a risk rating that is recorded, and employees who use it given relevant information and training. Data sheets or cards must be kept in an easily accessible place so staff can refer to them when needed. Measures must be taken to ensure that all staff understand these, with consideration given to those who do not speak English as their first language or who have other possible barriers to understanding the information.

Personal Protective Equipment at Work Regulations 1992

These regulations require employers to assess the need for and to provide suitable personal protective equipment and clothing (PPE) (see page 58). Employers must keep these items clean, in good condition and provide suitable storage for them. Employees must use them correctly and report any defects or shortages.

PPE is not provided instead of other safety measures; they are the final items in health and safety considerations.

Manual Handling Operations Regulations 1992

These regulations protect employees from injury or accident when required to lift or move heavy or awkwardly shaped items. Handling of objects can be more difficult in hospitality areas because they could be very hot, frozen or sharp.

A risk assessment must be completed, employees trained in correct manual handling techniques, and lifting or moving equipment provided where appropriate.

Fire Precautions (Workplace) Regulations 1997

These regulations state that premises with more than five employees must have a written fire risk assessment with details of the appropriate fire safety precautions in place. The fire safety precautions may include:

- provision of emergency exit routes and doors
- 'fire exit' signs, emergency lighting to cover the exit routes where necessary
- fire-fighting equipment, fire alarms and, where necessary, fire detectors, all regularly maintained
- fire training for employees in fire safety following the written risk assessment
- production of an emergency plan and sufficient trained people/equipment to carry out the plan
- employers must plan, organise, control, monitor and review the measures taken to protect employees and others from fire.

Gas

Gas Safety (Installation and Use) Regulations 1998

These regulations require employers to maintain gas appliances. It is vital that all gas equipment, and in particular Calor gas equipment, is properly and regularly serviced and adjusted. They also require any work to a gas fitting or gas storage vessel to be carried out by a 'competent person'. This includes installing, reconnecting, maintaining, servicing, adjusting, disconnecting, repairing, and purging the equipment of gas or air. The person must be Gas Safe registered and have a valid certificate of competence that covers the particular type of gas work to be carried out. For this reason, an agreement should be in place with a properly qualified gas installer or maintenance company.

An EU directive requires that all gas appliances sold since 1996, whether new or used, must be fitted with a fuel cut-out mechanism should the main pilot light be extinguished.

'Interlocking' describes the mechanical link between sensors in the extraction system and the main valve of the gas supply to cooking equipment. Should the carbon monoxide level in the ventilation system go up, the interlocker will turn off. All new commercial kitchens must have interlocking in the ventilation system, and any replacement, new installation or modification to existing ventilation systems must incorporate interlocking.

Electrical equipment

Electricity at Work Regulations 1989

These regulations introduced new, specific requirements for electrical appliances, extending the general duties of the Health and Safety at Work Act 1974. All electrical systems and equipment in the workplace, both fixed and portable, are covered by the regulations, requiring that:

- the design, installation and maintenance of electrical systems and equipment are carried out only by competent people
- equipment is suited to the job and the conditions in which it is used
- the manufacturer's instructions on the safe use and maintenance of equipment are followed
- employees use equipment safely, having been given the appropriate supervision, guidance and training, and report any faults or problems.

The safety of electrical equipment must be checked by an electrician at intervals, such as every six or twelve months. This is often known as portable appliance testing (PAT testing). After testing, a sticker is usually placed on the item noting the testing date, and the testing information is recorded and stored with other safety documentation.

A supervisor or other responsible person should also check these items on a regular basis and staff must remain vigilant too: electrical equipment can easily be damaged in kitchen areas – for example, an electrical flex burned by using it above a gas jet.

All equipment should be included in the health and safety risk assessment, and staff must have training in the safe use of the equipment.

Electrical equipment is mostly covered by a non-binding EU directive: the Low Voltage Directive. This was passed into UK health and safety law as the Low Voltage Electrical Equipment Safety Regulations.

WEBLINK

For more on electrical safety, go to:
www.sgs.co.uk

Computers and other display screen equipment

An employer must take steps to reduce the risks to health of those using a computer for work purposes under the Health and Safety (Display Screen Equipment) Regulations 1992.

The Health and Safety (Miscellaneous Amendments) Regulations 2002 widened the scope of the regulations to require all computers and other display screen workstations to meet health and safety specifications.

Legal requirements for safety signs

The employer has a duty to:

- provide and maintain any necessary safety sign
- give employees instructions and training in the meaning of the signs and what to do in connection with them.

The correct and safe use of signs is covered in the Safety Signs and Signals Regulations 1996

RIDDOR (Reporting Injuries, Diseases and Dangerous Occurrences)

These regulations require employers, and/or the person responsible for health and safety within a workplace, to report and keep records of any:

- work-related fatal accidents
- work-related disease
- accidents and injury resulting in the employee being off work for three days or more
- dangerous workplace events (including 'near miss' occurrences)
- major injuries, loss of limbs or eyesight.

In 2013 the reporting procedures were simplified and the list of incidents/diseases that need to be reported was shortened, but most requirements remain unchanged.

Accidents and incidents under RIDDOR need to be reported and can be done so in the UK by contacting the HSE by telephone on 0845 300 9923 or by completing the RIDDOR form on its website: www.hse.gov.uk/riddor/.

Other regulations

Some other relevant regulations that apply to the workplace are:

- Lifting Operations and Lifting Equipment Regulations (LOLER) 1998
- Noise at Work Regulations 1989
- The Health and Safety (First Aid) Regulations 1981
- Data Protection Act 1998 (plus Europe-wide updates, and general data protection legislation from 2003, 2011 and 2018)
- Working Time Regulations 1998.

European laws have strict guidelines or explicit instructions on topics as diverse as pressure in systems and the surface temperature of oven doors; these are implemented in the UK through UK health and safety legislation.

Enforcing health and safety legislation in the workplace

Health and safety law is of great importance and authorised bodies have the powers to enforce legislation.

In the UK, the Health and Safety Executive (HSE) regulates health and safety law in industry and public areas. The HSE gives local authorities delegated power to regulate health and safety law in premises including catering services, restaurants and hotels, etc.

Health and safety law is enforced by authorised officers, as follows:

- inspectors from the HSE, Environmental Health Officers/Practitioners (EHOs/EHPs), and technical officers from local authorities
- fire officers – in the majority of premises, local fire and rescue authorities are responsible for enforcing fire safety.

Inspections

Inspectors have the right of entry to premises to inspect them without prior notice. They have the power to serve legal notices requiring improvement work, or prohibiting work procedures or processes, and the use of work equipment. Inspectors may:

- enter premises at any reasonable time
- take a police officer or an authorised person or equipment to help with the investigation
- make necessary examinations and inspections
- take samples, measurements, photographs or recordings
- take possession of and detain/dismantle any article or substance for examination or to ensure that no one tampers with it

- require any person to give information to assist with any examination or investigation
- require documents to be inspected or copied
- require that assistance and facilities be made available to allow full investigation
- remove anything the inspector believes could cause danger or serious injury
- serve notices (see below)
- close the business, part of the business or a procedure immediately.

The employer or someone working for them such as a manager is likely to be asked to accompany an inspector during an inspection of their area. They will need to answer any questions, and make paperwork and records ready for inspection. The inspector may also discuss any improvements needed with the person accompanying them.

Improvement notices

If the inspector thinks there is a contravention of legislation – for example, health and safety or food safety legislation – an improvement notice may be served on the person responsible. The person responsible is the owner, director, manager, franchisor or supervisor in charge of the premises at the time of the inspection. The notice must state:

- that a contravention exists
- the details of the law contravened
- the inspector's reasons for his or her opinion
- that the person responsible must arrange to remedy the contravention
- the time given for the remedy to be carried out; this must not be less than 21 days.

If a person fails to comply with an improvement notice, he or she commits a criminal offence and there will be further action.

Prohibition notices

If an inspector believes that the premises or work activities involve a serious risk of personal injury, a prohibition notice may be served on the person in charge of the work activity. This will prevent further work being carried out in the premises or area deemed to be dangerous. This would also apply if an EHO/EHP considers there is imminent risk of injury if a business remains open. The notice must:

- state that, in the inspector's opinion, there is a risk of serious personal injury or illness
- identify the issues that create the risk
- give reasons why the inspector believes there to have been a contravention of the law
- direct that the activities stated in the notice must not be carried on, by or under the control of the person served with the notice, unless the matters associated with the risk have been rectified.

This notice closes the business immediately for three days. The inspector will then apply for an Emergency Prohibition Order to keep the premises closed. Notices/orders must be displayed in a visible place within the premises. The owner of the business must apply for a Certificate of Satisfaction before they can reopen.

Fines and penalties for non-compliance

Consequences for employers can include:

- magistrates' courts can impose fines of up to £5,000 for each offence, a six-month prison sentence or both
- for serious offences, such as knowingly making employees use dangerous equipment, magistrates could impose fines of up to £20,000 and/or six months' imprisonment.
- in a Crown Court unlimited fines can be imposed and/or two years' imprisonment.

If it can be proved that an incident or injury was caused by the negligence or wrongdoing of an employee or that the employee intentionally did not comply with the employers' procedures, this could result in:

- fines imposed appropriate to the offence
- compensation payments to an affected or injured person
- up to two years' imprisonment
- dismissal from employment.

➜ Health and safety management

Organisations should make everyone aware of the importance of high standards of health and safety. Making health and safety part of daily working practices will help.

All workplaces with five or more employees must have a written health and safety policy that is given to all employees and must have conducted a full risk assessment of premises and procedures (see below) then put controls in place to keep employees safe. Those with fewer than five employees still have a duty of care to keep their employees safe at work.

Ongoing and recorded training is also essential and should include information on hazards and incident procedures. Records of staff training, the topics covered and the dates they were completed should also be kept.

Managing health and safety should cover the usual management functions of:

- planning
- organisation
- control
- monitoring
- review.

Sources of support for managers and supervisors of health and safety

There are a number of helpful sources of health and safety information, including:

- workplace HR departments and health and safety representatives
- the Health and Safety Executive

- Environmental Health Officers employed by local authorities
- fire safety officers
- product manufacturers and the literature they produce
- health and safety publications, and hospitality textbooks
- trades unions.

WEBLINK

Health and Safety Executive:

www.hse.gov.uk/catering/

There is a wealth of information on this website, some of it specific to hospitality. This includes useful guidance and templates for risk assessments.

Health and safety and employee absence

Employee absence from work can be disruptive and costly to the business. Reasons for absence from work in hospitality businesses include all the reasons recorded in other industries, but in addition could involve:

- effects of working in constant heat or cold
- injury from equipment and the working environment
- stress from pressures caused by the nature of the work
- effects of anti-social or long working hours
- conditions such as contact dermatitis due to work area substances.

High standards of health and safety awareness can reduce many of these factors.

Risk assessment

It is required by law that an employer control the potential risks in the workplace (see above). To do this, they need to consider what could cause harm to people and if they are taking the reasonable steps to prevent any harm. This is known as risk assessment. Managing risk need not be complicated.

Definitions

A hazard is anything with the potential to cause harm. This could include a wide range of activities, such as, say, the use of chemicals or knives.

A risk is the possibility that someone could be harmed by the hazard.

Involve employees

These are people most at risk of having accidents, or experiencing ill health if correct procedures are not in place. They also know the most about the jobs they do so are in the best position to help managers develop safe systems that are effective in practice. All those involved with a work activity, managers, supervisors and operatives, can be engaged in assessing risks.

How to assess risk

There are five steps in a risk assessment, as follows.

1. Consider the hazards – what are the processes or procedures that could cause harm?
2. Decide who might be harmed and how.
3. Evaluate the risk and decide whether the existing precautions are adequate, or whether more should be done.
4. Record the findings so you have a formal record that can be checked.
5. Regularly review the risk assessment with regular and 'spot' checks to see that the standards set are being complied with, and revise the assessment when necessary.

The following points should be considered:

- determine preventative measures
- decide who carries out safety inspections
- decide frequency of inspection
- determine methods of reporting back and to whom
- detail how to ensure inspections are effective.

Risk assessment outcomes can be divided into four areas, as follows.

1. **Minimal risk:** safe conditions with adequate safety measures.
2. **Some risk:** acceptable risk, however attention must be given to ensure safety measures operate correctly.
3. **Significant risk:** safety measures are not fully in operation; requires immediate action.
4. **Dangerous risk:** processes and operations to stop immediately, and to be completely checked.

Risk assessment must be recorded and must remain a 'live document', regularly updated and changed as appropriate. It will be kept in the establishment's records as part of 'due diligence' and the overall health and safety policy. (Due diligence is when a person or organisation who may be subject to legal proceedings can establish a defence that they have taken 'all reasonable precautions and exercised due diligence' to avoid committing an offence.)

Should an incident occur, it is essential that the cause or causes are investigated and any defects in the system remedied at once to prevent further accidents.

All personnel need to be trained to be actively aware of the possible hazards and risks, and to take positive action to prevent accidents occurring.

When trying to identify risks, it may be helpful to consider the following points.

- What are the chances of people slipping or tripping?
- Do people work with, or come into contact with, dangerous items such as asbestos?
- Do people work with hazardous chemicals or other substances?
- Do people perform work at height and, if so, is this done safely?
- Has due consideration been given to training/retraining on all matters that could affect health at work?

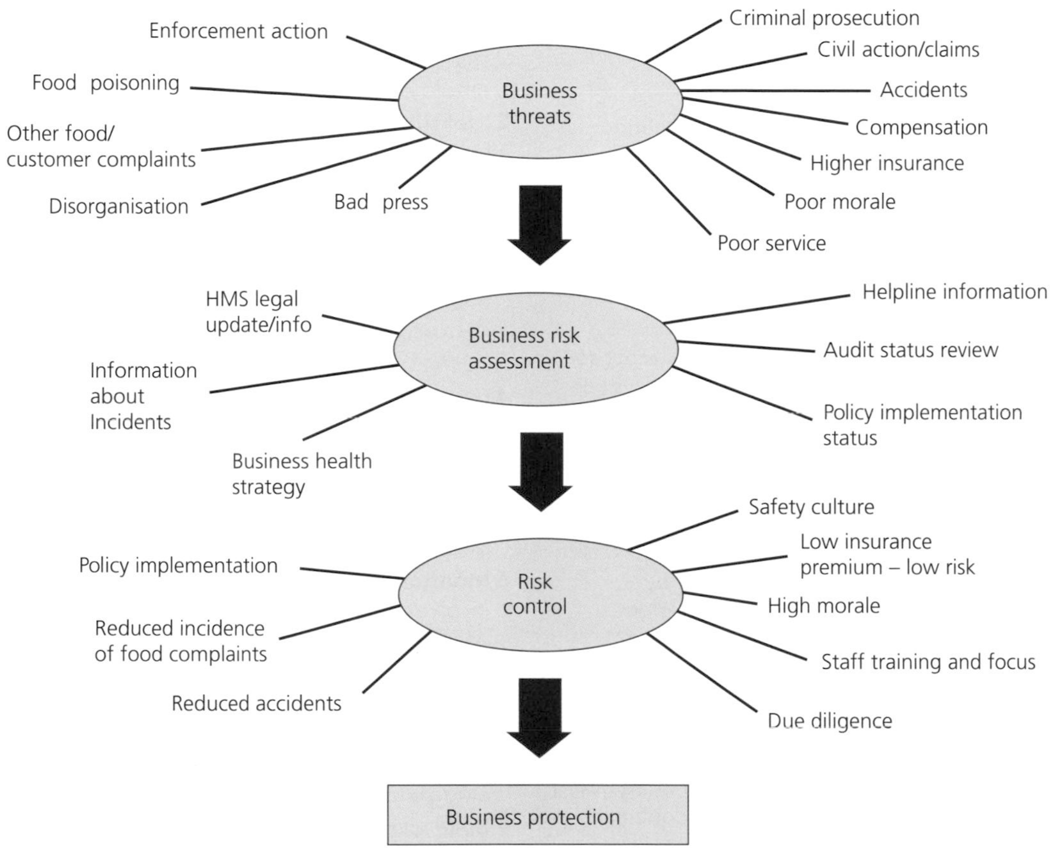

Figure 4.11 Protecting the business from threats

➜ Health and safety information for employees

All employees, including trainees, must be provided with information about the particular risks they may face in their everyday work, what to do in the event of a fire or other emergency, and the preventative and protective measures designed to ensure their health and safety, including the identity of the staff that would assist in the event of evacuation. The information needs to be presented in a way that can be understood by all, bearing in mind that a significant number of hospitality employees in the UK do not speak English as their first language.

Safety signage should be used as a way to control a hazard only when all other methods to reduce the risk have been exhausted. Safety signs must not take the place of other risk-control methods and should significantly decrease the likelihood of an accident occurring.

The employer has a duty to:

- provide and maintain any necessary safety sign
- give employees instructions and training in the meaning of the signs and what to do in connection with them.

Employees' duties

Employees must use all equipment provided by their employer correctly, and work in accordance with the training and instructions they have received.

Employees must immediately inform their employer, or person responsible for health and safety, of any work situation that might present risk of an accident or imminent danger. Also, employees should report any shortcomings in the health and safety protection arrangements in their work area.

Employee consultation

Under the Safety Representatives and Safety Committees Regulations 1997, the employer must consult employee representatives in health and safety matters. A recognised trade union must notify the employer in writing of the appointed health and safety representatives. Alternatively, an employer could create a health and safety function within the company, with one or more representatives.

The functions of a health and safety representative include:

- investigating potential hazards and dangerous occurrences in the workplace
- examining the cause of accidents, and investigating health and safety complaints by any employee
- making representations to the employer on matters affecting the health, safety or welfare at work of employees
- attending health and safety meetings.

If two or more health and safety representatives make a request in writing for a committee, the employer must set one up within three months, after consultation with those making the request.

Developing the health and safety policy

The written health and safety policy establishes how health and safety is managed in the organisation.

Implementing effective health and safety measures doesn't have to be expensive, time consuming or complicated. Developing a positive health and safety culture within the organisation, with ongoing training and updates, will help to maintain standards as well as saving time and money by the prevention of accidents and decreased absence from work. This requires effort to create a committed and well-organised management that understands the benefits of good health and safety practice, and knowledgeable staff.

The health and safety policy is the essential foundation on which to build. It need not be complex but should reflect the actual workplace and procedures, and so be meaningful and useful to all concerned. With a policy, control of hazards is possible through safe systems and procedures.

Periodic review of systems will be necessary to further develop health and safety procedures and include any updates. Reviews should take place on a regular basis but especially when workplace systems change, such as when new equipment is installed.

WEBLINK

For information on producing a health and safety policy go to the Health and Safety Executive's website:
www.hse.gov.uk

Ten ways to reduce health and safety risks at hospitality premises

1 **Understand the consequences:** many business owners and managers are oblivious to the sort of problems that can occur. Having a sound understanding of safety issues that can impact on the business and its employees is the first and most important step.
2 **Identify possible risks and how they can be managed:** whether this is just one person or a team of people from across the business, it is vital that they have the skills, knowledge, attitude and awareness to identify and manage risks properly.
3 **Enlist the help of experts:** look for experts that can develop the knowledge base within the team, and manage the areas of health and safety management the team may be too busy or not experienced enough to deal with.
4 **Create a clearly defined risk management system:** document all the risks that have been identified, who is responsible for dealing with them and how they will be monitored.
5 **Educate:** train all employees, in particular the key personnel, in risk awareness and risk reduction.
6 **Monitor:** make sure that the risk management system involves obvious checkpoints that are recorded and easily identifiable.
7 **Evaluate:** regularly review the risk management system to ensure that it is achieving the desired results.
8 **Change:** the hospitality industry is dynamic, so it is important that the risk management system changes along with the business.
9 **Build a knowledge base:** the problems that one hospitality business is experiencing will be similar to those of other establishments. Communicating with professional associations and groups can be a vital source of ideas.
10 **Keeping guests and customers safe:** poor safety standards, which could cause injury, will deter future guests/customers. Remember that, with social media, a bad experience at an establishment can be broadcast worldwide within seconds.

→ Staff facilities and welfare

The welfare of all employees at a place of work is the responsibility of the employer/business owner. Facilities must be provided that are both safe and beneficial. These include:

- sufficient working space (minimum of 11 cubic metres per person)
- easy evacuation in an emergency and regular training in this

- floors and exit routes are non-slip and in good repair
- efficient ventilation
- working temperature comfortable (normally around 16°C and not below 13°C, except when foods are to be kept cold, such as in a cold room preparation area where suitable clothing should be provided)
- provision of adequate toilets, hand-wash facilities and drinking water
- changing facilities and accommodation for outdoor clothes, separate ones for men and women
- provision of a rest-room facility.

Smoking

Smoking is banned in public places, workplaces and in vehicles used for work purposes. However, employees may want to smoke in their break times. Set rules about where this can take place outside of the building, considering the visibility of staff smoking and the proximity to the building, and about wearing workplace clothing outside. For example, chefs' clothing should be worn only in the kitchen to avoid contamination from outside. This can be difficult to enforce, so for practical reasons many establishments now say that chefs must remove their apron and hat, and wear a white coat over the rest of their uniform, before going outside.

It is up to employers to decide on a policy for e-cigarettes as they are not currently covered in the ban on smoking in workplaces as laid out in the Health Act 2006. Most employers are reluctant to allow e-cigarettes into a working environment, though, and will treat them in exactly the same way as conventional cigarettes.

Occupational health

Occupational health refers to protecting the safety, health and welfare of people relating to their work, including any illness or disease possibly caused by the employment. The aims of occupational health programmes include a safe and healthy working environment, and advising on working procedures and substances that could affect health – for example, frequent exposure to strong cleaning chemicals causing respiratory difficulties.

Occupational health departments may also offer health advice, pre-employment medical checks, fitness-to-work checks, and more. They frequently advise on safe working when there is a change in circumstances – for example, an employee who is pregnant. Health professionals, such as occupational health nurses, record cases of illness, take samples from contaminated areas and keep medical records. Awareness of possible early symptoms of illness may also be covered. Symptoms may not appear for years after the original contact with a procedure or substance – for example, exposure to asbestos leading to asbestosis.

Some problems can be detected early and before they become serious. Vulnerable employees should have regular check-ups, and occupational health departments can often arrange these. This may depend on their age, previous medical history and position within the organisation.

Increasingly, occupational health provision for companies is sourced from outside agencies.

Employees must cooperate with occupational health and safety programmes as these are designed to identify and control occupational health hazards.

An employee with health concerns that may be related to their employment should seek help according to the company policy. They may need to inform an occupational health department, a line manager or health and safety officer, after which seeking professional medical advice to allow for prompt action and treatment is essential.

Fire safety

Every employer has an explicit duty for the safety of employees in the event of a fire. The Regulatory Reform Fire Safety Order 2005 places responsibility for fire prevention and the safety of the occupants of premises on a defined responsible person, usually the employer.

The responsible person must:

- make sure that the fire precautions, where reasonably practicable, ensure the safety of all employees and others in the building
- make an assessment of the risk of fire in the establishment; special consideration must be given to dangerous chemicals or substances, and the risks that these pose if a fire occurs
- review the preventative and protective measures.

Fire safety requires constant vigilance, using the provision of detection and alarm systems, and well-practised emergency and evacuation procedures in the event of a fire. Businesses no longer need a fire certificate, but the fire and rescue authorities will continue to inspect premises and ensure adequate fire precautions are in place. They will also wish to check that the fire risk assessment is comprehensive, relevant and up to date.

An employer must consider workers' capabilities when asking them to carry out tasks or assignments relating to fire safety. This responsibility was clarified in the Fire Safety (Employees' Capabilities) England Regulations 2010.

Fire precautions

- Identified hazards must be removed or reduced so far as is reasonable without significantly affecting the business. All persons must be protected from the risk of fire and the likelihood of a fire spreading.
- All escape routes must be safe and used effectively.
- Means for fighting fires must be available on the premises.
- Means of detecting a fire and giving warning in case of fire on the premises must be available.
- Arrangements must be in place for action to be taken in the event of a fire, including the instruction and training of employees.
- All precautions provided must be installed and maintained by a competent person.

Fire risk assessment

A fire risk assessment will help determine the chances of a fire occurring and the dangers from fire for the people in the workplace. The five-step risk assessment approach used in general health and safety management can be used, as follows.

1. Identify potential fire hazards in the workplace.
2. Decide who (e.g. employees, visitors) might be in danger in the event of a fire, in the workplace or while trying to escape, and note their location.
3. Evaluate the risks arising from the hazards and decide whether your existing precautions are adequate or whether more should be done to get rid of the hazard or to control the risks (e.g. by improving fire precautions).
4. Record the findings and details of the action you took as a result. Inform employees about the findings.
5. Keep the assessment under review and revise it when necessary.

This could be combined with a general risk assessment if appropriate. A risk assessment is not a theoretical exercise: a tour of the workplace will be needed to confirm, amend or add detail to the initial findings.

➜ Security in the workplace

Security in hospitality premises is a major concern. The main risks are:

- theft – from customers or employees, or from the business (e.g. silver, wine or spirits, cash)
- burglary – theft with trespass
- robbery – theft with assault, such as when banking cash
- fraud – false claims for damage; counterfeit currency; stolen credit cards
- assault – fights between customers, while staff banking/collecting cash
- vandalism – malicious damage to property
- arson – setting fire to property
- undesirable persons – such as drug traffickers operating in the building
- terrorism – bombs, telephone bomb threats.

Theft

Theft from hospitality premises is often opportunist; individual losses may be small but they can add up to a significant loss to a business.

Eliminate or reduce cash handling as a preventative measure:

- use credit and debit cards and pre-paid internet bookings
- pay employees by bank transfer if possible.

However, it is still necessary for most businesses to use cash. Make sure that only the staff who actually need to know have relevant cash information. Larger-scale crime is generally well planned, so reducing the information available to the potential criminal limits the ability for the theft to be planned and committed.

Other measures include:

- notices that cash is not kept on the premises overnight or that safes are protected by time-delay locks
- strict stock control to reduce the amount of goods on the premises
- train staff in simple anti-fraud measures such as checking bank notes, checking credit cards against passports and checking that photographs on passports match the person.

It is impossible to remove all temptation, however. Therefore equipment – for example, computers, electronic tablets – should be security marked. Equipment and stock should be kept in secure storage.

With regard to employees, the first step is, wherever possible, to appoint honest staff by taking up references from previous employers and interviewing with care.

Security of the premises

Although hospitality premises may have open access, remain aware of any unauthorised person entering.

- Everyone reporting to reception should be registered in some way; guests by the usual registration processes and visitors or contractors signing in and being given a security badge to wear.
- Check that visitors all leave the building when they should.
- At the back door, everyone delivering goods must report to a security officer or someone else who can verify their visit.
- Check all areas regularly and make sure all staff understand the importance of vigilance.
- Make sure that any suspicious person does not re-enter the building.
- Night-time security staff may be used to maintain security in the quieter night periods.

Install equipment to improve security.

- Well-lit areas deter thieves. Use general lighting to illuminate areas seen by staff or passers-by, or movement-activated lighting where appropriate.
- Lock doors, with keypad codes or swipe cards, and windows too.
- Closed-circuit television (CCTV) cameras are used as a deterrent against crime. These have recording features that can be played back if specific incidents need to be investigated.

Security systems should be carefully selected according to the needs of the business and having taken advice from an independent expert.

Other security issues

The Health and Safety at Work Regulations require employers to conduct a risk assessment with regard to employee safety. Where staff come into close contact with the public, offer training in recognising and defusing volatile or difficult situations, and dealing with aggressive customers. However, staff should also be trained not to approach people who could pose a physical threat to them or that they suspect may lead to difficult situations.

All staff should be made aware of the potential threat from terrorists and remain alert at all times, reporting to security staff or a line manager if they have concerns.

Each business will have its own risks and threats. Observant and alert staff are very important to security. Make sure that security is an important part of their induction and training, and that retraining takes place periodically. This is especially important when changes are made to areas and systems.

Management of a security system

A security system needs to be managed. This involves:

- developing a policy for the establishment to cover security threats, bomb alerts, theft, policy regarding prosecution
- covering the cost of security staff, whether in-house or contract
- developing procedures for security risk assessment, dealing with breaches of security
- understanding the legal implications of, for example, vicarious liability for false arrest or imprisonment
- seeking a proper balance between the often conflicting demands of security and safety.

→ Health, safety and security: a summary

Managers must think positively about how they can sustain and improve health and safety in their establishment, to minimise the risk of incidents occurring. Accidents frequently happen because of acts or omissions by management rather than staff neglect.

The Management of Health and Safety at Work Regulations 1999 provide the basis for safety management requirements. This legislation requires:

- all involved in safety to think positively
- competence to be established
- risk assessment to be undertaken
- implementation of effective control.

Knowledge of and compliance with health and safety legislation is essential. Measures to reduce risk will always include ongoing staff training.

Case studies

Example A

In a large food production kitchen a new, white vinyl floor was laid. Unfortunately when kitchen workers walked across the floor their shoes left black marks that would not come off with the usual floor cleaning chemicals and equipment. A kitchen porter thought it would be a good idea to spray the floor with a strong oven-cleaning chemical. This did work and the floor was free of marks. However, in spraying the oven cleaner it made contact with the legs of some stainless-steel benching, making the legs porous and therefore weak. A chef carried and placed a large pan of hot soup to the table, which immediately collapsed, resulting in the soup pouring over the chef and causing burns to his face, arms and chest.

1 Write a list of good practice instructions for staff working in kitchens to prevent something like this happening.

Example B

A restaurant in an old building did not have enough power points in the right places. On a hot day the staff wished to place fans around the room. This involved using a number of extension cables from the same socket and running cables across the floor. The trailing cable in the main walkway was mainly covered with a service trolley, but when this was needed it was wheeled away. A waitress tripped on the cable and a pot of freshly made coffee flew from her hands covering a small child who was badly burned and needed hospital care.

1 What was done badly?
2 How could this restaurant have improved the situation?

Example C

A kitchen porter was handed a large used chopping board with two sharp knives to clean. Walking to the wash-up area, he slipped on some oil on that had been left on the floor. The porter fell backwards and the knives flew off the chopping board, one going into his eye.

1 What are the main health and safety issues that should have been observed to prevent this happening?

Further reading

Hughes, P. and Ferret, E. (2009) *Introduction to Health and Safety at Work*. Routledge.

Health and Safety Executive (2014) *Health and Safety Made Simple*. HSE.

Health and Safety Executive (2015) *A Recipe for Safety*. HSE.

Tolley (2015) *Tolley's Health and Safety at Work Handbook*. Tolley.

Chartered Institute of Environmental Health: www.cieh.org (the CIEH is a professional, awarding and campaigning body on environmental and public health)

Fire prevention advice: www.fireservice.co.uk (advice on fire prevention, risk assessments and training)

Highfield: www.highfield.co.uk (information provider and awarding body for health and safety, food safety, first aid and many more qualifications)

Institution of Occupational Safety and Health: www.iosh.co.uk (IOSH is the Chartered body for health and safety professionals)

Red Cross: www.redcross.org.uk

Royal Society for Public Health: www.rsph.org.uk (RSPH is dedicated to the promotion and protection of health and well-being; it also awards qualifications in areas relevant to health priorities)

Topics for discussion

1 Discuss the main causes of accidents in hospitality premises. What are the specific measures you could put in place to reduce accidents? How can a hospitality workforce be 'educated' to be safe workers?

2 There will always be a number of health and safety signs, posters, notices or stickers throughout hospitality premises. How are these categorised? Compile a list of notices and signs you would need for a hotel kitchen area, wash-up area and staff rooms.

3 There are a number of training courses for staff relating to health and safety, food safety and security. Find out what the relevant courses are and which would be suitable for different members of staff.

4 As an employer in a large restaurant what are your obligations under the Fire Precaution Regulations 1997? What are the processes and procedures you would need to put in place to comply with the regulations?

5 What provision should be made for the health and welfare of hospitality staff at work? Discuss this, bearing in mind costs and the fact that in the industry many employees are casual or part-time.

6 In a hospitality business there are a number of people with the authority to ensure that you comply with the law affecting the business. Who are they and how could you contact them for advice?

7 Under the Health and Safety at Work Act 1974 what are the responsibilities of (a) an employer, (b) an employee. What are eight other pieces of legislation that affect employers/employees?

8 What are the security measures that could be put in place in a hospitality business? In your area who could advise you about suitable security measures?

9 What is meant by COSHH and what are the employer's responsibilities in relation to this? Which items used in hospitality premises would be covered by COSHH? What information do you need to provide for employees?

10 What would be the implications of an employee having an accident resulting in serious injury in your workplace? If this happened, what are the actions you would need to take immediately and in the longer term?

5 Kitchen planning, equipment, services and energy conservation

Factors influencing design

Before a kitchen is planned, it is important to understand its goals and objectives in relation to market strategy. You also need to know the target numbers you intend to serve.

Design of the front-of-house areas is discussed in Chapter 11.

Services: gas, electricity and water

The designer must know or plan where the services are located and the maximum load that the gas and/or electricity can provide. This will assist in deciding how to make efficient use of the services, otherwise they become very expensive and may not work correctly – for example, blocked drains and insufficient water and gas pressure are common occurrences.

Staff

The number and skill level of the staff the company intends to employ needs to be decided upon quickly as it will have an impact on labour costs and equipment choices. Equipment can help less skilled staff with cooking consistency and efficiency, and replace labour-intensive kitchen operations. Equipment designed for the easiest possible maintenance and cleaning will also keep labour costs down.

The more prepared food is used, the more this will affect the skill level.

Amount of capital expenditure

Most design has to work with a detailed capital budget. It is not always possible to design, then consider the cost afterwards. Finance will often determine the overall design and acceptability.

Because space is at a premium, kitchens are generally becoming smaller. Equipment is being designed to cater for this trend, becoming multi-functional and streamlined.

Food production methods and equipment

A fast-food restaurant using prepared convenience food will require planning and equipping very differently than an à la carte or cook-chill kitchen.

Determine the following.

- Will sweets and pastries be made on the premises?
- Will there be a need for larder or butcher?
- Will fresh or frozen food, or a combination of both, be used?
- How much will be purchased prepared and ready to cook and serve?

The type, amount and size of the equipment will depend on the type of menu.

The equipment must be suitably sited. When planning a kitchen, standard symbols are used that can be produced on squared paper to provide a scale design. Computer-aided design (CAD) is often used to do this. In large public-sector projects – for example, education, health care or prisons – there is a new requirement for design known as building information modelling (BIM).

Hygiene and food safety

The design and construction of the kitchen must comply with the Food Safety Act 2005/2006/2013. The basic layout and construction should enable adequate space to be provided in all food-handling and associated areas for equipment as well as working practices, and frequent cleaning to be carried out.

Design and decor

The trend towards more attractive eating places has had an effect on kitchen planning and design. One trend has been that of bringing the kitchen area into view – for example, where grills or griddles are in full public view and food is prepared on them to order. Some restaurateurs are even moving the kitchen to the front, in full view of everyone walking by.

While there will be a continuing demand for the traditional heavy-duty type of equipment found in larger hotel and restaurant kitchens, the range of equipment available has become greater and more affordable. However, price will reflect the quality of the machine and therefore its life expectancy. Research the leading manufacturers and choose equipment designed to cope with change and redevelopment.

When thinking about interior design, it is very important that the colour, room temperature and type of seating are in keeping with the theme of the restaurant, the service and overall dining experience.

Multi-usage requirements

Round-the-clock requirements, such as in hospitals, factories where shift work takes place, the police and armed forces, have also encouraged kitchen planners to consider the design with a view to their partial use outside peak times. Kitchen equipment is being made more adaptable and flexible, so that whole sections can be closed down when not in use, in order to save on heating, lighting and maintenance. Staffing during those times will be minimal and some equipment should also provide for minimum operator effort.

➜ Kitchen design

Kitchens must be designed so that they can be easily managed. Managers must have easy access to the areas under their control and good visibility in the areas that have to be supervised. Large operations should work on separate work flows, for reasons of efficiency and hygiene:

- product – raw materials to finished product
- personnel – how people move within the kitchen; for example, staff working in areas of contamination should not enter areas of finished product or where blast-chilling is taking place
- containers/equipment/utensils – equipment should, where possible, be separated out into specific process areas
- refuse – refuse must be kept separated and should not pass through other areas to get to its storage destination.

The layout of the kitchen must focus on the working and stores area, and the equipment to be employed. These areas must be designed and based on the specification of the operation.

To get ideas on effective kitchen design:

- visit existing kitchens with a critical eye
- ask staff for comments on the suitability, and practicality, of layout
- seek professional advice from a number of manufacturers.

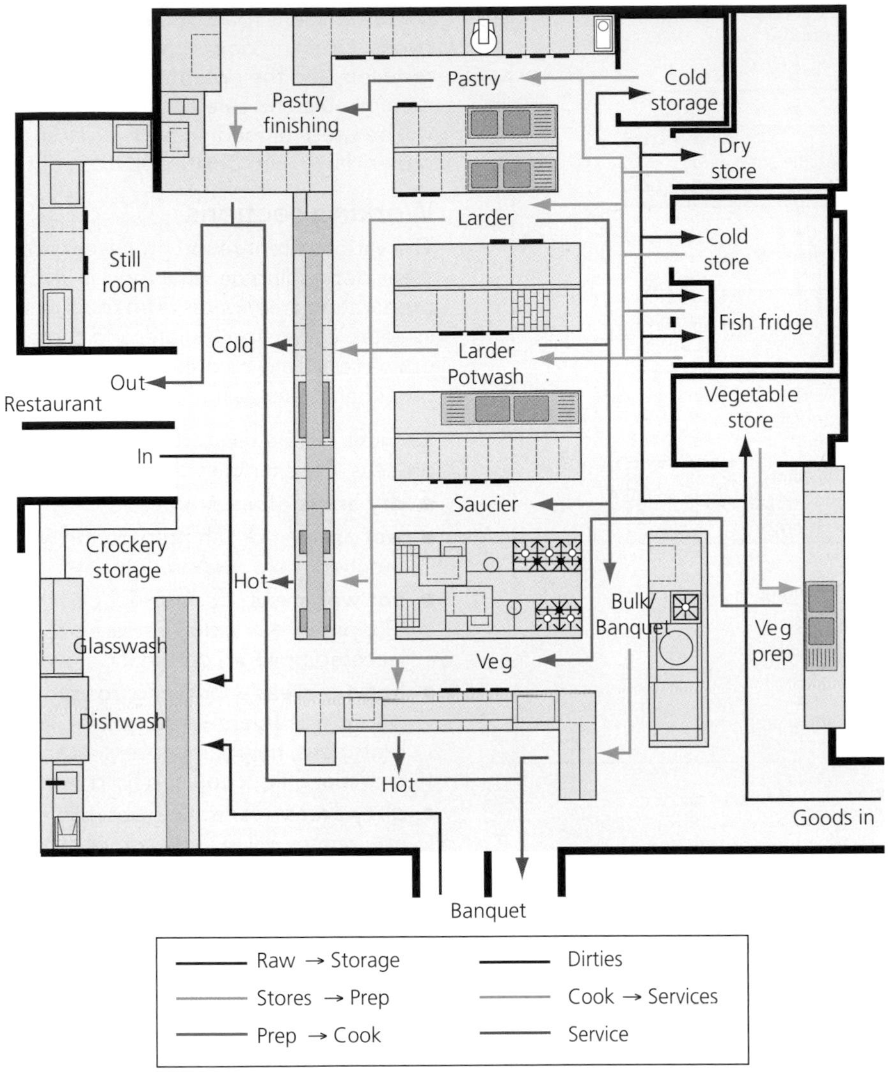

Figure 5.1 Kitchen design

Product flows

Proper design and layout of the preparation area can make a major contribution to good food hygiene. There are certain basic rules that can be applied that not only make for easier working conditions but help to ensure that food hygiene regulations are complied with. Staff generally respond to good working conditions by taking more pride in themselves, in their work and in their working environment.

The layout should be planned so that raw foodstuffs arrive at one point, are processed in the cooking section and then despatched to the servery. There should be a distinct progression in one direction. Back-tracking or cross-over of materials and product must be avoided. Vegetable preparation and wash-up areas should be separate from the actual food preparation and service areas. The staff should not hamper one another by having to cross one another's paths more than is absolutely necessary.

Each section should be subdivided into high-risk and contaminated sections. High-risk food is that which, during processing, is likely to be easily contaminated. Contaminated food is that which is contaminated on arrival before processing – for example, unprepared vegetables, raw meat (see Chapter 3).

Work flow

Food preparation rooms should be planned to allow a 'work flow' whereby food is processed from the point of delivery to the point of sale or service. The various processes should be separated as far as possible, and food intended for sale should not cross paths with waste food or refuse. A design that reduces wasteful journeys is both efficient and cost-effective.

The overall sequence of receiving, storing, preparing, holding, serving and clearing is achieved by:

- minimum movement
- minimal back-tracking
- maximum use of space
- maximum use of equipment with minimum expenditure of time and effort.

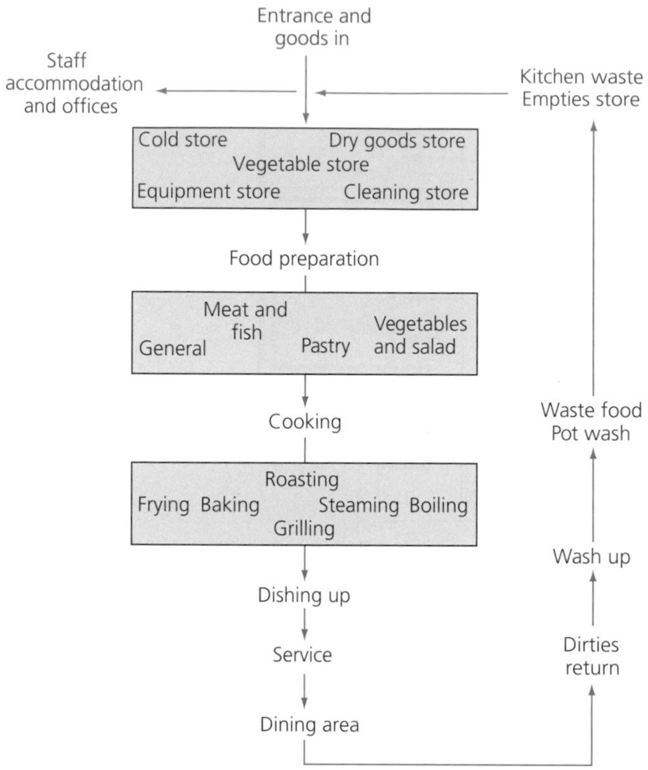

Figure 5.2 Work flow

The size and style of the menu and the ability of the staff will determine the number of sections and layout that is necessary. A straight-line layout would be suitable for a snack bar, while an island layout may be more suitable for a hotel restaurant.

The cooking section should contain no through traffic lanes used by other staff.

Work space

The size of the kitchen is also determined by purpose and function.

- The operation and its design and equipment are based on the menu and the market it is to serve.
- The management policy on buying raw materials will determine kitchen plans on handling raw materials.

Adequate work space must be provided for each process.

Approximately 4.2 square metres is required per person; too little space can cause staff to work in close proximity to ranges, ovens, steamers, cutting blades, mixers, and so on, thus causing accidents. A space of 1.37 metres from equipment is desirable, and aisles must be of adequate size to enable staff to move safely. The working area must be suitably lit, and ventilated with extractor fans to remove heat, fumes and smells.

Worktops should be adequate in size for the preparation processes necessary, and should be designed so that the food handler has all required equipment and utensils close to hand.

Allow sufficient space for access to equipment such as ovens. Opening doors creates an arc that cannot be reduced, and the operator must have sufficient room for comfortable and safe access. It is also likely that trolleys will be used for loading and unloading ovens, or rolling tables drawn into position in front of the oven.

Working sections

The various preparation processes require different areas depending on what food is involved. In a vegetable preparation area, water from the sinks and dirt from the vegetables will accumulate, and therefore adequate drainage should be provided. Pastry preparation, on the other hand, entails mainly dry processes.

Kitchens can be divided into sections based on this process. For example:

- **dry areas** – for storage
- **wet areas** – for fish preparation, vegetable preparation, butchery, cold preparation
- **hot wet areas** – for boiling, poaching, steaming; equipment will include steamers, bratt pans, steam jacketed boilers, combination oven
- **hot dry areas** – for frying, roasting, grilling; equipment will include fryers, salamanders, induction cookers, bratt pans, halogen cookers, roasting ovens, microwave, charcoal grills, cook and hold ovens
- **dirty areas** – for refuse, pot wash, plate wash; equipment will include compactors, dishwashers, refuse storage units, glass washers, pot wash machines.

Because 'raw materials' enter the cooking section from the main preparation areas (vegetables, meat and fish, dry goods), this section will be designed with a view to continuing the flow movement through to the servery. To this end, roasting ovens, for example, are best sited close to the meat preparation area, and steamers adjacent to the vegetable preparation area.

Equipment

Selection of equipment will be made after detailed consideration of the functions that will be carried out within the cooking area. The amount of equipment required will depend upon the complexity of the menus offered, the quantity of meals served, and the policy of use of materials – from the traditional kitchen organisation using only fresh vegetables and totally unprepared items, to the use of prepared foods, chilled items and frozen foods, where the kitchen consists of a regeneration unit only.

Prepared food will require different types of equipment and labour compared to part-prepared food or raw-state ingredients. Prepared food examples are sous-vide products, cook-chill, cook-freeze and prepared sweets. Part-prepared food examples are peeled and cut vegetables, convenience sauces and soups, portioned fish/meat. Raw-state food examples are unprepared vegetables, meat that requires butchering, and fish requiring filleting and portioning.

The kitchen operation must work as a system. It is advisable to site items of equipment used for specific functions together. This will help increase efficiency and avoid shortcuts.

To allow for the cleaning of wall and floor surfaces, stationary equipment must be positioned:

- 500 mm from the walls
- allowing 250 mm clearance between the floor and underside of the equipment.

Not only should the equipment be suitably situated but the working weight is very important to enable the equipment to be used without excess fatigue. Kitchen equipment manufacturers and gas and electricity suppliers can provide details of equipment relating to output and size.

The service policy – e.g. all-plate service, a mixture of plate and silver service, or self-service – will affect the volume and type of dishwashing required.

Other elements of the design

If satellite kitchens are served, it is desirable to have two loading bays: one for receiving and one for delivery. They should be adjacent to the relevant store to facilitate loading. The receiving bay should be adjacent to the prime goods store for purchased meat, vegetables, and so on, and the delivery bay near to the finished goods stores that contain items ready to go out to their end units. A good receiving area needs to be designed for easy receipt of supplies with nearby storage facilities suitably sited for distribution of foods to preparation and production areas.

Hygiene must be considered so that kitchen equipment can be cleaned, and all used equipment from the dining area can be cleared, cleaned and stored. Still room facilities may also be required (see Chapter 11).

Hand basins must be sited strategically to encourage frequent hand washing in all food preparation areas.

Allow for the storage of cleaning equipment.

Planning and layout of the cooking area

Island groupings

In an island arrangement, equipment is placed back to back in the centre of the cooking area. There will need to be sufficient space to allow for this, including adequate gangways around the equipment and space to place other items along the walls. Without careful thought, an island arrangement may result in the chef walking to the other side of the island, which is not practical.

Wall siting

An alternative arrangement involves siting equipment along walls. This arrangement is possible where travel distances are reduced, and normally occurs in smaller premises.

L- or U-shaped layouts

These arrangements create self-contained sections that discourage entry by non-authorised staff; they can promote efficient working, with distances reduced between work centres.

The kitchen environment

- **Space:** the Office, Shop and Railway Premises Act 1963 stipulates 11.32 cubic metres (400 cubic feet) per person, discounting height in excess of 3 m.
- **Humidity:** a humid atmosphere creates side effects such as food deterioration, infestation risk, condensation on walls and slippery floors. Anything higher than 60 per cent humidity lowers productivity. Provision for the replacement of extracted air with fresh air is essential.
- **Temperature:** no higher than 20–26°C is desirable for maximum working efficiency and comfort, with 16–18°C in preparation areas.
- **Noise:** conversation should be possible within 4 m.
- **Light:** the minimum legal level in preparation areas is 20 lumens per square foot, with up to 38 lumens preferable in all areas.

Ventilation systems

You will need to consider the following when deciding on ventilation.

- The **extract flow** rate required. This must always be based on the individual items of cooking equipment. You can find the details in HVCA Specification DW/172.
- Where in the building the extracted air can be discharged. If it can be discharged at roof level (which is 1 metre above the highest openable window), then there is no requirement to treat this exhaust air prior to discharge. If this is not possible, then local authority consent will be required. For approval to be granted you will need to put in place adequate pollution control measures, including odour, smoke and noise control.
- How to provide fresh air to replace that being extracted.

Consultants

There are a number of specialist consultants involved in kitchen design. Consultants are often used by companies to provide independent advice and specialist knowledge. Their expertise should cover:

- equipment
- mechanical and electrical services
- food service systems and methods
- drainage
- architectural elements
- ventilation/air conditioning
- statutory legislation (Food Act, Health and Safety Act, fire regulations)
- energy conservation

- recycling
- green issues/legislation (waste management)
- refrigeration.

Consultants should provide the client with unbiased opinions and expertise not available in their company. Their aim should be to raise the standards of provision and equipment installation, while providing an efficient and effective food production operation that also takes into account staff welfare.

Maintenance

Planning and equipping a kitchen are an expensive investment. Efficient, regular cleaning and maintenance are essential. It is quite normal that all the catering staff take responsibility for the cleanliness of the working environment, so following each meal service, the entire team should clean down together, pulling out all the equipment where possible.

Kitchen design

Industry trends

In most cases, throughout the industry, companies are looking to reduce labour costs while maintaining or enhancing the meal experience for the customer. Some trends in various situations are as follows.

- **Hotels:** greater use of buffet and self-assisted service units.
- **Banqueting:** move towards plated service, much less traditional silver service.
- **Fast food:** new concepts coming on to the market, more specialised chicken and seafood courts, more choices in ethnic food and international food cultures.
- **Roadside provision:** increase in number of operations, partnerships with oil companies, basic grill menus now enhanced via factory-produced à la carte items.
- **Food courts:** development has slowed down; minor changes all the time; most food courts offer an 'all day' menu.
- **Restaurants/hotels:** less emphasis on luxury-end, five-star experience.
- **Casual dining:** increasing with use of different concepts and themes.
- **Theme restaurants:** will continue to improve and multiply.
- **Hospitals:** greater emphasis on bought-in freezer and chilled foods; steam cuisine; reduced amount of on-site preparation and cooking; satellite kitchens; cook-chill; cook-freeze.
- **Industrial:** more zero-subsidy staff restaurants, increased self-service for all items; introduction of cashless systems will enable multi-tenant office buildings to offer varying subsidy levels.
- **Prisons, institutions:** little if any change; may follow hospitals by buying in more pre-prepared food; may receive foods from multi-outlet central production units, tied in with schools, 'meals on wheels' provision, etc.
- **University/colleges:** greater move towards providing food courts; more snack bars and coffee shops.

Chefs and managers are often asked to assist in the design of food service systems. In these circumstances there are various issues that need to be taken into account. If possible, all designs should be market-led in the first place.

- **Market expectations:** type of customer demand (including price), type of menu, type of meal, type of establishment, 'product life' and possibility of 'product' changes, customer participation.
- **Operational needs:** amount of space available, expected throughput/seat turnover, type of operation (e.g. call order, traditional).
- **Amount of basic preparation:** amount of regeneration, storage needs, flows of materials, people and equipment, availability of supplies, frequency of delivery, need for storage, availability of services – gas, electricity, water, waste disposal, energy costs, ventilation, extraction and induction systems.
- **Type and quantity of labour to be employed:** e.g. unspecialised staff using pre-prepared materials, traditional 'partie' system using basic ingredients, room for future expansion.
- **Finance:** objective (e.g. to make a profit, to provide a service), cost of space (i.e. cost per square metre), amount and type of finance (e.g. purchase, leasing, hire purchase), whether to use second-hand equipment, depreciation policy, life of investment.

Kitchen equipment trends

- **Refrigeration:** more focus on providing CFC-free equipment.
- **Environmental:** with an environmentally conscious society, energy conservation will feature higher in the development agenda; this will include heat recovery systems, recirculated air systems, improved working conditions and lighting systems.
- **Cooking:** more use of induction units, combination ovens, microwave and tunnel ovens.
- **Servery counters:** more decorative units being used.
- **Dishwasher/potwash:** greater economy of water, more mechanised and automated use of combination machines.
- **Ventilation:** moves towards integrated wash systems, recirculated air systems, integral air supply, integral fire suppression.

The general trend will be towards self-diagnostic equipment and automated service call-out. With the use of replacement components, there is less emphasis on repairs.

Towards the greener kitchen

Restaurants generally use much more energy than other commercial buildings; sometimes about two to five times more energy per square foot.

Investing in energy efficiency is the best way to protect the business from rising energy costs.

- **The stores area:** use PIR (passive infrared) low-energy lighting. This reduces the risk of lighting being left on when the areas are not in use.
- **Hand-wash facilities:** use sensor taps.
- **Refrigeration:** use drawer units in refrigerators – these can reduce the work of compressors and glass doors in upright cabinets as doors are opened less frequently. All refrigeration equipment should be checked against the Energy Technology List (ETL), which lists models that are 30 per cent more energy efficient than standard industry models.
- **Preparation sinks:** use pressure-reducing valves in taps, with inbuilt flow-limiting devices or aerators to reduce the volume of water used.
- **Cooking:** some ranges use pan sensors, which provide energy efficiencies, although energy is lost around the edge of the pan.
- **Fryers:** these burners work only when the range is being used. When the pan is removed from the cooking surface the flame is extinguished, leaving just the pilot light on, so no energy is used.
- **Induction hobs:** these also provide energy-saving benefits. Induction hobs are 50 per cent more efficient than halogen hobs, and 86 per cent more efficient than gas hobs.
- **Microwaves:** a combination of convection heat, impingement pressure and electromagnetic energy allows typical cook times from 15–90 seconds. A built-in catalytic converter eliminates the need for a ventilation hood so the oven can operate in any environment. This results in energy saving.
- **Combination ovens:** combinations of steam and convection can reduce energy costs by 50 per cent. A triple-glazed viewing door will save up to 40 per cent of energy compared to a single-glazed door.
- **Service pass:** use drawer warmers that have separate compartments, thermostat and humidity control to ensure food is held at the correct temperature and does not deteriorate. Each drawer is in its own separate compartment so when the drawer is open the temperature in the other drawers is not affected, and elements are mounted in the cabinet interior rather than the wall, giving faster production and recovery.
- **Waste management:** many local authorities and water companies record the use of water disposal units as this passes the problem down the line.
- **Bio-enzymatic fluid systems:** these break down fats, oils, and grease and starch, which can block kitchen drains. There are cost-effective solutions available to meet legislative demands.

Environmental targets

The built environment makes heavy demands on natural resources, can be energy intensive and, if poorly managed, can have an adverse effect on communities and businesses. Controls and measures implemented during the design, construction and operation of a facility can limit the environmental impact, reduce running costs, and help create better working and living conditions.
It is now mandatory for an environmental performance assessment to be carried out on all public-sector construction projects and it can also be requested for private projects.

Case study

Example environmental policy

The company recognises its responsibilities to reduce its impact on the environment as part of national and international efforts to stem the continued risk of global warming. It aims to operate in a sustainable way by minimising the use of resources, including energy and water, and by using sustainable resources wherever possible.

We aim to purchase our food and ingredients from sustainable and local sources wherever possible, and to do our utmost to use seasonable food in our kitchens.

We aim to minimise kitchen waste and to recycle wherever possible.

The company aims to harness the latest energy saving ideas and technology, and to improve the energy efficiency of all its properties, while maintaining their character.
In the short term, we recognise that much can be done through effective management, sub-meter monitoring and energy control, and will work with all staff to support the aims of this policy.

This policy will form the basis of actions that will lead to reduced risk of polluting incidents, full legal compliance and better support for a sustainable future. This is expected by our customers, our staff and everyone associated with our business.

Alongside our commitment to this policy, the company recognises the need to meet the expectations of customers. This will include levels of comfort, hospitality and service.

Chief Executive:

Date:

The catering team has a responsibility to ensure that energy consumption is reduced to a minimum. All staff must be made aware that, from arriving at the beginning of their shift to leaving the workplace, their actions will have a direct impact on the environment.

Environmental responsibilities of management

It is the responsibility of the manager to ensure that an environmental policy is in place for the operation of the services, and that all members of staff have a clear understanding of this policy at their induction.

Where the catering services are outsourced it is important for the environmental policy to be included within the tender specification and, where possible, maximum energy consumption levels identified to ensure the contractor takes responsibility for managing the use of utilities.

The management has a responsibility to produce energy consumption awareness through staff induction and training. Up to 30 per cent of energy savings can be attributed to operational standards within the commercial kitchen environment. Good, and ongoing, staff training is therefore essential.

A great deal of kitchen energy wastage occurs through simple operator actions such as appliances being switched on too far in advance of their being needed, or refrigeration plant being overworked due to chilled air escaping when doors are left open. In addition, equipment that is not routinely cleaned will become less energy efficient over time.

It is essential that kitchen staff understand the benefits of the kitchen's energy-saving strategy and their roles within it, and take 'ownership' of it.

It is important to match the capability and training of the workforce and the complexity of the equipment. For example, mistakes made with programmable ovens can result in food and energy wastage, as well as an increase in contaminants being processed through the drainage systems.

Regular staff appraisals will enable the identification of personal and group energy efficiency training needs.

Linking equipment to computers

Electronic point of sale (EPOS) terminals in restaurant bars can interface directly with back-of-house computers. Some EPOS systems with kitchen monitor hook-ups can optimise meal preparation by telling chefs when to start cooking particular components, thus allowing all the items that make up an order to be completed at exactly the same time.

A growing range of kitchen equipment, from cookers and refrigerated storage to large ware-washing systems, come with on-board computer control, and several products can additionally be specified with extra hardware and software to permit continuous monitoring of the main equipment functions. Some appliances can also be specified with a two-way interactive link, enabling programs subject to frequent change (such as recipes) to be downloaded to the appliance from a computer directly via cable or wireless hook-up, or via modem connection to the internet.

The temperature monitoring of all refrigerators and freezers within an establishment can be linked to a computer system. Several temperature readings are sent to the computer each day and it can also record temperature highs and lows, and any unusual trends. Temperatures outside the specified limits will be highlighted. Regular refrigeration temperature readings can be recorded as part of an operation's HACCP records.

Water management

In the UK, laws governing the use of water include the Water Industry Act 1991, the Health and Safety at Work Act 1974 and the Water Supply Bylaw 1989.

The purpose of water law is to:

- discourage undue consumption of water
- prevent contamination of the water supply.

Substantial savings can be made through the renewal and replacement of older water-using equipment. Self-closing taps, for example, reduce water consumption by as much as 55 per cent.

In many countries it is an offence for the owners or occupiers of buildings to intentionally or negligently allow any 'fitting to waste', or to unduly consume water – for example, taps constantly dripping or left running, overflows from storage and WC cisterns dripping, and water leaks not repaired.

There is evidence to show that the undertaking of a water-management audit can save money. Practical action to save water includes:

- water metering
- tap flow regulator – flow control
- urinals using less water
- shut-off devices and self-closing taps
- automatic or programmed mains shut-off device when buildings are not in use
- low-flow shower heads.

WEBLINK

To find out more about water management, visit the Water Management Society website:

www.wmsoc.org.uk

➜ Equipment design

The Food Safety (General Food Hygiene) Regulations 1995, and subsequent regulations (2006, 2013), require all articles, fittings and equipment with which food comes into contact to be kept clean, and to be constructed and maintained so as to minimise risk of contamination. Equipment must also be installed in such a way that the surrounding area can be cleaned.

The following equipment is preferable:

- tubular machinery frames
- stainless-steel table legs
- drain cocks and holes instead of pockets and crevices that could trap liquid
- dials fitted to machines having adequate clearance to facilitate cleaning.

Where practicable, equipment should be mobile to facilitate its removal for cleaning – that is, castor mounted and with brakes on all the wheels.

Preparation surfaces

The choice of surfaces on which food is to be prepared is vitally important. Failure to ensure a suitable material may provide a dangerous breeding ground for bacteria. Stainless-steel tables are best as they do not rust, and their welded seams eliminate unwanted cracks and open joints. Sealed tubular legs are preferable to angular ones because they eliminate the corners in which dirt collects. Tubular legs have often been found to provide a harbour for pests.

Preparation surfaces should be jointless, durable, impervious, of the correct height and firm-based. They must withstand repeated cleaning at the required temperature without premature deterioration through pitting and corrosion.

Working methods

Time-and-motion studies are essential for all tasks. Working in a hot environment – possibly against the clock, possibly leading to stress – it is necessary to conserve energy. A skilled craftsperson is one who completes the task in the minimum time, to the required standard and with the minimum effort.

The objective is to make work easier; this can be achieved by simplifying the operation, eliminating unnecessary movements, combining two operations into one or improving old methods. For example, if you are peeling vegetables and you allow the peelings to drop into the container in the first place, the action of moving the peelings into the bowl and the need to clean the table have been eliminated. This operation is simplified if, instead of a blunt knife, a good hand peeler is used, because it is simple and safe to use, requires less effort, can be used more quickly and requires less skill to produce a better result. If the quantity of vegetables is sufficient, then a mechanical peeler could be used, but it would be necessary to remember that the electricity used would add to the cost and that the time needed to clean a mechanical aid may lessen its work-saving value. If it takes 25 minutes to clean a potato-mashing machine that has been used to mash potatoes for 500 meals, it could be time well spent in view of the time and energy saved mashing the potatoes. It may not be considered worthwhile using the machine to mash potatoes for 20 meals, however. Note that it may be more efficient to buy vegetables already peeled and prepared.

Properly planned layouts with adequate equipment, tools and materials to do the job are essential if practical work is to be carried out efficiently.

The storage, handling of foods, tools and utensils, and the movement of food in various stages of production needs careful study. Many people carry out practical work by instinct and often evolve the most efficient method instinctively. Nevertheless careful observation of numerous practical workers will show a great deal of time and effort wasted through bad working methods.

Work must be planned carefully so that items requiring long preparation or cooking are started first. Where fast production is required, lining up will assist efficiency. Work carried out haphazardly, without plan or organisation, takes longer than work done according to plan. There is a sequence to work that leads to high productivity and an efficient worker should learn this sequence quickly.

Creative kitchen management

Executive chefs and head chefs are under increasing pressure to reduce costs and work within tight budgets. This means that chefs are looking to find innovative and creative ways to manage their kitchens effectively and efficiently within cost constraints. This often means experimenting with labour-saving equipment. Other creative approaches that could be taken include:

- rearranging staff rotas to keep the maximum input from staff while allowing sufficient time off work
- experimenting with different menus that require less preparation and, in some cases, less skill
- searching the market for different ingredients and prepared products that will save chefs time
- examining innovative ways to reduce wastage and increase yields
- developing a multi-skilled approach in the kitchens, e.g. kitchen porters are trained in basic food preparation skills; chefs are skilled enough to be able to take over any section in the kitchen, including pastry.

Kitchen equipment

Cooking equipment provides the backbone of any busy catering operation. It is the key to catering success and quality. In terms of food safety it controls the most critical step in the food production process. A mistake at the cooking stage, such as the undercooking of raw food, is likely to result in a mass food-poisoning incident.

Kitchen equipment is expensive, so initial selection is important. The following points should be considered before each item is purchased or hired.

- Overall dimensions in relation to available space.
- Weight – can the floor support the weight?
- Fuel supply – is the existing fuel supply sufficient to take the increase?
- Drainage – where necessary, are there adequate facilities?
- Water – where necessary, is it to hand?
- Use – if it is a specialist piece of equipment for certain foods or products, will there be sufficient use to justify the expense and investment?
- Capacity – can it cook the quantities of food required efficiently?
- Time – can it cook the given quantities of food in the time available?
- Ease – is it easy to handle, control and use properly?
- Maintenance – is it easy to clean and maintain?
- Attachments – is it necessary to use additional equipment or attachments?
- Extraction – does it require extraction facilities for fumes or steam?
- Noise – does it have an acceptable noise level?
- Construction – is it well made, safe, hygienic and energy efficient, and are all handles, knobs and switches sturdy and heat resistant?
- Appearance – if equipment is to be on view to customers does it look good and fit in with the overall design?
- Spare parts – are replacement parts easily obtainable?

Kitchen equipment may be divided into three categories:

1. large equipment – ranges, steamers, boiling pans, fish fryers, sinks, tables
2. mechanical equipment – peelers, mincers, mixers, refrigerators, dishwashers
3. utensils and small equipment – pots, pans, whisks, bowls, spoons.

Manufacturers provide instructions on how to clean and keep their apparatus in efficient working order, and it is the responsibility of everyone using the equipment to follow these instructions, which should be displayed in a prominent place near the machines.

Arrangements should be made with the local gas board for regular checks and servicing of gas-operated equipment; similar arrangements should be made with the electricity supplier. It is a good plan to keep a logbook of all equipment, showing where each item is located when servicing takes place, noting any defects that arise, and instructing the fitter to sign the logbook and to indicate exactly what has been done.

Large equipment

Ranges and ovens

Ranges can be operated by gas, electricity, solid fuel, oil, microwave or microwave plus convection.

Oven doors should not be slammed as this is liable to cause damage.

When a solid-top gas range is lit, the centre ring should be removed to reduce the risk of blowback, but it should be replaced after approximately five minutes, otherwise unnecessary heat is lost.

Convection ovens

In convection ovens, a circulating current of hot air is rapidly forced around the inside of the oven by a motorised fan or blower. As a result, an even and constant temperature is created, and food can be cooked successfully in any part of the oven. This means that the heat is used more efficiently, cooking temperatures can be lower, cooking times shortened and overall fuel economy achieved.

Forced air convection can be described as fast conventional cooking: conventional in that heat is applied to the surface of the food, but fast since moving air transfers its heat more rapidly than does static air. In a sealed oven, fast hot air circulation reduces evaporation loss, keeping shrinkage to a minimum, and gives the rapid change of surface texture and colour that are traditionally associated with certain cooking processes.

There are four types of convection oven:

1. where forced air circulation is accomplished by a motor-driven fan
2. where low-velocity, high-volume air movement is provided by a power blower and duct system
3. a combination of a standard oven and a forced convection oven designed to operate as either by the flick of a switch
4. a single roll-in rack convection oven with heating element and fan housed outside the cooking area; an 18-shelf mobile oven rack makes it possible to roll the filled rack direct from the preparation area into the oven.

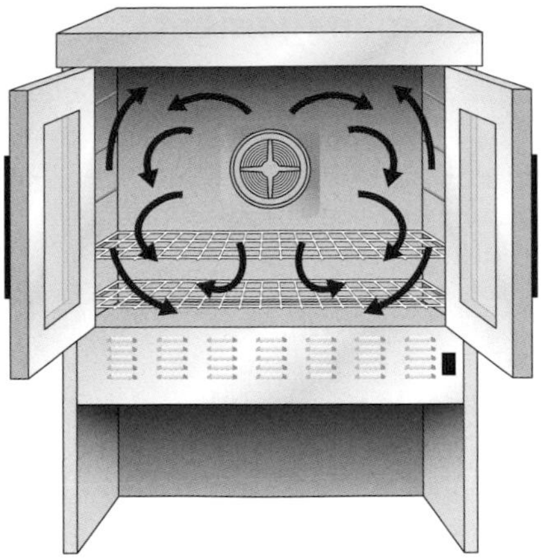

Figure 5.3 Forced air convection oven

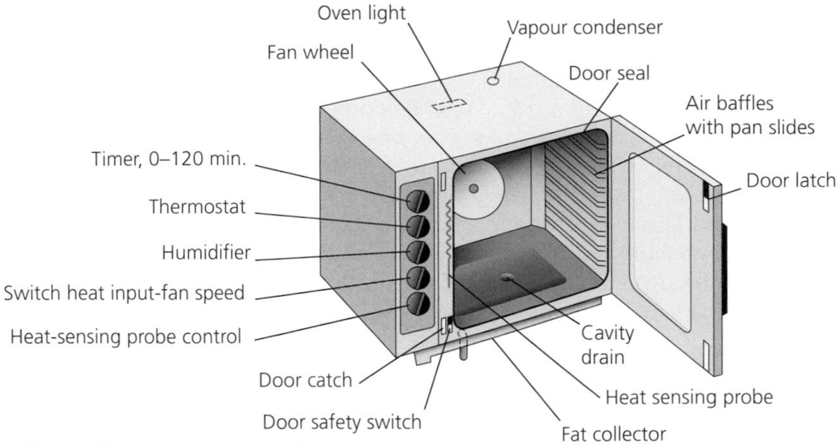

Figure 5.4 Hot air convection oven

Combination ovens

Combination ovens (combi-ovens), fuelled by gas or electricity, are widely used in most sectors of the catering industry, and especially in large banqueting operations.

Ovens can be programmed easily for exact cooking times and the regeneration of chilled food, allowing chefs to produce consistent products every time.

The special features of combination ovens are:

- they reduce cooking times
- they are fully automatic – desired browning levels and exact core temperatures can be achieved
- they are self-cleaning
- they allow more food to be produced in less space
- energy efficiency
- increased productivity.

A hybrid of fridge and oven, designed for use in cook-chill food systems for banqueting or industrial catering, is available. The chilled food is held until the predetermined moment when the chilling unit switches off and the oven facility kicks in, bringing the food safely up to eating temperature.

Rotary rack ovens

Rotary rack ovens operate on a different principle from roll-in convection or combi-ovens and deliver even more production capacity. These ovens accept one or two full racks loaded with bake pans, which are rolled in to the oven compartment. These ovens have either a mechanical lift system that suspends and rotates the rack during the cook cycle, or a floor-mounted platform that provides the rotation. Rack ovens are also equipped with a steam system, which provides the nice sheen to the crust required by many bread products.

Rotary rack ovens are available in both gas and electric heated models. Because of their size, they typically have an integrated ventilation hood system. They are used in large institutional kitchens, hotels and banqueting operations.

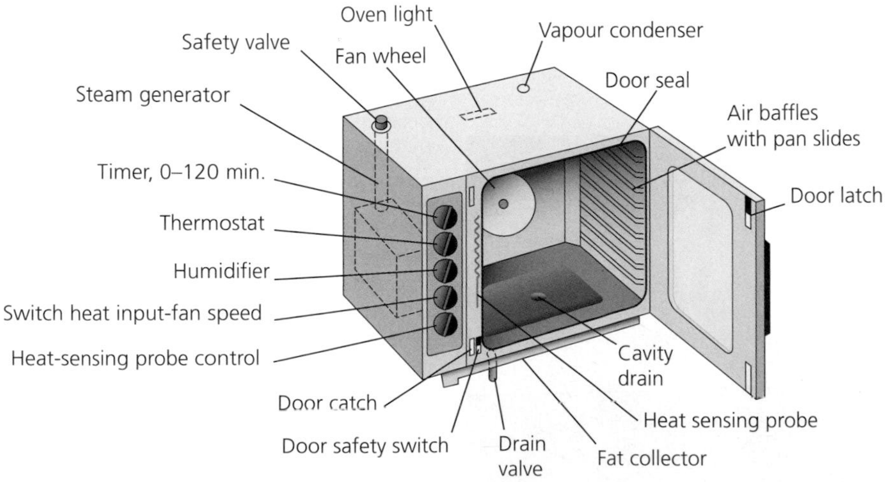

Figure 5.5 Hot air steamer oven

Mechanical ovens

Large mechanical ovens with trays evolved from conventional ovens. Rather than having to travel between ovens to load and unload product or check product being cooked, the chef or baker can do it all at one location. A convection oven has many operational and performance advantages, but it must be relatively small to control air movement. This is by design a batch production method. The moving tray oven has many of the benefits of a convection oven, but it is a continuous production method, with much higher production capabilities.

The revolving tray or reel oven (the 'Ferris wheel' oven) has been the mainstay of many bakeries for more than 50 years. Like a Ferris wheel (fairground 'big wheel'), pans are suspended from double wheels that revolve in a gas or electrically heated chamber. The pans are pivoted so that they remain level at all times, no matter what their position on the wheel. This type of oven has a reputation for turning out remarkably good products at relatively low labour and energy costs.

For greater capacity in a mechanical oven, trays are attached to chains that move from the front to the rear, horizontally. They then circle around the wheel or transfer arm, to a lower level. From there they return to the loading area at the front of the oven. In some ovens, the product being baked merely goes from one end of the oven to the other, where it is unloaded. Then the tray or belt returns to the front for product reloading. At the front of the oven, the tray is raised to the unload–load position. An item that is to be baked may take several trips through this style of oven before it has finished baking. Other mechanical ovens move in a circular, horizontal path up to three and five levels. These types of oven are known as rotary ovens.

Although mechanical ovens were designed for baking, they can be used for roasting as well. They are found in large institutional kitchens or commissaries, commercial and wholesale bakeries, and large restaurants that have separate baking areas.

Pizza ovens

Gas-fired and wood-burning ovens are now popular for cooking large numbers of pizzas.

Figure 5.6 Pizza oven

The cooking process management system

This links the combi-oven to a computer, which monitors the cooking process to help with HACCP. The software monitors not just the combi-ovens, but other items of equipment in the kitchen too, such as pressure bratt pans, steamers and boiling kettles. The chef inputs into the software what the day's food production is to be, and the computer works out the order in which the food should be cooked, and in what equipment, in order to deliver the food just in time for freshness.

The HACCP management part of this system can track food from goods delivery to the plate by using probes – for example, a chilled or frozen chicken can be probed to monitor and record temperatures before cooking so that if a problem occurs in the food cycle, the kitchen manager can check to see if there were any discrepancies in the goods storage procedures.

During cooking the probes will record any variations to the pre-set cooking programme. This means the software system can alert the kitchen management team not just that a problem has occurred during the cooking procedure, but where it occurred.

Smoking ovens

Smoking certain foods is a means of cooking, injecting different flavours and preserving. Smoking ovens or cabinets are well insulated with controlled heating elements on which wood chips are placed (different types of wood chips give differing flavours). As the wood chips burn, the heated smoke permeates the food (fish, chicken, sausages, etc.) that is suspended in the cabinet.

Microwave ovens

Microwave ovens are common in most commercial kitchens, handling everything from defrosting to self-steaming and rapid rethermalisation. Solid-state programmable controls make them easy to use, and today's microwave ovens offer more power, better warranties and greater durability.

A microwave is an invisible electromagnetic wave, which travels at the speed of light. The water and fat molecules that are found in food absorb the microwave energy. This energy causes these molecules to vibrate against one another (about 2.5 billion times per second), creating friction, which in turn creates heat, which in turn warms or cooks the food.

Microwave energy cooks faster than conventional cooking because a greater amount of heat is created in the outside portion of the food (the area 12.0 to 20.0 mm deep, which is penetrated by the microwave) so that the heat is transferred faster to the inside of the food.

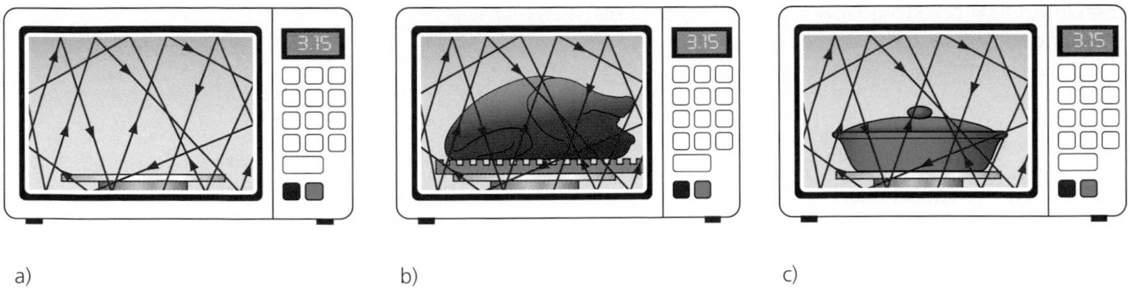

Figure 5.7 (a) Microwave energy being reflected off cooking cavity walls; (b) microwave energy being absorbed by food; (c) microwave energy passing through cooking container material

Metal dishes or aluminium foil should not be used in a microwave oven. The metal deflects the microwaves away from the food, preventing cooking. Paper, plastic, china, glass and ceramic are acceptable materials for use inside a microwave.

The technology that makes microwave ovens possible also creates a few disadvantages. For instance, standard microwave ovens do not brown foods. Food browns when amino acids and certain sugars are brought together under dry heat, at least 90°C, for a sustained period of time. Microwave cooking does not create these conditions.

To solve this problem, combination convection/microwave ovens have been introduced, which give the dry heat and air movement of a convection oven, plus the speed of a microwave oven. The result is a device with the advantages of both. This combination unit cooks up to 80 per cent faster than a standard convection oven, can accommodate metal cookware and delivers a fully browned product that looks good on the plate.

A microwave oven's power input will determine its function. The four basic types of commercial microwave ovens, and their intended uses, are as follows.

1. **Light-duty microwaves:** these units are generally in the 700- to 800-watt range. They are small, and are most often used for quick point-of-service heating applications such as a food service station. They are also used in low-volume restaurants where speed is not a critical factor.
2. **Heavy-duty microwaves:** most of these units are rated in the 900- to 2200-watt range. They all come with a stainless-steel cavity, and most have a stainless-steel exterior and are compact in their overall size.
3. **Bulk cookers and microwave steamers:** these large microwaves operate in the 2400- to 3700-watt range. Some of these units have been positioned to compete with countertop convection steamers. They rely on the water content of the food itself to generate some steam when heated by the magnetrons. These larger units are not normally used for single or small-portion heating. However, they work well for bulk applications, such as reheating and cooking products in cafeterias and other institutions.
4. **Convection microwave ovens:** these are actually small convection ovens with built-in microwave assistance.

WEBLINK

To find out more, contact the Microwave Technologies Association:

www.microwaveassociation.org.uk

Induction cooking

An induction cooktop holds a series of burners called induction coils, which generate magnetic fields that induct a warming reaction in steel-based pots or pans; it is the cooking vessels themselves that heat the food, not the stove elements. The cooktops may feel slightly warm to the touch after they are turned off, but they remain relatively cool.

Induction cooktops heat up faster than an electric range – water will boil in half the time as on an electric cooking surface. Because of this reduced cooking time, induction cooktops are 85–90 per cent more energy efficient than electricity-powered stoves and ovens, and use approximately half the energy of gas-sourced models.

Cleaning an induction cooktop is simple because the surface is flat and continuous; there are no spaces where food particles or spillovers can collect. Range-top mess is also reduced because the induction cooktops offer convenient safeguards; they turn themselves off if a pot has gone dry and, if there is a spillover, the cooking surface prevents the burning on and hardening of spilled food.

While induction cooktops will save money in the long run, there are some initial costs. The cooktops themselves, which range from a one-unit hotplate type to the traditional four-burner size, range in price from several hundred to several thousand pounds.

An additional expense can arise if you need to replace your cookware. Induction cooktops induct energy only into ferrous metal-based pots and pans. If you are using cast iron, steel-plated or certain types of stainless-steel pans, you should be able to use the cookware you already own. However, you cannot cook with materials such as copper, aluminium or glass. If in doubt, test your present cookware with a magnet – if the magnet sticks to the pot, the pot will work with an induction cooktop.

Try to find an induction hob that works using normal pans. Beware of induction hobs that need special pans or do not give constant performance from one type of pan to another.

Figure 5.8 An induction wok

Other advantages of induction cooking hobs are as follows.

- **Safety:** only the pan gets hot, therefore you cannot burn yourself on this type of hob.
- **Cool working environment:** very little heat escapes to the atmosphere, providing a cool working environment.
- **Less extraction:** the kitchen needs much less extraction, further reducing energy bills.
- **No combustion gases:** unlike gas hobs, induction hobs do not emit any combustion gases and are environmentally friendly.
- **Speed of cooking:** modern induction hob designs are faster than gas hobs.

WEBLINK

To find out more, see the Induced Energy Limited website:

www.inducedenergy.com

Halogen hobs

A halogen hob runs on electricity, and typically comprises five individually controlled heat zones, each of which has four tungsten halogen lamps under a smooth ceramic glass surface. The heat source glows red when switched on, getting brighter as the temperature increases.

When the hob is switched on, 70 per cent of the heat is transmitted as infrared light directly into the base of the cooking pan, the rest is conducted via the ceramic glass. Ordinary pots and pans may be used on the halogen hob, but those with a flat, dark or black base absorb the heat most efficiently.

WEBLINK

Further information about different types of hobs and stoves can be found at:

www.controlinduction.co.uk

Steam cooking equipment

Steam cooking equipment comprises many different and varied items, such as compartment steam cookers (both pressure and pressureless steamers), combination oven steamers, boiling kettles/steam-jacketed kettles, and tilting braising pans or bratt pans. In each of these general categories, there are numerous types, models, power inputs, etc.

What is steam?

What you see when you think you are seeing steam is water vapour, which is very small droplets of water carried by or mixed with the steam. Occasionally you will hear the terms 'dry steam' or 'wet steam' used in the kitchen. Wet steam carries significant water vapour. True dry steam carries little water vapour.

Steam is an efficient heat transfer medium, which gives up heat energy on contact with a cooler surface. Steam expands in volume more than 30 times when it is converted from its liquid (water) state, which helps it move in to and fill compartments, jackets and places where heat transfer can take place. This makes steam an excellent medium for cooking and warming foods.

Steam was first used within the confines of a (kettle) jacket, for the efficient conduction heating of products within a vessel. In addition, steam was introduced into a closed compartment, in direct contact with the food, resulting in the heating and cooking of those foods.

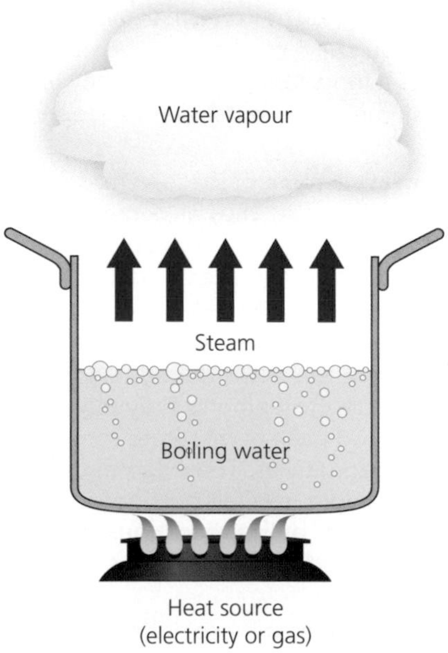

Figure 5.9 What is steam?

How steam cooking works

Steam carries six times as much energy as boiling water. Steam readily gives up that energy load when it condenses back into water (condensate) upon contact with food or any cooler surface. In the case of kettle cooking, that heat is transferred into the food by conduction, through the kettle wall.

Steamers

Steamers have been one of the fastest-growing equipment categories, driven by menu trends and the desire for healthier foods. There is a growing list of models, sizes and steam-generation methods available. The major categories and the key sub-categories are:

- pressureless steamers (convection or atmospheric steamers) – traditional convection steamers, connectionless steamers, 'boilerless' steamers
- pressure steamers – high-pressure steamers, low-pressure steamers
- pressure/pressureless steamers
- speciality steamers.

Pressureless steamers

In pressureless steamers, the heat is transferred from steam to food by forced convection, creating turbulence that reduces the insulating barrier of condensation on food.

When steam contacts the food's cooler surface, the steam transfers its energy load directly into the food. Because air and water diminish this heat transfer, a continuous venting system in pressureless steamers eliminates virtually all the air from the cooking compartment, as steam expands and fills the compartment. This results in fast, gentle cooking at a relatively low temperature of 100°C, in a steamer at sea level.

Pressureless steamers are well suited to a wide variety of foods, including fresh or frozen seafood and vegetables, including loose individually quick frozen (IQF), pack frozen or frozen block vegetables. Because the cavity is continuously vented and condensate drained, unwanted flavour transfer from one food product to another is eliminated. Perforated gastronorm pans are recommended for cooking most food items, but some foods, such as rice, scrambled eggs, and certain kinds of beef and pasta, are prepared in solid pans or a perforated pan nested in a deeper solid pan. These steamers are also effective for reheating vendor-prepared or cook-chill product.

Traditional cabinet base convection steamers can operate with direct steam from a central steam supply, a steam boiler that is remotely located or its own boiler mounted in the cabinet below the steamer compartments. Cabinet base boilers are most typical, and available in either gas or electric heated models.

Countertop units are popular for their compact size and smaller power requirements. They typically have their own self-contained steam generators, and can be stacked or banked for additional capacity and flexibility in the same footprint or hood space. They are available with three-, four- or five-pan capacity. Countertop steamers are electric or gas powered, and require a water line and drain line connection.

Connectionless steamers

The amount of steam generated by countertop models makes them especially prone to hard water service problems and failures, unless regular de-liming (descaling), and comprehensive water treatment and system maintenance are practised. Connectionless steamers don't have water or drain lines. They all generate steam inside, on the bottom of the steam compartment. The operator must pour 7–15 litres of water into the cook compartment. These units heat the compartment bottom or an adjacent open reservoir to generate steam in the cavity. These (all electric) models have heating elements clamped to the bottom of the compartment or reservoir and not immersed in the water. This design eliminates most water-related element failures, and the need for water treatment and regular de-liming with caustic chemicals.

'Boilerless' steamers do require water and drain connections but eliminate the need for operators to manually fill the compartment with water or deal with hot, nutrient-rich waste water, which must be drained from connectionless steamers after use. In addition, they employ the same non-immersion heating elements or under-fired gas burner designs, which reduce water-related component failure, and the need for heavy and frequent de-liming or descaling.

Regardless of the type or style of pressureless steamer desired, proper sizing is important for timely and efficient food preparation and production. Actual requirements will depend on the menu, customer count and the availability of alternative equipment such as steam combination ovens. While most steamers accept 65–200 mm deep 1/1 gastronorm pans, 65 mm deep pans are most typically used. Here are some tips for converting pan capacity into menu portions.

- A 1/1, 65 mm deep gastronorm pan holds 72 115 gram, 48 170 gram or 36 225 gram portions.
- A 1/1, 65 mm deep gastronorm pan is 2.54 cm full with 2.8 litres, 3.2 cm deep with 3.8 litres and 500 mm deep with 5.7 litres of liquid.
- A 1/1, 65 mm deep gastronorm pan comfortably holds 2.3 kg to 2.5 kg of frozen cut vegetables.

Large pans, boilers and fryers

Bratt pan

The bratt pan is one of the most versatile pieces of cooking equipment in the kitchen because it is possible to use it for shallow-frying, deep-frying, stewing, braising and boiling. A bratt pan can cook many items of food at once because of its large surface area. A further advantage is that it can be tilted so that the contents can, quickly and efficiently, be poured out on completion of the cooking process. Bratt pans are heated by gas or electricity; several models are available incorporating various features to meet differing catering requirements.

Boiling pans

Many types are available in different metals – aluminium, stainless steel, etc. – in various sizes (10-, 15-, 20-, 30- and 40-litre capacity) and they may be heated by gas or electricity. As they are used for boiling or stewing large quantities of food, it is important that they do not allow the food to burn; for this reason the steam-jacket type boiler is the most suitable. Many of these are fitted with a tilting device to facilitate the emptying of the contents.

After use, the boiling pan and lid should be thoroughly washed with mild detergent solution and then rinsed well. The tilting apparatus should be greased occasionally and checked to see that it tilts easily. If gas fired, the gas jets and pilot should be inspected to ensure correct working. If a pressure gauge and safety valve are fitted these should also be checked.

Pasta cooker

This equipment is fitted with water delivery and drain taps, and can be used for the cooking of several types of pasta simultaneously. It is electrically operated.

Deep-fat fryers

A deep-fat fryer is one of the most extensively used items of equipment in many catering establishments. The careless worker who misuses a deep-fat fryer and spills food or fat can cause accidents and waste money.

Fryers are heated by gas or electricity and incorporate a thermostatic control in order to save fuel and prevent overheating. There is a cool zone below the source of heat into which food particles can sink without burning, thus preventing spoiling of other foods being cooked. This form of heating also saves fat.

Pressure fryers

Food is cooked in an airtight frying vat, thus enabling it to be fried a lot faster and at a lower oil temperature.

Conveyor fryers

Conveyor fryers permit the operator to place the product in one end, typically in individual baskets attached to a conveyor system. The product is then carried through the oil-filled tank and dumped from the baskets at a collection station, after it has completed the cooking cycle. The conveyor rotates back, in a continuous loop, for reloading.

The speed of the conveyor can be increased or decreased, permitting the operator to control the cooking process. As with the previous fryers covered, proper frying results depend on the temperature of the oil, the condition of the oil and the amount of time food is immersed in the oil.

Conveyor fryers are excellent units to have for high-volume sites, such as theme parks, where concession stands need to produce a lot of product in a short period of time. Some conveyor fryers are capable of producing 45 kg of French fries per hour, from a compact countertop unit.

Air and speciality fryers

An air fryer is a small countertop unit that uses a small amount of oil in a rotating drum mounted inside a closed compartment to 'fry' single portions or small batches of product. They primarily use hot air convection heat transfer to cook fries and other fairly durable frozen product.

An advantage of these smaller units is that they typically don't require placement under a grease rated hood. They don't use or release significant amounts of grease-laden vapour, so they can be used in bars, snack shops, bowling alleys and other places without heavy-duty utilities and ventilation.

Hot cupboards

Commonly referred to in the trade as the hotplate and also known as the kitchen pass, hot cupboards are used for heating plates and serving dishes, and for keeping food hot. Care should be taken to see that the amount of heat fed into the hot cupboard is controlled at a reasonable temperature. This is important, otherwise the plates and food will either be too hot or too cold, and this could obviously affect the efficiency of the service. A temperature of 60–76°C is suitable for hot cupboards and a thermostat is a help in maintaining this.

Hot cupboards may be heated by steam, gas or electricity. The doors should slide easily, and occasional greasing may be necessary. The tops of most hot cupboards are used as serving counters and should be heated to a higher temperature than the inside. These tops are usually made of stainless steel and should be cleaned thoroughly after each service.

Figure 5.10 A waiter at the hotplate

Bains-marie

Bains-marie are open wells of water used for keeping foods hot; they are available in many designs, some of which are incorporated into hot cupboards, some in serving counters, and there is a type that is fitted at the end of a cooking range. They may be heated by steam, gas or electricity, and sufficient heat to boil the water in the bain-marie should be available. Care should be taken to see that a bain-marie is never allowed to burn dry when the heat is turned on. After use the heat should be turned off, the water drained and the bain-marie cleaned inside and outside with hot detergent water, rinsed and dried. Any drain-off tap should then be closed.

Figure 5.11 A water bath, used to cook delicate foods

Food distribution equipment

In situations requiring mobile equipment (e.g. hospitals, banqueting) wheeled items are essential to facilitate service, particularly of hot foods.

Grills and salamanders

The salamander or grill heated from above by gas or electricity probably causes more wastage of fuel than any other item of kitchen equipment through being allowed to burn unused. Most salamanders have more than one set of heating elements or jets, and it is not always necessary to turn them all on fully.

Salamander bars and draining trays should be cleaned regularly with hot water containing a grease solvent such as soda. After rinsing they should be replaced and the salamander lit for a few minutes to dry the bars.

For under-fired grills (see Figure 5.12) to work efficiently they must be capable of cooking food quickly and should reach a high temperature 15–20 minutes after lighting; the heat should be turned off immediately after use. When the bars are cool they should be removed and washed in hot water containing a grease solvent, rinsed, dried and replaced on the grill. Care should be taken with the fire bricks, if these are used for lining the grill, as they are easily broken.

Figure 5.12 An under-fired grill

Contact grills

Contact grills (double-sided or infragrills) have two heating surfaces arranged facing each other. The food to be cooked is placed on one surface and then covered by the other. These grills are electrically heated and can cook certain foods very quickly, so extra care is needed, particularly when using this type of grill for the first time. In many coffee shops and cafés, paninis are cooked using a form of contact grill.

Fry plates, griddle plates

These are solid metal plates heated from below, and are used for cooking individual portions of meat, hamburgers, eggs, bacon, etc. They can be heated quickly to a high temperature and are suitable for rapid and continuous cooking. Before cooking on a griddle plate a light film of oil should be applied to the food and the griddle plate to prevent sticking.

To clean griddle plates, warm them and scrape off any loose food particles; rub the metal with pumice stone or griddle stone, following the grain of the metal; clean with hot detergent water, rinse with clean hot water and wipe dry. Finally re-season (prove) the surface by lightly oiling with vegetable oil.

Griddles with zone heating are useful when demand varies during the day. These reduce energy consumption in quiet periods while allowing service to be maintained.

Mirror chromed griddles have a polished surface that gives off less radiated heat, which saves energy and makes for a more pleasant working environment.

Barbecues

Barbecues are popular because it is easy to cook and serve quick, tasty food on them, and the outdoor location, smell and sizzle create an atmosphere that many customers enjoy.

There are three main types of barbecue: traditional charcoal, gas (propane or butane) and electric. The charcoal-fired type can take up to an hour before the surface is ready; with gas and electricity the barbecue is ready to cook on almost immediately.

Gas is more flexible and controllable than electricity. Propane gas is recommended because it can be used at any time of the year. Butane does not work when it is cold. Propane is, however, highly flammable and safety precautions are essential. Anyone connecting the gas container must be competent in the use of bottled gas. The supply pipe must be guarded to avoid accidental interference, and the cylinder must be placed away from the barbecue. The cylinder must be upright and stable, with the valve uppermost and securely held in position. Connections must be checked for leaks.

Flame grills

Open-flame natural fuel is a new trend. Flame grills provide instant gas-fired cooking and even heat distribution. They can be used with charcoal or lump wood for extra aroma. There are several different varieties on the market.

Figure 5.13 Flame grill

WEBLINK

For more details about Josper charcoal ovens, which combine a grill and an oven in a single piece of equipment, see: **www.josper.es/en/josper/about/**

Other equipment and surfaces

Stainless steel is generally used for kitchen sinks for all purposes.

Tables and work surfaces

- Formica- or stainless steel-topped tables should be washed with hot detergent water then rinsed with hot water containing a sterilising agent. Alternatively, some modern chemicals act as both detergent and sterilising agents.
- Marble slabs should be scrubbed with hot water and rinsed. All excess moisture should be removed with a clean, dry cloth.
- No cutting or chopping should be allowed on table tops; cutting boards should be used.
- Hot pans should not be put on tables; protective triangles must be used to protect the table surface.
- The legs and racks or shelves of tables are cleaned with hot detergent water and then dried. Wooden table legs require scrubbing.

Wooden table tops should not be used. If a wooden butcher's block is used, a scraper should be used to keep it clean. After scraping, the block should be sprinkled with a few handfuls of common salt in order to absorb any moisture that may have penetrated during the day. Do not use water or liquids for cleaning unless absolutely necessary as water will be absorbed into the wood and cause swelling.

All types of storage racks should be emptied and scrubbed or washed periodically.

Mechanical equipment

If a piece of mechanical equipment can save time and physical effort and still produce a good end result then it should be considered for purchase or hire.

The performance of most machines can be closely controlled and is not subject to human variations, so it should be easier to obtain uniformity of production over a period of time.

The caterer is faced with two considerations:

1. the cost of the machine – installation, maintenance, depreciation and running cost
2. the possibility of increased production and a saving of labour costs.

The mechanical performance must be carefully assessed and all the manufacturer's claims as to the machine's efficiency checked thoroughly. The design should be foolproof, easy to clean and operated with minimum effort. Before cleaning, all machines should be switched off and the plug removed from the socket.

When a new item of equipment is installed it should be tested by a qualified fitter before being used by catering staff. The manufacturer's instructions must be displayed in a prominent place near the machine. The manufacturer's advice regarding servicing should be followed and a record book kept, showing what kind of maintenance the machine is receiving and when. The following list includes machines typically found in catering premises, which are classified as dangerous under the Provision and Use of Work Equipment Regulations 1998 (PUWER).

1. Power-driven machines:
   - worm-type mincing machines
   - rotary knife, bowl-type chopping machines
   - dough mixers
   - food mixing machines when used with attachments for mincing, slicing, chipping and any other cutting operation, or for crumbling
   - pie- and tart-making machines
   - vegetable slicing machines.
2. Potato peelers:
   - potatoes should be free of earth and stones before they are loaded into the machine
   - before any potatoes are loaded, the water spray should be turned on and the abrasive plate set in motion
   - the interior should be cleaned out daily and the abrasive plate removed to ensure that small particles are not lodged below
   - the peel trap should be emptied as frequently as required
   - the waste outlet should be kept free from obstructions.
3. Machines, whether power-driven or not:
   - circular knife slicing machines used for cutting bacon and other foods (whether similar to bacon or not)
   - potato-chipping machines.

Dough preparation equipment

The following pieces of speciality equipment have been designed to help the pastry chef/baker with all the repetitive but critical tasks involved in producing a wide variety of baked goods.

- **Dough extruder:** designed to dispense dough that has been prepared in bulk in predetermined sizes and/or shapes. The dough is rammed or forced through a die (a type of cutting mould) or openings of the desired shape and size.
- **Dough divider/rounder:** used to equally portion dough by size and weight. It can be either manually or hydraulically operated.
- **Dough/butter press:** a hydraulically run machine that is used to press and form bulk dough and/or butter into a shape that is suitable for use in sheeters, cutters and formers.
- **Former/moulder:** mechanical devices designed to give a final length, size and/or shape to yeasted dough, before it is placed in pans.
- **Depositor:** a machine that places pre-measured pieces of dough on or in bake pans.
- **Sheeter:** a machine that is used to flatten dough to the desired/required thickness and shape. It is also used to remove the gas from yeasted dough.
- **Sheeter/moulder:** sheets and moulds dough pieces in one simple process.
- **Sheeter/reversible sheeter:** a mechanical device that is used for rolling and layering dough into specific shapes and thicknesses. It is primarily used in the production of pastries and sweet goods.
- **Prover:** found in every bakery. In essence, a prover is a cabinet that allows yeasted dough products to leaven (ferment) in an ideal temperature- and humidity-controlled environment until the desired product volume is achieved. This process ensures the desired appearance and quality of the finished baked product. Leavening is a raising action that aerates dough or batters during mixing and baking, so that the finished product is greater in volume than the raw ingredients, with flavour characteristics that are superior to the same ingredients baked without leavening. Typical prover box temperatures range from 29°C to 46°C, with humidity levels ranging from 70 to 95 per cent. Provers are available in many sizes and often match the pan capacity of convection, rack and combi-ovens. Small provers are available for mounting below a half- or full-size convection oven, providing a compact baking centre in a small footprint. Large roll-in provers are sized by rack capacity, and can vary from 1 to 20 racks or more, depending on the size and number of ovens served.
- **Prover/retarder:** retarders are multi-function units. They are used to initially retard the rising of dough, then later prove the product prior to bake-off.

WEBLINKS

The Health and Safety Executive (HSE) has several publications on catering machinery.

The HSE's information page for people working in the catering industry:

www.hse.gov.uk/catering

HSE leaflet 'Maintenance priorities in catering':

www.hse.gov.uk/pubns/cais12.pdf

List of all HSE catering and hospitality publications:

www.hse.gov.uk/catering/guidance.htm

HSE leaflet 'Gas safety in catering and hospitality':

www.hse.gov.uk/pubns/cais23.pdf

Free leaflets for catering and hospitality:

www.hse.gov.uk/pubns/caterdex.htm

- **Prover/quick thaw:** a prover that decreases the normal dough thawing time through the introduction of heat, then continues with the standard proving cycle. It is used when frozen dough is employed.
- **Retarder:** another important piece of equipment found in most bakery operations. In essence, a retarder is a speciality refrigeration unit that is designed to maintain a high level of humidity.

Food-processing equipment

The **food mixer** is an important labour-saving, electrically operated piece of equipment used for many purposes: mixing pastry, making cakes, mashing potatoes, beating egg whites, for mayonnaise, cream, mincing or chopping meat and vegetables.

- It should be lubricated frequently in accordance with the manufacturer's instructions.
- The motor should not be overloaded; this can be caused by obstruction to the rotary components. For example, if dried bread is being passed through the mincer attachment without sufficient care the rotary cog can become so clogged with bread that it is unable to move. If the motor is then allowed to run, damage can be caused to the machine.
- All components, as well as the main machine, should be thoroughly washed and dried. Care should be taken to see that no rust occurs on any part.

Food processors are generally similar to vertical, high-speed cutters except that they tend to be smaller and to have a larger range of attachments. They can be used for a large number of mixing and chopping jobs but they cannot whisk or incorporate air to mixes.

Figure 5.14 A vertical, variable-speed mixer

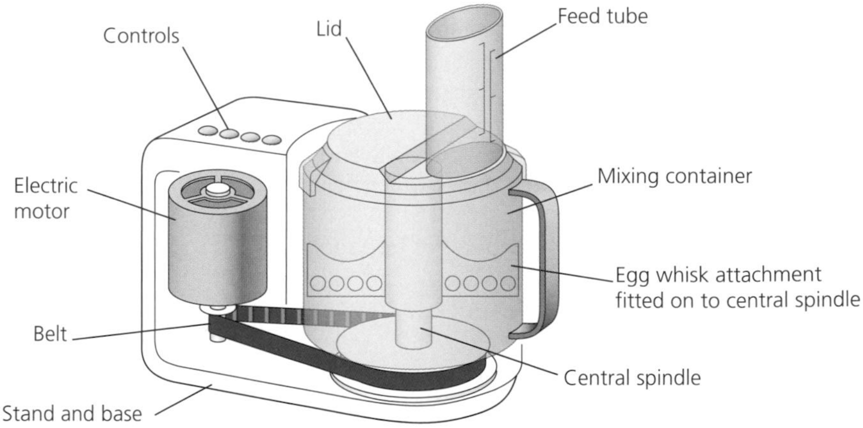

Figure 5.15 A belt-driven food processor

The **liquidiser**, or **blender**, is a versatile, labour-saving piece of machinery that uses a high-speed motor to drive specially designed stainless-steel blades to chop, purée or blend foods efficiently and very quickly. It is also useful for making breadcrumbs. As a safety precaution food must be cooled before being liquidised.

Food slicers may be manually or electrically operated. They are labour-saving devices, but can be dangerous if not used with care, so working instructions should be placed in a prominent position near the machine.

- Care should be taken that no material likely to damage the blades is included in the food to be sliced. It is easy for a careless worker to overlook a piece of bone that, if allowed to come into contact with the cutting blade, could cause severe damage.
- Each section in contact with food should be cleaned and dried carefully after use.
- The blade or blades should be sharpened regularly.
- Moving parts should be lubricated, but oil must not come into contact with the food.
- Extra care must be taken when blades are exposed.
- No one aged under 18 should complete these tasks.

Figure 5.16 A gravity feed slicer

The **electric chipper** should be thoroughly cleaned and dried after use, particular attention being paid to those parts that come into contact with food. Care should be taken to avoid any obstruction that prevents the motor from operating at its normal speed. Moving parts should be lubricated according to the maker's instructions.

The **hand masher** should be washed immediately after use, then rinsed and dried. The **electric masher** should have the removable sections and the main machine washed and dried after use, extra care being taken over those parts that come into contact with food. The same care should be taken as with electric chippers regarding obstruction and lubrication.

Juicers and **mixers** can provide freshly made fruit and vegetable juices, milk shakes and cocktails.

Ice cream machines and **sorbet machines** are available from 1-litre capacity, and enable establishments to produce ice cream and sorbet using fresh, frozen or canned fruits.

Figure 5.17 An ice cream machine

Boilers

Two main groups of water boilers are used to make tea and coffee.

1. **Bulk boilers:** boiling water can only be drawn from these when all the contents have boiled. They are generally used when large quantities of boiling water are required at a given time. They should be kept scrupulously clean, covered with the correct lid to prevent anything falling in, and when not used for some time should be left filled with clean, cold water.
2. **Automatic boilers:** these boilers have automatic water feeds and can give freshly boiled water at intervals. It is important that the water supply is maintained efficiently, otherwise there is a danger of the boiler burning dry and being damaged.

Pressure boilers

This is the type that operates many still sets, consisting of steam heating milk boilers and a pressure boiler providing boiling water. Care should be taken with the pilot light to see that it is working efficiently. Regular inspection and maintenance should be carried out by registered Gas Safe fitters.

Coffee and milk heaters

Water-jacket boilers are made for the storage of hot coffee and hot milk, with draw-off taps from the storage chamber. Inner linings may be of glazed earthenware, stainless steel or heat-resistant glass. It is very important that the storage chambers are cleaned thoroughly with hot water after each use and then left full of clean, cold water. The draw-off taps should be cleaned regularly with a special brush.

→ Refrigeration and freezing equipment

Location

As adequate ventilation is vital, locate refrigeration equipment in a well-ventilated room away from:

- sources of intense heat – cookers, ovens, radiators, boilers, etc.
- direct sunlight – from window or skylights
- barriers to adequate air circulation.

In large establishments it is necessary to have refrigerated space at different temperatures. The cold rooms may be divided into separate rooms: one at a chill temperature for storing salads, fruits and certain cheeses; one for meats, poultry and game; and one for deep-frozen foods. Refrigerated cabinets, thermostatically controlled to various desired temperatures, are also used in large larders. Deep-freeze cabinets are used where a walk-in deep-freeze section is not required: they maintain a temperature of -18°C. Chest-type deep-freeze cabinets require defrosting twice a year. It is important to close all refrigerator doors as quickly as possible to contain the cold air.

Figure 5.18 Refrigerated drawers

WEBLINK

Adande drawers are an example of versatile refrigeration equipment that can switch from fridge to freezer:

http://adanderefrigeration.com/product-range

Hygiene precautions

Refrigeration cannot improve the quality of foodstuffs; it can only retard the natural process of deterioration. For maximum storage of food and minimum health risk:

- select the appropriate refrigerator equipment for the temperature requirement of the food
- always ensure refrigerators maintain the correct temperature for the food stored
- keep unwrapped foods, vulnerable to contamination, and flavour and odour transfer, in separate refrigerators or in airtight containers and away from products such as cream, other dairy products, partly cooked pastry, cooked meat and delicatessen foods
- do not store foods for long periods in a good, general-purpose refrigerator because a single temperature is not suitable for keeping all types of food safely and in peak condition
- never keep uncooked meat, poultry or fish in the same refrigerator, or any other food that is not in its own sealed, airtight container
- never refreeze foods that have been thawed out from frozen
- always rotate stock in refrigerator space
- clean equipment regularly and thoroughly, inside and out.

Loading

- Ensure that there is adequate capacity for maximum stock.
- Check that perishable goods are delivered in a refrigerated vehicle.
- Fill frozen food storage cabinets only with pre-frozen food.
- Never put hot or warm food in a refrigerator unless it is specially designed for rapid chilling.
- Ensure that no damage is caused to inner linings and insulation by staples or nails in packaging.
- Air must be allowed to circulate within a refrigerator to maintain the cooling effect – do not obstruct any airways.

Cleaning

- Clean thoroughly inside and out at least every two months as blocked drain lines, drip trays and air ducts will eventually lead to a breakdown.
- Switch off power.
- If possible, transfer stock to available alternative storage.
- Clean interior surfaces with lukewarm water and a mild detergent. Do not use abrasives or strongly scented cleaning agents.
- Clean exterior and dry all surfaces inside and out.
- Clear away any external dirt, dust or rubbish that might restrict the circulation of air around the condenser.
- Switch on power, check when the correct working temperature is reached, refill with stock.

WEBLINKS

Further information can be obtained from the British Refrigeration Association:

www.feta.co.uk/bra/

and the Federation of Environmental Trade Associations Ltd:

www.feta.co.uk

Defrosting

This is important as it helps equipment perform efficiently and prevents a potentially damaging build-up of ice. The presence of ice on the evaporator or internal surfaces indicates the need for urgent defrosting; if the equipment is designed to defrost automatically this also indicates a fault.

Automatic defrosting may lead to a temporary rise in air temperature; this is normal and will not put food at risk.

For manual defrosting of chest freezers always follow the supplier's instructions to obtain optimum performance. Never use a hammer or any sharp instrument that could perforate cabinet linings – a plastic spatula can be used to remove stubborn ice.

Emergency measures

Signs of imminent breakdown include unusual noises, fluctuating temperatures, frequent stopping and starting of the compressor, excessive frost build-up and absence of normal frost.

Check that:

- the power supply has not been accidentally switched off
- the electrical circuit has not been broken by a blown fuse or the triggering of an automatic circuit breaker
- there has been no unauthorised tampering with the temperature control device
- any temperature higher than recommended is not due solely to routine automatic defrosting, to the refrigerator door being left open, to overloading the equipment or to any blockage of the internal passage of air
- there is no blockage of air to the condenser by rubbish, crates, cartons, etc.

If you still suspect a fault, call a refrigeration service engineer and be prepared to give brief details of the equipment and the fault. Keep the door of the defective cold cabinet closed as much as possible to retain cold air. Destroy any spoilt food.

Monitoring refrigeration efficiency

The Energy Technology Support Unit (ETSU) estimates that businesses could save 20–25 per cent of the energy currently consumed by refrigeration plants. Your local energy efficiency advice centre may be able to provide consultancy services at subsidised or no cost.

All types of refrigerators – walk-in, cabinet, with or without forced air circulation – should be fitted with display thermometers or chart recorders that will enable daily monitoring to check that the equipment is working correctly. Sensors that can set off available alarms must be placed in the warmest part of the cabinet.

Chilled display units include:

- multi-deck cabinets with closed doors, used for dispensing sandwiches, drinks and other foods; used if food needs to be displayed for more than four hours
- open and semi-open display cabinets where food is presented on the base of the unit and cooled by circulating cooled air
- gastronorm counters.

Because of surrounding conditions it is unsafe to assume that refrigerated display cabinets will maintain the temperature of the food below 5°C, which is why these units should never be used to store food other than for display periods of no more than four hours.

Maintenance and servicing should be carried out regularly by qualified personnel.

Figure 5.19 Chilled display unit

Dishwashers

The effective operation of the dishwasher plays a critical role in food service sanitation. A basic understanding of dishwasher operation will help ensure that clean and attractive tableware is always available. Most machines clean in a four-step process, as follows.

1 **Prewash stage:** in dishwashers with a prewash chamber, hot water sprays of around 45°C remove most of the 'easy' soil from the tableware. This soil is usually greasy and can't be removed effectively if the water is too cool. However, if the water is too hot, it may have a tendency to bake on other soils. For example, milk and fruit juice glasses should be prewashed in cold water. Dairy products bake on at high temperatures. A cool prewash is also necessary to remove fruit juice residues. If not properly removed, they may react with metal protecting agents in the wash water detergents to form an insoluble film.

2 **Wash stage:** a solution of hot water of around 55°C plus detergent first loosens the soil, then washes it down over perforated scrap trays designed to remove the gross soil. The water and detergent solution then returns to the wash tank. As it comes in contact with the tableware, the wash water should be a solid sheet, since drops of water in a spray do a poor job of soil removal. The temperature of the wash water should be in the 60–65°C range. Temperatures in this range soften soils and melt greases so they can be removed effectively.

3 **Rinse stage:** during this cycle, hot water at 65–75°C removes the detergent solution and any residual soils from the tableware. The action is similar to that described in the wash tank, without the addition of detergent.

4 **Final rinse stage:** in the final rinse stage, all trace of the wash solution is removed. The water temperature should be 82°C to allow the sanitising action to take place. Fast surface drying will also occur at these temperatures. A rinse additive is also injected into the final rinse water, to facilitate 'sheeting' and to prevent water spotting during this quick-dry stage.

For more information on the dishwashing process, see Chapter 11.

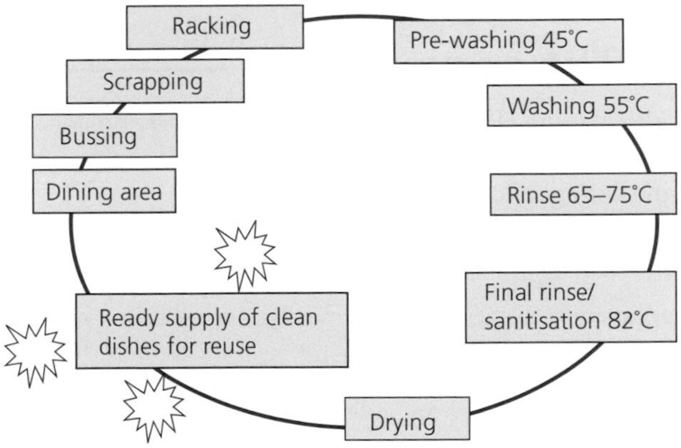

Figure 5.20 The dishwashing continuum

WEBLINK

Further information can be obtained from the Catering Equipment Suppliers Association:
www.cesa.org.uk/products/cesa-buying

Legislation affecting equipment in the professional kitchen

CE marking

All powered catering equipment sold in the UK and Europe must carry a small 'CE' (European Conformity) badge. This means that the manufacturer has certified that it meets EU safety, and in some cases performance, standards. The EU standards are strict and are drawn up to ensure that kitchen staff have the least possible risk of injury.

The regulation recognises that many kitchens have well-manufactured old equipment that pre-dates the introduction of CE marking, and the legal requirement for equipment to be CE marked applies only to equipment manufactured after 1995.

When manufacturers sell kitchen equipment and offer a guarantee, it comes with conditions of servicing. Kitchen equipment needs a trained and accredited service engineer to keep it in working order and comply with the terms of the guarantee. If equipment breaks down and a chef calls on the guarantee for cost-free repairs without evidence of accredited servicing the guarantee could be invalid.

Gas safety

The law is clear that only people registered with the Gas Safe Register can install and maintain a gas-powered piece of kitchen equipment (see Chapter 4).

Gas Safe regulations and British Standard 6173 both require a gas safety interlock system (described in Chapter 4) to be fitted in all commercial kitchens. This prevents a build-up of potentially poisonous gas combustion fumes.

If any gas appliances do not have flame failure devices (FFDs) fitted, then a gas proving system must also be fitted to comply with regulations.

WEBLINKS

For more information visit:

www.gassaferegister.co.uk

www.ventamsystems.co.uk/gassafety/gassafe.html

Health and safety regulations

The Health and Safety Executive (HSE) makes the rules covering the safety of kitchen staff using machines or equipment. Some are guidance notes, some are law, but to go against either can result in both prosecution and compensation claims.

The regulations are complex, but no chef can ignore them (see Chapter 4).

WEBLINK

Visit the website of the Catering Equipment Suppliers' Association (CESA):

www.cesa.org.uk

The servery area

Several factors affect the shape and size of serving lines:

- the volume, or anticipated volume, of sales
- the variety or complexity of the menu
- the size and shape of the available space
- the flow of traffic.

Simple, limited-choice menus may be served from either a permanently installed, continuous line cafeteria or one that is made up of mobile, modular units. This style of cafeteria is often referred to as an 'in-line' cafeteria.

Where a large number of people are to be served within a relatively short period of time, or when there is a wide variety of food choices, a cafeteria with multiple counters and points of service may be the best layout. Cafeterias designed around these operating premises are referred to as a hollow square or scrambled service cafeteria.

A scatter system provides multiple serving stations, easy access to beverages and condiments, and the grouping and physical separation of popular menu options, to reduce queues and hold-ups. This system lends itself to demonstration cooking areas, themed dining areas and more flexibility in changing menus to meet changing tastes.

Scrambled cafeteria plans and scatter systems are designed to speed up service by reducing the amount of time spent standing in line. Customers can pass others or go directly to the station that has their choice of food or beverage. During peak periods, short lines may form at some of the more popular service areas. Space should be allowed for people to pass one another with loaded trays. The layout should allow for easy resupply of service stations with food and tableware. When an area becomes crowded, it is difficult to supply food and replenish plates, flatware and disposables to centrally located stations.

Some key considerations when planning a scramble cafeteria layout include:

- what features would appeal to customers
- the ability to protect the quality of the food
- the ease and speed of supplying the food and dishes to various serving points
- the dishes that are to be promoted
- how to handle delay or back-up points in the service area
- the flow of traffic
- minimising hazards that could cause accidents

- the location of items that customers return for in the service area (e.g. condiments, flatware)
- the cost of labour
- the menu offerings – whether it is a simple, limited menu or complex, offering a wide variety of food
- any service time limitations.

Achieving a smooth flow of cafeteria traffic requires anticipation of the key items that will be sought by customers, then placing them at various stations within the cafeteria to achieve a good balanced flow. This is easier said than done. Food service design consultants have experience of cafeteria service operations and can recommend alternative layouts. If fixed serving lines and service stations are to be used, a good people-flow plan is critical and subsequent changes are costly.

The service-related equipment used in cafeterias is as varied as the food items offered. Some equipment needs are directly dependent on the cafeteria design (straight-line vs scramble service), the complexity of the menu, anticipated traffic flow and the amount of available space. The service equipment frequently found in cafeteria line-ups includes:

- sandwich prep tables
- salad bars
- dessert display case
- cold or hot food tables
- bains-marie
- beverage stations
- milk, soft-drink and cup dispensers
- grilled food unit
- menu boards
- cashier stand
- flatware and plate dispensers
- tray stands
- sneeze guards
- heat lamps
- tray rails.

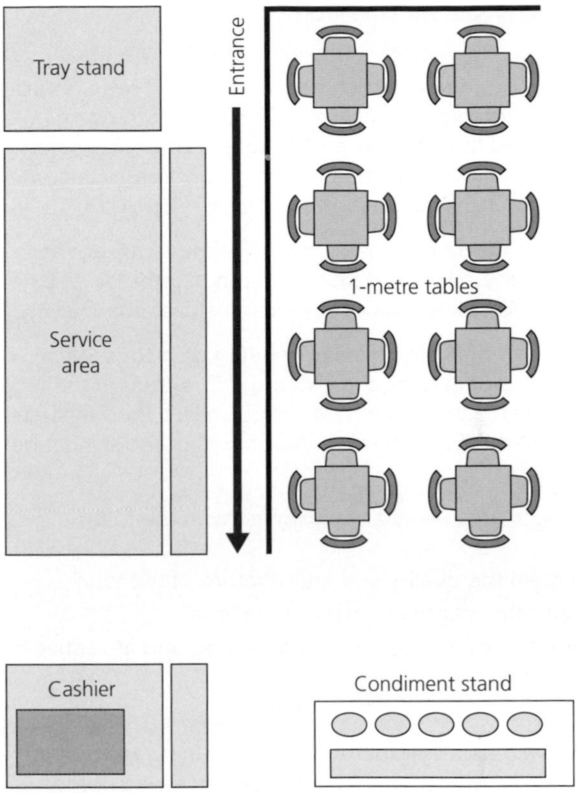

Figure 5.21 'In line' cafeteria service – a simple layout

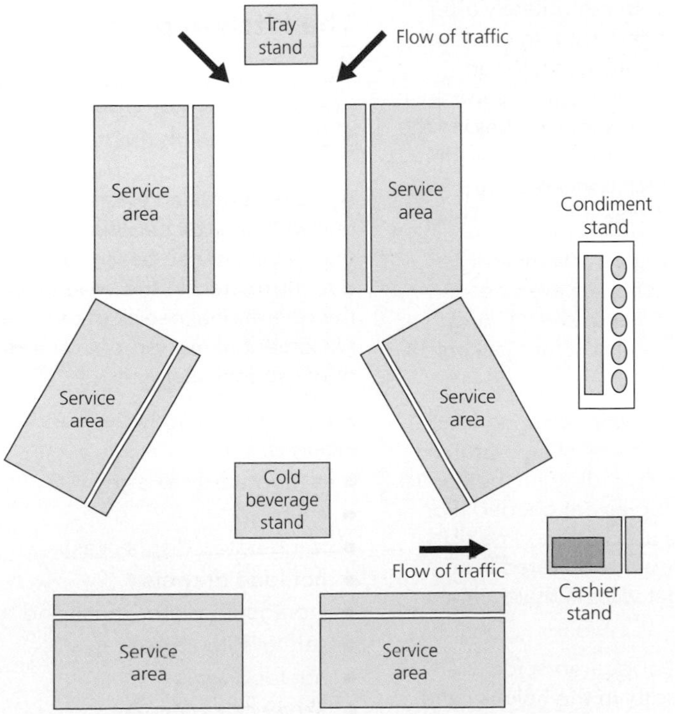

Figure 5.22 'Hollow square' or 'scrambled' cafeteria service

Hygiene and food holding

Hygiene is a major issue in the design and operation of all cafeterias. Appropriate equipment can help – for example, the use of sneeze screens where foods are openly displayed, and the use of serving utensils to discourage any hand contact with the food.

One of the most critical issues is ensuring that proper food-holding temperatures are maintained. These retard the growth of micro-organisms. When key menu items are prepared far in advance of plating and service, safe and effective means of holding that temperature become critical, and it should be monitored and recorded.

By law, hot food being held for service must be kept at or above 63°C. Hot food that has been held below this temperature for two hours or more must be thrown away.

Chilled food that is on display or being held for service should be kept at between 1°C and 4°C, although the legal requirement is to keep it below 8°C. Chilled food that has been held at 8°C or above for four hours or more must be thrown away.

The service area should be designed with the following aims:

- maintain the quality and temperature of the food
- ensure the microbial safety of the food
- present the food so that it is satisfying and attractive to customers
- provide fast and efficient service.

In typical cook-serve operations, maintaining the quality of cooked foods calls for limiting holding time prior to service. Equipment capacity needs to be planned around peak demand and how quickly food quality deteriorates – for example, meats are best served immediately after cooking. Vegetables under prolonged holding can lose their flavour, texture and important nutrients. When designing the service area, flexibility in holding capacity is desirable because different food items may be held in the serving area at different times. Different day-parts offering planned menu cycles and daily specials will require different holding times and conditions.

Larger kitchen operations often require advanced production and large batch production to even out the work flow, and to optimise the use of key cooking equipment such as ovens, steamers and steam-jacketed kettles.

Maintaining acceptable food quality and ensuring food safety require holding food at the proper temperature and humidity level. This will vary depending on the item(s), and various methods and technologies are needed. For example, infrared heaters may be used for a prime rib carving station, while soup may require a heated food well or self-serve display kettle that will maintain a higher temperature.

Some foods call for a fresh, moist appearance for presentation, with sufficient humidity in the holding and serving equipment to prevent drying and loss or change of colour. Vegetables should have a bright, natural colour, while bread and rolls should always have that 'just baked' texture and taste. Some items need moist air, while other items, such as fried foods, should be kept as dry as possible; dry heat from an infrared heat lamp is best for these items. Many holding cabinets allow the humidity level inside the cabinet to be adjusted, to match the food being held.

Hot and cold food tables, salad bars and bains-marie

This holding and serving equipment is designed to merchandise and display food and ingredients, maintain safe holding temperatures, and provide easy access for both patrons and the cafeteria employees that replenish them. The design and heating or chilling methods vary, depending on whether the product is pre-plated or held in bulk containers for portioning and plating by staff or the customer.

Hot food tables and bains-marie are rectangular tables designed with heat wells or support frames sized to hold steam table pans and other pan shapes. Typically a hot water reservoir is located under the pans. Electric heating elements or gas burners heat the water and provide the heat necessary to maintain a safe food serving temperature. For some products, heat lamps or strip heaters are added above the food pans to provide additional dry heat.

Cold food tables and salad bars use a small, integrated refrigeration system or ice to maintain safe holding temperatures.

The kitchen pass

The kitchen pass, or hotplate, is found in the service area of table service restaurants. The hot cupboard is usually found underneath the hotplate. After the preparation and cooking of the food, the next stop is normally the pass. A kitchen pass can be as simple as a standard bain-marie unit with an attached worktable, or a large custom-made unit. Most kitchen passes are outfitted with equipment directly related to the type of food service operation and the operational needs of their service area. The type and placement of equipment on a kitchen pass are critical for effective table service.

Equipment that may be found in a kitchen pass area includes:

- refrigerated storage
- ice bins
- refrigerated display case
- hot food drawers
- storage for plates, pans and trays
- self-levelling plate racks
- hot food wells
- server call systems

- order holders
- soup and roll warmers
- toaster
- microwave oven
- heat lamps
- cutting/carving boards
- bread dispensers
- beverage dispensing equipment
- coffee makers/warmers.

Infrared strip heaters and heat lamps are commonly used for keeping plated meals hot for short periods. They may be installed above pass-through windows between the kitchen and service area, or incorporated into the kitchen pass. These heaters have elements or lamps mounted directly above a shelf or plate landing area and typically are kept on. They provide instant radiated heat when a plate is placed under the warmer. They are available in a range of heat patterns, lengths and configurations designed to support all types of service method.

Refrigerated drawers and hot food drawers in both the service area and the production kitchen are common. While a reach-in refrigerator is often just steps away, those steps add up and slow down meal assembly. Locating small refrigerators or refrigerated drawers at the workstation, and even under cooking equipment such as ranges and griddles, can speed up production, reduce staff fatigue, and help ensure the safe holding of cooked products and raw ingredients.

The type of food service operation and the service offered will determine which beverages are offered and how those beverages are delivered to the customer (see Chapter 11). While there are some equipment and supply items used in fine wine table service (racking, wine chillers, decanting gadgets, etc.) as well as full bar service (glass washers, refrigeration, bar sinks, glasses, mugs and more), the main focus in designing a beverage system is very often the provision of water, tea, coffee and cold drinks.

→ Miscellaneous equipment

Food waste disposers are operated by electricity and take all manner of rubbish, including bones, fat, scraps and vegetable refuse. Almost every type of rubbish and swill, with the exception of rags and tins, is finely ground, then rinsed down the drain. It is the most hygienic method of waste disposal.

Care should be taken by handlers not to push waste into the machine with a metal object as this can cause damage.

New technology

New appliances regularly appear on the market. This is a response by equipment manufacturers to the demands of chefs who innovate and create new dishes incorporating different textures and food styles. Some of these new concepts and techniques are based on the principles of molecular cuisine.

Using lab equipment to experiment with food is part of a modernist cooking revolution.

The following are just a few examples of innovative equipment, some of them adopted from the lab environment.

- **Pacojet:** a kitchen appliance to assist with making sauces, mousses and ice creams while saving time, and food waste. Further details may be found at: www.pacojet.com.
- **Polyscience Vacuum Rotary Evaporation System:** prepares liquids for use in adding a variety of aromas and flavours to recipes. See http://polyscienceculinary.com/products/rotary-vacuum-evaporation-system-120v for more details.
- **Anti-Griddle Flash Freeze:** this removes heat quickly, to turn sauces or similar products into solids and produce different textures. Find out more at: http://polyscienceculinary.com/products/anti-griddle-flash-freeze-120v-60hz-12-amps.
- **Thermomix:** a kitchen cooker/processor with blades, a steel bowl and a heating element. See more at http://thermomix.vorwerk.co.uk.
- **Smoking Gun:** this offers an alternative to traditional smoking methods and allows you to use different types of combustibles when smoking dishes. For more information, visit: http://polyscienceculinary.com/products/the-smoking-gun.
- **Centrifuge machines:** the centrifuge is a piece of laboratory equipment that spins samples at extremely high speeds, separating them into liquid and solid components. For example, peas separate into three different parts: pea liquid, pea butter and pea solid. Read more about cooking using centrifuges at http://sciencecalling.com/2012/02/10/cooking-with-centrifuges.
- **Ultrasonic homogenisers:** this is a mechanical process to reduce small particles in a liquid so that they become uniformly small and evenly distributed. It could be used in the kitchen to produce emulsions. See more at http://seattlefoodgeek.com/2012/01/experimenting-with-the-polyscience-sonicprep-ultrasonic-homogenizer.
- **Vacuum filtration:** filtration is the process by which solid materials are removed from a fluid mixture, either a gas or liquid mixture. Filtration is carried out to capture the solid material suspended in a fluid or to clarify the fluid in which the solid is suspended. See how this could be used in the kitchen at www.studiokitchen.com/studio-kitchen/vacuum_filtration.
- **Dehydrators:** food dehydrators (Figure 5.23) gently preserve the nutrients and flavours in food with low-temperature drying. They can be used in kitchens to produce powders and to dry fruit and vegetable garnishes.

Figure 5.23 Food dehydrator

→ Small equipment and utensils

Small equipment and utensils are made from a variety of materials such as non-stick coated metal, iron, steel, copper, aluminium and wood.

Iron

Items of equipment used for frying, such as portable fat fryers and frying pans of all types, are usually made of heavy, black, wrought iron.

Frying pans are available in several shapes and many sizes. For example:

- omelette pans
- oval fish-frying pans
- pancake pans.

Baking sheets are made in various sizes, of black wrought steel. The less they are washed the less likely they are to cause food to stick. New baking sheets should be well heated in a hot oven, thoroughly wiped with a clean cloth and then lightly oiled. Before being used, baking trays should be lightly greased with a pure fat or oil. Immediately after use and while still warm they should be cleaned by scraping and dry wiping. Hot soda or detergent water should be used for washing.

Figure 5.24

Figure 5.25

Tartlet and barquette moulds and cake tins should be cared for in the same way as baking sheets.

Aluminium

(Note: minimum use of aluminium is recommended – stainless steel is to be preferred.)

Saucepans, stockpots, sauteuses, sauté pans, braising pans, fish kettles and large, round, deep pans and dishes of all sizes are made in cast aluminium. They are expensive, but one advantage is that the pans do not tarnish; also, because of their strong, heavy construction they are suitable for many cooking processes.

A disadvantage is that in the manufacture of aluminium, which is a soft metal, other metals are added to make pans stronger. As a result certain foods can become discoloured (care should be taken when mixing white sauces and white soups). A wooden spoon should be used for mixing, then there should be no discoloration. The use of metal whisks or spoons must be avoided.

Water boiled in aluminium pans is unsuitable for tea making as it gives the tea an unpleasant colour. Red cabbage and artichokes should not be cooked in aluminium pans as they will take on a dark colour, caused by a chemical reaction. Acid foods react with aluminium pans, so avoid using them to cook foods such as rhubarb or Bramley apples.

Steel

Heavy-duty stainless steel pans, incorporating an extra thick aluminium base that gives excellent heat diffusion, are available. They are suitable for all surfaces except induction hobs. Stainless steel is also used for many items of small equipment.

A number of items are made from tinned steel, including strainers, sieves and colanders.

Layered metal

No single metal or alloy makes a perfect pan, so the best cookware has always used layers of different metals.

All-Clad is a brand of cooking pan using a combination of materials designed to make the best use of the properties of them all. Each All-Clad pan is made of several layers of different metals and alloys, permanently bonded together (clad). The pans are designed to:

- heat evenly, with no hotspots, and cool evenly at a consistent rate
- be responsive to temperature changes
- not react with any foodstuffs or cleaning agents
- work equally well on any cooker type or in the oven.

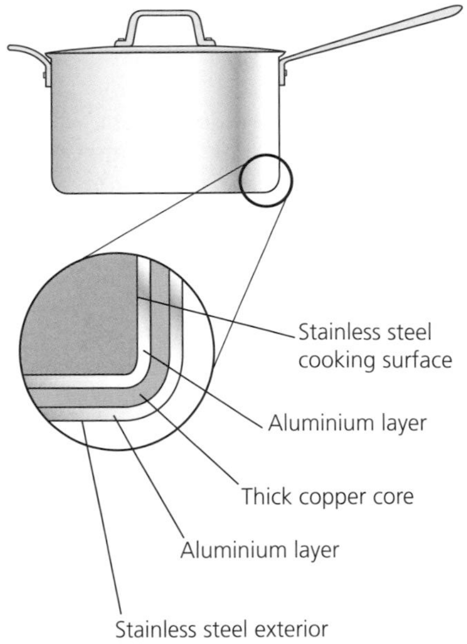

Figure 5.26 Structure of a layered pan

Non-stick metal

Non-stick saucepans, frying pans, baking and roasting tins are suitable for certain kitchen operations, such as small scale or à la carte. To protect the non-stick surface:

- excessive heat should be avoided
- use plastic or wooden spatulas or spoons when using non-stick pans so that contact is not made to the surface with metal
- extra care is needed when cleaning non-stick surfaces; the use of cloth or paper is most suitable; avoid using abrasive cleaning cloths and scouring pads.

Figure 5.27 Non-stick pans

Wood and compound materials

Cutting boards

These are an important item of kitchen equipment, which should be kept in use on all table surfaces to protect the table and the edges of cutting knives.

Bear in mind the following aspects when choosing cutting boards:

- water absorbency – soft woods draw fluids into them and, with the fluids, bacteria are also drawn in
- wooden cutting boards made of hard wood, if cleaned and sterilised, are perfectly acceptable in catering premises
- resistance to stains, cleaning chemicals, heat and food acids
- toxicity – the cutting board must not give off toxic substances
- durability – the cutting board must withstand wear and tear and must not split or warp; high-density plastic boards are recommended to avoid this from happening.

To avoid cross-contamination, it is important that the same equipment is not used for handling raw and high-risk products without being disinfected. To prevent the inadvertent use of equipment for both raw and high-risk foods, it is recommended that, where possible, different colours and shapes are used to identify products or raw materials used.

Plastic cutting boards

Plastic is the most popular material for cutting boards. It has the advantage of being able to be put through a dishwasher to clean and sterilise it, and can be colour coded so that high-risk foods are prepared only on the one cutting board, thereby reducing the risk of cross-contamination.

The accepted UK system is:

- **yellow** for cooked meats
- **red** for raw meats
- **white** for bread and dairy products (e.g. cheese)
- **blue** for raw fish
- **green** for salad and fruit
- **brown** for raw vegetables grown within the soil.

Wooden chopping boards

To comply with current regulations, wooden boards should not splinter or leak preservatives. They should be of close-grained hardwood, either in a thick, solid slab or separate pieces with close-fitting joints.

- Before using a new board, wash to remove any wood dust.
- After use, scrub with hot detergent water, rinse with clean water, dry as much as possible and stand on its longest end to prevent warping.
- Do not use for heavy chopping; use a chopping block instead.
- Appearances can be deceptive. Researchers at the University of Wisconsin found that wooden kitchen surfaces are good at decontaminating themselves. Left overnight at room temperature the bacteria on plastic surfaces multiplied, while the wooden surfaces cleaned themselves so thoroughly that the researchers could not record anything from them. This is because of the porous structure of wood. The bacteria stick to the wood's fibres and are 'strangled' by one of the anti-microbial chemicals with which living trees protect themselves.

Cutting boards of compound materials

There are several types available. When selecting compound cutting boards it is essential to purchase those with a non-slip surface.

One material used to make cutting boards is polyethylene. Cutting boards are also made of hard rubber and rubber compounds (rubber, polystyrene and clay). These are hygienic because they are solid, in one piece and should not warp, crack or absorb flavours. They are cleaned by scrubbing with hot water and then drying or passing through a dishwasher. High-density boards are the most hardwearing and least likely to warp.

Wooden items

Rolling pins, wooden spoons or spatulas should be scrubbed in hot detergent water, rinsed in clean water and dried. Rolling pins should not be scraped with a knife as this can cause the wood to splinter. Adhering paste can be removed with a cloth. Wooden spoons and spatulas are being replaced by a high-density plastic capable of withstanding very high temperatures. They are considered unhygienic unless washed in a suitable sterilising solution such as sodium hypochloride solution (bleach) or a solution of Milton. Metal piping tubes are being replaced by plastic; these can be boiled and do not rust.

When cleaning wood-framed sieves, care of the wooden frame should be considered, taking into account the previous remarks.

Mandolins

The blades of the mandolin should be kept lightly greased to prevent rust (stainless-steel mandolins with protective guards are available).

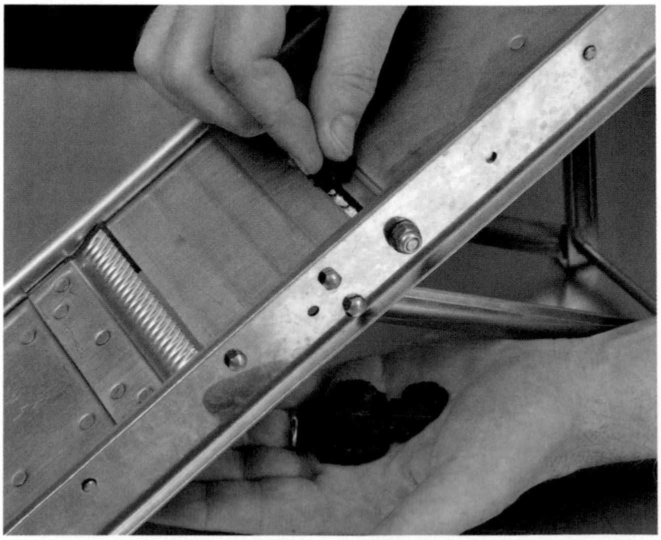

Figure 5.28 A vegetable slicer (mandolin) shown without the safety guard

China and earthenware

Bowls and dishes in china and earthenware are useful for serving a variety of foods, and for microwaved dishes. They should be cleaned in a dishwasher with mild detergent and rinse aid, or by hand, using the appropriate detergent for hand washing.

Materials (cloths, etc.)

All materials should be washed in hot detergent water immediately after use, rinsed in hot, clean water and then dried. Tammy cloths, muslins and linen piping bags must be boiled periodically in detergent water. Kitchen cloths should be washed or changed frequently, otherwise accumulating dirt and food stains may cause cross-contamination of harmful bacteria/germs on to clean food.

Muslin may be used for straining soups and sauces.

Piping bags are made from disposable plastic and are used for piping preparations of all kinds. Plastic piping bags are the most hygienic.

Kitchen cloths:

- general purpose – for washing-up and cleaning surfaces
- tea towel (teacloth) – for drying up and general-purpose hand cloths
- bactericide wiping cloths – impregnated with bactericide to disinfect work surfaces; these cloths have a coloured pattern that fades and disappears when the bactericide is no longer effective; they should then be discarded
- oven cloths – thick cloths designed to protect the hands when removing hot items from the oven; oven cloths must only be used dry, never damp or wet, otherwise the user is likely to be burned.

Paper products used in the kitchen include the following.

- **Greaseproof or silicone:** for lining cake tins, making piping bags and wrapping greasy items of food.
- **Kitchen:** white absorbent paper for absorbing grease from deep-fried foods and for lining trays on which cold foods are kept.
- **General purpose:** thick, absorbent paper for wiping and drying equipment, surfaces, food, etc.
- **Towels:** disposable, for drying the hands.

Clingfilm is a thin, transparent material for wrapping sandwiches, snacks, and hot and cold foods; it has the advantage of being very flexible and easy to handle and seal; due to risk of contamination, it is advisable to use a clingfilm that does not contain PVC or is plasticiser free.

Metal foil is a thin, pliable, silver-coloured material for wrapping and covering foods, and for protecting oven-roasted joints during cooking.

→ Energy conservation and efficiency

With the rising cost of fuel, pressure will be on all operations to look at efficient ways of saving money on fuel. There is a global emphasis on sustainability and maximising the use of resources. This is driven by political, financial, environmental and sustainable agendas.

Statistics issued by the Building Research Establishment (BRE) indicate that the UK's hospitality sector remains a major consumer of fossil fuels, greater than that in education, government or the health service. The major cost sectors for energy use are heating, air conditioning, cooking and refrigeration, lighting and production of hot water. It is estimated that most hospitality businesses could, however, save between 20 and 40 per cent of energy.

The main uses of energy are for providing catering services and hot water.

Chefs and managers have to take responsibility for energy management. Fuel tariffs have to be checked to ensure the most competitive rates are achieved. Assess the current fuel costs and identify any wastage. All staff should be trained to save fuel and monitor use.

WEBLINK

Visit the Department for Environment, Food & Rural Affairs (Defra) website for information about energy efficiency:

www.defra.gov.uk

Who benefits from energy efficiency?

- Hotel owners and management benefit because efficiently run buildings cost less to operate.
- Guests benefit because an efficiently controlled hotel satisfies their needs and leads to repeat business.
- Staff benefit through improved morale and better motivation, which in turn increase productivity.
- The environment benefits because using energy efficiently reduces adverse effects on the environment and preserves non-renewable resources for future generations.

Services and energy

The supply of gas, electricity and water is of vital importance to the caterer. Any information required is best obtained from the appropriate local board so that it will be up to date.

Water

Water authorities are required, by law, to provide a supply of clean, wholesome water, free from suspended matter, odour and taste, all bacteria that are likely to cause disease, and mineral matter injurious to health.

Electrical safety

All electrical products must meet safety criteria laid out in European and national regulations. It is essential that any electrical installation is undertaken by qualified engineers in accordance with British Standard 7671, and carried out by registered contractors of the National Inspection Council for Electrical Installation Contracting (NICEIC).

Gas

Gas is a safe fuel, but like all fuels it must be treated with respect in order to remain safe. If you smell gas:

- open all doors and windows
- check whether a gas tap has been left on, or if a pilot light has gone out; if so, turn off the appliance
- if in doubt, turn off the gas supply at the meter and phone emergency services.

Electricity and mains gas are the fuels most used in catering. Bottled gas (e.g. Calor) is also used in some operations. Before deciding on the fuel to use (if there is a choice) the following factors should be considered:

- safety
- constancy of supply
- cost
- cleanliness and need for ventilation
- efficiency
- cost of equipment, installation and maintenance
- storage requirements.

Energy conservation

The costs of energy use in hotel and catering establishments vary widely according to the type of fuel used, the type and age of equipment, the way in which it is used and the tariff paid.

The basic principles of energy management are:

- obtain the best tariff available
- purchase the most suitable energy-efficient equipment, referring to wattage and running costs
- reduce heat loss to a minimum
- match heat and cooling loads on environmental systems whenever possible to the demands
- maintain all equipment to optimum efficiency and cleanliness (particularly filters on ventilation and conditioning systems; refrigeration plant condensers; cooking and dishwashing equipment)
- ensure that the operating periods of systems and equipment are set correctly
- use heat recovery systems
- monitor energy consumption
- train staff to be energy efficient.

Table 5.1 Comparison of electricity and gas

Advantages	Disadvantages
Electricity	
Clean to use, low maintenance Easily controlled, labour saving Good working atmosphere Little heat loss, no storage space required Low ventilation requirements	Time taken to heat up in a few instances Particular utensils are required for some hobs, e.g. induction More expensive than gas
Gas	
Convenient, labour saving, no smoke or dirt Special utensils not required No fuel storage required Easily controllable with immediate full heat and the flames are visible Cheaper than electricity	Some heat is lost in the kitchen Regular cleaning required for efficient working For gas to produce heat it must burn; this requires oxygen, which is contained in the air, and as a result carbon dioxide and water are produced As a result, adequate ventilation must be provided for combustion and to ensure a satisfactory working environment

Figure 5.29 **A bank of modern equipment, with induction hobs built in**

Some factors to be considered are as follows.

- When replacing equipment, review the contents of the menu, and the cooking and storage methods that the menu requires. Can certain procedures be scaled down or omitted, or can alternative procedures be used?
- Check all pre-heating of equipment – overlong pre-heating wastes fuel.
- Constantly review all heating and cooking procedures.
- Is it possible to reduce operating hours?
- Regularly check ventilation systems.
- Regularly check that storage temperatures for hot water systems are not more than 65°C for central systems and 55°C for local units. (Also ensure that this temperature is not less than 55°C to avoid the risk of Legionnaires' disease.)
- Regularly check all lighting systems; where possible, use energy-efficient compact fluorescent bulbs.
- Train staff not to waste electricity or use lighting unnecessarily.

The savings quoted in Table 5.2 are the minimum you can expect to achieve from energy conservation measures. Small percentage savings can mean appreciable cash benefits.

Table 5.2 **Energy efficiency measures and percentage savings**

	Boilers, controls and hot water	Fossil saving %	Electricity saving %	Lighting, catering and other services	Fossil saving %	Electricity saving %
No cost	Ensure systems come on only when, where and to the extent they are needed	1	2	Switch off lights and other equipment whenever possible Label light switches	0	0.5
	Establish a daily routine for checking control settings, especially where they may have been overridden in response to unexpected circumstances	1	1	Make maximum use of daylight Place lights where they will be most effective Clean light fittings and use translucent shades Improve the reflection of light from walls and ceilings by using pale colours	0	0.5
	Use your existing equipment effectively Check that timers, programmers, optimum start controls and weather compensation controls are set up and operating correctly	3	1	Set illumination levels to the type of activity Reduce lighting levels where possible and remove surplus lamps (but do not compromise safety)	0	0.5
	Isolate parts of systems that are not in use – for example, seasonally Remove redundant pipework during refurbishment	1	0	Provide training for catering staff about energy costs and correct use of equipment Set energy targets for meals, monitor consumption and give feedback to staff	0.2	0.2

	Boilers, controls and hot water	Fossil saving %	Electricity saving %	Lighting, catering and other services	Fossil saving %	Electricity saving %
	Ensure plant is regularly and correctly maintained	0.5	0.5	Ensure regular maintenance of cooking utensils, all appliances, burners, timers, controls and taps Badly maintained equipment wastes energy	0.2	0.2
	Review hot water thermostat accuracy and temperature settings periodically Reducing temperatures will save energy – but take precautions to avoid the risk of Legionnaires' disease	1	0	Ensure optimum use of hot water, ventilation and lighting in the kitchen for various times of day and night Do not use hobs or ovens for space heating Run dishwashers only on full loads	0.2	0.2
Low cost	Fit draught stripping around windows and doors Fit heavy curtains to guest and public rooms	1	0	Where fittings allow, replace 38 mm fluorescent light tubes with 26 mm type, and install electronic starters and ballasts	0	0.5
	Check boiler efficiency periodically and make improvements as required	2	0	Consider replacement of tungsten lamps (including light fittings where necessary) with compact fluorescent types	0	6
	Provide temperature and time controls for domestic hot water	1	0	Consider installation of timers, dimmers, photocells and sensors so lighting operates only when, where and to the extent needed	0	1
	Install showers and flow restrictors where possible Reduce standing losses from hot water storage by lagging pipes and tanks	2	1	Consider installation of bedroom key fobs so lights and other electrical items operate only when rooms are occupied	0	1
	Consider direct fired water heaters for hot water in place of boiler serving calorifier	3	0	When replacing catering equipment, review current developments in appliance design to select the most energy efficient	1	1
	Establish a system for setting targets for energy consumption, monitoring actual consumption and assessing performance	1	2	If you have a swimming pool, provide and use a cover to reduce heat losses at night	0.5	0
	Modernise heating and ventilation plant controls	6	1	Ensure enough linen is available so that laundry equipment is run at full load	0.5	0
	Provide power factor correction, and consider load shedding to reduce maximum demand charges This will not save fuel but will reduce electricity charges	6	1	Use high-efficiency lights for all external lights, including car parking areas, controlled by timers and/or photocells	0	0.5

Controlling the carbon footprint of a catering operation begins with the selection of appropriate suppliers. When auditing potential suppliers, ensure that the company has an environmental policy that addresses the following issues:

- sourcing locally produced goods, wherever possible
- reducing unnecessary packaging
- employing energy-efficient delivery vehicles
- ensuring a structured delivery programme that minimises fuel consumption.

Excess packaging will increase the cost of recycling for the catering operation and will have an ongoing impact on the environment.

There is a balance to be struck between a reduction in the number of deliveries per week and the effect this will have on the cost of refrigerated storage within the catering department.

Further reading

Catering Equipment Suppliers Association (CESA) 'An introduction to the food service industry'. Handout to CFSP (Certified Food Service Professional) course delegates.

Katz, R.L. (1974) Skills of the effective administrator. *Harvard Business Review* 52(1).

Mintzberg, H. (1975) The manager's job: folklore and fact. *Harvard Business Review* 74.

Topics for discussion

1 Who should be responsible for planning a kitchen?
2 Discuss a kitchen you are familiar with and how it could be improved.
3 Compile a list of all the factors that affect the good design of a kitchen and discuss why they are necessary to enable efficiency.
4 Poor design may cause accidents in the kitchen. Discuss the ways in which accidents can be prevented.
5 List the essential requirements of kitchen equipment.
6 Discuss the respective advantages of a conventional oven, convection oven and a combination/steaming oven.
7 Compare induction cooking plates, halogen hobs and conventional cooking tops.
8 What are the advantages of pans made up of layers of different metals?
9 What are the benefits of the bratt pan?
10 Discuss the importance of sufficient refrigeration.
11 Discuss the design of equipment in relation to maintaining high standards of hygiene.
12 What factors should be considered by those designing kitchen equipment?
13 What are the advantages and disadvantages of induction equipment?
14 What are the advantages of gas or electricity for kitchen equipment?
15 Why is maintenance of all services is essential?
16 How can water conservation be achieved?
17 How could the sun and wind be used to reduce costs in small establishments?
18 Discuss how training could reduce wastage of water, gas and electricity.

6 Production systems

➔ A strategic and methodical approach to food production and service

Every chef's challenge is to ensure that the production of food is as safe, efficient, cost effective and consistent as possible. This is only possible when the chef can analyse the full process using a critical path and identify all areas of work.

Areas of risk include:

- suppliers
- the market
- cooking consistency
- the workforce
- non-compliance with food safety legislation (see Chapter 3).

All these areas hold potential risks that could lead to a fall in profits and perhaps increase staff turnover. Hospitality businesses that fail do so due to one or more of the above areas not being properly managed.

Food production systems

Table 6.1 shows the different types of food production system.

Table 6.1 Methods of food production

Method	Description
Conventional	Production utilising mainly fresh foods and traditional cooking methods
Convenience	Production utilising mainly convenience foods
Call order	Where food is cooked to order either from customer (as in cafeterias) or from waiter; production area often open to customer area
Continuous flow	Production-line approach where different parts of the production process may be separated (e.g. fast food)
Centralised	Production not directly linked to service; foods are 'held' and distributed to separate service areas
Cook-chill	Food production storage and regeneration method utilising principle of low temperature control to preserve the qualities of processed foods
Cook-freeze	Production, storage and regeneration method utilising principle of freezing to control and preserve the qualities of processed foods; requires special processes to assist freezing
Sous-vide	Method of production, storage and regeneration utilising a sealed vacuum to control and preserve the quality of processed foods
Assembly kitchen	System based on using the latest technology in the manufacturing and conservation of food products

In order to ensure high quality at all times it is essential that working conditions are maintained to the highest possible standards of hygiene (see Chapter 3). Consult with Environmental Health Officers when planning food production systems.

Centralised production

Why centralise?

Some specific problems faced by the catering industry are as follows.

- **Staff:** unattractive work conditions, limited numbers of skilled staff, mobility of labour.
- **Food:** high cost, wastage.
- **Equipment:** high cost of replacement and maintenance, under-usage.
- **Energy:** wasteful high-cost systems, availability.
- **Overheads:** wage increases, payments to National Insurance.
- **Space:** premises must be adequate for comfortable working while using space efficiently; space is very costly.

To resolve the shortage of skilled catering staff and a high turnover of employees:

- skilled staff should be more fully utilised and given improved working conditions
- certain catering tasks require deskilling so as to be carried out by a greater proportion of unskilled staff
- better conditions of employment must be provided for key staff in order to enhance job satisfaction.

The solution comes in the form of centralised production, using the skilled staff available to prepare and cook in bulk and then to distribute to finishing kitchens, which are smaller, employing semi-skilled and unskilled labour. It helps with the following areas.

- **Food cost:** greater control over waste and portion sizes; competitive purchasing through bulk buying.
- **Equipment:** intensive central use of heavy equipment and less equipment in individual units.
- **Product:** greater standardisation and quality control.
- **Labour strategy:** staff are employed at regular times (9 a.m. to 5 p.m.), which can eliminate or lessen the difficulty of obtaining staff who will work shifts and any additional cost this may involve.

When considering a centralised production system it is essential that a detailed financial appraisal is produced and reviewed, as profitability depends on features specific to each business, such as the product, the size of each unit, and the number of units.

Cook-freeze, cook-chill and sous-vide systems (described below) have been developed to meet centralised production requirements, each system having advantages depending on the size and nature of the overall operation.

Design

Centralised production systems can be designed in two ways:

1 using existing catering (operations) unit and modifying, etc.
2 purpose-built.

The central production unit may prepare and despatch fresh cooked foods, or make use of cook-freeze, cook-chill or sous-vide.

There are two types of operation in centralised food production:

1 weekly production run
2 daily total run.

Forecasts obtained from the end unit determine the quantity of the weekly production run. The weekly production run prepares items of a particular type on one occasion only. The quantity produced is based on forecasts. As soon as the run is completed the next run is then scheduled.

The main advantage of this type of production is in the comparative ease with which a control system may be installed and operated. However, in the event of an error in production scheduling, it is wasteful and costly to organise a further production run of small volume. Another disadvantage is that stocks, both finished and unfinished, can build up, affecting the profitability of the operation.

A daily total run is based upon the items required by the end unit per day. The forecast gap is shorter, so the end units are not able to estimate their requirements so accurately.

Small centralised operations

There are some very good examples of smaller centralised operations in the catering industry. Their purpose is to provide ready-prepared goods that may be served to banquets or supplied to grills/coffee shops.

The preparation of the food takes place during the kitchen 'slack' period, principally after the luncheon service. Cook-chill or cook-freeze processes are used. Refrigerators in the outlets are stocked up daily from the central store.

When an item is ordered it is reheated. The cooked items are placed on the plate, with the garnish and vegetables being added separately. There are also, of course, many other refinements: carefully calculated production schedules and coloured photographs of the dishes to guide presentation, for example.

Transport

Centralised production very often means that production is separated from the food service by distance, time, or both. An example is in hospital wards; here there are satellite kitchens or regeneration kitchens. Other examples exist in aircraft catering and banqueting.

The distribution of goods, routing and the maintenance of vehicles are very important to a centralised production operation. Transport is usually under the control of a senior manager, who also has the complicated job of batching up deliveries (normally weekly or bi-weekly). It is important that the senior manager has considerable administrative skill in order to prevent errors occurring.

➔ Cook-chill

Cook-chill is a catering system based on the normal preparation and cooking of food followed by rapid chilling and storage in controlled low-temperature conditions. The chilled food is regenerated in finishing kitchens, which require low capital investment and minimum staff, immediately before consumption. Almost any food can be cook-chilled provided that the correct methods are used.

The cook-chill system is used in volume catering, such as hospitals and schools, and in banqueting and conference catering. It is also used in vending machines, as well as services provided outside of main mealtimes, during nightshifts for example.

The main difference between cook-freeze and cook-chill is the degree of refrigeration and the length of storage life. Other than these differences the information given here relates to both systems. (For details of cook-freeze, see page 134.)

Foods suitable for the cook-chill process are as follows.

- **Meats:** all meat, poultry, game and offal can be cook-chilled. Meat dishes that need to be sliced, such as striploin of beef, are cooked, rapidly chilled, sliced and packaged for storage. The regeneration temperature must reach 70°C in the core/centre of the produce for two minutes. Therefore, it is not possible to serve undercooked meats.
- **Fish:** all precooked fish dishes are suitable for cook-chilling.
- **Egg dishes:** omelettes and scrambled eggs are now commonly used in this process, especially on airlines.

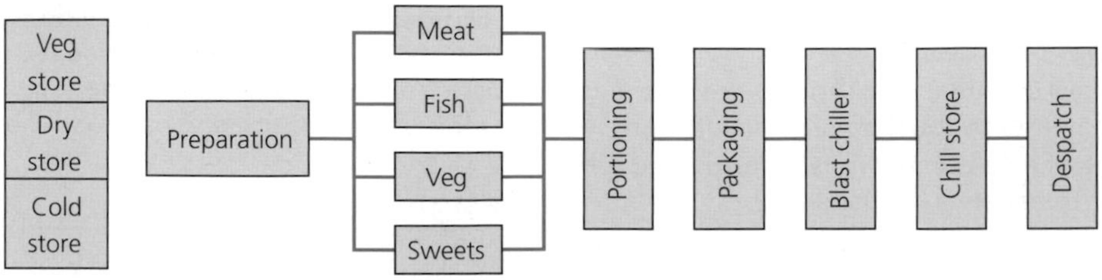

Figure 6.1 Production unit: cook-chill process

The quality of the end product has greatly improved and continues to do so as money is invested in product development.

- **Soups and sauces:** most soups and sauces can now be chilled successfully. Recipes with a high fat or egg yolk content need modification to prevent separation or coagulation on regeneration.
- **Desserts:** a large number of desserts chill well, especially the cold variety; developments continue with hot sweets, especially those that require a hot base and a separate topping.

It has been found that, during the storage period before reheating and consumption, certain products deteriorate in quality.

- The flavour of certain meat dishes – in particular white meats, veal and poultry – deteriorates after three days.
- Chilled meats without sauces can develop acidic tastes.
- Fatty foods tend to develop 'off' flavours due to the fat oxidising.
- Fish dishes deteriorate more rapidly than meat dishes.
- Dishes containing meat tend to develop a 'flat' taste, and if spices have been used these can dominate the flavour of the meat by the end of the chilled storage period.
- Vegetables in general may discolour and develop a strong flavour.
- Dishes that contain large amounts of starch may taste stale after the chilled storage time.

The following recipe modifications may have to be introduced during the preparation or cooking or both.

- **Battered fish:** the batter should be made thicker, using a mixture with a higher fat content. This type of batter does not easily break away from the fish and will give a crisper end product.
- **Stewed/braised items:** cut meat into smaller portions. To avoid undue thickness, flour-based sauces must be cooked thoroughly otherwise they will continue to thicken during regeneration.
- **Scrambled eggs:** cook until the egg begins to scramble, remove from heat and allow the product to continue to cook to a soft consistency. Chill immediately in shallow dishes and stir during chilling.
- **Creamed and mashed potatoes:** more liquid is added than normal, giving a loose and less dense product, as the potato absorbs more liquid when chilled.

Food safety and quality

The purpose of chilling food is to prolong its storage life. Under normal temperature conditions, food deteriorates rapidly through the action of micro-organisms and enzymic and chemical reactions. A reduction in the storage temperature inhibits the multiplication of micro-organisms, and slows down chemical and enzymic reactions (see Chapter 3).

Even where high standards of fast chilling practice are used and consistent refrigerated storage maintained, slow growth of spoilage organisms does take place at these temperatures and, for this reason, storage life cannot be greater than five days (including the day of production and consumption).

Food must be stored at 0–3°C to ensure both full protection from microbiological growth and the maintenance of maximum nutritional values in the food. Food chilled at 0–3°C will not last as long as frozen food, but it does produce a good product.

A properly designed and operated cook-chill system observes the following points.

- All food must be prepared quickly, avoiding any possible cross-contamination and at the correct temperature. It is important to have separate work areas for both cooked and uncooked food, especially high-risk foods such as raw meat and fish. Use different slicing machines for raw and cooked food.
- The food should be cooked sufficiently to ensure destruction of any pathogenic micro-organisms. The centre of the food must reach a temperature of at least 70°C, but preferably 75°C or even 80°C.
- Portioning should take place in a controlled environment, which is maintained to the highest hygiene standards. The depth of the food should be no more than approximately 5 cm. The containers must be labelled with the date of cooking, number of portions and reheating instructions.
- The chilling process must begin as soon as possible after cooking and portioning, within 30 minutes of cooking. The food should be chilled to 3°C within a period of 90 minutes. A higher temperature may be due to the food being packed too deep in the containers; the food may have been covered; there may be a malfunction in the equipment.
- Food containers must be sealed correctly before storage in order to protect the food from air-borne contamination, enhance the presentation of dishes, prevent the evaporation of moisture when heated, reduce the dehydration effects chilling has on food, avoid finishing products being tampered with.
- The food should be stored at a temperature of 0–3°C. Most pathogenic organisms will not grow below 5°C, but a temperature below 3°C is required to reduce growth of spoilage organisms and to achieve the required storage life.
- The chilled food should be distributed under such controlled conditions that any rise in temperature during distribution is kept to a minimum. This may be due to the journey taking too long using unrefrigerated transport; the refrigerated van not operating correctly; the insulated box (if used) not being precooled, or the lid not being properly fitted. Whatever the cause, it must be recorded and the appropriate persons informed. Should the temperature of the food exceed 5°C during distribution the food ought to be consumed within 12 hours (depending on the type of food); if the temperature exceeds 8°C it should be discarded. If in doubt, throw it out.

- For both safety and palatability the reheating (regeneration) of the food should follow immediately upon the removal of the food from chilled conditions.
- Reheating should raise the core temperature to a minimum of 70°C, ideally 75°C but preferably 80°C. Failure may be due to the label information not being followed correctly, the label information not being correct, the lid being taken off when it should have been left on, or faulty equipment. If the food temperature is unsafe, throw it away.
- In some systems the food is chilled in multi-portion containers then portioned and plated before reheating. The portioning should be done in a controlled environment within 30 minutes of the food leaving the chilled store and at a temperature of 8°C or below.
- The food should be consumed as soon as possible and not more than two hours after reheating. It is essential that unconsumed reheated food is discarded. Food not intended for reheating should be consumed as soon as convenient and within two hours of removal from storage.
- The critical safety limit for chilled food is 8°C. Should the temperature of the chilled food rise above this level during storage or distribution, the food should be discarded.
- All chilled cooked food must be stored in its own special refrigeration area. Never store cooked chilled food under the same conditions as fresh products. Monitor the temperature of the product regularly.
- Do not use food in damaged containers.

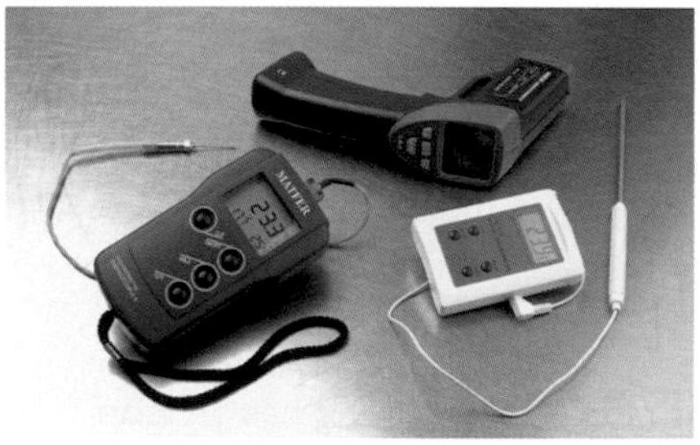

Figure 6.2 A selection of temperature measuring devices

Breaking food safety laws, and lack of due diligence can be very costly if legal action is taken against the caterer or food manufacturer (see Chapter 3). It is essential to:

- maintain and record the correct temperatures
- maintain high standards of food safety
- use fresh, high-quality ingredients, avoiding raw materials that may contain excessive numbers of micro-organisms.

To ensure quality product and a well-managed process, the following guidelines should be adhered to.

- Food should not be overcooked after reheating. This may be caused by the food being heated too long or the temperature being too high, or faulty equipment.
- Portions must be controlled when filling packages in order to ensure efficient stock control, control costs, ensure that sufficient food is delivered to regenerating/finishing kitchens.
- Protect containers of food from damage, which may be due to mishandling during transportation or badly stacked storage containers.
- All food purchased must be of prime quality and stored correctly at the required temperatures.
- Maintain a consistent process. Failure to adhere to just one procedure could result in disorganised production and reduced productivity.

Equipment and premises for cook-chill production

Cook-chill is generally planned within a purpose-designed, comprehensive, central production unit to give small-, medium- or large-scale production along predefined flow lines. Within an existing kitchen, where existing equipment is retained, chilling/post-chilling packaging and additional storage for cooked chilled food are added.

The equipment used will vary according to the size of the operation, but if food is batch-cooked then convection ovens, steaming ovens, bratt pans, jacketed boiling pans, tilting kettles, and so on, may be used. Certain oven models are available in which a set of racks can be assembled with food and wheeled in for cooking.

Chilling equipment

Only specially purpose-built and designed equipment can take the temperature of cooked food down to safe levels fast enough.

Blast-chillers or air blast-chillers use rapidly moving cold air to chill the food evenly and rapidly. Some models have temperature probes so that the temperature of the food can be checked without opening the door.

Cryogenic batch chillers use liquid nitrogen at a temperature of -196°C; this is sprayed into the chilling cabinet containing the warm food. In the warmer temperature of the cabinet, the liquid nitrogen turns to super-cold gas, absorbing the heat from the food as it does so. Fans move the cold gas over and around the food. Once the gas has become warm it is removed from the cabinet. Some equipment uses carbon dioxide instead of nitrogen.

Figure 6.3 A blast-chiller

Reheating, distribution and finishing

The following equipment may be used for regenerating cook-chill products.

- **Combination ovens:** these are ideally suited for bulk production and can be used with steam, which is very effective in producing quality products and retaining moisture in foods.
- **Steamers:** these may be used for certain foods, especially vegetables.
- **Microwave ovens:** these are used for small amounts of food.
- **Infrared ovens:** these may be used for small or large quantities of food.

Finishing kitchens can consist of purpose-built regeneration equipment plus refrigerated storage. Additional equipment, such as a deep-fat fryer, boiling pans and pressure steamer for chips, sauces, and so on, can be added to give greater flexibility.

Where chilled food is produced for supply on the same premises, with no transport involved, the meals should be supplied, stored and regenerated by exactly the same method as used when the production unit and finishing kitchens are separated by some distance.

Ensure the security of storage areas against unauthorised access in order to prevent pilferage or damage by unauthorised persons, and prevent unnecessary opening of store doors, which could destabilise the storage temperature and thus may affect the temperature of the product, rendering it unsafe.

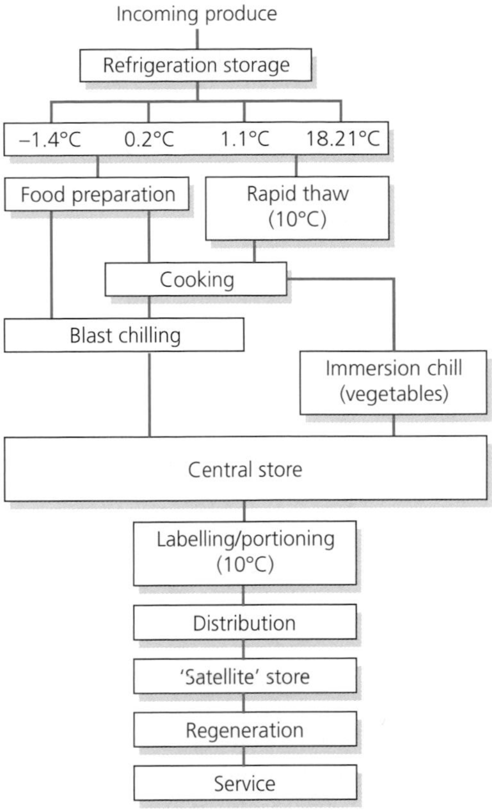

Figure 6.4 Refrigeration for cook-chill catering

Distribution of the chilled food is an important part of the cook-chill operation. The temperature below 3°C must be maintained throughout the period of transport for food safety (see above), so refrigeration during distribution is to be encouraged in all circumstances.

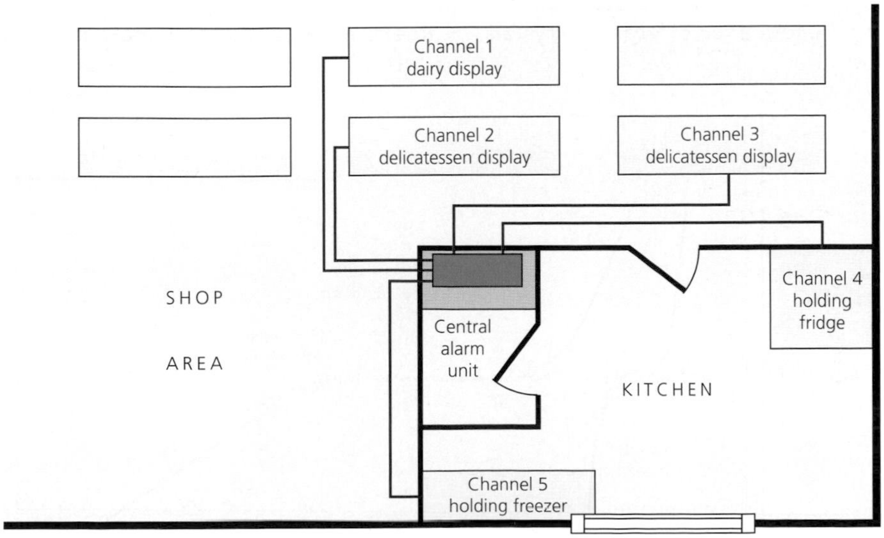

Figure 6.5 A central monitoring alarm unit and an example of the area it covers

In some cases the cook-chill production unit can also act as a centralised kitchen and distribution point. Food is regenerated in an area adjacent to the cook-chill production area, and heat retention or insulated boxes are used for distribution. During transportation and service the hot food must not be allowed to fall below 63°C.

Containers for cook-chill

The containers must protect, and in some cases enhance, the quality of the product at all stages; they must assist in rapid chilling, safe storage and effective reheating. Therefore the container must be:

- sturdy – to withstand chilling, handling and reheating
- safe – not made of a substance that will cause harmful substances to develop in the food, nor react with the food to cause discoloration or spoilage
- have an easy-to-remove lid – without damaging contents or causing spillage
- attractive – to enhance the appearance of the product when it is going to be displayed and served from the same container
- airtight and watertight – so that moisture, flavours or odours do not penetrate the food or escape during storage and transportation.

Single-portion containers can be of cardboard laminated with plastic, aluminium foil (unsuitable for microwave heating), plastic compounds or stainless steel and ceramic, which are durable and reusable (stainless steel is, however, unsuitable for microwave ovens).

Multi-portion containers can be of strong plastic compounds, stainless steel, ceramic or aluminium foil.

Labels must stick securely to containers and be easy to apply, clearly identifying the product. Colour coding is sometimes used to help identify the different days of production (Figure 6.6).

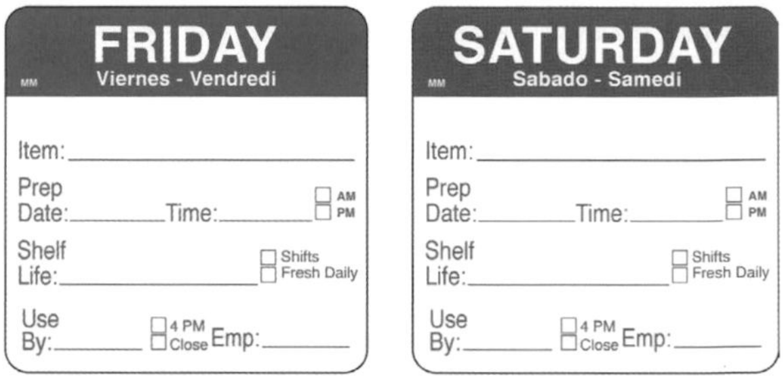

Figure 6.6 Labelling system

WEBLINK

For further information, contact the Chilled Food Association:

www.chilledfood.org

Cook-freeze

Cook-freeze is a production system similar to cook-chill, using blast-freezers rather than blast-chillers. The freezing must be carried out very rapidly to retain freshness and to accelerate temperature loss through the latent heat barrier, thus preventing the formation of large ice crystals and rupturing of the cells.

The frozen food can be stored at -18 to -20°C for up to six months. The ability to freeze cooked dishes and prepared foods, as distinct from storing chilled foods in a refrigerator or already frozen commodities in a deep-freeze, allows a caterer to make more productive use of staff.

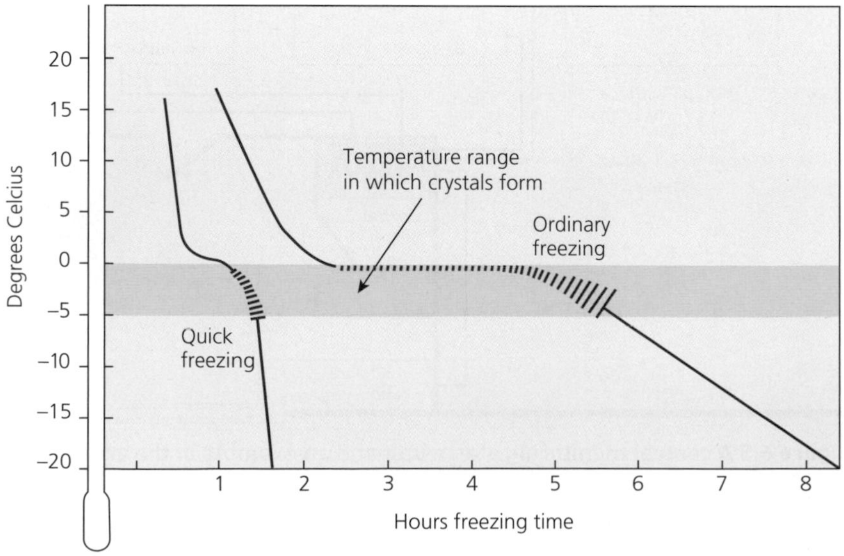

Figure 6.7 Speed of freezing and crystal formation

How freezing affects different foods

Freezer burn occurs due to badly packaged food or when food is stored for too long.

Meat, poultry and fish

The fat in meat will oxidise and go rancid, even in frozen storage, so lean meat is better than fatty meat for freezing. Chicken fat contains a natural antioxidant (vitamin E), and this will react to prevent rancidity occurring.

Fresh meat must always be used for cook-freeze dishes. Never use meat that has previously been frozen. This is because each time meat is thawed, even in cool conditions, there is a chance for food-poisoning bacteria to multiply.

Some loss of flavour in fish is unavoidable and any surfaces left exposed can oxidise, producing a rancid taste. Deep-fried fish in batter has to be modified so that the batter does not peel off as a result of the freezing process. The batter should be made thicker or with a higher fat content.

Freezing does not stop the enzyme activity in the meat, poultry or fish that makes the fat present in the flesh go rancid. This particularly affects the unsaturated fats in pork, poultry and fish. These items should therefore not be stored frozen for longer than two to three months. It is advisable therefore to trim off all fat before processing these items.

Fruit and vegetables

When fruit and vegetables deteriorate and turn brown, it is because of the action of enzymes present. These enzymes cause discoloration and gradually destroy the nutritional value of the fruit. Freezing will further slow this down but not stop it completely. Therefore, fruit and vegetables should be blanched or completely cooked prior to freezing, which will stop the enzymic processes.

Freezing also has a softening effect on the texture of fruit and vegetables. This is acceptable for hard fruits such as apples, unripened pears and so on; it is not, however, suitable for soft fruits such as strawberries. Fruits like these are suitable for freezing only if they are later to be used as a filling or in a sauce, but not for decorative purposes. The structure of such soft fruits breaks down during the freezing and defrosting process, and therefore they cannot be used afterwards in the same way as fresh fruit.

Only exceptionally fresh vegetables should be used for freezing. Avoid bruised vegetables, which may produce 'off' flavours. Blanch the vegetables to inactivate the enzymes, but avoid over-blanching, otherwise the vegetables will be overcooked. Blanch if possible in high-pressure steamers as this will help reduce vitamin C loss.

Recipe modification

Recipes have to be modified in order to be freezer stable. The exact adjustment of recipes to produce the best result is still being developed by chefs.

Normal starches will cause sauces, batters, thickened soups, and gravies to curdle or separate when thawed and reheated. An appropriate modified starch, capable of resisting the effects of freezing, must be used. Colflo and Purity 69 are two commercially manufactured starches used in cook-freeze recipes.

Jellies and other products containing gelatine are unsuitable because they develop a granular structure in the cook-freeze process, unless the recipe is modified with stabilisers.

WEBLINK

A tool used to rework recipes to reduce sugar, salt and saturated fat; it takes the stated ingredients and suggests healthier substitutes:

www.foodafactoflife.org.uk

The cook-freeze process

Preparation of food

The production menu for a month is drawn up and the total quantities of different foods required calculated. With poor production planning a backlog of food for freezing will occur. Supplies are then ordered, with special attention given to their being:

- of high quality
- delivered so that they can immediately be prepared and cooked without any possibility of deteriorating during an enforced period of storage before being processed.

Deep-freeze temperatures prevent the multiplication of micro-organisms but do not destroy them. If, therefore, a dish were contaminated before being frozen, consumers would be put at risk months later when the food is prepared for consumption. To ensure food safety:

- make sure that all preparation and cooking areas are clean and that the equipment is in working order
- have separate work areas for both cooked and uncooked food, especially high-risk foods such as raw meat and fish
- never use previously frozen food
- have separate refrigeration and separate slicing machines for both raw and cooked food
- avoid any delay between preparation and cooking
- always use temperature probes to check that the centre of the food has reached a safe temperature before the final cooking is complete.

Check on the cooking process for the food to ensure that it takes account of the overall effect on flavour, texture and nutritional value.

Portioning and packing

In order to achieve rapid freezing with a quick reduction of temperature to -18°C or below, the cooked food must be carefully portioned (with uniform portion sizes). Portions in individual disposable aluminium foil containers may conveniently be placed into aluminium foil trays holding from six to ten portions each, sealed and carefully labelled with their description and the date of preparation.

To maintain high standards of food hygiene when portioning:

- all reusable containers must be cleaned and sterilised thoroughly
- make sure that all assistants who portion and package wear food-handling gloves
- make sure that all general equipment used in this area is sterilised.

Portions must be controlled when filling, in order to standardise and control costs, facilitate stores control, assist in food service, and standardise the thawing and reheating process. Follow these guidelines:

- accurately portion the food according to the recipe
- do not pack the food to a depth greater than 5 cm; for food that is to be microwaved the depth should be less
- food containers must be sealed correctly before storage in order to prevent spoilage due to contact with the cold air, prevent spillage prior to freezing, allow for safe stacking, help prevent damage to containers
- cover the food before blast-freezing
- check and record the temperature of the food.

Label all food correctly with:

- production date, storage life and 'use by' date
- name of dish, description of contents
- number of portions
- instructions for reheating/regenerating – including type of oven, temperature, time, and whether lid should be on or off.

Correct labelling will enable quick and efficient stock-taking and indicate important information.

Freezing

Freezing should be done immediately after cooking and portioning.

Blast-freezing takes place when low-temperature air is passed over food at high speed, reducing food to a temperature of at least -20°C within 90 minutes. An effective procedure is to place the trays on racks in a blast-freezing tunnel and expose them to a vigorous flow of cold air until the cooked items are frozen solid and the temperature reduced to at least -5°C. There must be at least 2 cm air space between layers of containers in the freezer.

Blast-freezers can hold from 20 to 400 kg per batch, the larger models being designed for trolley operation. The quality of the final product depends on how quickly the food's temperature is reduced to below freezing. The capacity of the blast-freezer should be designed to achieve this reduction in temperature within a period of 60–90 minutes.

Storage of frozen items

Immediately after freezing the food must be transported to the deep-freeze storage at a maximum of -18°C. The ideal deep-freeze temperature range is -20°C to -30°C. Monitor deep-freezer temperatures and food temperatures regularly, and keep accurate records.

Store the food in the accepted manner on shelves and racks above the floor, away from the door and with enough space around to allow the cold air to circulate. Always wear protective clothing when entering the deep-freeze store.

A catering operation involving several dining rooms and cafeterias, some of which may be situated at some distance from the kitchen and frozen store, may need enough space to store four weeks' supply of cooked dishes.

Transport of frozen items to the point of service

Keep food, which has been frozen in the cooked state, frozen until immediately prior to its being served.

Cook-freeze meals have to be delivered to finishing kitchens at the same temperature as they were held in storage, although if the food is going to be regenerated within 24 hours, the permissible temperature range is between 0 and -18°C.

For short distances, insulated containers are used. These are cooled down before use. However, it is safer and more efficient to use refrigerated vans. If necessary, a subsidiary deep-freeze store should be provided for them on arrival.

Regeneration of frozen cooked portions

Specially designed equipment for reheating frozen food is also needed.

To reheat cook-freeze products:

- remove products from deep-freeze for regeneration; check the labels
- make sure equipment is at the correct temperature and in working order
- follow the regeneration instructions on the label
- the foods must be reheated to at least 70°C, but to 75–80°C immediately before service; check temperature has been reached by using a sterilised calibrated temperature probe
- serve the food as soon as possible after regeneration
- food that has not been eaten within two hours should be thrown away
- food that has been allowed to cool must never be reheated.

Coated food products will become soggy unless the lid is removed when regenerating.

Packaging for cook-freeze

Packaging affects the storage and regeneration of the product. Containers must protect the food against oxidation during storage, and allow for freezing and reheating. The containers must be:

- watertight
- non-tainting
- disposable or reusable
- equipped with tight-fitting lids.

There are a number of packaging materials available, which include plastic compounds, aluminium foil and cardboard plastic laminates. These are available as single-portion packs, complete meal packs and bulk packs.

Various factors will affect your choice of container.

- **Menu choice:** single packs provide the greatest flexibility, but tend to be the most expensive way to package and therefore purchase.
- **Food value:** the overheating of complete meal packs, or the edges of bulk packs, will damage the nutritional value.
- **Storage space:** large bulk packs make the best use of space.
- **Handling time:** after cooking, bulk packs are the quickest and easiest to fill, whereas complete packs are more difficult to fill. Bulk packs do, however, have to be portioned at the time of service and are therefore more time-consuming than single packs.
- **Quality of the food:** freezing time is affected by the depth of the food; therefore bulk packs, where the food is relatively deep, may not survive the freezing process as well as single-portion packs. Bulk packs also rely on trained service staff to present the food attractively and portion it accurately. Regeneration instructions can be complex if complete meal packs contain different food components that, in theory, may require different lengths of reheating time.

Freezing equipment

Specialist equipment is required in order to reduce the temperature of the food to the required storage temperature of -18°C.

- **Air blast-freezers or blast-freezers:** these take approximately 75–90 minutes to freeze food, depending on how it is packaged. Extremely cold air – between -32°C and -40°C – is blown by fans over the cooked food. The warm air is constantly removed and recirculated through the heat exchange unit to lower its temperature. In the larger cook-freeze units the food is pushed in on a trolley at one end and then wheeled out at the other end frozen.
- **Cryogenic freezers:** these use liquid nitrogen with the freezing time taking on average 25 minutes, depending on the food being frozen, provided the food is left uncovered. Liquid nitrogen at -196°C is sprayed into the freezing chamber. Fans circulate the nitrogen so that the foods freeze evenly. The warm gas is pumped out of the cabinet as more cold nitrogen is pumped in. Some freezers used liquid carbon dioxide.
- **Plate freezers and tunnel freezers:** these are used in food manufacturing and are less likely to be used in catering.

Finishing kitchen equipment

The blast-freezing system is effective because it is, in design, an especially powerful form of forced convection heat exchanger arranged to extract heat. It follows that an equally appropriate system for replacing heat is a forced convection oven, designed for trays of frozen portions. An oven with an efficient thermostat and adequate control of the air circulation system will allow standardised setting times for the controls to be laid down for the regeneration of the various types of dishes needed.

The following types of equipment may be used for regeneration.

- **Forced air convection ovens** are suitable for large quantities of food.
- **Thawing cabinets** are similar to a forced air convection oven, but use a temperature of 10°C.
- **Rapid thawing cabinets:** these are used to defrost containers of frozen meals before they are placed in the oven; this has the effect of halving the reheating time. The temperature of the food is brought from -20°C to 3°C in approximately four hours, under safe conditions. Warming is kept at a steady controlled rate by a process of alternating low-volume heat with refrigeration.
- **Combination ovens:** these are suitable for large quantities of food.
- **Microwave ovens:** these are suitable only for small amounts of food.
- **Dual-purpose ovens:** these are microwave ovens that have a second heat source – for example, an infra-red grill – and a defrost control that switches the microwave power on and off.

➜ Overall benefits of cook-chill and cook-freeze

To the employer, both systems provide:

- portion control and reduced waste
- controlled, precise production according to requirements of the business
- central purchasing with bulk-buying discounts
- full utilisation of equipment
- full utilisation of staff time
- savings on equipment, space and fuel
- fewer staff with better conditions – no unsociable hours, no weekend work, no overtime
- simplified, less frequent delivery to units
- solves problem of moving hot foods (EC regulations forbid the movement of hot foods unless the temperature is maintained over 65°C; maintaining 65°C is very difficult to achieve and high temperatures inevitably will be damaging to foods).

To the customer, this means:

- increased variety and selection
- improved quality, with standards maintained
- more nutritious foods
- services can be maintained at all times, regardless of staff absences.

The advantages of cook-freeze over cook-chill are:

- seasonal purchasing provides considerable savings
- delivery to units will be far less frequent
- long-term planning of production and menus becomes possible
- less dependence on price fluctuations
- more suitable for vending machines incorporating microwaves.

The advantages of cook-chill over cook-freeze are:

- regeneration systems are simpler – infrared and steam convection ovens are mostly used and only 12 minutes are required to reheat all foods perfectly
- thawing time is eliminated
- smaller-capacity storage is required – three to four days' supply as opposed to up to 120 days'
- blast-chillers are cheaper to install and run than blast-freezers
- chiller storage is cheaper to install and run than freezer storage
- cooking techniques are unaltered (additives and revised recipes are needed for freezing)
- all foods can be chilled so the range of dishes is wider (some foods cannot be frozen); cooked eggs, steaks and sauces such as hollandaise can be chilled (after some recipe modification where necessary)
- no system is too small to adapt to cook-chill.

Table 6.2 shows how cook-chill compares with fast-food systems.

Table 6.2 Characteristics of cook-chill and fast-food systems

	Cook-chill	Fast food
Types of equipment	Flexible, general purpose	Single purpose Single function
Design of process	Functional	Product flow
Set-up time	Variable	Long
Operatives	Variously skilled, partie system, limited flexibility	Low skill Flexible
Inventories for start of process	Vary, depending on 'foods in' required Limited in time by planning and forecasting Limited by pre-planning and forecasting	High to meet potential demand
Holding inventory	Five days max. Level forecasted	Ten minutes max. Level controlled
Lot sizes	Small to large (multiples of ten)	Individual
Production time	Variable depending on menu requirements	Short or constant
Product range	Fairly wide but within constraints of three- or four-course meals, lunch or dinner	Very restricted
System structure	Stock/customer/operation	Stock/queue/operation
Capacity	Variable	Highly variable
Scheduling	Externally orientated	Externally orientated

Case study

South Devon Healthcare Trust

Torbay Hospital's catering department has to provide around 1,900 meals for patients, staff and visitors every day. When South Devon Healthcare Trust needed to improve its catering operation in line with the recommendations of the Health of the Nation Report, it considered three options:

1. continuing with the existing central kitchen
2. moving to a cook-chill operation
3. moving to a cook-freeze operation.

After much consultation, and successful pilot studies, the hospital's patient catering operation moved to a cook-freeze system.

The brief

The catering operation had to be of the highest quality possible and consistent in terms of the service and the products. Flexibility was required with menu planning to avoid a system that was tied in to a fixed production cycle. In addition, two key concerns with the existing system had to be addressed: the poor presentation and varying temperature of food when it arrived on the wards.

The solution

A weekly menu cycle giving patients a choice of at least four main dishes every mealtime, compared to three offered previously. Patients make their choice and it is phoned through from the ward to the kitchen by 9.30 a.m. on the day of service. Frozen meals are then simply sent up the ward, where they are cooked in a regeneration trolley, heated through to the optimum temperature and served to the patients. This way the food is at its best at the point of service.

The frozen meals are stored in a walk-in freezer. The maximum six-month shelf life minimises waste and maximises convenience for the caterer. Wastage at ward level has been addressed by offering individual, twin and multi-portion pack sizes, so only the required number are sent up to the patients.

Torbay caterers can choose from more than 180 dishes, many of which have been approved by the Better Hospital Food Programme. In addition, there is a range of specially developed puréed meals, and meals suitable for patients on low-salt, diabetic, reducing, gluten-free or moderate-salt diets.

The results

South Devon Healthcare Trust has to date hosted more than 40 site visits as an example of an efficient and good-quality hospital catering operation.

Source: based on a case study at www.apetito.co.uk

→ Vacuum cooking (sous-vide)

Sous-vide is a combination of vacuum sealing food in plastic pouches, tightly controlled en papillotte cooking using steam or hot water, and rapid chilling. It is a form of cook-chill food production that can be used by almost any type of catering operation. The objective is to rationalise kitchen procedures without having a detrimental effect on the quality of the individual dishes.

All the basic principles of cook-chill (see above) also apply to sous-vide.

The process

Prime-quality ingredients should be used.

- Individual portions of prepared food are first placed in special plastic pouches. The food can be fish, poultry, meats, vegetables, and so on, to which seasoning, a garnish, sauce, stock, wine, flavouring, vegetables, herbs and/or spices can be added.
- The pouches of food are then placed in a vacuum-packaging machine, which evacuates all the air and tightly seals the pouch.
- The pouches are next cooked by steam or temperature-controlled water. This is usually in a special oven equipped with a steam control programme, which controls the injection of steam into the oven, to give steam cooking at an oven temperature below 100°C or in a water bath with a controlled temperature controlled. Each food item has its own ideal cooking time and temperature.
- When cooked, the pouches are rapidly cooled to 3°C, usually in an iced water chiller, or an air blast-chiller for larger operations.
- The pouches are then labelled and stored in a holding refrigerator at an optimum temperature of 3°C.
- When required for service, the pouches are regenerated in boiling water or a steam combination oven until the required temperature is reached, then cut open and the food presented. Meats, such as steaks cooked by water bath, are usually seared in a hot pan to caramelise the proteins and develop the meaty aromas and flavours associated with such products.

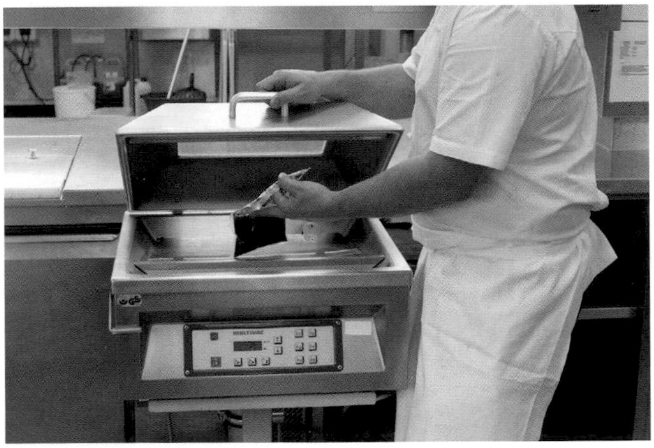

Figure 6.8 Vacuum packer

Vacuum pressures are as important as cooking temperatures with regard to weight loss and heat absorption. The highest temperature used in sous-vide cooking is 100°C, and 1000 millibars is the minimum amount of vacuum pressure used.

As there is no oxidation or discoloration involved, this method is ideal for conserving fruits, such as apples and pears (e.g. pears in red wine, fruits in syrup). When preparing meats in sauces the meat is pre-blanched then added to the completed sauce.

Advantages of sous-vide:

- long shelf life, up to 21 days, refrigerated
- ability to produce meals in advance means better deployment of staff and skills
- vacuum-packed foods can be mixed in the cold store without risk of cross-contamination
- reduced labour costs at point of service
- beneficial cooking effects on certain foods, especially moulded items and pâtés, reduces weight loss on meat joints
- full flavour and texture are retained as food cooks in its own juices
- economises on ingredients (less butter, marinade, etc.)
- makes pre-cooking a possibility for à la carte menus
- inexpensive regeneration
- allows a small operation to set up bulk production
- facilitates portion control and uniformity of standards
- has a tenderising effect on tougher cuts of meat and matures game without dehydration.

Disadvantages of sous-vide:

- extra cost of vacuum pouches and vacuum-packing machine
- unsuitable for foods where colours may 'bleed' into one another
- all portions in a batch must be identically sized to ensure even results
- most dishes require twice the conventional cooking time
- unsuitable for large joints as chilling time exceeds 90 minutes
- complete meals (meat and two vegetables) not feasible; meat component needs to be cooked and stored in separate bags
- extremely tight management and hygienic controls are imperative
- potentially adverse customer reaction ('boil in the bag' syndrome).

Food safety

When using sous-vide methods, high standards of food hygiene and personal hygiene must be observed. Where possible, sous-vide should operate in a temperature-controlled environment.

Remember that:

- all food contact surfaces and equipment must be clean and sanitised frequently
- different packaging machinery (and preferably areas) should be used for raw and cooked foods
- the supplier's list for sous-vide products, including food and packaging, must be recorded and available
- document safe methods for each product, including time, temperature and size, and how the methods have been validated to prove food safety
- calibration records for the probe and water baths must be kept
- temperature of the water, core time/temperatures of foods, cooling records, storage time/temperatures and reheating time/temperatures must be recorded and kept
- evidence must be available of ongoing staff training on the sous-vide process
- all aspects of food safety legislation must be adhered to (see Chapter 3).

WEBLINKS

Fusion Chef sous-vide collection:
http://fusionchefsousvide.com

SousVide Supreme:
www.sousvidesupreme.com

Other technological developments

Ganymede dri-heat is a method of keeping foods either hot or cold. It is used in some hospitals as it ensures that the food that reaches the patients is in the same fresh condition as it was when it left the kitchens.

A metal disc or pellet is electrically heated or cooled, and placed in a special container under the plate. The container is designed to allow air to circulate round the pellet so that the food is maintained at the correct service temperature.

This is used in conjunction with conveyor belts and special service counters, and helps to provide a better and quicker food service.

Used for food production in hospitals and schools, microsteam technology is a fast, healthy cooking system that maintains the freshness of food using steam cooking with regulated pressure. As soon as the pack goes into the microwave, energy waves create steam from the water in the raw ingredients, which gradually builds up in the container. The pack expands as it cooks, and pressure is gradually released so that it stays at the right level to cook the food perfectly. Each dish is ready in just a few minutes, with no preparation time involved. If packages are kept sealed they will retain their heat at 75°C for 20 minutes.

Microsteaming cooks the freshest ingredients from raw – from chicken to couscous, fish to fresh vegetables. Steam cooking has long been recognised as one of the healthiest ways to prepare food, retaining much more vitamin C and chlorophyll than traditional or cook-chill methods. With this system it is easier to manage the bulk production and cooking of fresh vegetables and other items for large-scale banqueting and industry events.

Case study

Compass Group and Sherwood Forest Hospitals NHS Foundation Trust

Steamplicity is based on complete meals with a nutritional mix of fresh and cooked ingredients, served in containers with patented steam release valve lids. The packs are microwaved to pressure steam the food for maximum retention of texture, colour and nutrients.

Patients choose from a menu of 20 hot dishes, with additional meals to cater for special dietary requirements. Each ward kitchen has a bank of five standard 1,000 W commercial microwave ovens and an upright refrigerator to hold the chilled meal packs, which are delivered daily. The total ward equipment cost is about £2,000, and the food itself must comply with the average hospital budget for patient's food. The staff hours on the wards do increase slightly overall, as hostesses take over the patient meal service from the domestic cleaning staff. However, alongside the labour savings from reduced service hours in the kitchens, the extra cost is broadly negated.

Patient care has improved as a result of removing the meal service role from the domestic cleaning service. Having two dedicated roles allows one to focus on maintaining high standards of cleanliness and the other to concentrate on the patient meal service. The system also allows space, which had formerly been used for in hospital meal preparation, to be converted to other purposes.

Measurable benefits

One of the roles of the Medirest management accountants was to demonstrate the costs and benefits compared to its existing system.

The main costs and benefits that were identified were: a change in the roles and responsibilities of staff on the ward; an increase in the cost of the meal itself; labour savings arising from a much simpler and smaller on-site kitchen arrangement; energy savings as a consequence of no longer cooking food on-site and using microwave ovens rather than the traditional regeneration trolleys; and much lower repair and maintenance costs than those generated from ageing kitchen equipment and facilities.

The shorter lead-time that this meal ordering system allows means that more patients order and receive exactly what they want. Research has shown that patients are leaving less food on their plates compared to previous catering arrangements and it is much easier to provide the same service to late admissions. However, providing such a variety of meals means that there will invariably still be some waste (despite a shelf life of two days). To minimise this, the on-site management accountant built a tracking system designed to inform the site meal ordering process.

Source: www.cimaglobal.com

Food production planning

The profitability of the production system depends largely upon the content of the end-unit menus.

When planning production schedules it is important to balance the forecast in order to have the exact amount of food, number of staff and amount of equipment to produce the volume required. This is necessary to achieve efficiency, profitability or surplus. It is necessary therefore to determine the correct amounts.

'Just in time' (JIT) scheduling is an inventory strategy used to increase efficiency and decrease waste. The company receives goods only when they are needed for food production, therefore reducing the cost of holding stocks of ingredients. This means neither over-ordering nor having to wait for ingredients that are needed to be delivered. The labour and skills requirements also need to be considered and in place.

Key elements of production scheduling:

- minimising machine downtime
- accurate stock-recording system
- maximum use of labour.

In the production plan it is important to balance resources with customer requirements. Therefore you need to consider orders from customers and from the forecasts. The priority is always bookings with any special requirements from customers; it should be ensured that the plan does not put unnecessary stress on staff and equipment.

The production plan must also take account of profit margins, food costs and labour costs.

Production control

The function of production control is to ensure that production is maintained in line with the timings on the production plan wherever possible, and to respond to the things that go wrong and rework the plan in order to get production back on schedule.

Production control is about quality, but it is not the same as quality assurance. Quality assurance refers to food safety, consistency of high standards and uniformity of presentation. Customer feedback can be useful in monitoring quality.

Operations management in food production

The chef or chef manager is responsible for the smooth running of the operation. This includes:

- materials (food) management and purchasing
- receiving, storing and controlling stock
- production planning
- production control
- maintenance of all equipment
- quality performance
- labour relations.

Production management focuses on maximum output with minimum or budgeted costs. Most important is keeping the plant operational.

Operational objectives will be set. For example:

- to achieve the projected rate of turnover in financial terms
- maximum use of space in kitchens and dining rooms
- achieving the minimum number output of meals at self-service counters per hour to achieve efficiency and profitability
- achieving the minimum amount of production in relation to labour and demand (customers vs labour available)
- the right numbers of waiting staff to customers, no under- or overstaffing
- gross profit, the precise ratio of return although flexibility should be allowed in order to ensure maximum use of space
- achieving the average spend per customer
- consider alternative use of space to achieve a high customer spend, e.g. a function room into a conference suite
- always consider and monitor the hours of business to achieve maximum footfall, customers and repeat business.

The **production manager** is responsible for ensuring that good-quality food is produced regularly and that the workforce is sufficiently trained, skilled and motivated to want to produce good-quality products.

The **budget** is an organised operational plan; it monitors and regulates the activities of a business in financial terms. It gives a total perspective of the organisation's needs and shows the interdependence of its commercial activities.

Planning for an operational budget:

- where possible, ascertain from records the general level of business and possible income for a set period
- determine the budget period
- always outline the commitments and expectations for the forthcoming period
- deal with variations from the set targets in the previous year
- deal with special considerations such as any wage increase forecasts, sick pay, etc.
- calculate the exact requirements of the operation
- always consider the kind of products and food the projected customers will want to eat
- anticipate the level of demand
- determine the pricing policy
- consider the method of presentation and service
- consider customers' probable time limit for lunch, dinner, etc.
- the need to respond to the customers' demands within a specific time.

A policy for establishing the standards of the operation may include:

- value for money – related to gross profit and net profit returns
- the quality of the product and its presentation
- the standard source of the supply chain
- codes of practice, purchase specification, standardised recipes and menu descriptions.

A policy for governing control procedures may include:

- the establishment of stock levels
- who is responsible for ordering
- who is responsible for the inspection of food (goods) delivered
- storage procedures
- requisitioning and interdepartmental transfer
- preparation control, wastage control, amounts used
- sales and revenue records
- trading statement.

➔ Fast food

Fast food is characterised by a smooth operation. The principal control adopted is 'door time': 3½ minutes is the control average, 1½ minutes queuing and 1 minute serving. Capital costs are high for production equipment. The menu range is narrow, with the equipment often being specially developed to do one job. This is essentially one cell.

A high volume required is met by increasing the speed of foods through the system. This is achieved by increasing labour and by duplicating the same cell. Workers are often of low skill but are multi-functional and can be moved to different parts of the process. This type of staffing can give high job satisfaction (although short term), similar to the rotation of chefs through the partie system.

This operation comes nearer to the continuous flow ideal and is often quoted as a classic just-in-time (JIT) system.

The principles of manufacturing exist in both fast-food and cook-chill systems. Other systems, such as cook-freeze and sous-vide, will take on a variety of cells relating to different parts of the meal. The fast-food system is primarily based upon one-cell systems. All systems use variations in the number of workers to control costs.

➜ Purchasing

Any organisation dependent on the economics of bulk purchasing must pay particular attention to the process of buying. The following are the main objectives of the buyer.

- Quality and price of goods must be equalled with the size of purchase order.
- All purchase specifications must be met.
- Buying practice must supplement a policy of minimum stock holding.

Careful purchasing of meat is essential and the menu must be planned carefully.

- The cut of meat required must be clearly specified in order to produce the exact dishes.
- Strict portion control must be adhered to.
- Trimmings/by-products must be fully utilised: for example, meat trimmings for cottage/shepherd's pie, bones for stock.

Because of increasing labour costs and difficulty in obtaining staff, a number of establishments now purchase prepared potatoes, which are washed, peeled and in some cases shaped, as well as prepared root vegetables, topped and tailed French beans and ready-prepared salads.

➜ The assembly kitchen

The assembly kitchen and purchasing

The 'assembly kitchen' incorporates the latest technological developments in the manufacturing and conservation of food products. The chef does not automatically buy his or her ingredients, but will carefully choose from the 'five product types' (see below) what is best for him or her by asking the following questions.

- Which fresh produce will I use?
- Which semi-prepared food bases will I use?
- Which finished products will I use?

The five product types are:

1. fresh (raw product), e.g. meat with bones, unpeeled vegetables, milk
2. shelf-stable products, e.g. pasteurised dairy products, dehydrated stocks
3. frozen ingredients, or products such as pastry or ice cream
4. chilled 'fresh' products, partly prepared, e.g. boned and portioned fish, peeled and cut vegetables
5. chilled products, normally cooked and packed or sous-vide, with or without sauce.

The assembly kitchen still relies on skilled personnel. It requires a thorough understanding of how to switch over from the traditional labour-intensive production method to a more industrial type of production, with some of the principles of the cook-chill, cook-freeze or sous-vide production systems taken on board. It makes use of modern kitchen equipment and high-quality convenience food.

The process includes:

- preparing the food component in the kitchen
- arranging everything cold (even raw) on the plate
- regenerating (even cooking) on the same plate as served
- if necessary, serving the sauce.

Very precise preparations (mise-en-place) are required.

Advantages include:

- fewer staff needed
- different types of plate can be regenerated at the same time
- new-generation equipment can be easy to clean and maintain
- storage rooms are needed for only five types of product (see above)
- less space and equipment needed for food preparation.

Inconveniences include:

- very hot plates
- some additional investment (equipment for cooking, chilling/freezing and regenerating)
- some products cannot be prepared (French fries, etc.).

Table 6.3 Planning schedule for an assembly kitchen

Up to 2 days before service	Cook and chill Label, date and store at 3°C
Up to 12 hours before service	Arrange food on plates Store at 3°C on trolley
2 minutes before service	Take out plates Finish, sauce and garnish Serve
After service	Clean equipment

Quality management

The key elements in quality management for most hospitality businesses include:

- management responsibility – policy, objectives, identification of key personnel
- quality system procedures
- auditing the system – it must be audited internally
- quality in marketing – honest promotional activities
- material control and traceability of supplies
- conformity – ensuring that faulty products/service do not reach the customer
- corrective action – identifying reasons for faults, and implementing measures to correct them
- after-sales service
- documentation and records, e.g. audit reports
- personnel – identification of training needs, provision and verification of training
- product safety and liability.

In a competitive marketplace, with many similar businesses, the level of service provided is important. It is the front-line staff that offer this service – their training and development are crucial to business success. Total quality management (TQM) offers a framework that gives staff the scope to treat guests as individuals, and thereby offer superior service.

European Foundation for Quality Management Excellence Model

The European Foundation for Quality Management Excellence Model is a non-prescriptive framework that recognises that there are many approaches to sustainable excellence. Nine criteria (see Figure 6.9) are each given a weighting, which is used to calculate the company's performance.

In this model, business performance can be improved by:

- leadership
- policy and strategy – and how they are put into action
- people – how the organisation gets the best out of its people
- partnerships and resources – how the organisation manages resources
- processes – how they are managed and improved.

Four areas assess what the organisation has achieved.

1. **Customers:** what do they think of the organisation? Levels of satisfaction.
2. **People:** what do employees think of the organisation? Levels of job satisfaction.
3. **Society:** how is the organisation seen by the community? What has it done to help the local community or the environment?
4. **Key performance:** against business targets.

British Standard EN ISO 9002: 1994

The British Standard scheme provides a method for organisations to assess the suitability of their suppliers' products. The British Standard Quality Award BS EN ISO 9002: 1994 is a quality kitemark (standard or benchmark) for the fitness for purpose and safety of services and/or products provided to customers. It identifies the systems, procedures and criteria within the business which ensure that a product or service meets a customer's requirements.

BS EN ISO 9002 can be important to food service operations for two reasons. First, a supplier with this award operates a quality system of a high standard. Second, food service operators, such as contract caterers, may not be considered for some tenders without the award. Additionally, BS EN ISO 9002 may provide evidence of due diligence – for example, in the event of a food safety prosecution.

However, the costs involved in attaining BS EN ISO 9002 can be high, and therefore it needs to be carefully assessed before implementation. On the other hand, many organisations have found it cost-effective overall.

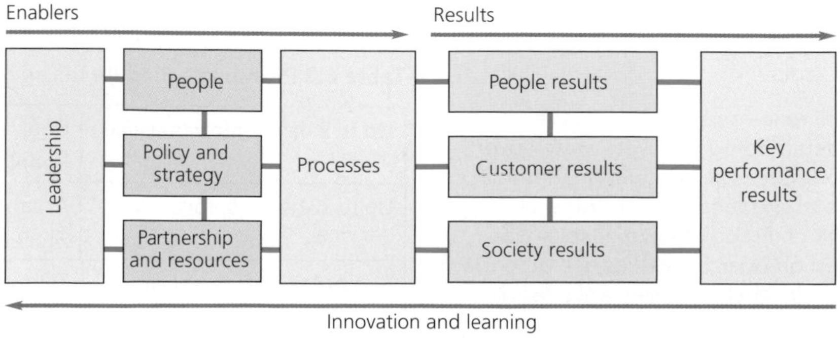

Figure 6.9 European Foundation for Quality Management Excellence Model

WEBLINKS

Further information on quality matters can be obtained from the following sources.

European Foundation for Quality Management:

www.efqm.org

The complete documents on BS EN ISO 9002: 1994 are available from the British Standards Institution:

www.bsi-global.com

Further reading

The following sources were used as the basis for this chapter.

Food Standards Agency (FSA) publications: *Safer Food Better Business* (England); *Safe Catering* (Northern Ireland); *CookSafe* (Scotland).

Visit www.food.gov.uk for advice and information.

Food Hygiene for Business, produced by the Food Standards Agency

Topics for discussion

1. The advantages and disadvantages of the cook-chill and cook-freeze systems.
2. Essential hygiene and food safety requirements for cook-chill and cook-freeze systems.
3. The reason for quality control, temperature control and microbiological control when producing cook-chill and cook-freeze foods.
4. Types of operation suitable for using cook-chill and cook-freeze foods.
5. For and against a centralised production system, with examples.
6. The food production system and its main advantages.
7. Discuss the importance of detailed specifications and traceability for cook-freeze and cook-chill products.
8. The difference between quality assurance and quality control.
9. The importance of preparing and producing food for customers with allergens in a separate area of the kitchen. Discuss how this should be designed and operated.
10. How performance and productivity can be improved in a centralised production kitchen.

7 Food commodities

→ The study of commodities

When studying commodities, explore markets to build your knowledge of the products available. Compare various brands of foods, and between convenience and fresh unprepared foods, considering the quality, price, hygiene, labour, cost, time, space required and disposal of waste.

Be cost conscious from the outset in your studies and form the habit of keeping up to date with the current prices of all commodities, equipment, labour and overheads. An inbuilt awareness of costs is an important asset to any successful caterer.

Seasonality

The following are some of the reasons why eating seasonally is a good idea.

- **Food tastes better in season:** seasonal food is more likely to be local and local food will have spent the minimum time in transit.
- **Seasonal food is better for the environment:** for example, air-freighted French beans imported from Kenya in the winter generate vast amounts of greenhouse gas. Seasonal food fits into traditional systems of farming, which don't need the same energy-intensive inputs of pesticides, herbicides and artificial fertiliser as intensive systems.
- **Seasonal food is often cheaper:** crop permitting, almost anything that's in season will be plentiful and therefore cheaper.
- **Seasonal food supports local agriculture:** buying locally offers another market for food producers, who are often squeezed between the demands of the powerful supermarket buyers and cut-price competition from overseas.
- **Seasonal food brings variety to the menu:** who wants to eat the same things all year round?

Food provenance

Food provenance means where the food comes from: where it is grown, raised or reared.

Consumers are increasingly demanding local, regional food. Food provenance information has been introduced to menus, informing the customer what they are eating and where it has come from.

In the UK there are strict regulations as to how farmers must rear animals in the food chain, and animals are continually tested to ensure they are healthy and comply with these regulations. (Regulations differ from country to country.)

Many reasons drive this interest in food provenance. For example, locally produced vegetables with traditional production techniques have a smaller carbon footprint. Ethical labels guarantee that products such as coffee were produced under decent working conditions, while promoting local sustainability, and fair terms of trade for farmers and workers in the developing world. Understanding the provenance of food has become an advantage to many restaurants, since it allows them to demonstrate quality in taste, carbon footprint and ethics.

Provenance and food safety

Governments and associated regulatory authorities are interested in food safety. EU law requires the traceability of food, food-producing animals, and any other substance intended to be or expected to be incorporated into the food or feed, to be established at all stages of production, processing and distribution. Similar laws, such as the US Bioterrorism Act, deal with the security aspect and the deliberate contamination of food by terrorists. Whenever contaminated food is discovered the ability to trace all the ingredients, suppliers and manufacturers involved is critical, as illustrated by the food scandals that regularly show up on the front pages of newspapers. For instance, the Sudan 1 scandal originated when it was found that there were traces of the carcinogenic dye found in 'spicy food', where red colours had been used to enhance the appearance of the product. The discovery of the dye resulted in the withdrawal of many products from supermarkets across Europe.

➜ Sustainable food

Sustainable farming and food:

- produces safe and healthy food
- is viable for producers who practise sustainable methods of land management, and have safe, fair working conditions
- is produced within the biological limits of natural resources such as soil and water
- uses as few resources as possible, and renewable energy where possible
- has high standards of animal welfare.

Benefits of sustainable food include:

- food is less highly processed and therefore can be healthier
- sustainable production methods produce food with fewer contaminants such as pesticide residues
- animals are treated humanely and therefore are less prone to disease
- damage to the environment, such as poor soil quality caused by badly managed farming, is reduced
- products and animals are transported over shorter distances, saving energy
- farm workers are paid fairly, boosting the local economy
- purchasing sustainably encourages relationships with local food producers.

Examples of sustainable food products include:

- foods that are produced under conditions that save on electricity and water
- food products made using environmentally friendly technology
- products packed in environmentally friendly packaging
- produce grown with a limited use of fertilisers and crop sprays, but not necessarily totally organic (see below).

In this way a trend may be expected in which industry slowly takes on the idea of organic production and increasingly begins to market environmentally friendly food products to the catering industry.

Some sustainability initiatives relevant to food purchasing are listed below.

- **Fair trade:** guarantees small-scale producers a fair financial return for their work.
- **Red Tractor Assurance:** a whole-chain assurance scheme that provides responsible production standards covering the environment, food safety, animal welfare and traceability for UK farmers and suppliers. The Red Tractor logo on a food product indicates that it has met these standards. To find out more, visit www.redtractor.org.uk.
- **Free range:** refers to food produced from animals that have access to outdoor spaces, usually free access to graze or forage for food. Unlike organic this is not a certification with legal requirements. (Organic food is certified, and one of the criteria is that animals are free range.)
- **Slow food:** a movement that links the pleasure of food with a commitment to nutritious food from sustainable local sources.

WEBLINK

For more information see the slow food website:
www.slowfood.org.uk

Sustainable fishing

Consumers are becoming increasingly concerned about sustainable fish supplies. Some fishing methods are environmentally damaging and can devastate fish populations. There are controls already in place to help prevent further depletion of fish stocks. Good restaurants do not purchase fish from overfished stocks or badly managed fisheries.

Organisations such as the Marine Conservation Society, the Worldwide Fund for Nature, and the Food and Agriculture Organization of the UN are keen to address the current problems by encouraging consumers to use fish that are plentiful and not at risk of depletion.

Organic foods

Organic farming restricts the use of pesticides, and avoids chemical fertilisers. It relies on crop rotation, crop residues, animal manures, and the biological system of nutrient mobilisation and plant protection. Organic farmers must follow high standards of animal welfare.

'Organic' is a term defined by European law, and all organic food production and processing is governed by strict legislative standards. Catering operations preparing and selling organic menus must be certified with a UK certification body – for example, Soil Association Certification Ltd.

Consumers are gradually becoming more interested in organic foods. Although there are no nutritional reasons for using organic produce, organic foods are said to contain fewer contaminants. However, global sources of contamination cannot be avoided by the organic farmer. Food inspection, particularly by the Department for Environment, Food and Rural Affairs (Defra), keeps a good check on the content of undesirable substances in conventional produce. The prospect of contamination, therefore, is not a good reason for using organically grown produce either. The main argument for using organic produce is that it supports environmentally sustainable farming. Some caterers have started using organic produce as they become more environmentally conscious.

Today's consumers have a natural expectation that insensitive use of the environment or resources should be avoided.

The quality of organic produce is variable.

Meat

Cattle, sheep and pigs are reared for fresh meat. The flavour of meat depends on the animal's diet and fat content; it is also affected by ageing (see below).

Conversion of muscle to meat

Glycogen is a carbohydrate energy reserve stored in the muscle of animals. It is used to provide energy in the living animal, and is broken down to water and carbon dioxide. In muscle after slaughter there is no supply of oxygen and therefore the glycogen is converted to lactic acid. The build-up of lactic acid reduces the pH from about 7.0 to 5.6 (i.e. it makes the meat more acidic). This natural acidity is important for the keeping quality of meat.

Under some conditions this process cannot follow the normal pattern. In particular, if there is insufficient glycogen present in the muscle at slaughter the pH does not fall to the same extent, and dark, firm, dry meat results. This is caused by insufficient feed prior to slaughter or a prolonged period of stress. Another condition, known as PSE (pale soft exudative), results if animals (especially pigs) are subjected to a period of acute stress prior to slaughter. This results in the pH fall occurring too rapidly, which gives rise to denaturation of the muscle protein.

Ageing and hanging of meat

Meat benefits from a period of ageing, or maturation, before it is consumed. This increases the tenderness as calpain enzymes, naturally present within the meat, break down key proteins. Flavour may be increased by the release of small protein fragments with strong flavour. Also, a short time after death, an animal's muscles stiffen – a condition known as rigor mortis. After a time chemical actions caused by enzymes and increasing acidity relax the muscles and the meat becomes soft and pliable. As meat continues to hang in storage, rigor mortis dissipates, and tenderness and flavour increase. Minimum ageing periods of seven days from slaughter to consumption are often recommended for beef, lamb and pork.

To age, meat is hung (held as carcasses) after slaughter, generally at a temperature of 1°C. Pork and veal are hung for three to seven days, depending on the temperature.

The method of carcass hanging used can give rise to marked differences in eating quality. Hanging the carcass by the hip bone (aitch bone) instead of the traditional Achilles tendon puts tension on the important muscles of the hindquarter. This 'stretching' effect in some muscles makes them more tender.

Alternatively, boning can take place as soon as 12 hours (for pigs), 24 hours (sheep) or 48 hours (cattle) after slaughter, provided that a period of ageing is allowed following butchery.

Purchasing and storage

Raw meat should be stored separately from cooked meat or meat products. Chilled meat must be used by the 'use by' date.

The temperatures of chillers and freezers should be checked and recorded regularly. Regulations state that meat must be stored below 8°C but it is widely recognised as best practice to store it at 1–4°C, or even lower. High-risk meat products that do not need any further cooking must be stored in the 1–4°C range. Any vacuum-packed meat should be stored below 3°C.

For economic reasons of saving on both labour and storage space, many caterers purchase meat by joints or cuts rather than by the carcass.

The Meat Buyer's Guide is a manual that has been designed to assist caterers who wish to simplify and facilitate their meat purchasing. It provides information and cutting guides.

Meat suppliers must be able to show the 'traceability' of the meat that they sell. This means that they can show where the meat came from, and where it was slaughtered and butchered.

Several methods of preservation are used for meat.

- **Chilling:** meat is kept at a temperature just above freezing point in a controlled atmosphere.
- **Freezing:** small carcasses, such as lamb and mutton, can be frozen; their quality is not affected by freezing. They can be kept frozen until required and then thawed out before use. Some beef is frozen, but it is inferior in quality to chilled beef.
- **Salting:** meat such as silverside, brisket and ox tongues can be pickled in brine. Salting is also used in the production of bacon and hams, before the sides of pork are smoked.
- **Canning:** large quantities of meat are canned; corned beef, for example, since it has a very high protein content. Pork is used for tinned luncheon meat and in canned hams. Prepared products such as beef stew or beef pie filling are also available canned.
- Many cuts of meat are now sold in **vacuum packs** (see below). This helps to preserve the freshness of the meat, but the packs must be kept in the refrigerator at less than 3°C.
- Meat cuts and products are also sold in **modified atmosphere packaging** (MAP). The meat is placed in a clear container sealed with a clear film top. The meat is surrounded with a modified gas mixture that slows down deterioration. These packs must be kept in the refrigerator.

Vacuum-packed meat

It is essential to store and handle vacuum-packed meat correctly. The storage temperature should be 1–3°C with the cartons the correct way up so that drips cannot stain the fatty surface. A good circulation of air should be allowed between cartons.

When required for use, the vacuum film should be punctured in order to drain away any blood before the film is removed. On opening the film, a slight odour is usually discernible, but this should disappear quickly on exposure to the air. The colour may also change: vacuum-packed beef has a deep-red colour, but when the film is broken the colour should change to its normal characteristic brown/red within 20–30 minutes. Once the film has been punctured the meat should be used as soon as possible.

WEBLINK

For further information about meat, contact the Institute of Meat:

http://instituteofmeat.org

Beef

Beef is hung at a chill temperature of 1°C for up to 14 days; this is essential as animals are generally slaughtered around the age of 18 to 24 months.

Large quantities of beef are prepared as chilled boneless prime cuts, vacuum packed in film. This process has the following advantages: it extends the storage life of the cuts; the cuts are boned and fully trimmed, thus reducing labour costs and storage space.

Quality

Lean meat should be bright red, with small flecks of white fat (marbled). The fat should be firm, brittle in texture, creamy white in colour and odourless. Meat of traceable origin is best.

Cuts and joints

A wide variety of cuts and joints are available; a selection is illustrated here. Some newer or less well-known cuts are:

- **tri-tip** – smallish 500 g–1500 g muscle from the bottom of the sirloin, roughly triangular
- **flat iron steak** – prepared from the feather blade; used for prime rib, Delmonico steak, rib steak, rib eye steak, rib eye roast
- **flank steak** – from the flank
- **Vegas Strip steak** – from the rib eye
- **bistro rump steak** – from the *gluteus medius* muscle of the rump
- **picanha steak** – cut from the rump removing the cap muscle, cut across the grain
- **centre cut steak** – cut from the tick flank/knuckle primal
- **Denver cut steak** – taken from the major chuck primal, the *serratus ventralis* muscle, which lies under the chuck eye roll
- **rustic-style brisket** – lean brisket muscle cut into individual pieces

- **shoulder brisket pavé** – this muscle is the extension of the rib cap muscle; the grain of the muscle is similar to brisket, requires slow and long cooking
- **feather steaks and blade steaks** – are both cut from the chuck
- **needle steaks** – cut from the skin
- **silverside steaks** – salmon-cut steaks cut from the silverside
- **goose skirt steak** and **flank skirt steak** – are both cut from the thin flank.

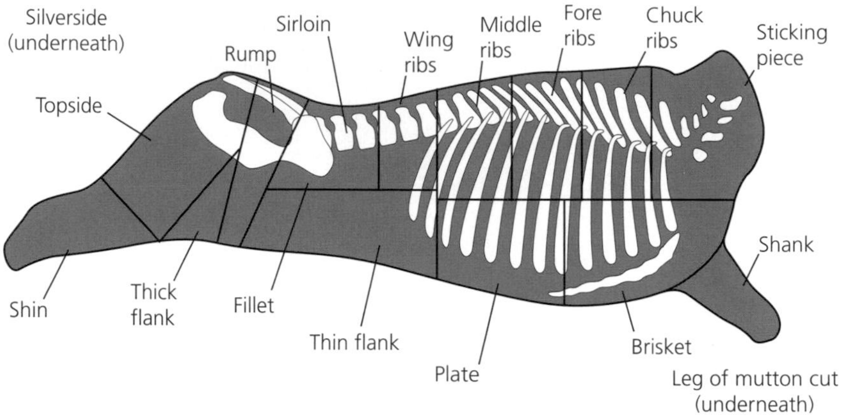

Figure 7.1 Side of beef

Figure 7.2 Beef, silverside (rolled)

Figure 7.3 Boned shin of beef

Figure 7.4 Forerib of beef

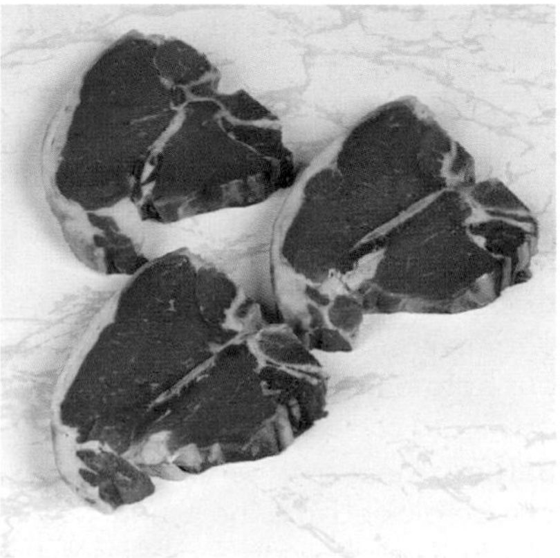

Figure 7.5 T-bone steaks

Figure 7.6 Sirloin steaks

Figure 7.7 Rib eye steaks

Veal

Originally, most top-quality veal came from Holland, but as the Dutch methods of production are now used extensively in Britain, supplies of home-produced veal are available there all year round, too. Good-quality carcasses weighing around 100 kg can be produced from calves slaughtered at 12–24 weeks. This quality of veal is necessary for first-class cookery.

The flesh of veal should be pale pink and firm, not soft or flabby. Cut surfaces must not be dry, but moist. Bones in young animals should be pinkish white, porous and with a small amount of blood in their structure. The fat should be firm and pinkish white. The kidney should be firm and well covered with fat.

'Welfare veal' comes from calves that are loosely penned. As a consequence, the colour of the meat is a deeper shade of pink.

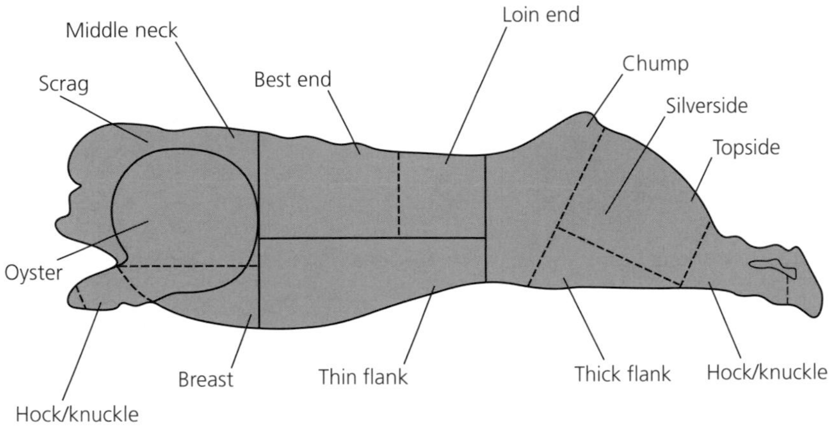

Figure 7.8 Side of veal

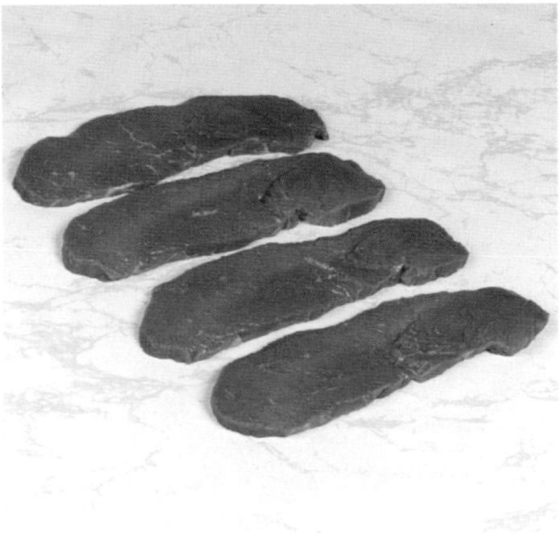

Figure 7.9 Veal escalopes

Pork and bacon

Pork is the meat of the pig, and bacon is the cured flesh of the pig.

Lean flesh of pork is usually pale pink. The fat is usually white, firm, smooth and not excessive. Bones are usually small, fine and pinkish. The quality of the skin or rind depends on the breed. Suckling pigs weigh 5–9 kg dressed and are usually roasted whole.

Cuts and joints

A wide variety of cuts and joints are available; a selection is illustrated here. Some newer or less well-known cuts are:

- **collar steaks** – a cut from the neck of the animal; it is used for a number of different cuts including boneless collar steaks
- **collar rasher steaks** – cut the same as collar rashers of bacon
- **loin eye rashers** – cut across the whole loin (bacon style)
- **loin T-bone steaks** – a large pork steak consisting of both loin and tender pork fillet
- **blade steaks** – cut from the feather blade muscles
- **loin medallions** – the round, lean part of the loin tied to form a round shape and cut into medallions; smaller medallions can also be cut from the fillet
- **valentine steaks** – same cut as lamb valentines
- **rib eye** – thick steaks cut from the boneless and rindless rib end of the loin
- **Bath chaps** – the lower half of a pig's cheek.

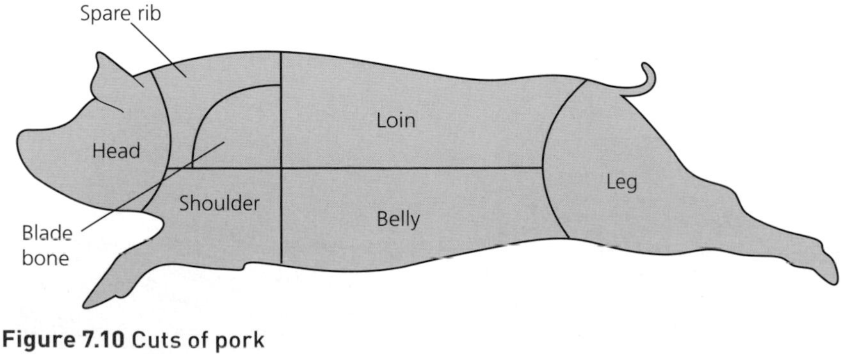

Figure 7.10 Cuts of pork

Figure 7.11 Boned leg of pork

Figure 7.12 Loin of pork

Figure 7.13 Pork chops

Figure 7.14 Suckling pig

Boars

Boars are uncastrated male pigs. Boar meat is available from specialist farms. Purchase good-quality animals from suppliers who are using as near as possible 100 per cent pure breeding stock. Animals that are free to roam and forage for food may have a better flavour than farm-reared ones that have been penned and fed. Animals are best between 12 and 18 months old, and weighing 70–75 kg on the hoof. Slaughtering is best done during late summer when the fat content is lower. Recommended hanging time is between seven and ten days at a temperature of between 1 and 4°C.

Marinating before cooking greatly improves the taste and texture of boar meat.

Bacon

Bacon is the cured flesh of a pig (60–75 kg dead weight) specifically reared for bacon because its shape and size yield economic bacon joints.

The curing process consists of salting either by a dry method and smoking, or by soaking in brine followed by smoking. Unsmoked bacon is brine cured but not smoked; it has a milder flavour but does not keep as long as smoked bacon.

There should be no sign of stickiness. There must be no unpleasant smell. The rind should be thin and smooth. The fat ought to be white, smooth and not excessive in proportion to the lean. The lean meat of the bacon should be deep pink in colour and firm, depending on the cure.

Bacon should be kept in a well-ventilated, preferably refrigerated, room. Joints of bacon should be wrapped in muslin. Sides of bacon are also hung on hooks. Cut bacon is kept on trays in the refrigerator or cold room. Bacon can also be vacuum packed ('vac packed'), as described above. Pancetta is rolled slices of cured pork belly. Pancetta is salt cured, flavoured with herbs and spices, and air dried. Lardo is an extremely fatty Italian bacon.

Lamb and mutton

Lamb is generally meat from sheep under one year old; mutton is the term for older animals.

The carcass should be compact and evenly fleshed. The lean flesh of lamb ought to be firm and of a pleasing dull-red colour, and of a fine texture or grain. The fat should be evenly distributed, hard, brittle, flaky and clear white in colour. The bones should be porous in young animals.

The factors influencing lamb composition, quality and value are very similar to those described above for beef.

Cuts and joints

A wide variety of cuts and joints is available; a selection is illustrated here. Some newer or less well-known cuts are:

- **lamb steaks** – cut from the leg, topside joint or from the whole leg
- **cannon skewers** – only the eye of the loin is used for this product.

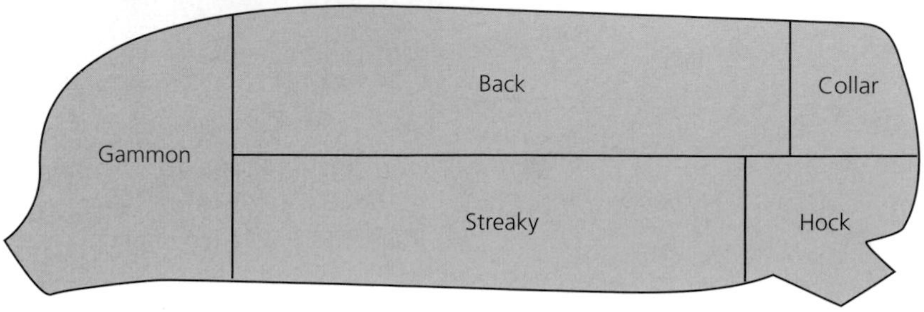

Figure 7.15 Side of bacon

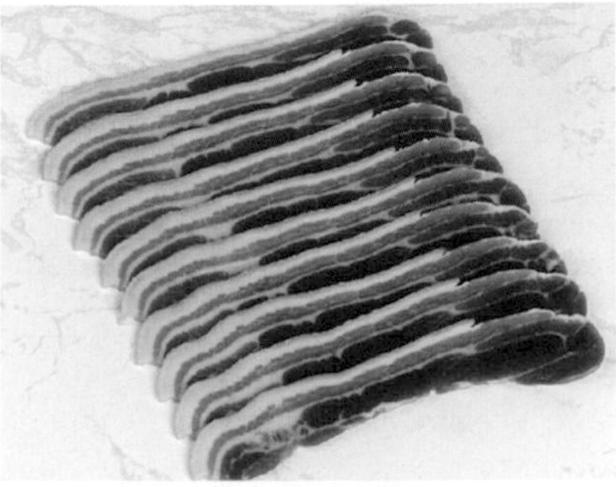

Figure 7.16 Streaky bacon

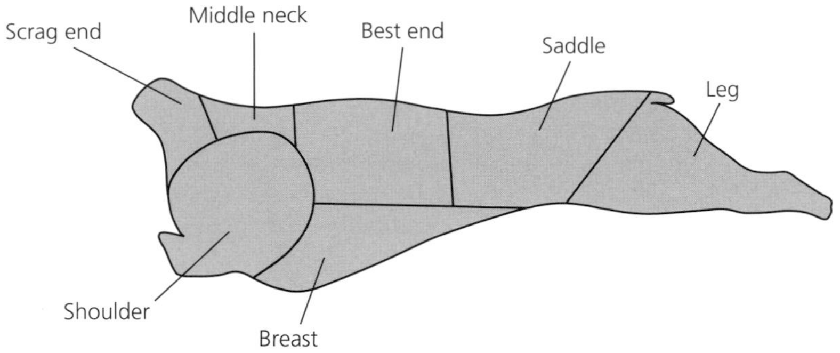

Figure 7.17 Cuts of lamb

Figure 7.18 Saddle of lamb

Figure 7.19 Shoulder of lamb

Figure 7.20 Best ends of lamb (racks, French trimmed)

Figure 7.21 Double loin chops (Barnsley chops) of lamb

Figure 7.22 Lamb cutlets

Figure 7.23 Lamb rosettes

Offal and other edible parts of the carcass

Offal is the name given to the parts taken from the inside of the carcass; edible offal includes liver, kidney, heart and sweetbread. Tripe, brains, oxtail, tongue and head are sometimes included under this term.

Fresh offal (unfrozen) should be purchased as required and can be refrigerated under hygienic conditions at a temperature of 1°C and at relative humidity of 90 per cent for up to seven days. Frozen offal should be kept frozen until required.

Tripe is the stomach lining or white muscle of beef cattle. Smooth tripe comes from the first compartment of the stomach. Honeycomb tripe is from the second compartment of the stomach and is considered to be the best. Sheep tripe, darker in colour, is obtainable in some areas. Tripe may be boiled or braised.

Oxtails should be 1.5–1.75 kg, lean and with no signs of stickiness. They are usually braised or used for soup.

Liver should appear fresh and have an attractive colour. It must not be dry or contain tubes. It should be smooth in texture. Calves' liver is the most expensive and is considered the best in terms of tenderness, and delicacy of flavour and colour. Lambs' liver is mild in flavour, tender and light in colour. Ox or beef liver is the cheapest and, if taken from an older animal, can be coarse in texture and strong in flavour. Pigs' liver is full-flavoured and used in many pâté recipes. Liver is valuable as a protective food; it consists chiefly of protein and contains high levels of vitamin A and iron.

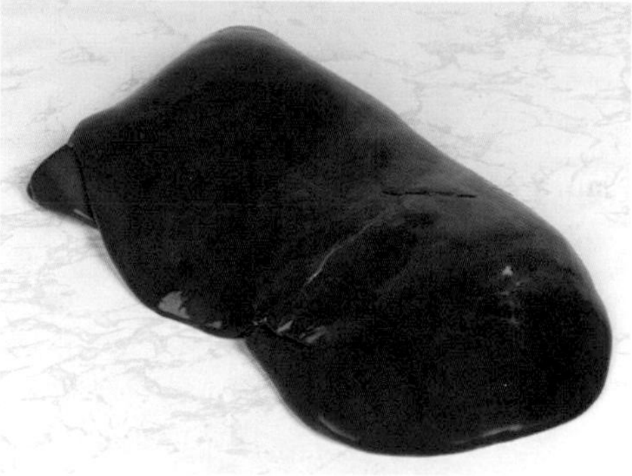

Figure 7.24 Calves' liver

Kidneys are also a rich source of protein, vitamin A and iron. Lambs' kidney is light in colour, delicate in flavour, and ideal for grilling and frying. It should be covered in fat, which is removed just before use; the fat should be crisp and the kidney moist. Calves' kidney is light in colour, delicate in flavour and can be used in a wide variety of dishes. Ox kidney is dark in colour, strong in flavour and is generally used mixed with beef, for steak and kidney pie or pudding. It should be fresh and deep red in colour. Pigs' kidney is smooth, long and flat by comparison with sheep's kidney; it has a strong flavour.

Figure 7.25 Lamb kidneys

Figure 7.26 Veal kidneys

Hearts should not be too fatty and should not contain too many tubes. When cut they should be moist. They have a high protein content. Ox or beef hearts are the largest used for cooking. They are dark coloured, solid, and tend to be dry and tough. Calves' heart, coming from a younger animal, is lighter in colour and more tender. Lambs' heart is smaller and lighter, and normally served whole. Larger hearts are normally sliced before serving.

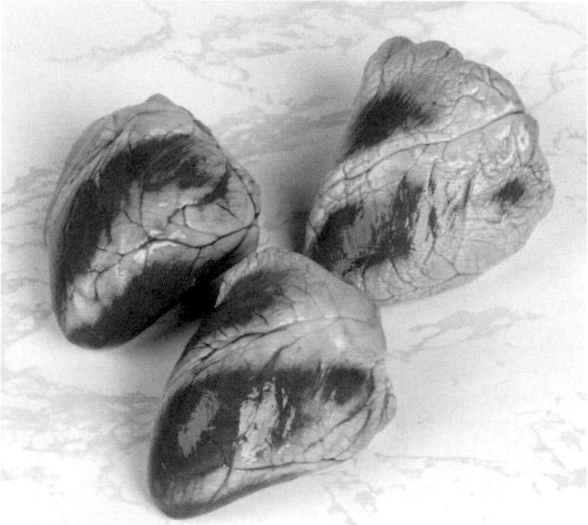

Figure 7.27 Lamb hearts

Tongues must be fresh. They should not have an excessive amount of waste at the root end. Ox tongues may be used fresh or salted. Sheep's tongues are used unsalted.

Sweetbreads are two glands: the pancreas and the elongated sausage-shaped thymus gland. The pancreas is undoubtedly the best as it is round, flat and plump. Sweetbreads should be fleshy, large and creamy white in colour. They are highly nutritious, as they are very easily digested and useful for building body tissues.

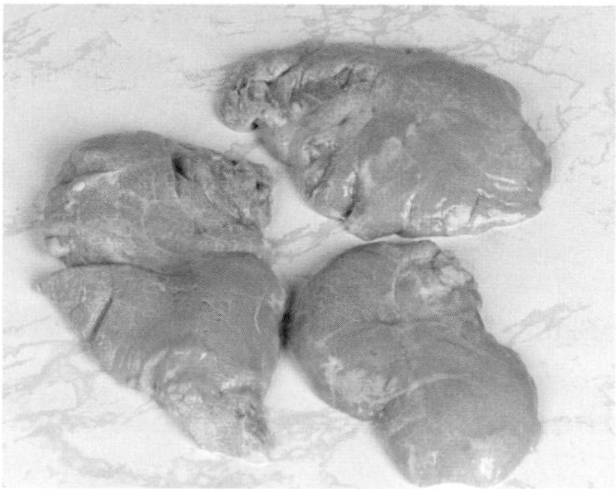

Figure 7.28 Veal sweetbreads

Suet is a type of fat that surrounds the kidneys. Beef suet should be creamy white, brittle and dry. It is used for suet paste. Other fat should be fresh and not sticky. Suet and fat may be rendered down for dripping.

Bones must be fresh, not sticky; they are used to make stock, which is the base for soups and sauces.

Meat substitutes

Textured vegetable protein

Textured vegetable protein (TVP) is manufactured from protein derived from wheat, oats, soya beans and other sources. The main source is the soya bean, due to its high protein content.

TVP is used chiefly as a meat extender, replacing from 10–60 per cent of fresh meat. Some caterers on very tight budgets make use of it, but its main use is in food manufacturing.

By partially replacing the meat in dishes such as casseroles, pies, sausage rolls, hamburgers and pâté, it is possible to reduce costs, provide nutrition and serve food that is acceptable.

Myco-protein

Myco-protein is produced from a plant that is a distant relative of the mushroom, by a fermentation process similar to yoghurt production. Myco-protein contains protein and fibre, and may be used as an alternative to chicken or beef, or in vegetarian dishes. Quorn is the brand name for myco-protein.

Tofu

Tofu (soya curd or bean curd) is made by curdling soya milk with a coagulant. There are two basic types of tofu:

- fresh water-packed tofu, which has to be refrigerated (firm and soft versions are available)
- silken tofu, which is packed in ascetic boxes and usually not refrigerated.

Tofu soaks up flavours, and is best when marinated with herbs and spices, oil and balsamic vinegar. It is rich in protein and B vitamins, and contains a high proportion of calcium.

Other meat substitutes

Tempeh is a traditional Indonesian food made from fermented soy beans and other grains. Unlike tofu, tempeh contains whole soybeans, making it denser. Because of its density, tempeh should be braised in a flavour liquid for at least an hour prior to cooking. This softens it and makes the flavour milder.

Seitan (wheat gluten) is derived from wheat and is a good source of protein.

Nalto is derived from fermented soy beans and is similar in appearance to overgrown kidney beans. The texture tends to be chewy and a bit stringy. It is known for its pungent smell, and is most commonly eaten with sushi rice or in a maki roll.

Quinoa is a grain crop with edible seeds. It is a complete protein, containing all eight of the essential amino acids, and is also rich in fibre, iron and magnesium.

Poultry

Poultry is the name given to domestic birds bred especially to be eaten and for their eggs. Poultry is Britain's most popular meat: almost twice as much poultry is consumed as beef.

Owing to present-day methods of poultry breeding and growing, poultry is available all the year round either chilled or frozen.

Storage

Fresh poultry must be hung by the legs under chilled conditions, otherwise it will not be tender; the innards are removed as soon as possible after slaughter.

Frozen birds must be kept in a deep-freeze cabinet below -18°C until required. To reduce the risk of food poisoning, it is essential that frozen birds be completely thawed, preferably in a refrigerator, before they are cooked. Chilled birds should be kept at between 1 and 4°C.

Chicken

Chicken is probably the most popular type of poultry. It comes in various types, with different uses:

- spring chickens (poussin) – four to six weeks old
- broiler chickens – three to four months old
- medium and large roasting chickens
- capons (castrated cock birds)
- old hens – used in soups and sauces.

Fresh chicken should have a plump breast, a pliable breastbone and firm flesh. The skin should be white with a faint bluish tint and unbroken. The legs should be smooth with small scales and spurs.

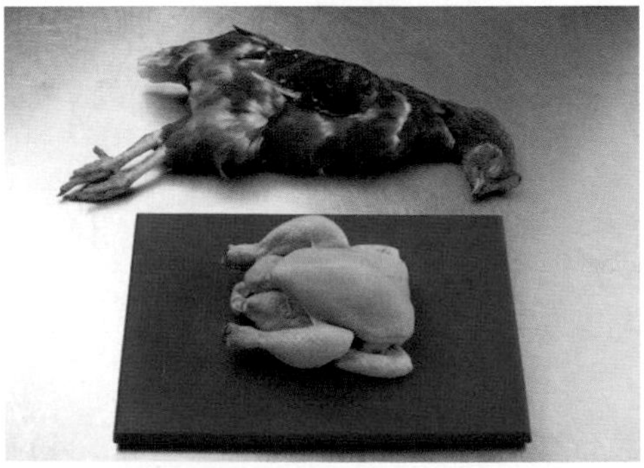

Figure 7.29 Chicken: whole and prepared for cooking

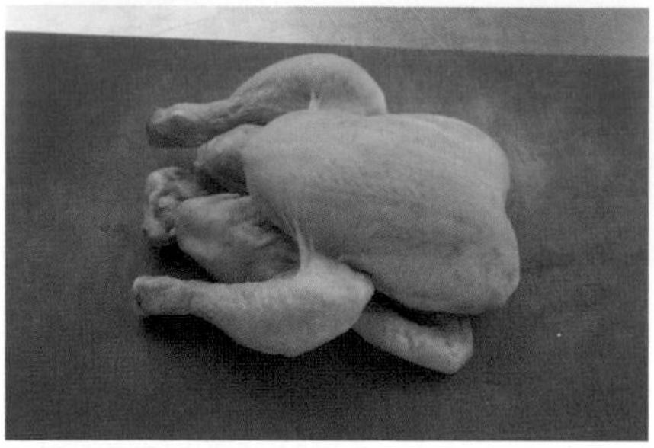

Figure 7.30 Corn-fed chicken

Duck/duckling and goose/gosling

The feet and bills of ducks and geese should be bright yellow. The upper bill should break easily. The webbed feet must be easy to tear. Ducks and geese may be roasted or braised.

In the UK, goose is traditionally in season from Michaelmas (29 September) until Christmas.

Turkey

Turkeys are usually roasted. When the whole bird is not required, turkey cuts are also popular. These include crowns (breasts left on the bone), breasts off the bone, legs, boned legs, drumsticks, wings, escalopes and mince.

The breast should be large, and the skin undamaged and with no signs of stickiness. The legs of young birds are black and smooth, the feet supple with a short spur. As the bird ages the legs turn reddish grey and become scaly. The feet become hard.

Other poultry

Guinea fowl are grey and white-feathered birds; when plucked, they resemble a chicken with darker flesh. The young birds are known as squabs. The quality points relating to chicken also apply to guinea fowl.

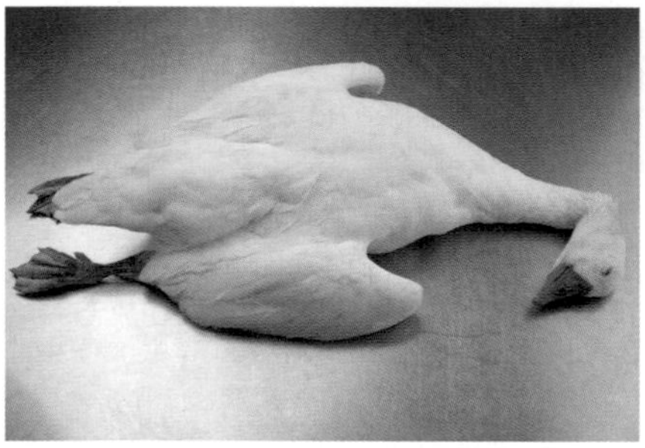

Figure 7.31 Goose

Figure 7.32 Goose prepared for cooking

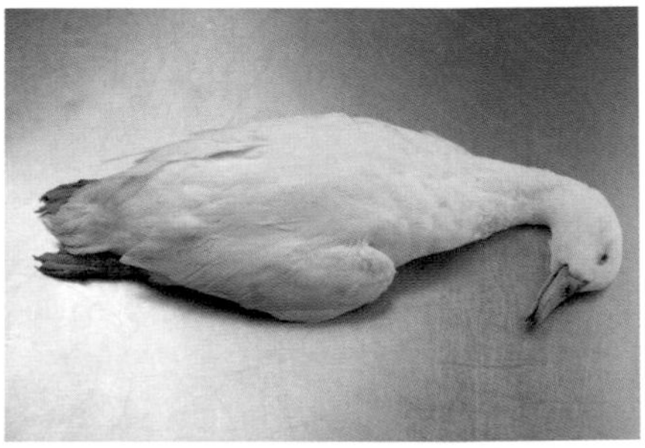

Figure 7.33 Duck: whole

Figure 7.34 Gressingham duck prepared for cooking

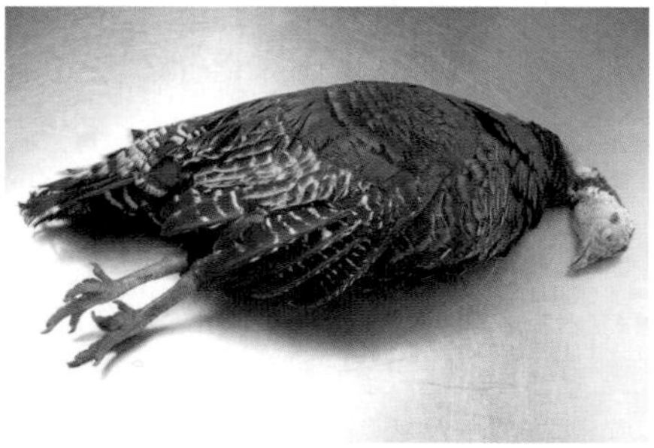

Figure 7.35 Turkey

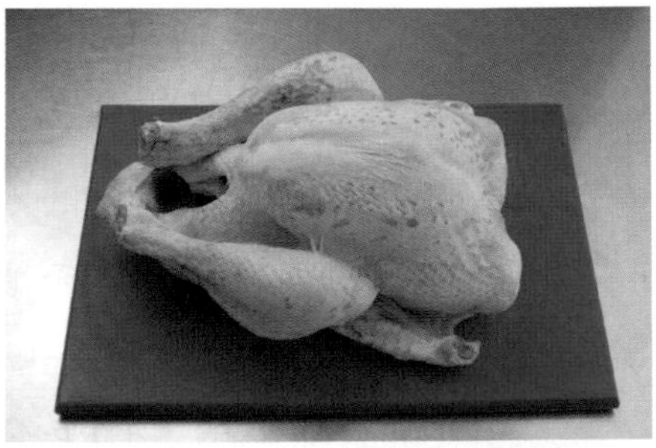

Figure 7.36 Turkey prepared for cooking

Pigeon should be plump, the flesh mauve-red in colour and the claws pinkish. Tame pigeons are smaller than wood pigeons. Squabs are young, specially reared pigeons.

Ostrich is usually sold as a fillet (taken from the thigh) or leg steak. The neck or offal is also available and is cheaper. It is often compared to beef, but it has a slightly coarser texture with less fat and lower cholesterol.

Figure 7.37 Guinea fowl: whole and prepared for cooking

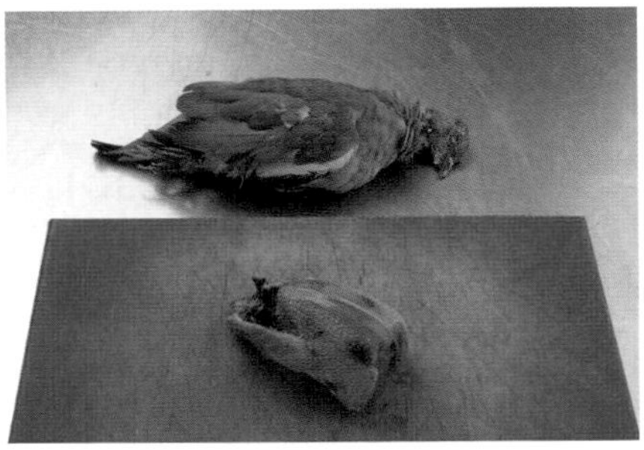

Figure 7.38 Wood pigeon: whole and prepared for cooking

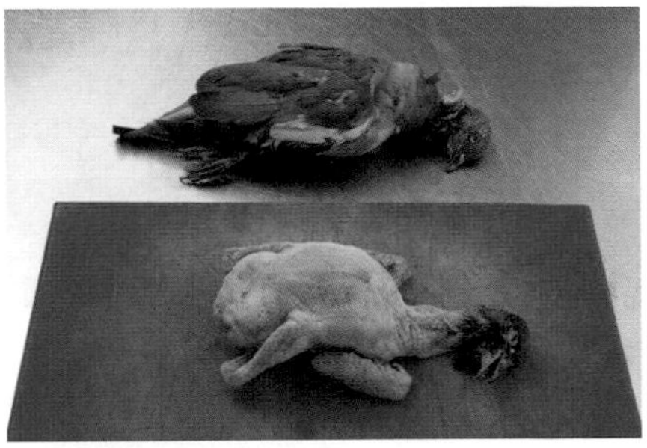

Figure 7.39 Squab: whole and prepared for cooking

Game

Game is the name given to certain wild birds and animals that are eaten. There are two kinds of game: feathered and furred.

Storage

Hanging is essential for all game. It drains the flesh of blood and begins the process of disintegration that is vital to make the flesh soft and edible, as well as to develop flavour. The hanging time is determined by the type, condition and age of the game, and the storage temperature. Old birds need to hang for a longer time than young birds. Game birds are not plucked or drawn before hanging. Venison and hare are hung with the skin on. Game must be hung in a well-ventilated, dry, cold storeroom; this need not be refrigerated. Game birds should be hung by the neck with the feet down.

Availability

In the UK, game is available fresh in season between the dates shown in Table 7.1, and frozen for the remainder of the year. Venison, hares, rabbits and pigeons are available throughout the year.

Table 7.1 Game in season (UK)

Grouse	12 August–10 December
Snipe	12 August–31 January
Partridge	1 September–1 February
Wild duck	1 September–31 January
Pheasant	1 October–1 February
Woodcock	31 October–1 February

Venison

Venison is the flesh from any member of the deer family, which includes elk, moose, reindeer, caribou and antelope. Red deer meat is a dark, blood-red colour; the flesh of the roe deer is paler and the fallow deer is considered to have the best flavour. Both farmed and wild venison are available.

Young animals up to 18 months produce delicate, tender meat. Meat from animals of more than 18 months in age tends to be tough and dry, and is usually marinated to counteract this.

Venison contains 207 calories per 100 g, and young venison has only about 6 per cent fat (compared to beef, lamb and pork at around 20 per cent fat). It is very suitable for a low-cholesterol diet because the fat is mainly polyunsaturated. The carcass has little intramuscular fat; the lean meat contains only low levels of marbling fat. Venison also has the highest protein content of the major meats.

Joints should be well fleshed and a dark brownish-red colour. Venison is usually roasted or braised in joints, served hot or cold with a peppery/sweet-type sauce. Small cuts may be fried and served in a variety of ways. Venison is available as: shoulder; haunch; prepared saddles and steaks; also as pâté, in sausages and burgers; and smoked.

Figure 7.40 Side of venison

Hare and rabbit

The ears of hares and rabbits should tear easily. In old hares the lip is more pronounced than in young animals. The rabbit is distinguished from the hare by its shorter ears, feet and body.

Hare may be cooked as a red wine stew thickened with its own blood, called jugged hare, and the saddle can be roasted.

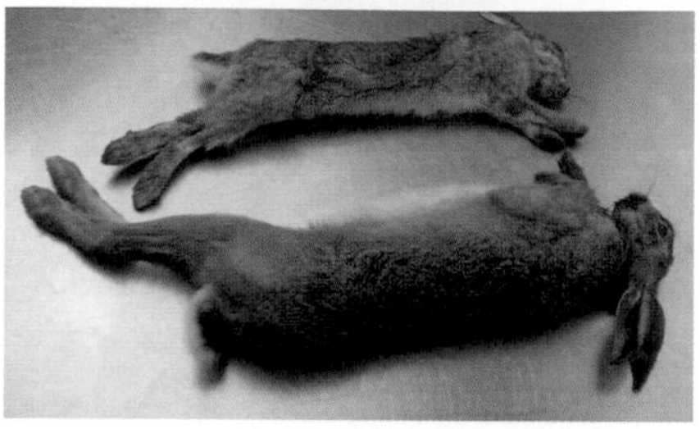

Figure 7.41 Rabbit and hare: furred

Figure 7.42 Rabbit and hare: skinned

Other meats

- **Alligator** is a white meat, with a veal-like texture and a shellfish-like flavour.
- **Bison** should be treated like a gamey, well-hung version of beef. However, because it is so lean it needs to be cooked quickly and served rare or medium rare.
- **Camel** is available as fillet, steak or diced. It is usually imported frozen from Africa.
- **Crocodile** has a firm-textured, light-coloured meat with a delicate fishy taste, that absorbs other flavours well. It is surprisingly fatty.
- **European wild boar** produces rich, dark-red meat with a dense texture.
- **Kangaroo** is similar to venison in flavour. It has a fine-grained meat that, once cooked, is similar in texture to liver; it is best served rare or medium rare.
- **Kid** usually comes from goats bred for their milk. However, the South African Boer goat, which is bred for its meat, has recently been introduced to the UK. It has a rich yet delicate flavour with very little fat.
- **Kudu** is a wild African antelope that is culled in a controlled way. The animals are very large and the meat has a stronger flavour than wild venison. It needs to be tenderised by marinating and cooking.

Game birds

The beak should break easily. The breast plumage should be soft. The breast should be plump. Quill feathers should be pointed, not rounded. The legs should be smooth.

The most common game birds used in catering, and the most frequently used methods of preparation, are as follows.

- **Grouse:** the red grouse is a famous and popular game bird. Average weight is 300 g. Young birds have pointed wings and rounded soft spurs. Hang for five to seven days. Use for roasting.
- **Partridge:** the most common varieties are the grey-legged and the red-legged partridge. Average weight is 200–400 g. Hang for three to five days. Use for roasting or braising.
- **Pheasant:** this is one of the most common game birds. Average weight is 1.5–2 kg. Young birds have a pliable breastbone and soft, pliable feet. Hang for five to eight days. Use for roasting, braising or pot roasting.
- **Quail:** these are small birds weighing 50–75 g, produced on farms and usually packed in boxes of 12. Quails are not hung. Serve roasted, grilled, spatchcock or braised.
- **Snipe:** weight is about 100 g. Hang for three to four days. The heads and neck are skinned, the eyes removed; birds are then trussed with their own beaks. Only the gizzard, gallbladder and intestines are removed; the birds are roasted with the liver and heart left inside.
- **Teal:** the smallest duck, weighing 400–600 g. Hang for one to two days. Usually roasted or braised. Young birds have small pinkish legs and soft down under the wings. Teal and wild duck must be eaten in season otherwise the flesh is coarse and has a fishy flavour.
- **Wild duck:** varieties include mallard and widgeon. Average weight is 1–1.5 kg. Hang for one or two days. Usually roasted or braised.
- **Woodcock:** these are small birds with long, thin beaks. Average weight is 200–300 g. Prepare as for snipe.

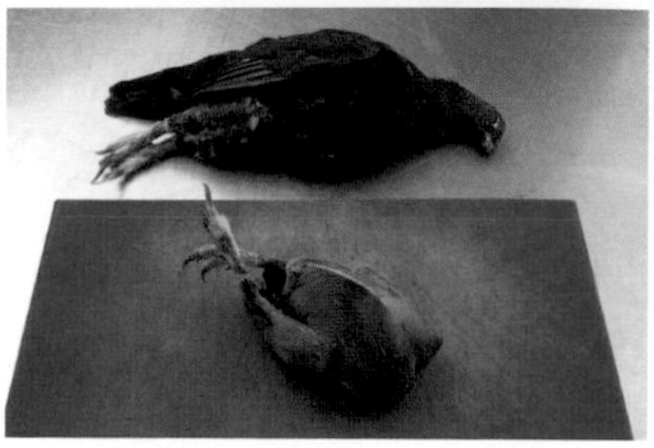

Figure 7.43 Grouse: whole and prepared for cooking

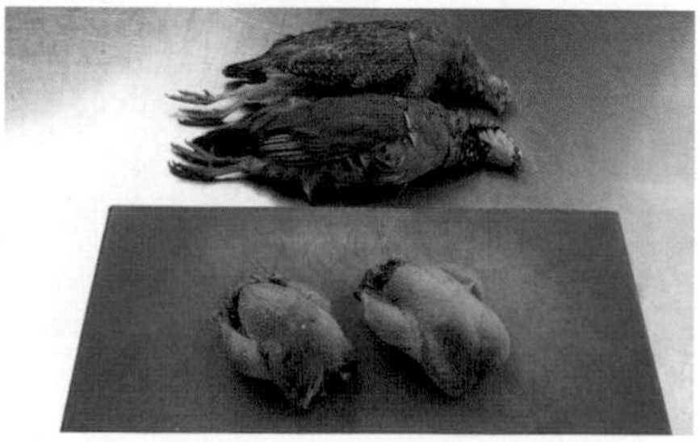

Figure 7.44 Red-legged and English partridge: whole and prepared for cooking

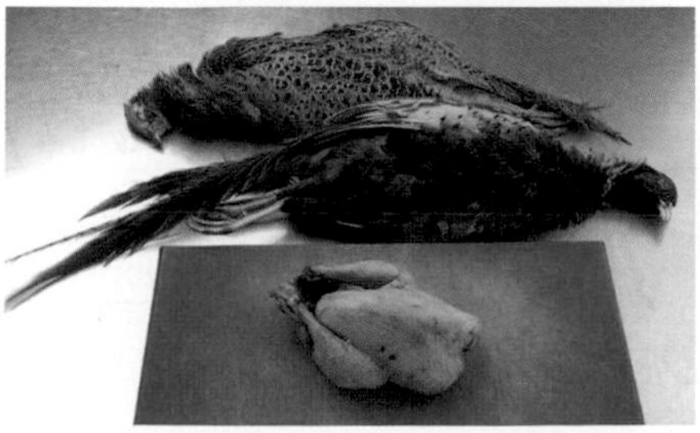

Figure 7.45 Male and female pheasants, and one prepared for cooking

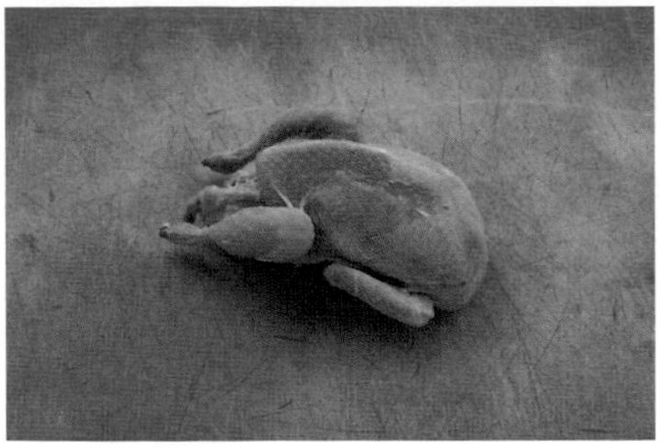

Figure 7.46 Quail: prepared for cooking

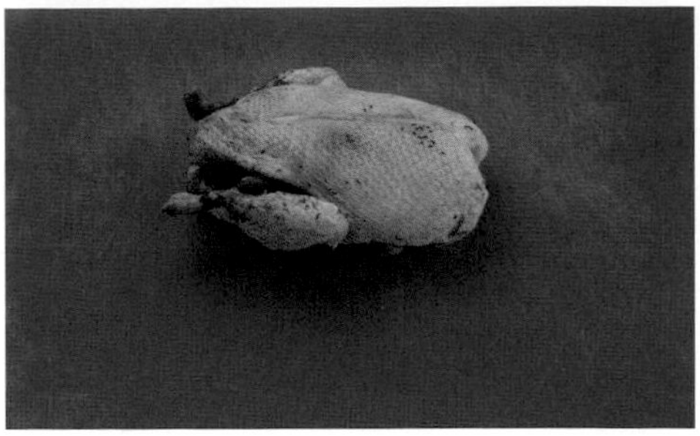

Figure 7.47 Wild duck: prepared for cooking

→ Fish

Fish have always made up a large proportion of the food we consume because of their abundance and relative ease of harvesting. However, because the fish supply is not unlimited, due to overfishing, fish farms (e.g. for trout, salmon, cod, sea bass, halibut and turbot) have been established to supplement the natural sources. Overfishing is not the only problem: the seas and rivers are increasingly polluted, affecting both the supply and suitability of fish, particularly shellfish, for human consumption.

Fish are not only a good source of protein, they can be cooked and presented in a wide variety of ways. The range of types of fish of varying texture, taste and appearance is indispensable to the creative chef.

Oily fish are round in shape (e.g. herring, mackerel, salmon). White fish can be round (cod, whiting, hake) or flat (plaice, sole, turbot).

Table 7.2 Seasons for fish (UK)

Variety of fish	Season
Oily	
Anchovy	Imported occasionally; June to December (home waters)
Common eel	All year, best in autumn
Conger eel	March to October
Herring	All year except spring
Kingfish	Check with supplier
Mackerel	September to July
Pilchard (mature sardine)	All year
Salmon	February to August (or farmed, all year)
Salmon (Pacific)	July to November
Salmon trout	February to August
Sprat	September to March
Sardines	All year
Trout	February to September (or farmed, all year)
Tuna	All year
Whitebait	When available
White, flat	
Brill	June to February
Dab	March to December
Flounder	May to February, best in winter
Halibut	June to March
Megrim	April to February
Plaice	May to February
Skate	May to February
Sole, Dover	May to March
Sole, lemon	All year, best in spring
Turbot (wild/ farmed)	All year
Witch	All year, best in spring
Round	
Barracuda	Check with supplier
Bass (wild/ farmed)	June to September
Bream, fresh water	August to April
Bream, sea	June to December
Carp (mostly farmed)	Fluctuates throughout year
Cod	All year, not at best in spring
Dogfish (huss, flake, rigg)	All year, best in autumn
Grey mullet	May to February, best in autumn and winter
Grouper	Check with supplier
Haddock	All year, best in autumn and winter
Hake	June to February
John Dory	September to May
Ling	September to July

Variety of fish	Season
Round	
Monkfish (anglerfish)	All year, best in winter
Pike	All year
Perch	May to February
Pollock (yellow, green)	May to December
Redfish	All year
Red gurnard	All year, best from July to April
Red mullet	Imported; best in summer and autumn
Sea bream	June to February
Smelt	Occasionally
Shark (porbeagle)	Occasionally
Snapper, red snapper	Check with supplier
Whiting	All year, best in winter

Purchasing and storage

Fresh fish is bought by the kilogram, by the number of fillets or by whole fish of the weight required. For example, 30 kg of salmon could be ordered as 2 × 15 kg, 3 × 10 kg or 6 × 5 kg. Store in a fish box containing ice, ideally in a separate refrigerator or part of a refrigerator used only for fish at a temperature of 1–2°C. The temperature must be maintained just above freezing point.

Frozen fish can be purchased in 15 kg blocks, as individual whole fish or as fillets, etc. Store in a deep-freeze cabinet or compartment at -18°C or below.

Fish may be bought on the bone or filleted in steaks or suprêmes. (The approximate loss from boning and waste is 50 per cent for flat fish, 60 per cent for round fish.) Fillets of plaice and sole can be purchased according to weight. They are graded from 45 g to 180 g per fillet, and go up in weight by 15 g.

Smoked fish should be kept in a refrigerator.

Oily fish

- **Anchovies:** small, round fish supplied in tins, filleted and packed in oil. They are used for making anchovy butter and anchovy sauce, for garnishing dishes, and for snacks and salads.
- **Common eel:** eels live in fresh water in Britain and Europe, and are also farmed. They grow up to 1 m in length. Eels must be kept alive until the last minute before cooking and are generally used in fish stews.
- **Conger eel:** a dark-grey sea fish with white flesh, which grows up to 3 m in length. It may be used in the same way as common eel, or it may be smoked.
- **Herring:** fresh herrings are used for breakfast and lunch; they are grilled, fried or soused. Kippers (split, salted, dried and smoked herrings) are served for breakfast and as a savoury. Average weight is 250 g.
- **Kingfish** come from the Spanish mackerel family; their flesh is orangey-pink coloured.
- **Mackerel** are grilled, shallow-fried, smoked or soused, and used regularly on breakfast and lunch menus. They must be used fresh because the flesh deteriorates very quickly. Average weight is 360 g.
- **Pilchards:** mature sardines that can grow up to 24 cm. They have a good, distinctive flavour.
- **Salmon:** perhaps the most famous river fish. It is caught in British rivers like the Tay, Severn, Wye and Spey, and farmed extensively in Scotland. A considerable number are imported to the UK from Scandinavia, Canada, Germany and Japan. Fresh salmon is used in a wide variety of dishes; it is also tinned or smoked.
- **Salmon trout (sea trout):** a sea fish similar in appearance to salmon, but smaller, and used in a similar way. Average weight is 1.5–2 kg.
- **Sardines:** small fish of the pilchard family, usually tinned and used for hors d'oeuvres, sandwiches and as a savoury. Fresh sardines may be grilled or fried.
- **Sprats:** small fish fried whole; they can also be smoked and served as an hors d'oeuvre.
- **Trout** live in rivers and lakes in the UK; they are also cultivated on trout farms. Trout may be poached, grilled or shallow-fried, and may also be smoked and served as an hors d'oeuvre. Average weight is 200 g.
- **Tuna** has dark reddish-brown flesh that, when cooked, turns a lighter colour. It has a thin texture and a mild flavour. If overcooked it dries out, so is best seared or cooked medium rare. It is used fresh for a variety of dishes, or tinned in oil and used mainly as an hors d'oeuvre and in salads.
- **Whitebait:** the fry, or young, of herring; they are 2–4 cm long and are usually deep-fried.

Figure 7.48 Herring

Figure 7.49 Kipper

Figure 7.50 Mackerel

Figure 7.51 Salmon

Figure 7.52 Side of fresh salmon

Figure 7.53 Sardine

Figure 7.54 Trout

Figure 7.55 Whitebait

White flat fish

- **Brill:** a large flat fish. Brill is oval in shape; the mottled brown skin is smooth with small scales. It is sometimes confused with turbot, but can be distinguished by its lesser breadth in proportion to length; average weight is 3–4 kg. It is usually served in the same way as turbot.
- **Dab:** an oval-bodied fish with sandy brown upper skin and green freckles. Usual size is 20–30 cm. It has a pleasant flavour when fresh and may be cooked by all methods.
- **Flounder:** oval, with dull brown upper skin (or dull green with orange freckles). Usual size is 30 cm. Flesh is rather watery and lacks flavour, needing good seasoning. It can be cooked by all methods.
- **Halibut:** a long and narrow fish, brown, with some darker mottling on the upper side; it can grow to 3 m in length and weigh around 20–50 kg. Halibut is much valued for its texture and flavour. It can be poached, boiled, grilled or shallow-fried. It is also smoked.
- **Megrim** has a very long slender body, sandy-brown coloured with dark blotches. Usual size is 20–30 cm. It has a softish flesh and an unexceptional flavour, so needs good accompanying flavours. It is best shallow-fried.
- **Plaice** are oval in shape, with dark-brown colouring and orange spots on the upper side. They are usually deep-fried or grilled. Average weight is 360–450 g.
- **Skate:** a member of the ray family. A very large fish and only the wings are used. It is usually served on the bone and either poached, shallow- or deep-fried, or cooked in a court bouillon and served with black butter.
- **Sole:** one of the best of the flat fish. Sole is cooked by poaching, grilling or frying (both shallow and deep). It is served whole or filleted and garnished in many ways.
  - **Dover sole** has excellent texture and flavour. Grilling and pan-frying tend to be the most popular methods for cooking it.
  - **Lemon sole** is broader in shape, and its upper skin is warm, yellowy-brown and mottled with darker brown. It can weigh up to 600 g, and may be cooked by all methods.
- **Turbot** has no scales and is roughly diamond in shape; it has knobs known as tubercles on its dark skin. In proportion to its length it is wider than brill; 3.5–4 kg is the average weight. Turbot may be cooked whole, filleted or cut into portions on the bone. It may be boiled, poached, grilled or shallow-fried.
- **Witch:** similar in appearance and weight to lemon sole, with sandy-brown upper skin. It is best fried, poached, grilled or steamed.

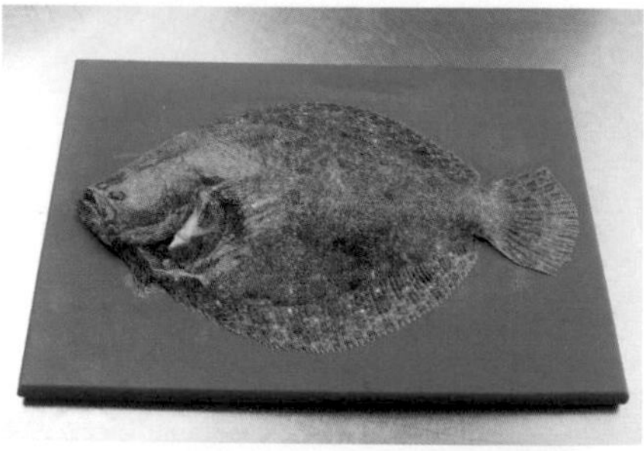

Figure 7.56 Brill

Figure 7.57 Halibut

Figure 7.58 Plaice

Figure 7.59 Skate

Figure 7.60 Dover sole

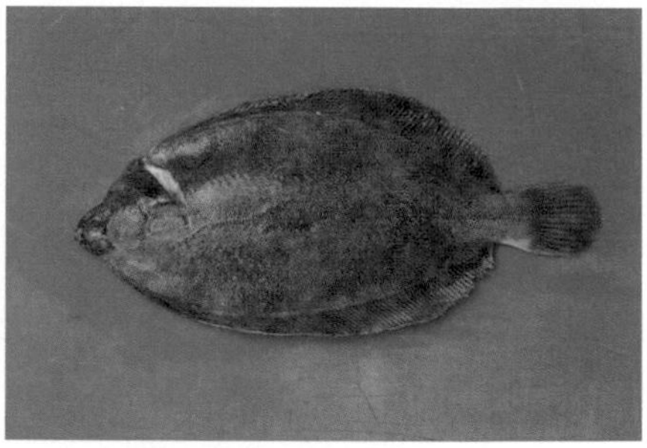

Figure 7.61 Lemon sole

Figure 7.62 Turbot

Round fish

- **Barracuda:** a game fish with reddish flesh that, when cooked, turns pastel white. A mild-flavoured fish, it should be cooked as a suprême with the skin left on to prevent drying out.
- **Bass** have silvery grey backs and white bellies; small ones may have black spots. They have an excellent flavour, with white, lean, softish flesh (which must be very fresh). Bass can be steamed, poached, stuffed and baked, or grilled in steaks. Usual length is 30 cm but they can grow to 60 cm. Bass is usually farmed in the UK, France and Greece, but sea bass is also available (also called wild or natural).
- **Bream:** a short, oval-bodied, plump, reddish fish, with large scales and a dark patch behind the head. It is used on many less expensive menus; it is usually filleted and deep-fried, or stuffed and baked, but other methods of cooking are also employed. Average weight is 0.5–1 kg, size 28–30 cm. Bream are caught fresh or farmed.
- **Carp:** a freshwater fish, usually farmed. The flesh is white with a good flavour, and is best poached in fillets or stuffed and baked. The usual size is 1–2 kg.
- **Cod** varies in colour but is mostly greenish, brownish or olive grey. It can measure up to 1.5 m in length. Cod is cut into steaks or filleted and cut into portions; it can be deep- or shallow-fried or poached. Small cod are known as codling. Average weight of cod is 2.5–3.5 kg.
- **Coley (saith, coalfish, blackjack)** is dark greenish-brown or blackish in colour, but the flesh turns white when cooked. It has a coarse texture and a dry undistinctive flavour, so is best used in mixed fish stews, soups or pies. Average size is 40–80 cm.
- **Dogfish (huss, flake, rigg):** a slender, elongated small shark. The non-bony white or pink flesh is versatile, and is usually served shallow- or deep-fried. It has a good flavour when very fresh. Length is usually 60 cm and weight 1.25 kg.
- **Grey mullet** has a scaly, streamlined body, which is silver-grey or blue-green. Deep-sea or offshore mullet has a fine flavour, with firm, moist flesh. It may be stuffed and baked or grilled in steaks. Length is usually about 30 cm and weight 500 g.
- **Grouper:** types include brown, brown spotted, golden strawberry and red speckled. Grouper has a light-pinkish flesh that cooks to a greyish-white, with a pleasant mild flavour.
- **Gudgeon:** small fish found in European lakes and rivers. They may be deep-fried whole. On UK menus the French term 'en goujon' refers to other fish such as sole or turbot, cut into pieces the size of gudgeon.
- **Gurnard:** a large family of tasty fish with many culinary uses.
- **Haddock:** distinguished from cod by the 'thumb mark' on its side and by its lighter colour. Every method of cooking is suitable for fresh haddock, and it appears on all kinds of menus. Smoked haddock may be served for breakfast and lunch, and as a savoury. Average weight is 0.5–2 kg.

- **Hake:** owing to overfishing, hake is not plentiful. It is usually poached and is easy to digest. The flesh is very white and has a delicate flavour.
- **John Dory** has a thin, distinctive body, flattened from side to side, which is sandy-beige in colour and tinged with yellow, with a blue/silver-grey belly. There is a blotch on each side, the 'thumbprint of St Peter'. It has very tough sharp spikes. The flavour is superb, and the fish may be cooked by all methods, but is best poached, baked or steamed. The large bony head accounts for two-thirds of the weight. Usual size is 36 cm.
- **Ling:** the largest member of the cod family, it is mottled brown or green with a bronze sheen, and the fins have white edges. Size can be up to 90 cm. Ling has a good flavour and texture, and is generally used in fillets or cutlets, as for cod.
- **Monkfish** has a huge flattened head, with a normal fish-shaped tail. It is brown with dark blotches. The tail can be up to 180 cm, weight 1–10 kg. It may be cooked by all methods, and is a firm, close-textured white fish with excellent flavour.
- **Perch** has a deep body, marked with about five vertical bars, and the fins are vivid orange or red. Usual size is 15–30 cm. It has an excellent flavour, and may be shallow-fried, grilled, baked, braised or steamed.
- **Pike** has a long body, usually 60 cm, which is greeny-brown, flecked with lighter green, with long toothy jaws. The traditional fish for quenelles, it may also be braised or steamed.
- **Pollock:** a member of the cod family, It has a similar shape and variable colours. Its usual size is 45 cm. It is drier than cod, and can be poached, shallow-fried or used for soups and stews.
- **Redfish** is bright red or orangey-red, with a rosy belly and dusky gills. Usual size is 45 cm. It may be poached, baked or used in soups.
- **Red gurnard (or grey and yellow gurnard)** has a large 'mail checked', tapering body with very spiky fins. Usual size is 20–30 cm. It is good for stews, braising and baking.
- **Red mullet** is on occasion cooked with the liver left in, as it is thought that this imparts a better flavour to the fish. Mullet may be filleted or cooked whole. Average weight is 360 g.
- **Rockfish:** the fishmonger's term for catfish, coalfish, dogfish, conger eel and the like, after cleaning and skinning. It is usually deep-fried in batter.
- **Shark:** the porbeagle shark, mako or hammerhead, fished off the British coast, gives the best-quality food. It is bluish-grey with a white belly and matt skin. Size is up to 3 m. It may be cooked by all methods, but grilling in steaks or kebabs is particularly suitable.
- **Smelt:** small fish found in river estuaries and imported from Holland; they are usually deep-fried or grilled. Before grilling they are split open. The weight of a smelt is 60–90 g.
- **Snapper:** there are several kinds of snapper, all of which are brightly coloured. Deep-red or medium-sized ones give the best flavour. Snapper may be steamed, fried, grilled, baked or smoked.
- **Swordfish:** popular grilled, barbecued, roasted or shallow-fried.
- **Whiting:** very easy to digest is therefore suitable for use in cookery for the unwell. It may be poached, grilled or deep-fried and used in stuffing. Average weight is 360 g.
- **Wrasse:** fish of variable colours, but usually tinged with red and blue, covered in white and green spots. Wrasse has a variety of culinary uses and can be baked and steamed.

Figure 7.63 Cod

Figure 7.64 Gurnard

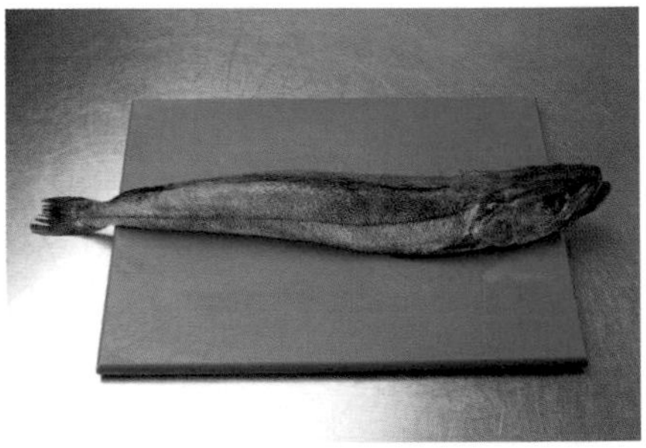

Figure 7.65 Hake

Figure 7.66 John Dory

Figure 7.67 Monkfish

Figure 7.68 Monkfish tail: prepared

Figure 7.69 Red mullet

Figure 7.70 Snapper

WEBLINK

For further information on fish, visit:
www.seafish.org.uk

Shellfish

Shellfish are of two types:

1. crustaceans (lobster, crabs)
2. molluscs (oysters, mussels).

Shellfish is a good body-building food. As the flesh is coarse and therefore indigestible, a little vinegar may be used in cooking to soften the fibres.

Table 7.3 Seasons for shellfish (UK)

Shellfish	Season
Clams	All year
Cockles	All year, best in summer
Common crab	All year, best April to December
Spider crab	All year
Swimming crab	All year
King crab, red crab	Check with supplier
Soft-shelled crab	Check with supplier
Crawfish	April to October
Dublin Bay prawn	All year
Freshwater crayfish	Mainly imported, some farmed in the UK, wild have short season
Lobster	April to November
Mussels	September to March
Oysters	May to August
Prawn and shrimp	All year
Scallop	Best December to March
Sea urchin	All year

Crustaceans

- **Crabs** are used in cocktails, salads and sandwiches. Soft-shelled crabs are eaten in their entirety. They have an excellent flavour and may be deep- or shallow-fried or grilled.
- **Crawfish:** like large lobsters without claws, but with long antennae. They are brick-red in colour when cooked. Owing to their size and appearance they are used on cold buffets, but they can be served hot. The best size is 1.5–2 kg. Dishes include langouste à la Parisienne (dressed crawfish Paris-style).
- **Crayfish:** a type of small freshwater lobster used for salads, garnishing cold buffet dishes and for recipes using lobster. They are dark brown or grey, turning pink when cooked. Average size is 8 cm.
- **Lobster:** served cold in hors d'oeuvre, salads, sandwiches and on buffets. They are used hot for soup, grilled and served in numerous dishes.
- **Prawns:** larger than shrimps, they may be used for garnishing and decorating fish dishes, for cocktails, canapés, salads and hot dishes such as curry. Prawns are also popular served cold with a mayonnaise-type sauce.

Figure 7.71 Crab

Figure 7.72 Crayfish

Figure 7.73 Lobster: raw

Figure 7.74 Lobster: cooked

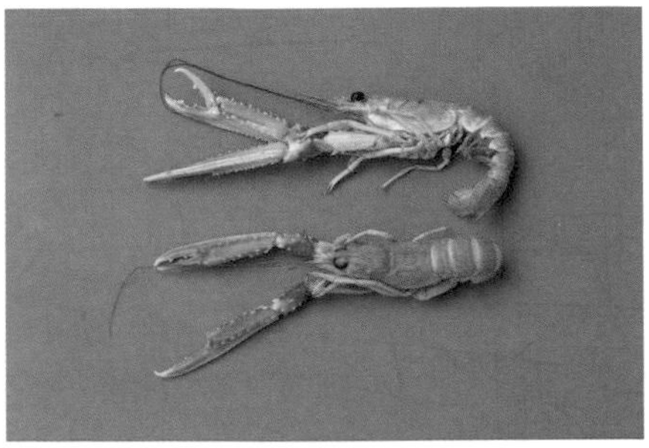
Figure 7.75 Langoustines

- **Scampi, Dublin Bay prawns and langoustines** resemble small lobsters, about 20 cm long, and only the tail flesh is used for a variety of fish dishes, garnishing and salads. Scampi are found in the Mediterranean. The Dublin Bay prawn, from the same family, is caught around the northern coasts of the British Isles.
- **Shrimps:** used for garnishes, in cocktails, sauces, salads, potted shrimps and savouries.

Molluscs

- **Clams:** there are many varieties; the soft or long-neck clams, such as razor and Ipswich, and small hard-shell clams such as cherrystones, can be eaten raw. Large clams can be steamed, fried or grilled and used for soups (chowders) and sauces.
- **Cockles** are enclosed in pretty cream-coloured shells of 2–3 cm. They are soaked in salt water to purge, and then steamed or boiled. They may be used in soups, salads and fish dishes, or served as a dish by themselves.
- **Mussels** are extensively cultivated on wooden hurdles in the sea, producing tender, delicately flavoured, plump shellfish. British mussels are considered good; French mussels are smaller; Dutch and Belgian mussels are plumper. All vary in quality from season to season. Mussels are usually stored in their original packaging, in the refrigerator.
- **Oysters:** some of the best oysters in the world are British – the Colchester native oyster from Mersea Island and the Whitstable oyster, for example. Since most oysters are eaten raw it is essential they are thoroughly cleaned before kitchens receive them. Oysters must be alive; this is indicated by their firmly closed shells. They are graded by size, and the price varies accordingly. Oysters should smell fresh. They should be purchased fresh daily. Oysters are in season in the UK from September to April (i.e. whenever there is an 'r' in the month). During the summer months oysters are imported to the UK from France, Holland and Portugal. Oysters are usually stored in their original packaging, in the refrigerator, to keep them moist and alive. The shells should be tightly closed; if they are open, tap them sharply and, if they do not shut at once, discard them. The most popular way to eat oysters is in their raw state. They may also be served in soups, hot cocktail savouries, fish garnishes, as a fish dish, and in meat puddings and savouries.
- **Scallops:** great scallops are up to 15 cm in size, bay scallops up to 8 cm, queen scallops are small-cockle sized and are also known as 'queenies'. Scallops may be steamed, poached, fried, baked or grilled.
- **Sea urchin,** or **sea hedgehog**, has a spine-covered spherical shell. Only the orange and yellow roe is eaten, either raw out of the shell or removed with a teaspoon and used in soups, sauces, scrambled eggs, and so on; 10 to 20 urchins provide approximately 200 g roe.
- **Winkles:** small sea snails with a delicious flavour. They may be boiled for three minutes and served with garlic butter or on a dish of assorted shellfish.

Figure 7.76 Clams

Figure 7.77 Mussels

Figure 7.78 Scallops

Cephalopods and fish offal

Cephalopods

The common squid has mottled skin and white flesh, two tentacles, eight arms and flap-like fins. Usual size is 15–30 cm. Careful, correct preparation is important if the fish is to be tender. It may be fried, baked, grilled or braised.

Cuttlefish are usually dark with pale stripes; their size can be up to 24 cm. They are available all year by number and weight. Cuttlefish are prepared like squid and may be stewed or gently grilled.

Octopus is available all year by number and weight. Large species are tough and need to be tenderised; they are then prepared as for squid. Small octopi can be boiled, then cut up for grilling or frying. When stewing, a long cooking time is needed.

Fish offal

The oil from the liver of cod and halibut is rich in vitamins A and D. This is used medicinally.

The soft and hard roes of herring, cod, sturgeon and the coral from lobster are eaten. Soft herring roes are used to garnish fish dishes and as a savoury. Cod's roe is often smoked and served as an hors d'oeuvre.

Caviar is the uncooked roe of the sturgeon, prepared by carefully separating the eggs from the membranes and gently rubbing them through sieves. It is soaked in a brine solution, sieved and packed. Caviar is produced in Russia or Iran; types are named after the type of sturgeon and include Beluga and Sevruga. Caviar is extremely expensive, and needs to be handled with care. It should be kept at a temperature of 0°C, but no lower otherwise the extreme cold will break the eggs down. Caviar must never be deep-frozen.

Red caviar (keta) is obtained from the roe of salmon, and 'mock caviar' from the lumpfish. These are considerably cheaper than genuine caviar.

The coral of lobster is used for colouring lobster dishes, and also as a decoration for fish dishes.

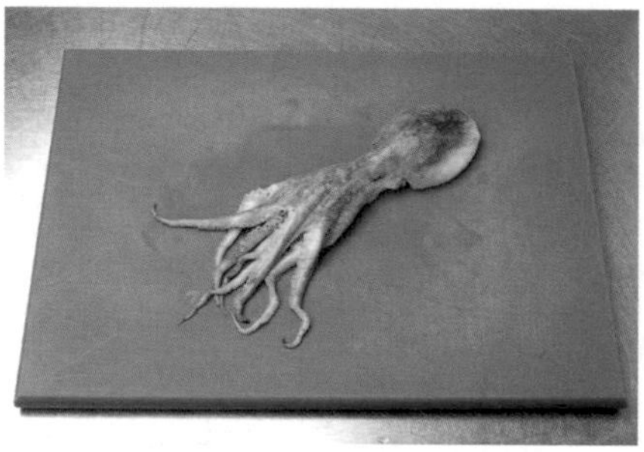

Figure 7.79 Octopus

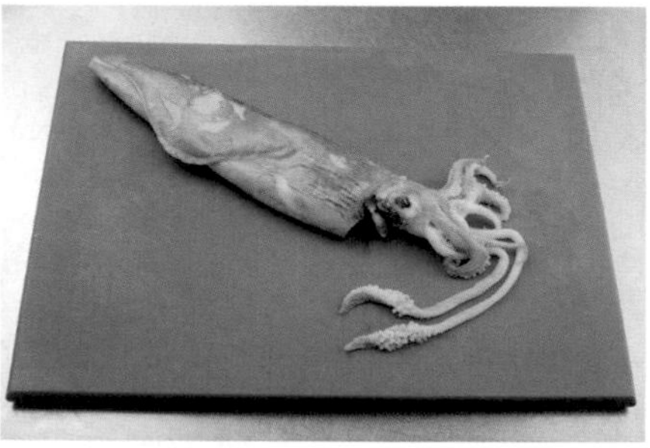

Figure 7.80 Squid

Figure 7.81 Cod roe

➜ Vegetables

Fresh vegetables and fruits are important foods, both from an economic and nutritional point of view. On average, each person consumes 125–150 kg per year of fruit and vegetables.

Composition

Most vegetables contain at least 80 per cent water: the remainder is made up of carbohydrate, protein and fat. The content varies depending on the type of vegetable: squashes contain a high percentage of water; potatoes contain a great deal of starch. Corn, carrots, parsnips and onions contain invert sugars.

Because of the high water content, most fruits and vegetables provide only minerals, certain vitamins and some fibre. However, these additions – particularly of vitamins such as ascorbic acid – can be of immense value in our diet.

A typical plant cell is like a balloon, not blown up with air but with water. The internal pressure in the cell is called turgor pressure. When plant tissues are in a state of maximum water content they are said to be turgid or in a complete state of turgor.

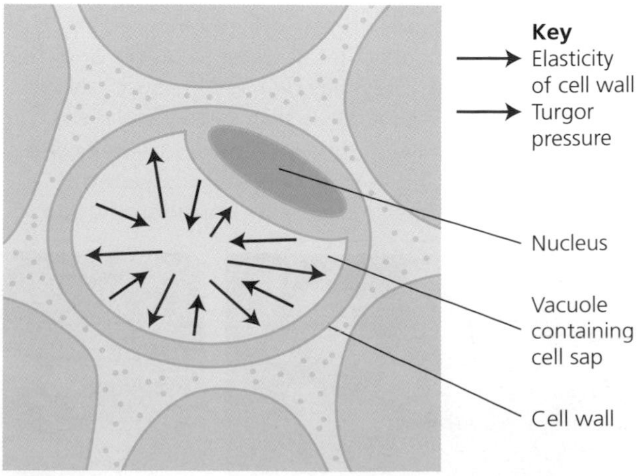

Figure 7.82 Equalised pressures within a plant cell

Once the supply of water is reduced or cut off to the cell, water is gradually lost from the plant by transpiration and the turgor pressure cannot be maintained. This causes it to wilt. The rate of wilting varies: harvested leafy vegetables such as lettuce, for example, last only short periods before becoming limp.

The cell wall of fruit and vegetable cells is made of carbohydrates, mainly cellulose and starch. As the cells age, a substance called lignin is deposited in the cell wall, making it tougher. Water evaporates and sugars become concentrated – old raw carrots, for example, are sweeter than young ones. Sugars change as soon as the vegetable is separated from the plant. A good example is corn, which is often rushed straight from the stalk to the pot in order to preserve its taste.

Cells are held together by pectins and hemicellulose; these change as the vegetable ripens, so that the cells part easily, giving a softer texture.

The composition of vegetables is also affected by the following factors.

- **Origin:** where vegetables are grown. The type of soil (acid, alkali, rocky, sandy or clay) is a factor.
- **Seasons and climate:** these affect the size of fruits and vegetables, and the yield per acre. Adverse weather conditions can reduce yields dramatically. Good weather conditions can increase yields and produce high-quality fruits and vegetables.

Purchasing, quality and preservation

Experience and sound judgement are essential for the efficient buying and storage of all commodities, but none probably more so than fresh vegetables and fruit.

The purchasing of these commodities is difficult because the products are highly perishable, and supply and demand vary. Fresh vegetables and fruits will lose quality quickly if not properly stored and handled. Improved transportation and storage facilities can help prevent loss of quality.

Automation in harvesting and packaging speeds the handling process and helps retain quality. Vacuum cooling – a process whereby fresh produce is moved into huge chambers, where, for about half an hour, a low vacuum is maintained, inducing rapid evaporation, which quickly reduces field heat – has been highly successful in improving quality.

There are four main quality classes for fresh fruit and vegetables in the EU:

1. Extra Class – top quality
2. Class I – good quality
3. Class II – reasonably good quality
4. Class III – low marketable quality.

Vegetables are preserved by the following methods (described in Chapter 3).

- **Canning:** e.g. artichokes, asparagus, sweetcorn, carrots, beans, peas, tomatoes, truffles.
- **Dehydration:** onions, carrots, potatoes and cabbage are shredded and quickly dried until they contain only 5 per cent water.
- **Drying:** the seeds of legumes (peas and beans) have their moisture content reduced to 10 per cent.
- **Freezing:** e.g. peas, beans, sprouts, spinach and cauliflower.
- **Modified atmosphere packaging (MAP):** prepared vegetables and salads are packed and surrounded by modified gases that slow down deterioration.
- **Pickling:** e.g. onions and red cabbage preserved in spiced vinegar.
- **Salting:** e.g. French and runner beans sliced and preserved in dry salt. Capers are also salted in this way.

Types of vegetables

Root vegetables include:

- **beetroot** – round or long varieties; used for soups, salads and as a vegetable
- **carrots** – numerous varieties and sizes; used extensively for soups, stocks, stews, salads and as a vegetable
- **celeriac** – large, light-brown, celery-flavoured root, used in soups, salads and as a vegetable
- **horseradish** – long, light-brown, narrow root, grated and used for horseradish sauce
- **mooli** – long, white, thick member of radish family, used for soups, salads or as a vegetable
- **parsnips** – long, white root, tapering to a point; unique nut-like flavour; used in soups, added to casseroles and as a vegetable (roasted, etc.)
- **radishes** – small summer variety, round or oval, served with dips, in salads or as a vegetable
- **salsify** – also called oyster plant because of similarity of taste; long, narrow root used in soups, salads and as a vegetable
- **scorzonera** – long, narrow root, slightly astringent in flavour; used in soups, salads and as a vegetable
- **swede** – large root with yellow flesh; generally used as a vegetable, mashed or parboiled and roasted; may be added to stews
- **turnip** – long or round varieties; used in soups, stews and as a vegetable
- **wasabi** – used in Japanese cooking, to make a sharp, pungent condiment; similar to horseradish.

Figure 7.83 Root vegetables (left to right: parsnip, carrots, celeriac, horseradish, radishes, mooli)

Tubers include:

- **Jerusalem artichoke** – potato-like tuber with a bitter-sweet flavour; used in soups, salads and as a vegetable
- **potato** – many varieties are grown and should be sold by name (e.g. King Edward, Desiree, Maris Piper); this is important as different varieties are best suited to specific cooking purposes; the varieties fall into four categories – floury, firm, waxy or salad potatoes; examples are Jersey royals (specially grown, highly regarded new potatoes), Purple Congo (a blue potato) and Truffle de Chine (a deep-purple potato grown in France)
- **sweet potato** – long tuber with purple or sand-coloured skin and orange flesh; flavour is sweet and aromatic; used as a vegetable (fried, puréed, candied) or made into a sweet pudding
- **taro** is the name for several varieties of tuber found in tropical areas – two common varieties are eddo and dasheen; they are all a dark mahogany-brown with a shaggy skin, looking like a cross between a beetroot and a swede
- **yam** – similar to sweet potato and used in the same way, usually cylindrical, often knobbly in shape.

Figure 7.84 Tubers (left to right: yam, sweet potato, potatoes, new potatoes, Jerusalem artichokes)

Bulbs include:

- **fennel** – the bulb is the swollen leaf base and has a pronounced aniseed flavour; used cooked as well as raw in salads
- **garlic** – an onion-like bulb with a papery skin inside of which are small individually wrapped cloves; used extensively in cookery; garlic has a pungent distinctive flavour and should be used carefully
- **leeks** – summer leeks have long white stems, bright-green leaves and a milder flavour than winter leeks, which have a stockier stem and a stronger flavour; used extensively in stocks, soups, stews and as a vegetable
- **onions** – there are numerous varieties with different-coloured skins and varying strengths; after salt, the onion is probably the most frequently used flavouring in cookery, in almost every type of food except sweet dishes
- **shallots** – have a similar but more refined flavour than the onion and are therefore more often used in top-class cookery
- **spring onions** – are slim and tiny, like miniature leeks; used in soups, salads, and Chinese and Japanese cookery; ramp looks like a spring onion but is stronger.

Figure 7.85 Bulbs (left to right: leek, garlic, onion, shallots, spring onions)

Leafy vegetables include:

- **chicory** – a lettuce with coarse, crisp leaves and a sharp, bitter taste in the outside leaves; inner leaves are milder
- **Chinese leaves** – long, white, densely packed leaves with a mild flavour resembling celery; a good substitute for lettuce; can be boiled, braised or stir-fried as a vegetable
- **corn salad** – sometimes called lamb's lettuce; small, tender, dark leaves with a tangy nutty taste
- **cress** – many varieties with different flavours, suitable for a large range of uses
- **culaboo** – leaves of the tero plant, poisonous if eaten raw, but widely used in Asian and Caribbean cookery
- **lettuce** – many varieties, including cos, little gem, iceberg, oakleaf, Webb's; used chiefly for salads or as a wrapping for other foods, e.g. fish fillets
- **mustard and cress** – embryonic leaves of mustard and garden cress with a sharp, warm flavour; used mainly in, or as a garnish to, sandwiches and salads
- **nettles** – once cooked the sting disappears; should be picked young, used in soups
- **radicchio** – round, deep-red variety of chicory with white ribs and a distinctive bitter taste
- **red salanova** – a neat, tasty lettuce; very suitable for garnish
- **rocket** – a type of cress with larger leaves and a peppery taste
- **sorrel** – bright-green sour leaves, which can be overpowering if used on their own; best when tender and young; used in salads and soups
- **spinach** – tender dark-green leaves with a mild musky flavour; used for soups, garnishing egg and fish dishes, as a vegetable and raw in salads
- **Swiss chard** – large, ribbed, slightly curly leaves with a flavour similar to but milder than spinach; used in the same ways as spinach
- **vine leaves** – all leaves from grape vines can be eaten when young
- **watercress** – long stems with round, dark, tender green leaves and a pungent peppery flavour; used for soups, salads, and for garnishing meat and poultry dishes.

Figure 7.86 Leafy vegetables (rocket and radicchio)

Brassicas include:

- **broccoflower** – a cross between broccoli and cauliflower
- **broccoli** – a delicate vegetable with a gentle flavour used in soups, salads, stir-fry dishes, and as a vegetable; various types include calabrese, white, green and purple sprouting; Chinese broccoli is a leafy vegetable with slender heads of flowers
- **Brussels sprouts** – small green buds growing on thick stems; can be used for soup but are mainly used as a vegetable
- **cabbage** – three main types, including green, white and red; many varieties of green cabbage available at different seasons of the year; early green cabbage is deep green and loosely formed; later in the season they firm up, with solid hearts; savoy is considered the best of the winter green cabbage; white cabbage is used for coleslaw; green and red as a vegetable, boiled, braised or stir-fried
- **cauliflower** – heads of creamy-white florets with a distinctive flavour; used for soup and as a vegetable
- **Chinese mustard greens** – deep green and mustard flavoured
- **kale and curly kale** – thick green leaves; the curly variety is the more popular
- **pak choi (bok choi)** – a leaf vegetable with many varieties; typically has long, smooth milky-white stems and dark-green foliage
- **Romanesco** – pretty green or white cross between broccoli and cauliflower.

Pods and seeds include:

- **broad beans** – pale-green, oval-shaped beans contained in a thick fleshy pod; young broad beans can be removed from the pods, cooked in their shells and served as a vegetable in various ways; old beans will toughen and, when removed from the pods, will have to be shelled before use

Figure 7.87 Brassicas (from left: broccoflower, Savoy cabbage, pak choi)

- **butter or lima beans** – butter beans are white, large, flattish and oval-shaped; lima beans are smaller; both are used as a vegetable, or salad or casserole ingredient
- **mangetout** – also called snow peas or sugar peas; flat pea pod with immature seeds that, after topping, tailing and stringing, may be eaten in their entirety; used as a vegetable, in salads and for stir-fry dishes
- **okra** – curved and pointed seed pods with a flavour similar to aubergines; cooked as a vegetable or in creole-type stews and curries
- **peas** – garden peas are normal size, petits pois are a dwarf variety; marrowfat peas are dried; popular as a vegetable, peas are also used for soups, salads, stews and stir-fry dishes
- **runner beans** – must be used when young; bright-green colour and a pliable, velvety feel; if coarse, wilted or older beans are used they will be stringy and tough
- **sweetcorn (maize, Sudan corn)** – available 'on the cob', fresh or frozen, or in kernels, canned or frozen; a versatile commodity used as a first course, in soups and salads, and as a vegetable
- **yard-long beans** – similar to French beans but three or four times longer.

Figure 7.88 Pods and seeds (clockwise from top left: okra, sweetcorn, runner beans, mangetout, peas, bean sprouts)

Pulses are the dried seeds of plants that form pods. Pulses are used extensively for soups, stews, vegetables and salads. They are good sources of protein and carbohydrate, and, with the exception of the soya bean, contain no fat. Examples include:

- **aduki beans** – small, round, deep-red, shiny beans
- **black beans** – glistening black skins and creamy flesh
- **black-eyed beans** – white beans with a black blotch
- **borlotti beans** – pink-blotched mottled colour
- **broad beans** (**fava beans**) – strongly flavoured beans
- **cannellini** – Italian haricots, slightly fatter than the UK version
- **chickpeas** – look like the kernel of a small hazelnut; the main ingredient of hummus
- **Dutch brown beans** – light brown in colour
- **flageolets** – pale-green, kidney-shaped beans
- **ful mesdames** (**Egyptian brown beans**) – small, brown, knobbly beans, also known as the field or broad bean in the UK
- **haricot beans** – white, smooth oval beans

- **lentils** – available in bright orange, brown or green; the grey-coloured puy lentils are considered the finest
- **mung beans** – chiefly used for bean sprouts
- **pinto beans** – pink-blotched mottled colour
- **red kidney beans** – used in chilli con carne; a black variety is also available
- **soissons** – the finest haricot beans
- **soya beans** – the most nutritious of all beans
- **split peas** – available in bright green or golden yellow.

All pulses should be kept in clean containers in a dry, well-ventilated store.

Stems and shoots include:

- **asparagus** – the three main types are white, with creamy white stems and a mild flavour; French, with violet or bluish tips and a stronger more astringent flavour; and green, with a delicious aromatic flavour; used on every course of the menu, except the sweet course
- **bean sprouts** – slender young sprouts of the germinating soya or mung bean, used as a vegetable accompaniment, in stir-fry dishes and salads
- **cardoon** – longish plant with root and fleshy ribbed stalk similar to celery, but leaves are grey-green in colour; used cooked as a vegetable or raw in salads
- **celery** – long-stemmed bundles of fleshy, ribbed stalks, white to light green in colour; used in soups, stocks, sauces, cooked as a vegetable and raw in salads and dips
- **chicory (Belgian endive)** – conical heads of crisp white, faintly bitter leaves, used cooked as a vegetable and raw in salads and dips
- **fallow wax beans** – similar to French beans
- **fiddleneck fern (ostrich fern)** – 5 cm long, a bit like asparagus and used in oriental dishes
- **globe artichokes** – resemble fat pine cones with overlapping fleshy, green, inedible leaves, all connected to an edible fleshy base or bottom; used as a first course, hot or cold; as a vegetable or in casseroles
- **kohlrabi** – stem that swells to turnip shape above the ground; those about the size of a large egg are best; may be cooked as a vegetable, stuffed and baked and added to casseroles
- **palm hearts** – the buds of cabbage palm trees
- **samphire** – the two types are marsh samphire (glasswort, sea asparagus), which grows in estuaries and salt marshes, and white rock samphire (sometimes called sea fennel), which grows on rocky shores
- **sea kale** – delicate white leaves with yellow frills edged with purple; can be boiled or braised, or served raw like celery
- **Thai beans** – similar to French beans
- **water chestnuts** – common name for a number of aquatic herbs and their nut-like fruit; the best-known is the Chinese water chestnut (Chinese sedge).

Figure 7.89 Stems and shoots (left to right: globe artichoke, celery, fennel)

Fruiting vegetables include:

- **aubergine** – firm, elongated, varying in size with smooth shiny skins ranging from purple-red to purple-black; inner flesh is white with tiny soft seeds; almost without flavour, it requires other seasonings, e.g. garlic, lemon juice, herbs, to enhance its taste; may be sliced and fried or baked, steamed or stuffed; varieties include baby, Japanese, white, striped and Thai
- **avocado** – fruit that is used mainly as a vegetable because of its bland, mild, nutty flavour; the summer variety is green when unripe and purple-black when ripe, with golden-yellow flesh; the winter ones are more pear-shaped with smooth green skin and pale green to yellow flesh; eaten as a first course, and used in salads and dips, and as garnishes to other dishes
- **courgette** – baby marrow, yellow or light to dark green in colour, with a delicate flavour becoming stronger when cooked with other ingredients, e.g. herbs, garlic; may be cooked in many ways
- **cucumber** – long, smooth-skinned, ridged and dark green in colour; used in salads, soups, sandwiches, garnishes and as a vegetable
- **exotic gourds** – include bottle gourds, chayotes (chow-chow), Chinese butter lemons; similar in texture to a squash
- **marrow** – long, oval-shaped edible gourds with ridged green skins and a bland flavour; may be cooked as for courgettes
- **peppers** – available in three colours, green peppers are unripened and then turn yellow to orange and then red (they must remain on the plant to do this); used raw and cooked in salads and many other dishes
- **pumpkins** – vary in size and can weigh up to 50 kg; associated with Halloween as a decoration but may be used in soups or pie
- **squash** – many varieties, e.g. acorn, butternut, delicate, kuboche, onion; flesh firm and glowing; can be boiled, baked, steamed or puréed
- **tomatoes** – along with onions, probably the most frequently used 'vegetable' in cookery; several varieties, including cherry, yellow, globe, large ridged (beef) and plum; used in soups, sauces, salads, sandwiches and as a vegetable; tomatoes are also canned, sundried or semi-dried (sunblush).

Figure 7.90 Fruiting vegetables (clockwise from top left: avocado, Italian aubergine, red pepper, yellow pepper, tomatoes)

Plantains are tropical fruits and include:

- **ackee** – used in Caribbean-style savoury dishes
- **breadfruit** – found on the islands of the South Pacific Ocean.

Mushrooms and fungi, both wild and cultivated, have a great many uses in cookery, in soups, stocks, salads, vegetables, savouries and garnishes. Wild mushrooms are also available in dried form. Types include:

- **mushrooms** – field mushrooms, found in meadows from late summer to autumn; creamy white cap and stalk, and a strong earthy flavour
- **cultivated mushrooms** – available in three types – button (small, succulent, weak in flavour), cap, and open or flat mushrooms
- **ceps** – wild mushrooms with short, stout stalks with slightly raised veins and tubes underneath the cap
- **chanterelles** or **girolles** – wild, funnel-shaped, yellow-capped mushrooms with a slightly ribbed stalk that runs up under the edge of the cap
- **horns of plenty** – trumpet-shaped, shaggy, almost black wild mushrooms
- **morels** – delicate, wild mushrooms varying in colour from pale beige to dark brown-black with a flavour that suggests meat
- **oyster mushrooms** – creamy gills and firm flesh; delicate with a shorter storage life than regular mushrooms
- **shiitake mushrooms** – solid texture with a strong, slightly meaty flavour
- **truffles** – black (French) and white (Italian) are rare, expensive but highly esteemed for their unique flavour; black truffles from France are sold fresh, canned or bottled; white truffles from Italy are never cooked, but grated or finely sliced over certain foods (e.g. pasta, risotto).

Figure 7.91 Mushrooms and fungi (clockwise from top left: girolles, chestnut, pieds du moutons, flat, button, chanterelle, shiitake)

Table 7.4 Seasons for vegetables in the UK

Spring	Summer	Autumn	Winter
Asparagus Cauliflower Cabbage Potatoes Broccoli – white and purple New carrots New turnips New potatoes Greens	Globe artichokes Turnips Asparagus Cauliflower Aubergine Cos lettuce Broad beans Peas Radishes French beans Carrots Sea kale Sweetcorn	Globe artichokes Parsnips Field mushrooms Jerusalem artichokes Aubergine Peppers Runner beans Cauliflower Red cabbage Broccoli Celery Shallots Salsify Swedes Marrow Celeriac Turnips	Brussels sprouts Chicory Cabbage Kale Celery Parsnips Cauliflower Broccoli Red cabbage Savoy cabbage Celeriac Swedes Turnips
All year round			
Although these vegetables are available all year, at certain times – owing to bad weather, heavy demand or other circumstances – supplies may be temporarily curtailed; however, owing to air transport, most vegetables are now available all year round.			
Beetroot Tomatoes Spinach	Mushrooms Leeks Watercress	Cucumber Carrots Lettuce	Onions

Fruit

With the exception of certain fruits (lemon, rhubarb, cranberries) fruit can be eaten as a dessert or in its raw state. Some fruits have dessert and cooking varieties (e.g. apples, pears, cherries and gooseberries).

For culinary purposes fruit can be divided into various groups: stone fruits, hard fruits, soft fruits, citrus fruits, tropical fruits and melons.

Fruits are preserved by the following methods.

- **Drying:** apples, pears, apricots, dates, peaches, bananas and figs are dried; plums when dried are called prunes; currants, sultanas and raisins are produced by drying grapes.
- **Canning:** almost all fruits may be canned; apples are packed in water and known as solid packed apples; other fruits are canned in fruit juice or syrup.
- **Bottling:** the process is very similar to canning and fruit is commercially preserved in this way; cherries are often bottled in maraschino.
- **Candied, glacé and crystallised fruits** are mainly imported from France.
- **Jam:** some stone fruits and all soft fruits can be used.
- **Jelly:** jellies are produced from fruit juice.
- **Quick freezing:** apples, berries, grapefruit and plums are frozen and must be kept below -18°C.
- **Cold storage:** apples are stored at temperatures of between 1 and 4°C, depending on the variety.
- **Gas storage:** fruit can be kept in a sealed storeroom where the atmosphere is controlled; the amount of air is limited, the oxygen content of the air is decreased and the carbon dioxide increased, which controls the respiration rate of the fruit.

Fruit juices such as orange, lemon and blackcurrant are canned. Syrups such as rosehip and orange are bottled. Fruit drinks are also bottled; they include orange, lime and lemon.

Table 7.5 Different fruits and their seasons*

Fruit	Season	Fruit	Season
Apple	All year round	Greengage	August
Apricot	May to September	Lemon	All year round
Avocado pear	All year round	Mandarin	November to June
Banana	All year round	Melon	All year round
Blackberry	September to October	Orange	All year round
Blackcurrants	July to September	Peach	September
Cherry	June to August	Pear	September to March
Clementine	Winter	Pineapple	All year round
Cranberries	November to January	Plum	July to October
Damson	September to October	Raspberry	June to August
Date	Winter	Redcurrants	July to September
Fig	July to September	Rhubarb	December to June
Gooseberry	July to September	Strawberry	June to August
Grapefruit	All year round	Tangerine	Winter
Grapes	All year round		

* Modern transportation and storage methods mean that imported fruits may be available all year.

Stone fruits

Damsons, plums, greengages, cherries, apricots, peaches and nectarines are used as a dessert; stewed (compote) for jam, pies, puddings and in various sweet dishes, and some meat and poultry dishes. Peaches are also used to garnish certain meat dishes. Varieties of plums include dessert, Victoria, Gamota, Mayoris, Burbank; for cooking, Angelina, Stanley, Beech Cherry and Reeves Seedling.

Stone fruits are best placed in trays for storage, so that any damaged fruit can be seen and discarded. Peaches can be refrigerated.

Figure 7.92 Stone fruits (clockwise from top: mango, plums, nectarines, dates)

Hard fruits

The popular English dessert apple varieties include Beauty of Bath, Discovery, Spartan, Worcester Pearmain, Cox's Orange Pippin, Blenheim Orange, Pink Lady, Laxton's Superb and James Grieve; imported apples include Golden Delicious, Braeburn and Gala. The Bramley is the most popular cooking apple.

The William, Conference and Doyenne du Comice are among the best-known pears. Other varieties include: Anjou, Beurre-Beth, Beurre-Bose, Beurre-Hardi, Beurre-Supersin, Forelle, Morton Poirde, Onwaide, Rocha, Housi and Perry Tientsin.

Apples and pears are used in many pastry dishes. Apples are also used for garnishing meat dishes and for sauce served with roast pork and duck.

To ensure quality, hard fruits should not be bruised, and pears should not be overripe.

Hard fruits are left in boxes and kept in a cool store.

Figure 7.93 Hard fruits (clockwise from top left: Comice pears, quinces, William pears, Braeburn apples, crab apples, Red Delicious apples)

Soft fruits

Raspberries, strawberries, loganberries and gooseberries are used as a dessert.

Gooseberries, blackcurrants, redcurrants and blackberries are stewed, used in pies and puddings, or may be used for decorative purposes. They are used for jam and flavourings, and in certain sauces for sweet and savoury dishes.

Other varieties of soft fruit include: dewberries, jam berries, young berries, boysenberries, sunberries, wineberries, blueberries and elderberries. Varieties of gooseberries include: Leveller, London and Golden Drop.

Soft fruits deteriorate quickly, especially if not sound. Care must be taken to see that they are not damaged or too ripe when bought. They should appear fresh; there should be no shrinking, wilting or signs of mould. The colour of certain soft fruits is an indication of ripeness (e.g. strawberries, dessert gooseberries).

Soft fruits, such as raspberries and strawberries, should be left in their punnets or baskets and refrigerated.

Figure 7.94 Soft fruits (clockwise from top: redcurrants, raspberries, blackberries, strawberries)

Citrus fruits

Oranges, lemons, limes and grapefruit are not usually cooked, except for use in marmalade. Lemons and limes are used for flavouring and garnishing, particularly of fish dishes. Oranges are used mainly for flavouring and in fruit salads, also to garnish poultry dishes. Grapefruit are served at breakfast and as a first course. Mandarins, clementines and satsumas are eaten as a dessert or used in sweet dishes. Kumquats look like tiny oranges and are eaten with the skin on; the flavour is more bitter than oranges. Tangelos are a cross between tangerines and grapefruit, and are sometimes called uglis. Pomelos are the largest of the citrus fruits, predominantly round but with a slightly flattened base and pointed top.

Citrus fruits are left in their delivery trays or boxes for storage, and can be refrigerated.

Figure 7.95 Citrus fruits (clockwise from top left: pink grapefruit, orange, lemons, limes, satsuma, white grapefruit)

Tropical and other fruits

- **Banana:** as well as being used as a dessert, bananas are grilled for a fish garnish, fried as fritters and served as a garnish to poultry (Maryland); they are used in fruit salad and other sweet dishes. Bananas should not be stored in too cold a place because the skins will turn black.
- **Bubaco:** hybrid of the papaya.
- **Cape gooseberry (physalis):** a sharp, pleasant-flavoured small round fruit, sometimes dipped in fondant and served as a type of petit four.
- **Carambola (starfruit):** has a yellowish-green skin with a waxy sheen; the fruit is long and narrow and has a delicate lemon flavour.
- **Cranberry:** these hard red berries are used for cranberry sauce, which is served with roast turkey, and cranberry juice.
- **Curuba (banana passion fruit):** has soft yellowish skin.
- **Custard apple:** heart-shaped or oval, light tan or greenish quilted skin; soursops (prickly custard apples) have dark-green skins covered in short spines.
- **Date:** whole dates are served as a dessert; stoned dates are used in various sweet dishes and petits fours.
- **Dragon fruit:** yellow or pink; pink are large, about 10 cm long and covered with pointed green-tipped scales.
- **Durian:** large fruit that can weigh up to 4.5 kg; round or oval, have a woolly olive-green outer layer covered with stubby, sharp pikes, which turn yellow as they ripen; contains creamy white flesh with the texture of rich custard.
- **Feijon:** member of the guava family, resembles small slightly pear-shaped passion fruit, with a dark-green skin that yellows as the fruit ripens.
- **Fig:** fresh figs may be served as a first course or dessert; dried figs may be used for fig puddings and other sweet dishes.
- **Granadilla:** largest members of the passion fruit family; like an orange in shape and colour, light in weight and similar to a passion fruit in flavour.
- **Grape:** black and white grapes are used as a dessert, in salads and fruit salad, and also as a fish garnish.
- **Guava:** vary from walnut-sized to apple-sized; ripe guavas have a sweet pink flesh and can be eaten with cream or mixed with other fruits.
- **Jackfruit:** related to breadfruit; the large, irregularly shaped oval fruits can weigh up to 20 kg; they have a rough spiny skin, which ripens from green to brown.
- **Jujube (Chinese jujubes/apples/dates):** small greeny-brown fruit.
- **Kiwano (horned melon, horned cucumber, jelly melon):** the oval fruits have thick, bright golden-orange skin covered with sharp spikes. The skin conceals a bright green, jelly-like flesh, encasing edible seeds, rather like a passion fruit.
- **Kiwi fruit:** have a brown furry skin; the flesh is green with edible black seeds that, when thinly sliced, gives a decorative appearance.
- **Kumquat:** about the size of an olive. The skin is edible, and tastes and smells distinctly orangey.
- **Longan:** very similar to lychees, they have translucent perfumed flesh and a central inedible stone.
- **Loquat (Japanese medlar):** has a sweet scent and a delicate mango-like flavour.
- **Lychee:** has a delicate flavour, obtainable tinned in syrup and also fresh.
- **Mango:** can be as large as a melon or as small as an apple; ripe mangoes have smooth pinky-golden flesh with a pleasing flavour; they may be served in halves sprinkled with lemon juice, sugar, rum or ginger; mangoes can also be used in fruit desserts and for sorbets.
- **Mangosteen:** apple-shaped with tough reddish-brown skin, which turns purple as the fruit ripens; they have juicy creamy flesh.
- **Maracoya (yellow passion fruit):** vibrant green with a thick shiny skin, which turns yellow as it ripens; inside has orange pulp enclosing hard grey seeds.
- **Nashi pear (Japanese pear):** firm white flesh, yellow to rosy-pink skin, very aromatic juicy fruit, shaped like a round pear.

- **Palm fruit:** harvested from the Palmyra or Toddy palm, which grows wild; the shiny nut contains oval gelatinous seeds that are opaque and very sweet.
- **Passion fruit:** the size of an egg but slightly rounder, with crinkled purple-brown skin when ripe; flesh and seeds are all edible but not the outer husk; has many uses in pastry work.
- **Pawpaw (papaya):** green to golden skin, orangey flesh with a sweet subtle flavour and black seeds; eaten raw sprinkled with lime or lemon juice; served with shellfish and mayonnaise as a first course.
- **Pepino (tree melon):** smooth golden skin heavily streaked with purple.
- **Persimmon:** a round orange-red fruit with a tough skin, which can be cut when the fruit is ripe; when under-ripe they have an unpleasant acid-like taste of tannin.
- **Physalis ('Peruvian cherry'):** tiny orange-coloured fruit, size of a gooseberry.
- **Pineapple:** served as a dessert; also used in many sweet dishes and as a garnish to certain meat dishes.
- **Pomegranate:** apple-shaped fruit with leathery reddish-brown skin, and a large calyx, or crown; inside is a mass of creamy-white edible seeds, each encased in a tiny translucent juice sac.
- **Pomelo:** largest of the citrus fruits, has a thick dimpled green yellow skin, shaped like a flat rugby ball.
- **Prickly pear ('Indian fig'):** fruit of the cactus; skin is covered in prickles; greenish-orange skin and orangey-pink flesh with a melon-like texture.
- **Quince:** golden-yellow skin, pear-like shape, highly aromatic, usually used in cooking with game, pork or in preserves.
- **Rambutan ('hairy lychee'):** related to the lychee.
- **Rhubarb:** forced, or early, rhubarb is obtainable from January, natural rhubarb from April to June; used for pies, puddings, fools and compotes.
- **Sapodilla:** oval fruit with light-brown skin, the flesh is sweet, with inedible hard black pips.
- **Sharon fruit:** a seedless persimmon tasting like a sweet exotic peach.
- **Snake fruit:** large member of the lychee family; the creamy flesh is divided into four segments each encasing a very large inedible brown stone.
- **Tamarillo ('tree tomato'):** large egg-shaped fruits with thick, smooth wine-red skins; each fruit has two lobes containing a multitude of black seeds.
- **Tamarind:** red, egg-shaped, flavour a mix of tomato, apricot and coconut, used in curries, sweet dishes and salads.
- **Ugli fruit:** closely related to the grapefruit, available March to October.

Figure 7.96 Tropical fruits (clockwise from top left: pineapple, papaya, coconut, kiwis, passion fruit)

Melons

There are several types of melon, including:

- **honeydew** – long and oval shaped with dark green or yellow skins; the flesh is white with a greenish tinge
- **charentais** – small and round with a mottled green and yellow skin; the flesh is orange coloured
- **cantaloupe** – large and round with regular indentations; the rough skin is mottled orange and yellow, and the flesh is light orange in colour
- **ogen** – small and round, mottled green skin, each suitable for one portion (depending on size); mainly used as a dessert, hors d'oeuvre or in sweet dishes
- **watermelon** – large and round with hard, green skin; the flesh is red, not particularly sweet and contains large brown pips.

Figure 7.97 Melons (clockwise from top: watermelon, cantaloupe, honeydew, ogen)

Care must be taken when buying as melons should not be over- or under-ripe. This can be assessed by carefully pressing the top or bottom of the fruit and smelling the outside skin for sweetness. There should be a slight degree of softness to cantaloupe and charentais melons. The stalk should be attached, otherwise the melon deteriorates quickly.

WEBLINK

For further information, visit the website of the Fresh Produce Consortium:

www.freshproduce.org.uk

Nuts

Nuts are the reproductive kernel (seed) of the plant or tree from which they come. Nuts are used extensively in pastry and confectionery work and vegetarian cookery, and also for decorating and flavouring. They are used whole or halved, and almonds are used ground, nibbed and flaked.

Some people have an allergy to some nuts, which can cause severe illness and possibly death.

There are different types of nuts. Tree nuts include almond, hazelnut, pistachio, cashew, walnut and Brazil nuts. These are not to be confused or grouped together with peanut, which is a legume, or seeds, such as sesame or sunflower.

Dessert nuts are in season in the UK during the autumn and winter.

Nuts are perishable and may easily become rancid or infested with insects. Dessert nuts, with the shell on, are kept in a dry, ventilated store. Nuts without shells, whether ground, nibbed, flaked or whole, are kept in airtight containers.

Purchasing points:

- nuts should be of good size and heavy for their size
- there must be no sign of mildew.

Types of nut include:

- **almonds** – salted almonds are served at cocktail parties and in bars; ground, flaked or nibbed almonds are used in sweet dishes and for decorating cakes
- **Brazil nuts** – served with fresh fruit as dessert; also used in confectionery
- **chestnuts** – used in certain stews, with vegetables (e.g. Brussels sprouts) and as stuffing for turkey; chestnut flour is used for soup, and as a garnish for ice cream; chestnut purée is used in pastries and gateaux; chestnuts are also available dried
- **cob** or **hazel nuts** – used as a dessert and in praline; chopped or ground, they have many uses in pastry work
- **coconut** – used in desiccated form for curry preparations, and in many types of cakes and confectionery; coconut cream and milk are also made and used in West Indian, Malaysian and Thai cookery
- **macadamia nuts** – expensive nuts with a rich, delicate, sweetish flavour; can be used in pasta dishes, savoury sauces, and in ice cream, sorbets and puddings
- **peanuts** and **cashew nuts** – can be salted and used as bar snacks; also used in some stir-fry dishes; peanuts are also used for oil and peanut butter
- **pecans** – usually roasted and may be salted; also used for desserts, various sweets and ice cream
- **pine nuts** – seeds of the stone pine; an important ingredient in pesto
- **pistachios** – small green nuts; popular eaten straight from the shell, and used for decorating galantines, cakes and petits fours; also used in ice cream and confectionery such as nougat
- **walnuts** – used as a dessert, in salads and for decorating cakes and sweet dishes; they are also pickled while green and unripe, and used for making oil.

Eggs

Around 26 million hens' eggs are consumed each day in the UK and approximately 85 per cent of these are produced in the UK. Turkeys' and guinea fowls' eggs may be used in place of hens' eggs. The eggs of the goose or duck may be used only if they are thoroughly cooked. Quails' eggs are used as a garnish, in soups and salads, or as an hors d'oeuvre.

The British Egg Products Association (BEPA) has a strict Code of Practice that covers all stages of production, from the sourcing of raw materials to packaging and finished production standards. Members of the BEPA can qualify to show a date stamp on their products, which signifies that the eggs have been produced to standards higher than those demanded by UK and European law. The aim of the date stamp is to reduce the risk of infection in hens, and to ensure that eggs are held and distributed under the best conditions.

Whole egg is used primarily for cake production, where its foaming and coagulation properties are required. Egg whites are used for meringues and light sponges where their foaming property is crucial.

The structure of eggs

The egg white is divided into a thick layer around the yolk and a thinner layer next to the shell. The thick layer anchors the yolk, together with the chalazae (two spiral bands of tissue that suspend the yolk in the centre of the white), in the middle of the egg, where it is less vulnerable to microbial attack. The egg white possesses special antibacterial properties, which under normal circumstances prevent the growth and multiplication of micro-organisms that have entered the shell. The yolk is rich in nutrients and is the part of the egg that is most vulnerable to micro-organisms.

Egg yolks are high in saturated fat, while egg whites are made up of protein and water.

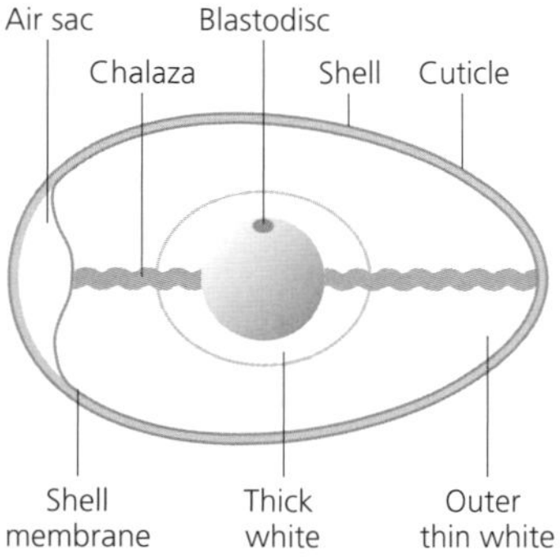

Figure 7.98 The structure of an egg

Table 7.6 The composition of eggs (approximate percentages)

	Whole egg	White	Yolk
Water	73%	87%	47%
Protein	12%	10%	15%
Fat	11%		33%
Minerals	1%	0.5%	2%

Purchasing and quality points

When buying eggs the following points should be noted.

- The egg's shell should be clean, well shaped, strong and slightly rough.
- When eggs are broken there should be a high proportion of thick white to thin white. If an egg is kept, the thick white gradually changes into thin white, and water passes from the white into the yolk.
- The yolk should be firm, round (not flattened) and of a good, even colour. As eggs are kept, the yolk loses strength and begins to flatten, water evaporates from the egg and is replaced by air.
- Cracked eggs should not be used.

Candling of eggs is a method that is used for checking the quality of eggs. The egg is illuminated with a light so the flaws can be seen, including the yolk position and size, the size of the air sac, and the presence of blood or meat spots.

Always purchase fresh eggs from sources where there is no salmonella contamination (see below) or from a low-risk supplier. In the UK, look for the 'Lion' quality mark on the egg shell and egg box – it shows that the eggs have been produced to the highest standards of food safety, including a programme of vaccination against *Salmonella enteritidis*. All egg boxes leaving the packing station are dated. Always buy eggs from a reputable retailer, where they will have been transported and stored at the correct temperature (below 20°C).

Under European law eggs are graded for quality using the following system.

- Grade A: naturally clean, fresh eggs, internally perfect with intact shells and an air sac not exceeding 6 mm in depth.
- Grade B: eggs that have been downgraded because they have been cleaned or preserved, or because they are internally imperfect, cracked or have an air sac exceeding 6 mm but not more than 9 mm in depth. Grade B eggs are broken out and pasteurised.
- Grade C: eggs that are fit for breaking for manufacturing purposes but cannot be sold in their shells to the public.

All Class A eggs have to be marked with a code showing the country of origin and the farm or unit where they were produced. The code also includes a number to indicate the farming method used: 0 means organic; 1 free range; 2 barn; 3 cage.

Hens' eggs are also graded in four sizes:

1. small, 53 g or under
2. medium, 53–63 g
3. large, 63–73 g
4. very large, 73 g and over.

WEBLINK

For more information on the British Lion quality mark, see:
www.lioneggfarms.co.uk

Eggs and salmonella

Hens can pass salmonella bacteria into their eggs and therefore cause food poisoning. Most infections cause only mild stomach upsets, but the effects can be serious in vulnerable people such as the elderly, the infirm, pregnant women and young children.

To reduce this risk, pasteurised eggs may be used where appropriate. (Pasteurised eggs are heat treated – see Chapter 3.)

In a number of salmonella food poisoning cases, raw eggs have been suspected as the cause. Consumers, particularly the more vulnerable, are advised to avoid eating raw and lightly cooked eggs, uncooked foods made from raw eggs, and products such as mayonnaise, mousses and ice creams. Caterers are advised to use pasteurised eggs. Dishes with an obvious risk of passing on contamination also include soft-boiled eggs, scrambled eggs and omelettes. The UK's Department of Health has issued the following guidelines, which apply to raw eggs.

- Grade B eggs are always broken out and pasteurised.
- There does not appear to be a similar risk with eggs that are cooked thoroughly.

- Eggs should be stored in a cool, dry place, preferably under refrigeration.
- Eggs should be stored away from possible contaminants such as raw meat.
- Stocks should be rotated: first in, first out.
- Hands should be washed before and after handling eggs.
- Cracked eggs should not be used.
- Preparation surfaces, utensils and containers should be cleaned regularly and always cleaned between the preparation of different dishes.
- Egg dishes should be consumed as soon as possible after preparation or, if not for immediate use, refrigerated.

Egg products

Many egg products are available in liquid, frozen or spray-dried form.

Convenience egg products, which will carry the date stamp, include:

- pasteurised whole egg, yolk or albumen*†‡
- salted whole egg, or yolk*†
- sugared whole egg, or yolk*†‡
- sugared albumen*
- egg granules†
- hard-boiled eggs*
- pickled eggs
- chopped hard-boiled egg with mayonnaise*
- scrambled egg*†
- omelettes†
- egg custard blend*‡
- quiche blend*†
- eggmilk blends*†‡

Key: * chilled † frozen ‡ dried

WEBLINK

For further information on eggs, visit:
www.egginfo.co.uk

Dairy products

Milk

Milk is a white, nutritious liquid produced by female mammals for feeding their young. The milk most used in that the UK is obtained from cows. Goats' milk and ewes' milk can also be used.

Milk is used in:

- soups and sauces
- puddings, cakes and sweet dishes
- the cooking of fish and vegetables
- hot and cold drinks.

Storage and packaging

Milk is a perishable product and therefore must be stored with care. It will keep for four to five days in refrigerated conditions. Milk can easily be contaminated and therefore stringent precautions are taken to ensure a safe and good-quality product for the consumer.

Unless milk is supplied directly from the farm, it will be heat-treated in one of the ways described below. Heat treatment will bring any bacteria present down to a safe level, or destroy them altogether.

- Fresh milk should be kept in the container in which it is delivered.
- Milk should be kept covered as it easily absorbs smells from other foods, such as onion and fish.
- Fresh milk should be ordered daily.
- Tinned milk should be stored in cool, dry, ventilated rooms.
- Dried milk is packaged in airtight tins and should be kept in a dry store.
- Sterilised milk will keep for two to three months if unopened, but once opened must be treated in the same way as pasteurised milk.
- UHT (ultra-heat treated) milk will keep unrefrigerated for several months. Before using, always check the date stamp, which expires six months after processing, and make sure to rotate stocks. Once opened it must be refrigerated and will keep for four to five days.

Bulk fresh milk can be supplied in a variety of packages. The most common is a plastic bag-in-box, with a capacity of between 12 and 20 litres. This should be placed in the appropriate refrigerated unit and the contents can be drawn off as required by fitting the correct tap device.

Other types of packaging include:

- polybottles (large plastic bottles) of fresh milk available in 1-litre, 2-litre and 3-litre sizes
- cartons of fresh milk available in 0.5-litre and 1-litre sizes.

Almost all milk is homogenised (see below), and available whole, semi-skimmed or skimmed. Channel Island milk from the Jersey and Guernsey breeds of cow usually has a higher fat content than whole milk; it is often non-homogenised.

Milk heat treatment and types of milk

Most milk is homogenised: milk is forced through a fine aperture that breaks up the fat globules to an even size so that they stay evenly distributed throughout the milk and therefore do not form a cream line.

Milk, including homogenised, is heat treated in one of several ways to kill any harmful bacteria that may be present.

Approximately 99 per cent of milk sold in the UK is heat treated by pasteurisation, sterilisation or ultra-heat treatment (UHT). See Chapter 3 for descriptions of these processes.

Types of cows' milk and milk products include:

- **whole milk** – has a fat content of an average 3.9 per cent
- **semi-skimmed milk** – has a fat content of between 1.5 and 1.8 per cent
- **skimmed milk** – contains just 0.1 per cent fat
- **organic milk** – comes from cows grazing on pastures with no chemical fertilisers, pesticides or agrochemicals, meeting the strict requirements of the Soil Association
- **Channel Islands milk** – comes from the Jersey and Guernsey breeds of cow, and has a particularly rich and creamy taste; it is not usually homogenised and has a distinct cream line; it contains, on average, 5.1 per cent fat
- **evaporated milk** – a concentrated sterilised product with a final concentration about twice that of the original milk
- **condensed milk** – concentrated in the same way as evaporated milk but with the addition of sugar; this product is not sterilised but is preserved by the high concentration of sugar it contains
- **dried milk powder** – produced by the evaporation of water from milk by heat, or other means, to produce solids containing 5 per cent or less moisture; available as a whole or skimmed product
- **dried milk** – skimmed milk powder to which vegetable fat has been added.

Alternatives to cows' milk, useful for people with an intolerance to it, include:

- **soya milk** (also suitable for vegan diets)
- **goats' milk** – nutritionally similar to cows' milk
- **rice milk** – heat stable, which makes it a good replacement for cows' milk in cooking, although it tends to have a sweeter taste; also suitable for vegan diets
- **coconut milk** – not to be confused with the 'milk' or juice found inside the fresh coconut; the coconut milk used for cooking is produced from the white flesh of the coconut; if left to stand, the thick part of the milk will rise to the surface like cream; coconut milk is high in saturated fats; it can be served as a drink but is more often used as an ingredient and a base for sauces.

Cream

Cream is the lighter-weight portion of milk, which still contains all the main constituents of milk but in different proportions. The fat content of cream is higher than that of milk, and the water content and other constituents are lower. Cream is separated from the milk and heat treated. Cream is that part of cows' milk rich in fat that has been separated from the milk.

Table 7.7 shows the most used types of cream. Other creams available include:

- extra-thick double cream (48 per cent) homogenised and pasteurised – will not whip
- spooning cream or extra thick textured cream (30 per cent)
- frozen cream (single, whipping or double)
- aerosol cream – heat-treated by UHT method to give a highly aerated cream
- soured cream (18 per cent) cream soured by addition of a 'starter' – a culture or lactic acid
- crème fraîche –made from double cream with the addition of buttermilk, soured cream or yogurt; lower-fat versions are now available.

Table 7.7 Types of cream and their fat content

	Minimum butterfat content per cent by weight
Clotted cream	55
Double cream	48
Whipping cream	35
Whipped cream	35
Sterilised cream	23
Cream or single cream	18
Sterilised half cream	12
Half cream	12

For cream to be whipped it must have fat content of 38–42 per cent. If the fat content is too low there will not be enough fat to enclose the air bubbles and form the foam. Conversely, if the fat content is too high, the fat globules come into contact too easily, move against one another and form butter granules before the air can be incorporated to form the foam.

The addition of stabilisers to cream prevents seepage (particularly important when cream is used in flour confectionery). Cream substitutes are, in the main, based on vegetable fats or oils, which are emulsified in water with other permitted substances.

Storage guidelines:

- fresh cream should be kept in the container in which it is delivered
- fresh cream must be stored in the refrigerator until required
- cream should be kept covered as it easily absorbs smells from other foods, such as onion and fish
- fresh cream should be ordered daily
- tinned cream should be stored in cool, dry, ventilated rooms, and refrigerated after opening
- frozen cream should be thawed only as required and not refrozen
- artificial cream made from vegetable oil should be kept in the refrigerator.

Ice cream and other frozen dairy products

Ice cream is made by churning (stirring), while freezing, a pasteurised mix of one or more dairy ingredients – milk, concentrated fat-free milk, cream, condensed milk – sweetening agents, flavourings, stabilisers, emulsifiers, and optional egg or egg yolk solids or other ingredients.

Other products include the following.

- Frozen custard (French ice cream, French custard ice cream) is similar to ice cream but contains a higher content of egg yolk solids.
- Reduced-fat ice cream, low-fat ice cream, light (lite) ice cream and fat-free ice cream all contain less fat per serving.
- Sherbet contains 1 to 2 per cent milk fat and 2 to 5 per cent total milk solids. Water, flavouring (e.g. fruit, chocolate, spices), sweetener and stabilisers are added. Sherbet has more sugar than ice cream.
- Frozen yoghurt is made by freezing a mixture of pasteurised milk, with or without other milk products, flavourings, seasonings, stabilisers, emulsifiers and lactic acid cultures.

Ice cream and frozen yoghurt can be nutritious foods providing high-quality protein, riboflavin (B2), calcium and other essential vitamins and minerals. The calorie and fat content varies depending on the type of milk used and the addition of cream, egg yolk solids or sweetening agents.

WEBLINK

For further information, contact the Ice Cream Alliance: **www.ice-cream.org**

Fermented milk products

Yoghurt is a cultured milk product. Differences in the taste and texture depend on the type of milk used (e.g. cows', goats') and the activity of the micro-organisms involved. A bacterial 'starter culture' is added to the milk, which causes the natural sugar 'lactose' to ferment and produce lactic acid. There are three types of yoghurt:

1. stirred yoghurt, which has a smooth fluid consistency
2. set yoghurt, which is more solid and has a firmer texture
3. Greek-style yoghurt, a smooth yoghurt that has been stirred then strained to remove some of the water content, resulting in a thick, heavy yoghurt.

All yoghurt is 'live' and contains live bacteria that remain dormant when kept at low temperatures, unless it clearly states on the packaging that it has been pasteurised, sterilised or ultra-heat treated. If stored at room temperature or above, the dormant bacteria become active again and produce more acid. Too high an acidity kills the bacteria, impairs the flavour and causes the yoghurt to separate. Yoghurt will keep refrigerated for up to 14 days.

Yoghurt is available plain (natural) or in a wide variety of flavours; it often has pieces of fruit added during manufacture. Yoghurt beverages are available in a variety of flavours.

Other fermented milk products include:

- **cultured buttermilk** – made from skimmed milk with a culture added to give it a slightly thickened consistency and a sharp taste; it contains less than 0.5 per cent fat and should be kept refrigerated
- **smetana** – a cultured product containing 10 per cent fat; it has a slightly sharp flavour and can be served chilled as a drink or used as an alternative to soured cream.

Table 7.8 The fat content of yoghurt

	% fat content per 150 g pot
Very low fat – plain (natural)/fruit	0.3
Low fat – plain (natural)/ fruit	1.1–1.2
Whole milk/creamy	4.2
Greek, Greek style	13.7, 2 or 0

Cheese

Cheese is made from milk protein coagulated by an enzyme such as rennet (an animal product). For vegetarian cheese a non-animal enzyme is used instead of rennet. It takes approximately 5 litres of milk to produce 0.5 kg of cheese.

Cheese is made worldwide. There are many hundreds of varieties, and most countries manufacture their own special cheeses.

It is used in soups, pasta, egg, fish and vegetable dishes, and savouries.

Storage, quality and hygiene

Quality points:

- cheese, when cut, should not give off an over-strong smell or any indication of ammonia
- hard, semi-hard and blue-vein cheese, when cut, should not be dry
- soft cheese, when cut, should not appear runny, but should have a delicate creamy consistency.

Cheese is a living product and should be handled carefully. It should always be wrapped in greaseproof or waxed paper or foil, or put in a closed container. Natural rind can be exposed to air, so it can breathe, but cut surfaces should be covered with film to prevent drying out.

All cheese should be kept in a cool, dry, well-ventilated store and whole cheeses should be turned occasionally if being kept for any length of time. If refrigerated, cheese should have plenty of air circulating around it.

The skin or rind of cheese should not show spots of mildew, as this is a sign of damp storage.

Remove cheese from the refrigerator about an hour before serving to allow it to return to room temperature.

Listeria can grow and multiply at a lower temperature than most bacteria, especially at 10°C or warmer, and this can be a risk in soft unpasteurised cheeses.

Mould-ripened cheeses should be separated from other cheeses. Cheese should be kept away from other foods that may be spoilt by the smell.

Figure 7.99 A selection of cheeses

Certain hard cheeses may be further preserved by processing. The cheese is ground to a fine powder, melted, mixed with pasteurised milk and poured into moulds (e.g. processed Gruyère, Kraft, Primula, Dairylea).

WEBLINK

To find out more about all dairy products, visit the Dairy Council's website at:

www.milk.co.uk

Types of cheese

British cheeses are usually named after the region where they are made. Most are made from cows' milk. Some examples are listed in Table 7.9.

Table 7.9 Examples of British cheeses

Name	Type	Appearance, flavour and other features
Barkham Blue	Blue	Creamy and rich mould rind
Beacon Fell	Semi-soft	Made from a three-day-old curd and matured for up to three months
Bowland	Hard	A type of Lancashire cheese mixed with apple, sultana and cinnamon prior to setting
Caboc	Cream	Made with double cream or cream-enriched milk. This rennet-free cheese is formed into a log shape and rolled in toasted pinhead oatmeal
Caerphilly	Hard	White in colour and flaky, with a fresh, mild, slightly salty flavour
Cheddar	Hard	Pale to golden colour with a close texture and a fresh mellow, nutty flavour, mild to mature
Cheshire	Hard	Orange-red or white, loose crumbly texture and a mild mellow, slightly salty flavour
Cornish blue	Blue	Creamy blue cheese
Cornish Yarg	Semi-hard	Made from the milk from Friesian cows. Before being left to mature the cheese is wrapped in nettle leaves to form an edible, though moulding, rind
Dorset Blue Vinney	Blue	A traditional blue cheese, hard and crumbly, made near Sturminster Newton in Dorset from skimmed cows' milk
Double Gloucester	Hard	Orange-yellow, a buttery open texture with a delicate creamy flavour
Dovedale	Semi-soft	Full-fat, blue-veined
Dunlop	Hard	A Scottish equivalent of Cheddar, milder and lighter in colour and texture
Lanark Blue	Blue	Made from unpasteurised sheep's milk
Lancashire	Hard	White in colour, soft and crumbly with a fresh, mild flavour
Leicester	Hard	Red colour; buttery open texture; mellow medium strength
Lincolnshire Poacher	Hard	Unpasteurised; its rind resembles granite in appearance
Sage Derby	Semi-hard	Mild flavour; mottled green with a hint of garden sage running throughout
Shropshire Blue	Blue	A blue cheese made from pasteurised milk with vegetable rennet
Stilton	Blue	Soft and close texture, and a strong flavour
Stinking Bishop		A washed rind cheese made from the milk of Gloucester breed heifers
Swaledale	Hard	Full-fat
Wensleydale	Hard	Moderately close texture with a fresh, mild, slightly salty flavour

Some examples of French cheeses are:

- **Brie** – white, round cheese with close, soft, creamy texture and delicate flavour
- **Camembert** – white, round with soft, close, creamy texture and full flavour
- **chèvre** – a generic name for a wide range of goats' cheeses
- **Fourme d'Ambert** – sometimes called a French Stilton; salty, full flavour
- **Roquefort** – blue cheese made from ewes' milk; rich, sharp flavour with salty aftertaste.

Some examples of Italian cheeses are:

- **bel paese** – round, firm, pearly-white texture and a fresh, creamy taste
- **Gorgonzola** – blue vein with a rich, sharp flavour; **dolcelatte** is a milder version
- **mascarpone** – rich, creamy, slightly acrid, used mainly in desserts
- **mozzarella** – traditionally made from buffalo milk; pale and plastic looking, sweet flavour with a little bite
- **Parmesan** – hard, low-fat cheese; grated and used extensively in cooking
- **ricotta** – fresh, white, crumbly and slightly sweet, similar to cottage cheese.

Some other cheeses from around the world are:

- Ireland – **Cashel blue**, a creamy rich blue cheese
- Netherlands – **Edam**, round, full flavoured with low fat content; covered in red skin
- Switzerland – **Gruyère**, firm, creamy white with a full fruity flavour
- Greece – **feta**, white, moist, crumbly with a refreshing salty-sour taste
- Cyprus – **halloumi**, a rubbery white cheese usually served grilled and hot so the cheese softens.

Soft curd cheeses

These are made from pasteurised milk, a milk-souring culture and rennet. They are soft, milk-flavoured, low-fat (11 per cent) cheeses; made from either skimmed or medium-fat milk. Some particular types of curd cheese are:

- **cottage cheese** – a low-fat, high-protein product made from skimmed milk; many varieties are available
- **fromage frais** or **fromage blanc** – a fat-free type to which cream can be added to give richer varieties; many types are available
- **quark** – a salt-free, fat-free type made from skimmed milk.

There is a range of hard cheese with half the fat of traditional cheese.

Fats and oils

Fats should be kept in a refrigerator.

Butter

Butter is a natural dairy product made by churning fresh, pasteurised cream. During churning, the butterfat globules in the cream coalesce to form butter and the excess liquid (buttermilk) is drained off.

There are two types of butter: lactic ('continental taste') and sweetcream. In lactic butter, the cream is ripened before churning with a lactobacillus culture. This produces a mildly acidic flavour. In sweetcream butter, produced in the UK, Republic of Ireland and New Zealand, the cream is not ripened.

Salt is added to sweetcream butter, between 1 and 2.5 per cent, to enhance its flavour and shelf life. The mild acidity in lactic butter extends its shelf life, so this butter is available with or without added salt.

Apart from the salt, there are no additives in butter. The colour is entirely natural, and varies slightly according to the type of butter, the breed of cow and the pastures on which they feed. Seasonal variations affect the colour slightly, as the cow's diet changes during the year.

Quality and storage

The flavour of butter is rich, creamy and mellow. The colour varies from a delicate pale yellow to a rich, bright colour. The texture is smooth and creamy, and butter remains firm when chilled.

It should be kept refrigerated, covered, below 5°C for optimum quality, where it can be kept for up to six weeks. Butter kept at room temperature soon deteriorates and exposure to light causes rancidity. Store butter away from strong flavours or smells that could taint its delicate taste.

Uses

The unique taste and texture of butter mean that it has many uses and improves the flavour and appearance of many foods.

Butter is used as a base for soups, sauces, compound butters and hard butter sauces like brandy butter. It is also used in cakes and pastries, icings and frostings. Sometimes unsalted butter is chosen for these recipes.

Butter is ideal for shallow-frying foods, but it is not suitable for stir-frying or deep-frying, where higher temperatures would cause the butter to burn. Melted butter is used to baste grilled foods, and can be combined with chopped fresh herbs, grated citrus rind, and so on, to vary the flavour.

For finishing cooked foods, butter can be used as a glaze.

In sandwiches, butter acts as a protective layer, preventing moist foods from permeating the bread. The butter also gives a delicious flavour.

Clarified butter can be made by gently heating butter until it has melted and separated. The milk solids can then be strained off and the resultant clarified butter used at higher temperatures. Ghee is a type of clarified butter, widely used as the basis of Indian cooking. A type of clarified butter known as concentrated butter is made by removing most of the water and milk solids. It is suitable for cooking and baking, but not for spreading or finishing foods.

Margarine

Margarine is produced from milk and a blend of vegetable oils emulsified with lecithin, flavouring, salt, colouring, and vitamins A and D.

There are several grades of margarine: block (hard or semi-hard); soft (butter substitute); semi-hard for making pastry; and cake margarine, which creams easily and absorbs egg. Some margarines are blended with butter; others are primarily produced as spreads.

Uses

Margarine can be used in place of butter, but the flavour and aroma of nut brown (beurre noisette) or black butter (beurre noir) cannot satisfactorily be produced from margarine.

The flavour of margarine is inferior to butter – it is therefore not so suitable for finishing sauces and dishes. However, is equally nutritious and is often cheaper than butter.

Alternatives

Vegetable shortening and high-ratio fat are available. They are used extensively in bakery products to achieve products with the desired finish.

Low-fat spreads have a similar composition to margarine but are lower in fat, with 40 per cent or, in very low-fat products, as little as 5 per cent fat. These spreads are blended with oils, water, skimmed milk or buttermilk. They may be fortified with vitamins A and D although this is not required by law.

WEBLINK

European Margarine Association:
www.imace.org

Animal fats

- **Lard:** lard is the rendered fat from pigs. It has almost 100 per cent fat content. It may be used in hot-water paste and with margarine to make short paste. It can also be used for deep- or shallow-frying.
- **Suet:** suet is the hard solid fat deposits in the kidney region of animals. Beef suet is the best, and is used for suet paste and mincemeat.
- **Dripping:** dripping is obtained from clarified animal fats (usually beef) and is used for deep- or shallow-frying.

Oils

Types of oil include:

- peanut (groundnut)
- cotton seed
- palm
- rapeseed
- olive
- coconut
- soya bean
- sunflower
- palm
- corn
- speciality (e.g. almond, grapeseed, hazelnut, walnut).

Oils are used for deep-frying, and to lubricate utensils and slabs. They are ingredients in mayonnaise, vinaigrette and hors d'oeuvres. Pasta, certain doughs and breads use olive oil.

The choice of an oil as a food ingredient or for cooking will depend on factors including:

- price – variations will occur according to supply and demand
- intended use – some oils are more versatile than others
- flavour – e.g. olive oil has a distinctive flavour, but sunflower oil tends to have a bland flavour
- durability – in use and in storage
- nutritional and health concerns
- flash point – for frying, an oil must reach a high temperature without smoking; food being fried will absorb the oil if the oil smokes at a low temperature; however, as oils are combustible they can catch fire at their flash-point temperature; in some cases the margin between smoking and the flash point may be narrow.

As oil has a very high fat content it is useful as an energy food.

Oils keep for a fairly long time but may go rancid if not kept in a cool place. If refrigerated, some oils congeal but will return to a fluid state when removed from the refrigerator.

Herbal oils are available or can be made by adding chopped fresh herbs to olive oil and keeping refrigerated in screw-top jars for about three weeks, then strained and rebottled. If fresh green herbs are used, blanching and refreshing them will enhance the colour of the oil, and kill any pathogens that may be present.

Polyunsaturated fats and monounsaturated fats

Polyunsaturates, and to a lesser extent monounsaturates, have been shown to lower blood cholesterol levels and therefore help in reducing the risk of heart disease.

It is better to eat foods rich in monounsaturates (olive oil and rapeseed oil) and polyunsaturates (sunflower oil and soya oil), than foods rich in saturates.

Rapeseed oil, which, like olive oil, contains mostly monounsaturated fat, is a good and cheaper alternative to olive oil. Sunflower, soya bean and corn oil all contain mostly polyunsaturated fat so are also good choices.

Some oils are labelled as vegetable oil or blended oils. All of these are also low in saturated fat and are generally cheaper.

WEBLINK

To find out more, contact the National Edible Oil Distributors' Association:

www.neoda.org.uk

Hydrogenated fats

Hydrogenation is the application of hydrogen to vegetable oils. It changes the unsaturated fatty acids to saturated, and changes the liquid oil into a solid or semi-solid fat. Hydrogenated fats are used in manufactured food products, but they may be linked to heart disease. In many cases, food packaging will state whether hydrogenated fats are present and in what proportion.

Cereals

Cereals are cultivated grasses, but the term is broadened to include sago, rice and arrowroot. All cereal products contain starch. The important cereals used in catering are wheat, oats, rye, barley, maize, rice, tapioca, sago and arrowroot.

Cereals are ground into flour for bread, cakes and so on (see below). Cereals can be used in other ways. Whole grains can be added to stews and casseroles, or cooked until soft. Cracked or kibbled grains are cut or broken pieces of whole grains (e.g. kibbled wheat and bulgar wheat). Meal, a coarse kind of flour, can be used to make porridge or thicken soups, or mixed with wheat flour to add interesting flavours and textures to ordinary breads, biscuits, muffins, etc. Barley, wheat, rice, bran and corn are also processed into breakfast foods. Whole grains (e.g. wheat grains, raw buckwheat and barley) can be sprouted, which enhances their nutritional value and produces a different flavour.

Store cereals in airtight containers in a cool, dark, dry place. Whole grains can be stored for up to two years; flaked, cracked grains and flours should be used within two to three months of purchase.

Whole grains should be washed thoroughly before use.

Wheat

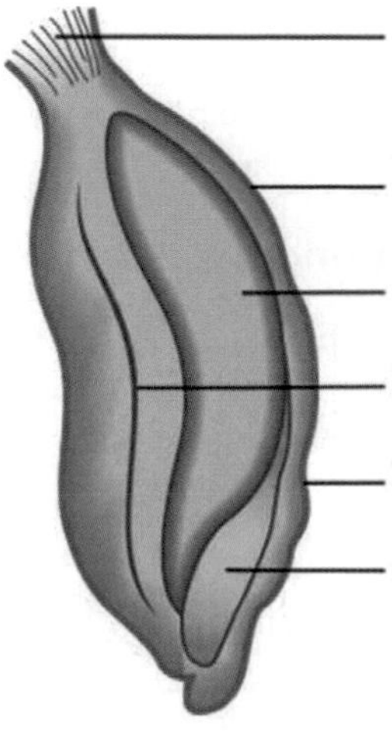

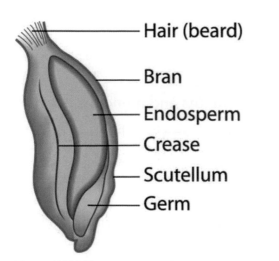

Figure 7.100 The structure of wheat

Wheat is the most common cereal produced in the western world; it is grown in most temperate regions. Large quantities are grown in the UK and a great deal, particularly in the form of strong flour, is imported from Canada.

Bulgar (steamed cracked wheat) is used in tabbouleh.

WEBLINK

To find out more, visit the Flour Advisory Bureau's website:

www.fabflour.co.uk

Wheat flour

Flour forms the foundation of bread, pastry and cakes, and is also used in soups, sauces, batters and other foods.

Flours vary in their composition and, broadly speaking, are defined by the quality of wheats used in the grist prior to milling. A mill can produce hundreds of different types of flour using a wide range of wheats.

Flour is graded by the percentage of whole cleaned wheat grain that is present, and the gluten content.

- White flour contains 72 to 85 per cent of the whole grain (the endosperm only).
- Wholemeal flour contains 100 per cent of the whole grain.
- Brown flour contains 85–95 per cent of the whole grain.
- High-ratio or patent flour contains 40 per cent of the whole grain.
- Self-raising flour is white flour with the addition of baking powder.
- 00 flour is a flour used to make pasta. (00 is its grading in the Italian system, which runs from 00 to 04, and indicates that it is very white flour.)

Semolina is granulated hard flour prepared from the central part of the wheat grain. White or wholemeal semolina is available. Semolina is used for couscous.

Flour is also described as soft (used for cakes, biscuits, most pastry, and for thickening and coating) or strong (used for bread, pasta, and puff, flaky and choux pastry). Wholemeal flour can be used to make wholemeal bread, pastry, and so on.

Store all types of flour with care.

- The storeroom must be dry, at 10–16°C and well ventilated.
- Flour should be removed from sacks and kept in wheeled bins with lids.
- Flour bins should be of a type that can easily be cleaned.
- Rotate stock rather than adding new deliveries to older stock.

Rye

Rye is the most important European cereal after wheat.

It is the only cereal apart from wheat that contains gluten proteins. However, these proteins are not of the same quality or quantity as those in wheat. Dough produced from rye flour has a sticky, dense consistency. The baked product has a low volume.

Rye flour is available as light, medium and dark rye; the colour and flavour of rye bread varies accordingly.

Oats

Oats are one of the hardiest cereals, and are grown in large quantities in Scotland and the north of England. Oats are either rolled into flakes or ground into three grades of oatmeal: coarse, medium and fine.

Because of the fat content, oat products need extra care. They should be kept in containers with tight-fitting lids, and stored in a cool, well-ventilated storeroom.

Oats are used for making porridge, thickening soups, coating foods, and in cakes, biscuits and haggis. Patent rolled oats have largely displaced oatmeal: they are already heat treated, and consequently more quickly and easily cooked.

Barley and buckwheat

The whole grain of barley is known as pot or Scotch barley and requires soaking overnight. Pearl barley has most of the bran and germ removed, and is polished. These products are used for making barley water for thickening soups and certain stews. Barley needs the same care in storage as oats.

Roasted barley becomes malt and is used to brew and distil vinegar.

Buckwheat is the seed of 'bran buckwheat'. The grain is usually roasted before cooking, and is also ground into a strong savoury flour for pancakes and baking.

Maize

Maize is also known as corn, sweetcorn or corn on the cob, and besides being served as a vegetable is processed into cornflakes. It yields a good oil suitable for cooking.

Cornflour is produced from the crushed endosperm of the maize grain, with the fat and protein washed out so that it is practically pure starch.

Cornflour is used for making custard and blancmange powders, because on boiling with a liquid it thickens easily, and sets when cold into a smooth paste that cannot be made from other starches.

Rice

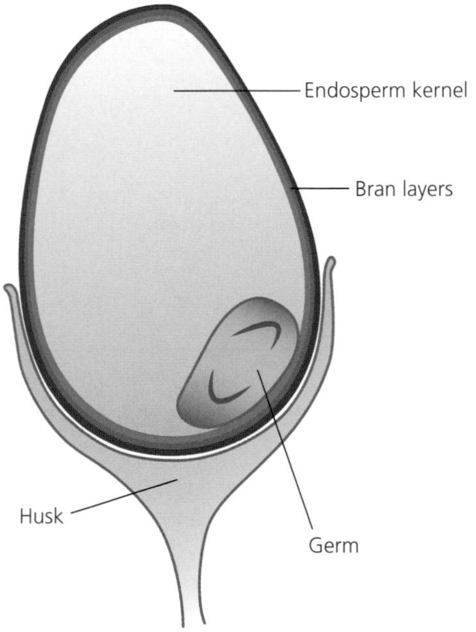

Figure 7.101 The structure of rice

Rice is the staple food of half the world's population. There are three main types:

1. long grain – a narrow, pointed grain, used for savoury dishes and boiling because of its firm structure, which helps to keep the grains separate (e.g. basmati, patna)
2. medium grain – an all-purpose rice suitable for sweet and savoury dishes (e.g. arborio)
3. short grain – a short, rounded grain, best suited for milk puddings and sweet dishes because of its soft texture (e.g. Carolina).

Some specific types and products are:

- **wholegrain rice** – whole and unprocessed rice
- **brown rice** – any rice that has had the outer covering removed but retains its bran and as a result is more nutritious, with a nutty flavour
- **basmati rice** – a thin, long grain rice which has a distinctive fragrance when cooking; the cooked rice is light and fluffy with the grains staying separate; served with curries

- **Thai fragrant rice (jasmine rice)** – used in Thai and Vietnamese dishes, this rice has a fragrant aroma; it is similar to basmati
- **wild rice** – seed of an aquatic plant related to the rice family; it has a nutty flavour and a firm texture
- **ground rice** – used for milk puddings
- **rice flour** – used for thickening certain soups (e.g. cream soups)
- **rice paper** – a thin, edible paper produced from rice, used with macaroons and nougat
- precooked instant and boil-in-the-bag rice are also available
- easy-cook rice has been partly boiled (with the husks on); this helps to keep the grains separate in the final cooking.

Rice should be kept in tight-fitting containers in a cool, well-ventilated store.

WEBLINK

To find out more about cereals, see:
www.cropsreview.com/cereal-crops.html

Alternatives to cereals

Tapioca is obtained from the roots of a tropical plant called cassava. Flake (rough) and seed (fine) are available. It is used for garnishing soups and milk puddings.

Sago is produced in small pellets from the pith of the sago palm. It is used in milk puddings and to garnish soups.

Arrowroot is obtained from the roots of a West Indian plant called maranta. It is used for thickening sauces, particularly when a clear sauce is required because it becomes transparent when boiled. It is also used in cakes and puddings. It is easy to digest. It must be stored in airtight tins as it is easily contaminated by strong-smelling foods.

Potato flour (fécule) is a preparation from potatoes, suitable for thickening certain soups and sauces.

Gram flour is made from ground chickpeas and has a unique flavour.

Raising agents

Mixtures can be aerated (made light) in several ways.

Baking powder

Baking powder may be made from one part sodium bicarbonate to two parts of cream of tartar. In commercial baking the powdered cream of tartar may be replaced by another acid product (e.g. acidulated calcium phosphate).

Under the right conditions, with a liquid and heat, it produces carbon dioxide gas. Only a small amount being given off when the liquid is added, the majority of the gas is released when the mixture is heated. Therefore cakes and puddings when mixed do not lose the rising property if they are not cooked right away.

Baking powder is used in sponge puddings, cakes and scones, and in suet puddings and dumplings.

Yeast

Yeast is used in bread and bun doughs, cakes and batters.

Yeast is a fungus form of plant life available as a fresh or dried product. It should be ordered only as required, and wrapped and stored in a cold place. Good-quality yeast should crumble easily and be fresh and moist. It is rich in protein and vitamin B.

→ Sugar

Three-quarters of the world's sugar is produced from sugar cane grown in tropical climates such as India, the Caribbean and Brazil. The rest is made from sugar beet, which is grown in more temperate climates in Europe.

There are many types:

- refined white sugars – granulated, caster, cube, icing
- unrefined sugar – brown sugar
- partially refined sugar – demerara
- syrups and treacle (liquid forms of sugar).

Sugar is not just a sweetener; it can be used:

- as a preservative – sugar helps to stop micro-organisms growing and so prevents food spoilage (for example, in preserves); this is why reduced-sugar jams spoil much more quickly than traditional jams
- to offset the acidity and sour flavour of foods from mayonnaise to tart fruits like gooseberries
- as a bulking agent – sugar gives a characteristic texture to foods including jams, ice cream and cakes
- to raise the boiling point or lower the freezing point; this is essential in some recipes (for example, ice cream)
- to speed up fermentation (by yeast) in baking
- to make cakes light and open-textured – when it is beaten with butter or eggs in a recipe.

Sugar should be stored in a dry, cool place. When purchased by the sack, the sugar is stored in covered bins.

See Chapter 8 regarding the nutritional value of sugar and its health impact.

WEBLINK

To find out more, visit the website of British Sugar plc:
www.britishsugar.co.uk

Alternatives to sugar

- Honey is a natural sugar made from the nectar of flowers and collected by bees. It comprises 80 per cent natural sugars, 18 per cent water, and 2 per cent minerals, vitamins, pollen and protein. There is a huge variety of types of honey, based on different plant sources, including acacia, avocado, macadamia and orange blossom.
- Agave nectar is a sweetener that comes from several species of the agave plant in Mexico. It is 1.5 times sweeter than table sugar.
- Xylitol is produced from trees, fruits and plants.
- Dextrose is a form of glucose (see Chapter 8) manufactured from corn.
- Stevia is a natural sweetener made from the leaves of the stevia plant, mostly grown in Brazil. It is 250–300 times sweeter than sucrose.
- Coconut palm sugar is a strongly flavoured, hard brown sugar produced from the sap of the coconut palm's flower buds. Contains amino acids, potassium, magnesium, zinc, iron and B vitamins.

→ Non-alcoholic beverages (drinks)

Water

Water varies from place to place in taste and character according to the substances dissolved or suspended in it. Soft water has a low content of lime. Hard water has an abundance of lime (if the flavour of lime is too strong, the water may have to be softened to remove the excess of lime). Water can also contain varying degrees of other substances (mineral waters – see below).

Coffee

Coffee is produced from the beans of the coffee tree, and is grown in regions such as South America, the West Indies, Africa and Sumatra. The varieties of coffee are named after the areas where they are grown, such as Mysore and Java.

The amount of caffeine in a cup of coffee can vary greatly, depending on the coffee, the method of brewing and the strength. Instant coffee generally contains less caffeine than roast and ground coffee, but may be consumed in greater volume.

Coffee beans – either unroasted, roasted or ground – are sold by weight. Coffee essence is obtained in bottles.

Different ways to prepare coffee

Coffee house or barista-style drinks are based on espresso, an intense strong coffee made by forcing hot water through ground coffee beans at high pressure. Drinks served include:

- espresso – served small in volume
- Americano – espresso with hot water
- latte – espresso with steamed milk
- cappuccino – espresso with steamed and foamed milk
- frappuccino – sweetened coffee blended with ice
- mocha – espresso and chocolate syrup with steamed milk
- flat white – pressurised steamed milk over espresso, achieving a thick foamy top
- skinny – made using skimmed milk.

Figure 7.102 A modern coffee machine for espresso-style coffee

Arabian or Turkish coffee is very strong and thick. It is made with finely ground beans, sugar is added and it may be flavoured with cardamom seeds.

In the **drip, or filter**, **method,** finely ground coffee is placed in a paper or reusable cone-shaped unit and nearly boiling water poured on top. The water filters through the coffee into the jug below. Individual one-cup filters are also available.

To make coffee in a **cafetière,** the pot is warmed, coarsely ground coffee is placed in the bottom, hot water is added to the grounds and stirred, then it is allowed to steep for three to five minutes before the plunger is pushed down to separate the coffee grounds from the coffee infusion. This is an efficient way to serve customers. Various sizes of cafetière are available, including single-serving pots.

The **percolator** used to be a very popular way to make coffee, but is now less common. It heats water so that it bubbles and filters through ground coffee in the top of the unit.

Semi-automatic **coffee machines** can complete the whole process, including grinding the coffee beans, or may force hot water through a pre-sealed pod of ground coffee. Because these produce a good product but are simple to use they are growing in popularity everywhere from restaurants to hotel bedrooms.

Figure 7.103 Cafetière and filter machine

Water that has been artificially softened should not be used for coffee or tea making. The mineral content of water used for brewing can significantly affect the final taste of the coffee or tea. A blend of coffee or tea brewed in the very hard water of London has a completely different taste to the same blend brewed in Edinburgh, where the water is very soft.

Although milk is not added to Arabian coffee, and coffee purists tend not to add milk, most people find coffee more palatable with its addition.

Coffee products

There is a diverse range of instant (soluble) coffee. It has a number of advantages over fresh brewed coffee, including convenience. It stays fresher longer, it is a robust product and, perhaps it is fast, less expensive and clean.

Today there are more than 100 different flavoured coffees available. The flavours are added to the beans by roasting them, then spraying them with a carrier oil followed by the particular flavouring.

Flavoured syrup can also be added to hot brewed coffee.

Tea

Tea is an evergreen plant of the camellia family, grown in more than 30 countries. It varies in flavour and quality due to the season, location and producer.

Most teas in the world end up blended; there are more than 1,500 blends with many different characteristics. A blend can contain as many as 35 different teas.

Tea comes in either tea bag or loose-leaf packs, which cover a wide variety of catering needs. It must be stored in an airtight container at room temperature.

Highly specialist teas or artisan teas come from very specific, single batches. These teas are served in a glass and carefully prepared at the optimum infusion temperature, which is often under 100°C. Examples include:

- **shade tea** – grown in Japan and picked in spring
- **premium Assam**
- **summer reserve Lakyrsiew Garden** – from Meghalaya, India.

Darjeeling Makaibari flavoured teas are blended with fruit, herbs or spices, whereas tisanes and fruit infusions do not contain any real tea.

Green tea varieties have half the caffeine of black teas.

WEBLINKS

Visit the website of the UK Tea Council:

www.tea.co.uk

For more information on speciality, single-batch teas, see:

www.lalaniandco.com

Preparing tea

In order to draw the best flavour out of the tea, the water must contain oxygen; this is reduced if the water is boiled more than once.

Use one tea bag or one carefully measured rounded teaspoon of loose tea for each cup to be served. Allow the tea to brew for the recommended time before pouring (see Table 7.10).

Table 7.10 Recommended brewing times for tea

	Type	Country of origin	Brewing time	Milk/black/lemon	Characteristics
Darjeeling	Black	India	3–5 minutes	Black or milk	Delicate, slightly astringent flavour
Assam	Black	India	3–5 minutes	Black or milk	Full-bodied with a rich, smooth, malty flavour

	Type	Country of origin	Brewing time	Milk/black/lemon	Characteristics
Ceylon blend	Black	Sri Lanka	3–5 minutes	Black or milk	Brisk, full flavour with a bright colour
Kenya	Black	Kenya (Africa)	2–4 minutes	Black or milk	A strong tea with a brisk flavour
Earl Grey	Black	China or India/ Darjeeling	3–5 minutes	Black or lemon	Flavoured with the natural oil of citrus bergamot fruit
Lapsang souchong	Black	China	3–5 minutes	Black	Smoky aroma and flavour
China oolong	Oolong	China	5–7 minutes	Black	Subtle, delicate, lightly flavoured tea

Case study

Tea at Claridge's

Today, our delicious, hand-picked and hand-prepared teas are as fine, rare and splendid as ever. Our carefully curated selection was put together with skill and expertise by world-renowned tea connoisseur Henrietta Lovell of Rare Tea Company and has been sourced from some of the oldest tea plantations in China, Sri Lanka, Africa, India and an idyllic corner of Cornwall to name but a few. We've also developed a delicious Claridge's Blend tea.

Among the highlights of this tea menu are a White Silver Tip from the mountains of Fujian in far eastern China and one of the most prized teas in the world; the rare Malawi Antler which is made from the shoots of the tea plant and cannot be found anywhere else in the UK, and an Earl Grey from Tregothnan, a walled tea garden in Cornwall that has been producing beautiful teas since the 14th century.

As for the preparation, we'll measure out the correct amount of tea, and make sure the water is at the perfect temperature before serving it at your table, steeped to your preferred strength. Once served, we'll drain off the water from the leaves ready for a second infusion – which experts regard as being even better than the first.

Source: Claridge's Tea Menu, reproduced by kind permission

Cocoa

Cocoa is a powder produced from the beans of the cacao tree, mainly in West Africa and South America. It contains some protein and a large proportion of starch. Iron is also present.

It should be kept in airtight containers in a well-ventilated store.

For hot drinks, cocoa is mixed with milk, milk and water, or water. Hot liquid is needed to 'cook' the starch and make it more digestible. Cocoa can be used to flavour puddings, cakes, sauces, icing and ice cream.

Drinking chocolate is ground cocoa from which less fat has been extracted, and to which sugar and milk have been added. It can be obtained in flake or powder form.

Mineral waters and soft drinks

A wide range of mineral waters is available, either natural (still or naturally carbonated) or treated with gas (carbon dioxide) to give a light fizz. The natural mineral elements in mineral water are regulated and must be present in consistent amounts.

Spring water is bottled water that does not conform to the mineral water regulations. It must meet the same regulations as tap water.

Manufactured soft drinks include tonic water, colas and ginger beer.

Fruit syrups and squashes

Fruit syrups are concentrated fruit juices preserved with sugar or manufactured from a range of compound colourings and flavours.

Squashes are concentrated, sweetened, fruit-flavoured drinks to be diluted with water. They may contain natural fruit juice.

Milk drinks

Milk can be offered plain, either hot or cold. Other milk drinks include:

- **milkshake** – made with ice cream and a flavouring syrup
- **ice cream soda** – fruit syrup with fresh cream and soda water, topped with ice cream
- branded products such as Bournvita and Ovaltine, from which beverages are made by the addition of hot water or milk.

Alcoholic drinks

Wine

Wine is the fermented juice of the grape and is available in many styles, including red, white, rosé and sparkling. Wines may be dry, medium dry or sweet in character, and according to the type and character they may be drunk while young (within a short time of bottling) or allowed to age (in some cases for many years).

Grapes have yeasts naturally present on their skins and their juice has high proportions of natural sugars, so when the fruit is crushed the yeast and sugars mix and fermentation takes place. This produces alcohol, which remains, and carbon dioxide, which escapes, although there are processes to keep some carbon dioxide in the liquid to produce sparkling wine. Making wine is a complex process but this initial fermentation is the key. Most wines contain 8 to 16 per cent alcohol by volume (ABV). Wines are a significant part of the overall alcoholic drinks market.

Bottled wines should always be stored on their sides so that the wine remains in contact with the cork. This prevents air from entering and spoiling the wine. The exceptions are champagne and sparkling wines, which should be stored upright, as should screw-top bottles.

Fortified wines are those that have been strengthened with additional alcohol, usually produced from grape juice; the best known are port, sherry and Madeira.

Aromatised wines are produced by flavouring a basic wine with ingredients (fruit, roots, bark, peel, flowers, quinine, herbs, etc.). Vermouth and Dubonnet are two examples served as aperitifs.

Rice wine is made in China and Japan, using rice instead of grapes. Mirin is a mild, sweet variety used in cooking; sake is a powerful fortified rice wine.

Spirits and liqueurs

Spirits are distillations of fermented liquids that are converted into liquid spirit; they include whisky, gin, vodka, brandy and rum. Most spirits have about 40 per cent ABV.

Liqueurs are spirits that are sweetened and flavoured with a wide range of agents (e.g. aniseed, peach, raspberry, rose petals, cinnamon, honey, coffee).

Cocktails are usually a mixture of a spirit with one or more ingredients such as liqueurs, fruit juices, cream, etc. Cocktails may be garnished.

'Mixed drinks' refers to an assortment including flips, fizzes, nogs, sours and cups. Cocktails and mixed drinks can also be made from non-alcoholic ingredients.

Beer

Beer is a term that covers all beer-like drinks such as ale, stouts and lagers. Beer is made from a combination of water, grain, hops, sugar and yeast. Types include bitter, mild, barley wine, porter and lager.

Beers contain high levels of carbohydrates and protein. Beers are richer in minerals than wines, but lower in alcohol at only 3–5 per cent.

Cider and perry

Cider is fermented apple juice. Also in this category are:

- pomagne – a sparkling cider
- scrumpy – strong, often cloudy cider.

Perry is fermented pear juice.

Herbs and spices

The leaves of herbs contain an oil that gives the characteristic smell and flavour. Herbs may be used fresh, but are dried to ensure a supply throughout the year.

Herbs have little food value but aid digestion because they stimulate the flow of gastric juices. Some examples are listed below.

- **Ajowan:** a plant used in Indian recipes, Bombay mix and breads such as parathas.
- **Basil:** a small leaf with a pungent flavour and sweet aroma. Used in cooked tomato dishes or sauces. Thai basil has an anise/liquorice flavour and is slightly spicy. It is more stable under high temperatures or longer cooking processes than sweet basil.
- **Bay leaves:** the leaves of the bay laurel or sweet bay trees. They may be fresh or dried, and are used for flavouring many soups, sauces, stews, fish and vegetable dishes, often in a bundle of herbs (bouquet garni).
- **Borage:** a plant with furry leaves that produces a flavour similar to cucumber when added to vegetables and salads.
- **Chervil:** small, neatly shaped leaves with a delicate aromatic flavour. It is best used fresh. Because of its neat shape it is often used for decorating chaud-froid work.
- **Chive:** a bright-green member of the onion family, resembling a coarse grass. It has a delicate onion flavour. It should be used fresh for flavouring salads, many cooked dishes and as a garnish. Chinese or garlic chives are used in Asian cookery.

- **Coriander:** a member of the parsley family. It is both a herb and a spice. The leaves have a distinctive pungent flavour.
- **Dill** has feathery green-grey leaves and is used in fish recipes and pickles.
- **Fennel** has feathery bright green leaves and a slight aniseed flavour, and is used for fish sauces, meat dishes and salads.
- **Kaffir lime leaves:** used like bay leaves, to give an aromatic lime flavour.
- **Lemon grass:** a tall plant with long leaves and a strong lemon flavour. A natural companion to fish, also used in stir-fries and salads, and widely used in Thai cookery.
- **Lovage** has a strong celery-like flavour; when finely chopped the leaves are used in soups, stews and salads.
- **Marjoram:** a sweet herb that may be used fresh in salads and many other dishes; when dried, it can be used for flavouring soups, stews and stuffings.
- **Mint:** there are many varieties of mint. Fresh sprigs are used to flavour peas and new potatoes. Fresh or dried mint may be used to make mint sauce or mint jelly for serving with lamb. Chopped mint can be used in salads.
- **Oregano** has a flavour and aroma similar to marjoram but stronger. It is used in Italian and Greek-style cooking, in a wide variety of dishes.
- **Parsley:** has numerous uses for delicate flavouring, garnishing and decorating a large variety of dishes. Flat-leaf, or French, parsley is also available.
- **Rosemary:** a strong fragrant herb that should be used sparingly, and may be used fresh or dried for flavouring stews, salads and stuffings. It can also be sprinkled on roast or grilled meat (particularly lamb), poultry and fish during cooking.
- **Sage:** a strong, bitter, pungent herb that helps the stomach to digest rich fatty meat; it is therefore used in stuffings.
- **Tarragon:** a bright-green, attractive leaf. It is best used fresh, particularly when decorating chaud-froid dishes. Tarragon has a pleasant flavour and is used in sauces, such as sauce béarnaise.
- **Thai parsley:** similar in appearance to spring onion but without the bulb.
- **Thyme** is used fresh or dried for flavouring soups, stews, salads and vegetables.
- **Toey leaves (pandanus):** long, flat blades, bright green in colour.

Figure 7.104 Herbs (clockwise from top left: coriander, oregano, parsley, flat-leaf parsley)

Figure 7.105 Herbs (clockwise from top left: rosemary, bay, lemon thyme, thyme)

Figure 7.106 Herbs (clockwise from top left: chives, chervil, tarragon, marjoram)

Figure 7.107 A selection of micro-herbs

Spices are natural products obtained from the fruits, seeds, roots, flowers or the bark of a number of different plants. They contain oils that aid digestion. They also enhance the appearance of food and add flavour. As spices are concentrated in flavour, they should be used sparingly, otherwise they can make foods unpalatable. Examples include those listed below.

- **Allspice (pimento):** so called because the flavour is like a blend of cloves, cinnamon and nutmeg. It is the unripe fruit of the pimento tree. Allspice is picked when still green, and dried when the colour turns to reddish brown. Allspice is ground and used as a flavouring in sauces, sausages, cakes, fruit pies and milk puddings. It is one of the spices blended for mixed spice.
- **Anise (pepper):** a strong, hot-flavoured red pepper.

Mustard

Mustard is obtained from the seeds of the mustard plant. There are three different types of seed: white, brown and black. It is sold in powdered form and is diluted with water, milk or vinegar for table use, or sold ready mixed in jars, in many variations.

Vinegar

Vinegar can be made from diluted alcohol products, the most common being wine, beer and rice. Vinegar is used as a preservative for pickles, rollmops and cocktail onions, and as a condiment on its own or with oil; it is used in mayonnaise and in reductions for sharp sauces (e.g. sauce piquante).

Speciality vinegars used in culinary work include:

- **apple cider vinegar** – made from pressed apples; allowed to ferment to produce alcohol and then vinegar
- **balsamic** – true balsamic vinegar is a product from Modena, Italy, and is made with concentrated grape juice that is allowed to ferment, then matured for 12 years; this is an expensive product and cheaper versions are available
- **Champagne vinegar** – this light vinegar is made with grapes grown in the Champagne region; the vinegar is left unfiltered and used in vinaigrettes
- **distilled white vinegar** – consists mainly of acetic acid and water; produced by fermentation rather than distillation, resulting in a clear vinegar suitable for pickling
- **malt vinegar** – made by malting barley, causing the starch to turn to maltose; an ale is brewed from the maltose and allowed to turn into vinegar; it is typically light brown in colour
- **red wine vinegar** – red wine ferments until sour; the vinegar is then strained or bottled, or is aged; the longer the vinegar ages, the better the flavour becomes; used in salad dressings and marinades
- **rice vinegar** – made from rice wine that is allowed to ferment; used in salad dressings and stir-fries; red or white
- **sherry vinegar** – produced from the fermented juice of sherry grape varieties such as palomino or muscatel; used in marinades and salad dressings
- **white wine vinegar** – made like red wine vinegar but from white wine; may not be aged in the same way.

WEBLINK

Read more about vinegar at the website of the Vinegar Institute:
www.versatilevinegar.org

Colourings, flavourings and essences

Colourings

Food colourings are available in powder or liquid form. Natural colours include the following.

- **Blackjack (commercial caramel) or browning:** a dark-brown, almost black liquid; it is used for colouring soups, sauces, gravies, aspics, and in pastry and confectionery.
- **Chocolate colour:** used in pastry and confectionery.
- **Cochineal:** a red colour, produced from the cochineal beetle, used in pastry and confectionery.
- **Coffee colour:** usually made from coffee beans with the addition of chicory.
- **Green colouring:** can be made by mixing indigo and saffron, or chlorophyll (the natural green colouring of plants) may also be used.
- **Indigo:** a blue colour seldom used on its own but mixed with red to produce mauve.
- **Yellow colouring:** obtained from turmeric, or by using egg yolks or saffron.

A large range of artificial colours is also obtainable; they are produced from coal tar and are harmless. Some mineral colours are also used in foodstuffs. All colourings must be pure and there is a list of those permitted for cookery and confectionery use.

Flavourings and essences

Essences are produced from a solution of essential oils with alcohol, for the use of cooks and confectioners. Among the many types are:

- almond
- anchovy
- lemon
- peppermint
- pineapple
- raspberry
- vanilla.

Essences fall into three categories: natural, artificial and compound. The costs vary considerably and it is advisable to try all types before deciding on which to use for specific purposes.

Natural essences are made from:

- fruit juices pressed out of soft fruits
- citrus fruit peel (e.g. lemon, orange)
- spices, beans, herbs, roots, nuts (e.g. caraway seeds, cinnamon, celery, mint, sage, thyme, clove, ginger, coffee beans, nutmeg and vanilla pod).

Artificial essences (such as vanilla, pineapple, rum, banana and coconut) are produced from various chemicals blended to give a close imitation of the natural flavour.

Compound essences are made by blending natural products with artificial products.

➔ Grocery, delicatessen

Delicatessen literally means 'provision store', but the name is commonly used to cover the place where a wide range of table delicacies may be bought. The following list includes some classic delicatessen products as well as store cupboard staples for Asian and fusion cookery.

- **Agar-agar ('vegetable gelatine'):** obtained from the dried purified stems of a seaweed; it is used in vegetarian cookery.
- **Annatto:** the seeds are washed and dried separately for culinary use. An orange food colour is made from the husk.
- **Aspic:** a clear savoury jelly, which may be the flavour of meat, game or fish. It may be produced from fresh ingredients or obtained in dried form. It is used for cold larder work, mainly for coating chaud-froid dishes, and may also be chopped or cut into neat shapes to decorate finished dishes.
- **Bamboo shoots:** mild-flavoured, tender shoots of the young bamboo. Widely available fresh, or sliced or halved in cans.
- **Blackbean sauce:** made from salted black beans, crushed and mixed with flour and spices (such as ginger, garlic or chilli) to form a paste. Sold in jars and cans.
- **Caviar:** see above, under 'Fish'.
- **Charcuterie:** cold meat preparations, usually hams, galantines, black puddings, pâtés, salamis, continental sausages and cured meats (e.g. bresaola).
- **Chilli bean sauce:** made from fermented bean paste mixed with hot chilli and other seasonings.
- **Chilli sauce:** a very hot sauce made from chillies, vinegar, sugar and salt.
- **Dashi:** light Japanese stock, available in powder form. The flavour derives from kelp seaweed.
- **Dried shrimps:** tiny shrimps that are salted and dried. They are used as a seasoning for stir-fry dishes.
- **Extracts (meat and vegetable):** extracts are highly concentrated forms of flavouring used in some kitchens to strengthen stocks and sauces (Bovril, Marmite, Maggi and Jardox are some examples).
- **Foie gras:** this expensive delicacy is obtained from the livers of specially fattened geese. It is available fresh and cooked (e.g. pâté).
- **Gelatine:** obtained from the bones and connective tissue (collagen) of certain animals; it is manufactured in leaf or powdered form and used in various sweets, such as bavarois.
- **Hams:** a ham is the hind leg of a pig cured by a special process, which varies according to the type of ham. York ham is cured by salting, drying and sometimes smoking. Bradenham ham is of coal-black colour and is sweet cured. These are all cooked before use. Continental raw hams (e.g. Bayonne from France, Parma from Italy and Serrano from Spain) are cut into thin slices and served raw.
- **Hoi sin sauce:** a thick, dark brownish-red sauce that is sweet and spicy.
- **Liquorice:** best known as a confectionery ingredient. The roots and rhizomes are cleaned, pulped, then boiled, and the liquorice extract is then concentrated by evaporation.
- **Mango powder:** unripe mangoes are sliced, sundried and ground to a powder, then mixed with a little turmeric. Used in vegetarian dishes, curries and chutneys.
- **Miso:** a fermented bean paste that adds richness and flavour to Japanese soups.
- **Noodles:** there are several types including egg noodles, rice noodles and Japanese udon noodles.
- **Nori:** paper-thin sheets of Japanese seaweed.
- **Oyster sauce:** made from oyster extract.
- **Papaya seeds:** can be used fresh or dried. Rich in the enzyme papain, which is an efficient meat tenderiser of commercial value.
- **Pickles:** vegetables or fruits preserved in vinegar or sauce, such as red cabbage, gherkins, onions, walnuts and capers. Mango chutney is a sweet chutney that is served with curries.
- **Red bean paste:** a reddish-brown paste made from puréed red beans and crystallised sugar.
- **Sambal kecap:** Indonesian sauce used as an accompaniment or dip. Dark soy sauce, lemon juice, garlic, red chilli, deep-fried onion slices.
- **Sambals:** an accompaniment that is spooned directly on to the plate. Made from deseeded red chillies puréed with salt.
- **Shrimp paste (terasi):** a dark, odorous paste made from fermented shrimps.
- **Smoked herring, anchovies and sardines:** these are preserved in oil and used as hors d'oeuvres.
- **Smoked salmon:** salmon weighing between 6 and 8 kg are used for smoking. A good-quality side of smoked salmon (see Figure 7.112) should have a bright, deep colour and be moist when lightly pressed with the fingertip at the thickest part of the flesh. It will remain in good condition for not more than seven days when stored at a temperature of 18°C, but refrigeration is recommended. This versatile food is used for canapés, hors d'oeuvres, sandwiches and as a fish course.

- **Snails:** edible snails are sold in boxes that include the tinned snails and the cleaned shells. The snails are replaced in the shells with a butter mixture, then heated in the oven and served in special dishes.
- **Soy sauce:** a major seasoning ingredient in Chinese cooking, made from fermented soya beans, combined with yeast, salt and sugar. Soy sauce falls into two main categories: light and dark. Light has more flavour than the sweeter dark sauce, which gives food a rich, reddish colour.
- **Spring roll and wonton wrappers:** paper-thin wrappers made from wheat or rice flour and water.
- **Tamarind:** the brown, sticky pulp of the bean-like seed pod of the tamarind tree.
- **Thai fish sauce (nam pla):** the most common flavouring in Thai food, in the same way soy sauce is used in Chinese dishes. It is made from salted anchovies and has a strong, salty flavour.
- **Thai nam prik sauce:** can be served on its own or used as a dip. Contains brown sugar, lemon juice, fish sauce, fresh red chillies, dried prawns, blanchan, cooked prawns, garlic and fresh coriander.
- **Yellow bean sauce:** a thick paste made from salted, fermented yellow soya beans crushed with flour and sugar.

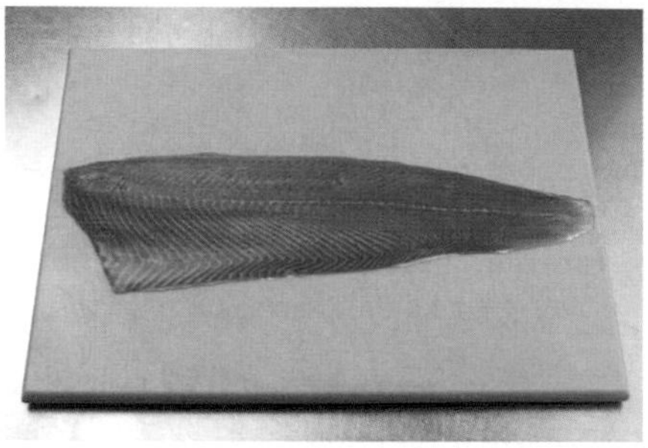

Figure 7.112 A side of smoked salmon

Confectionery and bakery goods

- **Cake covering:** produced from hardened vegetable fat with the addition of chocolate flavouring and colour.
- **Chocolate:** made from cocoa butter (from the cocoa bean), crushed cocoa beans and syrup. For commercial purposes, chocolate is sold in blocks of **couverture**. Pure chocolate couverture is made from cocoa mass, refined sugar and extracted cocoa butter; it is the additional cocoa butter that gives it its qualities for moulding, its flavour and therefore its higher price. With **baker's chocolate**, the cocoa butter is replaced by vegetable fat, giving a cheaper product that does not need tempering. Chocolate is used for icings, sauces, dipping chocolates and moulding into shapes. Drinking chocolate is made from cocoa (see above).
- **Chocolate vermicelli:** a ready-made preparation of small chocolate pieces used to decorate cakes and some sweets.
- **Cocktail cherries:** bright-red cherries preserved in syrup, often flavoured with maraschino liqueur.
- **Fondant:** a soft, white preparation of sugar that has many uses, chiefly for coating petits fours and gâteaux.
- **Gum tragacanth:** a soluble gum used for stiffening pastillage; only a very clear white type should be used. It is obtained from shrubs.
- **Jam:** preserve of fruit and sugar. Raspberry and apricot jams are those most often used in the pastry kitchen.
- **Marmalade:** a preserve of citrus fruits and sugar, used mainly for breakfast menus and for certain sweets.
- **Marrons glacés:** peeled and cooked chestnuts preserved in syrup. They are used in certain cakes, sweet dishes and as petits fours.
- **Marzipan:** a preparation of ground almonds, sugar and egg yolks used in the making of petits fours and pastries, and for lining large cakes. Marzipan may be freshly made or obtained as a ready-prepared commodity.
- **Mincemeat:** a mixture of dried fruit, sugar, spices, nuts, etc., chiefly used for mince pies.
- **Pastillage (gum paste):** a mixture of icing sugar and gum tragacanth (or gelatine), which may be moulded into shapes for set pieces or as baskets, etc., for serving petits fours.
- **Piping jelly:** a thick jelly of piping consistency obtainable in different colours and flavours. It is used for decorating pastries and gâteaux and cold sweets.
- **Redcurrant jelly:** a clear preserve of redcurrants used as a jam as an accompaniment and also in the preparation of sauces.
- **Rennet:** originally obtained from animal stomachs, but can now be obtained in synthetic form. Rennet is prepared in powder, extract or essence form, and is used in the production of cheese. Vegetarian rennet is also available.
- **Vanilla:** the dried pod of an orchid used for infusing mild, sweet flavour into dishes. It is usually the tiny seeds within the pod that are used to flavour the foods. After use rinse the vanilla stick, dry and store in a sealed jar of caster sugar. This will provide a mild flavour in the sugar.

Further reading

Foskett, D., Rippington, N., Paskins, P. and Thorpe, S. (2015) *Practical Cookery for Level 2 NVQs and Apprenticeships* (13th edn). London: Hodder Education.

Foskett, D., Rippington, N., Paskins, P. and Thorpe, S. (2014) *Practical Cookery for the Level 3 NVQ and VRQ Diploma* (6th edn). London: Hodder Education.

North American Meat Processors Association (2006) *The Meat Buyer's Guide*. Hoboken, NJ: John Wiley & Sons, Inc.

Topics for discussion

1. Factors that affect the quality of meat.
2. Pros and cons of using meat substitutes such as TVP and Quorn.
3. Purchasing of meat (by carcass, joints or portion-controlled cuts).
4. Much of today's poultry lacks flavour. How can this be remedied?
5. The rising popularity of fish compared to meat and poultry.
6. The best ways to purchase fish.
7. Buying policy for vegetables and fruit.
8. The importance of vegetables and fruit in the diet.
9. The importance of eggs to food production.
10. Compare the uses of butter, margarine and oil in cooking.
11. What is a sensible policy for selling cheese in a restaurant?
12. Is the average caterer sufficiently knowledgeable about the different types of flour and their suitability for specific purposes?
13. Should the caterer be offering a wider range of choice of teas and coffees?
14. The value of using pulses.
15. The value of using herbs, micro-herbs and spices.
16. What is meant by food provenance?
17. The UK government's definition of sustainable farming and food.
18. The politics of ethical trade.
19. State the advantages of using meat substitutes.
20. Can sugar alternatives really work and reduce our dependency on table sugar?

8 Basic nutrition, diet and health

What is nutrition?

Nutrition is all about food and its relationship to the maintenance of the body and to health. All foods are made up of nutrients in varying proportions; they are the components in food that provide energy, promote growth and maintain the body functions. A diet is the selection of foods someone eats, and a balanced diet provides all of the nutrients in sufficient quantities. Because of increased interest in nutrition people are more aware of the food they eat and the choices available to them. Therefore it has become more important than ever that those involved in producing food have knowledge of its nutritional value as well as the purchasing, storing, cooking and serving of it.

Nutrients

Nutrients provide energy, or kilocalories (kcals); there are around 50 nutrients, which are divided into the categories shown in Table 8.1.

- The **'macro' nutrients** such as protein, carbohydrates and fats provide the body with energy, growth and repair.
- The **'micro' nutrients** such as vitamins and minerals do not provide energy but are essential for good health and life processes.

The majority of foods are made up of a combination of nutrients, but some foods, such as sugar, have only one nutrient (carbohydrate in this case). Alcohol provides the body with 7 kcals per gram, but it actually has a similar effect upon the body as a drug so is not classified as a nutrient.

Water is essential for our health, to keep the body properly hydrated and for efficient maintenance of life systems.

We will now take a closer look at the main nutrients.

Table 8.1 Foods containing the various nutrients, the energy they provide and their uses in the body

Nutrient	Energy provided	Food in which it is found	Use in body
Protein	4 kcals per gram	Meat, fish, poultry, game, milk, cheese, eggs, pulses, cereals, vegetable-based proteins such as Quorn	For building and repairing body cells and tissues; can also provide some heat and energy
Fat	9 kcals per gram	Butter, margarine, cooking fat, oils, cheese, fat meat, oily fish and products made with any of the above	Provides a concentrated source of heat and energy; essential to the structure of body cells
Carbohydrate	4 kcals per gram	Flour, flour products and cereals, sugar, syrup, jam, honey, fruit, some vegetables and products made with the above	Provides heat and energy (primary source of energy)
Vitamin A	None	Oily fish, fish liver oil, dairy foods, carrots, tomatoes, greens	Stimulates growth; provides resistance to disease
Vitamin B1 – thiamin		Yeast, pulses, liver, whole grain, cereals, meat and yeast extracts	Stimulates growth and strengthens nervous system
Vitamin B2 – riboflavin		Yeast, liver, meat, meat extracts, wholegrain cereals	Stimulates growth and assists in the production of energy
Nicotinic acid (niacin)		Yeast, meat, liver, meat extracts, wholegrain cereals	Stimulates growth
Vitamin C – ascorbic acid		Fruits such as strawberries, citrus fruits, green vegetables, root vegetables, new potatoes, salad items	Stimulates growth and promotes good health
Vitamin D ('sunshine vitamin')		Fish liver oils, oily fish, dairy foods	Stimulates growth, and builds bones and teeth
Iron	None	Lean meat, offal, egg yolk, wholemeal flour, green vegetables, fish	Forming and maintaining healthy blood and preventing anaemia
Calcium (lime)		Milk and milk products, fish bones, wholemeal bread	Building bones and teeth, clotting the blood, the working of the muscles
Phosphorus		Liver and kidney, eggs, cheese, bread	Building bones and teeth, regulating body processes
Sodium (salt)		Meat, eggs, fish, bacon, cheese	Muscular activity and prevention of muscular cramp

Protein

There are two main kinds of protein.

1. Animal protein is found in meat, game, poultry, fish, eggs, milk and cheese: myosin, collagen (meat, poultry and fish); albumin, ovovitellin (eggs); casein (milk and cheese).
2. Vegetable protein is found mainly in the seeds of vegetables. The proportion of protein in green and root vegetables is small. Peas, beans and nuts contain most protein, and the grain of cereals such as wheat has a useful amount because of the large quantity eaten.

Proteins are formed of carbon, hydrogen, oxygen and nitrogen. They are made from long chains of amino acids. The way that these amino acids are arranged is how different proteins are formed, which is why the protein of cheese is different to the protein in meat. It is preferable to have both animal and vegetable proteins in the diet so that there are a variety of the necessary amino acids available.

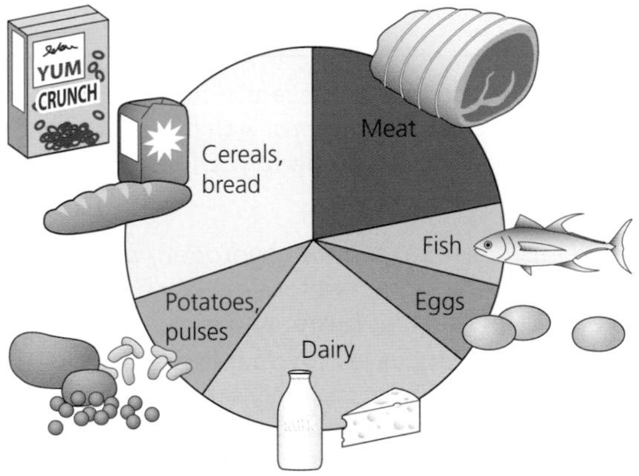

Figure 8.1 Main sources of protein in the average diet

Protein builds and repairs the body; it forms part of many enzymes, hormones and antibodies. It is also involved in maintaining body fluid, clotting the blood, and maintaining the body's acid and alkaline balance.

Table 8.2 shows the proportion of protein in some common foods.

Table 8.2 The proportion of protein in selected common foods

Animal food	Protein (%)	Plant foods	Protein (%)
Cheese, Cheddar	26	Soya flour, low fat	45
Bacon, lean	20	Soya flour, full fat	37
Beef, lean	20	Peanuts	24
Cod	17	Bread, wholemeal	9
Herring	17	Bread, white	8
Eggs	12	Rice	7
Beef, fat	8	Peas, fresh	6
Milk	3	Potatoes, old	2
Cheese, cream	3	Bananas	1
Butter	<1	Apples	<1
		Tapioca	<1

Source: Fox and Cameron, 1995

Because protein is needed for growth, growing children, and expectant and nursing mothers will need more protein than other adults, whose requirements are mainly for cell replacement and repair. Any excess protein is used for producing heat and energy. In diets where protein intake is minimal, it is important that there is plenty of carbohydrate available so that protein is used for growth and repair, rather than for energy purposes. The body's first need is for energy, and protein used for energy may deprive the body of protein when it is needed for other purposes.

Fats

Fats contain fatty acids that are essential to the diet. Edible fats are composed of glycerol with three fatty acids attached and are therefore called triglycerides.

There are three types of fatty acid.

1. Saturated fats are saturated with hydrogen, which makes them straight and therefore heavy, so they produce solid fats such as butter and lard.
2. Monounsaturated fats have one double bond, which means that they are not completely saturated with hydrogen. A monounsaturated fat such as olive oil can be liquid at room temperature but turn viscose (thick) when stored in the fridge.
3. Polyunsaturated fats have two or more points that are not saturated with hydrogen; they are found in corn, sunflower, soybean and sesame oil.

These factors give different properties to different fats.

Hard fats are mainly of animal origin and contain more saturated fatty acids, while, in comparison, oils and soft fats contain more polyunsaturated acids.

Table 8.3 Sources of saturated and unsaturated fats

High in saturated fats	Dairy products	Butter, cream, milk, cheese
	Meat	Liver, lamb, beef, pork (some cuts more than others, e.g. shoulders, belly)
	Others	Coconut oil, palm kernel oil, palm oil, hard margarine, lard
High in polyunsaturated fats	Vegetable oils	Corn (maize) oil, soya bean oil, safflower seed oil, sunflower seed oil
	Nuts	Most, except coconut and cashew nuts
	Margarines	Many soft varieties especially soya bean and sunflower seed

Source: Fox and Cameron, 1995

To be used by the body, fats have to be broken down into glycerol and fatty acids so that they can be absorbed; they can then provide heat and energy. The nutritive value of different fats is similar, although some animal fats contain fat-soluble vitamins A and D. The function of fat is to form a protective layer around vital organs of the body, and to provide heat and energy. Some fats provide a useful source of vitamins A and D; they also add flavours and textures to food as well as being a useful cooking medium such as in deep-fried food.

The two main groups of fats (animal and vegetable) can be divided into:

- solid fat
- oils – liquid at room temperature.

The contribution of animal fat in the western diet is gradually changing as healthy eating policies encourage a reduction in total fat intake, particularly animal fats. There has been a move towards skimmed milk, leaner cuts of meat, cooking with vegetable oils, and a reduced market for eggs, high-fat cheeses and butter.

Table 8.4 Percentage of saturated fat in an average diet*

Milk, cheese, cream	16.0
Meat and meat products	25.2
Other oils and fats	0.0
Other sources, including eggs, fish, poultry	7.4
Biscuits and cakes	11.4
The above 25.2% for meat and meat products splits down into:	
other meat products	9.1
beef	4.1
lamb	3.5
pork, bacon and ham	5.8
sausage	2.7

* A diet high in saturated fat is associated with an increased risk of heart disease

Fats should be eaten with other foods such as bread, potatoes, etc., as they can then be more easily digested and utilised in the body.

Certain fish, such as herrings, mackerel, salmon and sardines, contain oil (fat) in the flesh. A type of fat that is increasingly popular as a dietary supplement is omega-3, which can be found in the flesh of oily fish. Other fish, such as cod and halibut, contain the oil in the liver.

Vegetables and fruit contain very little fat, but nuts and seeds have a considerable amount.

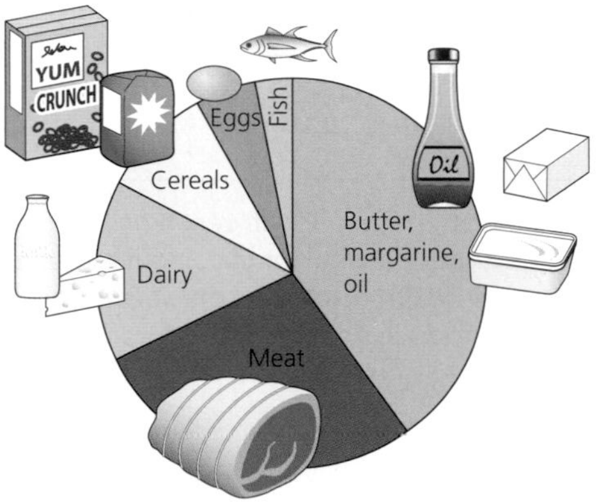

Figure 8.2 Main sources of fat in the average diet

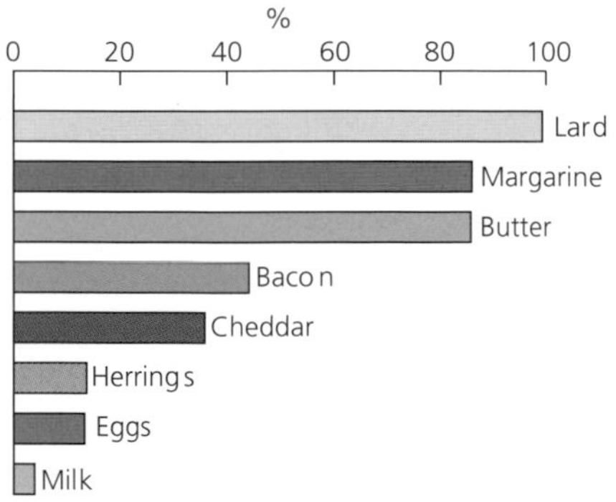

Figure 8.3 Proportion of fat in some foods

Hydrogenated fats

These are also known as trans fats and are produced when hydrogen is applied to liquid oils to turn them into a more solid fat. The process also turns unsaturated fats into a saturated form. These fats were popular for use in food manufacture but since information has been available linking hydrogenated fats to heart disease there has been a move to reduce or remove their use.

There is extensive research being carried out on the effect of high temperatures on fats and oils. It is thought that normal cooking temperatures may convert some unsaturated fats into a saturated version.

Carbohydrates

Carbohydrates are formed by plants as they grow and then either used by plants for their own energy or are eaten by animals or humans for energy. Carbohydrates are made up of sugar molecules.

There are three main types of carbohydrate:

1. sugar (saccharides)
2. starch (polysaccharides)
3. cellulose (fibre).

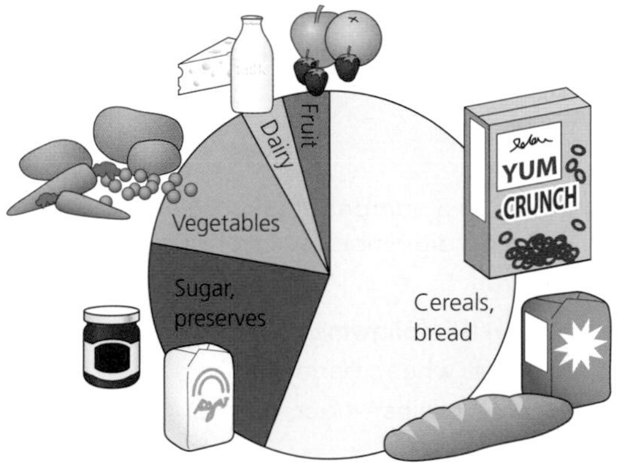

Figure 8.4 Main sources of carbohydrate in the average diet

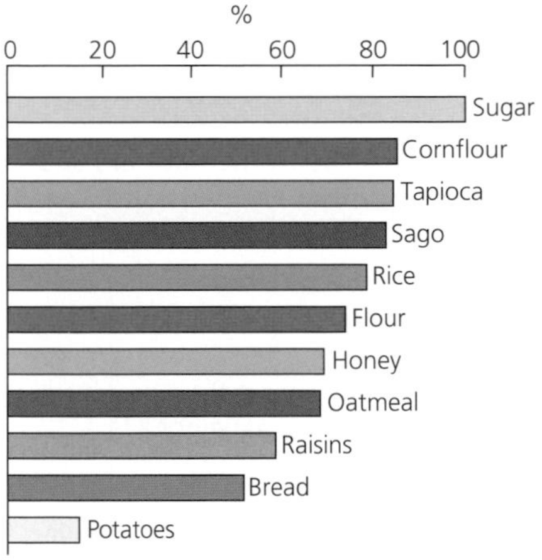

Figure 8.5 Proportion of carbohydrate in some foods

Sugar

Sugars are the simplest form of carbohydrate and are the end products of the digestion of carbohydrates. They are used to provide the body with heat and energy.

There are different kinds of sugar:

- glucose – found in the blood of humans/animals, and in fruit and honey
- fructose – found in fruit, honey and cane sugar
- sucrose – found in beet and cane sugar
- lactose – found in milk
- maltose – produced naturally during the germination of grain.

Simple sugars are called monosaccharides and are made of one unit, such as glucose, fructose and galactose. Disaccharides contain two monosaccharides joined together. They all contain glucose.

Monosaccharides	
Glucose	▲
Fructose	●
Galactose	◆

Disaccharides	
Sucrose	▲–●
Lactose	▲–◆
Maltose	▲–▲

Figure 8.6 Simple sugars are the building blocks: all carbohydrates are composed of single sugars, alone or in combination

Starch

Starch is composed of a number of glucose molecules (particles), and during digestion is broken down into glucose.

Starch is available in the following foods:

- whole grains – rice, wheat, barley, tapioca
- ground/powdered grains – flour, cornflour, ground rice, arrowroot
- vegetables – potatoes, parsnips, peas, beans
- unripe fruit – bananas, apples, cooking pears
- cereals – cornflakes, shredded wheat, etc.
- cooked starch – cakes, pastries, biscuits, bread
- pastas – macaroni, spaghetti, tagliatelle, etc.

Fibre (cellulose)

Fibre is formed in plants, vegetables, whole grains, nuts, seeds and legumes. There are two types of fibre.

1. **Soluble:** this fibre swells in water to form a gel-like substance that slows digestion and helps to control the release of glucose into the bloodstream. It also binds with cholesterol in the gastrointestinal tract, so reducing cholesterol levels. Soluble fibres are found in fruits and vegetables, and grains such as oats.
2. **Insoluble:** this is tougher, indigestible fibre such as the skin of fruits and vegetables, and the outer parts of seeds, wheat bran and brown rice. Insoluble fibre increases faecal weight, so assisting in the travel of waste, which prevents constipation.

Vitamins

Vitamins are chemical substances found in very small amounts in many foods. They are vital for life, and if the diet is deficient in any vitamin, ill health results. As they are chemical substances they can be produced synthetically. Vitamins can be fat soluble (A, D, E and K) or water soluble (B and C).

Vitamins assist the regulation of the body processes and help to maintain general good health. They will:

- assist in the growth of children
- promote good health
- help to protect against disease.

Table 8.5 Fat-soluble vitamins, their functions and sources in the diet

Vitamin	Functions	Sources
Vitamin A (can be made in the body from carotene, the yellow substance found in many fruits and vegetables)	Assists in children's growth Helps the body to resist infection May help to prevent the condition known as 'night blindness'	Halibut liver oil Cod liver oil Milk Cheese Herrings Kidney Liver Margarine (vitamin A is added in manufacture) Butter Dark-green vegetables such as watercress and spinach (the green colour mass is the yellow of the carotene) Carrots Tomatoes Apricots Eggs Notes: the amount of vitamin A in dairy produce varies. Because cattle eat fresh grass in summer and stored feedstuffs in winter, dairy produce contains the highest amount of vitamin A in the summer; at very high levels, vitamin A can be toxic
Vitamin D	Controls the use the body makes of calcium. It is therefore necessary for healthy bones and teeth	Action of sunlight on the deeper layers of the skin (approximately 75% of the body's vitamin D) Fish liver oils Egg yolk Margarine (vitamin D is added in manufacture) Oily fish Dairy produce

Vitamin	Functions	Sources
Vitamin E	Acts as an antioxidant, protecting cell membranes, helping to maintain skin and eyes, and protecting immune system	Plant oils (e.g. soya, corn, olive) Nuts, seeds and wheatgerm Many other foods
Vitamin K	Needed for clotting blood and to keep bones healthy	Green, leafy vegetables Vegetable oils Cereal grains

Vitamin B

Vitamin B consists of at least 11 substances, the two main ones being thiamin (B1) and riboflavin (B2).

Others include folic acid and pyridoxine (B6), and cobalamin (B12). B6 and B12 aid the formation of blood, so can prevent anaemia.

Vitamin B is water soluble and can be lost during cooking foods in water; it is required to:

- keep the nervous system in good condition
- enable the body to obtain energy from the carbohydrates and amino acid metabolism
- assist in the growth of children.

Table 8.6 Sources of vitamin B

Thiamin (B1)	Riboflavin (B2)	Nicotinic acid
Yeast	Yeast	Meat extract
Bacon	Liver	Brewers' yeast
Oatmeal	Meat extract	Liver
Peas	Cheese	Kidney
Wholemeal bread	Egg	Beef

Vitamin C (ascorbic acid)

Vitamin C:

- assists in the healing of cuts and the uniting of broken bones
- prevents gum and mouth infection
- makes collagen – a protein that makes skin and bones strong.

Vitamin C is water soluble and can be lost during cooking or soaking in water. It is also lost through poor storage (keeping foods for too long, bruising or storing in a badly ventilated place) and by cutting vegetables into small pieces. Vitamin C is also heat sensitive, and lost by heating and cooking above 70°C.

Sources of vitamin C include:

- blackcurrants
- potatoes, especially new potatoes
- Brussels sprouts and other green vegetables
- strawberries
- lemons, oranges and grapefruit
- tomatoes
- bananas
- fruit juices.

The major sources of vitamin C in the British diet are potatoes and green vegetables.

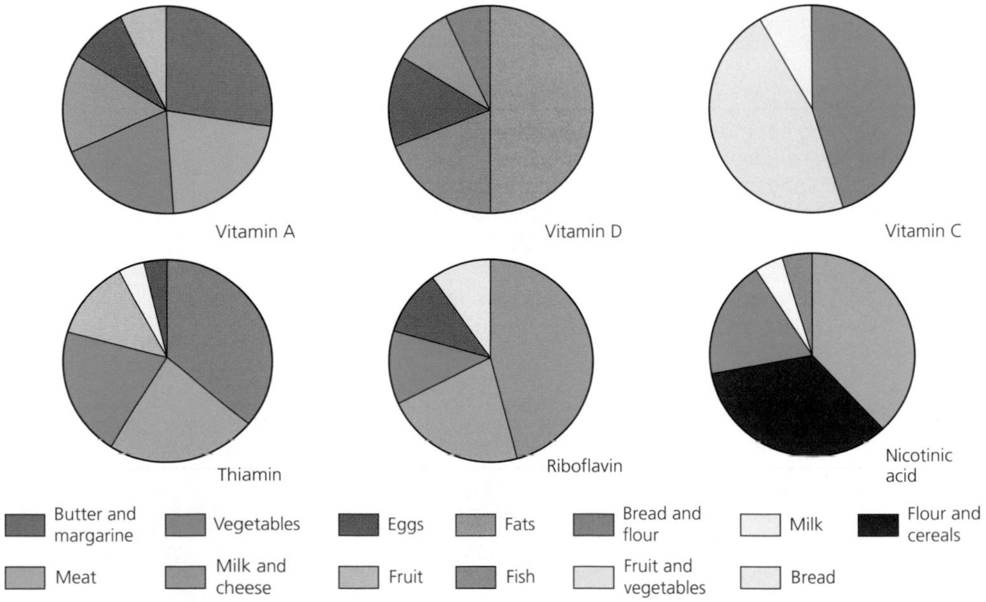

Figure 8.7 Main sources of vitamins in the average diet

Table 8.7 Cooking times and vitamin C retention for some common foods

Cooking time (minutes)	% retention of vitamin C during boiling			
	Brussels sprouts	Cabbage	Carrots	Potatoes
20	49	–	35	–
30	36	70–78	22	53–56
60	–	53–58	–	40–50
90	–	13–17		

Source: Fox and Cameron, 1995, reproduced by permission of Hodder Education

Mineral elements

There are 19 mineral elements, most of which are required by the body in very small quantities. The body has, at certain times, a greater demand for certain mineral elements and there can be a danger of a deficiency in the diet. Calcium, iron and iodine are those most likely to be deficient.

Table 8.8 Selected mineral elements, their uses and sources

Mineral element	Use in the body	Sources
Calcium	Building bones and teeth, muscle contraction, transmission of nerve impulses Because of the need for growth of bones and teeth, infants, adolescents, and expectant and nursing mothers have a greater demand for calcium	Milk and milk products, including cheese and yoghurt Bones of canned oily fish Green vegetables Tofu Wholemeal bread and white bread (to which calcium has been added) Although calcium is present in spinach and cereals, the body is unable to make use of it as it is not in a soluble form and therefore cannot be absorbed
Phosphorous	Building bones and teeth (in conjunction with calcium and vitamin D), for fluid acid balance (acts as a buffering agent), as a component of ATP (adenosine triphosphate), which provides energy for the body	Liver and kidney Eggs Bread Cheese Tofu Legumes Nuts Fish
Iron	Building haemoglobin in the blood, and therefore necessary for transporting oxygen and carbon dioxide round the body; haemoglobin in the blood should be maintained at a constant level and cannot be stored by the body The body requires more iron at certain times than others, such as after loss of blood	Lean meat Wholemeal flour (to which iron has been added) Offal Green vegetables Egg yolk Fish Iron is most easily absorbed from meat and offal; its absorption is aided by the presence of vitamin C Iron could also be obtained from the iron utensils in which food is prepared

Mineral element	Use in the body	Sources
Sodium	Sodium is required in all body fluids; excess salt is continually lost from the body in urine and the kidneys control this loss We also lose sodium in perspiring, a loss over which we have no control	Sodium is found in salt (sodium chloride) Many foods are cooked with salt or have salt added (bacon and cheese) or contain salt (meat, eggs, fish) Sodium levels in processed foods have been highlighted in recent years by the government as being too high; the Food Standards Agency (FSA) has now set added salt targets for processed retail foods in order to control amounts in food and the effect on health Excess sodium can cause hypertension (high blood pressure), which can lead to increased risk of health problems such as heart disease and stroke
Iodine	Functioning of the thyroid gland, which regulates basal metabolism	Sea foods Iodised salt Drinking water obtained near the sea Vegetables grown near the sea

Potassium, magnesium, sulphur and copper are some of the other minerals required in very small amounts by the body.

Water

Water is required for all normal body processes, including:

- regulation of body temperatures by evaporation of perspiration
- maintenance of body fluids
- metabolism
- digestion
- excretion
- absorption
- secretion.

Sources of water include:

- drinks of all kinds
- foods, such as fruits and vegetables, meat, eggs
- combustion or oxidation – when fats, carbohydrates and protein are used for energy, a certain amount of water (metabolic water) is produced within the body.

Table 8.9 Reference nutrient intakes (RNIs) for protein, vitamins and minerals

Age	Protein g/day	Vitamin A mg/day	Thiamin mg/day	Riboflavin mg/day	Niacin mg/day	Folate mg/day	Vitamin C mg/day	Vitamin D mg/day	Calcium mg/day	Iron mg/day
0–3 months	12.5	350	0.2	0.4	3	50	25	8.5	525	1.7
4–6 months	12.7	350	0.2	0.4	3	50	25	8.5	525	4.3
7–9 months	13.7	350	0.2	0.4	4	50	25	7	525	7.8
10–12 months	14.9	350	0.3	0.4	5	50	25	7	525	7.8
1–3 years	14.5	400	0.5	0.6	8	70	30	7	350	6.9
4–6 years	19.7	500	0.7	0.8	11	100	30	–	450	6.1
7–10 years	28.3	500	0.7	1.0	12	150	30	–	550	8.7
Males										
11–14 years	42.1	600	0.9	1.2	15	200	35	–	1000	11.3
15–18 years	55.2	700	1.1	1.3	18	200	40	–	1000	11.3
19–50 years	55.5	700	1.0	1.3	17	200	40	–	700	8.7
50+ years	53.3	700	0.9	1.3	16	200	40	**	700	8.7
Females										
11–14 years	41.2	600	0.7	1.1	12	200	35	–	800	14.8
15–18 years	45.0	600	0.8	1.1	14	200	40	–	800	14.8
19–50 years	45.0	600	0.8	1.1	13	200	40	–	700	14.8
50+ years	46.5	600	0.8	1.1	12	200	40	**	700	8.7
Pregnancy	16	1100	10.1*	10.3	10	1100	110	10	10	10
Lactation	111	1350	10.2	10.5	12	160	130	1		

Source: Department of Health, cited in Gaman and Sherrington, 1996

The effects of cooking on nutrients

Some foods are best eaten when freshly harvested, without further preparation or cooking (for example, fruits such as berries and vegetables such as lettuce). Cooking and storage over prolonged periods reduce the nutritional value of these foods.

Although some foods will always be best eaten raw and in their natural state, the digestibility of most foods is enhanced through cooking.

Protein

When protein is heated it coagulates and shrinks. Overcooking of some protein foods such as scrambled egg can spoil their appearance and texture. When overcooked the proteins harden and squeeze out water. Foods such as vegetables that are overcooked will lose certain vitamins.

On being heated, the different proteins in foods set, or coagulate, at different temperatures; above these temperatures shrinkage occurs; this is particularly noticeable in grilling or roasting meat. Moderately cooked protein is the easiest to digest: a lightly cooked egg is more easily digested than a raw egg or a hard-boiled egg.

Carbohydrate

Unless starch is cooked thoroughly it cannot be digested properly – for example, undercooked pastry or bread. Foods containing starch have cells with starch granules, covered with a cellulose wall that breaks down when heated or made moist, making the starch digestible. This is called gelatinisation of starch.

When browned – for example, the crust of bread, toast, roast potatoes or the skin of rice pudding – the starch forms dextrin and this produces a sweeter taste. This is known as the caramelisation of sugars.

On heating within a liquid, the starch gelatinises and causes the food to thicken. This can be seen with the thickening of a sauce when heated if a starch such as cornflour has been used.

Fat

The nutritive value of fat is not affected by cooking. During cooking processes a certain amount of fat may be lost from food when the fat melts, such as in the grilling of meat. However, fats are also added to foods in the cooking process such as with frying. Fat may also be absorbed by coatings such as breadcrumbs or batter.

Mineral elements

There is a possibility of some minerals being lost in cooking liquids, so reducing the mineral content in food. This applies to soluble minerals, such as sodium, but not to calcium or iron compounds, which do not dissolve into the cooking liquid.

- Iron may be acquired from foods cooked in iron utensils. The iron already present in foods is not affected by cooking.
- Cooking foods in hard water may very slightly increase the amount of calcium in food.

Vitamins

- Vitamins A and D withstand cooking temperatures, and are not lost during cooking.
- Vitamin B1 (thiamin) can be destroyed by high temperatures and by the use of bicarbonate of soda. It is soluble in water and can be lost in the cooking.
- Vitamin B2 (riboflavin) is not destroyed easily by heat, but bright sunlight can break it down.
- Vitamin C is lost by cooking and by keeping food hot for service. It is also soluble in water (the soaking of foods for a long time and bruising are the causes of losing vitamin C). It is unstable and easily destroyed in alkaline conditions so bicarbonate of soda must not be used when cooking green vegetables (this used to be a popular practice to keep vegetables green but is rarely used these days).

Digestion

Digestion is the process of breaking down food, assisted by the body's enzymes. Enzymes are proteins that speed up (catalyse) the breakdown processes and may take place:

- in the mouth, where food is mixed with saliva, and starch is broken down by the action of an enzyme in saliva
- in the stomach, where the food is mixed and gastric juices are added; these processes break down proteins
- in the small intestine, where proteins, fats and carbohydrates are broken down further and additional juices added
- in the large intestine, where bacteria attack undigested substances such as dietary fibre.

Absorption

To enable the body to benefit from food it must be absorbed into the bloodstream; this absorption occurs after the food has been broken down; the product then passes through the walls of the digestive tract and into the bloodstream. This occurs in:

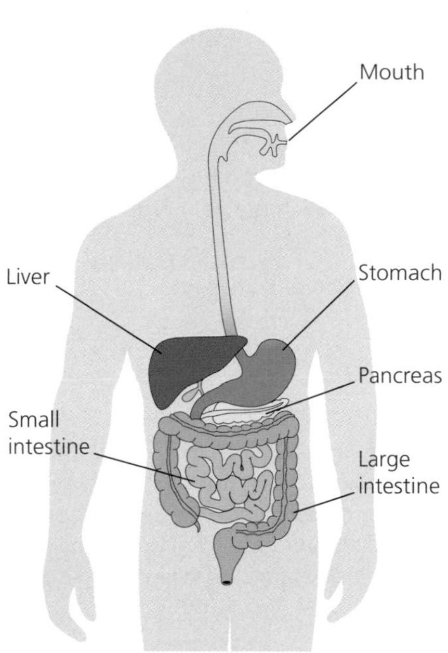

Figure 8.8 The digestive tract

- the stomach, where simple substances, such as alcohol and glucose, are passed through the stomach lining into the bloodstream
- the small intestine, where more of the absorption of nutrients takes place due to a further breakdown of the food
- the large intestine, where water is reabsorbed from the waste.

When food smells, looks and tastes appetising it helps to stimulate the flow of saliva and digestive juices in the body. This will enable the digestive process and ensure that most food is broken down and absorbed. If digestion and absorption are not efficient this could lead to a deficiency of one or more nutrients, and could lead to a state of malnutrition.

➔ Food and energy

Energy is required to enable the heart to beat, for the blood to circulate, the lungs and other organs of the body to function, for every activity such as talking, eating, standing, sitting, and for strenuous exercise and muscular activity.

The energy value of a food is measured by a term called a kilocalorie or calorie. This is the amount of heat required to raise the temperature of 1000 g of water from 15 to 16°C.

A new unit is now gradually replacing the calorie. This is the joule. Since the joule is too small for practical nutrition, the kilojoule (kJ) is used: 1 calorie = 4.18 kJ.

(Both units will be given here and, for ease of conversion, 1 calorie will be taken to equal 4.0 kJ.)

Foods contain certain amounts of the various nutrients, which are measured in grams.

The energy value of nutrients is as follows:

- 1 g carbohydrate produces 4 calories (16 kJ)
- 1 g protein produces 4 calories (16 kJ)
- 1 g fat produces 9 calories (36 kJ).

The energy value of a food, diet or menu is calculated from the nutrients it contains – for example, 28 g of food containing:

- 10 g carbohydrate will produce $10 \times 4 = 40$ calories (160 kJ)
- 2 g protein will produce $2 \times 4 = 8$ calories (32 kJ)
- 5 g fat will produce $5 \times 9 = 45$ calories (180 kJ)
- total = 93 calories (372 kJ).

Foods having a high fat content will have a high energy value; those containing a lot of water, a low energy value. All fats, cheese, bacon and other foods with a high fat content have a high energy value.

Men require more calories (kJ) than women; large men and women require more than small men and women; people engaged in energetic work require more calories (kJ) than those with sedentary occupations.

Basal metabolism

Basal metabolism is the term given to the amount of energy required to maintain the functions of the body, and to maintain body heat when it is still and without food. The number of calories (kJ) required for basal metabolism is affected by the size, gender and general condition of the body. The number of calories (kJ) required for basal metabolism is approximately 1,700 per day.

In addition to the energy required for basal metabolism, energy is also required for everyday activities, such as getting up, dressing and walking; the amount required will be closely related to a person's occupation.

The approximate energy requirements per day for the following examples are:

- office worker – 2,000 calories (8,000 kJ)
- carpenter – 3,000 calories (12,000 kJ)
- heavy physical work – 4,000 calories (16,000 kJ).

Nutritional value of foods in the diet

Dairy products

Dairy products are a very important group of foods. Not only do they contain protein, carbohydrates and fat, they are also a good source of calcium and vitamins.

Milk

Milk is designed by nature to be a complete food for young animals and humans. Cows' milk is almost the perfect food for humans due to its high nutritional value.

Milk contains protein, sugar (lactose), fat, vitamins and minerals. Because of its high water content, while it is a suitable food for infants, after the first few months of life it is not possible to consume enough milk for it to be the main source of protein and other nutrients. It is also deficient in iron and vitamin C.

The approximate composition of whole milk is as follows:

- 87 per cent water
- 3–4 per cent proteins (mostly casein)
- 3–4 per cent fat
- 4–5 per cent sugar
- 0.7 per cent minerals (particularly calcium)
- vitamins A, B and D (the vitamin content varies from season to season, and according to breed of cow and preservation method).

In Channel Islands milk (Jersey and Guernsey) the percentage of fat must be 4 per cent; in all other milk the minimum is 3 per cent.

Skimmed milk has had the cream layer removed. It provides a lower calorie intake for those watching their weight, but is also a healthy option for all adults because the animal fat has been removed. However, many people opt for semi-skimmed milk where half of the cream has been removed. It is recommended that children under the age of five have full-cream milk.

Soya milk is a popular alternative to cows' or goats' milk; it is low in saturated fat and cholesterol. Nut milk, made from almonds, is also available.

When milk is taken into the body it coagulates (sets) in the stomach when digestive juices that contain the enzyme rennin are introduced. Souring of milk is due to the bacteria feeding on the milk sugar (lactose) and producing lactic acid from it, which brings about curdling.

Cream

Cream is the fat of milk; the legal minimum fat content of single cream is approximately 18 per cent, for double cream 48 per cent and clotted cream 60 per cent. Cream is therefore an energy-producing food, which also supplies vitamins A and D. It is easily digested because the fat is in a highly emulsified form, which means that the fat globules are very small.

Butter

Butter is made from the fat (cream) of milk and contains vitamins A and D, the amount depending on the season. Like cream, it is easily digested. It is a very high-energy but also high-calorie food.

The approximate composition of butter is:

- 84 per cent fat
- 1 per cent salt
- 15 per cent water
- vitamins A and D.

Cheese

Cheese is made from milk; its composition varies according to whether the cheese has been made from whole milk, skimmed milk or milk to which extra cream has been added.

As an example, the composition of Cheddar cheese is approximately:

- 40 per cent fat
- calcium
- 30 per cent water
- vitamins A and D
- 25 per cent protein.

Hard cheese is high in saturated fat and can be high in sodium.

The nutritional value of cheese is exceptional because of the concentration of the various nutrients it contains. The minerals in cheese are useful, particularly calcium and phosphorus. Cheese is also a source of vitamins A and D.

It is a body-building, energy-producing and protective food because of its protein, fat and mineral elements, and vitamin content.

Cheese is easily digested, provided it is eaten with starchy foods and eaten in small pieces, as when grated.

Margarine and spreads

Margarine, which is made from animal and/or vegetable oils, and skimmed milk, has vitamins A and D added to it. The composition and food value of margarine are similar to those for butter; margarine is not inferior to butter from a nutritional point of view.

Yoghurt

Yoghurt is rich in nutrients containing protein, and a range of vitamins and minerals. It is particularly useful as a source of calcium.

Meat, poultry and game

Meat consists of fibres, which may be short, as in a fillet of beef, or long, as in silverside of beef. Generally, the shorter the fibre, the more tender and easily digested the meat.

However, it is the cooking method that makes the most difference. Meat is usually carved across the grain to assist chewing and digestion of the fibres.

Hanging meat helps to make the flesh more tender; this is because acids develop and soften the muscle fibres. Marinating in wine or vinegar prior to cooking also helps to tenderise meat so that it is more digestible. Expensive cuts of meat are not necessarily more nourishing or of better nutritional value than the cheaper cuts.

Meat, having a high protein content, is valuable for the growth and repair of the body and as a source of energy. It is an important source of several vitamins, minerals and other nutrients (e.g. vitamins B, A and D, zinc and iron).

The fat content of meat varies according to the type and the cut. In some meats, the fat surrounds the lean muscle; in other meat it appears as flecks of fat (marbling) in the lean tissue.

Bacon and pork, in general, are particularly valuable because of their thiamin content. Red meat is a good source of iron, while poultry generally has a lower fat content, especially once the skin has been removed. Meat, poultry and game of all kinds are therefore important as sources of protein.

Fish

Fish is as useful a source of animal protein as meat. Oily fish, such as sardines, mackerel, herrings and salmon, contain vitamins A and D in their flesh; in white fish, such as halibut and cod, these vitamins are present in the liver. Since all fish contains protein it is a good body-building food, and oily fish is useful for energy and as a protective food because of the vitamins it contains.

The amount of fat in different fish varies: oily fish contain 5–18 per cent, white fish less than 2 per cent.

When the bones are eaten, calcium is obtained from fish (canned sardines or salmon).

Oily fish is not so easily digested as white fish because of the fat content. However, oily fish is the best source of omega-3, an essential fatty acid. It is recommended that we consume oily fish twice a week. Shellfish are not easily digested because of the coarseness of the fibres they contain.

Eggs

The egg can store sufficient nutrients to supply a developing embryo chick with everything required for its growth.

Egg white contains protein called albumin (not to be confused with albumen, which is another name for the white of the egg itself) and the amount of white is approximately twice the amount of yolk.

The white is approximately 12 per cent protein and 88 per cent water. In comparison the yolk is about 35 per cent fats, 50 per cent water, 15 per cent protein, and a mixture of vitamins and minerals such as vitamins A and D, thiamin, riboflavin, calcium, iron, sulphur and phosphorus. All these factors make eggs a body-building, protective and energy-producing food. Eggs are also fairly high in cholesterol, although current research suggests that eating eggs does not necessarily raise cholesterol. Eggs are low in calories: two large eggs contain 180 calories. Eggs are easily digestible, which makes them useful for balancing meals.

Eggs may also be used as a main dish; they are a protective food, and provide energy and material for growth and repair of the body.

Fruit

The composition of different fruit varies considerably: avocados contain about 20 per cent fat, whereas most other fruits contain none. In unripe fruit the carbohydrate is in the form of starch, which changes to sugar as the fruit ripens. The cellulose in fruits acts as a source of dietary fibre.

Fruit is a valuable food because of the vitamins and minerals it contains. Vitamin C is present in certain fruits, particularly citrus varieties (oranges, satsumas, grapefruit), blackcurrants and other summer fruits. Dried fruits such as raisins and sultanas are a useful source of energy because of their sugar content and fibre, but they contain no vitamin C. The vitamin C in fruit is lost during storage. Frozen fruit maintains its vitamin C content during freezing.

The approximate composition of fruit is:

- 85 per cent water
- 0.5 per cent minerals
- 5–10 per cent carbohydrate
- varying amounts of vitamin C
- 2–5 per cent cellulose.

Very small amounts of fat and protein are found in most fruits, but more in avocados. Fruit is a protective food because of its mineral and vitamin content.

Nuts

Nuts are highly nutritious because of the protein, fat and minerals they contain, although much of the fat comes in monounsaturated or polyunsaturated form.

Nuts are not easily digested because of their fat and cellulose content. They are of considerable importance to vegetarians, who may use nuts in place of meat; they are therefore a food that builds, repairs and provides energy.

Vegetables

Green vegetables

Green vegetables are particularly valuable because of their vitamin and mineral content; they are therefore protective foods. The most important minerals they contain are iron and calcium. Green vegetables are rich in carotene, which is made into vitamin A in the body. Little protein or carbohydrate is found in green vegetables.

The greener the vegetable, the greater its nutritional value. Vegetables that are stored for long periods, or that are damaged or bruised, quickly lose their vitamin C value, therefore they should be used as quickly as possible after harvest.

Green vegetables and leeks also act as a source of dietary fibre in the intestines.

Root vegetables

Most root vegetables contain more starch and sugar than green vegetables; they are therefore a source of energy. They contain a small but valuable amount of protein, some mineral salts and vitamins; they are also a useful source of cellulose and water. Swedes and turnips contain a little vitamin C, and carrots and other yellow-coloured root vegetables contain carotene, which is changed into vitamin A in the body. They can be an excellent source of fibre.

Potatoes

Potatoes contain a large amount of starch (approximately 20 per cent) and a small amount of protein just under the skin. Because potatoes are eaten in relatively large quantities in the UK, the small amount of vitamin C they contain, especially in new potatoes, is of value in the diet.

Onions

Onions aid the good bacteria in the gut. They are used extensively in cooking, mainly for their flavour, and contain some sugar.

Peas and broad beans

These vegetables are significant nutritionally because they contain carbohydrate, protein, and a variety of vitamins and minerals, including vitamin C, B vitamins, vitamin K, calcium, magnesium, iron, zinc, phosphorus, potassium and magnesium. Peas in particular are important; they are popular and easy to use. In their frozen form they may be nutritionally superior to fresh peas.

Enzymes convert the natural sugars in peas to starch soon after harvest, and the peas can become grainy and starchy. Peas for freezing are picked and frozen at the peak of their condition; freezing halts the conversion to starch and can also halt some vitamin loss.

Cereals

Cereal crops include rice, wheat, corn/maize, barley, millet, oats, rye, wild rice, spelt, tapioca, sago, arrowroot and others in different parts of the world.

Cereals typically contain from 60 to 80 per cent carbohydrate in the form of starch and are therefore high-energy foods. They also contain 7–13 per cent protein, depending on the type of cereal, and 1–8 per cent fat.

The vitamin B content is considerable in stoneground and wholemeal flour, and B vitamins are added to other wheat flours, as are calcium and iron salts.

Oats contain good quantities of fat, protein and soluble fibre and have the highest food value of any cereal.

Of all cereals in the British diet, wheat for bread making is by far the most important. White flour is fortified with calcium, iron, thiamin and niacin to improve its nutritional value. However, wholegrain bread still contains the greatest number of nutrients and white bread the fewest. This is because the nutrients in the grain and bran are still present in wholegrain bread, but are removed to produce the white flour required to produce white bread.

Sugar

There are several kinds of natural and processed sugars, such as those found in fruit (glucose), milk (lactose), cane and beet sugar (sucrose).

Sugar, along with fat, provides the most important part of the body's energy requirements.

Saccharin and other manufactured sweeteners provide sweetness, but usually have no nutritive value. They are widely used to sweeten food and drinks without adding calories.

Sugar has been identified as the main cause of obesity and overweight; reduction in sugar consumption is strongly recommended for everyone. Sugar also causes tooth decay and dental problems.

Liquids

Water

Drinking water by itself is the most efficient way to provide for the body's needs. Certain types of water naturally contain mineral salts; hard waters contain soluble salts of calcium, and some spa waters in certain localities are known for their specific mineral salts. Fluoride may be present naturally in some waters, and makes teeth more resistant to decay. Bottled natural mineral waters and spring waters are sold worldwide for personal consumption. However, there has been a recent reduction in the popularity of bottled waters because of publicity about unnecessary 'food miles', i.e. transporting water over large distances, and also the possible migration of plastic traces from bottles to the water. Many hotels and restaurants now provide bottled water with their own establishment's label; this may simply be 'tap water', or could be filtered and can be aerated to provide sparkling water.

Fruit juices

The nutritional value of fruit juices is very similar to that of whole fruit when freshly squeezed, but without the fibre. Fruit juices can be high in sugars and are low in fibre, and because of the sugar content (even in its natural form) should be drunk in moderation.

Tea, coffee and cocoa

Tea and coffee have no nutritional value in themselves, but the caffeine in them acts as a stimulant on the nervous system. The ingredients added to tea and coffee, such as milk and sugar, do have nutritional values and some of the popular 'coffee shop items' such as latte and cappuccino can be high in calories. Herb teas, green teas and rooibos teas are caffeine-free. Green tea is an excellent antioxidant.

Cocoa contains some fat, starch and protein, also some vitamin B and mineral elements. Once again the preparation of cocoa as a drink will alter its nutritional value as milk and sugar are likely to be added.

Alcoholic beverages

Alcohol must be considered as a foodstuff because it provides calories. The energy value of wine is similar to that of whole milk, but without the nutritional benefit. Alcohol can affect the central nervous system, with effects ranging from mild stimulation to addiction, and even links with cancer of the liver, stomach and oesophagus. It is strongly recommended that alcohol be consumed in moderation.

➜ Food additives

There is an increasing trend in the UK towards simplifying recipes, and using as few artificial additives and including as many natural ingredients as possible. For this reason, the use of some additives (such as monosodium glutamate) is increasingly unpopular.

Additives can be divided into 12 categories and, except for purely 'natural' substances, their use is subject to certain legislation.

1. **Preservatives:** 'natural' preservatives include salt, sugar, alcohol and vinegar; synthetic ones are also widely used.
2. **Colouring agents:** natural, including cochineal, caramel and saffron, and many synthetic colouring agents.
3. **Flavouring agents:** synthetic chemicals to mimic or enhance natural flavours, such as monosodium glutamate.
4. **Sweetening:** saccharin (an organic petroleum compound), sorbitol and aspartame.
5. **Emulsifying agents** (to prevent separation of sauces, ice cream, etc.): examples are lecithin and glycerol monostearate (GMS).
6. **Antioxidants:** to delay the onset of rancidity in fats due to exposure to air; examples are vitamin E and butylated hydroxy toluene (BHT).
7. **Flour improvers:** to strengthen the gluten in flour, such as vitamin C.
8. **Thickeners:** animal (gelatine); marine (agar-agar); vegetable (gum tragacanth – used for pastillage – and pectin); synthetic products. Also a range of starch products are used for thickening.
9. **Humectants:** to prevent food drying out, such as glycerine (used in some icings).
10. **Polyphosphate:** injected into poultry before rigor mortis develops; it binds water to the muscle and thus prevents 'drip', giving a firmer structure to the meat. However consumer criticism about polyphosphates has reduced its use, especially in high-quality products.
11. **Nutrients:** vitamins and minerals added to breakfast cereals, vitamins A and D added to margarine, minerals added to white flour. This is a fast-growing area referred to as 'enhanced foods or products'. Examples are cholesterol-reducing agents in spreads, calcium-enhanced milk, vitamin- and mineral-enhanced water and juices.
12. **Miscellaneous:** anti-caking agents added to icing sugar and salt; firming agents (calcium chloride) added to canned fruit and vegetables to prevent too much softening in the processing; mineral oils added to dried fruit to prevent stickiness.

WEBLINK

Find out more about food additives from the Food Standards Agency:

www.food.gov.uk/science/additives-or-e-numbers

➜ Catering for health

A balanced diet

Food intake needs to provide the vitamins, minerals, protein and fibre the body requires, without too much saturated fat, sugar and salt. The government recommends that all individuals should consume a diet that contains:

- plenty of starchy foods, such as rice, bread, pasta and potatoes (choosing wholegrain varieties when possible)
- plenty of fruit and vegetables – at least five portions of a variety of fruit and vegetables a day
- some protein-rich foods, such as meat, fish, eggs, beans and non-dairy sources of protein, such as nuts and pulses

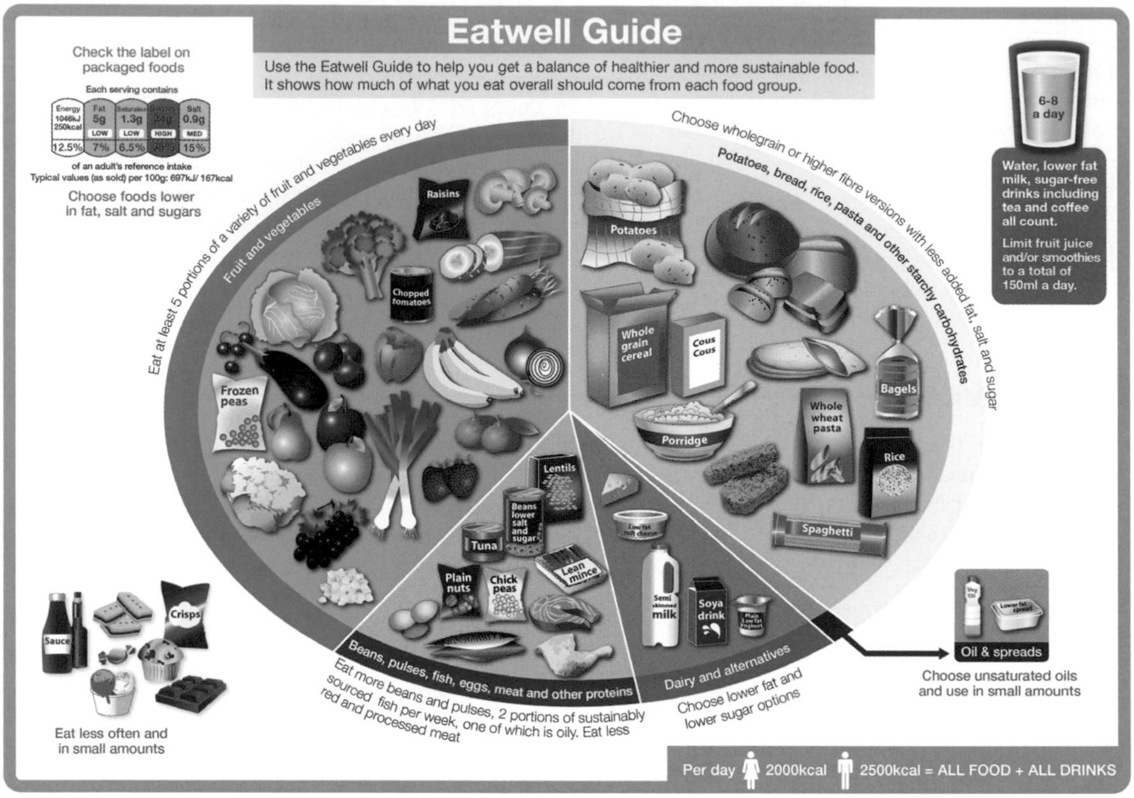

Figure 8.9 The Eatwell Guide

- some milk and dairy foods, choosing reduced-fat versions, or eating smaller amounts of full-fat versions or eating them less often
- small amounts only of saturated fat, salt and sugar.

The Eatwell Guide (Figure 8.9) is a pictorial representation of the contribution that different food groups should make to the diet. This representation of food intake applies to individuals over the age of five and provides an easy-to-follow guide for consumers.

Those in food businesses or food provision can assist customers to achieve a more balanced diet, while still enjoying the eating-out experience.

When the customer base is entirely or mostly 'captive', such as in a home for the elderly, hospital, boarding school or the armed forces, there are normally three meals a day, and a menu cycle that can be viewed over a week or fortnight. So, for example:

- the number of red meat main courses can be limited to two or three days a week
- fish is offered on one or two days a week, especially oily fish
- a variety of fruit can be included in all meals, with perhaps a glass of fruit juice or fresh fruit at breakfast; so can starchy foods, with cereals and/or porridge at breakfast, and bread rolls
- vegetables and salads can feature more prominently for midday and evening meals, and vegetable content can be increased, with meat content decreased
- dishes relatively high in fat and sugar can be limited to perhaps once a week.

When the customer base is transient – as in most restaurants, pubs, wine bars, hotels, cafés, and takeaways, the choices will be varied, with customers choosing just what they would like. The caterer can still assist the customer to eat healthily, and menu choice can be varied to offer something like a low-fat pasta dish, white meat and fish, as well as red meat, dishes that are low in fat, interesting vegetables and salads, and imaginative, appealing dishes based on these. Alternatives might be offered to the usual favourites, e.g. a baked jacket potato with a salad garnish, healthier alternatives to French fries with the main course.

Practical steps that can be taken are:

- offering accurate descriptions of dishes on menus
- avoiding general statements such as 'healthier'
- choosing suppliers that provide accurate information for their products or ingredients
- choosing and scrutinising the ingredients lists of prepared foods for any hidden ingredients
- training staff on the content of dishes so they can provide helpful, accurate information to customers; this is especially important for allergens
- employing policies for segregation of foods for diners with allergies, and prevention of cross-contamination, in the kitchen.

Customers' approach to food is based on their experience, education, background, sophistication, travel, advertising and peer groups. Some people enjoy experimenting, others don't. Healthy catering should not be introduced in such a way that it alienates people. Healthy catering by choice has more chance of being successful than any attempt to try to force customers into a better lifestyle, unless you are confident of reaching the quite specific market segment that wants only healthy dishes. Just as high-street retailers do with sandwiches and snacks aimed at the lunchtime market, it may work well to brand one or two dishes as healthy choices.

Even where there is quite strong customer resistance, subtle changes can be introduced over time, if necessary, to the content, presentation and service of favourite dishes. An example of this is where a number of food manufacturers and popular restaurants have committed to gradually reduce salt and sugar content in their popular items.

Marketing and presentation

Describe dishes and menu choices in ways that will appeal to customers. Choose descriptions with care and with your customers in mind. Terms like 'healthy', 'reduced fat', 'low in saturates' will be a selling point to some customers as people are becoming more health conscious but to others those terms would put them off the menu. Also as people are becoming more aware of health and nutrition it may be necessary to be much more specific about these terms – for example, why is it 'healthy', exactly how low in fat.

If unsure of the likely customers and their preferences, provide a balance of dishes or mark the healthy choices with a suitable symbol. Emphasise the positives on the menu: unusual flavours and combinations, freshly cooked, tasty, satisfying, interesting textures, colourful garnishes, exotic ingredients, associations with foreign travel, ethnic cuisines; equally popular are organic and locally sourced. Feature as dishes of the day, special promotions, house specialities, and on counters and buffets display those dishes that have been prepared and cooked according to healthy catering guidelines. Expand the choice of accompaniments and sauces to give appealing, healthier alternatives to those that are high in fat or sugar. Choose garnishes that increase the starch, fibre, vegetable and/or fruit content.

Include healthy additions in the price, such as a granary or wholemeal roll with soup, fresh fruit with a sandwich or lunchtime snack, rice or spiced vegetables with a curry. Select healthy choices for promotional offers.

Involve the staff: brief them on the dish content so that descriptions are appealing and accurate, and questions can be answered helpfully. Set chefs the challenge of producing favourite dishes in a healthier way and use this as a feature on the menu.

Be aware and take care not to use misleading or false descriptions, or terms that have a specific legal meaning under the food labelling regulations, such as 'lower fat', 'reduced fat', 'lower salt'.

Adapting recipes, preparation and cooking methods

With thought and skill, a substantial contribution can be made to a balanced diet without loss of flavour or texture, or restricting customer choice. Nor should it jeopardise the financial margins of the business. Indeed the process, by encouraging creativity, could lead to improved profits, with high added value yet less expensive ingredients.

There are many practical changes that can be made to the way food is prepared and cooked, which will lead to a healthier choice for the consumer. To get the best results, some trial and experimentation is recommended. Possibilities include the following.

- **Adapt recipes:** use alternative flavourings to salt and proprietary products high in salt; reduce quantities of fat/oil; replace butter with unsaturated oils or a mixture of butter and oils; thicken soups and sauces with purées of vegetables/fruit/pulses, or potatoes in place of a roux or butter-based sauces; use natural fruit juice to sweeten; use wholemeal with white flour for pastry.
- **Information on the menu:** which items are the low-fat/lower-calorie dishes; explanations about how you are making your menu healthier – this could well increase business.
- **Adjust preparation methods:** trim visible fat, remove poultry skin; leave skin on potatoes, vegetables and fruit (to increase fibre content and reduce vitamin loss); use chunky/thick cuts of vegetables (to reduce fat absorption/vitamin loss).
- **Selected ingredients:** lean cuts and joints of meat; skinless poultry; fish rich in oils beneficial to health, such as salmon, mackerel, herring or trout; use white fish, as it has very little fat; prepared dishes can be oven baked, grilled, steamed or poached instead of fried; sugar-free breakfast cereals; fruit juices and products in their natural juices/unsweetened; oils, fats and spreads that are high in monounsaturates or polyunsaturates; pre-prepared and convenience products that are low in salt/sugar/fat.
- **Change to low-fat cooking methods:** grill, bake, poach, microwave, stir-fry (quick cooking, minimum oil), using spray oils shallow-fry in non-stick pans (to use less oil), steam chips to blanch. Keeping the temperature of oil low can protect its structure and therefore preserve its health properties.
- **Change the balance on the plate:** less red meat and more vegetables.
- **For vegetables:** favour cooking methods that reduce vitamin loss – steam, microwave or stir-fry, cook in small batches (to reduce hot holding time).

WEBLINKS

You can find the honest food guide advice on healthy eating at:

www.honestfoodguide.org

Further information on nutrition and healthier catering practices can be found in the Food Standards Agency's *Catering for Health: A Guide to Teaching Healthier Catering Practices*. See:

http://tna.europarchive.org/20120419000433/

http://www.food.gov.uk/multimedia/pdfs/

cateringforhealthscot.pdf

Other useful sources of information on a balanced diet are as follows.

British Nutrition Foundation:

www.nutrition.org.uk

Nutrition Society:

www.nutritionsociety.org

Food Standards Agency:

www.food.gov.uk

Overweight and obesity

Body weight is influenced by energy intake (from food) and energy expenditure (needed for basal metabolism such as keeping the heart beating and for physical activity). If a person regularly consumes more energy (calories) than they use, they will start to gain weight and eventually become overweight or obese. If a person regularly consumes less energy than they use they will lose weight. Extra energy is stored in the body as fat. Balancing energy intake and output to maintain a healthy weight has many health and social benefits.

Obesity is a condition in which abnormal or excessive fat accumulation in adipose tissue impairs health. It is defined in adults as a body mass index (BMI) above 30. Obesity is now a worldwide public health problem, affecting all ages and socioeconomic groups. It is the most important dietary factor in chronic diseases such as cancer, cardiovascular disease and type 2 diabetes. It is second only to smoking as a cause of cancer. People who are overweight or obese are more likely to suffer from coronary heart disease, gallstones, osteoarthritis (of the knees) and high blood pressure. Obese women are more likely to have complications during and after pregnancy.

The latest NHS statistics on obesity show that in England:

- 24 per cent of men and 26 per cent of women aged 16 or over were classified as obese with a BMI of more than 30
- 42 per cent of men and 32 per cent of women were classified as overweight with a BMI of at least 25
- 31 per cent of boys aged 2 to 15, and 29 per cent of girls of the same age were classed as overweight or obese, with a steady increase since 2005
- 19.1 per cent of children aged 10–11 years were obese and a further 14.4 per cent were overweight; of children aged 4–5 years, 9.5 per cent were obese and another 13.1 per cent overweight; this means that a third of 10–11 year olds and over a fifth of 4–5 year olds were overweight or obese.

Source: Public Health England (http://phe.gov.uk)

Obesity is causing concern as statistics show rising levels of obesity year on year. This has a negative effect on the health of individuals and causes increasing public health problems.

It is not just a problem of excess fat, but where that fat is deposited. People who have extra weight (fat) around their middle – 'apple shaped' – are at greater risk of some of these diseases than those who have most of the extra weight around their hips and thighs – 'pear shaped'. Because the health risks of obesity are compounded by the influence of fat distribution, waist-to-hip ratios, or waist circumferences, are now commonly measured. In general, men are at increased risk of obesity-related diseases when their waist circumference reaches 94 cm (37 inches). For women, risks increase at 80 cm (32 inches). The risks of disease become substantially increased at 102 cm (40 inches) for men and 88 cm (35 inches) for women.

Obesity and diabetes

Obese people also have a higher risk of developing diabetes. The World Health Organization (WHO) has predicted that one of the consequences of the global epidemic of obesity will be 300 million people with type 2 diabetes by 2025.

Diabetes develops when the body cannot use glucose properly. Around 1.4 million people in the UK have been diagnosed with diabetes, of whom around 1 million have type 2 diabetes (which used to be called adult onset diabetes). By 2030, this figure is expected to rise to 4.6 million with 90 per cent being type 2 diabetes. In addition to this, there are a large number of people who may have unrecognised diabetes.

Eating a healthy balanced diet, taking regular physical exercise and maintaining a healthy body weight can help to prevent or delay the onset of type 2 diabetes. As well as following their medical advice, people with diabetes should try to maintain a healthy weight and eat a diet that is low in fat (particularly saturated fats) and salt, but eat plenty of fruit and vegetables, at least five portions a day, and starchy carbohydrate foods such as bread, rice and pasta (particularly the wholegrain types).

WEBLINK

To see a chart of healthy body weight go to NHS Choices:
www.nhs.uk/livewell/loseweight/pages/height-weight-chart.aspx

Case study

SuperSize Me

SuperSize Me was an American documentary directed by Morgan Spurlock, a US film-maker. His film follows a period from 1 February to 2 March, during which he ate only McDonald's food. The film documents this lifestyle's drastic effect on Spurlock's physical and psychological well-being, and explores the fast-food industry's corporate influence, including how it encourages poor nutrition for its own profit. The reason for Spurlock's investigation was the increasing spread of obesity throughout US society, which the Surgeon General had declared 'epidemic'.

Spurlock ate at McDonald's restaurants three times per day, eating every item on the chain's menu at least once. He consumed an average of 5,000 kcal (the equivalent of 9.26 Big Macs) per day during the experiment. An intake of around 2,500 kcal within a healthy balanced diet is more generally recommended for a man to maintain his weight. As a result, Spurlock gained 11.1 kilograms (24 lb), a 13 per cent body mass increase, increased his cholesterol to 230 mg/dL, and experienced mood swings, sexual dysfunction and fat accumulation in his liver. It took Spurlock 14 months to lose the weight gained from his experiment, using a vegan diet.

1 Do you think that Spurlock's experiment was a true representation of fast food?
2 Why do you think fast foods like McDonald's are so popular, especially with young people?
3 Do you think there would be a significant uptake of more healthy foods such as fresh fruit and vegetables if more of these were on the menu?
4 The fast-food chains are keen to say that they offer healthy choices as part of a balanced diet. What do you think is most important to them – the health of the nation or profit?

Case study

Growing Brits

Compared to statistics from 60 years ago the average British person is now taller, fatter and with bigger feet. All body measurements, including thighs, upper arms, hips, waist, chest and neck, are bigger – even fingers are bigger and old rings often don't fit (Victoria Lambert, 2009).

What are the factors that you think may have led to this? Consider the following:

- salaries and money available
- social aspects of eating out
- changing tastes
- influence of foreign travel on food
- fast food and more meals eaten away from home
- choices in supermarkets and online
- more car journeys made
- less time spent on cooking.

Salt and health

Yet another challenge for the hospitality industry is to reduce the amount of salt used in cooking. It is now well recognised that there is a link between salt and hypertension (high blood pressure). High blood pressure increases the risk of developing conditions such as heart disease and stroke. Around a third of the adult population in the UK has been diagnosed with hypertension; it is most common in older people, those with a family history of the condition and in some ethnic groups.

A number of lifestyle factors can help to prevent or treat high blood pressure – for example, not smoking, being physically active, maintaining a healthy body weight, avoiding or moderating alcohol, eating a balanced and varied diet that is low in fat (particularly saturated fats) and sodium (salt), and that includes low-fat dairy products.

As the main source of sodium in the diet is salt (sodium chloride), it has been recommended that people in the UK reduce their salt intake to a maximum of 6 g per day, which is about a teaspoon. For most people this will mean reducing their current salt intake by one-third and it must be remembered that this is not just added salt at the table, as salt is hidden in a wide range of foods.

- Salt added at the table and during cooking contributes around 10–15 per cent of our total salt intake.

- Naturally occurring salt in foods contributes another 10–15 per cent.
- On average, around 75 per cent of the salt in the diet comes from processed foods such as bread and cereal products, breakfast cereals, meat products, some ready meals, fast food, smoked fish, pickles, canned vegetables, canned and packet sauces and soups, savoury snack foods, and biscuits and cakes in which salt has been used as a preservative and flavour enhancer.
- Spreading fats and cheese also make a contribution to salt intake.

The FSA is working closely with the food industry to explore ways to lower the sodium content of processed foods, and a number of manufacturers and retailers have already taken action to achieve the necessary reduction. However, such activities will be successful only if there is consumer acceptance of these products. The FSA is playing its part by raising public awareness of the dangers of high blood pressure and the need to reduce the amount of salt in food. People can do this by using food labels to select lower-salt/sodium products and by persevering so as to adapt their palates to less salty tastes. Many food manufacturers and fast-food companies have committed to reduce the amounts of salt in their products gradually; such moves are considered the best way to change tastes and eating habits gradually.

A low-fat diet

A diet that is low in fat, and includes low-fat dairy foods, and fruit and vegetables, has been shown to lower blood pressure in people with or without previous high blood pressure. This diet reduced the amount of fat, saturates and cholesterol consumed, and increased the amount of potassium, magnesium and calcium.

The best effect was achieved when a reduction in salt and a reduction in fats were combined. This highlights the importance of improving the diet overall rather than focusing on single nutrients. Eating a healthy, balanced diet will also help to maintain a healthy body weight.

Potassium, calcium and magnesium

An inadequate dietary intake of potassium may increase blood pressure. A high potassium intake may, therefore, protect against developing hypertension and improve blood pressure control in people with hypertension. There is also evidence to suggest that the effect of sodium (salt) on blood pressure may be related to the amount of potassium in the diet, and that the ratio of sodium to potassium in the diet might be more important than the absolute amount of either. Potassium is found in meat, milk, vegetables, potatoes, fruit (especially bananas) and fruit juices, bread, fish, nuts and seeds. Celery is a good source of potassium; use it in salads, soups and stews or as crudités with hummus, guacamole or salsa.

Studies have also suggested that ensuring an adequate amount of calcium and magnesium in the diet is important to protect against high blood pressure, as well as for general health. Sources of calcium include milk and dairy products, soft bones in canned fish, bread, pulses, green vegetables, dried fruit, nuts and seeds. Foods containing magnesium include cereals and cereal products, meat, green vegetables, milk, potatoes, nuts and seeds.

Diet and cancer

It is now estimated that one-third of all cancers are related to poor diet. Epidemiological studies look at what people eat alongside the incidence of cancer. Studies over many years have shown a number of interesting links between different diets and cancers.

- The incidence of certain cancers, especially stomach and bowel, has increased as large-scale food processing and modern eating trends have replaced many of the wholegrain cereals, pulses and roots in our diet with white flour, refined cereals and sugars.
- Cancers of the stomach and oesophagus are much less common where the typical diet is high in cereals, tubers and starchy foods but low in animal proteins, the starches often providing half of the dietary energy needs. Diets in developed countries tend to be high in animal proteins, sugar and salt, but low in unrefined starches.
- There is a greater incidence of stomach cancer in countries where traditionally a lot of salty foods are eaten – for example, Japan, China and Portugal.
- In southern European countries, the consumption of fruit and vegetables is generally higher than in northern Europe, and the incidence of cancers of the mouth and throat, oesophagus, lung and stomach is lower in the south.

Some research may indicate only a possible link between diet and cancer, but where evidence is sufficiently strong, prestigious organisations such as the World Cancer Research Fund and the World Health Organization publish guidance to help people make dietary changes.

How can diet influence the development of cancer?

A damaged cell needs to replicate in order to grow into a group of cancer cells. Some substances in our diet may either encourage the replication process and promote cancer growth or slow it down, so protecting against cancer.

- **Carcinogenic agents:** these may directly influence DNA or protein in cells. Examples include alfatoxins or micotoxins, which are found in some mouldy food, alcohol and certain compounds produced by some cooking and food-processing methods.
- **Tumour promoters:** unlike carcinogens, tumour promoters do not act directly on DNA, but stimulate the genes and encourage replication. Some hormones may act in this way, and although the body produces these hormones naturally, diet can affect the level of components such as oestrogens in the body. Other tumour promoters include alcohol and a high-fat or a high-energy diet, which may promote the production of

harmful substances, such as free radicals. Free radicals are thought to influence DNA disorganisation.

But, just as we may introduce harmful elements into our bodies through our diet, there are also nutrients that may protect us.

- **Protective nutrients:** many foods contain protective substances that may reduce damage to tissues by free radicals, or potentially reduce cell growth.
- **Antioxidants:** antioxidants are important constituents of the diet, and are involved in DNA and cell maintenance and repair. They may reduce the production of free radicals, preventing early damage to cells and so reduce the chance that they will become cancerous. Antioxidants in the diet may be in the form of vitamins or minerals, such as vitamins C and E, beta-carotene and selenium, or they may be found in flavonoids in vegetables.
- **Phytoestrogens:** these have properties similar to oestrogens, but are much weaker than the oestrogens the body itself produces. They can be divided primarily into two groups: isoflavones and lignans. Isoflavones are linked to the protein part of food and lignans to the fibre. Table 8.10 includes examples of sources of phytoestrogens.
- **Other bioactive compounds:** many foods have functions beyond the vitamins and minerals they contain. Research is revealing that some of their chemicals and reactions may be beneficial to health. In laboratory experiments, for example, garlic extracts have killed *Heliobacter pylori*, a bacterium that can grow in the stomach and is known to increase the risk of cancer. Sulphur-containing compounds in garlic and onions may also reduce the formation of carcinogenic compounds that arise from the curing of meats.

Table 8.10 Protective nutrients: their sources and functions

Vitamins and minerals	Positive function	Sources
Carotenoids These are precursors of vitamin A; they include alpha-carotene, beta-carotene, xanthophylls (the main one is lutein), lycopene and cryptoxanthin	Antioxidant	Dark-green leafy vegetables, orange vegetables and fruit Lutein: kale, spinach, broccoli, corn Lycopene: tomatoes, watermelons, pink grapefruit, guavas Cryptoxantin: mangoes, papaya, persimmons, red peppers, pumpkins
Folate (folic acid)	Antioxidant; may affect division of cells in the colon	Beans, green leafy vegetables, liver, nuts, wholegrain cereals
Selenium	Stimulation of detoxification enzymes	Brazil nuts, wholemeal bread, eggs, fish, meat
Vitamin C (ascorbic acid)	Antioxidant	Broccoli, cabbage and other green leafy vegetables, citrus fruit, mangoes, peppers, strawberries, tomatoes and new potatoes
Vitamin D	May control cell growth through its effect on calcium	Effect of sunlight on the skin, fish liver oils, egg yolk, margarine and other spreads, oily fish, dairy produce
Vitamin E	Antioxidant	Nuts, seeds, vegetables oils, wheatgerm, whole grains
Other bioactive compounds	**Positive function**	**Sources**
Allium compounds (contain sulphur)	Stimulate detoxification enzymes	Chives, garlic, onions
Flavonoids (e.g. quercetin)	Antioxidant function within the plant	Berries, broad beans, broccoli, onions, tomatoes
Isothiocyanates	Stimulate detoxifying enzymes	Broccoli, Brussels sprouts, cabbage and other brassicas
Phytoestrogens (isoflavones and lignans)	May alter steroid hormone metabolism	Isoflavones: beans, chickpeas, lentils, soya Lignans: oils seeds (e.g. flax, soya, rape), legumes and various other vegetables and fruit, particularly berries, whole grains
Plant sterols	May bind with hormones in the gut and influence hormone metabolism	Cereals, fruit, nuts, seeds, vegetables
Terpenoid (e.g. D-limonene)	Stimulate enzyme systems	Oil of lemons, oranges and other citrus fruits

Source: Dr Clare Shaw, Royal Marsden Hospital

WEBLINKS

Vegetarian Society UK:
www.vegsoc.org

Vegan Society:
www.vegansociety.com

Food allergies and intolerances

It is estimated by the British Allergy Foundation and the Institute for Food Research that the proportion of the British population with an allergy to one or more foods or ingredients is between 1 and 2 per cent. Each year the number of allergy sufferers increases by approximately 5 per cent, half of all those affected being children.

Some recent allergy-related statistics include:

- 615 per cent increase in hospital admissions for anaphylaxis in the 20 years 1992–2012 (Turner et al.; JACI, 2015)
- in the last decade, cases of food allergies have doubled and the number of hospitalisations caused by severe allergic reactions has increased seven-fold (EAACI, 2015)
- more than 20,000 people admitted to hospital each year with allergy, 61.8 per cent (12,560) of admissions due to allergic reactions were emergencies, a 6.2 per cent increase (730) on the same period in the previous year (11,830) (HSCIC, 2014)
- 6–8 per cent of children have a proven food allergy (National Institute for Health Care and Excellence, 2014)
- allergy is a chronic disease that is expected to affect more than 50 per cent of all Europeans in ten years' time (EAACI, 2011)
- up to one in five allergic people suffer a serious debilitating disease, and are in fear of death from a possible asthma attack or anaphylactic shock (EAACI, 2011).

Food allergies occur when an individual's immune system sees certain foods or ingredients food as harmful and therefore a reaction takes place. The allergic reaction that some people have to certain food items can sometimes be fatal. Reactions include:

- tingling or itching, or a burning sensation in the mouth or throat
- an itchy red rash on the skin, with possible raised areas
- swelling of the face, mouth or other areas
- difficulty in swallowing
- wheezing or shortness of breath
- feeling dizzy and light-headed
- nausea or vomiting
- abdominal pain or diarrhoea
- hay fever-like symptoms, such as sneezing or itchy eyes.

The symptoms of a severe allergic response can be a sudden reaction and worsen very quickly. **Anaphylaxis** is frequently linked to people with a nut allergy (especially to peanuts) but nuts are not the only food that could cause a reaction. Initial symptoms of anaphylaxis may be the same as those listed above, but especially swelling in mouth, nose and throat. This can lead to difficulty in breathing, sudden fear and anxiety, rapid heartbeat, sudden drop in blood pressure, causing light-headedness, confusion and unconsciousness. Without quick treatment, it can be fatal and it is essential to seek medical attention immediately.

People who know they may be at risk of anaphylactic shock may carry an 'epi-pen'. This administers adrenaline (epinephrine) into the upper outer muscle of the thigh. It starts to work very quickly, reducing swelling, relieving breathing difficulties and improving blood pressure. However, medical attention should still be sought. The Anaphylaxis Campaign has warned caterers to be on the alert for foods containing flour made from lupin seeds as this can cause an allergic reaction similar to peanuts. Lupin flour is used as an ingredient in France, Holland, Portugal and Italy because of its nutty taste, attractive yellow colour and because it is guaranteed GM free.

Legislating for allergies and allergens

In December 2014 Regulation (EU FIC) came in to force in the UK and changed the way allergen information must be displayed on packaged food, non-packaged food, and in restaurants and other food outlets outside the home.

It is now a legal requirement for food providers to give details on request of specific allergens that are present within the food on offer (European Directives 2003/89/EC and 2006/142/EC). The EU identified 14 specific allergens and, where these appear, the food server or someone else in the establishment must be able to provide details. The details may be given in the menu, a separate leaflet, a notice in the restaurant or verbally. Where the food is packaged the allergen information must be printed or written on the packaging; most food producers do this by highlighting the allergenic ingredients in bold.

As well as providing accurate information to customers about possible allergens in the food being supplied it is essential to ensure that:

- all staff dealing with food are well informed about possible allergens in food and where they may be on the menu
- everyone is aware of the possibility of hidden allergens, especially in foods with a number of ingredients such as complex salads, soups and sauces
- any possible cross-contamination is avoided – for example, from food equipment or where different foods are presented together as they would be in a salad bar.

All food establishments need to check their menus to make sure there are some dishes suitable for allergy

WEBLINKS

The Food Standards Agency's allergy and intolerance information:

www.food.gov.uk/allergy

and its Allergy and intolerance guidance for businesses:

www.food.gov.uk/business-industry/allergy-guide

Resources for allergen information:

www.food.gov.uk/allergen-resources

You can receive alerts at:

www.food.gov.uk/about-us/subscribe

or follow:

#AllergyAlert

on Twitter and Facebook

Information on allergies from the National Health Service:

nhs.uk/conditions/allergies

Allergy Aware Kitchen provides training and support for allergy awareness:

www.allergyawarekitchen.co.uk

Food Allergy UK provides support for allergy sufferers:

www.allergyuk.org

Learn about testing for allergies at:

www.foodallergy.com

sufferers and that staff know exactly what they are so cross-contamination can be avoided. Alternatively, individual allergen-free dishes can be prepared to order. Many establishments are looking to partially overcome problems with allergens by providing non-allergenic ingredients in all of their dishes – for example, gluten-free flour, egg- and mustard-free mayonnaise – and carefully checking that dish garnishes are not on the allergens list.

The prevention of allergic reactions has legal status. Measures taken to provide information about allergens and also measures in place to prevent cross-contamination of non-allergenic foods with allergens must now form part of the HACCP plan and be part of due diligence. Authorised food officers have powers to take action against breaches in the legislation.

Please see the further information and information about the relevant legislation in Chapter 3.

Food intolerances

Food intolerance is different from an allergy because it does not involve the immune system. Nevertheless the symptoms can be significant in terms of causing illness, reactions and discomfort.

Food intolerance is much more common than food allergy. The reaction may be slower or delayed by many hours after eating the food. Symptoms could last for many hours, days or even longer. The intolerance could be to several foods or to a group of foods.

The symptoms of food intolerance can vary including fatigue, joint pains, darkness under the eyes, sweats, diarrhoea, vomiting, bloating, irritable bowel, skin symptoms such as rashes, eczema, and other chronic conditions.

Food intolerances include coeliac disease (intolerance to gluten) and lactose intolerance (intolerance to the natural sugar in milk).

Table 8.12 Special diets for those with food allergies and intolerances

Type of diet	Problems	Foods to avoid	Permitted foods
Coeliac	Not truly an allergy or intolerance but an autoimmune reaction to gluten; results in severe inflammation of the gastro-intestinal tract, pain and diarrhoea, and malnutrition due to inability to absorb nutrients	All products made from wheat, barley or rye; this includes bread; always check the label on all commercial products	Potatoes, rice and flours made from potatoes and rice; also cornflour, fresh fruit and vegetables; meat, fish, eggs and most dairy products
Lactose intolerance	A digestive problem where the body cannot digest lactose (natural sugar mainly in milk and dairy products)	Milk, dairy products and foods with these as an ingredient	Non-dairy foods and those where dairy products have not been included
Food allergies	Individuals can suffer severe and rapid reactions to any food they are allergic to, which can be fatal; common allergies are to peanuts and their derivatives, sesame seeds, cashew nuts, pecan nuts, walnuts, hazelnuts, milk, fish, shellfish and eggs	Peanuts, chopped nuts, fish and shellfish, sesame seeds, groundnut oil, eggs, mustard, peanut products and other nut products	Foods that do not contain the specific allergen, even in very small amounts, and where no cross-contamination with allergens has taken place

Type of diet	Problems	Foods to avoid	Permitted foods
Low cholesterol	High levels of cholesterol circulating in the bloodstream are associated with an increased risk of cardiovascular disease	Liver, kidney, egg yolks, fatty meats, bacon, ham, pâté, fried foods, pastry, cream, full-fat milk, full-fat yoghurt, cheeses, salad dressings, biscuits, cakes	Lean meat and fish (grilled or poached), fresh fruit and vegetables, low-fat milk, low-fat yoghurt, porridge, muesli
Diabetic	The body is unable to control the level of glucose in the blood	As above, plus high-sugar dishes; this can lead to comas and long-term problems such as increased risk of cardiovascular disease, blindness and kidney problems	Potatoes, rice and flours made from potatoes and rice; also cornflour, fresh fruit and vegetables wholemeal bread and grains, pasta, pulses; meat, fish, eggs, most unsweetened dairy products

Case study

Free school lunches

In September 2014 it became obligatory for all infant school children (children in reception classes, Year 1 and Year 2, plus 'disadvantaged' nursery-age children) in England to be provided with a free school lunch.

1 Do you think that this initiative is likely to have an impact on nutrition in young children?
2 Should it be offered to older children?
3 Suggest some foods that should go into these lunches to increase the vitamin intake of children. Why are vitamins important to growing children?

Further reading

Fox, B.A. and Cameron, A.G. (1995) *Food Science, Nutrition and Health* (6th edn). Hodder Arnold.

Gaman, P.M. and Sherrington, K.B. (1996) *The Science of Food* (4th edn). Routledge.

Henderson, L., Irving, K., Gregory, J. *et al.* (2003) *The National Diet and Nutrition Survey*. London: TSO.

Food Standards Agency, Scotland (2002) *Catering for Health: A Guide to Teaching Healthier Catering Practices* available online at www.food.gov.uk/multimedia/pdfs/cateringforhealthscot.pdf

Topics for discussion

1 What is meant by a balanced diet and why is it desirable that a balanced diet is achieved? How would you advise someone to achieve a balanced diet?
2 Why do you think preferences or fashions in food and eating change? How could a restaurant owner remain aware of changing trends while providing healthy choices on the menu?
3 What are the ways that food and diet can directly impact on health and well-being? What can be the relation between certain illnesses and food?
4 What issues are associated with nutrition at different times of life? What specific considerations are there for the diets of children, the elderly, nursing mothers and teenagers?
5 How may the nutritional value of foods be affected in preparation, cooking and holding food for service? Discuss examples of how to keep food in the best nutritional condition, preventing negative effects.
6 What are the main sources of nutritional information available to food providers, chefs and caterers? How could you best use some of the information available to inform customers on good food choices?
7 Do you consider that TV advertising and programmes, along with social media, affect how people eat? If so, is this a good thing?
8 Do restaurants/fast-food outlets, managers and owners need a good knowledge of nutrition when their clientele are not eating there on a daily basis?
9 How could a fast-food restaurant provide more 'healthy eating' options that would appeal to their young customers? Suggest six items you could introduce to the menu.
10 What effects have the latest legislation on allergens had on (a) restaurants, (b) school meals, (c) sandwich-making businesses, (d) large hotels, (e) airline caterers? Who will check that the legislation is being complied with?

9 Menu planning, events and banqueting

The development of the restaurant and the menu

A rough timeline of the development of restaurants and menus is as follows.

- Ancient world (e.g. China, Rome) – there were simple public eating places, in the form of roadside inns; commodities and methods of cookery from all over the Roman Empire were adopted and spread by the Romans.
- Middle Ages – in Europe, taverns and inns were the main eating establishments, and meat became the centre of the meal.
- Seventeenth and eighteenth centuries – classical French cuisine evolved.
- French Revolution (1789) – many chefs left France, taking the French approach to many other countries.
- Early nineteenth century – the first use of individual menus, as opposed to seemingly random lists of food). The first arrangement of a meal into different courses (e.g. hors d'oeuvre, fish, entrée, sweet) with up to seven courses on special occasions.
- Mid-nineteenth century – luxury hotels and grand restaurants evolved, with artistry and flair in their cooking, and often signature dishes (such as the peach melba, created at the Savoy Hotel, or the tarte tatin); new technologies developed (from the freezer to pasteurisation).
- End of the nineteenth century – Escoffier modernised the organisation of staff in the restaurant kitchen (the partie system).
- 1930s – the first franchised fast-food restaurants were opened in the USA, leading to the development of many other franchises during the twentieth century.
- Mid-twentieth century – more food service took place at work and in institutions such as schools or hospitals, requiring budget-conscious catering.
- Later twentieth century – easier and cheaper travel, including air travel, encouraged the spread of commodities (giving caterers more choice of produce) and types of cuisine (leading to the popularity of restaurants specialising in non-local ethnic styles of food.

La Trompette

Prix fixe

£22 three courses

Caesar salad
Cream of asparagus soup
Roast quail with green beans, griottines cherries and meat juices
Terrine de campagne with celeriac remoulade and toasted brioche
Glenarm salmon risotto with fresh herbs and champagne velouté
Deep-fried sand eels with garlic mayonnaise, lemon and parsley

Grilled andouillette with apple, chips and grain mustard sauce
Warm salad of duck magret with mushrooms and sablé potatoes
Grilled loin of veal with pasta salad, peas, broad beans and pesto
Sauté of free range chicken breast with lardons,
new potatoes and baby gem lettuce
New season's lamb with aubergine, courgette,
couscous, merguez sausage and salsa
Crisp fillet of sea bream with salt
cod brandade, summer beans and chorizo
Roast halibut with olive oil mash and aged balsamic vinegar

Lemon cheesecake
Chocolate profiteroles
Caramelised apple tart with caramel ice cream
Prune and Armagnac ice cream or white peach sorbet
Fresh strawberry salad with black pepper and basil
Cheese from the board (supp. £6.50)

Coffee £4.00
Mineral water £5.00 (75cl bottle)

A discretionary gratuity of 12.5% will be added to the total bill

Figure 9.1 Sample menu (prix fixe)

Menu

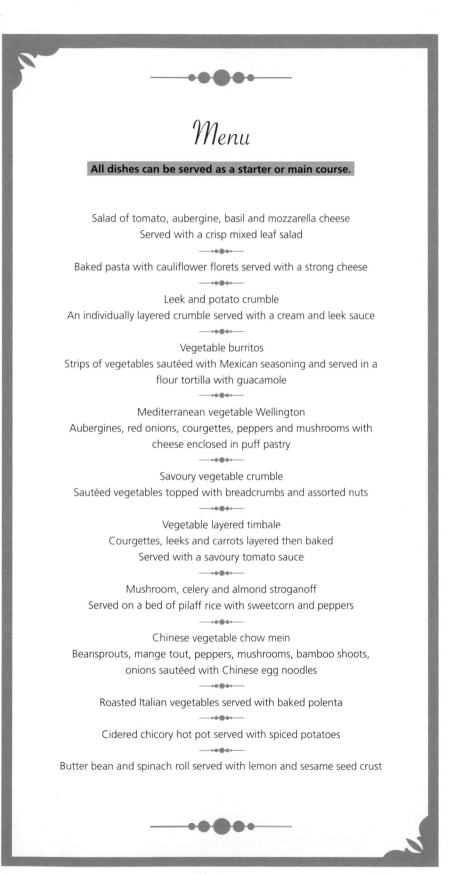

All dishes can be served as a starter or main course.

Salad of tomato, aubergine, basil and mozzarella cheese
Served with a crisp mixed leaf salad

Baked pasta with cauliflower florets served with a strong cheese

Leek and potato crumble
An individually layered crumble served with a cream and leek sauce

Vegetable burritos
Strips of vegetables sautéed with Mexican seasoning and served in a flour tortilla with guacamole

Mediterranean vegetable Wellington
Aubergines, red onions, courgettes, peppers and mushrooms with cheese enclosed in puff pastry

Savoury vegetable crumble
Sautéed vegetables topped with breadcrumbs and assorted nuts

Vegetable layered timbale
Courgettes, leeks and carrots layered then baked
Served with a savoury tomato sauce

Mushroom, celery and almond stroganoff
Served on a bed of pilaff rice with sweetcorn and peppers

Chinese vegetable chow mein
Beansprouts, mange tout, peppers, mushrooms, bamboo shoots, onions sautéed with Chinese egg noodles

Roasted Italian vegetables served with baked polenta

Cidered chicory hot pot served with spiced potatoes

Butter bean and spinach roll served with lemon and sesame seed crust

Figure 9.2 Sample menu (vegetarian)

- eggs – fried, boiled, poached, scrambled; omelettes with bacon or tomatoes, mushrooms or sauté potatoes
- fish – kippers, smoked haddock, kedgeree
- meats (hot) – fried or grilled bacon, sausages, kidneys, with tomatoes, mushrooms or sauté potatoes, potato cakes
- meats (cold) – ham, bacon, pressed beef with sauté potatoes
- preserves – marmalade, jams, honey
- beverages – tea, coffee, hot chocolate
- bread – rolls, croissants, brioche, toast, pancakes, waffles.

Some points to consider when compiling a breakfast menu are as follows.

- It is usual to offer three of the courses previously mentioned: fruit, yoghurt or cereals; fish, eggs or meat; preserves, bread, coffee or tea.
- As large a choice as possible should be offered, depending on the size of the establishment, bearing in mind that it is better to offer a smaller number of well-prepared dishes than a large number of hurriedly prepared ones.
- A choice of plain foods, such as boiled eggs or poached haddock, should be available for the person who may not require a fried breakfast.

A buffet breakfast offers a choice of as many breakfast foods as is both practical and economic. Customers can self-serve the main items with assistance from counter hands. Ideally, eggs should be freshly cooked to order and some other items, such as hot drinks, may also be served by staff.

Luncheon and dinner menus

Types of lunch and dinner menu include:

- a set-price one-, two- or three-course menu with ideally a choice at each course (table d'hôte)
- a list of well-varied dishes, each priced individually so that the customer can make up his/her own menu of whatever number of dishes they require (à la carte)
- buffet, which may be all cold or hot dishes, or a combination of both, either to be served or organised on a self-service basis; depending on the time of year and location, barbecue dishes can be considered
- special party, which may be either set menu with no choice; set menu with a limited choice, such as soup or melon, main course, choice of two sweets; served or self-service buffet.

Offer only the number of courses and number of dishes within each course that can be satisfactorily prepared, cooked and served.

	MONDAY	TUESDAY	WEDNESDAY	THURSDAY	FRIDAY
Soup of the day	Mushroom and chive (V) (L)	Roasted pepper (V) (L)	Parsnip and apple (V) (L)	Chilli and sweet potato (V) (L)	Leek and potato (V) (L)
Main meal 1	Aromatic chicken korma served with rice and poppadom (H)	Toad in the hole accompanied with onion gravy (H)	Roast turkey with bread sauce and cranberry (M)	Poached lemon and bay leaf chicken breast (L)	Breaded hake with chips and lemon (H)
Main meal 2	Boiled ham on the bone with a creamy parsley velouté (M)	Jambalaya with chorizo, prawns, rice and sweet peppers (M)	Beef and hoi sin with green peppers and noodles (M)	Pan-fried lambs' livers with redcurrant jus (M)	Hot chilli con carne with rice and sour cream (H)
Vegetarian meal	Vegetarian cottage pie with garden vegetables and a crusted potato topping (M)	Pesto roasted vegetables with chick pea couscous (M) (N)	Lightly spiced bean and tomato bruschetta (M)	Vegetable balti with coriander, cumin, mango and turmeric (M)	Sweet potato and mushroom pavé with tomato chutney (M)
Potatoes and vegetables	Rice or baby jackets Green beans provençale	Mashed potato Sauté courgettes	Roast potatoes Vichy carrots	Parmentier potatoes Buttered cabbage	Chips or new potatoes Mushy peas
Hot dessert	Bread and butter pudding with custard sauce (H)	Banana sponge with toffee sauce (H)	Apple and cinnamon crumble with custard sauce (H)	Pineapple upside down cake with custard sauce (H)	Orange sponge with chocolate sauce (H)
Some of our foods may contain GM soya or maize; please ask our staff for details. N =contains nuts, L =low fat content, M =medium fat content, H =high fat content, V =vegetarian					

Figure 9.3 Luncheon menu: staff restaurant

A vegetarian menu may be offered as an alternative to or as part of the à la carte or table d'hôte menus (see Figure 9.2).

Tea menus

The serving of 'tea' has become increasingly popular over recent years, in hotels, restaurants, teashops, department stores and even at events.

Traditional English afternoon tea may include:

- assorted small cut sandwiches
- bread and butter (white, brown, fruit loaf)
- assorted preserves
- scones with clotted cream, pastries, gâteaux
- tea (Indian, China, iced, fruit, herb or a house speciality).

High tea may have all the afternoon tea items but in addition something more substantial, probably something savoury and eaten with a knife and fork. For example, high tea might include:

- assorted sandwiches
- buttered buns, scones, cakes, Scotch pancakes, waffles, sausage rolls, assorted bread and butter, various jams, toasted teacakes, scones, crumpets, buns
- eggs (boiled, poached, fried, omelettes)
- fried fish, grilled meats, roast poultry
- cold meats and salads
- assorted pastries, gâteaux
- various ices, coupes, sundaes
- tea or fruit juices.

Light buffets

Light buffets for cocktail parties or other events can include:

- hot savoury pastry patties of, for example, lobster, chicken, crab, salmon, mushrooms, ham
- hot chipolatas; chicken livers wrapped in bacon and skewered
- bite-sized items – quiche and pizza, hamburgers, meatballs with savoury sauce or dip, scampi, fried fish en goujons, tartare sauce
- savoury finger toast to include any of the cold canapés; these may also be prepared on biscuits or shaped pieces of pastry
- game chips, gaufrette potatoes, fried fish balls, celery stalks spread with cheese
- sandwiches; bridge rolls, open or closed but always small
- fresh dates stuffed with cream cheese; crudités with mayonnaise and cardamom dip; tuna and chive catherine wheels; crab claws with garlic dip; smoked salmon pin wheels; choux puffs with Camembert
- sweets (e.g. trifles, charlottes, bavarois, fruit salad, gâteaux).

All food for a **fork buffet** must be prepared in a way that enables it to be eaten with a fork or spoon and with one hand.

Fast-food menus

Fast-food restaurant menus are planned to allow for fast turnover by providing a limited menu, planned preparation, limited cooking methods and rapid service.

In response to criticism about the nutritional elements of some fast foods and their contribution to obesity, some chains now include healthy options on their menus and a full nutritional guide for customers, along with special diet and allergy advice.

Banquet menus

When compiling banquet menus, consider the following points.

- The food, which will possibly be for a large number of people, must be prepared and finished in such a way that it can be served fairly quickly and efficiently. Heavily garnished dishes should be avoided.
- If a large number of dishes have to be dressed at the same time, certain foods deteriorate quickly and will not stand storage, even for a short time, in a hot place.

A standard menu is used, bearing in mind the number of people involved. It is not usual to serve farinaceous (starchy) dishes, eggs, stews or savouries. A luncheon menu could be drawn from the following and would usually consist of three courses. Dinner menus, depending on the occasion, generally consist of three to five courses.

- **First course:** soup, cocktail (fruit or shellfish), hors d'oeuvre, assorted or single item, a small salad.
- **Second course:** fish, usually poached, steamed, roasted or grilled fillets with a sauce.
- **Third course:** meat, poultry or game, hot or cold, but not a stew or made-up dish; vegetables and potatoes or a salad would be served.
- **Fourth course:** sweet – hot or cold.

Cheese may be served as an extra course.

LUNCH

Galvin

Bistrot de Luxe

Entrées

Steak tartare
Soupe de poissons, rouille & croûtons
Salad of endive with Roquefort, chives & walnuts
Matjes Harengs marines, pommes à l'huile
Oak smoked salmon, fromage blanc & blini
Salad of Dorset crab, apple dressing
Half dozen Fines de Claire oysters
Salad of buffalo mozzarella & caponata
Escargots bourguignon
Parfait of foie gras & duck liver
Rillette of black boar

Plats Principles

Grilled Crottin de Chavignol, morels, peas & asparagus
Confit of organic salmon, Bayonne ham, beurre de tomate
Roast tranche of cod, crushed Jersey Royals, étuvée of leeks
Pot roast Landaise chicken, tagliatelle of asparagus & morels
Grilled calf's liver, shallots aigre-doux, lardoons & flat leaf parsley
Roast pork fillet, Bayonne ham, black pudding & caramelised apples
Roast rump of lamb, broad bean risotto
Braised veal's cheek, fresh pasta, baby spinach & Madeira sauce
Tête de Veau, sauce Ravigote

Desserts

Oeuf à la neige
Délice of milk and dark Valhrona chocolate
Crème brûlée, coconut mousseline
Gariguette strawberries, crème Chantilly
Apricot & chocolate soufflé
Prune & Armagnac parfait
Baba au rhum
Tarte au citron
Assiette de fromages with walnut & raisin loaf

Menu Prix Fixé

Gravadlax of organic salmon or velouté of broad beans
Grilled sea trout, petits pois à la Française or Confit duck, honey & rosemary spring cabbage
Chocolate mousse, orange jelly or Brie de Meaux & walnut bread

Figure 9.4 Sample luncheon menu for a bistro

DINNER

The Grill Room at The Dorchester

Appetisers

Oak-smoked wild Scottish salmon
Lobster soup with flamed Scottish lobster
Squab pigeon and spring vegetable consommé with black truffles
Crisp red mullet and spring vegetable salad with sundried tomato cream
Seared scallops with cauliflower purée, citrus vinaigrette and mimolette crisps
Foie gras and duck confit terrine with onion marmalade and toasted brioche
Caramelised endive with goats' cheese, honey and winter truffles
Ham hock ravioli with white beans, trompettes and parsley
Denham Estate venison burger with quail's egg, griottine cherries, parsnips and Port
Warm Gressingham duck salad with glazed root vegetables, chestnuts and meat juices
Baby spinach salad with cashel blue, spiced pears and walnuts

Main Courses

Roast sea bass fillet with olive oil mash, red pepper relish and aged balsamic vinegar
Dover sole grilled or pan fried with brown butter and capers
Seared tuna with fennel, cherry tomatoes and Jersey Royals
Ragoût of John Dory, lobster and mussels with crème fraîche and chives
Free-range chicken breast with creamed morels, asparagus and tarragon
New season rack of lamb with aubergine caviar, couscous and confit garlic
Roast rib of Aberdeen Angus beef with Yorkshire pudding and roast potatoes
Rabbit leg with calf's sweetbread, ceps, smoked bacon and Lyonnaise potatoes
Saffron risotto cake with stuffed tomato, grilled vegetables and Parmesan

Specialities from The Grill

Served with either hand-cut chips or olive mash, sauce béarnaise, sauce bordelaise, green peppercorn sauce or rosemary butter
Veal chop
Rib eye steak
Calf's liver and bacon
Lobster (1 kg)

Desserts

Crisp apple tart with clotted cream and calvados
Lemon and blueberry millefeuille with blood orange sorbet
Hot ginger pudding with plums and crème fraîche sorbet
A plate of Valrhona chocolate desserts
Home-made vanilla and rhubarb yoghurt with churros
Strawberry ripple ice cream or mango sorbet
Honey roast pear with caramel sauce and cardamom custard
Iced passion fruit and bitter chocolate délice with chilli and coriander

Selection of Cheeses from the Board
***
Coffee and Petits Fours

Figure 9.5 Sample dinner menu for a hotel restaurant

Figure 9.6 Afternoon tea table

Avocado filled with cream cheese and two fruit sauces

* * *

Seafood-filled fish mousse with crayfish sauce

* * *

Butter-cooked fillet of beef with sliced mushrooms and tongue in Madeira sauce

A selection of market vegetables

Potatoes fried with garlic and thyme

* * *

Light soft meringue topped with fruit

* * *

Coffee

Sweetmeats

Figure 9.7 Sample banquet menu (note: sweetmeats may also be called petits fours)

The structure and design of menus

Length

The number of dishes on a menu should offer the customer an interesting and varied choice. In general, it is better to offer fewer dishes of good standard than a long list of mediocre quality.

Design and presentation

Ensure the menu is presented in a sensible and welcoming way. An offhand, brusque presentation (written or oral) can be off-putting and lower expectations of the meal.

The menu design should complement the image of the dining room and be designed to allow for changes (total or partial), which may be daily, weekly, monthly, etc. An inset for dishes of the day or of the week gives the customer added interest. The cover of the menu should reflect the identity or decor of the operation, and should ideally pick up the theme of the restaurant. The paper chosen must be of good quality, heavy, durable and grease resistant.

A good menu design emphasises certain items. If there are certain dishes that you would like to emphasise:

- draw a box around a group of items
- use different typography (although never anything that is difficult to read)
- use different colours or shading
- add drawings around the items
- place an asterisk beside the item(s).

Some menus break away from traditional food categories (for example, by focusing on a restaurant speciality). Decide what your menu wants to say prior to deciding on food groupings. It is important to accentuate your most profitable food items in every category, by listing the most profitable items first and listing the rest in descending order.

Regardless of what categorisation style or design you choose, always remember it is important that it must be easy for the customer to navigate the menu. Confusing or illogically organised menus will only annoy customers and could well affect sales.

Menu copy should be set in a style of print that is easily legible and well spaced. Mixing typefaces is often done to achieve emphasis; if overdone, however, the overall concept is likely to look a mess and therefore unattractive to the eye.

Price on menus

You must consider where to put the price on the menu. If prices appear in a column running along the side of the menu, customers may be inclined to compare items based solely on price and choose the cheapest item. This can be avoided by placing the price in the same line as the food and the description.

Extra information

These days, menus often provide additional information about where food has been sourced from, especially when it is locally sourced. Allergy information, vegetarian choices, suggested wines with certain foods and a range of other information may now be included on menus.

Alternative presentation styles

Menus may be presented on chalkboards, painted on windows or mirrors, on placemats, electronic screens or individual customer tablet computers, and in a range of other forms.

Language

Accuracy in dish description helps the customer to identify the food they wish to choose. The description should describe the item realistically and not mislead the customer. Items or groups of items should bear names people recognise and understand. If a name does not give the right description, additional copy may be necessary, but it is important to avoid over-elaboration and flowery choice of words. Wherever possible, use English language. If a foreign dish name is used then follow it with a simple, clear English version.

Some menus can be built around general descriptive copy featuring the history of the establishment or the local area in which the establishment is located. Descriptive copy can alternatively be based on a speciality dish that has significant cultural importance to the area or the establishment. In doing so the description may wish to feature the person responsible for creating and preparing the dish, especially if the chef is reasonably well known and has appeared on national or local television or radio. The chef may also have had his/her recipes featured in the local press. This too may be included in the menu to create further interest.

Menu flexibility

Customer demands change over time and therefore menus become outdated and obsolete. Some operations use a 'menu of the day' on a wall- or chalkboard to provide flexibility in items offered and pricing. Some establishments change part of their menus daily or weekly, while the main core of the menu remains the same. Changes can be made on a paper insert, which can be added to the printed menu. Hors d'oeuvre, side dishes, salads, desserts and beverages do not change frequently; these dishes are printed on the main copy, while the speciality dishes, which do change more frequently, are placed on the paper insert.

Nothing becomes obsolete faster to the regular customer than the same menu. Even fast-food establishments, which have a basic menu on offer year in year out, still have to create interest by adding certain new products or new recipes to existing products in order to keep interest alive. Menus should change at least every three months.

Use of part-prepared or fully prepared products

Do not rule out part-prepared and fully prepared products – it is about creating a menu that appeals to customers at a price they are prepared to pay and that will give a good return. The right combination will vary from restaurant to restaurant, and operation to operation, depending on the following factors.

- **Style of operation:** a fine-dining restaurant will use little in the way of convenience foods. Fine dining is often marked by skill in the variety of cooking, whereas a less skilled operation will very often use a high proportion of ready-prepared foods; this ensures a constant delivery of standards.
- **Volume:** where a chef is preparing for large numbers and staff have limited skills, there is often a reliance on pre-prepared and fully prepared food.
- **Type of customer:** the market for food prepared fully from new materials is small – for the mass market, expectations are driven by the different situations in which they find themselves. Those dining at their place of work are not necessarily concerned if all the food is not prepared on site. However, when they are dining out for a special occasion they will probably expect something quite different.
- **Price:** customers have a sense of what they are willing to pay. This often depends on the occasion and the type of operation. For example, some people are prepared to spend more on a celebration dinner than a casual meal at the local gastropub. The price must cover the costs of food and be calculated to take into account all the other variable and fixed costs.
- **Staff skills:** profitability will also depend on how you balance the level of skill in the kitchen, and the use of pre-prepared and fully prepared products.
- **Facilities (kitchen design):** where kitchens are on the small size for the number of customers to be served, there may be very little space to prepare food from new materials. Therefore there may be much more of a reliance on pre-prepared and fully prepared foods. Likewise there will not be such a need for highly skilled staff requiring high salaries.

Menus and consumer protection

All consumer protection starts with the basic contract: if a supplier fails to supply what a consumer has contracted to purchase, the supplier may be in breach of contract. However, because breach of contract cases can be difficult to prove and expensive, the government has introduced legislation to improve protection for the consumer.

Legislation concerned with protecting the consumer can be divided into three areas:

1. health and safety
2. economic protection, such as weights and measures
3. unfair contract terms.

Price lists and menu display

The Price Marking (Food and Drink Services) Order 2003 requires that prices must be displayed. The wording and pricing of food and drink on menus and wine lists must comply with the law and be accurate.

The act of displaying menus, food and drink or their prices does not oblige a hospitality operator to sell the goods. Nor is the hospitality operator under any specific obligation to have the goods available for sale.

By offering dishes on the menu there is no legal obligation to serve the customer if he or she may cause a nuisance to other customers or because, due to demand, the dish has sold out and is 'off' the menu. But for establishments offering accommodation there is an obligation to provide refreshment as long as the customer is able to pay and is in an acceptable state (e.g. sober).

Trade descriptions

The display of menus, price lists and tariffs comes within the scope of the Trade Descriptions Act 1968, which makes it a criminal offence to mis-describe goods or services. A false description means 'any materially false or misleading statement which is in any way displayed so that it is associated with the goods in the mind of the consumer'.

The chef or manager must be very careful when wording menus, and especially when describing menu items to customers. To describe a duck as Aylesbury duck when in fact the duck was imported would be an offence under the act. The menu must clearly state the conditions covering service charges, cover charges and any extras.

Under the Trade Descriptions Act 1968 there are required declarations, as follows.

- You must state if a food ingredient (e.g. soya) is genetically modified; if so, the food or ingredients must be labelled genetically modified. Alternatively, a general notice clearly displayed at the point of food selection may state words to the effect that some of the food contains genetically modified material and that further information is available from staff.
- Staff must be well trained, and know the menu and the ingredients so that they can advise customers effectively and accurately.

Anyone charged with an offence under the act may offer the defence that the false description:

- was because of a pure mistake made by the person charged
- resulted from the information provided by another person
- was the fault of someone else
- resulted from an accident or other cause beyond the control of the person charged
- occurred because the person charged with the offence could not reasonably be expected to know that the description was misleading.

Apart from offering one or more of the above defences, someone charged with an offence will have to prove that he or she took reasonable precautions to ensure that the description was not misleading.

Menu descriptions

Chefs and managers must be exceptionally careful with menu descriptions; for example, something must not be described as 'home-made' if you have not made the menu dish yourself from ingredients.

In terms of the provision of accurate information on menus, it is important to be aware of the sort of problems that may be encountered with food descriptions. Some examples are listed below.

- **Scampi:** refers to products made from complete scampi. When using products that are made from pure scampi but using off-cuts of scampi, the products must be advertised as 'reformed scampi', as they are not of the same high quality.
- **King prawn:** king prawns can be called king prawns only where the prawns are of one of three specific species of prawn and are of the correct size.
- **Tiger prawn:** tiger prawns can be called tiger prawns only when they are of this specific species.
- **Chicken fillet and breast:** this term can be used only where the chicken is chicken flesh, not chopped, shaped and reformed chicken.
- **Smoked:** this means that the food must have been through a smoking process. If smoke flavour is used, it must state 'smoke flavoured'.
- **Fresh:** 'fresh' can be used only for fresh food, not canned or frozen.
- **Vegetarian dishes:** can be labelled vegetarian only when they have been produced without any contact or contamination with meat, fish or shellfish.

Irradiated foods

Food that has been irradiated must be marked 'irradiated', or the words 'treated with ionising radiation' must be included. If the food contains an ingredient that has been irradiated, it needs to be labelled stating that it contains the ingredient and should be accompanied by the word 'irradiated'. Typical foods that may be irradiated include spices and shellfish.

Vegetarian dishes

Any vegetarian dish must be produced without any contact with meat, fish or seafood. This means that during the cooking process separate oils have to be used for frying vegetarian dishes. This also means checking all ingredients, such as stocks, sauces and cheese, to ensure that they too are free from any meat or fish extract.

Allergens

Restaurants now have to provide allergen information on menus. This is a requirement under EU Food Information for Consumers Regulations No. 1169/2011.

Always check that menu descriptions are correct and agree with the descriptions given by the suppliers. It is important to check all your suppliers for accurate information.

Sale and supply of goods and services

The Sale of Goods and Services Act 1982 aims to ensure that goods sold are of satisfactory quality and fit for the purpose intended. This applies especially to equipment as well as commodities. The act is concerned with ensuring that customers receive goods that are of satisfactory quality and are fit for purpose.

- Goods may be defined as of satisfactory quality 'if they are as fit for the purpose or purposes for which goods of that kind are commonly bought as it is reasonable to expect having regard to any description applied to them, the price (if relevant) and all the other circumstances'.
- Goods must also be fit for the purpose. This means that, if a purchaser makes known a specific purpose for their goods, then the goods should be able to satisfy that purpose.

It applies to the *sale* of goods and services only. From the caterer's viewpoint this act works mainly to his or her advantage, whereas the Supply of Goods and Services Act 1982 (see below) works mainly to the customer's advantage.

The Supply of Goods and Services Act 1982 is concerned with 'implied' terms in a contract.

The Sale and Supply of Goods Act 1994 is an amending act that mainly amends the Sale of Goods Act 1979.

Consumer protection

The Consumer Protection Act 1987 deals with three main areas, as follows.

1. **Liability for defective products:** a consumer may now claim directly against a producer for damages in respect of a defective product. Negligence no longer has to be proved. Consumers may bring an action for civil damages resulting from personal injury and loss of or damage to any property.
2. **Consumer safety:** it is an offence to supply goods that fail to comply with the general safety requirements. Goods must be safe for the purpose for which they are sold. The act does not include food, which is covered under food safety legislation.
3. **Misleading price indications:** the Act makes it an offence to give misleading price information about goods, services, accommodation or facilities, whether on the trader's own behalf or on behalf of another. If the statement asserts that:
   - the price is less than in fact it is
   - the price is independent of facts or circumstances when in fact it is not
   - the price covers matters for which, in fact, an additional charge will be made
   - the price will be increased (or reduced) (or maintained) when in fact it will not be
   - the facts which the consumer is relying upon are not what they are purported to be.

These rules apply to services as well as goods. The Consumer Rights Act 2015 consolidated UK consumer protection laws. It is similar to existing UK law, but there have been some changes, particularly in relation to services and unfair terms.

Code of Practice for Traders on Price Indications

The Code of Practice for Traders on Price Indications contains recommendations on service cover and minimum charges in hotels, restaurants or similar places where consumers must pay a non-optional charge, e.g. a service charge. Its recommendations include:

- incorporate the charge within fully inclusive prices wherever practicable
- state the fact clearly on any price list or priced menu, whether displayed inside or outside (e.g. statement like 'all prices include/do not include service')
- do not include suggested optional sums, for services or any other item, in the bill presented to the customer.

The code concedes that it is not practical to include some non-optional extra charges – for example, cover charges or minimum charges – in a quoted price. These charges should be shown as prominently as other prices in any list or menu, whether displayed inside or outside.

Data protection

See Chapter 2 for details of the Data Protection Act 1998.

Menu engineering

One approach to sales analysis that has gained in popularity is 'menu engineering'. This is a technique of menu analysis that uses two key factors of performance in the sales of individual menu items: the popularity and the gross profit contribution of each item. The analysis results in each menu item being assigned to one of four categories, as follows.

1. Items of high popularity and high cash gross profit contributions. These are known as Stars.
2. Items of high popularity but with low cash gross profit contribution. These are known as Plough horses.
3. Items of low popularity but with high cash gross profit contributions. These are known as Puzzles.
4. Items of low popularity and low cash gross profit contribution. These are the worst items on the menu and are known as Dogs.

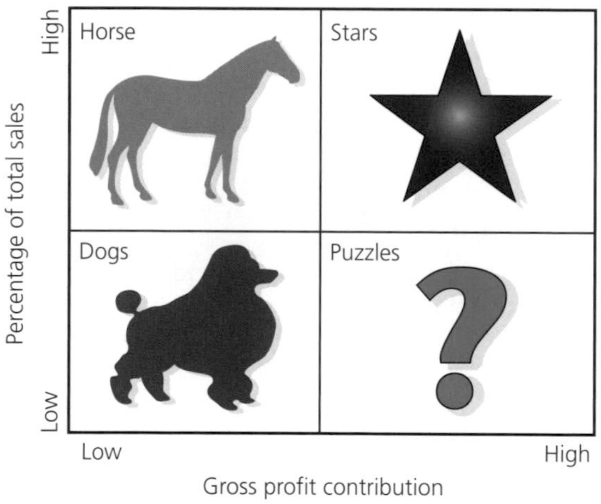

Figure 9.8 **Menu engineering matrix (based on Kasavana and Smith, 1982)**

Chefs and food and beverage managers operating in a competitive environment require knowledge of menu engineering in order to maximise business potential. The advantage of this approach is that it provides a simple way of graphically indicating the relative cash contribution position of individual items on a matrix, as in Figure 9.8.

There is a variety of computer-based packages that will automatically generate the categorisation, usually directly using data from electronic point of sale (EPOS) control systems.

In order to determine the position of an item on the matrix, two things need to be calculated. These are:

1. the cash gross profit
2. the sales percentage category.

The cash gross profit category for any menu item is calculated by reference to the weighted average cash gross profit. Menu items with a cash gross profit that is the same as or higher than the average are classified as high. Those with lower than the average are classified as low cash gross profit items. The average also provides the axis separating Plough horses and Dogs from Stars and Puzzles.

The sales percentage category for an item is determined in relation to the menu average, taking into account an additional factor. With a menu consisting of ten items, one might expect – all other things being equal – that each item would account for 10 per cent of the menu mix. Any item that reached at least 10 per cent of the total menu items sold would therefore be classified as enjoying high popularity. Similarly, any item that did not achieve the rightful share of 10 per cent would be categorised as having a low popularity. With this approach, half the menu items would tend to be shown as being below average in terms of their popularity. This would potentially result in frequent revision of the composition of the menu. It is for this reason that Kasavana and Smith (1982) have recommended the use of a 70 per cent formula. Under this approach, all items that reach at least 70 per cent of their rightful share of the menu mix are categorised as enjoying high popularity. For example, where a menu consists of, say, 20 items, any item that reached 3.5 per cent or more of the menu mix (70 per cent of 5 per cent) would be regarded as enjoying high popularity. While there is no convincing theoretical support for choosing the 70 per cent figure rather than some other percentage, common sense and experience tend to suggest that there is some merit in this approach.

Interpreting the categories

There is a different basic strategy that can be considered for items that fall into each of the four categories of the matrix, as follows.

- **Stars:** these are the most popular items, which may be able to yield even higher gross profit contributions by careful price increases or through cost reduction. High visibility is maintained on the menu, and standards for these dishes should be strictly controlled.
- **Plough horses:** these, again, are solid sellers, which may also be able to yield greater cash profit contributions through marginal cost reduction. Lower menu visibility than Stars is usually recommended.
- **Puzzles:** these are exactly that – puzzles. Items such as flambé dishes or a particular speciality can add an attraction in terms of drawing customers, even though the sales of these items may be low. Depending on the particular item, different strategies might be considered, ranging from accepting the current position because of the added attraction that they provide, to increasing the price further.
- **Dogs:** these are the worst items on a menu and the first reaction is to remove them. An alternative, however, is to consider adding them to another item as part of a special deal. For instance, adding them in a meal package to a Star may have the effect of lifting the sales of the Dog item and may provide a relatively low-cost way of adding special promotions to the menu.

The menu engineering methodology is designed to categorise dishes into good and poor performers. For dishes with high popularity and high contribution (Stars):

- do nothing
- modify price slightly – up or down
- promote through personal selling or menu positioning.

For dishes with high popularity and low contribution (Plough horses):

- do nothing
- increase price
- reduce dish cost – modify recipe by using cheaper commodities or reducing the portion size.

For dishes with low popularity and high contributions (Puzzles):

- do nothing
- reduce price
- rename dish
- reposition dish on menu
- promote through personal selling
- remove from menu.

For dishes with low popularity and low contribution (Dogs):

- do nothing (although this would be a waste of stock, labour and effort)
- replace dish
- redesign dish
- remove dish from menu.

Some potential limitations

- **Elasticity of demand:** one of the practical difficulties with price-level adjustment is not knowing enough about the elasticity of demand. The effect of demand (number of covers) of any one change in the general level of menu prices is usually uncertain. Also, what applies to one menu item applies equally to the menu as a whole. There is an additional problem of cross-elasticity of demand, where the change in demand for one commodity is directly affected by a change in the price of another. Even less is known about the cross-elasticity of demand for individual menu items than is known about the elasticity of demand for the menu as a whole. Any benefit arising from an adjustment in the price of one item may therefore be offset by resultant changes in the demand for another item. Price-level adjustments must therefore be underpinned by a good deal of common sense, experience and knowledge of the particular circumstances of the operation. (Price elasticity of demand is explained later in this chapter.)
- **Labour intensity:** in menu engineering the most critical element is cash gross profit. While this may be important, the aspect of labour intensity cannot be ignored. The cash gross profit on a flambé dish, for example, may be higher than on a more simple sweet; however, when the costs of labour are taken into account – especially at peak periods – it may well be that the more simple sweet is the more profitable overall.
- **Shelf life:** the food cost of an item used to determine the cash gross profit may not take account of cost increases that are the result of food wastage through spoilage, especially at slack times.
- **Fluctuations in demand:** another factor is the consistency of the buying of the consumer. The approach assumes that changes can be made to promote various items and that this will be reflected in the buying behaviour of the customer. The approach will work well where the potential buying pattern of the consumer is fairly similar over long periods. However, where customers are continually changing, as for instance in the restaurant of a hotel, popularity and profitability can be affected more by changes in the nature of the customer and the resultant change in demand than as a result of the operation's attempts to manipulate the sales mix.

Benefits of menu engineering

Although there are some difficulties, benefits can arise since the menu engineering approach requires the following:

- planning for continuous control of cash gross profit
- giving prominence to and controlling the determinants of menu profitability, i.e. the number of items sold, the cash gross profit per item and the overall composition of the menu
- application of an analytical approach, recognising that menu items belong to distinctly dissimilar groups, which have different characteristics and which require different handling in the context of cash gross profit control.

Further applications

While menu engineering technique is related to menu food items, the same technique can be applied to wine and beverages, as well as retail items. For example, in many instances house wine, although having the highest gross profit percentage contribution, often makes a very low contribution to the cash gross profit. Additionally, the principles of the technique underpin the approaches of the selling of hotel rooms and the rates that may be charged, now known as yield management.

'product' in a particular organisation being contracted. Arrangements should be made to show the client the facilities, and every effort should be made to create a good impression.

The function manager should devise a marketing plan based on the marketing policy for a given period. This plan should take into account the following factors.

- **Finance:** targets of turnover, profit for a given period.
- **Productivity:** targets of productivity and performance of the banqueting function department.
- **Promotions:** general – how to increase business and how this is to be achieved; special – specially devised promotions to be launched in a given period, often aimed at different groups, clubs, etc.
- **Facilities:** focused on selling certain facilities – for example, recently refurbished.
- **Development:** the promotion of a new development or concept; the launch of new conference/seminar rooms.
- **New product lines:** launch of weekend breaks for clubs, groups, etc., with special rates.
- **Research:** ongoing market research, project research, etc.

Every organisation needs to advertise and promote its functions. There are a number of ways in which an organisation can promote the business:

- special brochures
- photographs
- press releases about functions sent to local newspapers, magazines, etc.
- Online – social media, websites, etc.

Brochures have to be designed carefully using professional designers and printing. The menus should be clear and easily understood, with the prices stated. All photographs must be clear and accurate; they should be in no way misleading.

Brochures or folders should ideally display the company logo. The pack should also contain the following:

- a letter from the banqueting manager to the client
- rates and prices
- wine lists
- details of all function rooms, with size and facilities on offer
- maps
- sample menus.

Any menus included will have been carefully constructed by the chef, with predetermined gross profits, recipe specifications and purchasing specifications in mind.

Pricing

Function menus are usually pre-listed with the desired profit margins added to them. These menus will generally also include a standard set of purchasing and operational specifications. However, there is normally a flexible element as well. It is not unusual for a banqueting manager to offer additions to the menu at no additional cost to the client in order to capture the business in a competitive environment.

The relationship between price and value for money is an important aspect of pricing. Value for money extends far beyond the food to be served. It takes into account the whole environment in which the food is consumed: the atmosphere, decor and surroundings of the establishment, and the level of service.

In order to be successful and to obtain a satisfactory volume of sales, pricing has to consider three basic factors, as follows.

1. **The nature of demand for the product:** first, we have to think of the elasticity of demand (this means how sensitive demand is to the effects of pricing). Menus are said to have an elastic demand when a small decrease in the price brings about a significant increase in sales, and alternatively if an increase in price brings about a decrease in sales. If a menu is said to have an inelastic demand this means that a small increase or decrease in price does not bring about any significant increase or decrease in sales.
2. **The level of demand for the product:** most catering operations experience fluctuations in demand for their products. The change in demand affects the volume of sales, which results in the under-utilisation of premises and staff. Fluctuation in demand makes it necessary to take a flexible approach to pricing in order to increase sales. For example, at certain times of the year it may be possible to obtain deals on functions.
3. **The level of competition for the product:** establishments commonly monitor the prices in competitors' establishments, recognising that customers have a choice. Monitoring competition is not just about examining price, however, but also the facilities, decor, services, and so on.

The specific method of pricing used by an establishment will depend on the exact market in which it is operating. The price itself can be a valuable selling tool and a great aid to achieving the desired volume of sales.

Every business, whatever its size, can choose to set its prices above its proper costs, or at – or below – the prices of its competitors. More often establishments are forced to fix their price by the competition. This is the discipline of the marketplace. The challenge is to get the costs below the price that has to be set. The danger here is that managers tend to subconsciously alter the costs. This happens when fixed costs such as wages, heating, and so on, are split over all the sales, to arrive at the unit cost. It is always tempting then to overestimate the sales, thereby reducing the unit cost.

No one should attempt to sell anything until they have calculated the break-even point. This is the point the amount of sales (menus, portions) at a certain price have to reach to cover their variable costs and all the fixed costs. Profit starts only when the break-even point has been reached.

Pricing is as much about psychology as accounting. Establishments also need to market research price. Too low a price, although enabling them to produce profit on paper, may lead to failure as customers may perceive the product to be cheap and of poor quality. Some people expect to pay high prices for some goods and services.

Different services provided may be priced separately (e.g. menu price may comprise internal costs). For example:

- 30 per cent – food cost
- 30 per cent – labour
- 30 per cent – operational costs and overheads (e.g. linen, cleaning)
- 10 per cent – profit.

Overheads, labour and operational costs are the most significant costs and therefore establishments will want to reduce labour wherever possible and reduce food costs without compromising quality. This is achieved through more competitive purchasing in an attempt to reduce food costs to approximately 20–22 per cent and labour costs to 22–25 per cent. Reaching 10 per cent net profit is a good achievement.

- It is important to monitor energy costs, gas and electricity.
- Remain aware of costs of items such as laundry and flowers.
- Control food waste, and train staff to turn off stoves and equipment when not in use.
- Promotional costs, such as advertising, marketing and administration, all have to be calculated.

All revenue earned and costs are summarised on a weekly basis in the form of a weekly cost-breakdown report. This is then passed on to the control office, manager or director.

Expenditure for each function is usually controlled on a daily basis. The head chef must be aware of the total food expenditure target for each function. All costs must be controlled through the careful management of resources. Staffing needs to be kept to a minimum without compromising quality.

Considerations when planning functions or events

It is important to plan meticulously and well in advance of a function or event.

Depending on where the establishment is located, there will be a banqueting season; this is where the main business is concentrated – for example, from May to September is known as the 'wedding season' in the UK.

Collecting the function details: communication with the customer

A considerable amount of information is needed by the caterer in advance of the function. This includes:

- number of guests
- price per head or cover
- menu requirement
- drink required
- type of menu.

It is also important to clearly understand the purpose of the function and to define the budget. This information allows the manager to assess the resource requirement. For example:

- staffing
- linen
- food and drink
- space needed
- equipment.

The manager is then also able to assess the profit margins to be achieved. This will aid the control procedures and help to establish yardsticks against which the performance of a function may be measured.

Information, first, is obtained by the first point of customer contact (i.e. the event organiser or the food and beverage manager). At a later stage, more specialist information is gathered by the individual department heads.

All information relating to the needs of customers must be recorded throughout the booking process using appropriate documentation. This information is recorded in different stages:

- telephone enquiry
- bookings diary
- hire contract
- function sheet
- internal function sheet
- deposit
- invoice
- feedback form
- weekly report
- thank you letter.

Formal correspondence related to a client's function must be professionally presented and accurate, and must reflect the company's image.

Customers are usually invited for a detailed view of the venue; in some establishments this will include a menu tasting. During the menu tasting the customer is encouraged to discuss their requirements; the food and beverage manager will gather this information. The customer will also be advised of the different options available. For example:

- different room layouts
- choice of menu
- dietary requirements, e.g. vegetarian or allergy requirements
- order of service
- flowers
- cloakroom requirements
- technical requirements – overhead projectors, public address system, etc.

The customer requirements are then summarised on a function sheet and divided into departmental responsibilities. The function sheet may be issued to the customer one week before the function.

Ideally, function sheets should be colour coded for each department one week before the function. The date for confirmation of the final catering numbers is noted on the function sheet.

Internal communication procedures

Internal communication is especially important within any organisation. Information needs to be broken down and allocated to the appropriate departments, and it is vital that there is two-way communication between departments.

Frequent meetings are essential to inform staff of forthcoming events and the expected working hours for the following week. Often, more detailed and user-friendly internal function sheets are compiled so that the key people are aware of customer requirements. Information must be accurate and well presented so that staff are able to understand clearly what is expected of them. All instructions should be in detail, leaving nothing to chance or guesswork.

Internal function sheets should be given to the relevant staff at least one week in advance of the function. It is then up to each department to assess its own responsibilities and needs relating to the event so that the work can be planned in advance. These calculations will determine the amount of staff required for the function, and how much linen, crockery, glassware, and so on, is required. Such decisions will have to be made taking account of the price the customer is paying and the overall budget. Final attendance numbers should be confirmed with the client at least 48 hours before the event.

Any changes to the function must be communicated to all those concerned immediately.

Special requirements

In smaller establishments the services on offer can be tailored to the needs of the customer.

- Dietary needs must be catered for.
- If wheelchair access is required, it is made available.
- Where it is difficult to accommodate certain special requirements, the customer should be given alternatives where possible.

Food allergies

When planning menus for a large function the chef must think of the danger of any food allergies. All waiting staff must be informed of the contents of the dishes (e.g. shellfish, gluten, peanuts). Being able to provide adequate allergy advice is now a legal requirement (see Chapter 3).

Legal requirements

All functions must be planned within the legal framework. Consideration must be given to the welfare of staff by providing training in health, safety and hygiene. Employees must understand the fire regulations and evacuation procedures. Training is particularly important in risk assessment, handling dangerous equipment and handling chemical products.

Companies have a legal responsibility to the customer – for example, the customer needs to be aware of the maximum number of guests permitted in the building due to fire regulations and, similarly, whether or not a licence extension or evacuation procedures in the event of a fire or bomb threat are in place.

The issuing of a contract forms a legal bond between the customer and the venue.

Other considerations

When planning a conference, also consider the following:

- all aspects must be covered on the checklist
- always have a back-up plan in case of emergencies
- all staff must have clear roles and responsibilities
- the availability of all presenters, vendors, attendees and special guests must be confirmed
- registration forms have to be sent out; as they are returned, they must be recorded to get the confirmed number of attendees
- take care of logistics such as car booking, airport pick-ups, accommodation requirements, etc.
- the invites, agendas and brochures have to be designed
- sponsors' names and logos must be included in the leaflets, for advertising purposes
- make a note of all the extras needed – stationery, audio-visual equipment, name badges, seating arrangements, refreshments, catering, etc.
- make sure there is a registration table where the attendees can be checked in.

The event

Staff are required to familiarise themselves with the function sheets, identifying any special requirements that are needed by the organiser. Staff also require a full briefing so that they understand exactly what is required of them and to reconfirm the function details. It is important that the client feels they are being looked after and that they can feel at ease. The function must be executed as planned, in line with the client's needs.

Table layouts for functions, conferences and events

- **Classroom style:** rows of tables with chairs behind (Figure 9.12). This layout allows attendees to take notes while listening to a lecture-style presentation. All attendees have good visual line to audio-visual presentations. Limits the interaction between attendees.
- **Conference:** for small groups that require a lot of interaction, like committees, boards, breakouts (Figure 9.13).
- **Clusters:** clusters (Figure 9.14) can have varying numbers of attendees arranged in small groups.

- **Crescent rounds:** round banquet tables with chairs surrounding half to three-quarters of the table, facing the front (Figure 9.15). Useful for meetings where interaction and note taking are essential. All attendees have full view of the facilitator and any audio-visuals. Also good to use when the same room is booked for a meeting and meal with little turnaround time between.
- **Hollow square:** suitable for board and committee meetings.
- **Theatre style:** a set-up with just chairs, called auditorium seating (Figure 9.17).
- **U shape:** works well for group interaction and meetings with audio-visuals (Figure 9.18).

The importance of timing

The accurate timing of functions is vital, for the following reasons.

- Each department needs time to prepare for the function. Some departments will require more time than others. For example, the kitchen needs the most time to prepare the menu, while a technician may only require a few minutes to prepare the video playback machine.
- The timing of deliveries is most important as late deliveries can cause severe problems for the kitchen. It is also important that deliveries meet the required specification.
- In high-quality banqueting establishments much of the service and presentation is finished at the last minute.
- Any delays in the function will result in hourly paid staff being paid overtime, thus pushing up costs.
- Timing can affect the smooth running of the function, and whether it is possible to turn the room around in enough time for a second function (e.g. lunch, then dinner).

Figure 9.12 Classroom-style layout

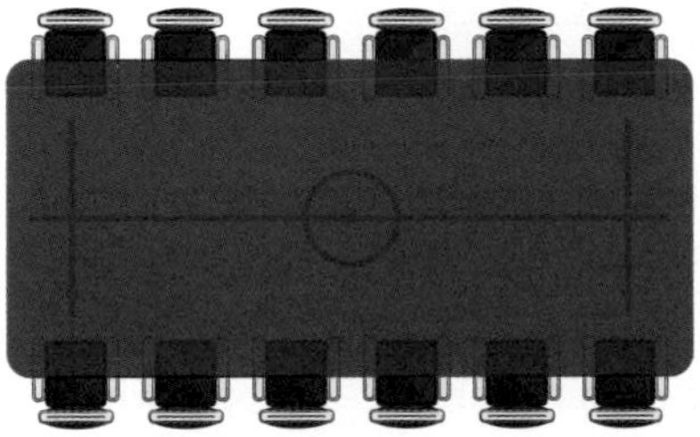

Figure 9.13 Conference-style layout

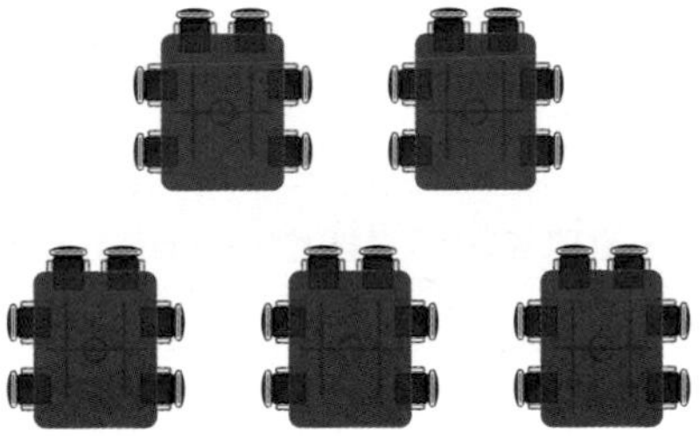

Figure 9.14 Clusters

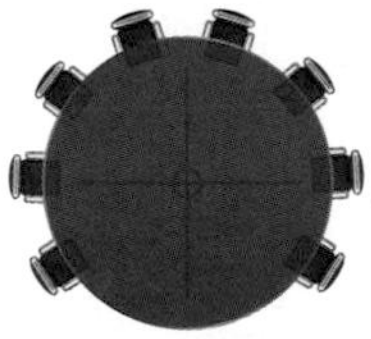

Figure 9.15 Crescent rounds

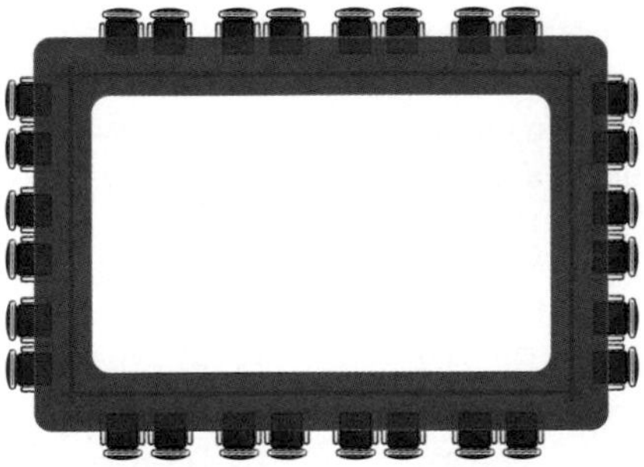

Figure 9.16 Hollow square layout

Figure 9.17 Theatre-style layout

Figure 9.18 U-shape layout

After the event or function

Feedback and evaluation

At the end of the function it is essential to gain feedback from the client to ensure that they were satisfied with the smooth running of the event, the contribution of the speakers, the suitability of the venue, the catering activities, timings, etc. Some companies will contact the client one to three days after the function to obtain constructive feedback, using a standard evaluation form for them to fill in. This may be done as a paper exercise, or online.

If the client was not satisfied, a follow-up letter apologising or offering some compensation can be sent. This client evaluation should then be passed on to the staff.

Well-organised functions that give customer satisfaction can not only be profitable but may also lead to repeat business. You may wish to consider social media – asking attendees and delegates to 'tweet' about their experience, etc.

Costs and invoices

A final calculation of the costs incurred by each department needs to be done to check the efficiency of budget management. Invoices are then raised.

Further reading

Kasavana, M.L. and Smith, D.I. (1982) *Menu Engineering*. Haworth Press.

Sprang, R. (2001) *The Invention of the Restaurant: Paris and Modern Gastronomic Culture*. Harvard Historical Studies.

Williams, E. (2005) *The Historic Restaurants of Paris: A Guide to Century-Old Cafes, Bistros and Gourmet Food Shops*. City Secrets.

www.restaurants.about.com

Topics for discussion

1. What are the advantages of using the English language in menus? When would you consider using another language?
2. What are the essentials of menu design and construction?
3. What are the implications of menu fatigue?
4. How would you promote your menu for a 50-seater high-street bistro in the centre of town?
5. Each member of the group should obtain a number of differing menus (e.g. breakfast, lunch, dinner, special party) from different types of catering area (e.g. school meals, industrial catering, small, medium and large hotels, and restaurants) for discussion and critique.
6. How have menus changed over the past 20 years? Discuss why they have changed.
7. What future menu changes do you envisage? Explain why you think they will occur.
8. How important is using local produce on a menu and why?
9. How important to the customer is the traceability of the ingredients in dishes?
10. Should a chef consider sustainability when planning a menu?
11. Discuss the origins of the word 'restaurant' and the different types of restaurant in the high street that break away from traditional concepts.
12. Do you consider menu engineering to be an advantage to a chef or manager when planning menus, or are there alternatives to this approach that could be much more effective?
13. How have the changes in culinary research influenced menu planning and menu descriptions?
14. Discuss the advantages of a cloud-based point-of-sale system. Do you consider there to be any disadvantages?

10 Food purchasing, storage and control

➜ Food purchasing

Purchasing is a highly significant process that contributes towards the achievement of financial targets and outcomes. The accuracy and reliability of information available to the purchaser can make a vast difference to the overall financial performance of a business.

Analysing historical data can help to predict future requirements. For example, analysing the sales history of various dishes can help to predict the likelihood of future sales. Certain menu items will be more popular than others, providing the purchaser with a reliable indication as to their likely requirements.

Other considerations include purchasing commodities at the most appropriate times. Buying commodities when they are at their peak (in high demand and price) or out of season, not only makes meeting financial targets more difficult, but it is also likely that the products themselves, particularly fresh and highly perishable products, are not of their highest natural quality.

➜ The purchasing cycle

The purchasing cycle is essential to business performance, and a robust purchasing policy is the initial control point of the catering business.

Once a menu is planned, a number of activities must occur to bring it to reality. One of the most important stages is to purchase and receive the materials needed to produce the menu items. Skilful purchasing and detailed checks upon receiving goods will contribute significantly towards the production of high-quality dishes on the menu.

There are six important steps in purchasing cycle, as follows.

1. Understand the market.
2. Design robust purchase procedures.
3. Determine purchasing needs.
4. Receive and check the goods.
5. Establish and use specifications.
6. Evaluate the purchasing task.

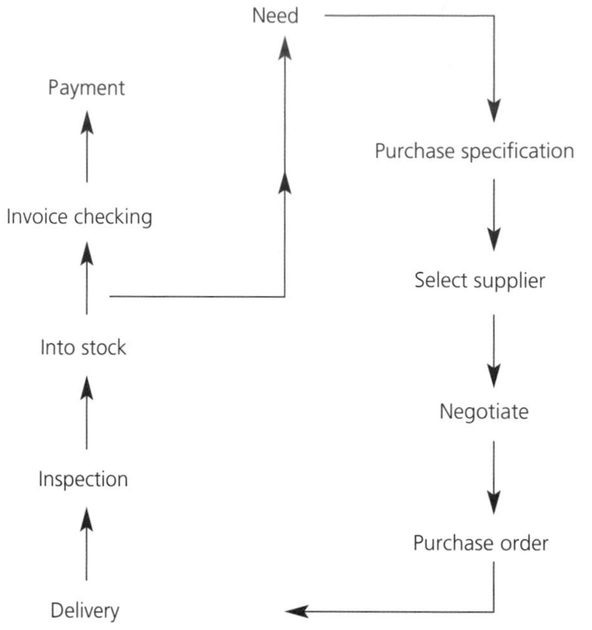

Figure 10.1 The purchasing cycle
Source: Drummond, 1998, reproduced by permission of Hodder Education

Understanding the market

A market is a place in which ownership of a commodity changes from one person to another through an agreed transaction. This could occur, for example, in a retail or wholesale outlet, over the phone or via the internet.

Since markets vary considerably, a food and beverage buyer must know the characteristics of each market. The buyer must also have knowledge of the items to be purchased, such as:

- where they are grown
- seasons of production
- approximate costs
- conditions of supply and demand
- laws and regulations governing the market and the products
- marketing agents and their services
- processing
- storage requirements
- commodity and product, class and grade.

The buyer

The buyer is the key person who makes decisions regarding quality, quantity, price, and what will satisfy customers. They must also consider the contribution to making profit. The buyer's decisions are often reflected in the success or failure of the operation. A buyer must not only be knowledgeable about the products, but have the necessary skills to deal with sales people, suppliers and other market agents. A buyer must be prepared for difficult and occasionally aggressive negotiations. In larger organisations and groups or chains, purchasing decisions are occasionally made by purchasing specialists; this is centrally managed and negotiated, and this officer will be responsible for general purchasing requirements – for example, those required in front-of-house areas, cleaning materials, disposables, etc. In smaller and medium-sized enterprises (SMEs), the executive/head chef is often the person purchasing supplies linked to the menu. A chef will often speak with suppliers on a daily basis, or even personally visit a wholesaler's premises.

A buyer must know the internal organisation of the company, especially the operational needs, and be able to obtain the products needed at a competitive price. Buyers must also acquaint themselves with the procedures of production and how these items are going to be used in order that the right item is purchased. The item required may not always have to be of prime quality – for example, tomatoes for use in soups and sauces.

A buyer must also be able to make good use of market conditions. For example, if there is an abundance of fresh salmon at low cost, can the organisation make use of extra salmon purchases? Is there sufficient freezer space? Can the chef create a demand on the menu?

Another key consideration is the scale of purchasing, or 'purchasing power'. A large organisation spending large amounts of money with a particular supplier is in a stronger position to negotiate terms and conditions than a smaller organisation placing low-value orders. Furthermore, large organisations and operators often negotiate fixed market prices to prevent future fluctuations (particularly rises) in price. This puts them in a better position to predict financial forecasts and control costs. However, suppliers will also try to build in contingencies to ensure that they are not affected by unforeseen fluctuations: they will try to raise their fixed price above the lowest current market price to protect them in the case of a future rise in price. If a supplier guarantees low market prices in the long term without a contingency, this could leave them in a position where they are supplying goods at a loss due to the contractual conditions of a long-term fixed-price contract.

Buying methods

Purchasing procedures depend on the type of market and the kind of operation. They are either formal or informal. Both have advantages and disadvantages. Informal methods are suitable for casual buying, where the amount involved is not large, and speed and simplicity are desirable. Formal contracts are best for large contracts for commodities purchased over a long period of time; prices do not vary much during a year once the basic price has been established, although some price flexibility may be built in. Prices and supply tend to fluctuate more with informal methods.

Informal buying usually involves oral negotiations, talking directly to sales people, face to face or on the phone. Informal methods vary according to market conditions.

Often referred to as competitive buying, formal buying involves giving suppliers written specifications and quantity needs. Negotiations are normally documented.

Selecting suppliers

The selection of suppliers is an important part of the purchasing process. First, consider how a supplier will be able to meet the needs of your operation. Consider:

- price
- delivery
- quality/standards.

Information on suppliers can be obtained from other purchasers. Visits to suppliers' establishments are to be encouraged. When interviewing prospective suppliers, question how reliable a supplier will be under competition and assess their stability under varying market conditions.

Liaising with suppliers

There are many important factors in a successful working relationship with food suppliers. Both parties have responsibilities to ensure proper food safety and quality. Food-borne illness incidents, regardless of their cause, have an impact on the reputation of caterers, and a suppliers' business could be at threat due to a food scare or poisoning outbreak. A good working relationship and knowledge of each other's responsibilities is a major factor in avoiding such incidents.

Suppliers must be aware of what is expected. They must also make the caterer aware of any food safety limitations associated with the product. These are usually stated on all labelling (see below). Such statements may simply instruct to 'keep refrigerated' or 'keep frozen', others may include graphics or a chart of the projected shelf life at different storage temperatures. Meeting these specifications is an important factor in a successful catering operation.

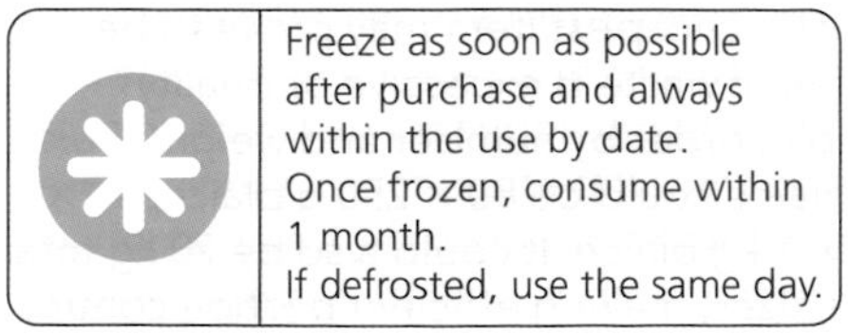
Freeze as soon as possible after purchase and always within the use by date.
Once frozen, consume within 1 month.
If defrosted, use the same day.

Figure 10.2 Shelf life of a food item at different storage temperatures

Principles of purchasing

A menu dictates an operation's needs. Based on this the buyer searches for a market that can reliably supply the company. Once the right market has been located, the various products available that meet the needs are investigated. The right product must be obtained to meet the need, providing the quality expected by the establishment. Factors that affect production needs include:

- type and image of the establishment
- style of operation and system of service
- occasion for which the item is needed
- amount of storage available (dry, refrigerated or frozen)
- finance available and supply policies of the organisation
- availability, seasonality, price trends and supply
- skills, experience and number of staff
- equipment and resources available.

The skill level of employees, catering assistants and chefs must be taken into account during the production process. The condition of the product is significant, as is control during processing in order to maximise the likelihood of the product resulting in the item or dish required. The storage life of the product is another factor that needs to be considered as part of this process.

Types of need

There are three types of need where product purchasing is concerned.

1. **Perishable:** fresh fruit and vegetables, dairy products, meat and fish; prices and suppliers may vary; informal needs of buying are frequently used; perishables should be purchased to meet short-term menu needs. Carrying a large stock of perishable items carries the risk of wastage, so careful assessment of supply is required to ensure all items are processed within use-by dates.
2. **Staple:** supplies that are canned, bottled, dehydrated or frozen; formal or informal purchasing may be used; because items are staple and can be stored easily, negotiation strategies are frequently used to take advantage of purchasing using 'quantity' as negotiating leverage. Staple commodities tend to have a long shelf life and best-before date, and can therefore be purchased to meet long-term needs based on storage capacities.
3. **Daily use needs:** daily use or contract items are delivered frequently on par-stock basis; stocks are kept up to the desired level and supply is often automated; supplies may arrive daily, several times a week, weekly or less often; most items are perishable, therefore supplies must not be excessive, only sufficient to get through to the next delivery.

What quantity and quality?

Determining the quantity and quality of items to be purchased is important. This is based on operational needs. The buyer must be informed of the products needed by their team of chefs or other members of the production team. The chef and his or her team must establish the quality and they should be required to inspect the goods on arrival. The buyer then checks out the market, seeking the best quality and best price. Delivery arrangements and other factors will be discussed and agreed at this point.

Conveniently portioned items are available, such as individual sachets of sugar, jams, sauces, salt and pepper, individual cartons of milk and cream, and individual butter and margarine portions. Such items can be expensive when categorised in terms of price per kilo, and individual packaging costs must be considered. However, by making use of these, portion control is simplified, wastage limited, and stock control more easily planned and managed.

There are certain items of equipment that can assist in maintaining control of the size of portions:

- scoops, for ice cream and sorbets
- ladles, for soups and sauces
- butter pat machines
- fruit juice glasses (75–150 ml)
- soup plates or bowls (14, 16, 17, 18 cm)
- milk dispensers and tea-measuring machines
- individual pie dishes, pudding basins, moulds and coupes
- standardised equipment, such as gastronorm trays
- pasta dishes made in specific trays, e.g. yielding 20 portions.

The following examples demonstrate how portion control can save money.

- If as little as 0.007 litres of milk was being lost per cup by spillage, a business selling 32,000 cups a year would lose 224 litres of milk. This adds up to a loss of hundreds of pounds per year.
- When an extra penny's worth of meat is served on each plate it mounts up to a loss of £3,650 over the year when 1,000 meals are served daily.

Portion amounts

The following is a list of the approximate number of portions obtainable from various foods.

General

- Soup: 2–3 portions to each half a litre (500 ml).
- Hors-d'oeuvres: 120–180 g per portion.
- Smoked salmon: 16–20 portions to the kg when bought by the side; 20–24 portions to the kg when bought sliced.
- Shellfish cocktail: 16–20 portions per kg.
- Melon: 2–8 portions per melon, depending on the type of melon.
- Pâtés and terrines: 15–30 g per portion.
- Caviar: 15–30 g per portion.

Fish

- Plaice, cod, haddock fillet: 8 portions to the kg.
- Cod and haddock on the bone: 6 portions to the kg.
- Plaice, turbot, brill, halibut, on the bone: 4 portions to the kg.
- Herring and trout: 1 per portion (180–250 g fish).
- Mackerel and whiting: 250–360 g fish.
- Sole for main dish: 300–360 g fish.
- Sole for filleting: 500–750 g.
- Whitebait: 8–10 portions to the kg.
- Salmon (gutted, but including head and bone): 4–6 portions to the kg.
- Crab or lobster: 250–360 g per portion (a 500 g lobster yields about 150 g meat; a 1 kg lobster yields about 360 g meat).

Sauces

For each type listed below, 8–12 portions to the half litre (500 ml):

- hollandaise or béarnaise
- tomato
- custard
- any demi-glace, reduced stock or jus-lié
- apricot
- chocolate.

For each type listed below, 10–14 portions to the half litre (500 ml):

- apple
- cranberry
- bread.

For each type listed below, 15–20 portions to the half litre (500 ml):

- tartare
- vinaigrette
- mayonnaise.

Meats

Beef:

- roast boneless – 6–8 portions per kg
- boiled or braised – 6–8 portions per kg
- stews, puddings and pies – 8–10 portions per kg
- steaks – rump 120–250 g per one portion; sirloin 120–250 g per one portion; tournedos 90–120 g per one portion; fillet 120–180 g per one portion.

Offal:

- ox liver – 8 portions to the kg
- sweetbreads – 6–8 portions to the kg
- sheep's kidneys – 2 per portion
- ox tongue – 4–6 portions per kg.

Lamb:

- leg – 6–8 portions to the kg
- shoulder, boned and stuffed – 6–8 portions to the kg
- loin and best end – 6 portions to the kg
- stewing lamb – 4–6 portions to the kg
- cutlet – 90–120 g
- chop – 120–180 g.

Pork:

- leg – 8 portions to the kg
- shoulder – 6–8 portions to the kg
- loin on the bone – 6–8 portions to the kg
- pork chop – 180–250 g.

Ham, sausages and bacon:
- hot ham – 8–10 portions to the kg
- cold ham – 10–12 portions to the kg
- sausages are obtainable 12, 16 or 20 to the kg
- chipolatas yield approximately 32 or 48 to the kg
- cold meat – 16 portions to the kg
- streaky bacon – 32–40 rashers to the kg
- back bacon – 24–32 rashers to the kg.

Poultry (from whole birds):
- poussin – 1 portion 360 g (1 bird), 2 portions 750 g (1 bird)
- ducks and chickens – 360 g per portion
- geese and boiling fowl – 360 g per portion
- turkey – 250 g per portion.

Vegetables:
- new potatoes – 8 portions to the kg
- potatoes – 4–6 portions to the kg
- cabbage, cauliflower or Brussels sprouts – 6–8 portions to the kg
- turnips, parsnips or swedes – 6–8 portions to the kg
- tomatoes – 6–8 portions to the kg
- French beans – 6–8 portions to the kg
- spinach – 4 portions to the kg
- peas – 4–6 portions to the kg
- runner beans – 6 portions to the kg.

Methods of purchasing

There are three main markets for buying, each dependent on the size and volume of the business.

1. **The primary market:** raw materials may be purchased at the source of supply (the grower, producer or manufacturer) or from central markets such as Smithfield (meat), Nine Elms (fruit and vegetables) and Billingsgate (fish) in London, or Rungis in Paris (the largest wholesale food market in the world). Most cities throughout the world have similar wholesale markets. Some establishments or large organisations will have a buyer who will buy directly from the primary markets. Also, a number of smaller establishments may adopt this method for some of their needs.
2. **The secondary market:** goods are bought wholesale from a distributor; the catering establishment will pay wholesale prices and obtain possible discounts.
3. **The tertiary market:** the retail or cash-and-carry warehouse is a method suitable for smaller companies. This method requires the user to have their own transport. Some cash-and-carry organisations require a VAT number before they will issue a membership card. Cash and carry is often an impersonal way of buying as there are often no staff available with whom to discuss quality and prices.

It is important to remember that there are added costs:
- running the vehicle and petrol used
- the person's time for going to the warehouse, if applicable.

Some cash-and-carry operators now offer an extensive delivery service for caterers.

WEBLINK

For more information, visit the World Union of Wholesale Markets website:

www.wuwm.org

Standard purchasing specifications

Standard purchasing specifications are documents that are drawn up for every commodity describing exactly what is required and expected. They assist with the formulation of standardised recipes. A determined specification is drawn up which, once approved, will be referred to every time the item is delivered. It is a statement of various criteria related to quality, grade, weight, size and method of preparation, if required (such as washed and selected potatoes for baking). Other information given may be variety, maturity, age, colour, shape, etc. A copy of the standard specification is often given to the supplier and the storekeeper, who are then very clear as to what is needed. These specifications assist in costing and control procedures.

Commodities that can be specified include the following.
- **Grown (primary):** butcher's meat; fresh fish; fresh fruit and vegetables; milk and eggs.
- **Manufactured (secondary):** bakery goods; dairy products.
- **Processed (tertiary):** frozen foods including meat, fish, fruit and vegetables; dried goods; canned goods.

Any food product can have a specification attached to it. However, the primary specifications focus on raw materials, ensuring the quality of these commodities. Without quality at this level, a secondary or tertiary specification is useless. For example, to specify a frozen apple pie, this product would use:

- a primary specification for the apple
- a secondary specification for the pastry
- a tertiary specification for the process (freezing).

However, regardless of how good the secondary or tertiary specifications are, if the apples used in the beginning are not of a very high quality, the whole product will not be of a good quality.

EXAMPLE OF A STANDARD PURCHASING SPECIFICATION

- Commodity: round tomatoes
- Size: 50 g, 47–57 mm diameter
- Quality: firm, well formed, good red colour, with stalk attached
- Origin: Dutch, available March–November
- Class/grade: super class A
- Weight: 6 kg net per box
- Count: 90–100 per box
- Quote: per box/tray
- Packaging: loose in wooden tray, covered in plastic
- Delivery: day following order
- Storage: temperature 10–13°C at a relative humidity of 75–80 per cent
- Note: avoid storage with cucumbers and aubergines

For most perishable items, rather than entering into a long-term contract, a daily, weekly or monthly quotation system is more common. This is essentially a short-term contract reviewed regularly to ensure that a competitive situation is maintained.

The standard recipe

The standard recipe is a written formula for producing a food item of a specified quality and quantity for use in a particular establishment. It should show the precise quantities and qualities of the ingredients, together with the sequence of preparation and service. It also enables the establishment to have greater control over cost and quantity.

The objective of the standard recipe is to predetermine the following:

- the quantities and qualities of ingredients to be used, stating the purchase specification
- the yield obtainable from a recipe
- the food cost per portion
- the nutritional value of a particular dish or product
- equipment requirements.

This facilitates menu planning, purchasing and internal requisitioning, food preparation and production, and portion control. It will also assist new staff in the preparation and production of standard products.

➜ Cost control

It is important to know the exact cost of each process and every item produced, so a system of cost analysis and cost information is essential.

The advantages of an efficient costing system are as follows.

- It discloses the net profit made by each section of the organisation and shows the cost of each meal produced.
- It will reveal possible sources of economy and can result in a more effective use of stores, labour, materials, and so on.
- Costing provides information necessary for the formation of a sound pricing policy.
- Cost records provide and facilitate speedy quotations for all special functions, such as parties, wedding receptions, etc.
- It provides a budgeting tool.

No one costing system will automatically suit every business, but the following guidelines may be helpful.

- The cooperation of all departments is essential.
- The costing system should be adapted to the business, not vice versa. If the accepted procedure in an establishment is altered to fit a costing system then there is danger of causing resentment among staff and, as a result, losing their cooperation.
- Clear, recorded, instructions must be given to staff who are required to keep records. The system must be made as simple as possible so that the amount of administration required is kept to a minimum. An efficient mechanical calculator or computer should be provided to save time and labour.

To calculate the total cost of any one item or meal produced, it is necessary to analyse the total expenditure under several headings. Basically the total cost of each item consists of the following three main elements.

1. **Food or materials costs:** known as variable costs because the cost will vary according to the volume of business; in an operation that uses part-time or extra staff for special occasions, the money paid to these staff also comes under variable costs.
2. **All costs of labour and overheads:** regular charges that come under the heading of fixed costs; labour costs in the majority of operations fall into two categories: direct labour cost, which is salaries and wages paid to staff such as chefs, waiting staff, bar staff, housekeeping, and where the cost can be allocated to income from food, drink and accommodation sales; and indirect labour cost, which would include salaries and wages paid, for example, to managers, office staff and maintenance staff who work for all departments

(so their labour cost should be charged to all departments). Overheads consist of rent, rates, heating, lighting and equipment.

3 **Cleaning materials:** an important group of essential items that are often overlooked when costing. On a regular basis, an outlet will use cleaning equipment and materials such as: brooms, brushes, buckets, cloths, drain rods, dusters, mops, sponges, squeegees, scrubbing/polishing machines, suction/vacuum cleaners, wet and wet/dry suction cleaners, scouring pads, detergents, disinfectants, sanitisers, dustbin powder, washing-up liquids, sacks, scourers, steel wool, soap, soda, kitchen paper, etc.

It is important to understand the cost of these materials and to ensure that an allowance is made for them under the heading of overheads.

It is important that management and control systems are implemented to maximise profitability within operations. For example, many establishments have introduced very simple control measures to monitor amounts of food waste. Examples include the use of clear bin liners to make waste highly visible, with other systems simply weighing amounts of food being discarded. Correctly managed electronic stores systems linked with accurately developed standardised recipes provide other examples of control measures that help to maximise profitability.

Costing and profit

Pricing

There are several different approaches to pricing products and services.

Table 10.1 Example breakdown

		Percentage of sales (%)
Food cost	£12,000	44
Labour	£6,000	25
Overheads	£3,000	18
	£21,000	
Net profit	£4,000	13
Sales	£25,000	

Competitive pricing

Using this method, prices are based on the prices charged by competitors for broadly similar products and services. The argument for this approach is that the consumer's choice is dependent largely upon price and that catering operations charging more than their competition price themselves out of business.

'Backward' pricing

This method bases prices on what market research indicates the consumer will be prepared and able to pay. Once the price has been determined, the cost of materials, labour and overheads is calculated in order to show a satisfactory profit. This method tends to be used by the more sophisticated operators.

Cost plus

This is the system used by many sectors of the industry. In order to arrive at the selling price, a percentage or ratio of cost price (e.g. 100 per cent/1:2/1:3) is added to cost of raw materials. This 'mark up' should set a level that meets costs and, in commercial businesses, makes a profit as well.

Gross profit: fixed percentage mark-up

The food cost of each dish is calculated and a fixed gross profit (e.g. 100 per cent) added. Gross profit refers to the difference between cost and selling price.

It is usual to express each element of cost as a percentage of the selling price. This enables the caterer to monitor and control profits.

Factors that can affect labour

The design and delivery of menus, alongside the level of services provided to customers, determines labour costs as a percentage of revenues. Generally, budget products and services will be low cost and relatively low in labour costs. Operating standards and procedures are designed in such a way that staffing levels (labour costs) are kept to a minimum. Automated check-in at budget hotels, ordering food from a point of sale positioned at the bar, and the provision of breakfast buffets (including hot products and dishes) provide clear examples of where operators have designed the delivery of products and services while reducing labour costs by lowering staffing requirements within the process. In all of these examples, the customer is performing some of the role that, more traditionally, would have been the responsibility of staff.

Design and level of service is critical in ensuring an efficient operation and one in which the customer's needs and expectations are met. Generally, higher levels of service generate higher costs, which result in a higher selling price. It is ultimately down to customers as consumers to decide upon the budget they have for the type of occasion or experience they are seeking or expecting. Generally, labour costs can vary from as low as 10 to 15 per cent in takeaway operations, for example, to 35 per cent in fine-dining restaurants and luxury hotels. The industry, generally, has a high reliance on agency staff in catering operations, which can be a more expensive option but is a necessity during peak business periods and in times of staff shortages.

Gross profit, sometimes referred to as kitchen profit, is the difference between the cost of the food and the net selling price of the food. Net profit is the difference between the selling price of the food (sales) and total cost (of food, labour and overheads).

Sales – food cost = gross profit (kitchen profit)

Sales – total costs = net profit

Food cost + gross profit = sales

Here is an example:

Food sales for 1 week	= £25,000
Food cost for 1 week	= £12,000
Labour and overheads for 1 week	= £9,000
Total costs for 1 week	= £21,000
Gross profit (kitchen profit)	= £13,000
Net profit	= £4,000

Food sales – food cost £25,000 – £12,000
= £13,000 (gross profit)

Food sales – net profit £25,000 – £4,000
= £21,000 (total costs)

Food cost + gross profit £12,000 + £15,000
= £25,000 (food sales)

Profit is always expressed as a percentage of the selling price.

$$\text{Net profit} = \frac{\text{£}4000 \times 100}{\text{£}25{,}000} = 16\%$$

A breakdown reveals the figures shown in Table 10.1.

If the restaurant served 1,000 meals, then the average amount spent by each customer would be:

$$\frac{\text{Total sales}}{\text{No. of customers}} = \frac{\text{£}25{,}000}{\text{£}1000} = \text{£}25.00$$

As the percentage composition of sales for a month is now known, the average price of a meal for that period can be further analysed:

Average price of a meal = £25.00 = 100%
25p = 1%

which means that the customer's contribution towards:

Food cost	= 25 × 48% = £12.00
Labour	= 25 × 24% = £6.00
Overheads	= 25 × 12% = £3.00
Net profit	= 25 × 16% = £4.00
Average price of meal	= £25.00

A rule applied to calculating the food cost price of a dish is to make the percentage of the cost the opposite of the expected gross profit target. As a percentage, the selling price is always 100 per cent. Therefore, if the gross profit target is 60 per cent, the food cost has to be 40 per cent. The higher the gross profit target, the lower the food cost becomes as a percentage of the selling price (as shown in Table 10.2).

Here is a worked example with a food cost of £4.00 and a gross-profit target of 60 per cent:

Cost of dish = £4.00 = 40%

$$\text{Therefore selling price} = \frac{\text{£}4.00 \times 100}{40} = \text{£}10.00$$

$$\text{That is, selling price} = \frac{\text{food cost} \times 100}{\text{food cost as a percentage of selling price}}$$

Selling the dish at £10, making 60 per cent gross profit (GP) above the cost price, is referred to as 40 per cent food cost.

For example: a 250 g entrecote steak at £10.00 per kg = £2.50. To fix the selling price so that it is 40% food cost and 60% GP:

$$\text{Selling price} = \frac{\text{£}2.50 \times 100}{40} = \text{£}6.25$$

More examples are shown in Table 10.2.

Table 10.2 Calculating the selling price of a dish with food costs of £2.50 (before adding VAT)

Gross profit required (% of selling price)	Therefore, food costs are: (% of selling price):	Calculation	Selling price
70	30	$\frac{\text{£}2.50 \times 100}{30}$	£8.33
60	40	$\frac{\text{£}2.50 \times 100}{40}$	£6.25
50	50	$\frac{\text{£}2.50 \times 100}{50}$	£5.00
40	60	$\frac{\text{£}2.50 \times 100}{60}$	£4.17
30	70	$\frac{\text{£}2.50 \times 100}{70}$	£3.57

If food costing is controlled accurately the food cost of particular items on the menu and the total expenditure on food over a given period is calculated. Finding the food costs helps to control costs, prices and profits.

An efficient food cost system will highlight poor purchasing practice and inefficient storage, and should prevent waste and the potential for theft. This will help to boost efficiency and enable a business to provide customers with value for money.

Table 10.3 The food and beverage manager's guide to factors affecting the gross profit % (1)

Area	Causes	Method of detection	Remedies
Purchasing 1 Suppliers and specifications	Poor specifications	Not fit for job in hand with regard to size, weight, standard, quality Goods disposed of or more used than necessary	Recheck all specifications against requirements
	Supplier unable to cope with volume or standard	As above	Change supplier
	Acceptance of minimum deliveries, which are in excess of daily requirements	Food wasted (kitchen bins checked)	Agree smaller deliveries or change supplier
	Not keeping close to agreed prices or checking market prices	Check market prices and competitors	Continually monitor suppliers' price lists
	Poor response following complaints	Items not changed immediately and credit note system not responsive	Change supplier
	Poor yields	Observation and physical checks	Carry out regular yield checks and introduce standard recipes
	Poor menu planning	Poor profitability Use of high-priced items out of season	Plan menus to take advantage of seasonal items Include realistic mix of high- and low-cost items
2 Ordering	Incorrect specification, quantity or price	Delivery note, visual check, invoice check	Increase control procedures Ensure orders are placed only by authorised staff Over-ordering, resulting in over-stocking
	Stock deteriorating Stock value high	Shortage of storage space	Closely monitor levels of business and establish trends Establish stock levels for non-perishable goods Eliminate standing orders Order as frequently as purchase contract allows to ensure lower stocks

Here is one further example: if a dish costs £2.80 to produce, what should its selling price be to achieve 70 per cent profit on sales?

$$\text{Selling price} = \frac{£2.80 \times 100}{30}$$

$$= £9.33$$

Add VAT (£7.00 × .20) + £1.87

Final selling price = £11.20

➜ Food cost and operational control

As food is expensive, efficient stock control levels are essential to help the profitability of the business. The main difficulties of controlling food are as follows.

- Food prices fluctuate frequently because of inflation and falls in demand and supply, through poor harvests, bad weather conditions, etc.
- Transport costs rise due to wage demands and cost of petrol.
- Fuel costs rise, which affects food companies' and producers' costs.
- Any food subsidies imposed by governments could be removed.
- Changes occur in the amount demanded by customers; increased advertising increases demand; changes in taste and fashion influence demand from one product to another.
- Media focus on certain products that are labelled healthy or unhealthy will affect demand; for example, butter being high in saturated fats, sunflower margarine being high in polyunsaturates.

Each establishment should devise its own control system to suit its own needs. Factors that affect a control system are:

- regular changes in the menu

Table 10.4 The food and beverage manager's guide to factors affecting the gross profit % (2)

Area	Causes	Method of detection	Remedies
Materials lost during delivery 1 Receipts short on delivery	Quantity not checked: • staff too busy • staff indifferent • staff unsuitable • staff untrained • insufficient time • staff failing to follow procedures • dishonesty • delivery times inappropriate Poor transportation of goods: • incorrect temperatures • incorrect packaging of goods • credit notes not checked	Inspection and observation of deliveries: • spot checks at delivery • unsigned delivery notes • staff shortages • observation • security checks • observation, goods arriving when stores unmanned • log temperatures of delivery vans • check condition of packaging • check credit notes	Establish procedures for checking orders on receipt of goods Constant spot checks Careful selection, training and monitoring of staff Report driver to supplier Visual checks Follow up on records
2 Change in source of supply and quantity	Inappropriate specifications issued Changes in supply standards not checked	Checking of material specifications against goods received	Establish appropriate purchase specifications
3 Poor stock rotation	Failure by staff Lack of training	Inspection and observation of storage areas and date-stamped goods Spot checks on stores Question staff on understanding of process	Establish stock rotation procedures (bin card system) Regular inspections Staff training Review stores layout Check best-before dates
4 Hygiene	Failure of staff to carry out procedures Training update (legal responsibility)	Regular inspection of stores area	Establish procedures (HACCP) Legal responsibilities Instigate and maintain staff training

- menus with a large number of dishes
- dishes with a large number of ingredients
- problems in assessing customer demand
- difficulties in not adhering to or operating standardised recipes
- raw materials purchased incorrectly.

Factors assisting a control system include:

- menu remains fairly constant (e.g. McDonald's, Harvester, Pizza Hut, Burger King)
- standardised recipes and purchasing specifications are used
- menu has a limited number of dishes
- centralised buying for very large purchasing operations, e.g. the National Health Service (NHS).

Stocktaking is therefore easier and costing more accurate.

In order to carry out a control system, food stocks must be secure, refrigerators and deep-freezers should be kept locked, portion control must be accurate. A book-keeping system must be developed to monitor the daily operation.

VAT (value added tax)

VAT in the UK is currently charged at the rate of 20 per cent, which has to be added to the value of any taxable sale.

VAT-inclusive price

The VAT-inclusive price is the price with VAT added. It may be calculated as follows:

Net VAT sale value £90.00

£90/100 × 120 = £108 or, more simply,

£90 × £1.20 = £108

Another way to calculate this is to take the selling price before tax and multiply it by 1 plus the rate of tax divided by 100. For example:

Selling price (SP) = £7.00

VAT = 20%

VAT/100 = 20/100 = 0.2

1 + 0.2 = 1.2

SP × 1.2 = £7.00 × 1.2 = £8.40

If VAT changes, carry out the calculation in the same way. For example, if VAT is 17.5 per cent:

Selling price (SP) = £7.00

VAT = 17.5%

VAT/100 = 17.5/100 = 0.175

1 + 0.175 = 1.175

SP × 1.175 = £7.00 × 1.175 = £8.225

VAT-exclusive price

If a price is quoted including VAT, you might want to work out what it was before the tax was added; this is the VAT-exclusive price. In order to calculate the VAT-exclusive element of a VAT-inclusive price of £108, it is not correct to take 20 per cent of the value of the inclusive selling price of £108 as this would also take 20 per cent from the VAT amount, giving an inaccurate answer. This would result in a net price of £86.40. Instead, the correct calculation is:

£108/120 (100 + 20) × 100 = £90.00
or, simply, £108/£1.20 = £90.00

Another way to calculate this is to take the selling price including tax and multiply it by 1 plus the rate of tax divided by 100. For example:

Selling price including tax (SP) = £8.40

VAT = 20%

VAT/100 = 20/100 = 0.2

1 + 0.2 = 1.2

SP/1.2 = £8.40/1.2 = £7.00

Example

If a dish costs £2.80 to produce, what should its selling price be to achieve 60 per cent profit on sales?

£2.00 cost = £5.00 selling price (exclusive of VAT)

£0.80 cost = £2.00 selling price

Selling price = £7.00

Or, more commonly, 2.80/40 (food cost as a percentage of sales) × 100 = £7.00

Add VAT (£7.00 × .20) = £1.40 (£7.00 + £1.40 = £8.40)

or £7.00 × 1.2 = £8.40

Either method results in the correct calculation and the final selling price of £8.40.

The control cycle of daily operations

Purchasing

It is important to determine yields from the range of commodities used, which will determine the unit costs. Yield testing indicates the number of items or portions obtained from a specific batch or production, and helps to provide the information required for developing specifications, purchasing details and production information.

If a specific portion size is agreed or specified, the number of portions from a scaled-up production should be possible. For example, a chef tasked with producing 100 portions of raspberry mousse should be able to quantify the portion size in conjunction with the volume of the moulds being used (e.g. individual/multi-portion moulds). A yield test will provide the chef with the quantities and batch size required. However, the attainment of a specified yield still relies on accurate weighing and measuring, etc., as well as the deployment of the correct skills and processes of the chef. In this example, it could be that, although the recipe and quantities are accurate, the mousse is not aerated sufficiently due to the inexperience or poor technique of the chef, resulting in an insufficient volume produced and therefore an insufficient number of portions.

Yield testing should not be confused with product testing, which is concerned with the physical properties of the food (e.g. texture, flavour, quality). In practice, tests are frequently carried out that combine these objectives.

Receiving

Goods must be checked on delivery to make sure they meet the purchase specifications.

Before items are delivered, it is necessary to know what has been ordered, both the amount and quality, and when it will be delivered. This is essential so that chefs and any other departments requiring stock items will know when foods will be available, particularly perishable items, so that on delivery they can be checked against the required standard. It is also helpful for stores staff to know when to expect the goods so they can plan the working day and also inform staff awaiting the arrival of items.

The procedure for accepting deliveries is to ensure that:

- adequate storage space is available
- access to the space is clear
- temperature of goods, where appropriate, is checked
- perishable goods are checked immediately and transported to cold/frozen storage without delay
- all other goods are checked for quantity and quality, and stored
- any damaged items are returned
- items past or approaching their 'use by' or 'best before' dates are not accepted
- receipts or amended delivery notes record returns
- one part (a copy) of the delivery note is retained, the other part kept by the supplier
- a credit note is provided for any goods not delivered
- should there be any discrepancies, the person making the delivery and the supplier are informed, to acknowledge and record the issue.

Most deliveries now arrive with a computerised delivery note, printed in the vehicle on arrival, stating details such as the temperatures of food/time of delivery. This is very important to file/record for HACCP and due diligence purposes.

Organisation of control

Control in every catering organisation is crucial – in every establishment. The role of supervisors and managers, from food and beverage managers and their assistants, to executive chefs, sous chefs and chef de parties, is to organise themselves, other people, their time and their physical resources.

Physical resources often include financial control, depending on the establishment. An essential factor of good organisation is effective control of all the above-mentioned elements. Successful control applies to all aspects of catering:

- purchasing of food, etc.
- security
- storage of food, etc.
- waste management
- preparation of food
- energy use
- production of food
- first aid
- presentation of food
- equipment
- hygiene
- food safety
- maintenance
- health and safety
- legal aspects.

Control of resources

The effective and efficient management of resources requires knowledge and experience. In addition, it is necessary to keep up to date. This may require attending courses on management, the use of IT packages, hygiene, legislation, etc. Membership of appropriate organisations, such as the Institute of Hospitality or similar trade/industry associations, can also be valuable, as is attending exhibitions and trade fairs.

How the control of resources is administered will depend partly on the systems of the organisation but also on the way the person in control operates. Apart from knowledge and experience, respect from those for whom one is responsible is earned, not given, by the way staff are managed in the workplace. Having earned the respect and cooperation of staff, a system of controls and checks needs to be operated that is smooth running and not disruptive. Training and delegation may be required to ensure effective control and, periodically, it is essential to evaluate the system to see that the recording and monitoring are being effective.

The purpose of control is to make certain that:

- supplies of what is required are available
- supplies are of the right quality and quantity
- they are available on time
- there is the minimum of wastage
- there is no over-stocking
- there is no theft
- legal requirements are met.

Means of control

Checks need to occur spontaneously, without prior warning being given. This should take place on a regular basis, which may be daily or weekly. These checks may involve one item, several items or a complete stock check. Records need to correspond with the physical items. It is necessary to know to whom any discrepancies should be reported and what action should be taken. Therefore the policy of the establishment should be clear to all members of staff.

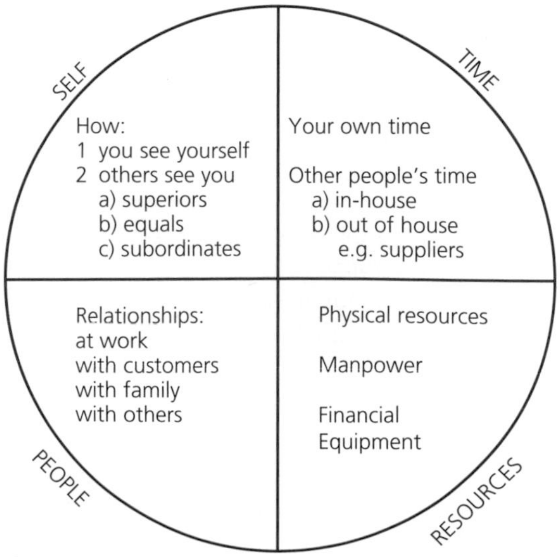

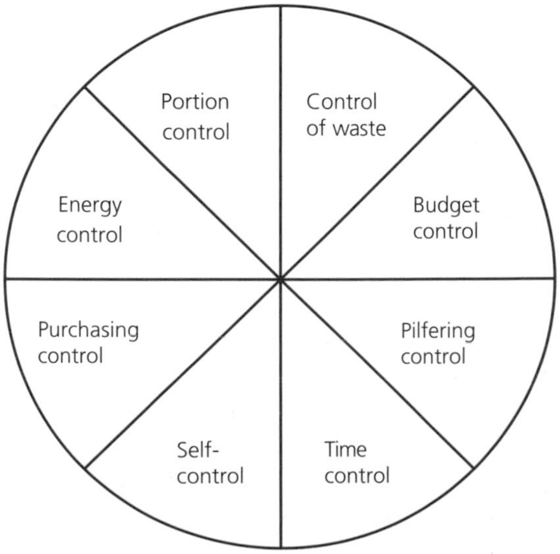

Figure 10.3 Organisation of resources

A system of authorisation regarding who may purchase, and who may issue goods to whom, needs to be established and inspected to ensure that the process operates satisfactorily. It is also essential to maintain documentation requirements and record-keeping procedures.

Checklist for control

- **Goods inwards:** are deliveries correct in terms of quality, quantity, food safety requirements, hygiene, temperature?
- **Storage:** items issued in rotation, accurate recording; correct standards of hygiene – temperature, security, minimum wastage.
- **Food preparation:** proper standards of hygiene and safety.
- **Production:** food safety requirements.
- **Presentation:** accurate portion control.
- **Exits:** measures to prevent theft.
- **Recording**.
- **Monitoring:** is it effective, adequate?
- **Checking**.

Introduction to the organisation of resources

Health and safety requirements

To comply with regulations it is essential to observe the following good practice requirements, not only for legal reasons but for the benefit of all who use the storage areas of the premises.

- Receiving areas must be clean and free from litter.
- Waste bins, empty return boxes, etc., should be kept tidy and safe.
- Waste bins (rubbish and food waste) must be kept with lids on, emptied frequently and kept clean.
- All storage areas must be kept clean and tidy.
- Trolleys and stacking shelves should be suitable for heavy items.
- Trolleys should not be overloaded; accidents can occur due to careless loading, such as heavy items on top of light ones.
- Lifting of heavy items should be done in a manner to prevent injury (e.g. assess job, bent knees, straight back).
- Cleaning equipment and materials must be available and kept separate from food items.
- All items should be stored safely, e.g. shelves not overloaded, heavier items lower than lighter items, suitable steps to reach higher items.
- Stores should have a hand-washing basin, towel, soap and nail brush.
- Unauthorised people should not have access to the stores or areas where goods are delivered.
- Be prepared for the unexpected – accidents can occur due to issues such as delivery vehicles and trolley movement, breakages of containers, glass jars, etc., undue waste left by delivery or storekeeping staff.
- Know the location(s) of first-aid boxes.
- Know the procedures to follow in the event of an accident.

Temperature of food on delivery

Procedures must be laid down for checking the temperature of foods on arrival at the establishment. Delivery vehicles are subject to legislation and food should be at the correct temperature when delivered. Current technology produces real-time information regarding the delivery, such as time and temperature of goods, which can be recorded for due diligence and HACCP purposes.

Documentation of deliveries

Goods are ordered from the supplier in the amounts required and when needed. The quality and details of the foods will have been specified by the establishment so that, when delivered, the goods should match the order.

Storing and issuing

Raw materials should be stored correctly under the right conditions, temperature, etc. A method of pricing the materials must be decided, and one of the following should be adopted for charging the food to the various departments. The cost of items does not always remain fixed over a period of time. Over a period of one year a stores item may have several prices. The establishment must decide which price to use:

- actual purchase price
- simple average price
- weighted average price
- inflated price (price goes up after purchase)
- standard price (fixed price).

Weighted average price example (of dried beans) where purchases have been made at different prices:

5 kg × £0.80	= £4.00
10 kg × £1.00	= £10.00
Total	= £14.00

Therefore: 14.00/15 kg = £0.93 per kg = weighted average price

Preparing

This is an important stage of the control cycle. The cost of the food consumed depends on two factors:

1. the number of meals produced
2. the cost per meal.

In order to control food costs we must be able to:
- control the number to be catered for
- control the food cost per meal in advance of production and service by using a system of pre-costing, using standardised recipes, indicating portion control.

Sales and volume forecasting

This is a method of predicting the volume of sales for a future period. In order to be of practical value the forecast must:
- predict the total number of covers (customers)
- predict the choice of menu items.

Therefore it is important to:
- keep a record of the numbers of each dish sold from a menu
- work out the average spend per customer
- calculate the proportion, expressed as a percentage, of each dish sold in relation to total sales.

Forecasting is done in two stages, as follows.

1. **Initial forecasting:** this is done once a week, for example, in respect of each day of the following week. It is based on sales histories, information related to advance bookings and current trends. When this has been completed, the predicted sales are converted into the food/ingredients requirements. Purchase orders are then prepared and sent to suppliers.
2. **The final forecast:** this normally takes place the day before the actual preparation and service of the food. It must take into account the latest developments, such as the weather and any food that needs to be used up. If necessary, suppliers' orders may need to be adjusted.

Sales forecasting is not a perfect method of prediction, but it does help with production planning. Sales forecasting, however, is important when used in conjunction with cyclical menu planning.

Pre-costing of dishes

This method of costing is associated with standardised recipes, which give the total cost of the dish per portion and often with a selling price.

Factors that affect profitability include:
- overcooking food, resulting in portion loss
- poor portion control
- too much wastage, insufficient use of raw materials; left-over food not being utilised
- theft
- inaccurate ordering procedures
- inadequate checking procedures
- no use of standardised recipes and yield factors
- insufficient research into suppliers
- inaccurate forecasting
- poor menu planning.

Food labels

A great deal of information can be obtained from a food product label. A number of regulations control what is permissible and compulsory on a food product label:
- name of food
- list of ingredients
- allergens highlighted
- conditions of use – special storage conditions
- indication of durability
- name and address of the manufacturer
- instructions for use, if necessary
- average weight of contents
- nutritional information
- use by/best before dates
- recycling of packaging.

If an ingredient is dehydrated or in a concentrated form, it may be positioned in the list of ingredients according to its weight before dehydration (i.e. when fresh). Similarly, reconstituted foods may be listed after reconstitution.

Water and volatile products used as ingredients must be listed in order of their weight in the finished product. Mixtures of ingredients like nuts, vegetables and herbs can be put under the heading 'in variable proportions', provided no single one dominates. The naming of ingredients is important (e.g. 'fish' can be used for any species, 'fat' for any refined fat, 'sugar' for any type of sucrose).

It is important to note that any allergenic ingredients must still be highlighted even if their presence is marginal; this is a legal requirement.

Flavouring is identified by the word 'flavouring'; the word 'natural' may be added for naturally occurring products. Additives can be listed by the principal function they serve, from this permitted list:
- acidic starch
- acidity regulator
- anti-caking agent
- anti-foaming agent
- antioxidant
- bulking agent
- colour
- emulsifier
- emulsifying salts
- firming agent
- flavour enhancer
- flour treatment agent
- gelling agent
- glazing agent
- humectant
- modifier
- preservation
- propellant gas
- raising agent
- stabiliser
- sweetener
- thickener.

The functional name is followed by the name or by the relevant E-number. An additive cannot be referred to as an emulsifier if it contains an allergen such as egg.

The 'best before' date indicates the potential quality of the food and how long it will remain in its first-class condition if stored correctly. Beyond the 'best before' date, the food may not retain the same qualities but may remain safe to consume. The way that the date is presented indicates the period of durability (see Table 10.5).

A 'use by' date indicates the date by which the food must be consumed. Beyond this date, the food is likely to be unsafe for human consumption. The use-by date should be indicated by the words 'use by', followed by the date – day/month or, for longer periods, day/month/year; details of necessary storage conditions must also be given.

Table 10.5 Indication of durability

Date to be declared	Period of durability
'Best before' – day/month	Within 3 months
'Best before end' – month/year	3–18 months
'Best before end' – month/year or year	18 months-plus

Nutritional labelling must be in the form of a table, like the example in Table 10.6.

Table 10.6 Nutritional labelling in tabular form

Per serving (g) and per 100 g	
Energy	kJ and kcal
Protein	g
Carbohydrate, of which sugars	g
Polyols	g
Starch	g
Fats of which saturates	g
Monounsaturates	g
Polyunsaturates	g
Cholesterol	mg
Fibre	g
Sodium	g
Vitamins*	Units as appropriate
Minerals	Units as appropriate

* Names of each vitamin and mineral to be given, and relevant units (e.g. vitamin C, ascorbic acid, 60 mg).

New types of labelling are being developed and introduced to the market in response to consumer demand for more environmental information and as a tool to encourage behaviour change. One example is a label developed by the British Retail Consortium and the government's Waste and Resources Action Programme to signpost the recyclability of packaging.

Labels developed in response to consumer demand are intended to drive up packaging recycling rates by signalling whether or not a product's packaging is collected for recycling. The Carbon Trust is also working with a number of companies, including food manufacturers and retailers.

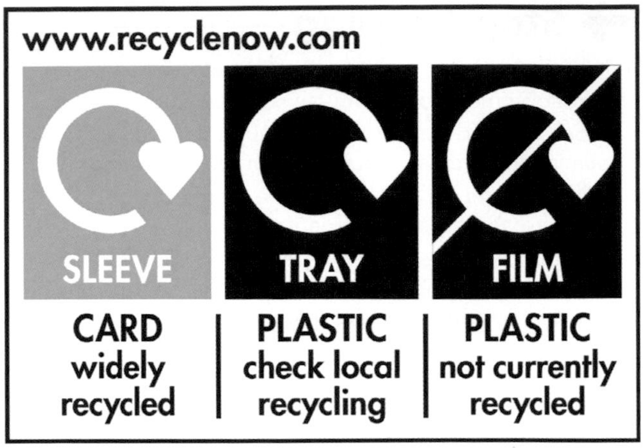

Figure 10.4 A new logo to explain the recyclability of food product packaging

WEBLINK

To find out more about food labelling, visit:
www.food.gov.uk/foodlabelling

Mislabelling

Food labelling is strictly governed by law, and part of the role of the Food Standards Agency (FSA) is to prevent the mislabelling or misdescription of foods.

Food authenticity is all about whether a food matches its description. If you, the buyer, are being deceived, then this deceit can be passed on to your customers by inaccurate wording on menus and/or incorrect answers given to customers in reply to questions about ingredients in certain dishes.

Listed below are some examples of misleading descriptions.

- **Health and safety:** e.g. people with an intolerance of, or allergy to, certain foods may suffer severe or life-threatening reactions.
- **Not having the necessary composition for a legal name:** e.g. if named 'chocolate' the food must contain a certain amount of cocoa solids; a sausage must contain a certain amount of meat.
- **Substitution with cheaper ingredients:** e.g. diluting olive oil with lower-quality vegetable oil.
- **Incorrect origin:** e.g. misleading descriptions of the meat species in a product or not declaring any other meat present; giving an incorrect region or country of origin of a food or wine. This could also be linked to describing something as local or referencing the production location of a product if this is not the case – for example, stating 'Cornish clotted cream' when the cream isn't from Cornwall.
- **Incorrect declaration of quantity:** e.g. giving the wrong amount of meat in a burger.

Storekeeping

A clean, orderly food store, run efficiently, is essential in any establishment for the following reasons.

- Stocks of food can be kept at a suitable level, so eliminating the risk of running out of any commodity.
- All food entering and leaving the stores can be properly checked; this helps to prevent wastage.
- A check can be kept on the percentage profit of each department of the establishment. (This control may be assisted by computer applications.)

A well-planned store should include the following features.

- It should be cool and face north, so that it does not have the sun shining into it. Internal stores may not have any direct, natural sunlight, avoiding this issue.
- It must be well ventilated, vermin-proof and free from damp (dampness in a dry store makes it musty, and encourages bacteria to grow and tins to rust).
- It should be in a convenient position to receive goods being delivered by suppliers and also in a suitable position to issue goods to the various departments.
- A hand-washing basin, soaps, nail brush, and hand drier or paper towels must be provided for staff, also a first-aid box.
- A good standard of hygiene is essential; the walls and ceilings should be free from cracks, and either painted or tiled, or of a non-porous material such as stainless steel, so as to be cleaned easily. The floor should be free from cracks and easy to wash. The junction between the wall and floor should be rounded to prevent the accumulation of dirt. A cleaning rota should clearly show daily, weekly and monthly cleaning tasks.
- Shelves should be easy to clean.
- Good lighting, both natural and artificial, is very important for health and safety purposes.
- A counter should be provided to keep out unauthorised persons, increasing security and reducing the risk of theft.
- The storekeeper should be provided with suitable working facilities, including IT access, facilities for documentation storage and desk space.
- There should be ample, well-managed storage space, with shelves of varying depths and separate sections for each type of food. These sections may include deep-freeze cabinets, cold rooms, refrigerators, chill rooms, vegetable bins and container stores. Space should also be provided for empty containers.
- Efficient, easy-to-clean weighing machines for large- and small-scale work should be supplied.
- Stores staff must wear clean clothing/overalls/jackets at all times, and suitable safety shoes to help prevent injury if a heavy item is dropped on the feet.
- Steps to help staff reach goods on high shelves and an appropriate trolley should also be provided.

Store containers

Foods delivered in flimsy bags or containers should be transferred to suitable storage containers. These should be easy to wash and have airtight-fitting lids. Glass or plastic containers are suitable for many foods, such as spices and herbs, as they have the advantage of being transparent; therefore it is easy to see at a glance how much of the commodity is in stock.

Bulk dry goods (pulses, sugar, salt, etc.) should be stored in suitable bins with tight-fitting lids. These bins should have wheels so that they can be moved easily for cleaning. All bins should be clearly labelled or numbered.

Sacks or cases of commodities should not be stored on the floor; they should be raised on duck boards so as to permit the free circulation of air.

Some goods are delivered in containers suitable for storage and these do not need to be transferred. Heavy cases and jars should be stored at a convenient height to prevent any strain in lifting or stretching.

Special storage points

- Always comply with 'best before' and/or 'use by' dates.
- Older stock should be brought forward with each new delivery.
- Commodities with strong smells or flavours should be stored as far away as possible from those foods that readily absorb flavour; strong-smelling cheese should not be stored near eggs, for example.
- Bread should be kept in a well-ventilated container with a lid. Lack of ventilation causes condensation and encourages mould. Cakes and biscuits should be stored in airtight tins.
- Stock must be inspected regularly, particularly dry goods such as flours, cereals and cereal products, to check for signs of mice or weevils.
- Tinned goods should be unpacked, inspected and stacked on shelves. When inspecting tins, check for:
  - blown tins; this is where the ends of the tins bulge owing to the formation of gases either by bacteria growing on the food or by the food reacting with the tinplate; all blown tins should be thrown away as the contents are dangerous
  - dented tins; these should be used as soon as possible, not because the dent is an indication of inferior quality but because dented tins will rust and eventually puncture.

  The storage life of tins varies considerably and depends mainly on how the contents react with the internal coating of the tin, which may corrode and expose the steel, which may then react with the contents.
- Due to the use of fewer preserving additives these days, many bottled foods now need to be refrigerated once they are opened.

- Cleaning materials often have a strong smell; therefore they should be kept in a separate store. Cleaning materials and powders should never be stored near food as, if they come into contact, they may chemically contaminate the food.

Storage accommodation

Foods are divided into three groups for the purposes of storage.

- **Perishable foods** include fresh meat, poultry, game, fish, dairy produce and fats, vegetables and fruit.
- **Dry foods** include cereals, pulses, sugar, flour, etc., bread and cakes, jams, pickles and other bottled and canned foods (cleaning materials can also be included in this section).
- **Frozen foods** must be placed immediately into a deep freeze at a temperature of –18°C to –20°C.

Table 10.7 Temperatures and storage times for freezers

Symbol	Maximum temperature	Safe storage time
*	-6°C	7 days
**	-12°C	1 month
***	-18°C	3 months
****	-18°C	3 months-plus

Storage of perishable foods

Perishable foods must be stored at the correct temperatures (see Table 10.7) and in the correct conditions.

Meat and poultry (unless frozen):

- in a large establishment, large joints of meat should be hung on hooks over a drip tray to collect any blood
- the humidity level should be approximately 90 per cent
- meat and poultry should ideally be stored in separate places
- cuts of meat may be brushed with oil or wrapped in oiled greaseproof paper, in clingfilm or vacuum packed
- drip trays and other trays used for meat or poultry should be changed and cleaned daily.

Fish (unless frozen):

- store on ice in a fish refrigerator or fish drainer
- keep different types of fish separated
- smoked fish should be kept separate from fresh fish.

Vegetables:

- ideally, in a cool, dry vegetable store with racks, or a well-ventilated refrigerator out of any packaging
- leave potatoes in sacks; as a safety precaution do not stack sacks too high
- place root vegetables, green vegetables, cauliflower and broccoli on racks
- store lettuce leaves as delivered in a cool, well-ventilated environment
- remove any vegetables that show signs of decay
- leave onions and shallots in nets and place on a rack
- leave courgettes, peppers, avocado pears and cucumbers in unwrapped delivery containers
- leave mushrooms in containers.

Fruit:

- do not refrigerate bananas as they will turn black; if possible, hang by the stems to slow down ripening
- there are details of the different types of fruit and their storage requirements in Chapter 7.

Eggs:

- keep away from other foods; their shells are porous and they can absorb strong smells
- keep in their delivery boxes; handle as little as possible
- use in rotation – first in, first out.

Milk and cream:

- partially used containers should be kept tightly closed
- use in rotation.

Cheese and butter:

- cut cheeses should be wrapped in clingfilm
- use in rotation.

Bread, etc.:

- use in rotation
- store in a well-ventilated cool store
- bread should by sealed in airtight containers or packaging to avoid drying out
- avoid over-stocking
- take care that biscuits are stacked carefully to avoid breaking
- frozen gateaux should be kept frozen and thawed before use
- cakes containing cream must be refrigerated.

Storage of dry goods:

- storage must be cool, well lit and well ventilated
- storage should be off the floor or in bins
- issue goods in rotation – first in, first out
- stack items so that a stock rotation system is simple to operate
- arrange items in such a way that they can easily be checked.

Storage of frozen goods

Store immediately on receipt.

- Storage temperature must at or below -18°C.
- Use in rotation.
- Keep chest freezer lid closed as much as possible.

Cleanliness and safety of storage areas

High standards of hygiene are essential in the store.

- Personnel must:
  (a) wear clean clothing
  (b) have high standards of personal hygiene
  (c) be particular with regard to hand washing
  (d) have clean hygienic habits.

- Floors must:
  (a) be kept clear
  (b) be cleaned of any spillages at once
  (c) be in good repair.
- Shelving must:
  (a) be kept clean
  (b) not be overloaded.
- Cleaning materials must be:
  (a) kept away from foods
  (b) stored with care and marked 'dangerous' if they are dangerous chemicals.
- Windows, and where appropriate doors, must be fly- and bird-proof.
- Walls should be clean and, where any access by rodents is possible, sealed.
- Equipment such as knives, scales, etc., must be:
  (a) cleaned thoroughly
  (b) stored so that cross-contamination is prevented.
- Cloths for cleaning should preferably be of the disposable type to avoid cross-contamination; ensure clean cloths are used on a regular basis
- Surfaces should be cleaned with an antibacterial cleaner.
- All bins should have lids and be kept covered.
- All empty bins should be stacked in a safe area with care.
- Waste and rubbish should not be allowed to accumulate.
- Empty bottles, waste paper, cardboard and all other types of waste should be recycled where possible.

Costs are now levied based on quantities of commercial waste. It is important that businesses review their recycling policies and procedures, particularly in defining and identifying different categories of waste and how they manage this within their business operations.

The cold room

A large catering establishment may have a cold room for meat storage, possibly also with a deep-freeze compartment where supplies can be kept frozen for long periods. The best temperature for storing fresh meat and poultry (short term) is between 1 and 5°C with controlled humidity. Fish should have a cold room/area of its own so that it does not affect other foods. Game, when plucked, is also kept in a cold room.

The chill room

A chill room is not the same as a walk-in refrigerator. It keeps food cold without freezing, and is particularly suitable for those foods requiring a consistent, chilled, temperature, such as dessert fruits, salads and cheese. Fresh fruit, salads and vegetables are best stored at a temperature of 4–6°C with a humidity that will not result in loss of water from leaves, causing limpness. Green vegetables should be stored in a dark area to prevent leaves from discolouring. Certain fruits, such as peaches and avocados, are best stored at 10°C, while bananas, as noted above, must not be stored below 13°C otherwise they will turn black. Dairy products (milk, cream, yoghurt and butter) are best stored at 2°C. Cheese requires differing storage temperatures according to the type of cheese and its degree of ripeness. Fats and oils are best stored at 4–7°C, slightly higher than standard refrigeration, otherwise they are liable to go rancid (particularly fats). In more restricted organisations, where resources such as refrigeration are shared across a range of commodities, systems and policies have to be implemented to ensure that foods and commodities are maximised in terms of their quality, flavour and texture, without affecting or jeopardising food safety controls and standards.

Refrigeration

Because spoilage and food-poisoning organisms multiply most rapidly in warm conditions, there is a need for refrigeration through every stage of food delivery, storage, preparation, service and, in certain situations, onward distribution. Refrigeration does not kill micro-organisms but prevents them multiplying. Many cases of food poisoning can be traced back to a failure to control food temperatures, or to store or chill food properly.

Temperature control is so important that, in Britain, statutory measures have been extended through the Food Hygiene Regulations, whereby all food must be stored at or below 8°C, though in practice most food businesses use the range of 1–4°C, and some foods at lower temperatures. Chilling at 0–3°C and freezing at -18 to -22°C are the easiest and most natural ways of preserving food and maintaining product quality, as this:

- cuts down on wastage (reducing operating costs)
- allows a wider variety of food to be stocked
- gives flexibility in delivering, preparation and use of foods.

To maintain the quality and freshness of food, refrigeration at the correct temperature must be ensured:

- upon delivery
- during preparation
- for onward distribution
- for holding, display and service
- during storage.

There are different types of refrigeration, as detailed below.

- **Mise-en-place:** these are smaller refrigerators placed near to or under specific working areas. Some types have bain-marie-style containers that allow for the storage of the many small prepared food items required in a busy à la carte kitchen.
- **Separate cabinets** are essential for such foods as pastry items, meat and fish, and cold buffets where food is displayed for more than four hours.
- **Blast-chillers:** as the slow cooling of cooked food can allow rapid bacterial growth, fast-working blast-chillers are available to cool food quickly.
- **Display cabinets** incorporate the forced circulation of chilled air.

In addition to the legal requirements for food to be stored at the correct temperature, the maintenance of correct temperature display should be specified on each cabinet and should be monitored regularly, with the use of probes, thermometers, etc. Temperatures and recommended storage times are listed earlier in this chapter.

Other points to note on refrigeration

- All refrigerators, cold rooms, chill rooms and deep-freeze units should be inspected and maintained regularly by qualified refrigeration engineers.
- Defrosting should take place regularly, according to the manufacturer's instructions. Refrigerators need to be defrosted regularly. If this is not done, their efficiency is reduced. Some have automatic cycles for defrosting.
- While a cold unit is being defrosted it should be cleaned thoroughly, including all the shelves.
- Hot foods should never be placed in a refrigerator or cold room because the steam given off can affect nearby foods and the temperature of the cabinet will be raised, endangering the safety of other foods.
- Peeled onions should never be kept in a cold room because their smell can taint other foods.

Vegetable store

This should be designed to store all vegetables in a cool, dry, well-ventilated room, with bins for root vegetables and racking for others. Care should be taken to see that old stocks of vegetables are used before new ones; this is important as fresh vegetables and fruits deteriorate quickly. If it is not convenient to empty root vegetables into bins they should be kept in their sacks on racks off the ground. Many establishments will refrigerate fresh fruit and vegetables. It is important that they have good air circulation and that they are stored, unwrapped, on clean aerated shelves or cabinets. To keep salad items moist and to prevent them from drying out, a clean, damp cloth can be placed lightly over the top of the tray while storing in the refrigerator.

Ordering of goods within the establishment

In a large catering establishment the stores carry a stock that, for variety and quantity, often equates to a large grocery store. Its operation is similar in many respects, the main difference being that requisitions take the place of cash or external ordering procedures. The system of internal and external accountancy should be simple but precise.

The storekeeper

The essentials that go to making a good storekeeper are:

- experience
- knowledge of how to handle, care for and organise the stock in their charge
- a tidy mind and sense of detail
- a quick grasp of figures
- computer literacy
- clear handwriting
- a liking for their role
- honest and security aware.

Many departments draw supplies from these stores, e.g. kitchen, still room, restaurant, grill room, banqueting, floor service. A list of these should be given to the storekeeper, together with the signatures of heads of department or those who have the right to sign requisition forms.

All requisitions must be handed to the storekeeper in time to allow the ordering and delivery of the goods on the appropriate day. Different-coloured requisitions may be used for the various departments, if desired.

The duties of a storekeeper are to:

- keep a good standard of tidiness and cleanliness
- arrange proper storage space for all incoming foodstuffs
- keep up-to-date price lists for all commodities
- ensure that an ample supply of all important foodstuffs is always available
- check that all orders are correctly made out, and despatched in good time
- check all incoming stores – quantity, quality and price
- keep all delivery notes, invoices, credit notes, receipts and statements efficiently filed
- keep a daily stores issue sheet and a set of bin cards
- issue stock only upon receipt of a signed requisition
- check all stock at frequent intervals
- see that all chargeable containers are properly kept, returned and credited – that is, all money charged for packaging (e.g. crates, boxes) is deducted from the account
- obtain the best value at the best price
- know when foods are in or out of season
- monitor temperatures of all refrigeration and freezers, make sure stock is used in rotation and food in the store is within use by/best before dates.

Types of record used in stores control

Bin card

There should be an individual bin card, or stock management record, for each item held in stock. It should record:

- the name of the commodity
- issuing unit
- date goods are received or issued
- from whom they are received and to whom issued
- minimum and maximum stock
- quantity received
- quantity issued
- balance held in stock.

BIN CARD

UNIT (kg, tins, etc.) ______________ PRICE

COMMODITY ______________________ MAX STOCK ____

MIN STOCK ____

DATE	RECEIVED	ISSUED	STOCK IN HAND	

Figure 10.5 Example of a bin card

In large catering operations, the traditional bin number system has been computerised. Beverages are often managed through systems such as the Fidelio Food and Beverage (F&B) system. This is a fully integrated software system with the following key features:

- stock control – pricing, recipe function for cocktails, stock-take store values, variances are automated
- breakdowns per outlet
- purchase orders
- interface with point-of-sale system (e.g. MICROS systems, Fidelio Front Office for charging and Fidelio F&B for consumption).
- invoice management – interfaced with a system (e.g. Oracle) for financial reporting.

Fidelio is an example of an operating system that forms a key component of food and beverage control systems.

Stores ledger

Traditionally, this was a loose-leaf file giving one ledger sheet to each item held in stock. Once again, such records are now more likely to be stored on a computerised system. The following details are found on a stores ledger sheet/file:

- name of commodity
- classification
- unit
- minimum and maximum stock
- date of goods received or issued
- from whom they are received and to whom issued
- invoice or requisition number.

Example of an operation of the stores ledger/departmental requisitions

- Process – outlets produce a requisition according to the outlet par stock (minimum stock levels) and forecasted two-day expected levels of trading.
- Cellar/stores supervisor allocates the request; this entails completing orders from stock, and managing par stock levels in accordance with outgoing requisition.
- Order requests are transferred to purchase orders and communicated to the supplier for delivery.
- To minimise stock-holding values, and efficiently utilise space within the property, daily deliveries are negotiated with main suppliers.
- In some organisations, one supplier is identified, from whom it is compulsory for the entire estate to purchase 99 per cent of all beverages.
- Monthly stock-take and variance reports are produced.
- Value of the stock for recording on the balance sheet is automatically calculated.
- Quantity received or issued and the remaining balance held in stock is established.
- Unit price is clear.
- Cash value of goods received and issued, alongside the balancing cash total of goods held in stock.

		Stock in hand	Monday		Tuesday		Wednesday		Thursday		Friday		Total purcha-ses	Total issues	Total stock
Commodity	Unit		In	Out	In	Out	In	Out	In	Out	In	Out			
Butter	kg	27		2						3				5	22
Flour	Sack	2		1			1						1	1	2
Olive oil	Litres	8		1						1/2				1 1/2	6 1/2
Spices	30g packs	8		4			6						6	4	12
Peas, tin	A10	30		6						3				9	21

______ CANTEEN Week ending ______ No. meals served ______ Cost per meal ______

		Stock received during week						Stock used during week									
Commodity	Hand B/F	M	Tu	W	Th	F	Total	M	Tu	W	Th	F	S	Total	@*	Cost	In hand C/F
Apples, canned																	
Apples, dried Apricots, etc. – dried																	
Baking powder																	
Baked beans																	

* The cost of stock used can be checked by using two extra columns

Figure 10.6 Example of a daily stores issue sheet

BIN No DESCRIPTION CLASSIFICATION CODE UNIT MAXIMUM MINIMUM

Date	DETAIL	Invoice or Req. No.	QUANTITY			UNIT PRICE	VALUE		
			Recvd	Balance	Issued		Received	Balance	Issued

Figure 10.7 Example of a stores ledger sheet

DEPARTMENTAL REQUISITON BOOK 267

Date __________ Class __________

Description	Quan.	Unit	Price per Unit	Issued if different	Quan.	Unit	Price per Unit	Code	£	

Figure 10.8 Example of a stores requisition sheet

Every time goods are received or issued, the appropriate entries should be made on the necessary stores ledger sheets and bin cards. In this way, the balance on the bin card should always be the same as the balance shown on the stores ledger sheet. In automated software packages, this will be deducted once the entry is made.

Departmental requisition book

A departmental requisition book should be issued to each department that needs to draw goods from the store. These books can be of different colours or have departmental serial numbers. Every time goods are drawn from the store a requisition must be filled out and signed by the necessary head of department – this applies regardless of the number of items that are needed from the store. When the storekeeper issues the goods he or she will check them against the requisition and tick them off; at the same time the cost of each item is filled in. In this way the total expenditure over a period for a certain department can be found quickly. The following details are found on the requisition sheet:

- serial number
- price per unit
- issue number, if different
- quantity of goods required
- name of department
- cash column
- quantity of goods issued
- unit
- date
- signature
- price per unit
- description of goods required.

Such functions can be performed using tablets and other hand-held devices. These are linked to a central system, and all of the functions that would traditionally be performed through a paper system are achieved automatically, with complete details of the requisition and transaction as live data for all who require access to it.

Order book

Traditionally, this was in duplicate and filled in by the storekeeper every time they wished to have goods delivered. Whenever goods were ordered, an order sheet was filled in and sent to the supplier, and on receipt of the goods they would be checked against both delivery note and duplicate order sheet. All order sheets were signed by the storekeeper. Once again, such functions are now usually done through purchasing software systems with the details stored electronically.

Details found on an order sheet or system are:

- name and address of catering establishment
- description of goods to be ordered
- name and address of supplier
- date
- serial number of order sheet
- signature
- quantity of goods
- date of delivery, if a specific day is required.

Stock sheets

Stock should be taken at regular intervals of either one week or one month. Spot checks are advisable about every three months. The stock check should be taken where possible by an independent person, thus preventing the chance of theft and 'losses' taking place. The details found on the stock sheets and stock control systems are as follows:

- description of goods
- price per unit
- quantity received and issued, and balance
- cash columns.

The stock sheets will normally be printed in alphabetical order.

All fresh foodstuffs, such as meat, fish and vegetables, will be entered on the stock sheet in the normal manner, but as they are purchased and used up daily, their stock will always appear as less on their respective ledger sheets.

Commercial documents

Delivery notes are sent with goods supplied as a means of checking that everything ordered has been delivered. The delivery note should also be checked against the duplicate or matching order sheet.

Invoices are bills sent to clients, setting out the cost of goods supplied or services rendered. An invoice should be sent on the day the goods are despatched or the services rendered, or as soon as possible afterwards. At least one copy of each invoice is made and used to inform accounts, stock records, etc. (see Figure 10.9).

INVOICE		
Phone: 0208 574 1133 Fax: 0208 574 1123 Email: greend@veg.sup.ac.uk Website: www.greend.com Messrs. L. Moriarty & Co., 597 High Street, Ealing, London, W5		No. 03957 Vegetable Suppliers Ltd., D. Green 5 Warwick Road, Southall, Middlesex Terms: 5% one month
Your order No. 67 dated 3rd September, 20...		£
Sept 26th	10 kg Potatoes bag 6.00	6.00
	5 kg Sprouts, net 8.00	8.00
		14.00

STATEMENT		
Phone: 0208 574 1133 Fax: 0208 574 1123 Email: greend@veg.sup.ac.uk Website: www.greend.com Messrs. L. Moriarty & Co., 597 High Street, Ealing, London, W5		Vegetable Suppliers Ltd., D. Green 5 Warwick Road, Southall, Middlesex Terms: 5% one month
20...		£
Sept 10th	Goods	45.90
17th	Goods	32.41
20th	Goods	41.30
26th	Goods	16.15
		135.76
28th	Returns credited	4.80
		130.96

Figure 10.9 Example of an invoice and statement

Invoices contain the following information:

- name, address, telephone numbers (as a printed heading), fax numbers of the firm supplying the goods or services
- name and address of the firm to whom the goods or services have been supplied
- the word 'invoice'
- date on which the goods or services were supplied
- particulars of the goods or services supplied, together with the prices
- a note concerning the terms of settlement, such as 'Terms: 5% one month', which means that if the person receiving the invoice settles his or her account within one month, a deduction of 5 per cent discount will be applied for timely payment.

Credit notes are advice to clients, setting out allowances made for goods returned, or adjustments made through errors of overcharging on invoices. They should also be issued when chargeable containers such as crates, boxes or sacks are returned. Credit notes have exactly the same format as invoices except that the words 'credit note' appear in place of the word 'invoice'. To make them more easily distinguishable they are usually printed in red, whereas invoices are printed in black. A credit note should be sent as soon as it is known that a client is entitled to the credit of a sum with which the company has previously been charged by invoice.

Statements are summaries of all invoices and credit notes sent to clients during the previous accounting period (usually one month). They also show any sums owing or paid from previous accounting periods and the total amount due. A statement is usually a copy of a client's ledger account and does not contain more information than is necessary to check invoices and credit notes.

Cash or incentive discount

This is a discount allowed in consideration of prompt payment. At the end of any length of time chosen as an accounting period (such as one month) there will be some outstanding debts. In order to encourage customers to pay within a stipulated time, sellers of goods frequently offer a discount. This is often referred to as a cash discount or prompt payment discount. By offering such a discount, the seller may induce his or her customer to pay more quickly, so turning debts into accessible money. Cash discount varies from 1.25 to 10 per cent, for example, depending on the seller and the time: 2.5 per cent if paid in 10 days; 1.25 per cent if paid in 28 days, etc.

Trade discount

This is discount allowed by one trader to another; a deduction from the catalogue price of goods made before arriving at the invoice price. The amount of trade discount does not therefore appear in the accounts. For example, in a catalogue of kitchen equipment, a machine listed at £250 less 20 per cent trade discount shows:

- catalogue price – £250
- less 20 per cent trade discount – £50
- invoice price – £200.

£200 is the amount entered in the appropriate accounts.

In the case of purchase tax on articles, discount is taken off after the tax has been deducted from the list price.

Gross price is the price of an item before discount has been deducted.

Net price is the price after discount has been deducted; in some cases a price on which no discount will be allowed.

Cash account

The following are the essentials for the keeping of a simple cash account:

- all entries must be dated
- all monies received must be clearly named and entered on the left-hand, or debit, side of the book/record
- all monies paid out must also be clearly shown and entered on the right-hand, or credit, side of the book/record
- at the end of a given period – either a day, week or month or at the bottom of each page – the book must be balanced – that is, both sides are totalled; the difference between the two is known as the balance; if, for example, the debit side (money received) is greater than the credit side (money paid out), then a credit or right-hand-side balance is shown, so that the two totals are then equal; a credit balance then means cash in hand
- a debit balance cannot occur because it is impossible to pay out more than is received.

An example is given in Table 10.8.

The general rule is:

- debit = monies coming in
- credit = monies going out.

Table 10.8 Cash account

DR.	First week				CR.
Date	Receipts	£	Date	Payment	£
Oct	to lunches	400	Oct	by repairs	80
3	" teas	100	1	" grocer	100
4	" tax rebate	60	2	" butcher	120
5		560	6	" balance c/fwd	260
					560
DR.	Second week				CR.
Date	Receipts	£	Date	Receipts	£
Oct	to balance b/fwd	260	Oct 8	by fishmonger	50
9	" sale of pastries	100	10	" fuel	50
11	" goods	200	11	" tax	40
		560	12	" balance c/fwd	420
					560
DR.	Third week				CR.
Date	Receipts	£	Date	Receipts	£
Oct	To balance b/fwd	420	Oct 19	By butcher	80
15	" teas	120	21	" grocer	60
17	" pastries	110		" balance c/fwd	710
24	" goods	60			850
26	" goods	80			
29	" goods	60			
		850			

Statement

This is received monthly, and verified by cost control, which will ensure all invoices have been accounted. Copy of invoices and credit notes are requested from the supplier.

Cash accounting

In larger organisations, it is rare to have a cash account, – in which case, a cash flow reconciliation will be used, similar to the one shown in the activity in the box.

ACTIVITY: CASH FLOW RECONCILIATION

Make out a cash account and enter the following transactions:

Oct.	1	Paid for repair to stove	£109.00
	2	Paid to grocer	200.00
	3	Received for lunches	750.00
	4	Received for teas	200.00
	5	Received tax rebate	97.84
	6	Paid to butcher	120.00
Oct.	8	paid to fishmonger	72.60
	9	Received for sale of pastries	112.90
	10	Paid for fuel	80.00
	11	Paid tax	60.00
	11	Received for goods	500.00
	12	Paid to greengrocer	112.36
Oct.	15	Received for teas	150.20
	17	Received for pastries	150.00
	19	Paid to butcher	100.80
	21	Paid to grocer	95.00
	24	Received for goods	130.00
	26	Received for goods	150.00
	29	Received for goods	140.00

Here follows a description of how the invoice statement process might work in a large hotel.

- Delivery notes received and checked in loading bay against delivery and purchase order – delivery note input into Fidelio on the basis of the purchase order; discrepancies identified to supplier and purchasing department.
- Delivery note and purchase order transferred to Food and Beverages 'Accounts Payable', invoice will follow.
- Invoice checked against delivery note and purchase order, discrepancies will be corrected in Fidelio; outstanding credit notes will be requested from supplier.
- Invoice control – invoice details entered to Fidelio, this closes the purchasing and delivery process.
- Information is interfaced with Oracle (accounting system) for recording and payment.
- Oracle will automatically pay in line with pre-agreed payment terms, regardless of input date of data.
- On completion of input, statement is considered paid even though the payment or bank transfer (BACs payment) may not have been expedited.
- From date of input, statement recorded as a cost of sale on ledger for the month.

Note that cash payments are quite a rarity in the modern industry. Most payment systems are automated and provide clearer auditing control, particularly when subject to statutory audits, etc.

Further reading

Drummond, D. (1998) *Purchasing and Costing for the Hospitality Industry*. Hodder Arnold.

Topics for discussion

Food purchasing

1. A food-purchasing policy.
2. Is there a need for portion control?
3. The relationship between food quality and price.
4. The reasons for using standard purchasing specifications.
5. The use of standardised recipes.
6. How would you implement a cost control system?
7. The advantages of a computerised stock-keeping system.
8. How the role of the storekeeper may change in the future.

Storage and control

1. Why control of goods from receipt (delivery) to final destination (the customer) is essential.
2. What controls are needed regarding goods, staff and the preparation and service of food.
3. The need to be knowledgeable regarding the cost and quality of foods in relation to selling price.
4. The implications of setting the selling price too low, and also of setting it too high.
5. How do you consider a fair profit percentage is arrived at? Does this exist? Specify an establishment you have in mind.
6. What do you understand to be a 'suitable portion'? Give examples and explain your reasoning.

11 The service of food and beverages

In any hospitality establishment, the service of food and beverages is an essential link between the menu, those producing the food and drinks, and the customer. Service staff have an essential customer service role because they communicate and interact closely with the customers. They perform a selling role, as well as providing information, answering questions and dealing with comments, concerns and complaints immediately. The skills, knowledge and qualifications gained by food service staff are transferable between different establishments and sectors of the industry, and throughout the world.

The type of customer, their requirements, amounts they wish to spend, the location and the type of establishment will all have an impact on customers' expectations and the style of service provided. For example, in a quality restaurant attracting people with high expectations the service would be attentive, personal and skilled, but in a fast-food restaurant the emphasis would be on efficiency and speed of service. (See Chapter 9 for more information on menu planning.)

For any food and beverage operation, how the food and beverage service is designed, planned, undertaken and controlled will depend on factors including:

- the type and style of the operation
- the nature of the customers – are they resident, booked/non-booked or 'captive', such as in an aircraft?
- prices to be charged
- production processes in place
- volume of custom
- volume of throughput
- space available
- availability of skilled, semi-skilled and unskilled staff
- hours of operation
- booking requirements
- types of payment accepted
- legal requirements.

Food and beverage service is not just a system of delivering food and drinks to customers. If this were the case the requirements of the operation itself would determine how the service was designed, planned and controlled. However, the customer is central to the process and an active participant within it. Food and beverage service actually consists of two separate systems operating at the same time:

1. the **service sequence**, which is concerned with the delivery of the food and beverages to the customer
2. the **customer process**, which is concerned with the whole customer experience.

The service sequence

The service sequence is the essential link between the food production system, beverage provision and the customer experience. The service sequence typically consists of:

- preparation of service areas
- meeting and greeting
- presenting the menu, and taking food and beverage orders
- the service of food and beverages
- billing
- clearing
- dishwashing
- clearing following service.

Preparation for service

Within the service areas, tasks and duties that need to be carried out in order to ensure preparedness for the expected volume of business include:

- taking and checking bookings from a variety of sources
- checking and ensuring the cleanliness and suitability of glassware, crockery, flatware and cutlery
- dealing with linen and disposable items
- housekeeping duties
- arranging and laying up the service areas
- checking deliveries
- stocking hotplates, workstations and display buffets
- setting up bar and lounge areas
- briefing staff to ensure that they have adequate knowledge of the product and the service requirements, as well as the day's bookings and business.

Meeting and greeting

This is a very important part of the food and beverage service role, allowing the server to provide customer care that will reflect well on the establishment. It is the opportunity for initial communication with the customer, when first impressions of the establishment are formed. Important information can be gained at this point, such as seating preferences and any allergy advice that is needed.

Presenting the menu and taking orders

Taking food and beverage orders from customers takes time. It may involve explanations of the menu, allergen advice, dish or wine recommendations, and more. The order-taking process provides information to the food production or bar areas, and provides essential information for billing. Whatever system is used, whether manual or electronic, it will be based on one of the following basic methods.

- **Duplicate:** order taken, copied to supply point and second copy retained by server for service and billing.
- **Triplicate:** order taken, copied to supply point and cashier for billing, third copy retained by server.
- **Service with order:** order taken and service provided at one point – for example, in a bar or takeaway establishment.
- **Electronic, with either a hand-held or desktop device:** the hand-held version will send the order direct to kitchen areas, bars and electronic billing systems; with a desktop device, the server writes the order manually then transfers it to the device, which then informs the necessary areas.
- **Self-order from another area:** customers order their food and drinks away from the food service area – for example, room service in a hotel, or pre-ordering a meal by telephone or email.
- **Self-order:** the customer can self-order on an electronic device on the table or by ticking boxes on an order sheet; these choices are then entered electronically by a server. This system removes a complete layer of service; it is used in many sectors of the industry, particularly fast food and pubs. Service staff still collect and serve the food, but these may be bar or kitchen staff.

While taking orders there are opportunities for personal selling by service staff. Personal selling or upselling refers to the ability of staff to contribute to the promotion of sales. Upselling is especially important where there are specific promotions, special offers or new items on the menu. Service staff need to be trained in selling techniques to make this helpful rather than 'pushy'. They must also be fully informed about special promotions, new dishes, etc.

Figure 11.1 **Taking an order with an electronic device**

Technology and electronic devices

The introduction of these has made a huge difference to food service operations across all types of establishment.

- The food service teams can monitor on screens the exact status of the area – for example, which tables are in use and the stages of their service.

- Food and drinks can be ordered electronically from hotel rooms, with this being linked to guests' bills.
- Orders may be taken on or transferred to electronic devices (as noted above). These orders can be placed with the kitchen instantly, which is much more efficient than paper, and can also be directly linked to billing, automatically making additions such as service charge.
- Menus can be displayed on electronic screens or individual customer tablets. Ordering can be done directly by the customer to the kitchen or bar, or may go through a front-of-house server first. Some restaurants have a system where menus are projected on to table tops.

The service of food and beverages

The various methods for serving food and beverages are outlined below. The choice of service method will depend on the customer service specification (see below) as well as on the capability of staff, the capacity of the operation and the equipment available. Differing service methods affect the speed of service and the time the customer takes to consume the meal, which in turn affects the throughput of customers. In general much more time will be allowed in fine dining establishments where throughput is not expected to be high but standards of service are paramount.

Good food and beverage service is achieved where management continually reviews, reinforces and supports service staff in the maintenance of good standards. Good service is also very dependent on teamwork, not only among service staff, but among and between staff in all other areas.

Billing

The various billing methods found in food service operations are as follows.

- **Order used for billing:** second copy of the order used as a bill.
- **Separate bill:** bill made up from the duplicate order and presented to customer.
- **Bill with order:** service staff take order and bill at the same time, as with takeaway orders.
- **Prepaid:** customer purchases ticket, voucher or card in advance, for specific meal or specific value.
- **Voucher:** customer has credit issued by a third party, such as a luncheon voucher for a specific meal or value. Prepayment deals booked online are increasingly popular.
- **No charge:** customer not paying – for example, if an employer provides a free-of-charge staff restaurant.
- **Deferred:** this could be function catering, where the bill is paid by an organiser, or a corporate event, where billing takes place after the event and the food is included in the package.

The choice of billing method will depend on the type and style of the operation. Electronic, cashless payment has become the most popular method but there is still a significant place for cash sales. Whichever method is used for payment, billing will always be part of a longer process linked to the order-taking method and the revenue-control procedures.

Clearing

Clearing needs as much thought, attention and planning as every other part of the food service process. Efficient clearing allows for the smooth running of the restaurant as well as maintaining its appearance, tidiness and hygiene. The main clearing methods are as follows.

- **Manual:** used dishware and cutlery collected by waiting staff, taken to dishwash area or loaded on to trolleys for transportation to dishwash area.
- **Semi-self-clear:** used dishware and cutlery placed by customers on conveniently placed trolleys or stands, for removal by staff.
- **Self-clear:** used trays, dishware and cutlery placed by customers on to a conveyor belt system for mechanical transportation to dishwash area.
- **Self-clear and load:** used dishware and cutlery placed into conveyorised dishwash baskets by customers. These are transported automatically through the dishwashing machine.

The choice of clearing method will depend not only on the type and standard of the operation but also on the nature of the demand being met.

Dishwashing

The capacity of the dishwashing system should always be greater than the operational maximum required, to allow for efficiency in the busiest periods. Slow and inefficient dishwashing increases the amount of equipment required to be in use at a particular time and therefore the storage space required for it. Service may also be slowed down waiting for clean items to be ready for use.

The main dishwashing systems are those described below.

- **Manual:** physical washing by hand or brush machine. This is slower than machine methods and usually less hygienic because lower water temperatures may be used and drying cloths may be used for reasons of speed (this is discouraged for food safety reasons – see Chapter 3 for more information).
- **Semi-automatic:** manual loading by operators into a free-standing dishwashing machine. Detergent is added in liquid, tablet or powder form.
- **Automatic conveyor:** items are often pre-rinsed using a hand-held spray, then manually loaded into baskets on a conveyor for automatic transportation through the dishwashing machine.
- **Flight conveyor:** similar to an automatic conveyor, but items are loaded vertically on to pegs on a conveyor.
- **Deferred wash:** this occurs when there are no immediate dishwashing facilities, such as at an outside event. For reasons of hygiene and to avoid attracting pests, debris should be scraped from plates and they should be neatly stacked, preferably in a container with a lid.

The volume that can be accommodated, and the efficiency of the dishwashing process, increases from the manual method to the flight conveyor, and the choice will depend largely on the scale of the operation. It is often necessary to employ more than one method, especially where there is more than one food service area or satellite areas.

For best practice with dishwashing the recognised requirements are a good supply of hot water at a temperature of 52–60°C for general cleansing, followed by a sterilising rinse at a temperature of 82°C for at least one minute. Alternatively, low-temperature equipment is available that disinfects by means of a chemical: sodium hypochlorite.

For more information on dishwashing machines, see Chapter 5.

WEBLINKS

Further information on dishwashing equipment can be obtained from the following sources.

Lever Industrial:

www.globalsources.com

Hobart:

www.hobartcorp.com/products/commercial-dishwashers

Electrolux Professional:

www.professional.electrolux.co.uk

Clearing following service

Clearing will take place throughout service periods, but there are additional tasks that need to be completed at the end of service to clear from the service that has just finished and to prepare for the next service. The efficient management of the clearing stage can have an immediate impact on the potential reuse of an area.

Cleaning programmes require planned management. Detailed cleaning schedules need to be developed to ensure that all cleaning activities are coordinated and occur so they are least disruptive to business. Planned cleaning tasks may be completed on a daily, weekly or monthly basis – or, for some items, over longer periods; for example, a chandelier may be cleaned once a year. Alongside these cleaning schedules, it is necessary to incorporate maintenance checks for all equipment. Maintenance checks, together with regular cleaning, can help to ensure that equipment and facilities are always available and in working order, and these regular checks are likely to prolong their usable life.

Figure 11.2 **Self-service salad bar**

Figure 11.3 **Fine dining**

Service methods and the customer process

(This section has been adapted from Cousins and Lillicrap, 2010.)

Many different service methods are found in the hospitality industry. These fall into the five groups of customer processes identified in Table 11.1 and described in more detail below.

The 'customer process' is the process of fulfilling the customer's requirements and striving to exceed their expectations. If food and beverage service were to be viewed only as a delivery process, then the systems and procedures of an establishment would be designed and viewed only from the delivery perspective. However, for a food and beverage operation to work well, the customer must be seen as central to the whole process.

Table 11.1 Simple categorisation of the customer processes in food and beverage service

Service method	Service area	Ordering/selection	Service	Dining/ consumption	Clearing	Customer processes
Table service	Customer enters and is seated	From offered menu	By staff to customer	At laid table/ cover	By staff	1 Waiter service 2 Bar/counter service
Assisted service	Customer enters and is usually seated	From menu, buffet, service trolleys or passed trays	Combination of both staff and customer	Usually at laid table/cover	By staff	3 Assisted
Self-service	Customer enters	Customer selects items on to a tray	Customer carries	Dining area or takeaway	Various	4 Cafeteria service
Single-point service	Customer enters	Orders at single point	Customer carries	Dining area or takeaway	By staff or customer clearing to central points	5 Consume on premises 6 Takeaway 7 Vending 8 Kiosks 9 Food court 10 Bar
Specialised or in situ service	Where the customer is located	From menu or predetermined	Brought to the customer	Served where the customer is located	By staff or customer clearing	11 Tray service 12 Trolley 13 Home delivery 14 Lounge service 15 Room service 16 Drive-in

The customer processes mentioned in Table 11.1 are defined as follows:

1 Waiter service
   - (a) Silver/English service: presentation and service of food on to a customer's plate by waiting staff from a food flat or dish.
   - (b) Family service: main courses such as fish or meat are plated. Vegetables are placed in multi-portion dishes on tables for customers to serve themselves. Any sauces are offered separately.
   - (c) Plated/American service: food is pre-plated by chefs in the kitchen.
   - (d) Butler/French service: food on a food flat or dish is offered individually to each guest. Using the serving spoon/fork the guests serve themselves. Sauces and accompaniments may be offered separately.
   - (e) Russian service: table laid with food for customers/ guests to help themselves.
   - (f) Guéridon service: food served on to a customer's plate from a side table or a trolley at the customer's table. May include the preparation of salads, carving, simple cooking and flambé dishes.

2 Bar/counter service: service to customers seated at a bar counter.

3 Assisted service
   - (a) Some parts of the meal are served to seated customers; the customers collect other parts. Used for breakfast and carvery service.
   - (b) Customers are assisted to select food and drink from displays, buffet tables or passed trays; the meal is eaten either at tables, standing or in lounge area.

4 Cafeteria service
   - (a) Counter: customers collect their food choices from a service counter, at different points or even separate counters. The customer places the items on a tray, may collect cutlery, condiments, etc., and may proceed to a cashier desk to pay before going to the seating area. Some establishments may use a 'carousel' – a revolving, stacked counter area that saves space. These are popular for plated desserts and salads.
   - (b) Free flow: food selection occurs as in counter service. Customers move at will to various areas and service points, exiting via a payment point.
   - (c) Echelon: the arrangement of counters within a large or busy free-flow area at angles to the flow of customers, to save space and speed up the flow.
   - (d) Island service points – separate 'islands' with different food and beverage items within a free-flow area.

   Note: call order – cooking individual items to order – may also feature in some self-service areas.

5 Consume on premises: this is the service of customers at a single point, where they consume food and drinks on the premises. Examples include ordering at a pub bar, or ordering and collection at a service point in a fast-food restaurant.

6 Takeaway: customer orders are served from a single point, usually at a counter, service hatch or stand; the food is normally consumed off the premises, although some takeaway establishments provide limited seating. This category also includes drive-thrus, where the customer drives a vehicle past order, payment and collection points.
7 Vending: automatic retailing of food and beverage products from a specialist machine, usually coin or card operated.
8 Kiosks: service provided in outstations during peak demand in specific locations, such as at festivals or sport events.
9 Food court: a group of autonomous counters where customers may either order and eat in a central eating area, or buy and take away. These are very popular in places such as shopping centres and airports.
10 Bar: a selling point for the consumption of alcoholic and non-alcoholic drinks in licensed premises or with special licences at events.
11 Tray service: service of a meal or part of a meal on a tray to the customer in situ, such as in hospitals or in an aircraft.
12 Trolley: service of food and beverage from a trolley to customers not in dining areas – for instance, at their seats on aircraft or trains, and at their desks in offices.
13 Home delivery: food and beverage delivered to a customer's location, such as pizza delivery to a home or sandwiches to offices.
14 Lounge service: service of food and beverages in a lounge or garden area – for example, afternoon tea in a hotel lounge.
15 Room service: service of food and beverages in hotel guest rooms or in meeting rooms. There is often a more limited menu than in the restaurants, but the service is popular for early-morning beverage trays, and for late-night food and drinks. Smaller establishments provide a limited service along with in-room mini bars, and tea and coffee facilities.
16 Drive-in: customers are served food and beverages to their vehicles.

Other customer processes and related terms include those described below.

- **Banquet/function catering:** food and beverage operations that are providing service for a specific number of people at specific times in a variety of dining layouts. Service methods also vary, with plated service and silver service being the most popular. The term banquet/function catering therefore refers to the organisation of service rather than a specific service method.
- **In-room dining:** this has increased in popularity as part of the service provided in luxury hotels. It differs from room service in that a full menu and choice of wines are offered. These are then served within a guest's suite at a fully laid dining table or at a portable laid table brought to the suite. The service is completed by hotel butlers or by specific in-room dining waiters. This service offers fine dining along with privacy, which would not be available in an open restaurant. A similar service may be offered in in some restaurants and hotels that offer private dining rooms.

Service of food when travelling

Food provision is offered in a wide variety of ways for people using different modes of transport. The food service provision will vary greatly according to the types of food being served and the facilities available.

- **Aircraft:** provision varies from elaborate meal choices to snacks sold from a trolley. The significant challenges are those of space and weight restrictions.
  - At the higher end of the market, menus will be presented by cabin crew, and food assembled or finished to order. Simple cooking may also be completed within the constraints of the facilities on the airliner.
  - For most passengers, trays of food are prepared by specialist providers within the airport. Cold items are kept in a chiller and hot items are reheated in specific ovens in the aircraft before being distributed from a trolley by cabin crew.
  - Some budget airlines have a limited offer of sandwiches and other simple items that can be purchased from cabin crew.
  - Airports also have a wide variety of food and service provision.
- **Ships and ferries:** food service provision and style will vary depending on prices charged and customer expectations. Cruise ships will have a number of different restaurants and dining areas, with varying food and service styles to choose from. They will also have in-room/cabin service offers. Ferries and other ships may have facilities from cafés to fine dining. Fast-food outlets may also be seen on ferries and in ferry ports.
- **Trains:** these vary hugely in terms of types of food service offered. Generally, train restaurant cars offering waiter service have been replaced by either a trolley service or a self-service counter, but on luxury train services fine dining is part of the experience. Larger stations offer a wide variety of coffee shops and fast-service restaurants. The provision is usually by recognisable high-street/franchise names.
- **Motorway service areas:** rather than one large food and drinks service area these now tend to be different and smaller franchised outlets that are almost always self-service with payment at the point of sale. They are supported by shops selling food and drinks.

For more on different food outlets in a variety of places, please see Chapter 1.

Roles in food and beverage service

Although the types of establishment and the skills required from staff will vary greatly, there are some key elements that are required from all staff serving food and beverages:

- sound knowledge of the menu and products they are offering, including allergy information
- competence in the relevant food and beverage service skills
- good communication and social skills
- the ability to work effectively as part of a team.

While there have been changes in food and beverage service, with less emphasis on the high-level technical skills in some sectors, these key requirements remain for all staff (although the emphasis on each varies according to the type of establishment and the service methods being used).

Figure 11.4 Working in food service

Food and beverage service is never just about delivering food from the point where it is cooked to the customer. Service staff play an important role in providing the overall customer experience. As well as product/menu knowledge and service skills, time must also be invested in developing customer care skills. They must have the ability to anticipate and respond to customer requirements, and to play a part in the overall dynamics of a restaurant. Well-trained food and beverage staff with the required experience should be able to predict the individual needs of customers and read their body language. Customers respond well to individual attention and being given a personalised service. With time customers may not remember everything about the meal they had, but they do tend to remember exceptional service and the person who provided it.

The most frequently used job titles and descriptions are identified below. In smaller establishments job roles may be combined and tasks distributed in different ways.

Because much of fine food and drinks service was based on traditional French style cuisine the roles often had French titles. This is less common now, but may still be seen in fine and traditional establishments. French titles are shown in brackets in the list.

The **food and beverage manager**:

- depending on the size of the establishment, is either responsible for implementing food and beverage policies or actually contributes to setting the policies of the business (the larger the organisation, the less likely the manager is to be involved in policy setting)
- ensures required profit margins are achieved for each area within a specific financial period
- updates and compiles new wine lists according to availability of stock, current trends and customer needs
- compiles menus, in liaison with senior chefs, for food service areas, events and banqueting
- purchases all materials and stock for food and beverage service areas
- ensures quality and standards are maintained
- determines portion size, along with chefs, in relation to selling price
- ensures staff training, sales promotions and maintenance of the highest professional standards
- employs staff and deals with staff issues
- organises regular meetings with section heads to ensure all areas are working effectively and efficiently, and are well coordinated.

The **restaurant manager** (or **supervisor**):

- has overall responsibility for the organisation and administration of specific food and beverage service areas (this may include not just restaurants but lounges, in-room dining, function suites, etc.)
- sets the standards for service, and is responsible for staff training and development
- manages staff rotas, holiday lists and individual working hours
- contributes to all operational matters so that all the service areas run efficiently and smoothly.

The **reception head waiter**:

- accepts and deals with bookings
- keeps the booking diary up to date
- reserves tables and allocates reservations to particular areas
- greets customers/guests on arrival, deals with outdoor coats and takes guests to the table to be seated.

The **head waiter** (**supervisor**, *maître d'hôtel*):

- has overall charge of the staff team
- is responsible for all the preparation duties necessary before service being efficiently carried out and ensures nothing is forgotten
- aids the reception head waiter during the service
- possibly takes some orders if the station head waiter is busy
- helps with the compilation of duty rotas and holiday lists
- may relieve the restaurant manager or reception head waiter on their days off.

Larger restaurants may be organised into groups of tables called stations or sections. The **station head waiter** or **section supervisor**:

- has overall responsibility for a team of staff serving a section of the restaurant
- must have a good knowledge of menus and wine lists, as well as food and wine in general and correct service methods
- provides some instruction and training to other members of staff.

The **station waiter** (*chef de rang*):

- provides service to a set of tables
- will normally have less experience than the station head waiter.

The **assistant station waiter** (*demi-chef de rang*) assists the station waiter and is directed by him or her.

The **waiter** or **server** (*commis de rang*):

- works on instruction from the more senior staff
- collects and carries food and other items into the restaurant (for this reason the waiter is often called a runner)
- lays tables and prepares the restaurant
- may serve vegetables or sauces, bread and accompanying items
- helps to clear the tables after each course and at the end of the meal.

A **trainee** (*commis*, **apprentice** or *debarrasseur*):

- keeps the sideboard well stocked with equipment, and service trolleys or tables replenished with the relevant food during service
- serves items such as cheeses from these areas
- helps to fetch and carry
- carries out some cleaning and preparation tasks during pre-opening times
- is usually just starting their career.

Carving at the table is now rarely seen, but hot buffet tables where meat is carved for customers to collect remain popular. This service may be provided by a specially trained **carver** and **buffet carvery server** (*trancheur*), or chefs may come in to the restaurant to do it.

A **floor or room service waiter** will be responsible for one floor or set of rooms within a hotel.

A **lounge waiter**:

- serves morning coffee, afternoon teas, and aperitifs, liqueurs and coffee before and after meals
- sets up the lounge in the morning, and maintains its cleanliness and presentation throughout the day
- will be employed within larger hotels (in a smaller establishment, members of the food service staff take over these duties on a rota basis).

A **sommelier**:

- is a knowledgeable wine professional, who normally works within restaurant areas and specialises in wine service
- advises customers on wine to accompany specific foods
- researches and develops wine lists along with a food and beverage manager
- may decide on stock of other drinks for the bars
- may supervise or manage wine waiters and bar staff, as well providing training and staff development
- may also be a member of staff with specialist knowledge of another area, such as cigars.

A **wine waiter**:

- works alongside the sommelier (where there is one) to the standards directed by them
- presents the wine list and advises on wine choices
- serves wine correctly and replenishes wine throughout the meal
- needs a good knowledge of wines and of pairing wines with food on the menu
- may (along with the sommelier) manage the stock and cellars, order wine and ensure correct storage of drinks
- sells wine (wine sales are very important to the profits of a hotel or restaurant).

Bar staff are increasingly referred to as **bar tenders** or **mixologists**. They:

- prepare and serve drinks, including wine, spirits, mixed drinks/cocktails and soft drinks
- need thorough knowledge of all alcoholic and non-alcoholic drinks offered within the establishment, and the ingredients for mixed drinks
- need to serve alcoholic drinks responsibly and know enough about licensing law to ensure legal compliance.

A **mixologist** tends to be an employee who mixes and serves alcoholic or non-alcoholic beverages at a bar. This term is often used for people who prepare any mixed drinks, but usually cocktails. (Cocktails have significantly increased in popularity and those who are skilled in making them are in demand.)

A **barista** typically works behind a counter, serving both hot and cold beverages, and occasionally alcoholic beverages. Barista does not necessarily just mean a coffee maker, although it is often used in this way, especially in popular coffee shops.

A **counter server**:

- assists in serving food at a counter or service table
- may work in areas such as hotel/restaurant buffets, events, fast-food restaurants, staff restaurants, school meals and more
- serves or portions food for customers
- may complete some cooking or finishing tasks.

Where functions, events and banqueting take place, the food and beverages may be served by permanent, casual or agency staff. An events company may manage and staff the whole event in the client's premises. Where banqueting and events are managed in-house, staff will usually include a banqueting and conferencing manager, assistant managers, and a food and beverage service team including bar staff. Depending on the size and type of event a number of casual staff may be engaged as required on a casual basis.

A **cashier**:

- makes up bills from food and drink orders
- takes payments and records sales
- charges to a specific room number or, in a self-service area, charges customers for their food
- deals with cash, vouchers, credit or debit cards, and a range of non-cash options.

A **table clearer**:

- works in self-service/buffet service areas
- clears tables using trolleys specially designed for stacking crockery, glassware, cutlery and disposable items efficiently.

Figure 11.5 Presenting wine

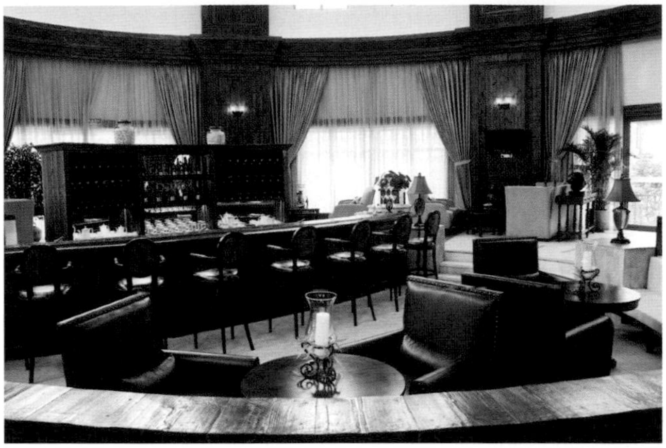

Figure 11.6 A hotel bar

Provision of drinks

The drinks offered by any establishment will depend on its type and its clientele. For example:

- a fine dining restaurant will need a good wine list to enhance and complement its food offer; it will also need a good selection of quality soft drinks and bottled water, aperitifs, spirits, beers, and possibly ingredients for mixed drinks and cocktails.
- a family restaurant may include more soft drinks that appeal to both adults and children, and a range of more budget wines and beers
- a city-centre bar would have a range of wines to sell by the bottle or glass, spirits, beers, ciders, and ready-mixed or ingredients to produce cocktails
- a fast-food restaurant would have a good range of soft drinks with perhaps a few types of wine or even individual bottles of wine (25 cl) and one or two beers.

Alcoholic drinks

Alcoholic beverages account for a significant part of the overall offer and revenue in a wide range of hospitality establishments. Wines may enhance menus, and bar areas can bring in their own custom and revenue. Alcoholic drinks may also be provided for purchase in hotel rooms and as part of banqueting or in-room dining.

An alcoholic beverage is a drink containing ethanol (a type of alcohol). To produce an alcoholic drink, a liquid (water) along with grains, fruits or vegetables may have sugar and yeast added (if these are not present in sufficient quantities naturally), and they will then go through a process called fermentation. Fermentation produces ethanol and carbon dioxide. For more on different types of alcoholic drinks, see Chapter 7.

Alcoholic drinks are a detailed and complex subject and those working in front-of-house hospitality areas are strongly advised to increase their own knowledge.

WEBLINKS

The Wine and Spirit Education Trust offers different courses in wines and spirits:

www.wsetglobal.com

Plumpton College Wine Research:

www.plumpton.ac.uk

Christies:

www.christies.edu/continuing-education/subject-wine.aspx

The nature of alcohol and how it affects the body

Alcohol can be classed as a drug because, when consumed, it can alter the physical, mental and emotional state of the drinker.

Alcohol is absorbed into the blood and reaches all parts of the body. Most of the alcohol is absorbed rapidly into the bloodstream. Nearly all the alcohol has to be burned up by the liver, and the rest is disposed of either in sweat or urine. A person becomes drunk when alcohol is consumed faster than the body can eliminate it, to a point where it affects the body.

The amount of alcohol in the bloodstream is measured by the blood alcohol concentration (BAC). BAC varies according to a person's gender, weight, body composition and speed of drinking. BAC is measured in milligrams (mg) of alcohol in millilitres of blood. A BAC of 80 mg of alcohol in 100 ml of blood is the level above which it is an offence to drive in England. This measurement has an equivalent in terms of micrograms in ml of breath (35 micrograms in 100 ml of breath). This can be measured using a breathalyser.

The amount of alcohol that gets into the bloodstream, and the speed with which it does, depends on the following factors.

- **Quantity:** how many drinks a person consumes and how strong the drinks are.
- **The size of a person:** the same amount of alcohol will produce a higher BAC in women than men.
- **Food eaten:** the presence of food in the stomach slows down the rate at which alcohol enters the bloodstream.

Usually about 20 minutes after the last drink, BAC starts to fall. As a rough guide, it takes about one hour to remove one unit of alcohol from the body.

The strength of an intoxicating drink depends on how much alcohol it contains. The amount of alcohol contained is expressed as percentage of alcohol by volume (ABV). The formula for expressing ABV on labels is alc % vol or % vol. So a fortified wine, such as sherry or vermouth, labelled as alc 18% vol means that 18 per cent of any given quantity is pure alcohol. Where the alcohol by volume (ABV) is more than 0.05 per cent, the drink is classed as alcohol for the purpose of licensing law.

- Most spirits are around 40 per cent ABV.
- Wines vary from 8 per cent to 16 per cent ABV.
- Beers range from 3 per cent to 9 per cent ABV; ciders range from 3 per cent to 8.5 per cent ABV.

To be classified as alcohol-free, a drink must contain no more than 0.05 per cent ABV; to be classified as low alcohol, more than 0.05 per cent but no more than 1.2 per cent ABV. Both must be labelled accordingly.

Units of alcohol

A unit is 8 grams (g) or 10 millilitres (ml) of alcohol. Any quantity of drink that contains 8 g or 10 ml of alcohol is said to contain one unit. Both of the following drinks, for example, contain about 8 g of alcohol, and therefore one unit:

- half a pint of beer of 3.6 per cent ABV
- one 25 ml measure of whisky of 40 per cent ABV.

Recommended safe limits of alcohol

When drinking alcohol everyone is advised to consume in moderation or not at all. Excessive drinking can be detrimental to health and even extremely harmful.

In 2016, at the request of the UK's Chief Medical Officers, experts evaluated evidence from all over the world about the health harm that can be caused by alcohol, and its effects on health and life expectancy. For the first time, consumption by men and by women was considered together, rather than separately. Recommendations were made under three headings:

- A weekly guideline on regular drinking: this recommends the maximum amount of alcohol to be consumed over a week, with consumption spread over more than one day, and with some alcohol-free days.
- Advice on single episodes of drinking: this advises on consumption of alcohol on a single occasion, recommends limiting the amount, and provides

Figure 11.7 Units of alcohol in different drinks

strategies such as alternating alcoholic drinks with water, consuming alcoholic drinks with food, and remaining safe when drinking alcohol.

- A guideline on pregnancy and drinking: the guideline is to drink no alcohol at all when pregnant or planning for pregnancy, in order to avoid the risk of a range of problems referred to as foetal alcohol spectrum disorders (FASD).

At the time of going to press, the related documentation is still under review. More information is available at: www.gov.uk/government/consultations/health-risks-from-alcohol-new-guidelines

Soft drinks and water

A good range of soft drinks should be provided. People may choose soft drinks because:

- they prefer not to drink alcohol
- they are under 18
- they have been refused alcohol
- they are going to be driving or operating machinery
- for religious or cultural reasons.

Having a good and interesting selection available will be beneficial for overall sales.

Water is often automatically set at the table, along with eating utensils, plates and the menu. Environmental sensitivity has made it common to ask customers if they require water service. This step can also reduce dishwashing and glass inventory requirements. If water is desired, a source of ice and clean, clear water is needed in the primary (table) service area and/or remote wait stations located closer to the customer/tables.

When bottled water is offered to customers, the only equipment required will be the necessary refrigerated storage space.

Licensing

The sale of alcoholic drinks is in England and Wales is subject to the Licensing Act (2003). Other areas and regions may have different regulations. Businesses, organisations and individuals who want to sell or supply alcohol in England and Wales must have a licence or other authorisation from a licensing authority, usually a local council.

The licensing requirements outline four key objectives:

1. the prevention of crime and disorder
2. public safety
3. the prevention of public nuisance
4. the protection of children from harm.

The usual requirements of the act are:

- the display of a summary of the premises licence, including the days and times of opening, the name of the registered licence holder, the licence number and a valid date
- drinks price lists to be displayed
- restrictions on under-aged persons (under the age of 18) being served alcohol and employed to serve alcohol
- the need for an authorised person (or the personal licence holder) to be on site at all times.

A personal licence is required by anyone authorising the sale of alcohol from a licensed premises. All licensed premises must have an allocated personal licence holder, known as the Designated Premises Supervisor (DPS). The DPS must authorise every sale of alcohol.

Temporary Event Notice

Sometimes alcohol is served away from the usual licensed premises at special events and functions. An authorisation – Temporary Event Notice (TEN) – would need to be applied for from the local authority and the personal licence holder must be present at all times.

The event must:

- have fewer than 500 people at all times, including staff running the event
- last no more than 168 hours (seven days).

You must be at least 18 to apply for a TEN.

- A TEN is needed for each event on the same premises.
- Those with a personal licence to sell alcohol can be granted up to 50 TENs a year.
- A single premises can have up to 12 TENs applied for in one year, as long as the total length of the events is not more than 21 days.
- If organising separate but consecutive events, there must be at least a 24-hour gap between them.
- Contact your council to apply for a TEN. You must do this at least ten working days before your event.
- You can apply for a TEN only as an individual, not an organisation.

Other licences

Other types of licence may include licences for music (live or pre-recorded), dancing, gambling, theatrical performance and television display. In all cases the supervisor and the staff should be aware of the provisions and limitations of the licences to ensure compliance.

Alcohol sales and young people

There is a responsibility placed on those selling alcohol not to sell it to those under the age of 18. It is advisable to ask for ID as proof of age. If no ID can be provided, refusal is the best option. Acceptable forms of ID include:

- a photo driving licence
- a passport
- a proof of age card, such as the PASS card from the national Proof of Age Standards Scheme.

It is illegal for someone else to buy an alcoholic drink for someone under 18. The only exception to this is that young people who are 16 or 17 years old and accompanied by an adult can consume – but not buy – beer, wine and cider on a licensed premises if it is consumed with a proper meal eaten at a table.

Refusal of alcohol

The service of alcohol should be refused to:

- anyone under the age of 18 years
- someone already intoxicated
- outside of permitted licensing hours (this may vary according to the establishment)
- where associated with rowdy or disruptive behaviour.

Individual establishments may have their own additional rules on the service and non-service of alcohol.

WEBLINKS

Further information regarding licensing in UK can be found by visiting:

www.gov.uk/guidance/alcohol-licensing

Wine and Spirits Trade Association:

www.wsta.co.uk/resources/facts-figures

PASS cards:

www.pass-scheme.org.uk

UK legislation for sales of alcohol

In the UK the measures of alcoholic drinks are controlled and monitored by the Trading Standards Authorities. Everyone selling alcoholic drinks must comply with legislation for measure sizes, as follows.

- **Spirits:** a whole bottle, or measure sizes of 25 ml, 35 ml, 50 ml or multiples of these.
- **Wine:** a whole bottle, or measure sizes of 125 ml, 175 ml or multiples of these.
- **Fortified wine:** a whole bottle, or measure sizes of 50 ml, 70 ml, or multiples of these.
- **Beer (on draught):** pint, half pint, third/two-thirds of a pint (multiples of half a pint); bottles and cans are also sold.

Matching food to wine/drinks

Food and its accompanying wine/drink should harmonise well, with each enhancing the other's flavours, strength and textures. However, the most successful combinations are those that appeal to the individual and provide what the customer wants.

When matching food and wine there are guidelines, but there will always be some exceptions. General guidelines are summarised in Table 11.2.

Table 11.2 General guidelines for matching wine and food

Characteristic	Food considerations
Acidity	Can be used to match, or to contrast, acidity in foods – for example, crisp, dry wines to match lemon or tomato, or to cut through creamy flavours
Age/maturity	As some wine ages and develops it can become delicate, with complex and intricate flavours; more simple foods, such as grills or roasts, work better with older wines than stronger-tasting foods, which can overpower the wines
Oak (wine matured in oak barrels or sometimes flavoured using oak chips)	The more oaked the wine, the more robust and flavoursome the foods need to be; heavily oaked wines can overpower more delicate foods
Sweetness	The wine should be sweeter than the foods or it will taste flat or thin; sweet dishes need contrast for them to match well with sweeter wines – for example, acids in sweeter foods can harmonise with the sweetness in the wines; savoury foods with sweetness such as carrots or onions can match well with ripe fruity wines; blue cheeses can go well with sweet wines, also sweeter wines can go well with salty foods
Tannin	Tannic wines match well with red meats and semi-hard cheeses such as Cheddar; tannic wines are not good with egg dishes and wines with high tannin content do not work well with salty foods
Weight	Big, rich wines go well with robust (flavoursome) meat dishes, but can overpower lighter-flavoured foods

Source: Cousins and Lillicrap, 2014

There has been increasing demand for beers with food, either alongside or as an alternative to wines, especially in popular chain or budget restaurants and also in pubs. As with wines it is a question of trial and error to achieve harmony and match between particular beers and foods. Generally, considerations for the pairing of beers and foods are similar to those for matching wines with foods; in particular, take account of acidity, sweetness/dryness, bitterness, tannin, weight and complexity of the taste. Cider has also increased in popularity and is often requested with food; similar considerations apply.

Making recommendations to customers

A few general points of advice are set out below for advising the customer on which drinks to choose to accompany a meal. However, customers should be given complete freedom in their selection of wines or other drinks.

- Aperitifs are usually alcoholic beverages that are drunk before the meal. If wine will be consumed with the meal, then suggest that the aperitif should be a grape (wine based) rather than a grain (spirit based) aperitif, since the latter may spoil or dull the palate. Grape aperitifs are more common. Aperitifs are meant to stimulate the appetite and therefore should not be sweet: dry and medium-dry sherries, dry vermouths, and Sercial or Verdelho Madeira are all good examples.
- Starter courses are often best accompanied by a dry white or dry rosé wine.
- National dishes should normally be complemented by the national wines of that country – for example, Italian red wine with meat-based pasta dishes.
- Fish and shellfish dishes are often most suited to chilled dry white wines.
- Red meats such as beef and lamb blend and harmonise well with red wine.
- White meats such as veal and pork are acceptable with medium white or rosé wines.
- Game dishes require the heavier and more robust red wines to complement their full flavour.
- Sweets and desserts are served at the end of the meal, and here it is acceptable to offer well-chilled sweet white wines that may come from the Loire, Sauternes, Barsac or Hungary. These wines harmonise best with dishes containing fruit.
- The majority of cheeses blend well with port and other dry, robust red wines. Port is fortified wine traditionally served with Stilton cheese.
- Grain- and fruit-based spirits and liqueurs all harmonise well with coffee.

Serving wine

Some guidelines when selecting and serving wines are given below.

- Dry wines should be served before sweeter wines.
- White wines should usually be served before red wines.
- Lighter wines should be served before heavier wines.
- Good wines should be served before great wines.
- Wines should be at their correct temperature before serving.
- Wine should always be served to customers before their food.

Cellar management

Alcoholic drinks may form a significant amount of the revenue and expenditure of an establishment, and managing, monitoring and controlling the stock is essential.

The term cellar may be used for any room or area where drinks are stored. This may be a central storage area from where restaurants, bars and other areas dealing with alcoholic drinks draw their stock.

The traditional cellar book or ledger has generally been replaced by electronic systems for monitoring cellar stock and these may form part of a wider system in an establishment such as a hotel.

Information that needs to be kept and updated as part of the cellar management will include:

- goods received
- name and contact details of supplier
- order number
- date of delivery
- delivery note/invoice number
- units and total quantity delivered
- unit cost, total cost and any discounts
- charge made on any returnable containers.

Cellar stock ledger (or file)

This should show movement of all stock in and out of the cellar area; deliveries as received would be recorded along with issues out to the various bars, restaurants, room service areas, etc. – if cost of stock is recorded here it is usually at cost price rather than selling price. Information from the stock ledger and/or bin cards informs the cellar manager of when new stock needs to be ordered. See Chapter 10 for an example of a stores ledger sheet.

Bin cards

Bin cards show the physical amounts held of each stock item. See Chapter 10 for an example of a bin card.

Ullage

This is the recording of cellar wastage, which could be due to cleaning and changing barrels, broken bottles, unusable stock, etc.

Storage of alcoholic beverages

Because of the high costs of alcoholic beverages, careful and efficient storage is essential.

- The cellar should always be clean and well ventilated; a room that is dark when not in use is ideal.
- Temperatures should be kept even at around 13–15°C; there should be no vibration or draughts, and humidity of 70 per cent is about right.
- Store most wines horizontally on racks with the label uppermost. Horizontal storage keeps the wine in contact with the cork, which prevents the cork from drying out. Horizontal storage also makes it easier to select wines in stock and for stock-taking. Champagne and sparkling wine is often stored upright.
- On delivery, beer casks should be placed where unnecessary moving will not be needed.

The security of these areas is also very important, to avoid unnecessary loss of stock.

- Limit the number of people who have access to the cellars.
- Invest in secure locking systems and maybe CCTV with recording.
- Use recording systems/ledgers to keep track of stock arriving and leaving the cellar, and investigate any discrepancies promptly.
- When stock is issued to different areas, have a proper ordering system (paper or electronic) and record any returns.

Designing a food service business

The process of designing a food service facility is complex. It involves many facets of business planning, right through to the development of layout drawings, interior designs and equipment specifications. It is certainly not unusual for an operator to consider or actually open a new restaurant without knowing what type of facility will have the best chance of success and a failing business may be the result. A potential operator may have sufficient money to invest, a location or a theme in mind, and a great amount of enthusiasm, but they may not have adequately considered the total concept of the operation – and that is vital.

The concept and business plan

Concept development in the food service industry means planning the menu, developing a theme for the decor and developing a method of serving food to an identified target market to achieve an acceptable level of profit. Concept development should also encompass a strategy for growth and for a reasonable financial return on investment.

In order to have a successful food service operation, an operator must combine several elements into a comprehensive and cohesive plan: the menu, market, finance, and methods of management and operation.

The menu

The importance of getting the menu right cannot be overemphasised. The menu design and concept could be the deciding factor between success and failure. The menu must appeal to the anticipated clientele and be within their expected price range. (See the section on menu engineering in Chapter 9.) The dishes must be within the capabilities of cooking and serving staff, and must be achievable in the time available, even at busy times. The following are some of the major operational and design factors influenced or driven by the menu:

- the selling price of the food
- the type of preparation and cooking equipment that will be needed
- the production capacities of the various pieces of cooking equipment that will be used
- the size of refrigeration and storage areas required
- the size of the dishwashing area, as well as the capacity of the machines
- the total amount of floor space that will be needed
- the type and capacity of tables and seating
- the design and type of service area(s)
- the total financial investment needed.

The market

Conduct market research before developing a concept and constructing a food business. Some of the basic questions that should be addressed include those listed below.

- What is the target market or potential customer base?
- Is the identified market large enough to generate acceptable sales and profits?
- What are the tastes, preferences and motivations of the target market?
- What are the best methods of marketing communication to reach the target customers?
- What are the appropriate messages that will influence and motivate the target audience to listen and act?
- Will the target audience need or want the facility and menu items that are being planned?
- Will the operation's internal and ongoing marketing strategies be successful in selling the customer additional products and services?

For more on market research, see Chapter 13.

Finance

One of the primary causes of the high failure rate of food service operations is lack of available finance or money – in particular, lack of money set aside as working capital. The operator may have sufficient funds to get the proposed business off the ground, but unfortunately fail to plan for the day-to-day cash requirements of product purchases, maintenance, repairs and payroll. As a result, they quickly find themselves in a working capital deficit position.

In addition to sufficient working capital, the business must have sufficient funds for:

- professional planning and design
- new building construction or the renovation of an existing building
- professional interior design and decorating
- various pieces of equipment and supply items
- furniture and fixtures.

Finance for these items must be identified and committed before any serious planning can begin. However, such commitments may not be made simply because all of the costs are not known or may change. Therefore, the planning process for capital funds needs two phases.

1. In the initial phase, the financial needs of the business set-up are estimated and, if the prospective operator or owner does not have sufficient personal funds, then sources of financial support should be contacted to determine the possibility of raising the necessary finance.
2. Next, lenders and investors make firm financial commitments after the concept development has taken place, preliminary designs and construction estimates have been made and market research has been completed.

Management

The quality and style of management in any food service business are the most important elements in achieving success. The following questions need to be addressed by any owner and investor.

- Who will actually run the day-to-day affairs of the facility? Will it be the owner or majority shareholder, or will an outside 'professional' manager be hired?
- What kind of educational background and food service experience must the manager and management team have?

- What level of assistance will be available to the manager? Who will assist the general manager in covering the long hours often required to operate a food service facility?
- What level of salary will the manager and the other staff members receive?
- Will the remuneration package contain an incentive for performance?
- How will operational policies be established, and by whom?
- How will these policies be communicated to the management team?
- How will the management team communicate with the rest of the operation's employees?

The answers to these and related questions will help determine the organisational structure of the operation and the kind of management team needed.

Many successful restaurants are owned and operated by one individual whose personality becomes a part of the guests' dining experience. On the other hand, the food and beverage department of a large hotel, or the food service in a large hospital or events company, may be under the management of more than one person and is usually part of a more complex organisational structure. In these cases, the policies and procedures of the food service facility should be laid out in an operations manual, to ensure consistent implementation of management policies.

Method of execution

The final step in the concept development process concentrates on operational issues. The areas that need to be addressed deal with methods of production, control systems and personnel issues.

Methods of food production raise questions such as 'Will fresh food and traditional cooking methods be used, or will prepared or semi-prepared foods be used?' This decision will have a major influence on the size of refrigerated and dry storage areas, and on the size of the kitchen. The chosen production method will also greatly influence the number of employees in the kitchen, as well as the skill levels of these employees and the amounts of organisation needed. Areas that should be looked at include:

- cash control
- sales analysis
- control of the guests' bills and receipts
- food production forecasting
- control over stock levels and the various storage areas, including refrigeration
- purchasing and receiving control
- portion control and control of wastage
- ongoing quality control.

How management deals with key staffing issues can significantly affect the success of any operation. Areas that need to be addressed include:

- determining the amount of labour required to run the business successfully
- employee work schedules and hours of work
- business operating hours
- staffing patterns
- benefits and enhancements that will be offered to employees
- provision for ongoing education and training for employees
- the varying skill levels and skills mix needed among employees
- levels of qualifications initially needed by employees
- the level of supervision that will be required
- payment levels for staff.

These, plus associated issues, must be addressed as part of the concept development process.

Running a feasibility study

Once the concept development process has been completed satisfactorily, the next phase assesses the feasibility of the concept: whether the proposed operation is likely to generate sales and make a profit.

This will in turn have a direct impact on the ROI (return on investment) analysis, which is critical to each investor.

This is often termed a feasibility study and consists of many components. One of these is the market feasibility study. This analyses all the issues associated with the marketplace, including:

- the demographics of the geographical area where the business is to be placed; this would be comprehensive and should include age, gender, income level, size of household, occupation, ethnicity, and anything else relevant to the area
- the buying and eating-out habits of the individuals in the area; information could be obtained through a questionnaire, survey, or by simply looking at what already exists in the area and which are most popular
- the traffic patterns of the area, including an assessment of roadway access, congestion at certain times of day, future street development, availability of public transportation and parking facilities
- general economic factors, such as employment statistics, industry growth, future economic development plans, tax structure, and commercial growth/new housing development in the area
- the competing businesses, to include size (number of seats), estimated customer counts, menu items, pricing, decor or theme, and professionalism of the staff at existing food service operations
- projected sales, based on an estimated customer count over a specific period of time, as well as an estimation of what the average spend per customer might be.

Understanding and properly responding to the target market are important factors in the success of any food service operation.

Once the feasibility study is complete, it is up to all concerned to make the critical decision. If, after a careful analysis of the findings and projections, the project looks financially sound, the market is identified and can be reached easily, a need for the proposed food service facility exists, and sufficient funding and working capital is available, the decision to proceed can be made with confidence.

However, if one or more of the critical elements is uncertain, one of the following options may be considered.

- The proposed facility may be too large, so consider something smaller.
- The staffing cost estimates may have been too high, so a different style of service may work.
- The menu may be wrong for the identified market, which can be solved by changing the menu.
- The proposed prices may be too high based on the customer demographics. The price structure and menu need to be changed.
- The local competition may be stronger than originally thought. This may mean selecting an alternative location or concept.

The second option is to abandon the project altogether. If the projections and conclusions in the feasibility study do not paint a positive picture, then there is no point in trying to 'force' the numbers.

The third option is to delay the decision until a later date. This is the least desirable option as the project will lose its momentum, initial findings may change, costs could rise, premises could be lost and there may be costs just to keep the proposed project alive.

The design process

Assuming that a 'yes' decision is made, the design process moves into an entirely new phase: the hiring of a professional food service facility designer or a food service design consultant. Restaurants are complex and expensive. For the operation to run smoothly and effectively the facility has to be designed properly, taking into consideration numerous factors, such as labour, space, equipment and energy requirements, traffic flow and menu, as well as other factors. This requires the services of a professional who understands the intricacies of food service operations, so prospective operators rely on food service design consultants to provide their expertise.

The operator should have a constant dialogue with the consultant throughout the design process, to ensure that requests are being handled to their satisfaction. Excellent communication will mean that mistakes and misunderstandings are less likely.

The design function may progress through nine phases. All phases are critical and are totally interdependent on the other stages. Table 11.3 outlines the natural sequence of events that takes place between the design consultant and the operator/owner.

Table 11.3 The sequence of events between design consultant and food service facility operator/owner

Phase 1: initial contact and proposal	The operator explores with the consultant the services they can provide, and the costs; this initial phase establishes the working relationship between the design consultant and client
Phase 2: feasibility study (see above)	The food service design consultant assists the prospective operator/client in conducting a proper feasibility study; this will assist with various aspects of the work
Phase 3: programming	This describes the function of each area and how each space will be used, and the number of square metres required. A typical programme includes: ● the room number/name of the room (i.e. kitchen) ● the relationship of this room to the other rooms ● a description of use ● the amount of square metres required ● the finishes for floors, walls and ceilings The key element in this phase is the establishment of space relationships among the areas of the facility once the total square metre space requirements are discussed with the client; if changes need to be made for any reason, they are initiated
Phase 4: initial design and cost estimates	This will show the shape of the building, the various entrances and flow patterns, plus the location of all the functional areas; these drawings will show elevations of the outside of the building (if applicable), site plans for the building plot, and the location of roads, parking areas, etc. In addition, and if required, schematic drawings are often used to gain preliminary approval from local authority planning departments
Phase 5: design development, equipment specification and engineering	This phase starts the detailed work; working drawings – the detailed plans that will guide and be used by contractors who build the facility – are developed during this phase of the process; the selection of all the important equipment to be used in the facility, the assembly of equipment literature, writing performance specifications and the development of utility schedules will be accomplished; from a design consultant's perspective, the 'best' piece of equipment is the piece that matches the specification exactly
Phase 6: bidding and awarding the contract	This is a process that can vary in length of time taken, depending on the complexity and size of the project under consideration

Phase 7: project construction	During this phase, the role of the food service design consultant is primarily to: • work closely with the general contractor and architect • inspect the fabricated equipment to make sure it has been built to specification and that it meets all of the requirements written into the specification documents
Phase 8: inspection and acceptance	The new food service facility will be inspected at least twice by the design consultant, owner/operator, equipment dealer and all other parties who may have been involved in the process
Phase 9: implementation and training	Demonstration of all the equipment found in the facility, along with thorough and specific training sessions designed to explain the layout and design of the equipment to all employees, is an important function

Source: Catering Equipment Suppliers' Association

When a food service operation is part of a group, or chain, of establishments some of the design procedures may be done centrally and then adapted for the individual outlets. Smaller businesses would probably have a simplified version of the process or may hand the whole procedure to a consultant company.

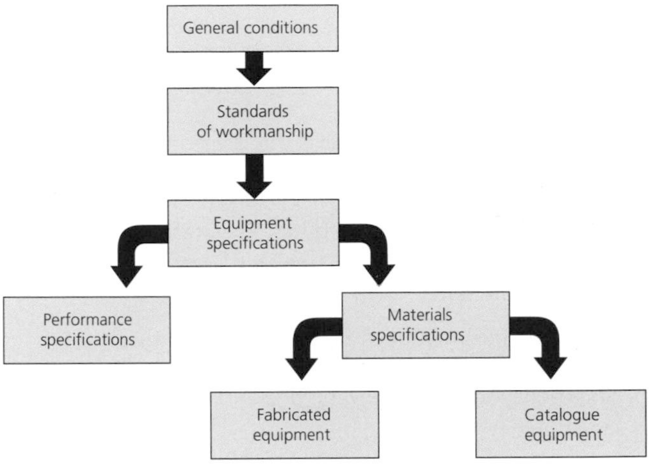

Figure 11.8 **Types of specification**

Designing the restaurant

In any establishment a customer may be gained or lost on their first impressions alone. The creation of a welcoming atmosphere, by the right choice of decor, furnishings and equipment, is therefore a major factor in the success of the food service operation.

Although there are significant differences in the physical layout, menu and method of service between the various types of food service facility, there are some underlying design principles that are consistently followed by all food service design consultants. Every food service project design should:

- have flexibility and modularity built in to it
- be designed for simplicity and ease of understanding
- be designed so that there is an efficient flow of materials and personnel
- have ergonomic design of fittings and equipment in mind
- facilitate the ease of sanitation
- make it easy to supervise the employees of the facility
- make efficient use of the space and services available.

Careful selection of items in terms of shape, design and colour enhances the overall decor or theme, and contributes to a feeling of total harmony. The choice of layout, furniture, linen, tableware, small equipment and glassware will be determined by considering:

- the type of clientele expected
- the site or location
- the layout of the food and beverage service area
- the type of service offered
- menu items
- the finance available.

Customer expectations of their 'dining experience' vary greatly according to type of restaurant. In most cases, the customer has made a personal choice about the type and level of service desired, as well as the atmosphere in which they wish to dine. Sometimes speed of service is paramount; sometimes they want a friendly bar with plenty of noise and comfort food. On special occasions, they may want an intimate booth or table, a great wine list, impeccable service and classic cuisine. All customers expect a clean dining area, adequate seating, appropriate heating, air conditioning and lighting, plus clean plates and cutlery, or service-appropriate disposables.

Behind the scenes

The service areas behind the scenes are often referred to as 'back of house'. These areas are usually between the kitchen and the service areas and are important parts of the design of the operation. These areas are meeting points for staff of various departments as they carry out their duties, and therefore there must be close liaison between the departments to ensure the smooth running of the operation.

In general – especially in large operations – five main back-of-house service areas can be identified. These are:

1. **Still room:** the area directly between the production area and the service area, and where certain food items – such as cold sauces, accompaniments and beverage items – are prepared that are not catered for by the other major departments, such as the kitchen, larder and pastry. Hot beverages are usually prepared in this area.
2. **Silver or plate room:** for the storage of all metal service equipment.
3. **Wash-up:** needs to be convenient for used items being returned from the restaurant and close to the still room area.
4. **The pass or hotplate:** this is the division between food service areas and kitchen, and is where orders are received (manually or electronically) and collected from the food production area by service staff.
5. **Linen store:** used for all restaurant linen, and disposable items.

A well-designed layout of all these areas is important to ensure an even flow of work by the various members of staff. The layout itself will vary, depending on the type of operational needs.

The general considerations for the planning of the back-of-house service areas are:

- appropriate siting and logical layout of equipment
- ease of delivery access
- ease of service
- meeting food safety standards, and following health and safety requirements
- ease of cleaning
- sufficient storage space for service equipment and food items
- secure storage.

A smaller establishment is unlikely to have all of the above as separate areas so for practical and operational requirements may need to use space as available. For example, serving equipment may be stored in the wash-up or kitchen area or linen/disposable items may be in a restaurant cupboard.

For more information on layout of these areas, see the section on product flows in Chapter 5.

Front of house

The 'front of house' is one of the most critical components of any commercial food service operation. If the kitchen is the manufacturing plant, the dining area is the showroom where 'the food meets the customer', and the 'stage' where good food, personal service and atmosphere come together to deliver a memorable dining experience. The establishment's success depends on equal attention being paid to these vital components.

The front-of-house areas are used by both customers and staff, and include:

- food service areas such as restaurants
- reception – the place for taking bookings, receiving customers and processing bills
- licensed bar with or without additional seating
- coffee lounge (bar facilities may be used for this)
- customer cloakroom/washroom facilities – cloakrooms, powder rooms, etc., will be staffed in a large establishment; in small businesses facilities may be shared between staff and customers because restricted space may not allow for separate facilities.

Figure 11.9 **Restaurant reception area**

The general considerations for planning the front-of-house areas will vary, but include:

- style of decor and lighting
- heating and ventilation needs
- noise level (consider noise from wooden flooring, uncovered wooden tables, etc.)
- the size and shape of the areas
- the style of establishment – fine dining establishments generally allow for more space
- size of furniture, fittings and equipment.

Important features of a food service area are as follows.

- **Proximity of the service and kitchen areas to the dining room:** a shorter distance between the service and kitchen areas can reduce labour costs and provide a higher-quality food product. It also reduces staff fatigue, which improves their attitude and the impression they make on the customer. A greater distance between these functional areas increases the cost of labour and makes it more difficult to deliver foods at an optimum serving temperature.
- **Proper equipment to maintain quality and temperature of food, and to ensure microbial safety:** both hot and cold foods must be held for service at the correct temperatures. In a properly designed and functioning service area, appropriate holding equipment should be used to ensure that these temperatures are maintained. Temperatures should be monitored and recorded.

In most food service operations the back-of-house and front-of-house areas are quite separate so that customers cannot see in to the back-of-house areas, especially the kitchen. More recently, some restaurants are making the cooking area a central feature – it is in full view of the customer, and the cooking aromas and bustle of the operation contribute to their meal experience.

A further development has been 'the chef's table', where in some establishments a table can be booked at the edge of the kitchen so the customer feels very much part of the whole process.

Space considerations

The amount of space required per customer varies. The customer's comfort has to be offset against the number of customers you are trying to fit in to the restaurant to generate maximum revenue. The more upmarket the restaurant, the more comfortable and spacious it should be in order to fulfil customer expectations.

Space allocation requires consideration of not only the construction costs but also the resulting operational costs. While allocating less space for some areas may reduce building costs, insufficient space can increase operating costs, reduce efficiency and affect profitability.

Some of the major decision criteria that any facilities designer or operator should consider include the following.

- How many individual customers are to be served, and over what period of time?
- What are their typical food requirements?
- How many customers will need service at any one time?
- What types of food are to be offered and what preparation methods will be used in the dining area, if any?
- What kind of service will be provided and on what schedule?
- What type and amount of storage space will be needed?
- What are the space requirements for maintenance, offices, employee facilities, toilets, and so on?
- Is there enough space allocated or left over for checkout, waiting, a cloakroom and service areas?

Space requirements should take into consideration customers' comfort, and the type and quality of service. The amount of serving equipment to be used in the dining area, and in the case of a cafeteria the queuing space, will impact the space allocated for each seat.

Table 11.4 provides some generally accepted 'space allowances per seat' for various types of food service operation.

Other factors that should be taken into consideration include those listed below.

- **The use of service stations:** estimate based on one small unit for every 20 seats or a large central service station for every 50–60 seats. Service stations are important when the production area or kitchen and dining areas are on different floors or located at some distance from each other.
- **Table size:** this will have an influence on the comfort of the patron and the efficient use of space. For example, in a cafeteria where patrons are more likely to dine from trays, it is important that tables are large enough to accommodate the size and number of trays expected.
- **Aisle space:** carefully calculate the aisle space between tables and chairs to include the passage area, plus the area occupied by the individuals seated at the tables.

Table 11.4 **Space allowances per seat for various types of food service operation**

Type of operation	Space allowance per seat
Commercial cafeteria	1.5–1.7 m^2
College	1.1–1.4 m^2
School cafeteria	0.8–1.1 m^2
Counter service restaurant	1.7–1.9 m^2
Table service at a hotel, club or restaurant	1.4–1.7 m^2
Table service (minimum)	1.0–1.3 m^2
Banquet room	0.9–1.0 m^2

The size and configuration of the dining room or rooms will have a major impact on the atmosphere and, ultimately, the dining experience. New facilities offer an opportunity for control and creativity in the room layout. Existing buildings and room layouts often place fundamental limitations on seating capacity, seating type and room configuration. A good consultant or interior designer can generate creative solutions.

Lighting considerations

Lighting is a very important component of the overall dining room design. The amount of light required is dictated by the area and the activity that occurs there. Lighting design in a restaurant or commercial dining facility should encompass five basic principles:

1. space relationships
2. perspective
3. contour
4. special details of intrinsic beauty
5. imaginative and subtle qualities.

These five principles apply to the three general types of illumination found in all food service facilities.

1. **Overall general illumination:** general lighting is designed to perform and function day and night. It must achieve a perfect balance. If it doesn't, 'dark spots' or 'dead spots' will occur, creating a 'misreading' of the space.
2. **Sparkle and excitement:** a burst of colour or a strategically placed light can enhance an otherwise monotonous lighting plan, making certain areas stand out. This kind of lighting is appropriate for reception areas, windows, cathedral ceilings, partitions, special flooring or changes in flooring.

3 **Specific focal points:** subtleties of light placement can direct the patron's eyes away from 'trouble spots' or create an illusion of extra space. Special-effect spotlights, uplights, etc., can highlight artwork, a table, the patrons, a bar, a stairway or the food. The various methods include:
   - silhouetting, allowing interesting objects to be emphasised
   - grazing light, used to emphasise various textural qualities
   - modelling, designed to give depth and character to objects.

The design of cafeteria and serving areas, and equipment for the hot and cold holding of food, is discussed in Chapter 5.

Creating a customer care specification

Increasingly, quality of the service and the customer experience have become the main differentiators between similar establishments seeking customers. Understanding how the customer is involved in the process, their needs and expectations, and identifying the experience they are likely to have is critical to the success of the business.

Like the food, beverages and other product specifications used in hospitality businesses, there must also be a customer service specification, frequently referred to as Standard Operational Procedure. For food and beverage operations, the customer service specification is focused as much on identifying the procedures that need to be followed as on the way they are carried out. This is because food and beverage is more than a delivery system; it also needs to be completely customer focused from the time the customer makes their booking until the time they leave. Much is achieved by good communication and positive interaction between staff and customers.

A customer care specification needs to consider the entire experience the customer has within the establishment, and needs to be supported by planners and management at all stages. A customer service specification takes account of five key characteristics.

1. **Levels of service:** the service methods, and the extent of the individual care and personal attention that is given to customers.
2. **Availability of service:** days and times at which the service is available, the variation in the menus and how often menus change, extent of wines and other drinks lists on offer.
3. **Level of standards:** quality of food and drinks, surroundings and decor, furniture and equipment costs, staffing and professionalism.
4. **Reliability of the service:** the extent to which the product is consistent in practice, and especially at busy times.
5. **Flexibility of the service:** the provision of alternatives or variations in the standard product, including variation of service locations such as bar service, room service, garden, etc.

In designing a food service operation to meet a customer service specification, care needs to be taken to ensure the profitability of the operation through efficient use of the available resources. The resources used in food service operations are as follows.

- **Materials:** commodities and equipment.
- **Labour:** staffing and staff costs.
- **Facilities:** the premises and the volume of business that the premises are physically able to support.

Managers must therefore take account of the effect of the level of business on the ability of the operation to maintain the required service. At the same time they need to ensure maximum productivity, and the best and most efficient use of resources.

The operation must be physically capable of supporting the desired customer service specification. In addition, the staff must be capable (through support and training) of delivering the intended customer service specification. This takes account of the technical and interpersonal skills, product knowledge and team-working capability of the staff.

As well as customers, service staff also interact with staff from other areas, such as the kitchen, reception, accounts office, stores, and many more. It is important that the provision of the food and beverage product is seen as a joint effort between all departments, with each understanding the needs of the others in order to provide the best possible service and meet (and possibly exceed) customers' expectations.

In order to avoid any problems with customer relations, careful attention needs to be given to the physical aspects of the service and how it is operated, along with the care and interaction between customers and staff. Knowing what the potential for customer satisfaction is from the food and beverage product can help to ensure that there are procedures in place for dealing with any difficulties that might arise. The potential for satisfaction should already have been built in to the initial design of the product so that it meets the expectations the customers may have. However, there will always be a potential for dissatisfaction and customer complaints, and these may be considered in two categories, as follows.

1. **Tangible:** those that can be controlled by the establishment, such as untidy areas, unhelpful staff or overcrowded conditions.
2. **Intangible:** those that are uncontrollable, such as the behaviour of other customers, the weather or transport problems.

Being able to identify all of these possibilities enables an operation to develop procedures to deal with them when they occur. Suitable staff training on how to deal with certain situations effectively will prove to be a good investment. See also Chapter 13, on sales and marketing, and Chapter 14, on customer service.

Case study 1

A country house hotel wishes to extend its food service provision. It has a good-sized, well-equipped kitchen and a large dining room that presently provides breakfast and dinner mainly for residents.

1. What else could it offer to increase its food provision within and outside of the hotel?
2. How could it publicise its new offers?
3. Should any new legal requirements be considered?

Case study 2

After successfully completing their hospitality qualifications, three friends decided to open a small restaurant in the high street of a market town. The premises they chose to lease already had an equipped kitchen though some of the equipment was quite old and not working properly. Finance for everything else was sourced through a loan and advertising for the new venue was all done on social media.

Because they wanted to reflect a variety of world foods the menu was large with a number of choices of each type of food supported by an extensive list of world wines. After a promising start in the opening week numbers started to decline, with some evenings seeing no customers at all. A large loss started to accumulate and the friends could not agree on what to do to put it right.

1. What mistakes were made with the set-up of this restaurant?
2. How could it have been done better?
3. Should the friends try to save the business? If so, what steps should they take?

Case study 3

A busy hospital has a large staff dining area that, at peak times over lunch, is having difficulty coping with the pressure. The kitchen has problems keeping up with demand for food on the hot counter, long queues form and it can take a long time to get through the payment point. There are numerous complaints, especially as there is nowhere else in the immediate area to buy food and some staff get only short breaks not allowing them time to queue.

Make a list of suggestions that may help to solve the problems in this dining area. Underline or highlight a selection of your proposed solutions that could be used together to solve the problem.

Further reading

Catering Equipment Suppliers' Association (CESA) *An Introduction to the Food Service*. Online at www.cesa.org.uk.

Cousins, J., Lillicrap, D.R. and Weekes, S. (2014) *Food and Beverage Service*. London: Hodder Education.

Topics for discussion

1 In a large, busy restaurant what are the measures you could introduce to develop good working relationships between kitchen staff and food service staff?

2 Suggest a suitable method of food service for each of the following:
- a fine dining restaurant in a luxury hotel
- a city-centre brasserie
- an events company dealing mainly with weddings
- a large staff restaurant.

Give reasons for your choices.

3 Discuss the main reasons why food service staff need to be knowledgeable about the food dishes they will serve. How can staff be given this knowledge?

4 In a newly refurbished country house hotel with 60 bedrooms/suites, an à la carte restaurant seating 100 covers and a 40-seat bar/lounge, what are the food service staff and bar staff you would require? What would their job titles be?

5 When deciding on wines for a new restaurant's wine list what should your main considerations be? Suggest 12 suitable wines to include, based on your considerations.

6 Discuss some of the technological developments used in food service areas (such as use of electronic devices) to make service faster and more efficient. List and describe some current ways in which technology is used and how these enhance service.

7 In a bar area when would you refuse to serve a customer with alcoholic drinks? Is it the responsibility of bar staff to encourage customers to drink alcohol responsibly? How could you do this?

8 Describe five important factors that need to be considered when designing a food service system.

9 As a hotel food and beverage manager, what are the various areas of legislation that may affect the food service operation? How can these be communicated to food service staff?

10 What is meant by a feasibility study and how would it apply to the opening of a new high-street brasserie?

12 Front office and accommodation services

To accompany high-quality food and beverage, a high standard of accommodation management is vital to any hospitality operation. Although not all hospitality operations provide rooms, a warm welcome, and clean, safe and well-maintained premises are imperative in attracting and retaining customers.

The purpose of this chapter is to introduce some of the key areas of importance within accommodation management – moreover, to highlight the importance of good-quality accommodation management for customers, employees and operational profits. It details the challenges that operators face in managing accommodation, and provides examples of tools, systems and approaches that can be used to deal with these challenges. The accommodation sector is highly competitive and constantly evolving, and so requires high-quality, motivated employees and managers to ensure that the delivery of the accommodation product meets customers' expectations every time.

Figure 12.1 Page boys at the Peninsula Hong Kong

Classifications of accommodation

Accommodation can be categorised into either private or public, or commercial or non-commercial operations. Some public-sector operations are run by independent commercial companies under contract (known as contract catering). Accommodation can be classified in different ways to include star rating, sector, geographic location, target market, ownership and size, to name a few.

For details of the classifications used in private accommodation, see Tables 12.1 to 12.6. Table 12.7 describes other types of accommodation.

Table 12.1 Private accommodation (commercial)

Type	Description (can vary from property to property)	Target customers
Five-star hotels	Can be part of a large hotel chain, consortia or independent. Can be fully owned, franchised or operated under a management contract agreement. A very high standard of facilities may include food and beverage outlets, conferences and banqueting, leisure facilities, spa and retail outlets. Room categories normally include suites, executive and standard. Rooms are spacious, comfortable, well equipped, high tech and designed to a luxurious standard. Front-office operations are extensive, providing a wide range of personal services, from personalised check-in to executive check-out	Monday to Friday Corporate CEOs and executives Business travellers Frequent independent travellers (FITs) Airline crew Some leisure business Corporate groups Leisure groups (off-season) Government officials Leisure customers (families, shoppers, weekend visitors) Conference attendees Customers attending banqueting functions (e.g. wedding party customers)
Boutique hotels	A sub-sector of the hotel industry that focuses on design, lifestyle and personal service. Traditionally four or five star, independent or chain, with between 20 and 150 rooms, with each guest room featuring a different and unique decor. Independent but can also be part of a small chain	Visitors looking for a more personalised, unique service
Four-star hotels	Can be part of a large hotel chain, consortia or independent. A good standard of facilities that may include restaurant, bar, coffee shop, conference and banqueting, leisure and retail outlets. The majority of accommodation consists of standard rooms, followed by executives and a few suites. Rooms are comfortable and well equipped	Business and leisure customers

Type	Description (can vary from property to property)	Target customers
Serviced apartments/ residences	Some large properties, particularly in Asia and the Middle East, allocate a small percentage of their accommodation to serviced apartments. In some cases in the USA, whole properties consist of exclusively serviced apartments. The main difference between a serviced apartment and a normal hotel room is that its facilities will include a dining area; a small, equipped, functional kitchen; laundry facilities; and TV relaxation area. Operators achieve satisfaction from customers due to having a larger space that is more flexible, with the opportunity to self-cater and hold small meetings. Also termed 'extended stay' and 'corporate housing'	Long-stay executives
Budget hotels	The British Hospitality Association (BHA) defines a budget hotel as a strongly branded offer with generally compact rooms, and a small food and beverage operation with limited facilities and services. Both the UK and other countries have seen a rise in the growth of budget properties in the past ten years. The characteristics of a budget hotel are: ● often chained and franchised ● in city-centre or motorway locations ● two or three-star standard ● competitive rates ● food and beverage services are limited (breakfast buffet and maybe a bar) ● branded internal decor throughout ● services are limited, with 'no frills' ● services are highly standardised, little flexibility ● rooms are compact and feature the basics (some have no bathtubs, only showers) ● front office features only a reception (no concierge, guest relations) – some self-check in terminals ● services such as housekeeping and maintenance are normally outsourced (see below) Examples of budget hotels include Holiday Inn Express (UK) and Jinjiang Inn (China)	Budget-conscious travellers Independent business people
Motels	Properties situated close to motorways in the budget category	Motorists
Guesthouses/ bed and breakfast (B&B)/ pension	Typically operated by the owner, who deals with the front-office procedures. These small businesses provide limited but comfortable room accommodation. A small team of in-house personnel clean the rooms. Facilities are limited, and may feature a small public area for breakfast and a bar	Budget-conscious travellers Independent business people Tourists
Public house or inn	The core focus is to provide food and beverage in a relaxed environment. In some cases landlords also provide basic accommodation at a reasonable price on the same premises. Some large establishments will also have a function room, where weddings, meetings or social get-togethers can be hosted. Customers travelling to or through an area may also find pubs a good low-budget alternative. In-house personnel carry out the preparation and cleaning of the rooms. Pub managers can look at the sales of accommodation for additional revenue opportunities	Tourists Those visiting friends, family and relatives (VFR)
Youth hostel/ backpackers	Budget accommodation can be located centrally or on the periphery of cities. Prices are low and rooms can be provided in different configurations, i.e. single, double or shared dormitories. Rooms are very basic, and fittings may include a wardrobe and TV. Bathroom facilities are normally separate	Students Tourists Backpackers
Timeshare	Tourists purchase the right to access an apartment or villa for a specific period each year over a set number of years	Tourists
Private clubs	Some private members' clubs provide some accommodation on their premises. These rooms consist of basic facilities	Members from affiliated clubs

Table 12.2 **Hotel sub-segments**

Hotel	Description	Target customers
Resort hotels	Located in scenic locations. Resort customers traditionally seek rest, relaxation and recreation. Nowadays companies increasingly select resorts to combine training and team building for executives. Resorts can provide extensive facilities, e.g. swimming pools, tennis courts, spas, miniature golf, children's play area and gardens. Resorts normally occupy more land, which requires lots of maintenance. Rooms are spacious and comfortable A growing trend is in the area of eco resorts, where the central theme is to provide accommodation in a natural setting with a sustainable operation. Similarly, with the growth in health and nutrition, wellness resorts are becoming more prominent	Vacationers Conference and banqueting customers Meetings, incentives, conference, events (MICE) customers Weddings Voucher holders from promotional websites
City-centre hotels	City-centre properties are located in central, city locations. Due to space being at a premium, these are normally high-rise structures. Leisure and recreation facilities such tennis courts, swimming pools and gardens are less prominent	Monday–Friday (business and MICE) Saturday and Sunday (leisure)
Airport hotels	Located in close proximity to airports, these can be either large, with between 200 and 1,000 rooms, or budget properties. Some major airports now provide private pods for sleepers that can be rented by the hour	Short-stay travellers in transit (half-day let) Passengers of cancelled/ delayed flights Airline crew Conference attendees
Casino hotels	These properties act as support for the casino, which is the main focus. Many properties (such as those in Las Vegas, Macao and Singapore) are very large, with more than 1,000 rooms. Front office areas are often vast: large Las Vegas hotels can have 20+ check-in counters. In addition, a large space is allocated to retail outlets, dining, recreation and entertainment. Rooms are luxurious and spacious	Gamers Tourists Pre-wedding parties
Conference/ convention hotels	These properties provide facilities to delegates or visitors attending an event. Normally located on the periphery of a city	Meetings, incentives, conference, events (MICE) delegates Banquet customers
Themed hotels	Themed properties provide entertainment; they target enthusiasts looking for a particular experience. They can be stand-alone or connected to a tourist attraction	Individuals looking for a fun and different experience
Portable pods/ containers	An emerging trend is the use of mobile pods that can be set up anywhere; equipped with beds and bathing facilities	Eco travellers
Lodge or villa	Normally located in scenic areas with several rooms and home-like facilities	Families and small groups looking for a relaxing getaway

WEBLINKS

Example of a boutique hotel chain:
www.firmdalehotels.com

Ascott is an established serviced apartment company in Asia that specialises in this type of accommodation:
www.the-ascott.com/en/index.html

Marriott Hotels:
www.marriott.com/default.mi

Shangri-La luxury hotels and resorts:
www.shangri-la.com

Jumeirah hotels:
www.jumeirah.com

Example of a casino hotel:
www.bellagio.com

Themed music and entertainment:
www.hardrockhotels.com

Themed experiential hotel:
www.icehotel.com

Family fun theme:
http://disneyland.disney.go.com

Hotel booking sites are also now providing awards to the best-performing properties as rated by customers – for example, the TripAdvisor.com Travellers' Choice awards:
www.tripadvisor.co.uk/TravelersChoice-Hotels-cTop-g1

Condé Nast annual awards featuring the best properties worldwide:
www.cntraveler.com/travel-awards

The UK's Automobile Association (AA) provides a star rating system to classify accommodation. This assists customers in selecting accommodation and provides standards for hotel operators (see Table 12.3).

Table 12.3 **AA requirements at each hotel star rating level**

Star rating	Description
*	Courteous staff provide an informal yet competent service. All rooms are en-suite or have private facilities, and a designated eating area serves breakfast daily and dinner most evenings
**	A restaurant or dining room serves breakfast daily and dinner most evenings
***	Staff are smartly and professionally presented. The restaurant or dining room is open to residents and non-residents
****	Professional, uniformed staff respond to your needs or requests, and there usually are well-appointed public areas. The restaurant or dining room is open to residents and non-residents, and lunch is available in a designated eating area
*****	Luxurious accommodation and public areas, with a range of extra facilities and a multilingual service available. Guests are greeted at the hotel entrance. High-quality menu and wine list

Source: AA, 2015

Table 12.4 **Non-serviced accommodation**

Type	Description
Caravan park or campsite	Individuals occupy tents, caravans or mobile homes. Communal bathrooms, leisure and entertainment facilities can be provided
Villas/lodge/apartments	Individuals or companies privately own these. Fully furnished, they feature bedroom, living, kitchen and outdoor spaces. Customers rent for vacation and self-cater. Cleaning does not take place until the customers vacate, when the company's personnel clean and prepare for the next customers
Domestic accommodation/home swap	A growing trend is for individuals looking for a slightly cheaper alternative to commercial accommodation in cities to rent the spare room or whole apartment of a landlord, for a single night or a longer stay

Table 12.5 **Transport and accommodation**

Type	Description
Cruise ship	Cruise ship passengers enjoy a large range of facilities while on board. These can range from restaurants, bars and nightclubs to conference rooms, gymnasiums and spas. Sleeping accommodation (cabins) can range from deluxe to basic. Different cruise companies offer standard cabins in a range of sizes, but the average cabin is around 150 square feet. Cabins feature beds (berths), bathroom and in some cases balconies
Rail	Some trains in Europe and Asia provide beds (berths) for sleepers on long train journeys. These beds can in some areas of Europe be referred to as 'couchettes'. Normally this accommodation is communal, with travellers sleeping in up to six berths per cabin. Blankets and pillows are provided
Air	Most international airlines now offer some kind of sleeping facility for 'upper class' passengers. Etihad Airlines, for example, provides a service called 'The Etihad Residence' (see Figure 12.2), where customers have their own hotel-type accommodation, with living room, bedroom, en-suite bathroom and butler service

Figure 12.2 **The Etihad Residence – a new suite experience on Etihad Airlines, which is leading the way in this type of travel experience**

Table 12.6 **Examples of accommodation specific to a particular country/area**

Country	Type	Description
Spain	Paradors	State-run properties, which are normally located in old buildings, castles or monasteries
Portugal	Posadas	Small family-run guesthouses
Japan	Ryoken	Small, friendly, owner-operated inns with authentic Japanese design. Rooms are equipped with tatami mats and futon beds, and normally situated close to a hot spring bath
Japan	Capsule	High-rise accommodation located in central city areas. Rooms are around 6 feet long by 3 feet wide (and high). Customers access the accommodation through a hatch-like door with room only for lying down. Customers check in via a vending machine and leave their luggage in a locker. Capsules include a television, mattress, bedding and light control. A similar concept and example of space optimisation has been created in the UK with a more comprehensive range of facilities and larger cabins (see 'Weblinks', below)

Table 12.7 **Accommodation within the non-commercial sector**

Type	Description
Hospitals	Accommodation for patients staying in overnight can vary. Public-sector hospitals provide 'wards' where patients share accommodation. In private hospitals, patients are provided with single (or twin) roomed accommodation, which is very comfortable, featuring own bathroom, refrigerator and television. To minimise the risk of infection the standard of hygiene is paramount in any hospital, so cleaning is carried out frequently by a well-trained team of cleaning personnel
Military	Accommodation can vary for military personnel depending on the rank and situation of the individual. For personnel who are with their families, fully furnished accommodation would be provided on or close to the military base. Single living accommodation (or barracks) is also provided on or close to base and consists of fully furnished en-suite accommodation. For new recruits, multi-occupancy barracks are commonly used. This style of accommodation is non-private and can accommodate up to 20 personnel at one time. Each individual has a single bed and wardrobe. Bathing facilities are communal. Depending on rank, military personnel are responsible for maintaining the cleanliness of their accommodation on a day-to-day basis
Prisons	Prisoners are accommodated, for most of the time, in cells. Cells measure 6 by 8 feet in size and in most cases accommodate two inmates on a vertical standing 'bunk bed'. Furniture and fixtures are limited apart from a lavatory, which may be provided. Shower facilities are separate. The prison provides cleaning personnel to clean cells as and when required
University halls of residence	Most universities provide halls of residence for students in close proximity to the university. Student rooms are small and feature a single bed, desk, television and shower. Communal kitchens are provided where students can prepare meals. The university, in most cases, outsources the cleaning of rooms and public areas to a specialist cleaning company. Public areas include lobby, corridors, food and beverage areas, and other areas the public frequent
Welfare or nursing homes	Many residential homes provide private comfortable rooms for all residents. Homes are in most cases developed as a single-storey unit so all rooms are easily accessible. Rooms may feature pleasant views, double beds, own bathroom, television and air conditioning/heating. Residents dine together in in-house restaurants. In-house employees clean rooms and public areas on a daily basis

WEBLINKS

Website offering domestic accommodation for travellers to stay in:

www.airbnb.co.uk

Example of a cruise ship operator:

www.carnival.com

UK take on a capsule hotel:

www.yotel.com

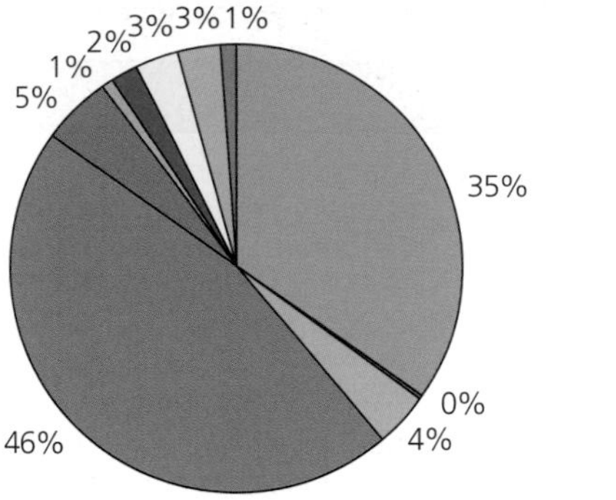

Figure 12.3 Breakdown of accommodation type used by tourists visiting the UK in 2012

Different data are collected on accommodation users. For example:

- type of accommodation used
- length of stay
- domestic or overseas
- nationality of guest
- age
- gender
- spend
- reason for visit.

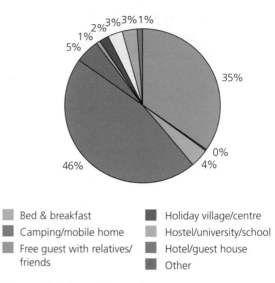

International travel, as presented in Table 12.8, drives the demand for accommodation.

Table 12.8 Top tourism destinations in 2013, compared with previous years (source: UNWTO/Visit Britain)

2013 rank	Destination	Arrivals (m)	2012 rank	2011 rank	2010 rank	2009 rank	2008 rank	2007 rank	2006 rank	2005 rank	2004 rank
1	France	84.7	1	1	1	1	1	1	1	1	1
2	USA	69.8	2	2	2	2	2	3	3	3	3
3	Spain	60.7	4	4	4	3	3	2	2	2	2
4	China	55.7	3	3	3	4	4	4	4	4	4
5	Italy	47.7	5	5	5	5	5	5	5	5	5
6	Turkey	37.8	6	6	7	7	8	9	n/a	n/a	n/a
7	Germany	31.5	7	8	8	8	9	7	7	8	9
8	UK	31.2	8	7	6	6	6	6	6	6	6
9	Russian Federation	28.4	9	n/a	n/a	n/a	n/a	n/a	n/a	n/a	n/a
10	Thailand	26.5	n/a	n/a	n/a	n/a	n/a	n/a	n/a	n/a	n/a

Quality management

It is imperative that hospitality operators ensure that each guest has a pleasant experience during their visit. When customers are satisfied, they are more likely to return, and will pass on their positive experiences online and by word of mouth, to friends and colleagues. However, as detailed in Table 12.9 hospitality operators are provided with many challenges that are unique to service providers.

Table 12.9 **Characteristics of the service industry**

Characteristic	Challenges	Solutions
Consistency	Most customers demand consistency, but due to the intangible element of the accommodation product, this is a challenge – for example, as humans, our moods can change easily due to a combination of factors, such as illness, bad news and difficult customers	Job specifications Job descriptions Effective recruitment Standardise tasks Supervision
External variables	The industry is faced with many external variables that can impact the running of the business. These can include weather, competitors and PESTLE factors (see Chapter 13)	PESTLE analysis (political, economic, social, technological, legal and environmental) Contingency
Heterogeneity	Each service experience is different; service delivery can vary in the same organisation due to different producers, and different consumers with different needs and wants	Understand target market's needs and wants Standardise tasks Flexibility
Intangibility	A large part of the hospitality product is made up of intangible elements such as service, ambience and other customers; these elements can provide many challenges for the operator as they are hard to standardise and can create inconsistencies	Regular employee training Develop service standards and monitor
Imitation is easy	Competitors easily observe the service process; no patents	External monitoring Differentiate Constantly review
Ownership	When purchasing a hospitality product the consumer owns that product only for that period of time; bedrooms are rented not owned	Customer care Customer retention
Perishability	The accommodation product, as in most service industries, is highly perishable. This means that certain products, such as bedrooms, cannot be stored. If a bedroom is not sold tonight, the revenue will be lost. Unused hospitality services cannot be returned, claimed or resold (see also Table 12.16 Key performance indicators in the front office)	Sales-orientated employees Internal budgeting External monitoring Revenue management Yield management
Simultaneous production and consumption	The uniqueness of the hospitality product is that it is produced and consumed simultaneously in most cases; this means limited time for quality control	Standardise tasks Simplify tasks Supervision Empowerment
Seasonality	Many hospitality businesses operate in a seasonal marketplace, which creates many challenges for operators in relation to staffing and expenses	Market research Forecasting Budgeting Yield management
No guarantees	As with most other industries there is little post-consumption aftercare or service	Loyalty schemes Customer care Follow-up evaluation Refunds Incentives
No pre-trial	Sampling as part of the pre-purchase decision is more difficult with hospitality products as no pre-trial is available	Accurate and effective information brochures and websites

Quality tools that can be used in accommodation management include:

- continually monitor and review service standards
- completed 'customer questionnaires' for every customer
- speak to customers face to face throughout their visit
- focus groups with customers
- mystery customers (or shoppers) to evaluate the accommodation product and services
- employ external consultants to evaluate product, service and systems
- adopt external quality assurance programmes
- good leadership and supervision (management by walking around – MBWA)
- effective 'service recovery' and complaint handling
- recruit good people, and invest in training and development
- source good products
- review trade and academic literature for latest trends and research
- ongoing review and utilisation of internal management information
- conduct internal surveys with employees for feedback and to determine satisfaction.

WEBLINK

Hospitality Assured (an example of an external quality assurance programme):
www.instituteofhospitality.org/hospitality-assured

The continual desire to meet the core functions is essential to the success of the accommodation product. As detailed in Table 12.10, the link to the market mix details the main areas that need to be carried out in order to successfully sell your product. (For more on the market mix, see Chapter 13.)

Table 12.10 The market mix's link to accommodation

Market mix	Linkage
Product	Both tangible and intangible products need to be aligned to continuously meet the needs of the target customer at all times. Tangible products can include the exterior, the interior furnishings, bedrooms, restaurants and bathrooms. Examples of intangible elements could include lighting, air temperature, music and service. The product is managed by accommodation managers through ongoing research with customers, employee training, monitoring of service standards and external scanning
Price	Price is of great importance in service industries due to the high perishability of the product. Revenue normally generated from rooms yields the greatest profitability of all departments within the hotel. It is important that the price is positioned correctly to meet the demands of customers and cover operational expenses To achieve and set the correct price, accommodation managers need to consider a wide range of internal and external information that will guide their decisions. If prices are too high, managers risk losing customers, while pricing too low can result in loss of profits and damage to the brand
Place	Place is 'where' the organisation distributes or 'sells' its room product. For example, if a guest wants to book a room in a four-star branded hotel, this can be purchased through various channels, including a travel agent, the hotel's website, the group's central reservations office (CRS), a third-party website or over the counter. Alternatively, a small bed and breakfast operation may distribute its rooms only over the counter or on its website. Therefore, the key is for accommodation operations to increase the amount of channels available where individuals can purchase rooms. The more distribution channels, the more opportunities to sell your accommodation. This, however, requires careful management to ensure the best occupancy rates and financial returns are achieved from each channel
Promotion	Once a good standard of accommodation has been achieved, the operator needs to create awareness to attract buyers and effectively sell its product. Many hospitality businesses operate in a seasonal environment; they often create promotions during the 'low season' to attract demand

The rooms division

The task of providing hospitality and services to customers in a friendly and efficient manner falls mainly to the property's room division. The overall success of an operation depends on the profitability of the rooms division, which generally accounts for a large share of hotels' sales, while generating a gross profit percentage from 70 to 80 per cent of the revenue (Casado, 2012).

At the core of the rooms division department are front office and housekeeping, with maintenance and security acting as valuable support departments. Rooms division and food and beverage are the two main revenue-generating departments within the hotel. It is often the case that rooms provide more profit than food and beverage due to lower operating costs. The size and scope of the rooms division can depend on the type of hotel (see Figure 12.4).

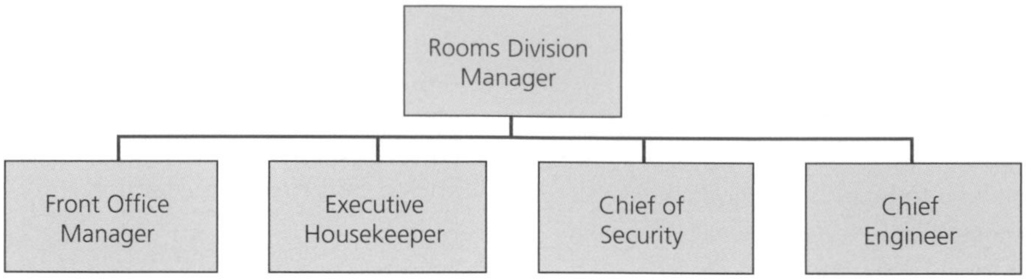

Figure 12.4 Typical rooms division structure in a large four-star hotel

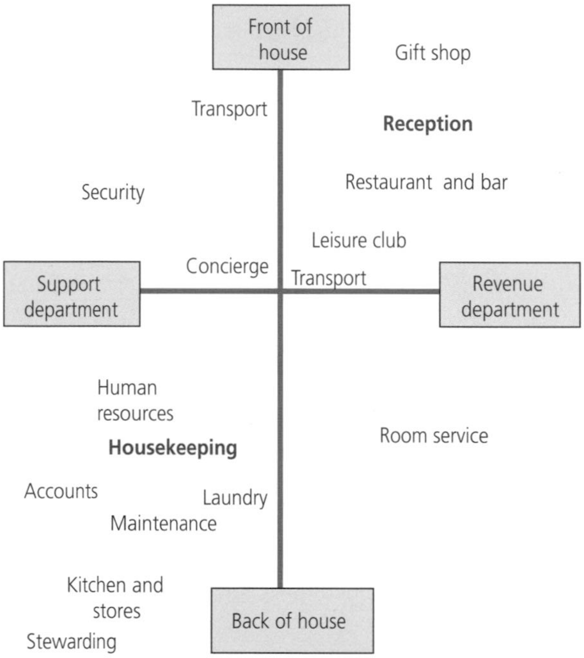

Figure 12.5 Revenue and support centres in a typical four-star hotel

The front office department

The hotel's front office is the busiest area within the hotel. It is the visitor's first impression on arrival and their last on departure. It is a hub of activity, where individuals may be attending meetings, requesting information from the concierge, having refreshments, shopping, waiting for transport, or just sitting in the lobby reading newspapers or using their mobile devices. Individuals that come into contact with front office personnel may include customers staying in the hotel, guests of customers, non-residents visiting the hotel's restaurants, conference and banqueting attendees, and individuals meeting with hotel executives. The times with the heaviest footfall tend to be the morning (10 am to 12 pm), when customers are checking out, and late afternoon, when arrivals are due (4–7 pm).

The objectives of the front office are to:

- maximise profits through the effective management of room inventory
- ensure that, at each stage of the customer cycle, expectations are met
- effectively channel and process information between the front office and other departments and stakeholders.

Figure 12.6 The lobby at the Renaissance Kuala Lumpur

In order to achieve the front office objectives there are many challenges and variables to contend with, as detailed in Table 12.11.

Table 12.11 Key challenges in the front office

Challenge	Meeting the challenge	Skills
Financial control	The front office deals with a large number of financial transactions each day. These could include processing cash and credit card transactions from customers or selling the correct rooms to the correct customers	Accuracy Sales orientated
Communication effectiveness	With front office acting as the main communication hub that channels information throughout the hotel, it is essential that processes and standards are in place to ensure that effective communication is achieved between customers, the front office and all departments	Computer literate (e.g. Microsoft Word, email) Knowledge of Fidelio and Opera Communicative/adaptive/reactive/ability to read people/confident/outgoing/general enthusiasm to meet people/patient/good body language and composure Problem solving and complaint handling
Complex distribution network (distribution channels)	Customers need to be reassured that they are buying at a fair price, and that the information on availability and price is consistent regardless of the distribution channel they have used. The distribution channel is the method used to purchase the hotel room, i.e. travel website, travel agent or tour operator. The management of various distribution channels is a complex and demanding task for operators. This is compounded by the fact that supply and demand patterns can change quickly. The manager must be able to assimilate a great deal of information quickly and make appropriate decisions while maintaining consistency across the distribution network	See also Table 12.15
Fixed capacity and perishability	The hotel has a maximum quantity of rooms that it can sell. On occasion, demand exceeds supply and the hotel fails to meet those demands due to a fixed quantity of rooms. This fixed capacity sometimes places limits on opportunities to sell more rooms and achieve greater sales. Unsold rooms equate to lost revenue. It is therefore important for front office managers to be aware of demand trends and to capitalise on them when they arise	Sales orientated
Diverse environment	With an increase in numbers of international travellers, the front office needs to be able to meet their needs and expectations. International employees and cultural awareness training is essential to achieving this aim	Multilingual Culturally aware Sensitivity towards different cultures, values and norms
Major interface for customers and departments	The front office department is a highly visible one. It is for this reason that all employees must be well trained and able to meet the myriad of demands that confront them in their day-to-day exchanges with customers, managers and other departments. See also Figure 12.12, on front office communications, and Table 12.2 on inter-departmental communications	Excellent personal presentation Good posture and body language Good body language
Automated work environment	Internet systems – PMS software (e.g. Fidelio, Opera, Remanco, Galileo, Delphi, GDS). See also Tables 12.18 and 12.19 on front office technology	Computer literate Knowledge of PMS systems Basic understanding of how to connect customers' mobile devices to the hotel's wifi network

Staffing and structures

Front office structures and staffing

The organisational structure of a hotel front office can depend on many factors (these may include those listed in Table 12.12). Employee positions in this area can be diverse (see Table 12.13) and require a myriad of skills to deal with this fast-paced environment.

Table 12.12 Factors affecting the organisational structure of a hotel front office

Factor	Example
Star rating/ standard/ price	The standard of the hotel drives the headcount. A budget hotel's front office may consist of only a reception supervisor and a receptionist, while in contrast a five-star hotel may have employees including door attendants, lobby hosts, guest services and concierge. See also Table 12.3
Size of hotel	Depending on whether a hotel has 50 rooms or 5,000, it will of course require different manning levels
Management structure	Management requiring close control may have a centralised, tight structure that will require more employee positions. Alternatively, a more open, decentralised management approach may require fewer employees, but they should be cross-trained and more flexible
Target customer	The type of customer can also be a factor in some circumstances. Some properties that cater to business clientele may provide separate executive check-in desks. Properties attracting business customers may also require a higher employee-to-customer ratio and individuals who are more experienced and more highly educated

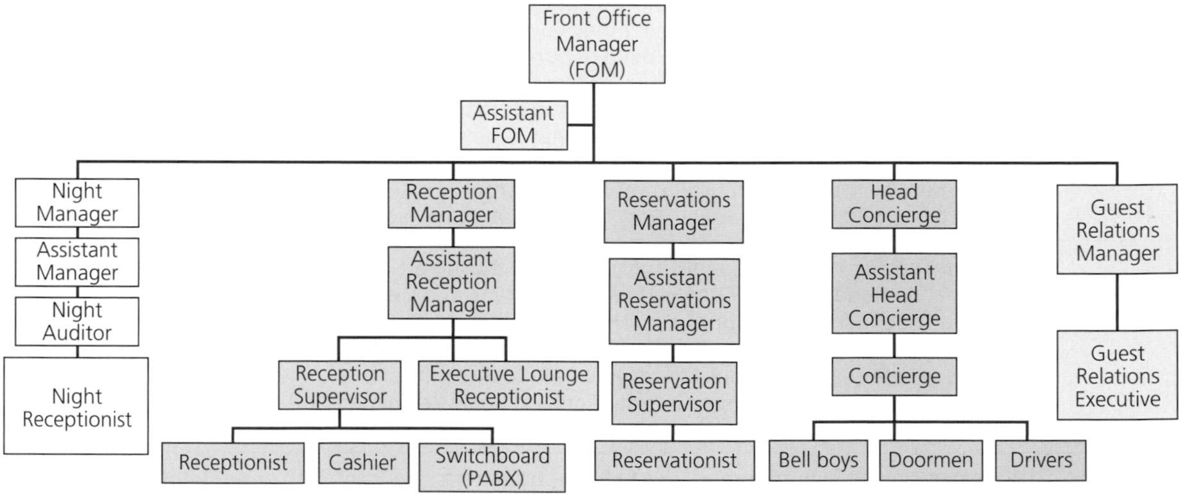

Figure 12.7 A standard four-star hotel front office organisation

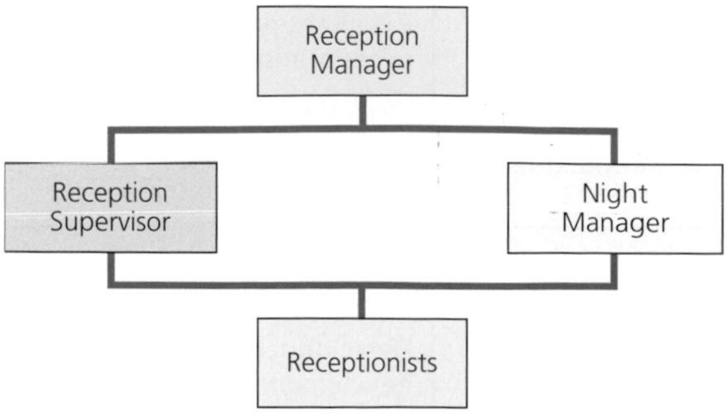

Figure 12.8 The front office structure in a budget hotel

The role of the front office manager

The front office manager is the leader of the team and responsible for the day-to-day running of the front office department. They oversee all front office sub-departments in their operations and ensure that each customer's needs are met throughout the guest cycle (see box for a sample job description).

FRONT OFFICE MANAGER: SAMPLE JOB DESCRIPTION

Job title: Front Office Manager

Report to: General Manager

Key functions

Maximising sales, minimising costs and maintaining standards simultaneously at all times.

Major responsibilities and duties

- Be responsible for the smooth, effective, efficient and professional operations of all front office areas.
- Conduct daily briefings, outlining daily targets, areas for improvement and VIPs.
- Ensure all front office personnel comply with hotel's standard guidelines.
- Attend daily management morning briefing, sales strategy meeting and other meetings as required; prepare all relevant reports to managers.
- Review and respond to any online comments (e.g. Facebook, TripAdvisor).
- Ensure all daily VIPs are pre-registered and greeted, and escorted to their rooms on arrival.
- Ensure all VIP room allocations are checked prior to customers' arrival.
- Train all front office employees to be fully acquainted with the property management system (PMS).
- Coordinate with the housekeeping department to ensure that there is a maximum number of rooms available for sale at all times.
- Develop a close and effective working relationship with all other department heads.
- Plan and hold meetings with employees and department managers.
- Ensure that costs are minimised at all times.
- Ensure that customer satisfaction is achieved, through constant monitoring.
- Implement systems to minimise and manage customer complaints.
- Manage and monitor room occupancy and average room rates throughout the day.
- Recruit and select front office personnel.
- Motivate employees and set incentives.
- Plan, organise and deliver training.
- Constantly evaluate service standards.
- Write and monitor budgets.
- Train and develop employees to the quality and consistency of service standards.
- Ensure that all front office employees are fully conversant with all hotel facilities, activities, and points of interests and attractions in the city.
- Train all front office employees in how to identify frequent customers, to know their preferences, ensuring all customers' needs are met.
- Train all front office employees to understand and be familiar with cultural differences of guests.
- Be fully conversant with all emergency procedures and train all front office employees to know how to act upon them.

Figure 12.9 A hotel doorman

Table 12.13 Roles and responsibilities of front office personnel

Position	Responsibilities
Receptionist	A key front-of-house position. Receptionists are responsible for all interactions between the customer and the front desk. This includes, check-in and check-out, cashiering, upselling, dealing with enquiries, dealing with complaints and any general assistance
Shift duty manager	A supervisory position at the front office that deals with any operational issues that may arise. A duty manager is normally available 24 hours
Reservationist	A reservationist is most importantly a sales position. They are responsible for attending to customers' room reservation enquiries, providing information, upselling and administering any bookings
Guest relations officer (GRO)	A guest relations officer provides a more personal front desk service to guests. Duties include check-in and check-out, tours, accompanying to room, organising special amenities, dealing with any enquiries and generally making sure the guest leaves satisfied
'Executive lounge' receptionist	An executive lounge is a private lounge to which customers paying a higher room rate have exclusive access. This employee assists with check-in and check-out, service of food and beverages, and deals with customer enquiries
Night receptionist/ auditor	A night receptionist deals with all front office activity throughout the night – check-in and check-out, night audit duties and assisting with any security issues
Cashier	Deals with deposits and bill payments, foreign exchange, and all financial transactions between customers and departments
Switchboard operator (PABX)	The PABX operator deals with all inbound and outbound telephone calls in the hotel
Personal host	Customers are greeted by a personal host who will know the customers needs, wants and plans for their stay in advance. This personal, bespoke attention provides a unique customer experience.
Lobby Hosts	Some properties provide lobby personnel for the sole purpose of welcoming visitors and assisting with any requirements relating to the purpose of their visit. Pullman Hotels have employees called 'Welcomers' who do only this
Door staff	A friendly face, who is the first and final contact in large hotels. Also assists bell desk with traffic management around hotel entrance
Concierge	Provides information to customers on the hotel facilities and on local areas, e.g. food and beverage, shopping, social, cultural and physical attractions, and hours of operation. Assists with reservations for tours, restaurants and any transport
Luggage porter/bell boy	Responsible for the safe storage, delivery and retrieving of guests' luggage to and from rooms
Hotel transportation/ driver	Responsible for the safe collection and transportation of customers and visitors between the airport, other locations and the hotel
Valet parker (in some deluxe properties)	Responsible for the safe parking of guests' vehicles

Revenue manager

The revenue manager is a position that must be included even though it is more of a strategic position than an operational one. Legoherel, Poutier and Fyall (2013) note that the revenue manager function is a new one, compared to traditional functions such as marketing, finance or human resources management. The revenue manager function is central in the organisational chart, and viewed as an essential and strategic function. The objective of the yield/revenue management unit, placed at an operational level, is site optimisation. It is responsible for market awareness, forecasting, budget fine-tuning of a site (e.g. hotel), pricing arbitration and sale quotas related to price levels, decisions to open or close fares, and distribution network management (see also Table 12.16 Key performance indicators in the front office).

Operations (front office, housekeeping and facilities)

The front office process

The front office exchange moves through four main phases, known as the 'guest cycle'. These phases are pre-arrival, arrival, occupancy and departure (see Figure 12.10). The guest cycle details the different stages that the majority of customers with reservations go through when dealing with the front office. Throughout the cycle, front office personnel carry out specific functions (shown in Figure 12.11) to ensure customers have a positive experience.

Although most customers advance through the cycle, this can change in certain situations, e.g. when properties receive 'walk in' customers who have not pre-booked. Each stage of the cycle provides opportunities and challenges. It is the front office manager's responsibility to ensure that all departmental objectives are met and the process is free from defects.

More specific functions are included for different customer types, such as business guest, leisure, international, family, disabled and groups.

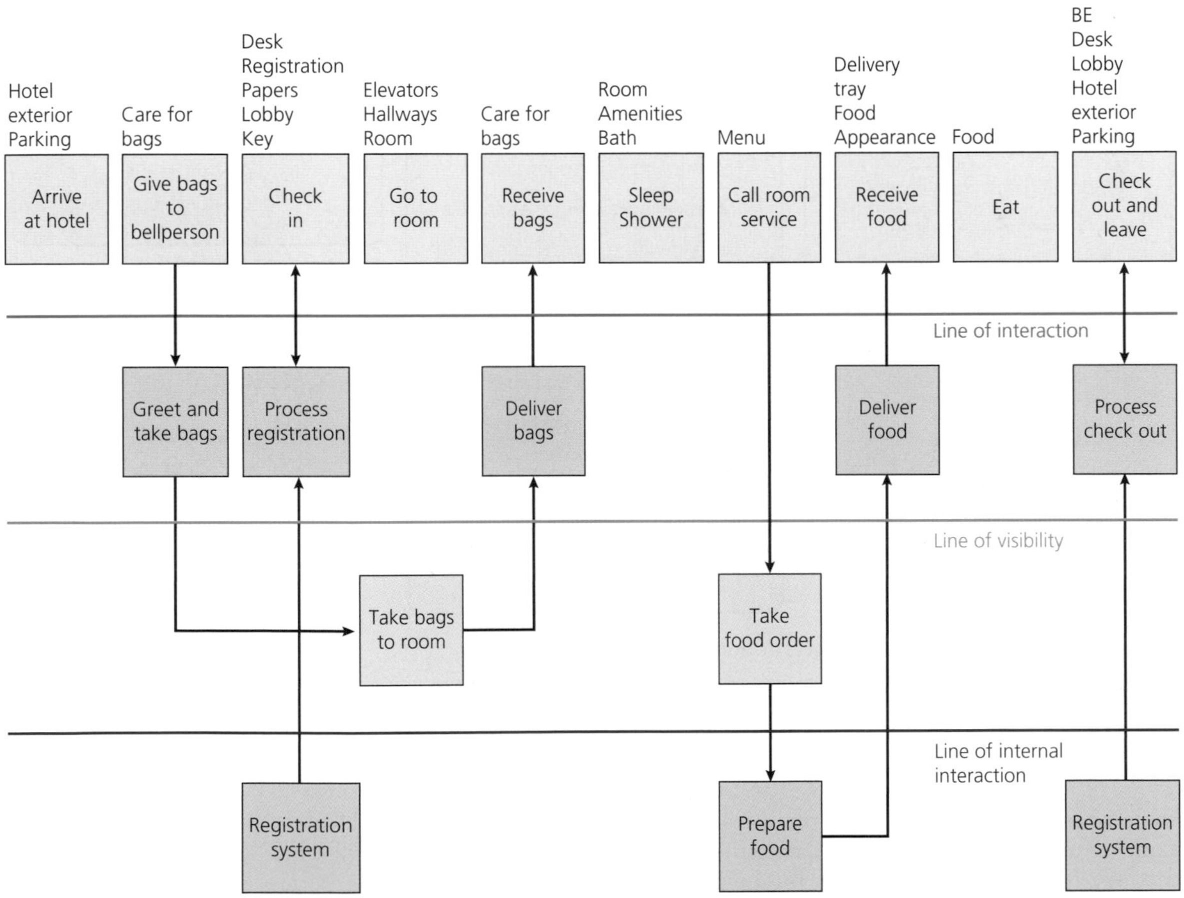

Figure 12.10 The flow of guest activity from arrival to departure

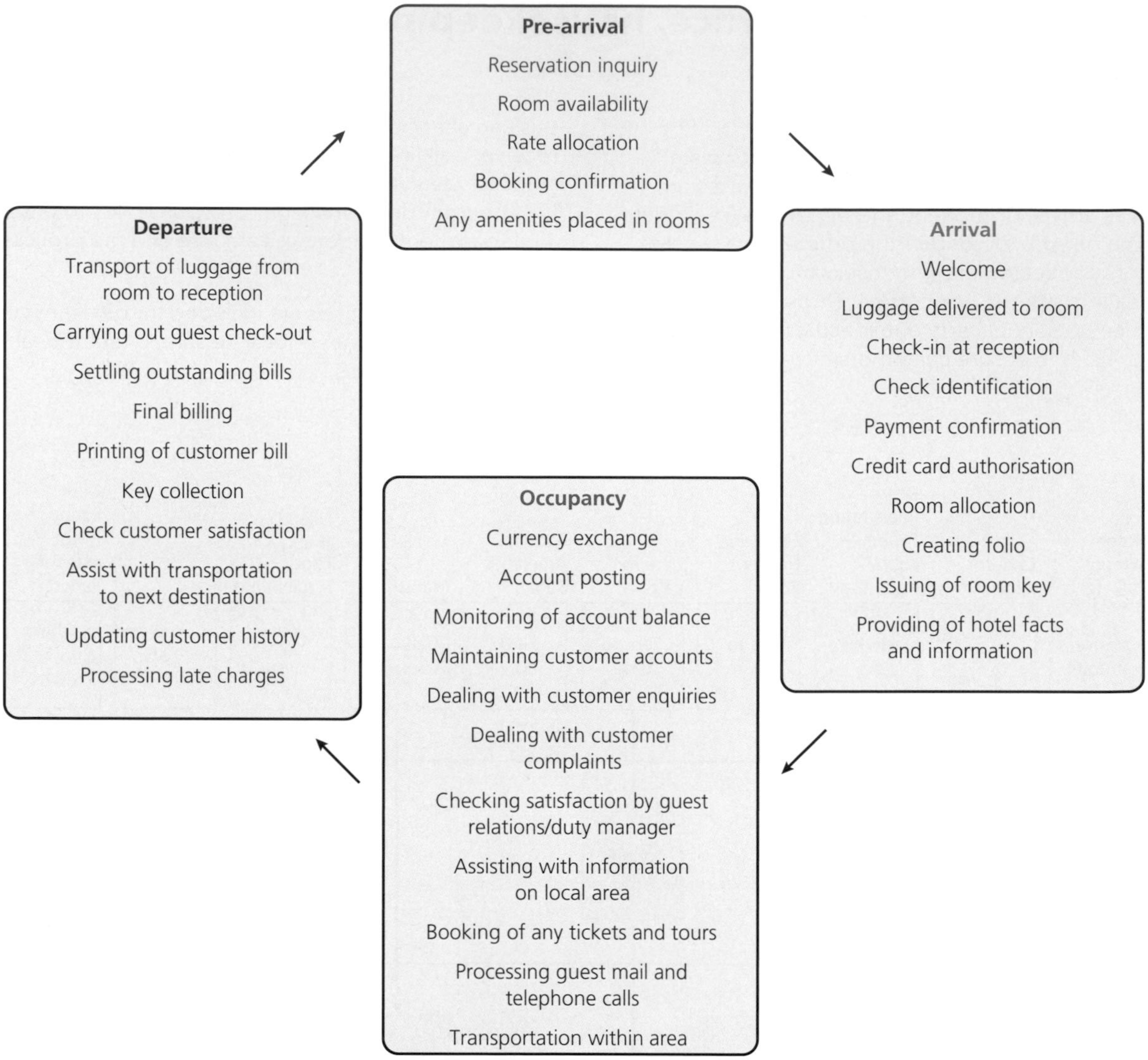

Figure 12.11 Key functions and interactions during the guest cycle

Meeting the needs of customers in the front office

All customers have different needs and requirements; it is the goal of the hotel to ensure that these specific needs are met, not only during their stay but before they arrive. Using past experience, profiling and information on consumer trends, properties are able to meet customer needs on arrival, e.g. a business guest may require a limousine pick-up from the airport, express check-in, a particular room of their choice and a particular newspaper. If their needs are anticipated then there is a greater opportunity to achieve satisfaction. Another method is to use 'guest histories'. Each time a guest stays at a hotel, data are collected on their preferences, which can be used to enhance satisfaction on their return, e.g. a customer who stays quarterly at the hotel always prefers a room with a view and the *Financial Times* newspaper, and always requests extra hangers. This information would be flagged (alerted) when the customer makes another booking, and these preferences put in place. The key is in reducing the customer's opportunity 'to ask' for services or products by anticipating and fulfilling their needs.

Departmental communication

While the guest is in-house a large amount of information is communicated between the front office and other departments (see Figure 12.12). Although the front office communicates with many departments, the department with which it has the closest relationship is housekeeping. The availability of rooms as customers check out and check in requires constant communication to ensure that customers receive a clean, ready-prepared room on check-in.

Table 12.14 Meeting customers' specific needs in accommodation

Customer type	Front office needs	Room needs
Large groups	Rooms allocated Room key cards prepared before arrival Pre-registration and separate check-in area Additional bell boys scheduled to deal with high volume of luggage	Rooms located together
Business customers or frequent independent travellers (FITs)	Airport limousine pick-up Check-in either en route, in room or executive lounge Business centre and club lounge	In-room (effective Wi-Fi and connectivity, desk, satellite TV with business/news channels, trouser press, safe) Financial/business newspapers and magazines
Female customers	Discreet service when informing of room number at reception Floors that are located closest to reception	Room on segregated female floor (if available) Non-interconnecting room Secure lock (double lock and chain) Extra wardrobe space/extra hangers, large vanity/full-length mirror/female amenities/female magazines Softer colours used in design and furnishings
Families	Interconnecting rooms Low-level floor Information on baby-sitting service	Rollaway or sofa bed available Gaming on in-room TV or for rent No sharp furniture edges Effective Wi-Fi
Tourists	Currency exchange Local maps Sightseeing information	Wi-Fi Tourist information brochures
MICE	Meeting room facilities	Wi-Fi
People with disabilities or physically challenged	Wheelchair-bound customers – ramps, low reception desk Hearing impaired – hearing loop	Wide entry door Special bathrooms and bedrooms (e.g. adapted for wheelchair customers) Vibrating pillows (hearing impaired) Information in Braille (visually impaired)

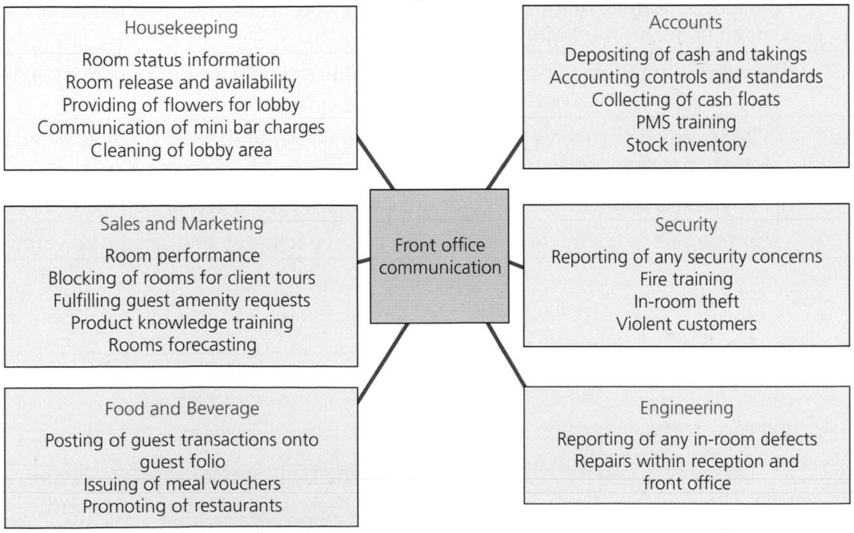

Figure 12.12 Front-office communications

Reservations and distribution channels

Customers have the choice to reserve rooms in a variety of ways (known as distribution channels) (see Table 12.15). Accommodation managers use these channels in different ways depending on different circumstances, which may include room demand, season, rate of commission and overall customer strategy. It is good practice for accommodation managers to evaluate the performance of each distribution channel regularly, to measure profit per channel and to achieve overall efficient performance within the rooms department. For example, you may be receiving a high quantity of bookings through travel agents at a low commission, but the type of customer is not your target market and requires more work. Alternatively, research from customers details that they find it difficult to book online through the hotel's website, a channel that is relatively cost-effective.

Table 12.15 Appraisal of distribution channels

Channel	Explanation
Third-party, price comparison websites (e.g. Expedia, Trivago)	This popular method allows properties to sell rooms to third-party websites, which then sell to customers booking through the websites Some disadvantages for the operator may include commissions paid to channels, and competitiveness
Social media channels (e.g. Facebook)	Properties can receive reservations direct from their Facebook page; social media is changing how we market to customers, creating a powerful media for them to interact with other customers and with organisations (Kotler, Bowen and Makens, 2014)
Company/hotel website	Many properties develop their own websites to attract customers. Websites allow potential customers to view products, services, availability and rates Not always the best rate for the customer
Central reservations	The central reservations system (CRS) is normally used by large hotel chains Reservationists are off-site and deal with reservations for properties within a particular region; employees are highly skilled in sales and very knowledgeable
Travel agents	Hotels use travel agents to sell room inventory on their behalf; very good for segments that don't use internet or social media
Corporate travel agents	Large corporate companies develop links with corporate travel agents to book reservations for their employees when travelling for business purposes
Over the counter (walk-ins)	Customers have no prior booking and walk in to purchase a room
Marketing consortia (see, e.g., www.slh.com)	Groups of independent properties with the same target market form a coalition and develop a CRS to compete with the large chains
Airport desk	Airports feature hotel desks to advertise hotel rooms to individuals arriving at destination in need of accommodation
Competitors' 'overflow'	Agreements formed between competing properties or sister properties to send overflow customers to one another when capacity is exceeded
Strategic partnerships (e.g. airlines)	Properties can receive reservations from individuals who have accrued air miles from airline loyalty programmes
Hotel loyalty scheme	Individuals book direct through the hotel's loyalty scheme
Vouchers	Companies (e.g. vouchercloud) offer room packages at discounted rates

Revenue and yield management

For hotels and other providers of room accommodation, it is imperative that they develop strategies to effectively sell their room's inventory. Room sales are important in terms of:

- meeting budgeted financial targets and achieving a return on investment
- avoiding wasted capacity
- providing owners with financial returns
- remaining competitive
- reducing expenses.

With the help of computer programs, managers are using price, reservation history and overbooking practices to develop a sophisticated approach to demand management called revenue management, a methodological approach to allocating a perishable and fixed inventory to the most profitable customers (Kotler *et al.*, 2014).

Front office managers are required to invest lots of time in research and forecasting to achieve these financial objectives. Possibly the most important planning function is the development of the room's budget. Budgeting is a management tool that forecasts departmental revenues, expenses and profit, by asking specific questions.

- What rates shall we charge for our rooms?
- How much demand will we have for our rooms on each day?
- How much profit is required?
- What will our operational costs be?
- What prices are our customers prepared to pay?
- What events will create demand?
- What is our room supply on each day?
- What are our strengths and weaknesses within our rooms operation?
- How much supply and demand will our competitors have?
- How can we create additional demand through room promotions?
- What are our competitors' strengths and weaknesses?
- What strategies and tactics can we use to sell more rooms?
- How can we achieve a competitive advantage with our rooms?
- How can we leverage our room's product to achieve the highest rate possible?
- What is our current position within the marketplace?
- Which customers yield the most profit?
- What changes in external forces will impact how we deliver our rooms products?
- Which reservation channels yield the most profit?
- Are there any ways in which we can increase supply?
- Is this budget realistic and achievable?

Yield management

A modern approach, commonly used in large international hotel operations, is yield management (YM). The concept of this approach is to maximise profitability with careful forecasting tactics – more simply put, selling the right room to the right customer at the right time. Through studying past history and future demand, reservation managers can use this information to determine whether room rates should be increased or decreased, or if a booking should be accepted or declined to achieve the greatest profit on the room sale.

YM is based on supply and demand. Prices tend to rise when demand exceeds supply; conversely, prices tend to fall when supply exceeds demand.

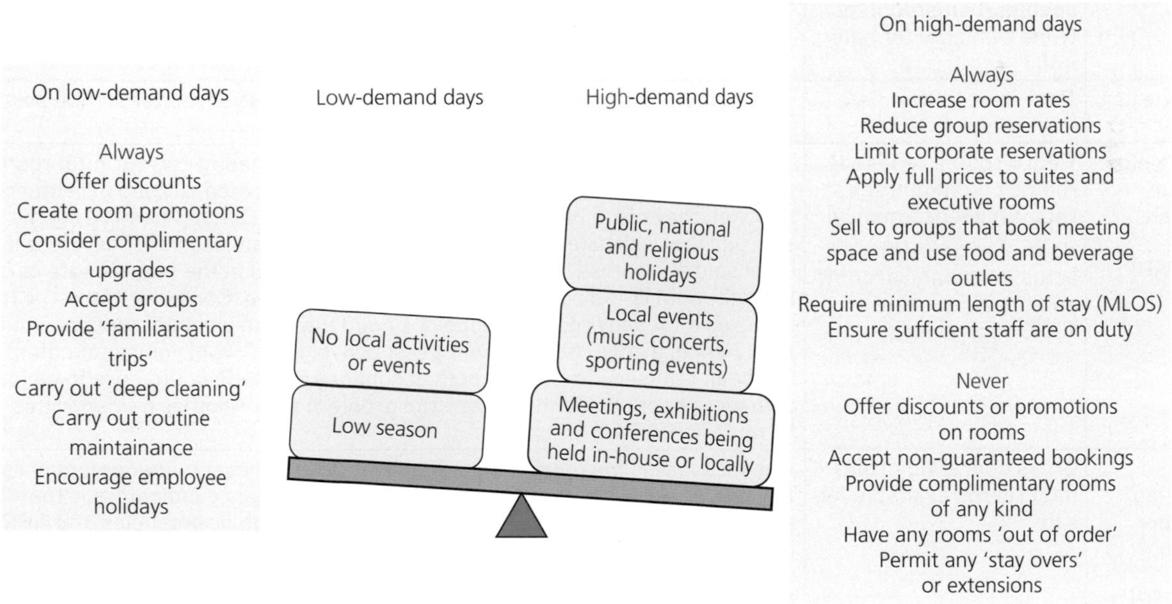

Figure 12.13 Examples of yield management strategies

Performance indicators

It is essential that front office managers evaluate the performance of resources within their department. The use of a variety of formulas can assist with this (see Table 12.16). This ongoing measurement will assist in improving profits and the hotel's positioning overall within the marketplace.

Table 12.16 **Key performance indicators in the front office**

Measure	Formula	Considerations
Rooms occupancy and average room rate (ARR)	Rooms occupancy = total number of rooms occupied/total number of rooms available for sale × 100 ARR = total rooms revenue/total rooms sold or total rooms revenue/total number of rooms occupied	Rooms occupancy measures the quantity of rooms occupied in the hotel. Although it measures total capacity of room stock, this formula has a number of weaknesses. On its own it is ineffective as a hotel can have 99% occupancy, but if the hotel's average room rate is very low then its performance is poor. Therefore, it is really effective only when combined with the average room rate (ARR) formula. In addition, if room occupancy is 80% one might also consider this to be relatively good. However, if the target daily occupancy of the hotel was 95% on that same day, it has failed to meet the target. Therefore, it is important to always measure against the target occupancy. Another consideration with this formula is that one should consider who is occupying the rooms. If the rooms are being occupied by individuals on a complimentary basis – for example, employees, managers and travel agents – then no sales are being achieved. Therefore, as a financial measure, a more accurate formula to be used is total number of rooms sold, as opposed to rooms occupied: total number of rooms sold/total number of rooms available × 100
Performance per room type or category	Suite occupancy = total suites occupied/total suites available for sale × 100 and suite ARR = total suite revenue/total suites sold	In many hotel properties there are several different room categories that may include suites, executive and standard rooms. It is therefore important for front office managers to measure the performance of these categories individually. This breakdown of room category performance will also help in identifying any particular weaknesses in occupancy and ARR
Bed or sleeper occupancy and double occupancy	Total number of beds occupied/total number of beds available for sale × 100 doubles/twins let as doubles/twins/doubles/twins available for sale × 100	To evaluate how well you are utilising your beds, consider the number of sleepers per room. Many hotel rooms have a configuration of two beds per room (twin) and if only one sleeper is allocated to the room this may be considered waste. Although the room price may be the same if either one or two sleepers occupy the room, one should consider the potential for spend on other facilities within the hotel – e.g. food and beverage, spa and leisure
Revenue per sleeper	Total rooms revenue/total sleepers	This formula is slightly different from ARR as it looks at room revenue per individual and not per room
Room yield/revenue per available room (REVPAR)	Yield = rooms realised/rooms potential (rack rate × 100% occupancy) Rooms actual ARR × actual occupancy/rooms potential (rack rate × 100% occupancy)	The room yield formula looks at how well you are managing your total room capacity. It investigates how well your rooms performed (actual) in relation to how well they could have performed (potential), e.g. a hotel has 100 rooms for sale and the rack rate (published rate, or highest rate) is £100. Therefore if the hotel sold all rooms (100%) and each room was sold at the highest rate of £100, the total yield is 100 rooms × £100 = £10,000 revenue. Consider this: if the hotel achieved total daily room revenue of £7,600 the room yield percentage would be 76%. Hence, from a management perspective, only 76% of your total potential has been realised. Therefore, both occupancy and ARR would have to be looked at in more depth to identify where the problem was. Another name for this formula is REVPAR
Gross operating profit per available room (GOPPAR)	Gross operating profit/total rooms available for sale	This measure is the only formula that evaluates the cost management of rooms. The one weakness with many other rooms performance indicators is that they do not measure profit, e.g. the hotel can achieve high occupancies and ARRs, but if management is failing to maintain costs, then ultimately profit is reduced. The gross operating profit per available room (GOPPAR) formula assists front office managers in measuring this. Accommodation managers need to ensure that a strict eye is kept on operating costs, such as staffing and cleaning, to ensure that profit is achieved. This formula is used less frequently due to the difficulties in measuring costs on a daily basis

Front office design

When designing a front office area there are many factors to consider to achieve a functional and appealing environment (Table 12.17). Many of these can be applied to the overall design of public areas and rooms.

Table 12.17 Key considerations in front office design

Considerations	Rationale
Aesthetic appeal	To enhance the appearance of the area, careful attention should be given to the coordination of colours, textures and fabrics of furniture and fittings. If colours are in stark contrast or very different it does not look attractive to the eye
Atmosphere and layout	To achieve the desired atmosphere, attention must be given to certain aspects, e.g. space, colours, aromas and sounds. Four- and five-star properties may use chandeliers, fountains, aquariums, staging for musicians, and flora and fauna to achieve this experience. Artificial fragrances pumped out across public areas are also becoming more common Some properties are transforming the traditional single-use lobby to one that is multifunctional, allowing for small meetings and collaborative workspaces
Branding	In some chain properties (particularly budget) the colours of the brand are introduced into the overall design to maintain theme and brand image. This may include lighting, fabric colour, carpets and employee uniforms
Cleaning	Furniture should be durable, functional, easy to clean and easy for housekeeping personnel to move
Comfort	Comfort can be achieved through the use of soft furnishings, appealing furniture, art, background music, carefully positioned televisions, and well-regulated heating, ventilation and air temperature control
Communication	To increase access for customers and efficiency for employees it is important to locate the sub-departments of reception, concierge and bell desk as close together as possible. Effective telecommunication is essential for the exchange of information between employees and to customers. This can be enhanced with front office areas being supplied with email, intranet, internet, touch-dial telephones, pagers and mobile phones. Ibis hotels, for instance, feature separate front office pods that make it easier for front office employees to assist customers
Competition	Many customers will select one hotel over another if they prefer the design
Cost and procurement	When purchasing you need to consider funds available for furniture, fixtures and equipment (FFE), and the potential return on investment. Ensure three quotations are obtained from different suppliers to get the best deal. On selecting items, consideration needs to be given to the amount of usage the item will have. Purchasing cheap, flimsy products will not withstand commercial use and therefore it is better to purchase durable, strong, simple products
Environmental	Energy-reducing design considerations can include natural light, energy-efficient equipment, energy management systems (EMSs), air blowers and revolving doors. Many consumers are now interested in how products are produced and made, such as purchasing fair trade items, organic cotton, and using local tradespeople as opposed to flying products in from overseas
Fashion	To remain contemporary, properties should attempt to integrate modernity into their design. This may include fashionable colours, art or technological advances
Flow and layout	Guest flow is important when designing a front desk operation. Queuing should be avoided on check-in; therefore sufficient check-in counters should be available. Outside, there should be sufficient space for vehicles to arrive, drop off and depart without causing any bottlenecks
Geographic location and culture	Location plays a big factor, with local features being integrated to create a more authentic, sustainable and cultural customer experience. For example, some properties in Bali incorporate local design and materials into their architecture and have employee uniforms in the traditional *kebaya* design. Properties in the Middle East may feature a small Bedouin seating area and in Malaysia prayer rooms, or *Surau* In warmer climates FFE would be installed to better suit hot and humid temperatures, e.g. tiled floors instead of carpets and air ceiling fans instead of heaters
Health, safety and security	The safety and security of customers, employees and the hotel's assets need to be considered. Closed-circuit television (CCTV), controlled access to room floors and task lighting are some examples. Similarly, ergonomics and the design of employees' workplaces to maximise efficiency and personal safety should also be considered. See also Table 12.33 Security risks and prevention
Legislation	Legislation should be considered. For example, in accordance with Disability Discrimination Act (DDA) legislation, the front office entrance should have a ramp for wheelchair access and a lowered desk to allow for easy check-in. Similarly, some properties in Europe and the USA have to abide by no-smoking laws
Sales opportunity	The opportunity for the hotel to maximise sales should not be missed, e.g. gift shop, window boxes, posters of partner properties, literature on loyalty programmes, and clear signage to other facilities and services
Technology	Technology to be integrated to improve guest service, financial control and communication (see Table 12.19)

WEBLINKS

Information on how to implement the requirements of the Disability Discrimination Act:
www.nidirect.gov.uk/tourism-and-the-disability-discrimination-act
Marriott hotels loyalty programme:
www.marriott.co.uk/Channels/rewards/rewards-program-uk.mi

Technology in the front office

A myriad of technology can be found in the front office area to assist employees and guests. High-speed internet, broadband Wi-Fi/WLAN wireless networks, biometric cellular smartphones, intelligent cameras and high-definition 3D touch-screen interactive televisions are defining how customers interface with hotel services. These new advancements are augmenting what have become conventional technologies such as computerised check-in, automatic wake-up calls, electronic guestroom locks, satellite television and teleconferencing (Penner, Adams and Robson, 2012).

Table 12.18 Technology in the front office

Technology	Description
Call accounting system (CAS)	Software that captures telephone charges for in-room customers calling numbers outside the hotel. The system captures rate per minute, minutes called and numbers called; this charge then appears on the guest's folio
Central reservations system (CRS)	A service developed by chains and consortia. Customers can call toll-free numbers and speak to a reservations agent 24 hours a day. Agents are trained in sales techniques, and knowledgeable on any of the properties, products and services within the organisation
Electronic locking system (ELS)	Many properties now feature electronic locks on hotel room doors, offices and storage areas. The locks provide additional security for customers and capture data on when the room was accessed and by whom. These systems are eco friendly as the keys turn on or off utilities when entering or leaving the room
Folio management and billing	Software that captures and manages all guest billing information
Global distribution system (GDS)	According to Nyheim and Connolly (2012), the term global distribution can be defined as attaining the broadest possible reach to the largest available audience, meeting a company's target market segments at the most affordable cost and with the highest potential for winning conversion
Point of sale (POS)	In a hotel, the POS is the main interface to all other systems listed here
Property management system (PMS)	The PMS is the central hardware hub that interfaces with all other hotel systems

New and emerging trends in hotel room technology

Hospitality executives must continually look towards the strategic opportunities technology offers, and use technology as a competitive method – or as a tool – to differentiate and create competitive advantage (Nyheim and Connolly, 2012).

Table 12.19 **New technological trends in accommodation**

Electronic signage or digital board	Programmable screens in hotel lobbies that facilitate the visual promotion of facilities, promotions and information on in-house conferences
Electronic concierge	Automated, interactive, self-service terminals that provide 24-hour, multilingual information on hotel and local services
Smartphones	The smartphone is a versatile tool for travellers; they can book and check on reservations, register at a hotel, and use it as a key access to the hotel room (Kotler *et al.*, 2014) Smartphone technology is increasingly being used to improve the overall customer experience while staying at the hotel. Examples include: ● applications to check in remotely and purchase hotel services ● mobile check-in terminals ● smartphone technology that replaces room key cards and in-room TV remote controls
Tablets	Used by employees to: ● check in customers en route to their rooms to save time ● as a tool for concierge to scan local businesses ● to carry out satisfaction surveys with customers And for customers: ● a specific reception counter with built in iPad for customers who want a less personalised check-in option Some properties provide iPads to customers during their stay to allow them to: ● search for in-house hotel services ● review room balance, and check in and out ● book wake-up calls ● make reservations and onward bookings ● control in-room services such as lighting and TV channels
Intelligent technologies	Customer fingerprints, retina scanning and voice recognition software to facilitate more convenient and secure room access Starwood (see 'Weblinks', below) appear to be pioneering the use of technology. With some properties already adopting many of the above initiatives, in hotel gyms it also uses treadmills that allow customers to check emails and the internet, and mirrors that allow customers to check weather and headlines while exercising

WEBLINKS

'The technology treats found in Starwood Hotels' Concept Lab':

http://skift.com/2015/05/20/the-technology-treats-found-in-starwood-hotels-concept-lab

'The hotel room of the future':

http://news.bbc.co.uk/2/hi/7795601.stm

Housekeeping

The housekeeping department's key focus is responsibility for the overall cleanliness and appearance of the facilities. The responsibility for cleaning an operation can vary depending on its size, standard and type of operation. Small independent restaurants and bars may employ a part-time cleaner, whereas a four-star hotel may employ a whole team of cleaning staff. Many operations now outsource their cleaning to improve quality and reduce expenses (see 'Outsourcing of services', below).

Challenges for the housekeeping department include:

- responsibility for the largest volume of area within the hotel
- the largest departmental employee headcount in the hotel
- difficult to attract, motivate and retain employees.

Objectives for the housekeeping department include:

- ensure all areas are clean at all times
- improve the appearance of the operation
- promote a healthy and safe environment
- make customers feel comfortable
- minimise any disruption to customers while cleaning
- clean at the most convenient times in the most efficient way
- minimise the build-up of dirt
- reduce any opportunities for infestation
- use good-quality, safe cleaning chemicals
- prolong the life of furniture, fixtures and fittings.

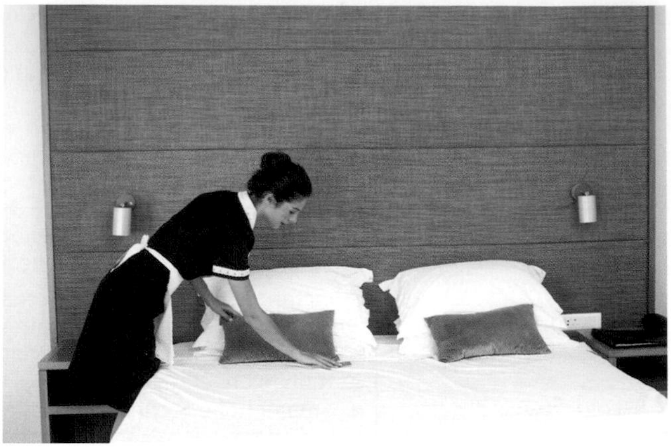

Figure 12.14 **Hotel room attendant at work**

Hotel housekeeping

Within a hotel, the housekeeping is overseen by the executive housekeeper, who manages a large team of employees, as detailed in Table 12.20.

Table 12.20 **Housekeeping structures and services: accommodation**

Organisation	Employee structure	Housekeeping services offered
Five-star hotel	Large team of employees	High standard of cleanliness Longer and more in-depth room cleaning times with own team of housekeepers Evening turn-down service (prepares the room for the customer to sleep – closes curtains, dims lights, leaves out slippers and turns down bed cover) High-quality room amenities, linen, furniture, furniture and fixtures Luxury internal design Public area cleaners more visible
Four-star hotel	Similar to a five-star, but butlers may not be used	A good standard of room and public area cleaning
Budget hotel	Room attendants may be outsourced to minimise costs and keep in line with main mission of hotel No in-house laundry, therefore linen is outsourced	A basic standard of room and public area cleaning In some new budget properties disposable linen is sold to customers
Bed and breakfast (B&B)	Owner employs part-time employees to assist when busy Linen may also be cleaned in-house	A basic standard of room and public area cleaning

SAMPLE JOB DESCRIPTION

Job title: Executive Housekeeper

Major responsibilities and duties

- Ensure that all areas are kept clean and as per standard at all times.
- Have in place an inspection programme that checks rooms, corridors, public areas, back-of-house areas, laundry and external surroundings.
- Ensure each area has cleaning specifications and that these are adhered to at all times.
- Ensure, through efficient employee rostering, that there are always the correct quantity of employees on duty at all times in relation to business demand.
- Create housekeeping budget detailing forecast consumption of each housekeeping item, and ensure budget is met each month.
- Ensure all employees follow health and safety legislation at all times.
- Ensure employees follow maintenance 'work order' system and keep rooms free from defects at all times.
- Successfully recruit all new housekeeping employees and carry out departmental inductions.
- Implement strategies to retain employees and reduce labour turnover.
- Motivate and guide employees at all times.
- Be visible throughout hotel and meet with customers as often as possible.
- Implement systems to collect feedback on housekeeping products and performance.
- Liaise with other department heads and communicate effectively.
- Ensure that par levels of housekeeping supplies and equipment are maintained.
- Constantly be proactive in looking for ways to improve the housekeeping product.

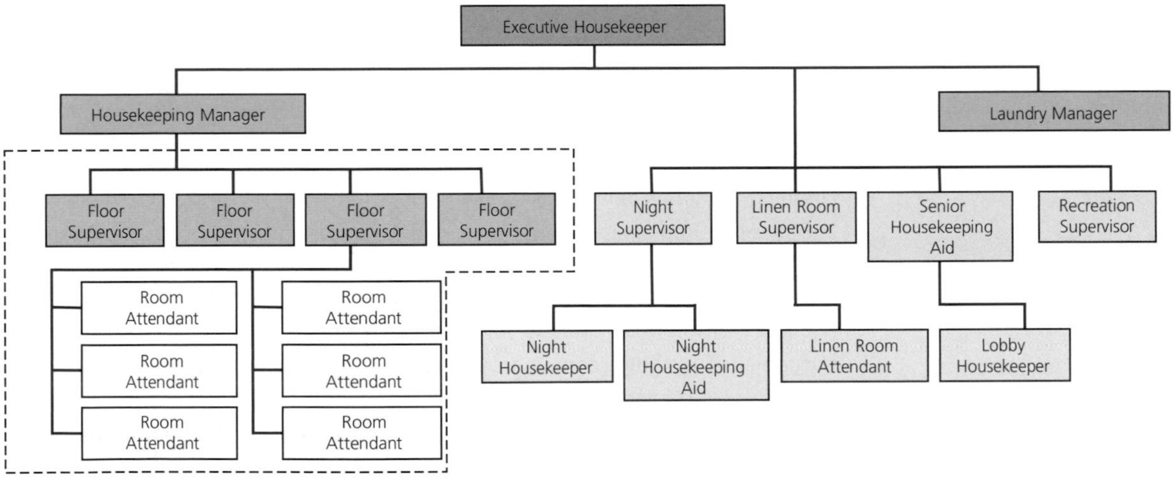

Figure 12.15 Typical organisational chart for housekeeping in a large four- or five-star hotel

Table 12.21 Examples of employees within the housekeeping department

Position	Responsibilities
Assistant housekeeping manager	Deputises for executive housekeeper
Room floor supervisor	Conducts shift briefings Reviews guest lists and VIP reports Checks rooms prior to arrival, during occupancy and after departure Verifies room discrepancies Releases clean rooms to reception Organises and schedules rooms and suites maintenance (e.g. spring clean, wall and ceiling washing, dusting, high dusting and under-bed vacuuming) Communicates any issues regarding rooms and suites with the housekeeping office coordinator and senior housekeepers Carries out weekly and monthly stock-takes to maintain par levels Ensures all keys (master and floor) are controlled tightly Motivates and monitors employees accordingly Reviews 'out of order' rooms Ensures all storage rooms are clean and stocked at all times

Position	Responsibilities
Room attendant	Attends daily briefings Replenishes service trolleys Cleans rooms and suites to the set standards Completes turndown service Maintains pantry areas Communicates with floor housekeeper on room status, issues, defects Greets and assists customers whenever necessary
Public area (PA) cleaner	Cleans public areas, to include lobby, lifts, corridors, public toilets, spa, offices and service areas Greets and assists customers whenever necessary
Housekeeping porter	Assists with floor housekeepers' and room attendants' requests Assists with any guest room changes Delivers and collects 'special requests' to rooms (e.g. cots, blankets, extra towels) Transports dirty laundry to linen room from floors Moves furniture in and out of rooms and suites as per floor housekeepers' instructions Assists room attendants during peak times Assists room attendants in deep cleaning activities Assists floor housekeepers with inventories
Valet (laundry runner)	Sends and receives customers' dry-cleaning items Washes and irons guests' laundry items
Linen/uniform room attendant	Sends out and receives all employees' laundry and dry-cleaning items on a daily basis Organises and puts all employees' laundry and dry-cleaning items in place, as per department, on a daily basis Delivers all linen to the maid service on each floor as per floor housekeepers' requests
Laundry attendant	Washes and irons in-house laundry items Sends and receives in-house dry-cleaning items Organises the chute room and delivers all linen items to the laundry room Separates all types of linen and laundry items before the items are processed Receives, sorts, cleans, dries, folds and stores linen and laundry items Carries out some basic sewing duties when required Ensures equipment and storage areas are clean at all times Adheres to safety standards at all times
Butler (this position is normally found only in very high-quality properties) Also employed on cruises, yachts, airlines, private jets, and chartered trains	Renewed interest in butlers has arisen due to increased work pressure and busy lifestyles, making a lifestyle manager a necessity. Increased personal wealth in some parts of the world means some people see a butler as a necessity. Corporate and leisure events now often include butlers to raise the perceived status of the event. With ever increasing numbers of luxury and five-star properties a butler service is seen as providing an extra service that competitors may not. However, many luxury properties (e.g. The Goring – www.thegoring.com) provide all of the butler services without having anyone called a butler Some of the butler's responsibilities include: ● unpacks on arrival and then re-packs guests' belongings for departure ● hangs, folds and organises customers' belongings (wardrobe management) ● sends and receives guest laundry and dry-cleaning items from the valet (also carries out some pressing duties) ● shoe shine ● service and clearance of food and beverages to the room ● provides information and some concierge services ● personal shopping

Like the front office, the housekeeping department is required to communicate with various departments to ensure the customer experience is of a high standard (see Table 12.22).

Table 12.22 Housekeeping communication with other departments

Department	Housekeeping contact
Front office	Communication of room status Transfer of calls by switchboard to customers' rooms Delivery and collection of luggage by bell desk to guest rooms Delivery of messages to customers' rooms
Maintenance	Scheduled, routine, preventative and emergency maintenance Refurbishments, renovations and restorations Deep cleaning Out of order rooms
Food and beverage	Decor for annual events (Christmas, Easter, Chinese New Year, Ramadan) Supply of table linen Pest control Uniforms for food and beverage (F&B) personnel Supplying of flowers and maintaining of plants in F&B areas Guest cloakrooms Deep cleaning of furniture in F&B outlets
Security	Suspicious packages, room burglaries/theft, fire, in-room damage by customers, disturbance issues, employee theft, customer fatalities, employee uniforms, lost property and CCTV
Sales and marketing	Guest tours and show rounds Familiarisation ('fam') trips Rooms product needs to be in good condition to drive return business and positive word of mouth VIP amenities Media photos for online and other marketing collateral
Leisure club and spa	Cleaning of leisure areas, e.g. gym/sauna Providing towels and linen Providing employee uniforms
Administration	Office cleaning, recycling of waste, payroll

Case study

Housekeeping

The Globe Hotel is a three-star budget hotel in Hong Kong's central business district. Peter Chan is the front office manager, a position he has held for three years. He is well liked by the customers for his friendly approach but in recent months he has been experiencing a lot of pressure from his rooms division manager due to a decrease in room rate and occupancy, and increase in complaints. Some of the complaints included long waiting times for check-in, rooms not ready for customers, and a lack of concierge and porter services. In addition, recent TripAdvisor comments also showed poor ratings for customer service at the front office and in-room cleanliness. The executive housekeeper, Winnie Tan, also raised in her recent appraisal that the front office employees are very inexperienced and lack good communication skills with the HK department.

Imagine you are Peter Chan. Answer the following questions.

1 What five possible actions would you take to improve the quality of service and communication on the front desk?
2 What five actions could you take to improve the profitability of the rooms inventory?
3 What could be some of the contributing factors to poor room cleanliness?
4 Write a 100-word standard statement that could be uploaded to TripAdvisor to address negative comments.

Outsourcing of services

Outsourcing can be defined as the transfer of tasks and/or services to an external, third-party specialist. Some of the drivers behind this trend are cost reduction, difficulties in attracting professional employees, increase in demand for quality, and technology. For hotels and other hospitality operators it is being used in many cases as a strategic choice to gain a competitive advantage. Traditionally, hotels delivered all services using their own in-house teams, i.e. food and beverage, leisure and spas (see below), cleaning and maintenance. However, attracting, retaining and training these personnel was challenging. It was then identified that the core focus for hotel operators was rooms and that trying to deliver everything was outside their real focus and core objective. This has led to the trend in outsourcing specialists carrying out many of the functions that were previously delivered in-house.

Leisure, recreation and spa facilities

It is common for four- and five-star hotels to feature some type of facility for leisure and relaxation. This has become more prominent with the global shift towards healthier lifestyles. Hotel facilities can consist of gymnasiums, exercise rooms, walking and running tracks, tennis courts and swimming pools. In recent years there has been a growth in spa facilities in the higher-end properties. Treatments include skin care, water therapies, massage, acupuncture, and manicures and pedicures. Increasingly, these facilities and services are provided by external specialists. Customers include hotel guests and external visitors.

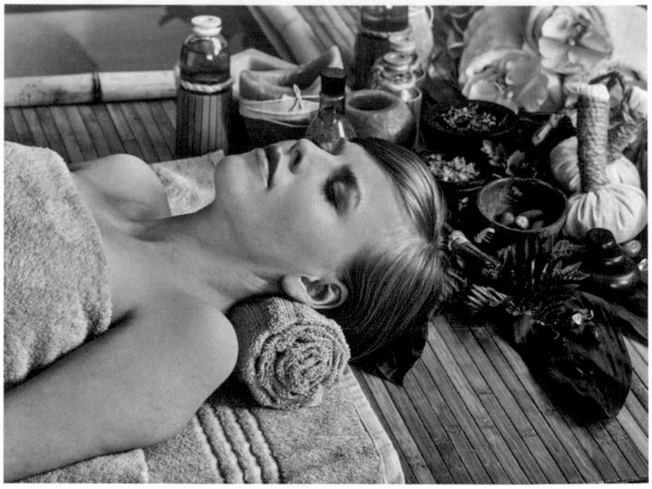

Figure 12.16 Spa treatment at a hotel

Functions that could be outsourced by the rooms division include:

- room cleaning
- security
- health club and spa
- laundry and linen
- floristry
- specialised maintenance
- pest control.

Table 12.23 Evaluation of outsourcing

Advantages of outsourcing	Challenges of outsourcing
Greater specialisation of talent	Hands over control to contractor
Reduction in HR tasks (advertising, recruiting, training, holidays, etc.)	Once a function has been outsourced this is very difficult to reverse
Less responsibility overall, facilitating a focus on the core product and objectives of the hotel	Many contractors have several clients, so priority may be a problem
In-house employees freed up to carry out more relevant tasks	Reduction in number of in-house employees can have an impact on morale of existing workforce; large employee reductions are not good for corporate culture or image
Cost reduction and higher profits	Some functions are difficult to outsource
Increased productivity	In hospitality, where personal service is key, it can be a challenge when different workers enter the hotel
More innovation and more current resources	
Less capital investment in equipment	

Cleaning

The importance of cleaning

Clean facilities are critical to the success of any hospitality operation. A clean environment can attract and retain customers, encourage return visits, and reduce sickness and accidents, thus avoiding waste and legal claims.

Tools for achieving and maintaining a high standard of cleanliness include:

- cleaning schedules and checklists
- performance standards, e.g. 'how to clean'
- ongoing training and monitoring

- provide the right tools
- good-quality chemicals and equipment
- productivity standards
- follow cleaning principles
- good leadership and supervision
- comply with the law.

Dirt, or soil, is generated in the workplace in different ways, as outlined in Table 12.24.

Table 12.24 Soil generated in the workplace

Cause	Examples		Solutions/prevention
Humans and employees	Poor hygiene	Poor hand washing	Signage, training, education, supervision, adequate bathing facilities
	Litter		Dustbins, signs
	Mistakes	Spillages	Training/prompt removal by cleaning
	Deliberate	Vandalism, graffiti	Code of conduct/rules
	Natural	Shedding skin, hair loss, perspiration	Personal grooming
	Disease	Sneezing, coughing	Hand-washing facilities/hand gel/disinfectant
Employees	Bringing in soil from outside	Dirt on clothing	Changing rooms, standards, employee rules and regulations
Weather	Rain/snow	Water/sludge	Doormats/temporary entry carpets/umbrella holders/umbrella disposable bags/floor mats
External matter/ foliage	Leaves, earth, dust, litter, debris	Visitors/employees bring in on footwear	Entry mats, foot grinders
Equipment	Machinery	Grease, dust, heating ventilation and air conditioning (HVAC)	Regular cleaning/cleaning schedules
Insects, vermin and pests	Cockroaches, rats, flies	Pests enter through the atmosphere, deliveries, luggage, cracks in delivery areas, and due to poor food hygiene, storage and disposal	Cover bins, keep doors closed, thorough checks on delivery
The atmosphere	Smoke, exhausts, dust	The atmosphere deposits soil	Regular cleaning, good ventilation and extraction
Natural	Decay/deterioration	Interior and exterior – buildings, paintwork, stone	Regular maintenance

There are two main types of soil.

1 **Organic (loose, dry):** commonly referred to as dust. It can usually be removed with direct mechanical action, as long as it stays dry. It can be swept, dust-mopped, wiped, vacuumed or wet-mopped with little or no chemical action required. Any surface that has not been cleaned in 12 hours will have dust accumulated on it. The longer dust remains on a surface, the better chance it has of becoming oily, sticky soil from contamination with other substances, even from moisture in the air or from air-conditioning units.

2 **Inorganic (oily, sticky):** soil or dirt is almost always mixed with grease or other oily materials. Grease and oil make the dirt stick to a surface. The longer dirt remains on a surface, the more it tends to bond to the surface and the harder it is to remove.

Soil build-up can be prevented by:

- reducing the opportunity for soil to enter the establishment
- minimising the build-up of soil within the establishment.

Types of cleaning include:

- daily/nightly – ongoing cleaning in high-usage areas
- routine – as and when required
- periodic/scheduled – cleaning of areas that don't require daily cleaning
- deep cleaning – may include carpet shampooing or laundering curtains.

Cleaning agents

To assist in the removal of soil, a selection of chemicals is available. When using cleaning agents one should remember to:

- use the right chemical and method
- always read the label
- follow the cleaning specification fully and read instructions

- use the correct quantity
- apply in the correct way
- apply safely and with care.

According to Raghubalan and Raghubalan (2007), examples of cleaning agents include:

- detergents
- organic solvents
- carpet cleaners
- glass cleaners
- floor sealers
- water
- polishers
- disinfectants and bleaches
- floor strippers
- laundry aids
- toilet cleaners
- deodorisers
- abrasives
- reagents.

Cleaning agents are applied using different methods, including:

- vacuuming
- mopping
- wiping
- scrubbing
- spotting
- buffing
- steam extraction
- polishing
- dusting.

Table 12.25 Cleaning equipment

Manual equipment	Mechanical equipment
Applicators	Vacuum cleaners
Brushes	Wet vacuums
Chamois leather	Wet extractors
Dusters	Rotary machines
Dustpan and brush	Steam cleaners
Mop and bucket	High-pressure jet sprays
Ladders	
Trolleys	
Squeegees	
Sprayers	

The principles of cleaning

When cleaning objects, the following principles should be applied.

- Remove all surface soil and obstructions before cleaning.
- Follow the least obtrusive and disturbing methods of cleaning, especially early in the morning.
- Restore all surfaces to as near perfect condition as soon as possible.
- Always use the simplest method of cleaning and the mildest cleaning agent.
- Beware of safety hazards.
- Remove all dust and dirt – do not transfer to another area.
- Carry out cleaning in the quickest possible time.

Quality of cleaning

Performance standards are used to ensure items are cleaned correctly. They detail:

- steps involved in cleaning each item
- what cleaning equipment is required (and how to use it)
- what chemicals or cleaning solutions should be used, quantity and application
- time to clean
- health and safety directives, e.g. gloves, mixing of chemicals.

It is these standards that are used by the housekeeping supervisor to measure cleaning standards.

Bedroom cleaning

The cleaning and servicing of bedrooms in properties is a major part of housekeeping's function. In four- and five-star hotels, housekeepers can clean up to 15–20 rooms a day. Rooms can be cleaned for guests due to arrive, while customers are in-house and after they depart. In each room there are different items that need cleaning, placing and replenishing (see Table 12.26). Housekeepers clean rooms in a particular order to ensure cleaning is effective and efficient.

Figure 12.17 A Grand Luxe bedroom at the Peninsula New York

Table 12.26 Typical bedroom items

Furniture	Fixtures and fittings	Equipment	Linen	Other
Upholstery (sofa, armchair, easy chair, chaise longue) Bedroom (wardrobe and hangers, drawers, luggage rack, dressing table/desk, dining/coffee table, bedside table, bed, mattress, hotel art) Bathroom (toilet, bidet, shower cubicle, vanity unit, bathtub)	Lighting (ceiling and surround, lamps, emergency) Fixtures (doors, handles, bed headboard, fire alarms, sprinklers, locks, windows, HVAC units and controls, ceiling fans, blinds, shades, shutters, speakers, key card unit) Fittings (flooring and carpet, wall coverings, pictures and decoration, mirrors, plug points and signage) Bathroom (bath tub, shower unit, mirror, faucets, towel fittings, shower fittings, hairdryer, hose, wall phone)	Television and remote control, trouser press, tea- and coffee-making facilities, iron and ironing board, minibar, telephone, safe, alarm clock, docking station, Wi-Fi router, radio, crockery and glassware) Wellness – Pullman hotels, for example, now provide lightweight dumbbells and a yoga mat in each room	Bed linen (sheets, pillowcases, blankets, bedspreads, mattress protectors, pillows, duvets, duvet covers, electric blankets and quilts) Bathroom linen (face, hand, bath towels, bath mats, bathrobe) Window curtains/ drapes and nylon curtains (bathroom) Soft furnishings – cushions, loose covers	Sales and marketing literature (welcome letters, directory of services, menus, minibar tariff, pillow menus, product takeaway list) Guest supplies (notepads, pens, dry cleaning bags and menu, environmental literature, TV channel menu) Guest amenities (slippers, moisturisers, shampoo, soap, shoe shine, tissues, toothbrush, razor, comb, shower cap, conditioner, shower gel, cotton buds, facial tissue, sewing kit, water, tea, coffee)

Table 12.27 Bed sizes

Name	Width (cm)	Length (cm)
Single	90	190
Double	135	190
King	150	200
Super king	180	200

Room status report

The room status report (as detailed in Table 12.28) is the report maintained by housekeeper to inform reception of the status of each room. This then assists with room allocation for check-in guests.

Table 12.28 Room status

Term	Description
Checked out (or departed)	The guest has settled his or her account, returned the room key cards and left the hotel
Complimentary	The room is occupied, but the guest is assessed no charge for its use
Did not check out (DNCO)	The guest made arrangements to settle his or her account but has left without informing the front office
Do not disturb (DND)	The guest has requested not to be disturbed
Due out	The room is expected to become vacant after the following day's check-out time
Late check-out	The guest has requested, and is being allowed, to check out later than the hotel's standard check-out time. There is sometimes an additional charge for this service
Lock-out (or double locked)	The room has been locked so that the guest cannot re-enter until he/she is cleared by a hotel official
Occupied	A guest is currently registered to the room
On-change (or vacant, dirty)	The guest has departed, but the room has not yet been cleaned and readied for resale
Out of order (OOO)	The room cannot be assigned to the guest. A room may be out of order for a variety of reasons, including the need for maintenance, refurbishment and extensive cleaning
Skipper	The guest has left the hotel without making arrangements to settle his/her account
Sleeper	The guest has settled his/her account and left the hotel, but the front office employees have failed to properly update the room's status from occupied
Sleep-out	A guest is registered to the room, but the room has not been used
Stay over	The guest is not checking out today and will remain at least one more night
Vacant and ready (or vacant, clean and inspected)	The room has been cleaned and inspected, and is ready for an arriving guest

Laundry

Although many newer properties do not have in-house laundries, some older properties and those in more remote locations do. Many properties now choose to outsource their laundry. Figure 12.18 and Table 12.29 detail the wash cycle and the linen cycle, respectively, and the stages that these cycles go through from dirty to clean.

At each stage, housekeeping managers need to consider quality and cost. The loss through shrinkage of linen in a lodging property can be staggering. Wear and tear, permanent stains, theft by guests and employees, and linen misuse are the main causes of linen loss.

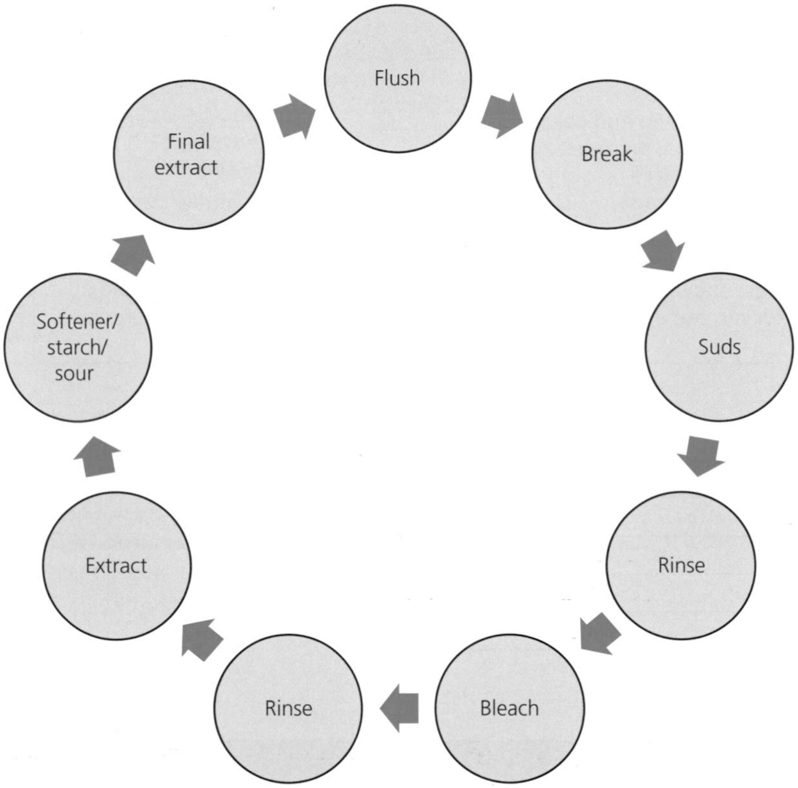

Figure 12.18 The wash cycle

Table 12.29 The linen cycle

Activity	Description
Transport of dirty linen to linen room	Room attendants collect soiled linen, which is placed into a laundry bin or trolley. Housekeeping porters then transport this laundry to the linen room; in some properties linen is simply bundled and deposited by means of a laundry chute
Counting and sorting of linen	On arrival at the linen room the laundry room attendants: ● count each item of linen ● separate linens into size, type and colour ● check for any damaged or heavily soiled items (damaged linen is removed from the operation and heavily soiled linen treated separately, as described below) ● ensure that the same amount of clean linen stock is returned to the attendant Each floor has its own 'pantry', which contains a par stock of linen, a sufficient quantity to replenish all rooms. This stock is put on to the room attendants' trolleys in the morning in preparation to go into the bedrooms. The system of 'clean for dirty' linen makes room attendants more accountable for the retention of their linen stock. If they are asking for more stock than they have deposited, why is this? At this stage the laundry is either collected and sent to an external laundry contractor or washed in-house

Activity	Description
Washing of linen	When loading, the machines should not be too empty or too full, and the operator should: ● ensure the correct laundry chemical is used, in the right quantity for the load/weight ● ensure the wash temperature is correct ● ensure colours are not mixed Many large machines nowadays are computerised, and chemical quantities and washing temperatures are calculated automatically
Drying	After washing, the laundry is dried in large commercial dryers: ● the machine should not be too full or too empty ● the machine's drying temperature should not be too hot or too cold ● drying time should be correct for the laundry load, not too short or too long Computerised dryers now calculate the time and temperature required based on load/weight
Pressing and folding	For linen to be crisp and to appear professionally laundered the next stage is for it to be pressed. Laundries have different ways of doing this, including: ● steam cabinets ● flatwork ironers ● pressing machines ● folding machines ● rolling equipment
Storing	After folding, the linen will be stored; the main linen room will have a par stock level for all linen items to ensure that the hotel has sufficient quantities of linen at any one time to accommodate the needs of its departments The linen should ideally rest in storage for at least 24 hours before being issued; this helps increase the useful life of linens and makes the linen smoother Linen rooms need adequate ventilation, and should be humidity-free and lockable
Issuing	Linen is issued from the linen room to housekeeping porters, room attendants and other departments throughout the day. Most linen rooms practise some form of control at this stage, such as employees signing for any linen types and quantities received. Other properties may have a system whereby Housekeeping porters and room attendants restock their linen pantries as and when required; the important element is tracking who has taken what linen and to which area

Environmental considerations in accommodation management

Hotels are the largest consumers of energy, not only in building construction but also as establishments with complex installations providing customers with high levels of multifaceted comfort, and exclusive amenities, treatment and facilities. Many of the services provided to hotel customers are highly resource intensive, whether in terms of energy, water or raw materials (Sloan, Legrand and Chen, 2012).

Common problems

These include:

- inefficient use of water and energy
- excessive solid waste generation (rubbish, plastics, etc.)
- limited involvement and tie-in by employees
- poor (or no) monitoring
- capital investment in new eco-friendly machinery/ equipment can be costly.

A hospitality business might be motivated to 'go green' for a variety of reasons, including:

- economic (cost reduction)
- marketing (corporate social responsibility, and reaching the green consumer)
- asset protection
- environmental accreditation/awards
- social responsibility
- regulatory (legislation)
- to build community trust.

Over the past few years, hotel companies have made a determined effort to deal with the impact their business activities have on the environment, particularly by measuring and reducing their carbon and water footprints (Sloan *et al.*, 2012).

The 'reduce, reuse, recycle' model is well known, easy to follow, and used as a basis for individuals and organisations to be more environmentally friendly. Various other initiatives can also be adopted by catering and hospitality establishments, including:

- fluorescent instead of incandescent lighting, dimmers, sensors
- double-glazing
- linen reuse

- ethical suppliers, organic products, fair trade linen, recycled stationery
- environmentally friendly/biodegradable cleaning chemicals
- flow restrictions and sensors for hand washing, half-flush toilets
- electronic locking systems linked to room utilities
- energy-efficient equipment
- rechargeable batteries for remote controls
- newspapers provided only on request
- signage for employees, e.g. 'Switch off lights'.

WEBLINK

'Reduce, reuse, recycle' – for more information on environmental practices in hotels, see:

www.greenhotelier.org

Case study

Environmental considerations

The Al Habibi Hotel in Dubai is a four-star, 220-room hotel, built in 1980, offering a wide range of services and facilities to tourists visiting Dubai. Some of the facilities include a large garden area with open-air swimming pool, leisure club, Jacuzzi, steam room and gymnasium. In addition, it has three restaurants, large conference facilities and 120 full-time, hard-working employees.

Due to the age of the hotel, the maintaining of these facilities is becoming quite expensive and as some of the systems are dated, they are also proving very costly compared with newer, more cost-effective equipment and systems. Water and electricity bills are very high overall, and this is not helped by the hotel having its own in-house laundry.

With the vast growth in hospitality in the Gulf region over the past ten years, newer and more modern hotels with new facilities are gaining market share and impacting the overall business of the Al Habibi. Furthermore, in recent years there has been pressure from local government and hotel owners to implement environmental initiatives to meet the needs of a more socially responsible customer base.

All of these factors have forced the management of the hotel to look at environmental practices within the hotel.

As the hotel manager, detail how you would deal with the following.

1. You will soon be updating the hotel bedrooms to make them more contemporary and eco friendly. Draw a floor plan of a bedroom that is eco friendly, detailing the different types of furnishings, furniture, fixtures and equipment that can be used to make the bedroom more environmentally friendly.
2. The water bill is increasing substantially each quarter. List five initiatives that can be implemented to reduce water consumption within the bedrooms and laundry.
3. The owner has identified that many of the newer hotels outsource their laundry to an external provider. What are the advantages and disadvantages for the hotel of doing this?
4. Consider what could be reused, recycled and reduced in the swimming pool and leisure club areas.
5. When all the above has been completed, you are required by the marketing department to write a press statement of 300 words for the media, communicating the actions you have taken at the hotel and your reasons for doing so.

Health and safety within accommodation

When cleaning facilities employees are confronted with many risks. See Table 12.30 for some typical health and safety risks for housekeeping employees, and how to prevent them.

Table 12.30 **Typical health and safety risks for housekeeping employees**

Risks	Examples	Prevention
Back problems	Turning mattresses, pushing carts, bending, stretching	Training in lifting techniques, ask for assistance
Broken glass/china	Room attendants and public area cleaners can come into contact with broken glass	Training/awareness/standards for correct disposal/broken glass containers
Contamination from infected needles/blood	Use of controlled substances in rooms by customers/non-disposed used needles; hepatitis B virus or HIV are found in blood and spread when infected blood or certain body fluids get into the body	Special training and standards in the correct, safe disposal of needles/blood stains/sharps box

Risks	Examples	Prevention
Dealing with hazardous chemicals	All housekeeping employees will have to deal with chemicals at some point; the correct use of these chemicals is paramount and failing to do this can lead to serious injury	COSHH (Control of Substances Hazardous to Health) training, protective clothing, chemical label fact sheets
Defective equipment	Shorts in equipment	Maintenance repair/preventative maintenance programme/purchase safe, tested equipment/portable appliance testing/risk assessment
Equipment flexes	Room attendants frequently use equipment with long flexes (for example, vacuum cleaners/polishers), and can be at risk of trips and falls	Training/operating procedures
Fire	Fire can be a risk in accommodation, with the potential for equipment fusing and cigarettes still permitted in some parts of the world	Tested and commissioned fire equipment Fire training and emergency teams Fire procedures communicated to customers and employees
High floor/ladder work	Some high dusting may require the use of ladders (for example, cleaning high balconies, artwork or chandeliers)	Training/ensure ladder is safe/colleague to hold ladder/attempt only if qualified/ Working at Height Regulations 2005/never use chair instead of ladder
Office work	Managers/operators who work at computers can suffer from back pain and repetitive strain injury (RSI)	Provide an ergonomic workplace environment
Wet/slippery floors	When floors are wet after mopping or wet weather	Non-slip work shoes, wet floor signs, grit
Work stress	All employees can be subject to additional workload and pressures, which can lead to stress	Good scheduling, regular breaks, job chats, fair distribution and allocation of work, observation, 'management by walking around' (MBWA), ergonomic workplaces

Maintenance and facilities

The responsibility of the maintenance and facilities department (sometimes referred to as 'engineering') is to ensure that all structural, equipment, fixtures and furniture are in good order and free from defects at all times. In the situation that these are not maintained, complaints can take place, sales can be lost and accidents can occur.

The objectives of the maintenance department include:

- maintain the operation's internal and surrounding facilities
- prompt repair of any defective furniture, equipment or fittings
- plan and oversee any major refurbishments, renovations or redecorations
- contract external specialists to perform maintenance works as and when required
- provide safe premises and environment for visitors, customers and employees
- actively work towards reducing energy costs.

Table 12.31 Types of maintenance

Maintenance	Description
Preventative	Inspections, minor corrections and work order initiations
Scheduled	Preventative maintenance sometimes identifies problems and needs beyond the scope of a minor correction; these problems are brought to the attention of engineering through a work order system, which maybe manual or automated
Routine	Related to the general upkeep of the property; can occur on a regular (daily or weekly) basis, and require relatively minimal training or skills
Emergency	As and when an emergency occurs, maintenance is required – electrical faults, floods, lift breakdowns, power cuts, etc.

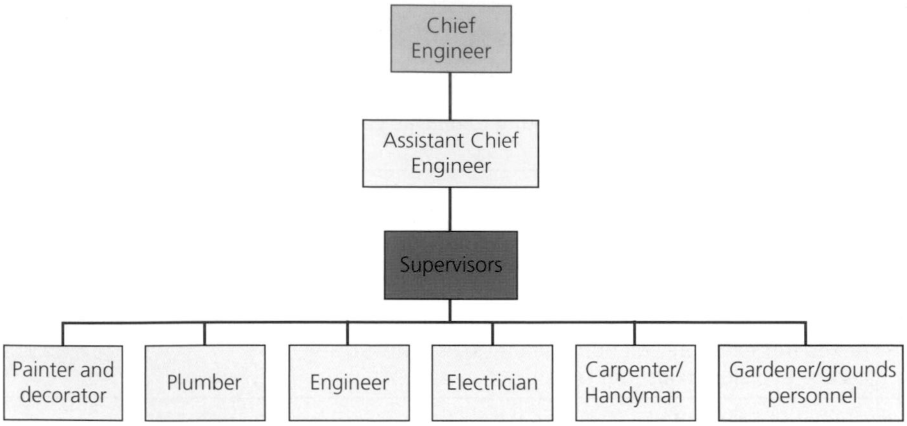

Figure 12.19 Organisational chart for the maintenance department of a large four- or five-star hotel

Very few properties employ a full team of specialised maintenance personnel to cover all areas. Many have general employees who work in the maintenance department, who may specialise in one area but are also cross-trained to carry out other maintenance tasks. For example, an employee who is a qualified plumber may also have had training on how to operate the energy management system. Another approach would be to have general 'handy people', who can deal with day-to-day tasks but, when a specialised piece of work needs to be done, a local contractor can be employed at an hourly rate to carry out the work.

Table 12.32 Categories of maintenance

Category	Examples
Building's exterior	Roof, walls, foundations, drainage, structure, sewers, water features, insulation, windows
Car park and grounds	Presentation, security, lighting, maintenance, irrigation, management and general upkeep
Design	Renovation, refurbishments, interior, comfort, fashion, health and safety, Disability Discrimination Act
Electrical	Equipment, lighting, batteries, generators, meters, energy management
Energy management	Cost control, employees, customers, law, comfort, utility pricing
Food service equipment	Kitchen equipment, refrigeration, ovens, buffet units, cook-chill units, storage, dishwasher, ice machines, coffee machines, vending machines
HVAC (heating, ventilation and air conditioning)	Temperatures, comfort, extraction, refrigeration, cooling systems, air supply
Laundry	Laundry equipment, energy management, wastewater
Lighting	Natural, in-room, public areas, task, emergency, exterior, colour, mood, ambience, decoration, energy saving
Plumbing and water systems	Central heating, boilers, spa, pool, sanitation, filtration, cleaning, irrigation, laundry, guest rooms, fountains, drainage
Safety and security	Signage, equipment, testing, electronic locking systems, alarm system, security lighting, perimeter fences, fire system, sprinklers, CCTV, in-room safes, fingerprint recognition
Telecommunications and internet	Internet, switchboard (PABX), facsimile, intranet, Wi-Fi, website, email, in-house pagers, mobile telephones
Waste management	Recycling systems

Security

Both customers and employees need to feel secure while on the premises. The size and complexity of the security department can vary depending on the operation. City-centre properties in volatile political locations require more security, as do casinos. It is common for security personnel to be outsourced from a security company. There is normally one individual in the hotel that is responsible for security – this person could be the chief of security or security manager.

The objectives of the security department are to protect:

- customers and their assets while on the premises
- employees and their assets while on the premises
- the hotel's assets
- the data of both the hotel, employees and customers.

The key responsibilities of security personnel include:

- monitor CCTV and be alert at all times
- escort cash-drops
- follow up on incidents
- respond rapidly to security requests
- make frequent walk-arounds of the premises
- work closely with local police
- create awareness of security issues in all employees
- escort suspicious or undesirable people
- assist in dealing with difficult or intoxicated customers
- assist in making security checks on personnel
- complete security paperwork.

Table 12.33 Security risks and prevention

Security risk example	At risk?	Risk prevention
Any verbal or physical violence directed at front desk personnel	Employees, assets	Security training for employees on what to do in the event of such a situation, panic alarm, CCTV, security personnel, drop safe
Cyber attack	Data	Firewalls, antivirus
Employee theft of cash and assets	Hotel	Reference checks, police checks, POS system, CCTV, good supervision, employee bag checks, security personnel
Employees attempting to defraud customers/identity theft/customer information	Customers	Employ good employees – references, police checks, effective supervision, CCTV, standards, data protection
Handbag thieves (pickpockets)	Customers	In-house security, informing customers to be aware, CCTV, handbag safety hooks
Harassment from customers	Employees	Visible in-house security guards
Potential in-room theft from intruders	Customers	Effective in-house security, awareness by employees, educating customers, electronic locking system (ELS), use of in-room safes, safety deposit box, CCTV (closed-circuit television) surveillance system, signing in and out for all visitors, lift key cards to provide access to floors and bedrooms
Suspicious packages	Customers, employees, assets	Visible in-house security, crisis planning, awareness by employees

Further reading

AA hotel quality standards: www.theaa.com/resources/Documents/pdf/business/hotel_services/aa_hotel_quality_standards.pdf

Casado, M.A. (2012) *Housekeeping Management*, 2nd edn. Wiley.

Guide to AA ratings and awards: www.theaa.com/travel/accommodation_restaurants_grading.html

Kotler, P.T., Bowen, J.T. and Makens, J. (2014) *Marketing for Hospitality and Tourism*, 6th edn. Pearson.

Legoherel, P., Poutier, L. and Fyall, A. (2013) *Revenue Management for Hospitality and Tourism*. Goodfellows.

Nyheim, P.D. and Connolly, D.J. (2012) *Technology Strategies for the Hospitality Industry*, 2nd edn. Pearson.

Penner, R.H., Adams, L. and Robson, S.K.A. (2012) *Hotel Design*, 2nd edn. Norton.

Raghubalan, G. and Raghubalan, S. (2007) *Hotel Housekeeping*. Oxford University Press.

Sloan, P., Legrand, W. and Chen, J.S. (2012) *Sustainability in the Hospitality Industry*, 2nd rev. edn. Routledge.

Social Media Revolution: www.youtube.com/watch?v=jottDMuLesU#action=share

Visit Britain (2015) *Britain and Inbound Market Report*. Visit Britain.

Visit Britain: www.visitbritain.org

Topics for discussion

Front office

1. Carry out research to identify some of the hotel applications (apps) available to enhance the customer reservation and arrival experience.
2. Discuss what may be the difference for a hotel receptionist when treating a first-time customer compared to a returning, regular customer.
3. Note down five reasons that budget hotels are able to provide such economical rates to their customers.
4. Considering the different types of accommodation available, list down those present in your city, detailing star rating, customer type and number of rooms.
5. The AA rating system is commonly used to determine standard of accommodation. Draft a table, and detail the advantages and challenges of using such a system for both accommodation managers and customers.
6. As a receptionist you are faced with a very angry regular customer whose room is not ready for them to check in. The customer is becoming increasingly angry, as they have just arrived on an overnight flight from New York. Detail:
   - why the customer may be angry
   - the impacts for the hotel of this dissatisfied regular customer
   - the steps you would take to deal with this customer.
7. Carry out internet research to determine some good examples of how hotels are meeting the needs of visitors with disabilities. Consider the booking, check-in and occupancy stages of the guest process.
8. Websites such as TripAdvisor.com have become very popular. Detail the advantages and challenges for both managers and customers of such sites.
9. A large group of tourists from mainland China are due to check in to a large hotel in your city. Consider the cultural differences, and list what specific services and facilities you can provide to them to make their stay more enjoyable.
10. List the benefits to which a loyalty card member would be entitled.
11. This list includes a selection of hotel brands.
    - Dorsett Hotels
    - Ibis Styles
    - Jumeirah
    - Dusit
    - Pullman
    - Rotana
    - Shangri-La
    - Morgans
    - Pan Pacific
    - Peninsula
    - Tune
    - W
    - Jin Jiang
    - Regent
    - Aloft
    - Armani

    Carry out research and establish the region in which each brand operates and its standard.

Housekeeping

1. Create a visual diagram and present the practices or incentives within the housekeeping department that can provide a cleaner and more sustainable environment.
2. Filling and retaining housekeeping attendant positions can be a challenge due to the physical nature of the work and the environment. As an executive housekeeper, detail how would you make the job of a room cleaner more attractive and comfortable.
3. Many of the assets found in a hotel's housekeeping department can be used at home, e.g. towels and chemicals. Consider ways to reduce the potential for theft of such items by employees.
4. Visit a local hotel. List down the different surfaces around the hotel – for example, ceramic or marble. Carry out library research to find out the most appropriate method for cleaning each surface.
5. As a hygiene inspector working for the local authority, create a checklist that can be used to inspect the hygiene standards in a food and beverage outlet (restaurant). Visit a local restaurant or fast-food outlet and use the checklist to evaluate its level of hygiene. From this, create a short PowerPoint presentation that could be used to demonstrate your findings to the manager/owner. The presentation should detail visual evidence, concerns and recommended areas for improvement.
6. Customer questionnaires have detailed that many customers are unhappy with the cleanliness of your hotel's bedrooms. As an executive housekeeper detail some of the possible causes of this and some recommendations to overcome the issue.
7. A group of your hotel residents have enjoyed a local football game and have returned to the hotel bar to celebrate. Over a number of hours a few of the group members have become quite intoxicated and rowdy. The barman is concerned and has called you, the duty manager. Detail the steps you would take to deal with this situation.
8. Go online and research hotels that demonstrate environmental practices. Describe the practices, the benefits and the challenges.

13 Marketing and sales

Marketing and sales are two different functions. Marketing looks at all the elements required to provide the right product and service to the right customer, at the right price, in the right place and at the right time. When all of these are delivered effectively it is then that the sales function can work effectively selling products either face to face, over the telephone or online.

Marketing

The Chartered Institute of Marketing (CIM) defines marketing as 'the management process responsible for identifying, anticipating and satisfying customers profitably'.

Marketing is necessary for the long-term survival of any business. It is the whole complex of business behaviour that identifies customer needs and trends in buying behaviour, and carefully monitors and interprets the business environment in which the establishment or business is operating. Factors include the amount of disposable income people have, the economic environment and exchange rates. There are also political factors, such as changes in government policy, that can affect the way we operate our businesses; these are referred to by the acronym PESTLE, which stands for political, economic, social, technological, legal and environmental. Market research relies on a systematic approach and there are a number of different approaches to researching a particular market.

In large organisations marketing departments will have positions that look at market research, public relations (PR), communications, branding, online marketing and advertising, to name a few. Market research can be done online, over the telephone or in the field, and it can be centralised and off-site. Increasingly, online promotion and advertising is outsourced to specialist agencies that advise, implement and manage all online marketing activity. In smaller organisations the owner or manager may handle all of these functions.

This chapter will cover the key models illustrated in Figure 13.1. Although these models will be presented separately it is important to note that they all work simultaneously within the marketing environment to achieve the desired goal.

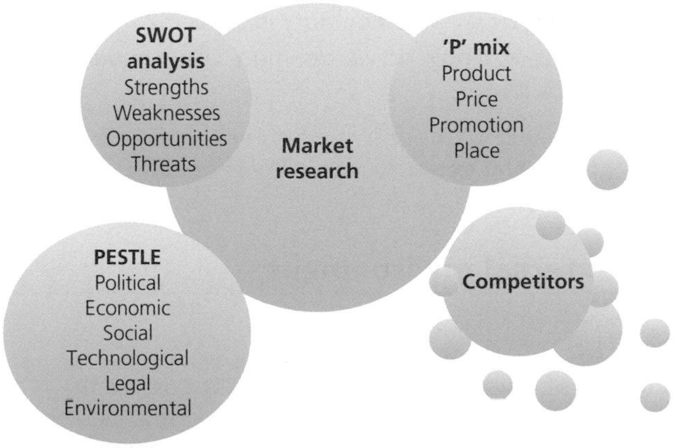

Figure 13.1 The marketing environment

Market research

Kotler, Bowen and Makens (2014) define market research as 'a process that identifies and defines marketing opportunities and problems, monitors and evaluates marketing actions and performance, and communicates the findings and implications to management'. It is important for any business to know the marketing environment in which it operates. Some catering and hospitality business will do their own market research, while others will bring in consultants. This research will assist the company in knowing potential and current customers, and the competition, bringing the company closer to knowing its own positioning.

Researching the market is something that happens at the start of the development of a concept or product, and needs to be carried out continuously throughout the life of the business. At the beginning, for example, if an entrepreneur wants to start a restaurant in a particular area, how do they know what kind of restaurant to open? Chinese? Italian? Fine dining? Fast casual? Therefore, in order to make the right decision, the entrepreneur should carry out research to assist in creating the business concept that the consumers in the market need and want without entering a saturated market. There are many market research tools available to assist in this.

Why market research?

Market research assists in:

- establishing needs and wants, e.g. what do customers want from a hotel bedroom?
- helping to solve a problem, e.g. how do we increase customer satisfaction?
- evaluating a product or service, e.g. what do our customers think about our website?
- helping with decision making, e.g. shall we open a bistro or a fine dining restaurant?
- answering a question, e.g. how do we get more walk-in business for our breakfast buffet?
- assisting in planning and management, e.g. how many employees do we need on duty in January?
- improving, e.g. how do we get more Likes on our Facebook page?

Typical research methods include survey, interviews, focus groups and external secondary information, such as industry reports.

The external environment

PESTLE

One area of research to be carried out is to assess the external environment in which a business operates. The PESTLE model (PESTLE stands for political, economic, social, technological, legal and environmental) examines the six external factors that can impact the business. Examples of these include those listed below.

- **Political:** inter-country relationships, wars, terrorism, pressure groups, elections, government leadership and trading policies, tax, visa and labour laws.
- **Economic:** internal finance and cash flow, seasonality, weather issues, industry factors, competition, unemployment/job growth, exchange rates and consumer confidence index.
- **Social:** brand image, consumer buying behaviour, ethnic and religious factors, ethical issues, attitudes to work, work changes, staff attitudes and management culture.
- **Technological:** consumer technological needs, obsolescence, internet and social media trends.
- **Legal:** legislation relating to HR, consumer protection, health and safety, future legislation, competitive regulations and the environment.
- **Environmental:** local issues, regulations, market values and attitudes, and employee values, targets and policies for energy use and recycling.

These factors are uncontrollable, but operators still need to be aware of what factors may impact their businesses and to what extent. For example, an increase in the number of consumers eating vegetarian food in the UK will not impact smartphone developers but will impact food service operators.

The questions that need to be addressed are as follows.

- What are the PESTLE factors that may impact the business?
- How much of an impact – high, medium or low?
- Who or what is impacted?
- Positive or negative impact?
- If any, what response if needed?

Data relating to the external environment can be accessed through visiting relevant local websites, industry trend reports and local media.

Competitor analysis

Another form of research that is required is a review of the competition. The first step is to identify who is/are the competition? A competitor can be defined as another business that provides a similar product or service to the same target customers. Competition can be minor or very fierce, with many establishments fighting for customers. It is important for businesses to both know and keep a close eye on their competitors as, if competitors have an improved offer, they can achieve a competitive advantage and erode one's business. As competitors may change their offerings regularly it is important to ensure that monitoring is carried out frequently. Such monitoring can be carried out by visiting the competitor directly as a customer or, more discreetly, by viewing the offerings on its website or customer comments on sites such as TripAdvisor. Competition is healthy and good for customers; it will drive up standards and poor operators will potentially not survive.

The key objectives while monitoring the competition are to evaluate your own organisation's 'P' mix (see below) and compare it with that of competitors. By looking at competitors, the organisation can establish the positioning of its business in relation to competitors. From this research the business can respond, develop strategic objectives and differentiate accordingly. Kotler *et al.* (2014) state that 'A product's position is the place the product occupies, relative to competitors' products, in consumers' minds.'

Buyers make purchase decisions in different ways. Some make them based on price, product, special promotion or service. Some will choose one hotel over another just because of the in-room amenities; similarly, another buyer will go to a particular bar because the bar staff treat them well, use their name and make them feel special. Buyers will want different things at different times – however, if operators know what are important considerations for buyers when making a purchase decision the more of these the operator can provide, the greater its chances of being selected over the competition. It is this mix of motivations that must be observed when monitoring competition. Measuring in which areas and to what extent their proposition is better is important. Achieving differentiation is key, as if all products and services are the same or very similar, the competition intensifies and the pool of potential buyers is diluted. However, if businesses can identify areas where they can achieve a differentiated advantage, this increases their chances of attracting more customers. Areas where you have a differentiated product or service offer can be termed 'unique selling points' (USPs).

WEBLINK

Hospitality operations are using sophisticated technology to better understand customers, with the aim of achieving a competitive advantage. See:

www.revinate.com

Buyer motivations when visiting a restaurant

What motivates a buyer to visit a restaurant? It might be:

- food quality
- value
- service quality
- location
- convenience and facilities (e.g. car parking)
- atmosphere
- special promotions (e.g. happy hour).

SWOT analysis

Another tool that can be used to evaluate competition in terms of product or service is the SWOT model. It investigates strengths, weaknesses, opportunities and threats. The strengths and weaknesses focus on internal aspects of the business, while the opportunities and threats evaluate the external environment. Managers should regularly evaluate their businesses, at least every quarter.

Why use SWOT?

SWOT analysis can be used:

- to examine the positioning of one's business
- to respond and improve
- to remain competitive
- to set goals and objectives.

Table 13.1 Examples of SWOT areas

Strengths refer to the positive aspects of the establishment. For example:	Opportunities could include:
good reputation good location attractive environment comfortable restaurant	economic environment – people with high disposable incomes geographical – good, attractive area, good parking facilities attractive area good transport links demographic – increasing numbers of young professional people moving in to the area technological – availability of new equipment, good control systems available competition – little competition in the area
Weaknesses could refer to:	**Threats could include:**
declining market lack of staff training lack of investment no parking spaces	technological – out-of-date equipment competition decline in demand for product geographical – area becoming rundown, poorly kept area, difficult parking legislation – impact of new legislation, which means more bureaucracy

→ Market segmentation and the target market

When developing a business, an organisation needs to decide what type of individuals it is targeting to purchase its products and become customers. Is it looking for business or leisure? Male or female? People who are on a budget, or not? Once the desired customer has been established, then the business can develop its products and services to attract such individuals. Next, it should consider who is the target consumer, and what do they want and need from the business. For example, providing an expensive menu if you are targeting students will not work. When there is a mismatch between the target customer and product/service, dissatisfaction often occurs.

Some businesses have one product that attracts different segments, such as a business hotel that attracts business guests Monday to Friday and families at weekends. Similarly, some organisations, such as Accor, develop different types of hotels and brands to cater to the needs of different segments.

WEBLINK

Accor Hotels:

www.accorhotels-group.com/en/brands.html

Why segment?

Segmenting a market helps in:

- providing a clear focus for the business
- designing the product more precisely to match the needs of the target consumer
- creating price to meet income levels
- designing appropriate promotional campaigns and distribution policies
- identifying and understanding competitors
- effectively selecting and using available resources.

When identifying target segments the following factors should be considered.

- Who is my target customer? What is their profile?
- Accessibility – where can they be reached (Facebook, newspaper, etc.)?
- Adequate size (quantity) – is the pool of target consumers big enough to sustain a business?
- Is it sufficiently different – uniqueness, sustainable, competitive advantage?
- Durability and life cycle – how long will customers have a demand for the product?
- Qualification – will these consumers be profitable?
- Which competitors also target this type of consumer?
- Are there any external factors that may impact a decline in this target consumer?

Types of customer segment include:

- business
- 'MICE' – meetings, incentives, conference and exhibition delegates
- leisure/tourists – for the purpose of culture, history, conference, medical
- 'VFF' – visiting friends and family
- 'bleisure' (customers who combine both business and pleasure)
- 'SMERF' – social, military, educational, religious and fraternal.

As detailed in Table 13.2, there are different ways to segment a market.

Once the target customer has been identified, the organisation then develops its 'P' mix (product, price, promotion, place – see below) to cater to their specific needs. An example is provided in Table 13.3.

Table 13.2 Some market segmentation approaches

	Type of segmentation	Example	Organisations that may target this type of segment
Demographic	Age, gender, nationality, occupation	Organisations target predominantly males, between the ages of 30 and 55, who are at manager or director level with a bachelor's degree	City private dining clubs Mercedes Armani Samsonite
Geographic	Global, regional, national or local	Targeting people globally	Marriott Hilton McDonald's
Psychographic	Particular needs	People who are looking to be more healthy or to lose weight	Leisure clubs Diet products Organic restaurants

Table 13.3 An example of customer segment fit to 'P' mix

Customer type	Product	Price	Promotion (reach)	Place (distribution)
Business	Efficient and personalised standard of customer service High-quality products	High	Business magazines Business newspapers Business TV channels (e.g. CNN)	Corporate travel agents

The 'P' mix

The 'P' mix – also known as the marketing mix – covers the areas a business needs to focus on to effectively sell its product. These elements are driven and developed around the organisation's target customer. Traditionally there were four areas (the so-called '4Ps', as in Table 13.3), but as highlighted in Figure 13.2, this has now expanded to cover more 'Ps' (people, publicity, physical evidence and process have been added). The key aim is to ensure that all of these areas are delivered effectively to both attract and retain customers.

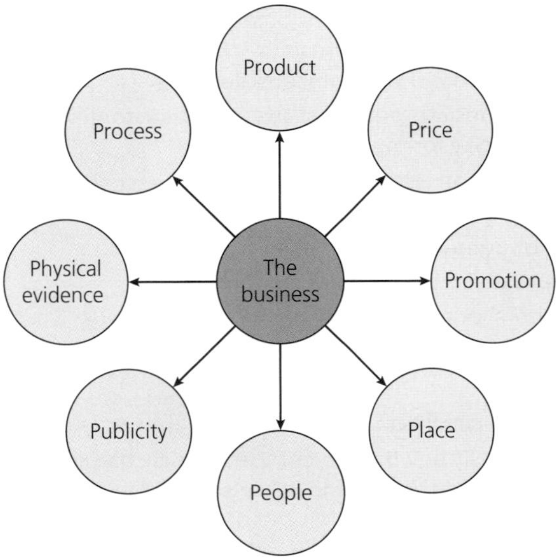

Figure 13.2 The new 'P' mix

These elements need to be continually monitored, evaluated, compared and adjusted to meet the internal and external requirements of the organisation. All of them need to be delivered effectively and simultaneously to successfully sell products and services. You can have effective products, at the right price and distributed in the right place, but if you are not promoting them effectively they will not sell.

The product

If you consider a restaurant, the product consists of three elements (see Figure 13.3), which are both tangible and intangible – tangible being the food, beverage, tables, decor, uniforms, toilets and the WiFi connection (actual product), intangible being the service, music, smells, other customers, plants, etc. (augmented). The core product in a restaurant is fulfilling the individual's basic need of hunger.

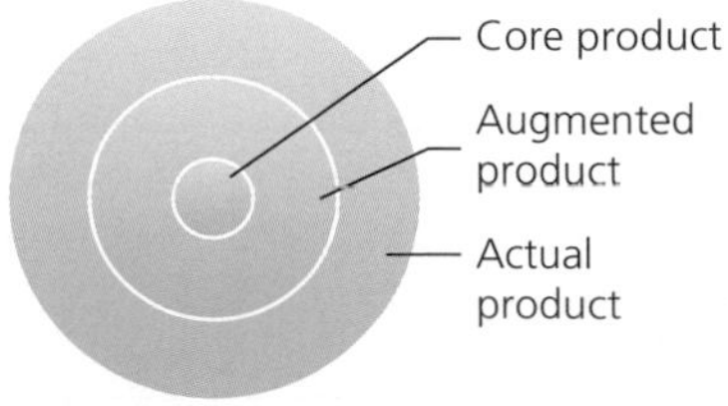

Figure 13.3 The product breakdown

It should be noted that to deliver a consistent and efficient product is a challenge for catering and hospitality operators as there are so many products that make up the total product offer. For example, a customer may have an excellent chicken curry, but if when they visit the toilets they are dirty, unhygienic and poorly equipped this will affect the customer's overall satisfaction with the whole visit. Similarly, an unstable, wobbly table can be very annoying. Therefore, operators need to put controls in place to ensure the product is 100 per cent at all times and without defect. Tools to assist in achieving a quality product include:

- constant evaluation of the product with customers, employees and external consultants
- standards of performance (SOPs)
- effective internal process – i.e. hazard analysis critical control point (HACCP)
- good leadership and supervision
- satisfied employees and a happy working environment
- a good understanding of your customers.

The product life cycle

When considering the product, another model to use is the product life cycle (PLC). This looks at the four different stages that all products progress through in the business cycle. It can be applied to any product – for example, a restaurant, hotel or even a mobile phone. All products go through four stages, as detailed in Figure 13.5: introduction, growth, maturity and decline. Imagine a new French restaurant in Dubai. During the introductory stage everything is new, shiny, up to date and in good working order. In the growth stage business increases and the physical product is well utilised (this can be the furniture, equipment and the employees). In the mature stage business has levelled off due to new competitors. The product is now looking a bit old in comparison with that of the competitors, who are at the introduction stage with more up-to-date products and facilities. During the decline stage the product starts to look dated, and the business struggles hard to attract customers and retain employees. Consider the mobile phone you bought three years ago; there are now newer phones being introduced to the market, which has moved your phone on a few stages. The goal for any product manufacturer or business is to be in the growth stage for as long as possible as this is when revenues are high and they are generating a profit. At the decline stage, they need to decide to either take the product off the market, or reinvest in it to make it more competitive and move it back into the growth stage. There are several hotels in London that in recent years have closed when they have reached the decline stage (such as the Savoy Hotel in the Strand), and have undergone extensive refurbishment to reopen and compete with other newer hotel properties in the luxury market.

WEBLINK

The Savoy, London:
www.fairmont.com/savoy-london

Products can change at any stage, based on the following factors.

- Competition – e.g. if a competitor lowers its prices the business may have to change its own product in order to compete.
- PESTLE factors – e.g. if there is a food scare in the market it may impact what product is offered.
- Seasonality – e.g. menus may change during winter and summer to reflect consumer needs.
- Availability of resources – e.g. perishable products may not be available and may have to be replaced.
- Usage – e.g. products also change from their initial condition with a high usage.
- Delivery – e.g. products can alter based on their delivery. For example, one chef may prepare a chef's salad differently to another.
- Obsolescence – this takes place when a product or service is no longer required by a group of consumers.

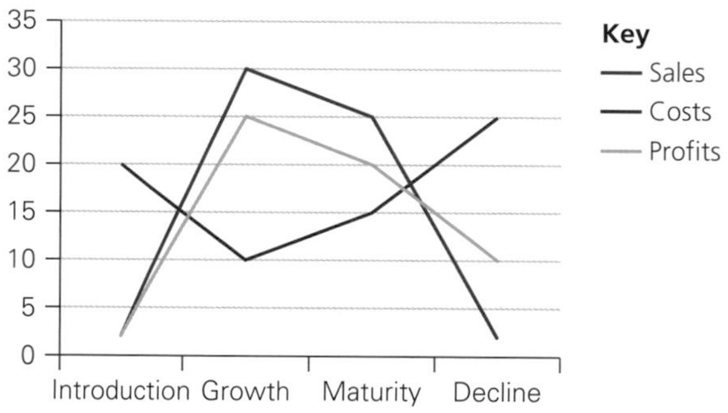

Figure 13.4 Trends in the product life cycle

Price

Good products need to be accompanied by a well-executed pricing strategy. Price can be defined as the amount a business charges to its customers in exchange for its products and services.

Different companies have different pricing strategies based on different factors. Some will implement a very high price and some very discounted. Generally, the basic premise with pricing is that if the product is priced too high in the minds of target consumers then it will potentially be a struggle to sell it. Similarly, if it is sold too low it may appear cheap and will be hard to achieve profits. Therefore the price positioning has to be right to achieve the desired business results. When setting prices the following factors should be considered:

- provide the desired price that the target customers are prepared to pay for the product
- cover production and operating costs
- achieve the desired profit
- achieve budgeted sales
- provide value in the minds of customers
- competitors' pricing strategies.

Pricing approaches

Competitive pricing

This looks carefully at what the competition is charging and aims to price at the same level, or sometimes at a slightly lower price. It is vital that the prices charged and the cost structure are compatible, otherwise this exercise is counteractive, unless it aims to damage the competition in the short term and grow customer loyalty.

Backward pricing

This requires an accurate estimate of what people are likely to spend in the future. The product and services are then designed to match what the market will bear – in other words, what the customer is prepared to pay for the product or service within that particular market segment.

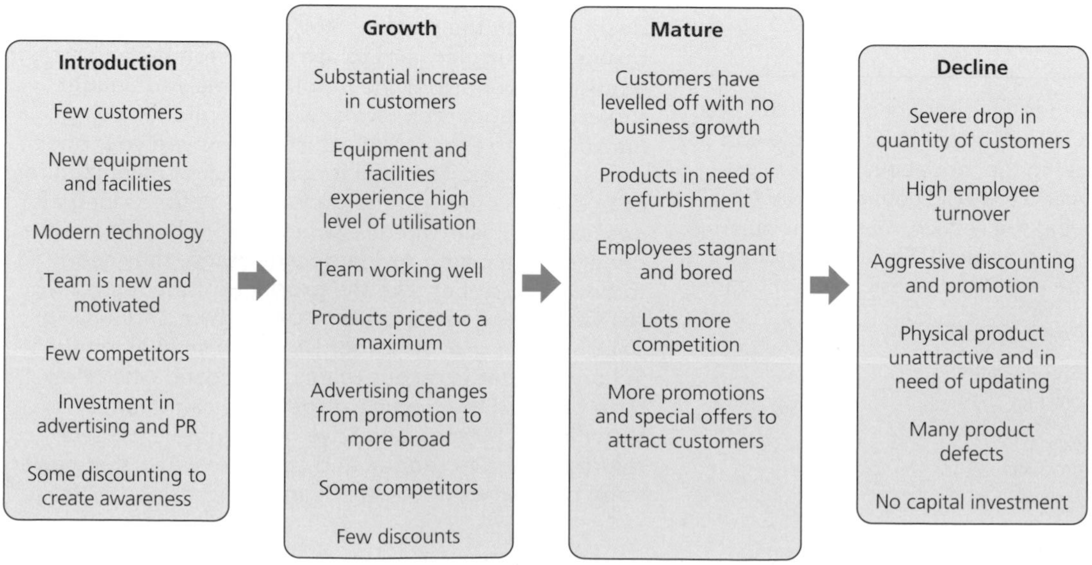

Figure 13.5 Changes in the product life cycle

Cost plus

This is where a set mark-up or a set percentage is added to basic costs. This approach is reasonably high risk. For example, if the price of the raw materials rises, then a cost-plus approach will mean that the price of the product or service will also have to rise – in some cases beyond the reach of the customer. For this reason many businesses adopt the backward-pricing approach.

Marginal pricing

This takes into account the actual costs a customer incurs in using the product or service; these costs include materials and energy costs. These are the direct costs. The customer is charged just over the direct costs, and so a contribution is made to the overhead costs. Overheads such as capital, insurance and staff costs have to be incurred whether or not the customer uses the product or service. This pricing is often used at weekends and off-season to sell hotel rooms, in the hope that the customer will purchase other products at a realistic price.

Discounts

Discounting is used to sell hotel rooms and hospitality products. It is used to maintain customer loyalty, increase the business, to attract repeat business, increase demand in off-peak periods and to encourage the prompt settlement of accounts.

Revenue management

With revenue management the concept is that the product price is not fixed and can vary according to demand. Consider a hotel that is situated close to a conference centre. When the conference centre hosts a large exhibition this attracts a high number of delegates from out of town that require accommodation. Therefore, if demand is predicted in advance the hotel can increase the price of the rooms to optimise revenue. Similarly, when demand is low (no conferences) room rates can be reduced to attract other segments. The basic concept is that, as rooms are highly perishable, it is best to sell a room even at a low price than to have an empty room.

However, this approach has been relatively slow to get off the ground in restaurants and food service operations. It should be remembered that restaurant seats are as perishable as hotel rooms and, if they are not sold, they cannot be re-sold, however the variable costs of the food, etc., remain the same unless deliberately reduced.

One of the biggest challenges with food and beverage operations is having fixed capacity but variable dining patterns, i.e. breakfast, lunch and dinner. Outside of the meal periods the operators are still required to pay for rent, staff and utilities, however there are few customers during this period. Therefore, attracting customers outside of these traditional meal periods will provide more of a curve in relation to customer business.

For example, one way to potentially overcome this challenge of perishability is for menu items to be adjusted depending on daily business trends. Figure 13.6 provides an example of a restaurant whereby a menu item is priced at £10. In a traditional restaurant this price remains the same throughout the day. However, if the price of the menu item were changed during low demand periods there is the potential to attract more customers. A similar case can be presented for food service operations to increase their menu prices during peak seasonal dates such as Christmas, Easter, Ramadan and Chinese new year, when demand for the dining product is high.

Promotion

During the promotion process the opportunity has to be generated whereby the buyer and seller come together.

Promotion is an activity that must be carefully planned and controlled. The main objective of the promotional campaign is to stimulate demand by using persuasive messages to attract new customers and past users of the establishment. Such messages must convince prospective customers that the product on offer represents good value for money. Promotion is concerned with the product. This product constitutes a total package on offer, and includes some of the following concepts:

- the image of the establishment
- the prices charged
- the quality of the product and service

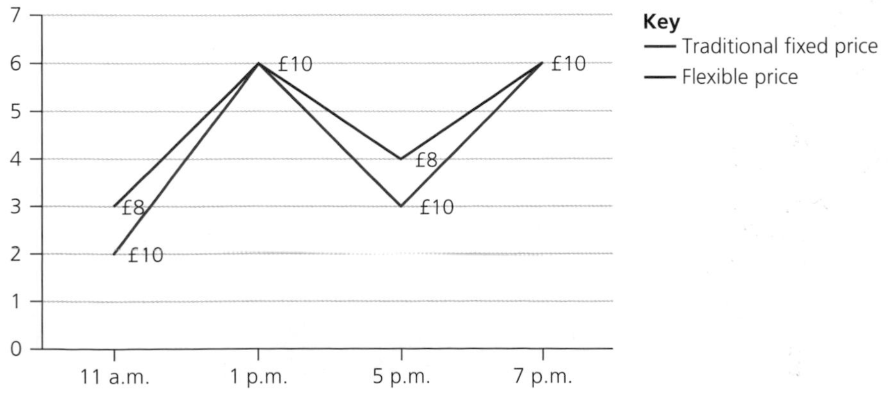

Figure 13.6 Traditional restaurant pricing versus revenue management approach

- the environment, facilities and services
- the style of management and staff.

Promotion should inform customers of the establishment, make them aware of its existence, persuade them to buy, and convince them of the image and quality of the product. This is done through the following methods.

- **Sales promotions:** short-term incentives encouraging the purchase or sale of a product or service.
- **Advertising:** paid form of non-personal presentation and promotion of ideas, goods or services.
- **Direct marketing:** interacting directly with consumers through various advertising media.
- **Public relations:** building good relations with various publics by obtaining favourable publicity in terms of image, rumours, stories, events.
- **Personal selling:** oral presentation to prospective purchasers to initiate sales, and to build and maintain relationships.

Why sales promotion?

Sales promotion is necessary for the following reasons:

- the perishability of the catering and hospitality product means demand must be manipulated
- most effective tool in the short-term manipulation of demand
- essential for the marketing of products
- use on a temporary basis to avoid price wars and the erosion of product quality
- shortfalls in demand – PESTLE factors, weather, exchange rate movements
- featured offers/special deals
- adding value, e.g. tangible advantages
- intention to achieve marketing objectives.

Some examples of sales promotion activities are:

- price cuts
- discount vouchers
- social media competitions
- Air Miles
- BOGOFs (buy one get one free)
- free gifts – e.g. Subway, McDonald's
- joint promotions between brands with the same target market
- free samples – tasters.

All promotions need to be well planned, with a clear business plan that addresses the following factors:

- promotion type and dates it will run
- promotion rationale
- promotion objectives
- costs and predicted sales
- measurement and evaluation.

Figure 13.7 An example of a promotion

Advertising

Advertising is paid communication to target customers with the aim of:

- informing
- persuading and altering beliefs
- reminding consumers and limiting post-purchase anxiety
- encouraging word-of-mouth or online communications to increase sales immediately
- creating greater public awareness of the location and existence of the promotion or organisation
- concentrating on the benefits and focusing on how the product differs from that of competitors.

Many organisations will have advertising budgets that detail:

- advertisement objective and rationale
- medium – e.g. online, radio, newspaper
- dates to be run
- target reach
- measurement
- cost and return on investment (ROI).

Advertising campaigns should:

- be creative and innovative
- be closely focused and targeted
- seize attention
- arouse curiosity
- be eye-catching
- be credible and truthful
- provide clear, tangible benefits
- be well written.

Advertising media

Kotler *et al.* (2014) explain that, 'Social media is changing how we market to customers, creating a powerful media for customers to interact with other customers and with organisations.' Businesses' advertising media have changed a lot since the introduction of the internet and social media. Traditional forms of print advertising (newspapers and magazines) are being eroded by online formats such as Facebook, Instagram, Pinterest, Twitter and YouTube, for example.

The selection of media depends on:

- objective – type of message
- advertising budget available
- target customer (where to reach them?)
- historical effectiveness of medium, e.g. last time we used radio how many enquiries and customers did it generate?
- competitors' advertising strategies.

Advertising media include:

- social media, e.g. Facebook, Instagram, LinkedIn, Twitter
- online, e.g. blogs, YouTube
- newspapers and periodicals
- posters and billboards
- flyers and brochures
- radio, TV, cinema and interactive TV
- transport, e.g. buses
- merchandising, e.g. pens
- banners and bunting
- text messages (SMS).

Social media and online marketing trends

Recommendations for catering and hospitality operators

Figure 13.8 details some of the key recommendations for catering and hospitality operators to adopt when using social media.

- Operators should be serious about social media – social media is not a fad.
- Operators need to advertise on social media networks where target customers are active.

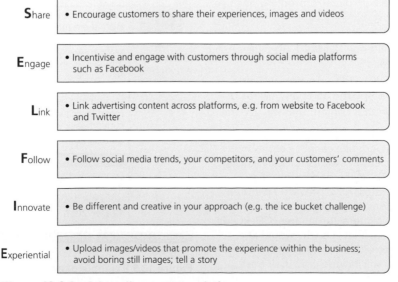

Share	• Encourage customers to share their experiences, images and videos
Engage	• Incentivise and engage with customers through social media platforms such as Facebook
Link	• Link advertising content across platforms, e.g. from website to Facebook and Twitter
Follow	• Follow social media trends, your competitors, and your customers' comments
Innovate	• Be different and creative in your approach (e.g. the ice bucket challenge)
Experiential	• Upload images/videos that promote the experience within the business; avoid boring still images; tell a story

Figure 13.8 Social media recommendations

- Content marketing – operators to set up Instagram, Flickr, Facebook, Twitter and other mobile apps, and encourage customers to like, check in and share.
- Get customers to use their smartphones to create user generated content (UGC) – have incentives for customers to create and upload/share visual content (Facebook, YouTube, etc.) such as photos and videos while visiting.
- Photography – provide competitions for customers and employees to create, edit, upload and share stylish pictures of the establishment.
- Engage – engage customers and followers on social media through asking questions and using stimulating content.
- Location based applications (LBAs) – use LBAs such as Foursquare to encourage customers to check in.
- Select hashtags (#) relevant to the company's brand.
- Pinterest – get customers to visually show off their images and videos.
- Online travel agents (OTAs) – be visible and promote across several OTAs.
- Customer-to-customer recommendations – be proactive in getting customers who have had positive experiences to go online and post an evaluation of their visit. This is known as the 'TripAdvisor effect' (see below) because the information comes from customers rather than from the establishment promoting itself.
- Response – ensure prompt response to any online comments, whether positive or negative.
- Create moving media – website should feature snippets or vignettes of videos communicating 'the experience' instead of boring, staged stills. Moving media creates more interest.
- Blog – create an online blog that tells a story.
- Good WiFi – do not compromise on WiFi connection and strength; today's consumers demand WiFi that is reliable and strong.
- Link – cross-post all postings across platforms (website, Facebook, blogs, etc.).
- Employee content – encourage employees to upload and share images of the workplace, promoting positive experiences.
- Optimisation – ensure content is optimised to work with different smartphones (iPhone, Android, BlackBerry), tablets and other devices.
- Invest in pay per click (PPC) – PPC provides valuable information on who is visiting the company's website.
- Be creative – be creative with content that will go viral.

One of the biggest challenges in catering and hospitality is that a travel or dining experience cannot be pre-trailed. For example, if a customer wants to book a hotel room they cannot go and lie on the bed before they purchase. In the past, operators have provided pictures accompanied by descriptions of the product on their websites and advertising collateral (brochures, CD-ROMs, etc.). However, the concern with this is why would any operator put negative descriptions or bad photos on their advertising material? They will include only their best photos and content to provide the best impression to motivate the shopper to reserve or book that restaurant seat or hotel. But is this really a truthful representation of the organisation? There are many reports of customers arriving and saying that a venue is not like the advertising on the brochure or website. TripAdvisor (see below) and other travel booking sites have reduced the amount of risk when booking a trip or reserving a restaurant seat.

WEBLINK

The Consumer Protection from Unfair Trading Regulations 2008 (CPUT) protect consumers against unfair or misleading marketing practices by organisations:

www.legislation.gov.uk/uksi/2008/1277/pdfs/uksi_20081277_en.pdf

The TripAdvisor effect

Kotler *et al.* (2014) explain: 'A growing part of the new customer dialogue is consumer generated marketing, by which consumers themselves are playing a bigger role in shaping their own brand experiences and those of others. This might happen through uninvited consumer to consumer exchanges in blogs, video sharing sites, and other digital forums.'

Third-party sites such as TripAdvisor now encourage customers after their stay or visit to post comments online. These comments can be either positive or negative, and can provide insight into areas such as service, quality, facilities and value. Similarly, customers can rate their experience on a sliding scale, which then provides an overall average rating from all customers.

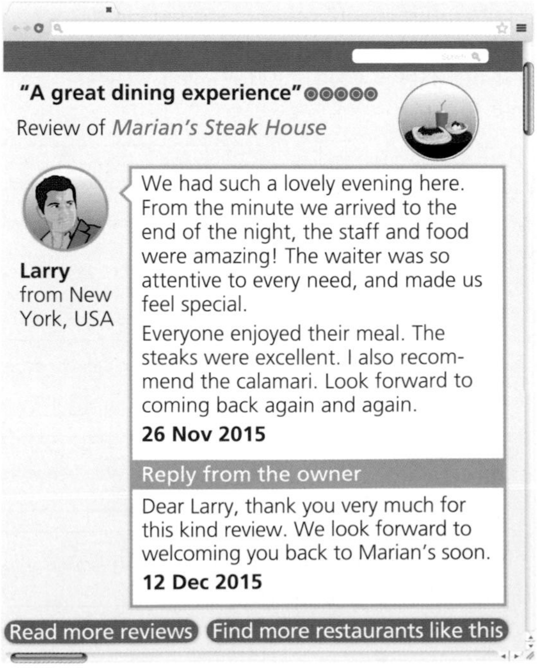

Figure 13.9 Example of an online customer hotel review

Table 13.4 Evaluation of customer online reviews

Advantages for customers	Challenges for customers	Advantages for organisation	Challenges for organisation
For customers – the power to reflect and leave feedback at post-purchase stage For buyers – the ability to make more informed purchase decisions based on customer feedback	Not always truthful	If positive, can be an effective marketing tool for the organisation Very influential tool when customers are deciding whether to book or not Power of this feedback potentially improves overall standards within the industry Useful feedback to either improve or as a promoter Can use feedback to identify strengths, weaknesses, opportunities and threats (from feedback in competitors' reviews)	Often feedback is provided when the customer has left the premises, so it can be too late to fix a problem face to face Competitors can view feedback and create strategies to take advantage of strengths and weaknesses The need to respond promptly to feedback and attempt service recovery

What is becoming apparent is that online shoppers trust these customer-to-customer posts more than company websites. This therefore, reduces the level of risk for a bad experience and assists in informing potential customers with a better, more accurate image and overview of the company.

In addition, a trend towards providing feedback is now being used more inside the organisation. For example, an app on a tablet can be used to showcase a wine list in a restaurant and customers can leave online reviews immediately. For example:

> **1978 Chablis – 'This wine was excellent and goes very well with the restaurant's seafood fricassée. Highly recommended and great value.' Peter – London, UK**

Place

Place refers to the channel of distribution of the product. It focuses on 'where' potential consumers can purchase the product or service. For example, when booking a hotel room consumers can purchase it through social media, hotel websites (i.e. Google Hotel Finder, TripAdvisor, Trivago, KAYAK and Expedia), travel agents, over the counter, tourist offices or via central reservations systems (CRS).

The simple formula is that, the more channels of distribution a business has, this increases the opportunity for consumers to purchase the product. If a hotel sells only over the counter then it is limiting its potential to be seen. Each channel has strengths and weaknesses, with different costs involved that will impact both the organisation's profit and the customer's pocket.

Global marketing and development

With the rise of the global markets, many catering and hospitality organisations are expanding overseas following in the steps of companies like McDonald's. Examples include Starbucks, Nando's, Zuma, Hilton and many more.

Some of the benefits for catering and hospitality organisations that internationalise are as follows:

- develop brand awareness in new destinations
- access to new revenues that may have been absorbed in the home economy (see Table 13.5)
- achieving economies of scale
- competitive advantage
- new customers
- familiarity for existing customers who travel.

Some challenges to internationalisation may include poor acceptance in the new market and the need to adapt the product to cater to the local market's needs, which may impact the brand standards.

As detailed in Figure 13.10 and Table 13.5, the Ansoff matrix highlights the different strategies that organisations can adopt when selling their products.

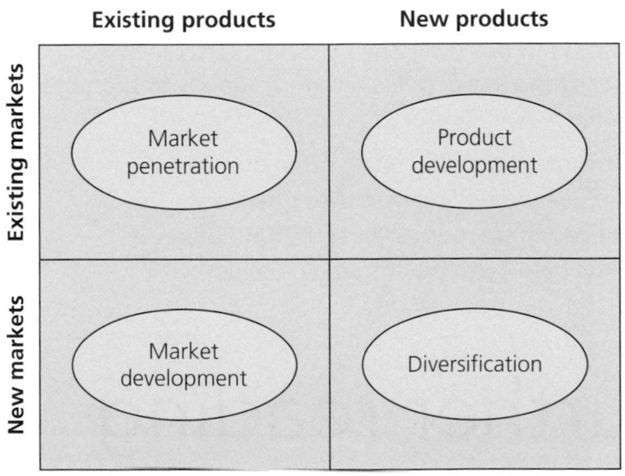

Figure 13.9 The Ansoff matrix

Table 13.5 Ansoff matrix breakdown

Strategy	Rationale	Risk
Company sells existing products to existing customers	Market penetration – this is a low-risk strategy as the company focuses purely on providing good products to customers that it knows well	Low
Company sells existing products to new markets	Market development – the reason for this is that perhaps demand at home is saturated and so a company looks for new markets; many hospitality and catering companies have adopted this strategy – for example, Nando's, Pizza Hut, Domino's Pizza, who can be seen in many international destinations	Medium
Company sells new products to existing customers	Product development – current product sales are in decline so the company decides to create and sell new products to its existing customers; as highlighted previously in the PLC model, all products have a life cycle and so organisations need to adjust their product mix to ensure they are providing products that their customers want. The McCafé (a brand of McDonald's) is an example of this; when the coffee culture started, McDonald's saw an opportunity and created a new café brand, which it sold to existing customers	Medium
Company sells new products to new markets	Diversification – company is innovative and diverse in its products, continually creating new products in new markets; examples of companies that follow this strategy are Accor and Virgin	High

Sales

When the 'P' mix has been analysed and delivered effectively, selling the product is much easier.

Personal selling

Personal selling is done through contacts with local businesses and committees, for example, or, more directly, through senior restaurant staff talking to clients. All employees who are in contact with customers must be made aware of the importance of selling the products to increase profits and provide a satisfactory experience for the customer.

Some large organisations will have a dedicated sales team that prospect and follow leads, contact and visit potential customers. In addition, all staff must therefore gain a good knowledge of the company's products and services, and develop good social skills, having an ability to promote and sell.

The advantages of personal selling are:

- effective in building up buyer preference
- involves interaction and assessment of needs
- builds long-term trusting relationships
- buyer feels a greater need to be attentive and respond.

The disadvantages are:

- developing an effective sales team requires long-term strategic planning
- sales personnel can be expensive.

Upselling and suggestive selling

It is the responsibility of all employees to sell in the workplace. In some positions it is the core focus, whereas with others it is just one part of their job description. Upselling and suggestive selling are used interchangeably, with the purpose of increasing customer spend. Examples include:

For just an extra £20 you can have a deluxe bedroom – *Receptionist*

Do you have any clothes for dry cleaning? – *Room maid*

Our in-house Spanish restaurant is excellent. Can I make a reservation for you? – *Concierge*

Is that a large gin and tonic, sir? – *Barman*

Can I suggest a lovely pavlova to complete your meal this evening? – *Restaurant server*

Further reading

Kotler, P., Bowen, J. and Makens, J. (2014) *Marketing for Hospitality and Tourism*, 6th edn. Pearson.

The most important hotel marketing trends to watch:

www.slideshare.net/kornfeind/the-most-important-hotel-marketing-trends-to-watch-in-2015?qid=201170b9-17fa-439a-87dd-71ee14a3de23&v=qf1&b=&from_search=1

CIM definition of marketing:

www.slideshare.net/stephendann/chartered-institute-of-marketing-definition?qid=6d1b7d2c-b2e2-48e9-b54e-e80fcf681d1a&v=default&b=&from_search=4

Topics for discussion

1 Carry out research and identify the key PESTLE factors impacting a city hotel in your home town.
2 As manager of a local nightclub you are under pressure to attract more customers on weeknights. Using IT, create an eye-catching promotional advert that could be used to attract more customers.
3 Visit the Facebook page of a local restaurant. Identify five ways in which it could be improved in order to, in turn, improve the restaurant's 'P' mix.
4 Visit five hotel websites. Looking at the websites, note down profiles of the types of customer they are attracting.
5 List five ways that YouTube could be used to promote a small independent restaurant.

14 Customer service

The importance of good customer service, and how to achieve it

Many employees in hospitality and catering may have the opportunity to come into contact with customers. For some, such as receptionists and food servers, it will be a regular aspect of their job. Employees called upon to serve and interact with customers need to be aware of how to achieve customer satisfaction.

The first thing to remember is that a smile gets both the customer and the employee off to a good start. Take a food service situation, whereby it is important to realise that excellent food is only the first essential to satisfy the customer: the finest food can be spoiled if served by uncaring employees. Technical skills and techniques are very important, but equally (or perhaps more) important are sincere caring attitudes and manners, with the food served in an environment that has an atmosphere that makes customers feel at ease, wanted and welcome.

Remember:

- put the customer first
- make them feel good
- make them feel comfortable
- make them feel important
- make them want to return to your restaurant or establishment
- make them comment positively about their experience.

As indicated in Table 14.1, achieving customer satisfaction is paramount to the growth and profitability of any business. If operators fail to deliver a good level of customer service this can result in negative word of mouth, a drop in profits and potential closure.

Table 14.1 Contrast between the impacts of good and poor customer service

Good customer service	Poor customer service
Fewer complaints	More complaints
Customer satisfaction	Customer dissatisfaction
Customer retention	Lose customers to competitors
Attract customers	Challenge to attract
Staff satisfaction and high retention	Staff dissatisfaction and low retention
Greater productivity	Less productivity
Good reputation and image	Bad reputation and poor image
Positive online reviews and word of mouth	Negative online reviews and word of mouth
Lower costs	Higher costs
Increase market share	Lose market share
Brand growth	Brand devalues
Profit	Loss
Growth	Decline
Open	Close

Customer dissatisfaction occurs primarily when the service provider does not meet the customer's expectations. The level to which the organisation meets the customer's expectation determines the extent to which satisfaction is achieved, as highlighted in Figure 14.1.

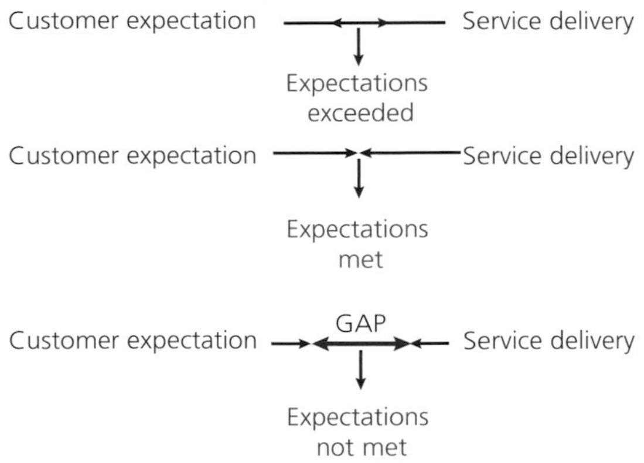

Figure 14.1 Customer satisfaction

'Wow moments'

As highlighted in Figure 14.1, there are three main outcomes in customer satisfaction: not satisfied, satisfied and extremely satisfied. When customers' expectations are exceeded these are sometimes termed 'wow moments' or 'moments of truth'. These can occur in budget and mid-range establishments, but are experienced more frequently in high-quality operations such as five-star hotels or Michelin restaurants. The objective for any operator is to achieve this level of satisfaction as often as possible.

➜ Quality challenges in hospitality and catering

Meeting the needs of customers in hospitality and catering is a challenge, as Table 14.2 highlights.

Table 14.2 Challenges in achieving customer service

Challenge	Explanation	Potential solutions
Customers are all different, with different expectations based on past experiences, culture and particular situations	Carry out research to establish the needs, wants and expectations of your target customers	Create service standards to meet these needs and expectations Employees to be empowered to adjust standards to achieve customer satisfaction
Employees can be inconsistent	Employees can impact customer satisfaction through their moods and inconsistencies. For example, one day the receptionist can provide great customer service as she has just received some good news from home. Similarly, the same employee can provide less than good service the next day, as she is feeling unwell	Recruit the most qualified individuals Train and employees in service standards, and monitor them
Simultaneous production and consumption	In hospitality and catering the time between production and consumption is very short, which provides challenges in relation to quality control. For example, a customer could order a dish at 1pm and it could be served at 1.20pm. Therefore, the product has been created in 20 minutes, which can leave little time for quality control	Standards of performance Quality control checks Good supervision
No pre-trial	When consuming hospitality and catering products it is not always possible to pre-try the product. For example, a customer wanting to order a burger cannot try the burger first and then decide whether they will order it or not. There are exceptions. For example, it is often possible to have a small sample of a craft beer before making an order	Communicate honestly and accurately about the product being provided. Product pictures and videos assist with this

Challenge	Explanation	Potential solutions
Volatile business levels due to external environment	Many external factors can impact the business levels of operators. These may include increased competition, external events, promotions and weather. For example, a coach full of tourists may stop randomly and decide to have lunch in your restaurant. This may cause service problems, as there may not be sufficient staff on duty	Have contingencies in place Good management and supervision Employee cross-training Positive, responsive work ethos
Uncertainty	In most situations customers can order anything from the menu	Managers/supervisors/chefs must have a good understanding of their business levels/trends Good internal processes, effective employees and mis-en-place
Other customers	Other customers sharing the facility can also cause existing customers to be dissatisfied. This for example maybe a group of intoxicated customers behaving rowdily on the next table	Procedures for handling difficult guests and difficult situations

Table 14.3 details some of the common issues that cause customer dissatisfaction when staying in hotels or dining in catering outlets.

Table 14.3 Common areas of dissatisfaction in hospitality and catering

Restaurant	Service: long waits to be seated, poor welcome, poor table location, slow service, too fast service, inattentive service, rude service, menu items not available Food: not what was expected, poor taste, wrong temperature, undercooked or overcooked, disappointed with portion size or presentation Atmosphere: too hot, too cold, too smoky, too loud, too crowded Facilities: old or damaged furniture, fixtures and facilities, dirty utensils and tables, sticky menus, poor hygiene, dirty toilets, poorly equipped (no toilet paper or hand soap) Value for money: too expensive, not worth the money, service charges when poor service has been received
Front office	Reception: long waits, slow check-in, room not available due to overbooking, room not ready, type of room not suitable, slow check-out, incorrect bill, inattentive service
Accommodation	Bedrooms: too small, smelly, dirty, stuffy, old, noisy, poor view, uncomfortable, poorly maintained

Considering these challenges, it is therefore imperative that organisations use a selection of methods, tools and strategies to assist in achieving customer satisfaction. These might include:

- good products
- high standards of performance
- external quality schemes
- leadership and supervision
- internal processes
- customer complaint handling and service recovery
- employee recruitment and ongoing effective training
- internal and external research.

Although, as noted in the list above, effective complaint handling is essential, it is preferable to avoid cause for complaint in the first place, for the following reasons:

- 96 per cent of dissatisfied customers do not go back and complain, but they do tell between 7 and 11 other people how bad your restaurant or service is
- 13 per cent will tell at least 20 other people
- 90 per cent will never return to your restaurant
- it costs roughly five times as much to attract a new customer as it does to keep an existing one.

Attracting customers costs a great deal in terms of investment in advertising and marketing, so to lose them is a big loss financially. Customers nowadays have so many choices to switch to competing organisations that retaining them must be treated as a key goal in customer service management.

Customer complaint handling

Complaints can be channelled to operators face to face, via email, telephone or online. Figure 14.2 details the recommended steps for employees to follow when dealing with a customer complaint.

When following the LEARN process illustrated in Figure 14.2 is it important to also note the guidelines detailed in Table 14.4.

Service recovery

Service recovery is the process of converting an unhappy customer into a happy customer. Following the LEARN steps in Figure 14.2 will assist in achieving this goal. If the customer is still not satisfied with how the complaint has been dealt with, the employee should inform a senior staff member immediately. It is then that individual's responsibility to assess and try to do whatever it takes to ensure the customer leaves satisfied.

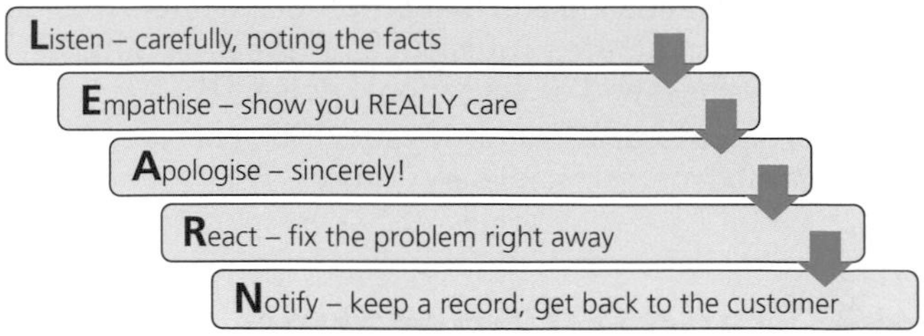

Figure 14.2 Steps in dealing with customer complaints

Who deals with complaints?

In most establishments it is the supervisor or manager who deals with complaints. However, this is sometimes not practical as they may not always be available due to other commitments, such as meetings etc. It is therefore good practice to train subordinates in complaint-handling procedure. This way the customer's grievance is dealt with immediately, without adding further anxiety to the situation.

Table 14.4 Dos and don'ts when dealing with complaints

Do:	Don't:
show empathy and use appropriate body language (e.g. show concern on your face, nod)	say 'It's not my fault'
use their name, when possible	say 'You're the fifth today to complain about that'
stop talking and listen, and use body language to show that you are listening (e.g. eye contact)	interrupt – it will only add to their upset
take notes	jump to conclusions
let them make their case	accept responsibility until you are sure it's your organisation's fault
ask questions to clarify the details	be patronising
recapitulate; confirm with them that you've got it right	argue
sympathise (regardless of where the blame lies)	lose your temper
gather together your version of the facts before replying	blame others
apologise profusely if your company is at fault	
tell them what you propose to do	
give them alternatives to choose from, if your company is at fault	
offer more than the bare minimum (e.g. make some concession on 'future business')	
get their full agreement that this will resolve the issue	
make sure that it is done properly and that they are kept fully informed	
contact them very soon afterwards to make sure they are happy	
see it as an opportunity to cement the relationship and encourage more business	

Employee recruitment and management

Considering the reliance on employees within hospitality and catering, effective human resource management is critical in achieving customer satisfaction. Some initiatives to assist in achieving this are:

- effective recruitment and right employee fit – selecting applicants based on job specification, reference checks, multiple hurdles strategy (see Chapter 15)

- employee readiness – ensure employees are equipped with the right skills to perform the job
- effective scheduling and manpower planning – supervisors to ensure sufficient employees on duty to meet business and organisational demands
- supervisors to deal promptly with employee dissatisfaction or disciplinary issues
- employee satisfaction – ongoing training, autonomy (empowerment), safe and friendly environment, sufficient tools to perform duties, regular evaluation, recognition and competitive remuneration
- build strong teams – sharing and consultative culture, social events, bottom-up culture, ethical practices, opportunities for progression.

Standard operating procedures (SOPs)

Imagine you visit your local sandwich bar and, each time you order the same club sandwich meal, it is served differently: sometimes on brown bread, sometimes on white, sometimes with French fries, sometimes with jacket potatoes, sometimes with ketchup, sometimes accompanied with mayonnaise ... How would you feel as the customer?

A lack of standardised procedures can cause many organisations to fail as a result of a lack of consistency and control, which ultimately leads to dissatisfied customers. Companies such as McDonald's have achieved their success due to the standardisation of all processes. However, some organisations feel that having standards constrains employees in terms of their ability to respond to different situations outside the set standards. For example, if the standard for a tuna sandwich is to serve it on white bread but the customer requests brown, what should the employee do?

Standard operating procedures (SOPs) are standardised procedures for operational and administrational tasks, put in place by the organisation to achieve greater consistency in achieving set goals. The benefits of SOPs are as follows.

For managers/supervisors.

- detailed steps for individual tasks, which allows for greater control in the service process
- procedures to enforce, train and monitor
- measuring employee performance
- financial control in relation to time and resource cost allocation per task
- procedures for internal and external parties to evaluate against.

For employees:

- clear guidelines and steps to follow on the job.

For customers:

- greater consistency
- greater satisfaction.

Most established and chain organisations have a large manual of standards for all of their operational tasks. This is the key document that underpins the whole philosophy and mission of the organisation, and that drives the success of the business. It details all tasks pertaining to running the business and would need to be continually adjusted to reflect their changing operating environments. Some areas in which standards are created with the aim of achieving success include:

- customer satisfaction
- sales maximisation
- cost minimisation
- administration and procedures.

Examples where SOPs may be created include:

- how to wear your uniform correctly
- how to answer the telephone
- how to set up a lunch buffet
- how to deal with an online customer complaint
- how to carry out an employee appraisal
- how to reconcile departmental accounts at the end of a shift
- how to prepare a chicken curry
- how to prepare a Coca-Cola
- how to serve a mojito cocktail.

Some of the challenges of SOPs include:

- considering the amount of tasks in any hospitality and catering operation, the task of writing and developing standards is a time-consuming job
- SOPs do not guarantee quality – they need to be delivered correctly and monitored regularly in order to achieve quality
- SOPs are sometimes too rigid and can cause frustration for customers – for example, a customer may want to swap the French fries for salad with a burger; therefore organisations and employees need to have guidelines with regard to how to deal with such situations while still achieving consistency and customer satisfaction.

Internal and external research

Ongoing research is imperative to:

- identify customer needs and wants
- create and evaluate service standards
- assist in identifying service defects.

Through research, organisations can establish the needs and wants of their target customers. This can be carried out internally through methods such as questionnaires and observations, or externally through market trend information and reports. Customer needs change over time so it is important that organisations continually monitor their customers to ensure that they are kept satisfied. For example, consumers nowadays have a high dependence on technology and so organisations need to provide facilities that allow their customers to stay connected. Similarly, more and more UK residents are now vegetarian or following other specific diets, so menus should reflect this trend. Failing to provide what customers want will result in a drop in customer numbers. In addition, business customers have different needs to leisure customers, as detailed in Table 14.5. Similarly, Chinese customers, for example, have different needs to customers from the Middle East because there are differences of culture and habit. Many organisations have different target customers, so this sometimes becomes a challenge.

In order to find out customers' needs and wants various methodologies can be used. Table 14.6 provides an overview and evaluation of some of these approaches.

Table 14.5 Examples of customer expectations of a hotel

	Price	Service	Food and beverage needs	Accommodation needs
Business guests	High	High standard, fast and discreet	High level of food and beverage on menus, personalised service, fine dining option, conference rooms	Wi-Fi, express check-in/check-out, executive room, access to executive lounge, leisure club
Families (with teenager and young infant)	Average	Good standard	Kids' meals, healthy and nutritious food options, set menus	Interconnecting rooms, Wi-Fi, rollaway bed, baby-sitting service
Budget travellers, e.g. students	Low	Basic	Promotions, happy hours	Shared, basic, Wi-Fi

Table 14.6 Evaluation of research methods

Research tool	Description and application	Strengths for operators	Weaknesses
Customer Surveys/ questionnaires	Questions are created to gain feedback on the product, service and overall experience Frequently used to evaluate food service or accommodation Most effective when anonymous	Can be designed quickly to evaluate any service Relatively easy and affordable to create Nowadays, e-surveys can be created and emailed direct to customers Many customers would prefer to write than speak out	Very common so completion rate can be poor Unhappy customers have normally left before feedback is received Time constraints (people in a rush) can result in customers providing unreliable feedback
Focus groups	Groups of individuals participate to discuss a product, service or theme; can be used to gain feedback, new ideas or opinion	Can be informative if executed well with the right group of individuals	Can take time to organise participants Data collected can be a bit challenging to analyse
Observations	Observation of customers, employees and the operation by managers/supervisors while on the job (See also garbage survey, page 350)	Useful to establish quickly the strengths and weaknesses in the operation, and the customer's experience Managers/supervisors to identify service and product problems/improvements while in outlets	Lack of evidence
Face-to-face interviews/verbal exchanges	Common interactions between employees and customers	An instant way to acquire customer feedback during or at the end of a customer's visit	When dissatisfied, customers may not be truthful as it is easier to just leave without a fuss but never return This feedback frequently does not get recorded and passed on to managers

Research tool	Description and application	Strengths for operators	Weaknesses
Online customer reviews/comments, e.g. Tripadvisor.com	Customers write comments based on their experience (see Figure 14.2)	Very influential with potential customers as comments tend to be more truthful than marketing information on organisations' websites	Need to be monitored closely by employee in organisation and dealt with promptly It is important to keep up to date with social media to show other customers that the organisation is responsive
Employee feedback	Managers/supervisors talk to employees to acquire feedback on how the customer service experience went and can be improved	Can be ongoing and informative Examples include end-of-shift briefings and service meetings	Normally quite informal and therefore undocumented
Management data	Internal, secondary data such as reports on customer discounts, voids/refunds, tips and bestselling items	A quick way to get a picture of a trend, problem or opportunity Can flag up issues and provide important feedback on performance	The data are quantitative in nature so may lack the depth to explain why something is happening

Garbage or waste survey

This is a useful management tool to establish how satisfied restaurant customers are with their food. Food service or kitchen managers position themselves by the dish-wash area to observe what food is being returned on the plates. Whatever is left on plates can be a useful form of feedback – for example, too many vegetables being left may mean too big a portion, bad taste, too much salt or poor cooking. With this knowledge, managers can then approach customers to ask more probing questions relating to why they have left the food on their plates.

Personalised service: knowing your customers

Knowing the needs and wants of your target customers, as detailed in Figure 14.3, is essential. However, many high-class hospitality and catering organisations are taking this a step further and collecting details of the specific needs and wants of their regular customers. Over time, data on customer behaviour and consumption are stored to provide a more personalised and bespoke service during their next visit. Knowing your customers' specific needs can enhance customer satisfaction, increase loyalty and positive word of mouth, and lead to more 'wow moments'.

Table 14.7 Examples of research tool uses in hospitality and catering

Research tool	Uses in food and beverage	Uses in rooms division
Customer survey	Can be used to evaluate customer satisfaction in the areas of restaurant, bar, room service, conference and banqueting Specific areas measured are normally product, service, atmosphere, cleanliness and value for money Typically the survey is left for the customer to complete in the area where consumption has taken place	Can be used to evaluate customer satisfaction in the areas of reception, concierge, housekeeping and laundry Specific areas to be measured are normally product, service and cleanliness Typically the survey is left for the customer to complete in the room or on check-out Increasingly surveys are automatically generated on check-out and sent to customers' via email to complete
Focus groups	Useful when planning new menus; groups of individuals can be organised to discuss current menu, its strengths and weaknesses Group members can also be invited back during tasting to comment on portion size, presentation, taste and value for money	Useful when planning the design of new room facilities, e.g. new bedrooms. Individuals can provide feedback on current room design strengths and weaknesses. Similarly, they can contribute ideas around what they would like to see in the new bedrooms in relation to layout, theme, colours, fabrics, furnishings and equipment
Face-to-face interview	Both waiters and chefs have the opportunity during and at the end of a meal to ask the customer to what extent they were satisfied with their meal	Receptionists and duty managers, during a customer's visit and on check-out, can ask them to what extent they were satisfied with their stay

Title	First Name	Last Name	Birthday	Email	Likes	Dislikes	Notes
Mr	Robert	Allsworth	16/04/1962	rallsworth@imc.ie	Room 204, The Times newspaper, Budweiser beer, extra portions of Earl Grey tea in room	Seafood, bedspread, allergic to fresh flowers so remove from room	Hard of hearing
Mr	Ashley	Abbott	12/02/1968	ashley68@ipg.com	Room 201, duck pillows, extra decaffeinated coffee in room, extra towels	Completing registration card on check-in, slow service, desk near the corner (HK to move closer to the window)	Works for large hotel company so expects a high standard of service and knows the business well
Mrs	Jane	Lee	22/12/1962	lee88@24455.com	Extra hangers in wardrobe, Chinese tea sachets in room, USA Today newspaper	None	Frequently gets late flight to SF so often needs a late check-out

Figure 14.3 Example of a customer database

Other information that may be included on a customer database is employer name, Twitter account, Facebook page, Skype address and number of visits. All this information could be used by the organisation for sales and marketing purposes.

As detailed in Table 14.8, external sources can also be used to assist in providing better service to customers.

Table 14.8 External data tools to assist with customer service

Research tool	Description and uses	Strengths	Weaknesses
Trade articles and reports	To identify current trends that may have an impact on the organisation, e.g. more people eating healthy food or ordering online	Reliable research	Some trend data are costly and hard to access
Mystery customers/ shoppers	External experts employed to discreetly evaluate the organisation's products and service from a customer perspective To measure any gaps in the service standards	Valid, unbiased, reliable and informative reviews by industry experts Can be bespoke for a particular organisation Reports that can be disseminated and used as an improvement tool	Can be costly

Ongoing and effective training

As detailed in Chapter 15 employee training is imperative to any hospitality and catering organisation. Dealing with people is a highly complex skill; we train people to use complicated machinery but we do not often consider training employees to deal with the most complex machinery of all: the human being.

There are many reasons why training needs to take place – for example, as new employees join the company, or when new processes or standards need to be implemented. Training can be structured or ad hoc (i.e. as and when required). For example, if a young chef has prepared some food that resulted in a customer complaining then corrective action should be taken and on-the-job training offered immediately to prevent the same error taking place again. It is good for customers to see training in the workplace as it demonstrates professionalism, investment in employees and general care. Training also needs to be effective, and managers/supervisors should be qualified in how to train their subordinates effectively.

Customer service training

In addition to day-to-day, ongoing training, more specific customer care training should be carried out with all employees. The following areas could be covered.

- **Personal presentation and grooming** – How you look immediately creates an impression. Creased and stained uniform, untidy hair and body odour will make a negative impression. Always be neat and tidy. Remember, you never get a second chance to make a first impression. What you wear and how you look are part of how potential customers judge your organisation. You are part of the company's image.

- **Smile** – Working in an international industry, a genuine smile will always be well received when greeting or dealing with customers. If dealing with a complaint, a smile can immediately help the situation.
- **Attentiveness** – Attend to customers' needs promptly and with a sense of urgency. No customer likes waiting and time wasting, so try to attend to questions and solve problems efficiently. If you are attending to someone else when another customer needs your assistance, simply acknowledge their presence and inform them that you will be with them shortly.
- **Friendliness** – Talking to customers about their visit or experience is a good way to relax them.
- **Helpfulness** – Eagerness to help when you see customers disorientated or unsure is what hospitality and catering is all about. First-time visitors may need extra help to assist them in familiarising themselves with the facilities and services.
- **Manners** – Always say 'please' and 'thank you'; be courteous and polite in your dealings. Treat customers as you would like to be treated yourself.
- **Use the customer's name** ('Good evening, Mr Tan') – When engaged in a conversation make an effort to use the customer's name as much as possible. Discreetly referring to credit cards, luggage tags and business cards can help with this.
- **Communication** – Remember, good verbal and written communication is important when dealing with customers. When talking face to face be clear, not too loud, and never condescending or too close. When messaging, texting or emailing, consider tone, grammar and spelling. Avoid emoticons, slang and jargon.
- **Distance** – Each person, according to their culture, has around them an area they regard as their personal space. Beware of intruding into a customer's personal space. Although some customers may regard this as friendliness, you may make others feel uncomfortable.
- **Attitude and behaviour** – When dealing with customers, behaviour should be:
  - welcoming – it can satisfy a customer's basic human desire to feel liked and be approved of
  - caring – make each customer feel special
  - confident – it can increase a potential customer's trust in you
  - empathy – understanding what it is like to be a customer
  - enthusiastic – it can be contagious
  - helpful – customers warm to helpful employees
  - patient – learn to be patient with all customers
  - understanding – customers in a restaurant want a service and are paying for it; learn to understand their needs.

Examples of good customer care phrases may include:

- 'I'll take care of that for you right away'
- 'I'll go and get it for you myself'
- 'I would be glad to help you'
- 'I don't know, but I'll find out now. Please take a seat for a moment'
- 'I'm sorry to hear about that. Let's find out what went wrong and I'll put it right'
- 'I'm sorry for the delay. I'll check with the kitchen to see how long your order will be'
- 'Let me show you to the elevators. Please follow me sir/madam'
- 'Is there anything else I can help you with?'
- 'We are here to improve, so please tell us about your visit today'

Body language

Body language includes unconscious signals that tell us what people really think/feel. If someone is telling a lie, for instance, their body language will usually give them away. By focusing on other people's body language you can discover their true feelings towards you and what they think about what you are saying. It has a clear value in business situations and is therefore very important in customer care.

Body language includes how you dress, your posture and distance from others, how you sit, facial expressions, movements, eye contact, gestures and eye movements. Avoid slouching, leaning and negative facial expressions such as frowning. Upright body language shows professionalism, confidence and openness. Similarly, learn to read customers' body language, observing when they are tired, in a hurry, upset etc.

Learn to:

- recognise how to use body language
- control it and use it to your advantage, so that you give the right positive message to people
- recognise other people's body language so you are able to 'read' them better.

Remember that body language is not universal and can mean different things in different cultures.

Signs and meanings

A gesture doesn't always reveal exactly how a person is thinking. For example, arms folded may mean that:

- the person is being defensive about something
- the person is cold
- the person is bored or upset, or
- the person is comfortable.

Some gestures are open, expansive and positive. For example, leaning forward with open hands, palms facing upwards, shows interest, acceptance and a welcoming attitude, while leaning backwards, arms folded and head down, says closed, defensive and negative, uninterested, rejection. Using plenty of gestures usually indicates warmth, enthusiasm and emotion, while using gestures sparsely may indicate that a person is cold, reserved and logical.

External quality schemes

Quality schemes involve the use of external companies to assist in implementing quality control processes to improve the organisation's overall performance.

Figure 14.4 shows how this process might work. Table 14.9 presents an evaluation of quality schemes.

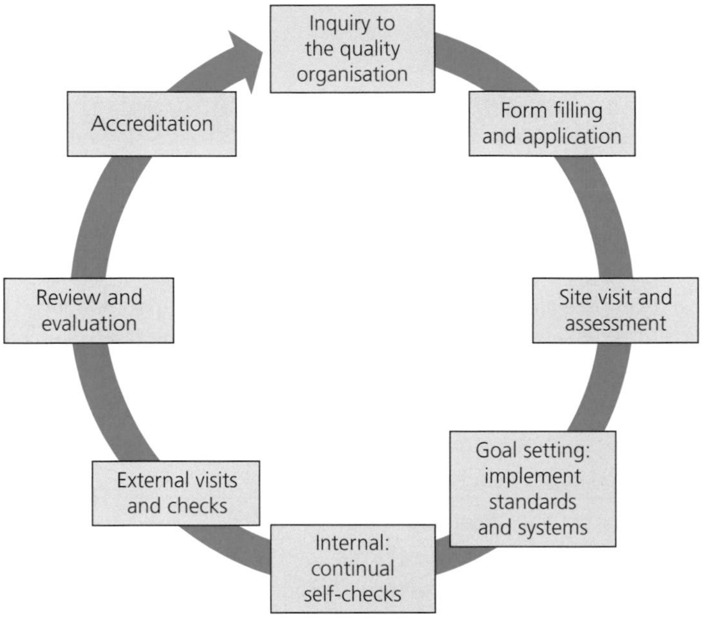

Figure 14.4 Process of quality scheme accreditation

Table 14.9 Quality scheme analysis

Advantages of quality schemes	Challenges of quality schemes
Higher standards Customer retention Fewer complaints More profits Happier employees Self-marketing – a stamp of quality Competitive advantage	Can be costly for small and medium-sized enterprises Difficult to achieve Lots of paperwork No guarantee of quality – complaints can potentially still occur

WEBLINKS

Examples of quality schemes

Information about the Hospitality Assured quality scheme:
www.hospitalityassured.com

Information about the Investors in People scheme:
www.investorsinpeople.co.uk

Information about ISO 9001 (type ISO 9001 in the search box on this page to go to the relevant information):
www.bsi-global.com

Good products

Good products make the first and last impression when visiting a hospitality and catering establishment. Good-quality, functioning and well-maintained facilities contribute highly to guest satisfaction. In addition, good products and a good working environment also make a major contribution to employee satisfaction. If employees do not have good tools to do their job and feel unsafe in their environment they will be dissatisfied, which will affect their mood and motivation. This subsequently impacts the service they provide to customers.

Typical product problems might include:

- worn and old products, e.g. stained carpets, old furniture

- defective products, e.g. broken lamps, faulty televisions, cracked floor tiles
- poor quality, e.g. new products but bad quality (not durable and won't last long).

Table 14.10 details what should be considered when dealing with products.

All products go through a cycle from introduction to decline. See Chapter 13 on Sales and Marketing for further details of this cycle.

Table 14.10 Quality control considerations

Product category	Quality control
Food and beverage	Research suppliers and visit them to establish hygiene standards Look for suppliers with quality awards – ISO etc. Products with quality stamps Use purchase specifications On receiving, check product against product specification Effective storage procedures and management (including stock rotation) Date-stamp stored foods Menu specifications for correct preparation and service of menu items Strict hygiene standards – e.g. HACCP Good supervision and monitoring
Furniture, fixtures and equipment	Product specifications Product cleaning procedures SOPs on how to correctly use product Scheduled maintenance Effective maintenance repair systems
Heating, ventilation and air conditioning (HVAC) Utility systems	Testing and commissioning during installation Employee training Scheduled and preventative maintenance

Internal processes

These are another integral element in the customer service process. Standards alone are not sufficient. For example, you may have standards of how to greet a customer and offer a menu, but there needs to be a process of steps, as outlined in Figure 14.5. In a restaurant these are referred to as the service sequence.

Leadership and supervision

As highlighted in Chapter 15, good leadership is extremely important when it comes to achieving customer satisfaction. Leaders need to incorporate customer focus in the organisation's overall strategy and objectives. It needs to be incorporated as a strategic objective, which can be seen in all aspects of the organisation.

Managers and supervisors are responsible for the day-to-day monitoring of standards and processes to ensure customer satisfaction is being achieved. In order to do this they must be very visible within the operation to allow them to observe to what extent standards are being delivered. This process of being visible in the operation can be termed 'management by walking around' (MBWA) and can be extremely effective, particularly in a fast-paced operation where there are so many different aspects to monitor.

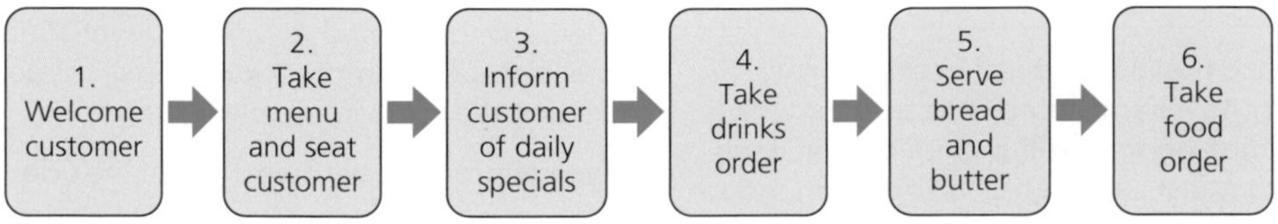

Figure 14.5 The customer service process

Case study

Figure 14.6 presents a complaint letter sent by a customer to a restaurant owner. Review the complaint and then complete the questions that follow it.

Mr John Wallace
20 Kingscroft Road
Cheltenham CH2 4PQ

5th May 2016

To whom it may concern,

I made a reservation for dinner for six people at your restaurant last Saturday, 27 April. The party consisted of my wife, my mother, two teenage daughters, my three-year-old son and myself. We had made the reservation to celebrate my mother's 70th birthday. I am a bank manager and one of my employees in the office had recommended your establishment.

The reason I am writing is that there were several things on the evening that caused me and my guests much disappointment, and I would like to bring these to your attention.

1 As it was my mother's 70th birthday, I had passed by in advance and given the supervisor some balloons to be put around the table. Unfortunately at our scheduled arrival time, 7pm, this had not been done. When I brought it to the attention of a supervisor he was not very helpful and just blamed the other supervisor I had dealt with.

2 On being seated at the table we then waited ten minutes for a server to come to our table. I understand it was busy, but ten minutes?

My son Joey had brought his iPad and so we asked for the Wi-Fi password. The server said that there was no Wi-Fi. Why in today's society is there no Wi-Fi for customers?

While ordering the food we asked if there was a children's menu. The waitress said there was no menu specifically for kids but we could simply order a half portion of one of the main courses. My wife, Heather, is on a diet and asked for salad instead of French fries with her chicken spatchcock. However, we were told by the server that the chef would not change the menu as you have set standards of performance.

We received our appetisers promptly, but my mother's dish did not arrive. I asked the server to follow up but another customer then distracted her. It appeared that the restaurant was short staffed, as everyone else seemed to be complaining.

My daughter also slipped in the toilets, as they were not being attended to.

We received the rest of our food but it was all very average.

I really wanted this evening to be special but it was very disappointing. I do not believe that we will be returning to your establishment after this experience.

I look forward to hearing from you on these matters.

John Wallace
email: wall1234@telecom.net.ie

Figure 14.6 Example letter of complaint

Consider the following.

1 What do you think about the way Mr Wallace has written this letter? Consider his tone and approach.
2 List some of the possible causes of these incidents.
3 Write an email of reply to Mr Wallace dealing with each of his points. Then write an email to the management team detailing the incident and your recommended solutions to prevent a reoccurrence.

Further reading

Cracknell, H.L. and Kaufmann, R.J. (2002) *Practical Professional Catering Management*. Thomson Learning.

www.bsi-global.com

www.hospitalityassured.com

www.investorsinpeople.co.uk

www.ipsos.com/loyalty/sites/ipsos.com.loyalty/files/Ipsos_Loyalty_Myth_8_Excerpt_0.pdf

www.mrgoodacre.com/plc---product-life-cycle.html

Topics for discussion

1 Detail five challenges to achieving quality for hospitality and catering operators, and some strategies for overcoming them.
2 Create a ten-question customer survey that could be used to evaluate a fast-food restaurant of your choice.
3 Note down a situation whereby, as a customer, you have received bad customer service.
   - What happened?
   - Possible causes?
   - Possible solutions that the management could take to prevent this problem from reoccurring.
4 As a customer, consider and list what you would expect from a local fast-food operation. Then visit the operation and measure to what extent your original expectations are met.
5 As a front-desk receptionist how would you deal with the following situations?
   - A customer had requested an early-morning room call but they didn't receive it. They are now very angry as they are running late to get to the airport.
   - A customer has come to front desk to report seeing a cockroach in their bedroom.
   - A customer is complaining that the heating in the bedroom is not working.
   - While settling their room bill the customer's credit card is not working.
6 Using a mind-map approach, outline the most effective methods (and why) to avoid customer complaints.
7 Visit a travel review website (e.g. Tripadvisor.com) and search for three-, four- and five-star hotels. Create a spreadsheet to detail the following:
   - current customer rating
   - positive customer comments
   - negative customer comments
   - whether you would stay there or not.

   Then visit each establishment's own website, and compare and contrast the online review site comments with the marketing information on each hotel's website.
8 In a group, discuss how the internet has changed the way today's consumer provides feedback, and the advantages and challenges this presents.
9 Do all food and beverage operations have standards of performance? If not, why not?
10 As the training manager of a large chain of restaurants you have been asked by your general manager to prepare a PowerPoint or Prezi presentation on customer service. Create a ten-slide presentation that could be used to train subordinates on the most important aspects of customer service.
11 MBWA is a style of management that is more visible in the operation. How much of a manager's time do you think should be allocated to office work and time spent in the operation, e.g. 10% office and 90% in the operation? Discuss this with a colleague. Detail how a manager's time should be split and give reasons for your answer.

15 Human resource and talent management

Leadership and management

Effective leadership at the top and from departmental managers is key to the success of any business. 'Management is doing things right; leadership is doing the right things' (Drucker).

Leadership styles

Seen as strategies, leadership styles become the tools to create the conditions in which employees become motivated to achieve department goals. Examples of leadership styles include the following.

- **Autocratic leadership:** a classical approach. Supervisors make decisions without input from their employees. They give orders without explanations, and expect those orders to be obeyed. Often, employers use a structured set of rewards and punishments to ensure compliance.
- **Bureaucratic leadership:** a supervisor focuses on rules, policies and procedures, acting more like a police officer than a leader. These supervisors manage by the rules and rely on higher levels of management to make decisions. Normally, this enforcement style is adopted only when all other leadership styles are inappropriate, or when employees can be permitted no discretion in decisions.
- **Democratic (participative) leadership:** almost the reverse of the autocratic style. The supervisor keeps employees informed on all matters that directly affect their work, and shares decision-making and problem-solving responsibilities. This supervisor emphasises the employees' roles in the organisation, and provides opportunities for employees to develop a sense of job satisfaction. The supervisor seeks the opinions of employees and seriously considers their recommendations.
- **Laissez-faire (free-rein) leadership:** a hands-off approach in which the supervisor actually does very little leading. The supervisor provides little or no direction and allows employees as much freedom as possible. In effect, the supervisor gives all authority (power) to the employees, and relies on them to establish goals, make decisions and resolve problems. While there are relatively few times when this approach can be used effectively, it may be appropriate with highly skilled or experienced employees who have been trained in decision-making and problem-solving techniques.

Key skills for management

Self-management

Effective management starts with how you see yourself, how superiors see you and how those you are responsible for see you.

Consider what constitutes a good manager: what qualities, attitudes and values are desirable? These may include:

- honesty and integrity
- being orderly and having a neat appearance

- loyalty and conscientiousness
- ability to lead and set an example
- willingness and cooperativeness
- enthusiasm and punctuality
- being courteous and caring.

Direction

To progress it is essential to be able to clarify roles, to focus on key issues, and to specify targets and standards – that is, to know in what direction you are going and how you intend to get there.

Teamwork

When working in a team it is essential to plan, to use the ideas of the team members so that you can be effective.

Here are some guidelines for good leadership of a team.

- Look at tomorrow's problems and issues today to detect signs of changes and potential pitfalls.
- Learn to adapt to change, and turn it to positive advantage.
- Set high standards and clear objectives.
- Think clearly, allowing intuition to influence rationality.
- Create a sense of value and purpose in work, so that team members believe in what they do and do it successfully.
- Act decisively, but ensure decisions made are soundly based and not just on impulse.
- Set the right tone by your actions, creating a clear, consistent and honest model to be followed.
- Choose the right time to make decisions and take action.
- Create an atmosphere of enthusiasm in which individuals are stimulated to perform well, gain self-respect and play an integral role in meeting the organisation's overall goals.
- Be sensitive to individual team members' needs and expectations.
- Define clear responsibilities and structures.
- Recognise what motivates each team member, and work with these motivations to achieve standards and objectives.
- Set boundaries within which team members can work freely.

Actions

Actions need to be taken. Prevarication, hesitancy and lethargy do not help decision making (see below). However, before acting, ensure that priorities are right, and use resources, manpower, finances, equipment and commodities efficiently.

Results

Analyse problems, give and receive feedback and use the information to persuade others, thus improving your own performance.

Positive balanced management

To improve performance, clear positive thinking and the ability to generate enthusiasm may be helpful. A flexible approach, sensitive to others' feelings and expectations, and capable of inspiring them may well develop confidence in one's own ability.

Table 15.1 Different types of people as managers

Category or type of person		Management skills that may need improving
Confident Bold Arrogant	Self-centred Authoritative Independent	May be too bossy and aggressive, needs to develop patience
Optimistic Cheerful Enthusiastic	Sociable Articulate Persuasive	May be too friendly and require greater self-discipline in difficult management situations
Relaxed Patient Laid back	Stable Passive Calm	May be unwilling to change and lacks any sense of urgency to change
Careful Neat Perfectionist	Self-disciplined Accurate Aggressive	May find difficulty in delegating, worry too much and be defensive
Agreeable Self-effacing Frustrated	Peaceful Unassuming Easily discouraged	May find leadership hard and become discouraged in difficult situations
Reserved Quiet Pessimistic	Distant Imaginative Remote	May be shy and unsociable, and not good at dealing with people
Restless Erratic Tense	Impetuous Quick Highly strung	May be seen as impatient, intolerant and aggressive, may need to learn to calm down
Independent Stubborn Argumentative	Informal Uninhibited	May be an effective delegator but unreliable and not good at making decisions

Decision making

The decision-making process moves through five stages, as follows,

1. Define the aim.
2. Collect the information.
3. List possible courses of action.
4. Evaluate the pros and cons, examine the consequences and make the decision.
5. Act on the decision, monitor and review it.

First, know why a decision has been made, and consider the situation and possible solutions. Evaluate how the aim will be achieved, how long it will take and what is its cost. Moreover, is it acceptable? If it is not acceptable, reconsider.

Effective thinking and decision making require all of the following aspects.

- **Analysing:** breaking the whole into small parts and the complex into simple elements.
- **Holistic thinking:** thinking of the entirety; the opposite to analysing.
- **Valuing:** the judgemental and critical aspect.

Intuition, instinct or emotion will not produce logical decision making. Before making a decision, ensure you have the facts. Value judgements are effective only if you are aware of any prejudices you have that may affect your decision; acknowledge them and learn not to be prejudiced. Also you need to know of any codes of values that are needed by the establishment, such as legal requirements, and any social behaviour codes and company procedures.

Time management

To organise yourself efficiently so as to be an effective manager, you need to control your time effectively. Determining priorities is an essential step and can be aided by producing lists and categorising jobs to be done, as well as using a diary effectively. Time needs to be allocated for tasks such as thinking and planning, as well as actions. A good organiser plans both for the expected and the unexpected. Be prepared for problems but allow time to prevent them if possible, and allot time for solving them.

Good managers need adequate-quality sleep and exercise, so as to be healthy and alert at work. Time is also needed for leisure and self-development. Good eating and drinking habits may not be easy in the catering industry, but they require time to be allocated sensibly – not too long, too short or erratic.

An efficient manager can organise his or her own time advantageously, as well and that of those he or she is responsible for. Always be punctual and expect others to be so too. Be well organised before a meeting, know what you expect from it and what others expect from you. If no time limit is stated then time could be wasted. Ideally, agree with each person the objectives that apply to them, as well as the time required to fulfil these objectives.

- Plan each day, and decide on priorities.
- Identify immediate, short-term and long-term goals.
- Organise office and paperwork.
- Avoid distractions, prevent interruptions.
- Delegate, make lists and delete things as they are done.
- Be organised, develop routines.
- Do important jobs when you are at your best. Set time limits and keep to them.
- Do not put off unpleasant or difficult tasks. Let others know when you are having quiet time.
- Do one thing at a time and finish it if possible; plan phone calls.
- Arrange breaks; keep a notebook for ideas.
- Learn to say no, and think before acting.

Communication and information

It is important to communicate effectively with senior management and other departmental managers, and with those for whom you are responsible. It is essential that what is communicated is understood in the way it is intended. Likewise it is very important that information, suggestions, commands, decisions, and so on, are clear, unambiguous and cannot be misconstrued. Listening is an art and a vital aspect of effective communication.

Information may be communicated by oral or visual means, depending on the establishment's policy, personal preference and the matter to be conveyed.

- The advantage of **speech** is that questions and discussions can clarify the issues immediately, and intonation and emphasis convey more accurately what is intended.
- While the **telephone** is invaluable, there is no eye contact or body language, which makes **face-to-face communication** more effective.
- **Written** instructions, reports, and so on, have the advantage that there is tangible evidence of what is communicated. However, care must still be taken that what is written is understood by the recipient; it may be clear to the writer but misunderstood by the reader, so it is essential that it is specific, unambiguous and not too wordy.
- Although **emails** are a popular form of communication, they also bring with them the risk of losing the value of face-to-face contact and oral skills.

Important points to consider with email communication.

- Do not treat an email like a conversation. In normal conversation we use the feedback of body language to modify our message, pace, tone, and emphasis in order to stay out of trouble. In email we do not have this real-time feedback.
- Keep messages short. A good email should take only 15–30 seconds to read and absorb. Less is more in online communication. Try to have the entire message fit on to the first screen. When a message goes 'over the horizon', the reader does not know how long it is, which creates a psychological block.
- Establish the right tone upfront; email messages have a momentum – if you start on the wrong foot, you will

have a difficult time connecting. The subject line and the first three words of a note establish the tone.
- Remember the permanent nature of emails. Using email to praise helps people remember the kind words. Using email to be critical, however, is usually a bad idea because people will re-read the note many times.
- Keep your aim in mind. Establish a clear objective of how you want the reader to react to your note. For sensitive notes, write the objective down. When proofreading your note, check to see if your intended reaction is likely to happen. If not, reword the note.
- Do not write notes when you are not yourself. This sounds simple, but it is really much more difficult than meets the eye. Learn the techniques to avoid this problem.
- Avoid 'email grenade' battles. Do not take the bait. Do not respond to edgy emails in kind.
- Be careful with use of pronouns in email. Pronouns establish the tone. The most dangerous pronoun in an email is 'you'.
- Avoid using 'absolutes'. Avoid words such as never, always, impossible and cannot. Soften the absolutes if you want to be more credible in emails.
- Avoid sarcasm. Humour at the expense of another person in an email will come back to haunt you.
- Learn techniques to keep your inbox clean (down to zero notes each day) so you are highly responsive when needed. Adopting proper distribution rules in your organisation will cut email traffic by more than 30 per cent instantly.
- Understand the rules for writing challenging notes so you always get the result you want rather than create a need for damage control.

Source: www.leadergrow.com

Managing labour as a resource

Managers have different resources available to them. These resources need to be planned, organised, coordinated, controlled and evaluated.

The different types of resources in hospitality and catering establishments include:
- space (rooms, restaurant, bar)
- data and information
- employees/labour
- utilities (water, gas, electricity)
- budgets
- equipment
- time
- food, beverage and supplies
- cash
- waste.

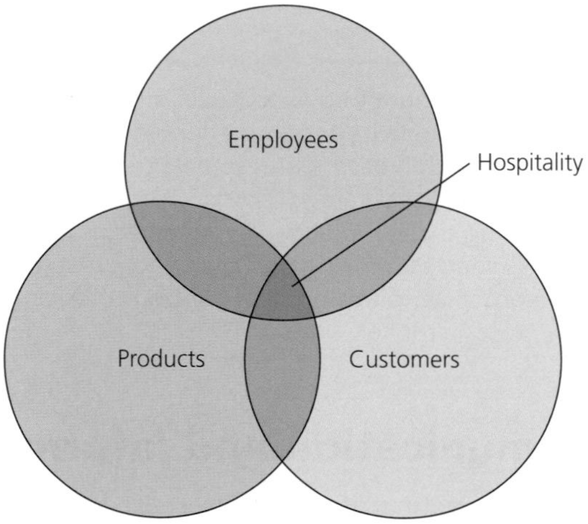

Figure 15.1 The hospitality mix

Management of many of these resources is discussed in other chapters. The sections that follow examine the management of labour as a resource in more detail. Labour is one of the biggest and most important costs for most hospitality organisations. Hospitality relies on labour to deliver a good product to customers.

Effective human resource (HR) management will provide:
- satisfied customers due to improved service and products
- fewer complaints and more positive word of mouth (WOM)
- cost reduction due to less recruitment and turnover
- the ability to attract new talent more easily
- employee retention and stronger teams
- competitive advantage and a differentiator
- organisational growth and expansion of market share
- increased profits and positive financial returns for shareholders.

Core functions of HR management

The key areas and disciplines in human resource (HR) management include planning and recruitment, training and development, evaluation, retention, legislation and discipline.

The core function of HR is to:
- attract and recruit the most talented and suitable candidates
- provide a working environment that stimulates, motivates and satisfies them
- manage labour to maximise HR efficiency and minimise waste.

HR planning

The resourcing of employees very much depends on supply and demand.

- The **supply** is the amount of positions available within the market at any point in time.
- **Demand** is the pool of labour available to recruit from, and candidates' suitability. At any point in time similar positions may be available in competing organisations, which will ultimately provide more options for the individual seeking employment.

The big questions to ask when HR planning include:

- How many employees do we need?
- What skills, qualifications and experience should they have?
- Do our employees have the right knowledge and the skills to overcome the challenges that the new economy demands; and how do we build a competitive advantage based on knowledge and skills?
- When do we need them?
- How can we attract them?
- Where will we find them?
- What will they do?
- How can we ensure we attract and recruit the best talent?
- What are their needs, wants and expectations from an employer?
- What can we do to retain them for as long as possible?

Simply put, the right number of employees, at the right time, in the right place, doing the right job, are the key considerations.

Labour resourcing and management vary from organisation to organisation, depending on such factors as:

- supply and demand for positions within the market
- leadership and management structure of the organisation
- type, standard and size of operation
- business levels or seasonality
- location
- local legislation
- organisational culture
- customer type and market
- budgets and manning levels
- technology.

HR strategies

Organisations need to be strategic in the way they position themselves in the HR marketplace and make themselves the preferred choice for employment. Some strategies to support this are listed below.

- Select the most appropriate channels to promote available positions, to achieve the right fit between job and candidate.
- Research current labour market needs and expectations for various positions, and meet these as much as possible.
- Research competitors' HR strategies and provide a better proposition than them.
- Nurture future talent through school and college visits. Provide tours, corporate social responsibility (CSR) projects and campaigns (see Figure 15.6).
- Provide a positive work environment that generates positive word of mouth from employees.
- Carry out regular internal research with your workforce. Communicate the best features of your workplace in your job advertising.
- Develop strategies and goals for the recruitment and retention of new staff, and training and development of all staff.
- Research how the organisation is positioned in the minds of your target employees, including competitors' employees.
- Put in place succession planning – this involves identifying internal successors for positions and providing them with the training to develop them into those positions.

The HR cycle

Due to their very nature, hospitality organisations rely heavily on a team of well-trained, competent employees to run the operation, ensuring that customer satisfaction is achieved at all times. The HR team plays an important role in ensuring that recruitment standards, monitoring and evaluation controls are in place and followed at all times.

The HR cycle comprises the steps involved in the turnover of employees within an organisation (see Figure 15.2). HR manages each stage to ensure that standards, controls and costs are maintained. This cycle can vary depending on employee and company situation. Some individuals can be recruited in weeks, with other positions taking months to fill. The duration of this cycle can also vary, with some employees staying only days and others providing many years of loyal service to the organisation.

Should an individual stay for only a short period of time, many of the costs will still be present. Therefore, one of the main goals of HR managers is to reduce the frequency of completing this cycle, as each time it is done it can be costly and labour intensive. One key performance indicator for HR is labour turnover. This measurement looks at the level of unwanted (and wanted) turnover within the workforce. Retaining employees in their positions for as long as possible is the main goal. A high turnover can be damaging for employee morale, teamwork and customer service, and make it difficult to both attract and retain employees.

Nickson (2013) suggests that, for 'the overall process of recruitment and selection to be considered successful, it is important that it is: considered fair by candidates; cost effective; user friendly; acceptable to both the organisation and the candidates; and reliable and valid'.

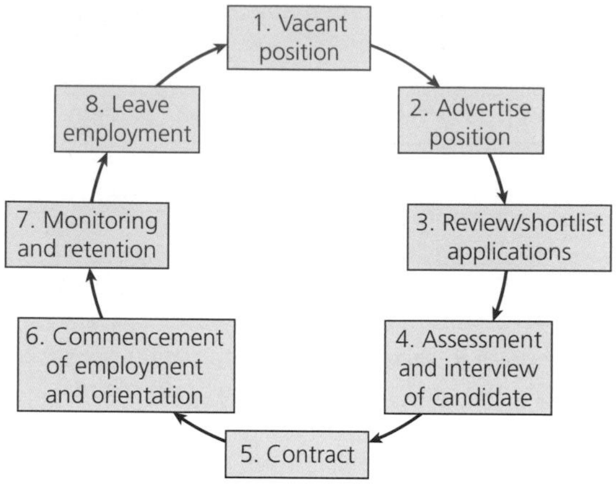

Figure 15.2 The HR cycle

1. Vacant position

Employment positions become available for different reasons, e.g. resignations, end of contract, dismissal, retirement or restructuring (including new departments/ operations opening).

As part of their contract most employees work a notice period and it is during this time that the process to find a replacement would commence. The notice period would normally be shorter (weeks) for lower-level employees and longer for managers (one to three months). Some employees may not give any notice and may simply not return the next day, leaving a real gap and problem in the department.

Each position is budgeted for and necessary. Therefore, not having an individual in a slot can create challenges in the completion of tasks and customer service. Often, until these positions are filled, the responsibilities will need to be redistributed to other cross-trained employees. If this is not possible, a product or service may need to be adjusted. For example, if a pastry chef is being recruited and it is taking time to fill the position, perhaps the pastries will need to be bought in already prepared. Unfortunately, organisations cannot employ back-up employees just in case gaps arise as this would be too costly. Therefore, the time between employees leaving and being replaced needs careful attention and should be managed as a priority.

2. Advertise position

To attract the best people:

- understand the needs and wants of prospective employees
- provide better conditions and benefits than the competition
- communicate the organisation's USP to the market
- advertise in the most appropriate media.

There are many challenges for hospitality managers and recruiters when attracting talent.

- Work can be unsociable – a lot of employees are required to work during the busy holiday periods (Christmas, Ramadan, Chinese new year, etc.).
- Fluctuations in business levels can result in some organisations requiring their employees to work split shifts.
- Due to the nature of work, long hours are common, and the work can be physical and tiring.
- Pay can be low at entry levels, particularly in competition with other industries.

Nickson (2013) notes: 'In the recruitment process organizations are seeking to attract and retain the interest of suitable candidates, while at the same time also seeking to portray a positive image to potential applicants.'

To recruit and attract individuals to work in hospitality the positives should be emphasised. For example:

- variety – every day is different
- multicultural environment – you will work with colleagues and meet customers from different cultures
- fast paced and energetic – no day will be boring
- interesting customer interactions – customers can be challenging, interesting, successful and famous
- challenging situations – hospitality can be challenging due to its fast-paced, diverse nature
- 24-hour environments – this develops the individual's inner character, strength, stamina and ability to respond, make decisions and problem solve
- travel – many multinational organisations provide opportunities to transfer around the globe
- transferable skills – many of the skills that you acquire in hospitality are transferable to other sectors
- responsive – the industry constantly researches employees to determine satisfaction levels, and responds accordingly
- positions for all personalities.

Job description and job specification

Positions are planned around tasks, standards and business levels. Each position must have a job specification and a job description.

The objective of the job description is to clearly communicate what the candidate will have to do if successful. It can be used for the following purposes.

- **Recruiting:** can assist managers to develop the job specification and the media advertisement to recruit employees.
- **Selection:** can help the manager to develop selection requirements and interview questions.
- **Orientation:** serves as an excellent guide when familiarising a new employee with the requirements of the job.
- **Training:** comparing an employee's job skills with the requirements outlined in a job description helps managers determine what kind of training an employee needs.
- **Employee evaluations:** performance appraisals are often developed directly from job descriptions, which provides a basis for evaluating employee performance.

- **Promotions and transfer:** job descriptions provide the information necessary to determine whether a current employee can perform the functions of a new job.
- **Discipline:** in situations where the employee is not performing the job tasks on his/her job description, this can be used as a reference by managers during a disciplinary hearing.
- **Protection:** a job description protects the employee from abuse of too many additional responsibilities being added to his/her job role.

Nickson (2013) suggests that 'the person specification provides a framework to assess how close candidates come to being the ideal'.

The primary objective of a job specification is to increase the chances of finding the right candidate, most suited to the position. It is a set of criteria that the candidate should meet in order to be considered. A job specification should detail position, qualifications required, experience required and any other particular skills. Anther objective is to ensure that there is a clear link between what is needed and what is advertised, and to reduce the amount of applications from individuals that do not meet the desired criteria.

GLOBAL Hotel

JOB DESCRIPTION

Front Desk/Concierge

To promptly attend to all guest enquiries in a friendly and attentive manner, making them feel welcome at all times.

RESPONSIBILITIES would include, but are not limited to: ·

- Welcome all guests on entry into the hotel.
- Answer telephones, take reservations, and direct incoming calls to necessary departments and co-workers.
- Provide outstanding guest services including, but not limited to, making restaurant reservations, booking tours, transport and providing general information.
- Provide information to customers on local attractions, dining and entertainment.
- Attend to customers' baggage as and when required.
- Transport baggage to customer's room as and when required.
- Assist transport employees as and when required.
- Develop a thorough knowledge of the properties, their rooms and amenities.
- To make reservations as and when required.
- To assist with onward bookings.
- Read and initial log book and memos daily; be aware of the current activities, meetings and groups taking place on the properties.
- Have a good personal appearance and follow uniform requirements provided by supervisor.
- Exhibit friendly, courteous, helpful behaviour at all times; be able to react calmly and professionally when solving the problems and/or concerns of our guests.
- Be able to handle a stressful, hectic atmosphere and follow through on duties after numerous interruptions; develop problem-solving and decision-making skills related to the front-office operation.
- Attend job-related seminars and meetings when requested by supervisor.
- Be able to work various shifts, weekends and holidays; be flexible with scheduling and assist co-workers with scheduling conflicts whenever possible; be on time for scheduled shifts.
- Complete recurring tasks as assigned by supervisor, including, but not limited to, filing, payment collection and cancellations, drawer checks, sorting mail and inventorying keys.
- Perform any other task, either written or verbally requested, for the overall good of the operation.
- Help managers with projects and site tours when needed.
- Deliver mail, packages and messages to units, and deliver cribs and rollaway beds as requested.
- Provide basic trouble-shooting support for in-room services such as internet, cable TV and DVD use.

Figure 15.3 Example job description for a hotel concierge

Table 15.2 Example of a job specification

Position:	Head Concierge	
	Essential	**Desirable**
Qualifications	Diploma in Hotel/Hospitality Management	Degree in Hotel/Hospitality Management
Experience	3–5 years' experience in similar position	5 years' experience in similar position (preferably a 5-star hotel)
Technical skills	Opera, Microsoft programs	
Other	Knowledge of local area Physically fit Knowledge of email Excellent telephone manner Immaculate appearance	Member of Golden Keys Additional language

Advertising

Once the job specification and job description are in place, the organisation will create an advert to promote the position. The objective of the advertisement is to generate suitable applications from candidates. It should be truthful and informative, should comply with local legislation and be eye catching so that it stands out among other adverts.

Adverts should include category (full-time, part-time, casual), position title, application criteria, contact details, submission information, USP, deadline and name/brand of organisation.

Organisations have a variety of channels in which to place the advertisement. The channel used would depend on factors such as target audience, budget, urgency and historical effectiveness to produce applicants.

Figure 15.4 Example of a job advert

Internal and external recruitment

Some organisations have to decide whether to recruit internally or externally, or both (see Table 15.3).

To reach internal employees the following methods could be used:

- company web page, intranet, Facebook page
- post on bulletin boards or announce current job openings in e-newsletters
- reward employees with promotions and target employees for future promotions
- internal transfers from partner properties.

External recruitment sources include:

- industry web pages – e.g. eHotelier (ehotelier.com/jobs)
- internet job sites and apps
- professional networks (e.g. LinkedIn)
- employment agencies
- industry/trade publications
- ads in local newspapers
- TV, radio, cinema.

HR managers can also promote their organisations with the aim of attracting future potential employees (i.e. hospitality students), targeting the likes of:

- schools or colleges (see Figure 15.6)
- education and recruitment fairs and exhibitions.

Table 15.3 Advantages and disadvantages of internal/external recruitment

	Advantages	Challenges
Internal	Improves the morale of the promoted employee and the morale of the employees who see opportunities for themselves Provides managers with a better assessment of the abilities of the candidate since their performance has been observed over time Is lower in cost than external recruiting (reduced advertising and recruitment costs) Reduces training costs, as the company does not need to train an employee that already has knowledge of company standards, etc.	Diminishes the opportunity to bring new ideas into the company Causes morale problems among those employees who miss out on the promotion Has political overtones – some employees attribute promotions to friendships and relationships with managers and supervisors Creates a critical gap in one department
External	Brings new blood and new ideas into the organisation Provides recruiters with an opportunity to see how things are on the outside Provides a fresh look at your department and organisation Serves as a form of advertising for the company	It is more difficult to find a good employee that can fit with the organisation's culture and management philosophy Morale problems can develop if the current employees feel that they have no opportunity to advance within the organisation Job orientation for external recruitment takes longer than internal recruitment Political problems and personality conflicts can result when employees believe that they could do the job as well as the external recruit

WEBLINKS

Many larger organisations promote the benefits of working for them and advertise their positions through their company website. See, for example:

www.kimptonhotels.com/careers

www.shangri-la.com/corporate/careers/career-opportunities

www.mcdonalds.com/us/en/careers.html

www.carnival.com/careers.aspx

Some organisations invest in videos to communicate the benefits of working for them. These can be uploaded on to sites such as YouTube and their own websites.

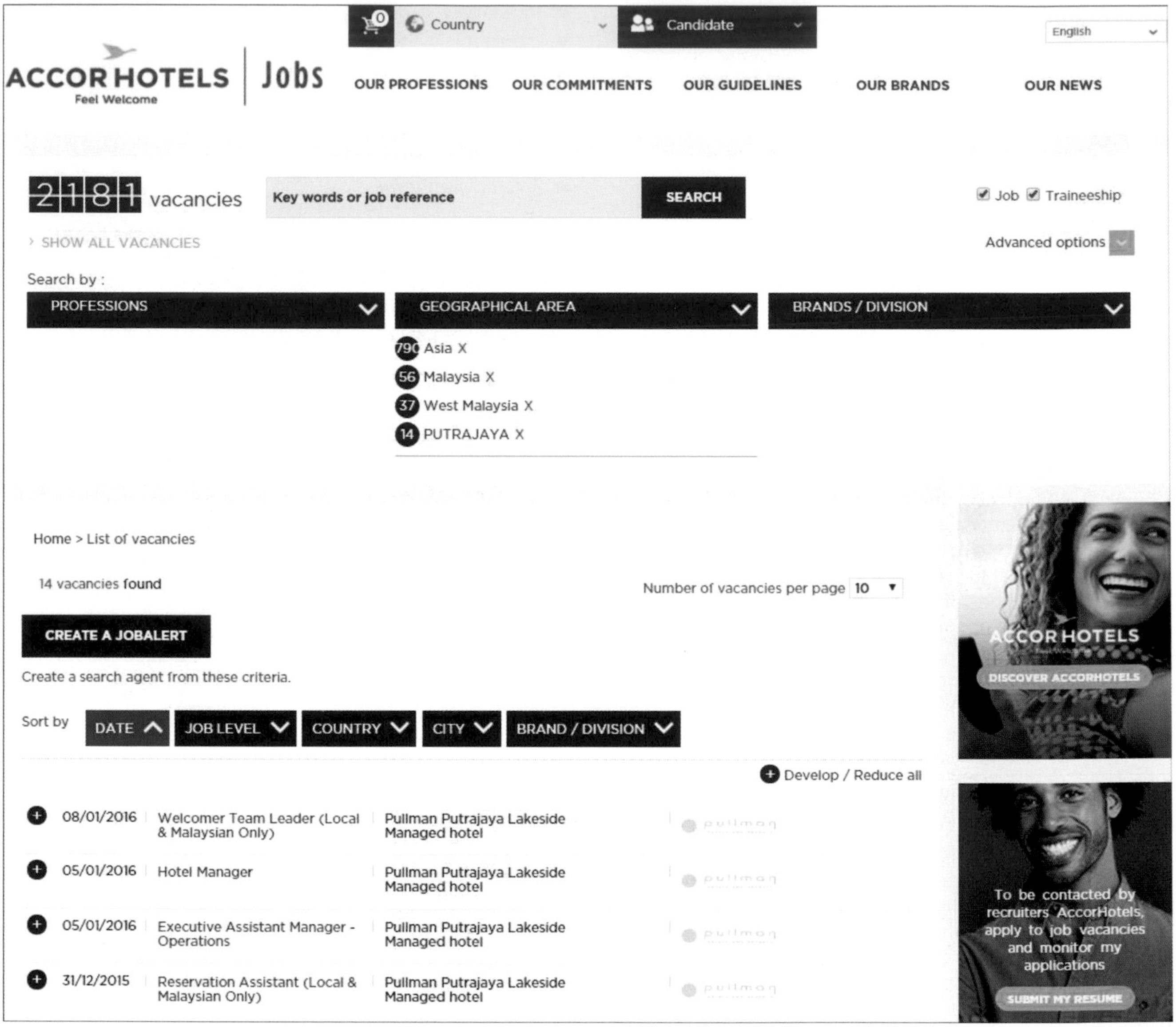

Figure 15.5 Company web page recruitment: Accor

Evaluating advertising channels

As advertising is a cost it is good practice for HR managers to evaluate the cost effectiveness of the channels they use (see Table 15.4).

Table 15.4 Template for evaluating advertising methods

Method	Cost	Number of applications generated	% employed	% retained
Hotel website				
Recruitment agency				
Job site				
Local newspaper				

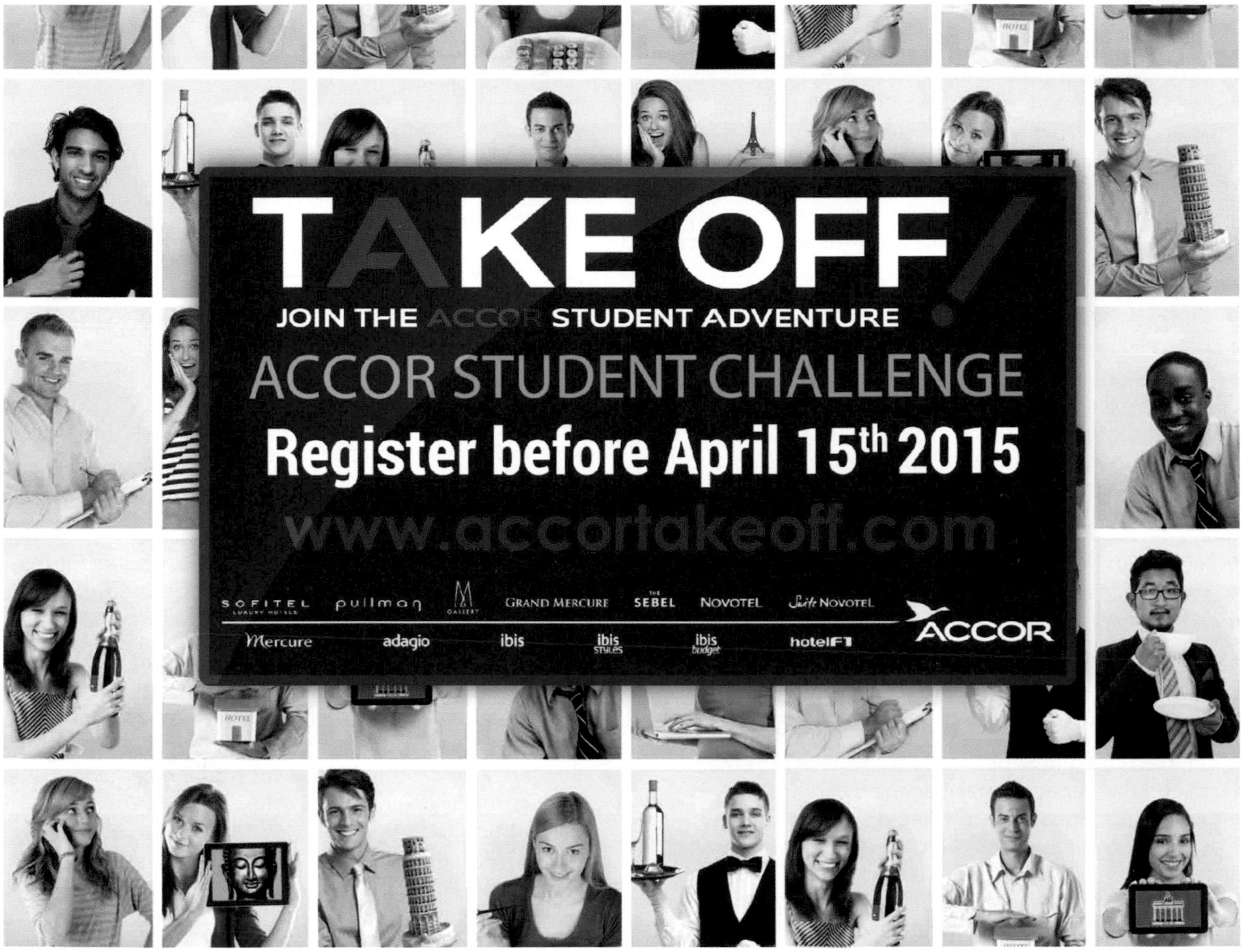

Figure 15.6 An example of a hotel company working with further and higher education: Accor Student Challenge

Attracting candidates and generating applications

The key goal of advertising employment positions is to generate suitable applications from candidates, and so hospitality organisations need to consider the needs of applicants, such as:

- competitive salary and benefits
- opportunities for progression
- flexibility
- wellness facilities
- individual and organisational learning
- interesting and challenging work environments
- sustainable work culture – sense of purpose, contribute to society
- respect for their talents
- open communication with management
- ethical values.

Staff recruitment is affected by the following drivers:

- work–life balance
- an embedded culture of employee learning and development
- integrated, connected work environments
- an embedded sustainability culture
- ethical practices
- opportunities for remote/virtual working
- recruitment of older workers.

WEBLINK

Accor PLANET 21 program:
www.accorhotels-group.com/en/sustainable-development/the-planet-21-program.html

3. Review and shortlist applications

The objective of reviewing applications is to ensure that only those candidates who best meet the criteria are shortlisted for interviews.

Candidates, in most cases, respond to advertisements by completing application forms or submitting a curriculum vitae (CV) (also termed a resumé).

CVs

A CV (resumé) is a sales tool to showcase your skills and experience. It is the first impression a potential employer will see. Therefore, it needs to be brief, informative, accurate, professional, well designed and honest. The CV is something that you will add to throughout your career as you gain more skills and experience. Candidates can also showcase their credentials through personal blogs, video pitches and links to professional websites such as LinkedIn.

A CV should include:

- professional photo (head shot)
- personal details (name, date of birth, nationality)
- contact details (home address, mobile phone, Skype address, email address, LinkedIn address)*
- qualifications (institution, qualification, grade)
- work experience (organisation, dates of employment, position, responsibilities and work achievements)
- technical skills (PC skills, systems, software)
- languages
- special achievements (awards, e.g. academic, sports)
- voluntary/community work.

* Facebook profiles are sometimes requested by employers, so ensure that they portray the right impression of you.

Submitted CVs and applications are reviewed by the HR team and the departmental manager. Candidates are either invited for an interview, kept in view or rejected. If application numbers are low or of poor quality other approaches, such as reviewing previous applications and using other channels, may be an option. Lowering the criteria or 'panic recruiting' (interviewing and recruiting a candidate even when they are not fully qualified for the position) should be avoided as employing the wrong individual may result in their needing more training, investment and monitoring, and could lead to defects on the job.

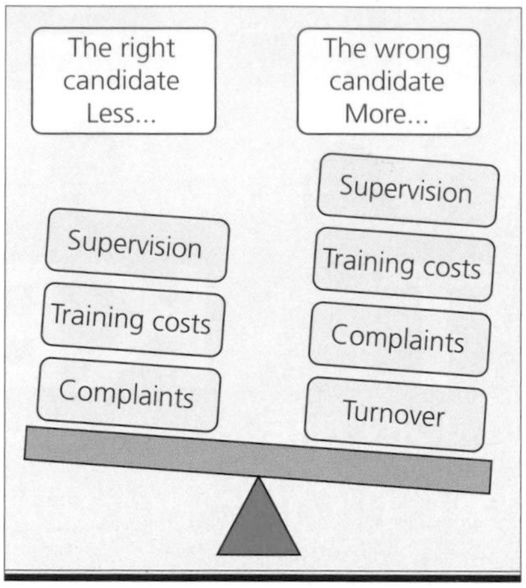

Figure 15.7 The importance of selecting the right candidate

4. Interview and assessment

To judge whether the candidate is the best person for the job a variety of assessment methods can be used. Table 15.5 outlines some of the different approaches.

When assessing candidates it is important that the process is accurate and fair. Bias is one of the challenges when interviewing candidates. There are different types of bias, as outlined below.

- **Similarity error:** the interviewer sees the candidate as having similar personal characteristics, experience or background to themselves.
- **Halo effect:** the interviewer looks favourably on a candidate, perhaps because of his/her appearance or the way they smile.
- **Devil's horns:** the opposite to the halo effect; the interviewer gets a negative impression from the candidate (perhaps they were a little late for the interview or are from a town that is not liked by the interviewer).

Table 15.5 Recruitment assessment methods

Assessment	Method
CV or resumé	Candidates submit their qualifications and experience on a document to apply for the position
Interview	Candidate is interviewed either face to face, via Skype or by telephone
Paper-and-pencil test	Tests the knowledge and understanding required on the job description or behaviour/character of candidate
Psychometric testing	Numerical, verbal, diagrammatical and behavioural tests; used for high-level positions
Computerised simulation	To reduce labour cost when interviewing, candidates are first assessed in front of a PC; simulations are designed to test knowledge, character and decision-making skills
Practical demonstration	Candidates applying for more practical positions (e.g. chef, restaurant, accommodation and training) are invited to carry out practical demonstrations
Service trial	Required to work a shift to determine capabilities and fit with job and team

- **The Heisenberg effect:** many candidates will tell the interviewer what they think he or she wants to hear. For the candidate the objective is to get the job and so they do what they have to do, even if it means exaggerating their experience. The candidate will, in this situation, be selected on the basis of information that is not 100 per cent accurate.
- **The Hawthorne effect:** when an individual changes their behaviour when they know they are being observed. For example, during a pre-work trial when a candidate knows that their supervisor is watching, they are likely to perform better than their normal standard.

It should be noted that, with all of these errors, the key question is, 'Does the candidate meet the criteria?'

To increase the reliability of the selection consider a multiple-hurdle strategy (Figure 15.8), where candidates are required to demonstrate various skills or each stage is more difficult.

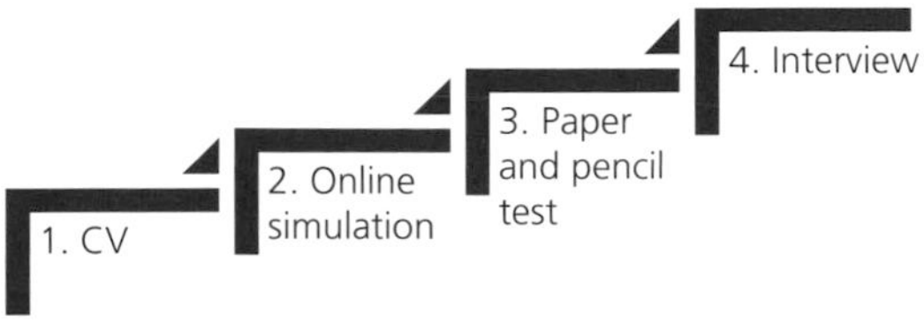

Figure 15.8 Example of a multiple-hurdle recruitment strategy

The interview

The main objective of the interview is to judge the suitability of the candidate for the position. The interviewer should try to get the candidate to talk as much as possible – probably in the range of 30 per cent interviewer to 70 per cent interviewee. The aim is to get the candidate to present themselves, their knowledge and their personality. If the interviewer does all the talking, it is difficult to get a valid representation of the candidate. Tables 15.6 and 15.7 offer some tips for interview preparation and procedure, while Table 15.8 includes some common interview questions.

Table 15.6 Preparation before the interview

	1 week before
Candidate (interviewee)	Carry out research on the organisation, products and services; try to obtain a brochure or carry out research on its website Practise answers to standard questions Create a few questions to ask, based on your research or personal requirements Research location and travel route Prepare formal dress
HR manager (interviewer)	Notify candidate of interview date, time, location and type of interview Review CV and draft questions Book interview room Block off in diary

Table 15.7 The WASP interview process for the interviewer

Welcome	Put the candidate at ease Greet the candidate and appraise promptly; do not make him/her wait Introduce yourself, smile, make eye contact and shake hands Begin by discussing something of interest to the candidate, which will help them to relax State the purpose and structure of the interview If you expect the interview to be 30 minutes long, say so Once you have broken the ice, move on to the main body of the interview, which is discussing the job
Acquire	Use a conversational tone throughout Speak on the candidate's level without talking down to them Control the topics discussed and the direction of the interview, but allow the candidate to set the pace If the candidate is shy or speaks slowly, the pace will be slower Begin questioning the candidate (see Table 15.8) Use encouraging facial expressions and body language; nod your head, maintain eye contact, lean towards the candidate Listen carefully as the individual responds, if the candidate hesitates before answering a question, they might be uncomfortable with the topic Listen for vague responses or changes in subject, which could indicate the candidate's desire to hide something Listen with sincerity and interest If the candidate asks questions, be honest and direct when you reply Ask questions in one major topic area at a time
Supply	Provide information on the company position and package Explain what you expect of the employee and why Answer the candidate's questions, and describe the next step in the process
Part	Before ending interviews, ask candidates if they have anything they want to add Allow the candidates to ask questions or further explain their skills and experiences Remember, what they say will give you further insight into their personalities, requirements and concerns If you are seriously considering hiring a candidate, explain the job accurately and thoroughly (sell it to them!) Let the candidate know when you will contact them After you have ended the conversation, stand up, shake hands and thank the candidate for their interest Notify all candidates of their status and, if unsuccessful, explain why the candidate won't be considered

Table 15.8 Interview question techniques

Personal Tell me about yourself What do you like and dislike about your present job? Can you describe a typical day on your last job? What do you look for in a position? Tell me what you know about our organisation Why should we employ you, and how would you add value to our company? Provide me with three strengths and weakness that you have
Education What subjects did you enjoy the most (or the least) in high school (or college)? What did you learn from your high school (or college) experience that is important today? Did you have any part-time jobs while attending high school (or college)? Which jobs were the most interesting? Why?
Employment What job pressures did you experience in previous jobs? Why? What kind of people do you like (or dislike) working with? Why? What were the main advantages (or disadvantages) of your last job? Do you prefer working alone or in a group?
Goal What are your career goals in the next two years? The next ten years? What are your salary goals and objectives? How do you evaluate this organisation as a place to help you achieve your career goals? If you are successful in one year (five years, ten years), what will be happening?
Awareness Which of your good qualities are most outstanding? Which of your qualities need the most improvement? Are you a self-motivated individual? Explain why How do you react to criticism from an employer? A guest? A staff member? Have you engaged in any self-improvement activities recently? What were they?
Product Why do you want to join our organisation? Tell me about the restaurants that we have here You spent a few minutes in the lobby when you arrived. How would you improve the product or service?
Situational If a customer complained to you because his soup was cold how would you handle this? If you observed a colleague taking money from the till and putting it in her pocket, what would you do? How would you handle the following situation?

Post-interview

After interviewing candidates:

- seek more information about those who seem especially promising
- analyse information the candidates supplied on their job application forms, job performance review forms and during interviews
- check at least two references that candidates supply
- check and validate any certificates
- if applicable, discuss candidates with other interviewers
- you may want to consider conducting a follow-up interview
- reject or offer employment.

5. Contract

When all the interviewing has been carried out, candidates will either be informed that they have been unsuccessful or be offered a position with the organisation. For candidates who have not been successful, it is good practice to keep their details on file for future reference.

A letter of offer and the main contract are sent. The letter congratulates the candidate, offers them a position, and asks them to review and sign the contract. The letter will include date of commencement, term, salary, holidays, notice period, legal clauses and job description.

The contract is a formal document intended to protect both employee and employer. The candidate should

Table 15.9 Full-time versus part-time work

	Advantages	Challenges
Full-time	More familiar with the job Possibility of cross-training More stability Improved quality of work and guest service Increased productivity Known to loyal guests Build a team	Possibility of boredom Costs of statutory benefits
Part-time	Lower wages Flexibility (employ as and when required) Fewer statutory benefits Fresh ideas	Can lack commitment and consistency May not fit in No relationship with loyal guests Not always available

spend time reviewing the contract to ensure that they are happy with all terms. Should they require any clarification or want to change any of the terms they must contact the HR office to discuss. The contract is also a tool for negotiation for both the candidate and the organisation. (Two copies of the contract are usually sent.)

Once the candidate is satisfied with all terms, the contract is signed by both parties, and kept by the employee for reference and also on file within the organisation. By signing, the employee agrees to all the terms.

Should the negotiations break down then the search for an employee to fill the position continues.

Within hospitality and catering both full- and part-time positions are common. Part-time employees are required for peak service times in restaurants, and for events in conference and banqueting. Table 15.9 provides an evaluation of both types of contract.

6. Commencement of employment and orientation/induction

Starting a new job is a daunting task that involves learning a new environment, building relationships and gaining trust, which some new employees find too much. Turnover in the first few weeks is common, and therefore HR should monitor and connect during this period to ensure the employee is settling in well. The induction process settles new employees in to their new positions. It is important for the company to make a good impression as this will influence the person's attitude to the job. The new employee needs to be aware of their responsibilities. This will include not just their day-to-day procedures but also their role in food hygiene, health and safety.

Orientation

On the first day, new employees usually attend a new employees' orientation/induction with HR. This often includes:

- an icebreaker
- tour of facilities and introduction to key employees
- presentation on the company – who's who, mission and overall philosophy
- employee handbook briefing and signing (rules and regulations)
- disciplinary regulations and process
- fire, health and safety procedures
- issuing of uniforms, name tags and access card
- paperwork (bank details, photos, passport copies, etc.)
- passwords for access to systems.

The new employee is also likely to have a departmental orientation, which is likely to involve:

- meeting with immediate supervisor
- tour of own department and introductions to colleagues
- introduction to mentor/buddy
- provision of locker key
- information on departmental standards
- review of job description
- issuing of rota/schedule
- addressing any questions the employee may have.

During the first few weeks of employment the following topics need to be explained to the new employee:

- organisational aims and objectives
- performance appraisal
- grievance procedures
- staff development.

The orientation is very important as an opportunity to connect with the employee early on, communicate all relevant information and assist with any questions. Some organisations will also do a pre-orientation online before new employees start.

7. Monitoring and retention

Retention is the length of time an employee stays with an organisation. The goal is for organisations to retain their employees (as discussed earlier). However, there are also risks with low employee turnover:

- employees get too comfortable and know too much
- breeds internal politics and groups
- difficult to change mentality with introduction of new services and products
- employees become stale and resistant to change
- too powerful
- a challenge to manage.

Tools for motivating and retaining employees include:

- competitive benefits
- ongoing training and development
- respect and trust from supervisors
- recognition of achievements, and opportunities for promotion
- empowerment, consultation, involvement in decision making and a 'voice' with management
- regular social activities
- SMART objectives.
- departmental incentives.

Motivation and the team

Understanding what motivates employees is crucial to the creation of productivity and the realisation of profits. People's needs and wants are complex and often difficult to define. Money and status are important but they cannot be relied upon exclusively.

A leader must motivate his or her team by making their work interesting and challenging. People must know what is expected of them and what the standards are.

Rewards should be linked to effort and results; if pay and prospects within the establishment are bad, they should be improved and performance should be recognised. Therefore, the leader should attempt to intercede on behalf of his or her employees. This will help to increase their motivation and their commitment to the team.

For the leader to manage his or her employees effectively, it is important to get to know them well, understand their needs and aspirations, and help them achieve their personal aims.

Behavioural scientists have provided useful ways of thinking about people's needs and wants. F.W. Taylor (1911) established a scientific management approach that involved breaking jobs into simple but repetitive tasks, providing training, isolating individuals from distractions and each other, and paying good wages, including bonuses for productivity over target levels. Abraham Maslow (1954) concentrated on human needs, which he defined as a five-stage hierarchy, as follows.

1. **Physiological needs:** the need for food and shelter.
2. **Safety needs:** the security of home and work.
3. **Social needs:** the need for a supportive environment.
4. **Esteem needs:** gaining the respect of others.
5. **Self-fulfilment:** the need to realise your own potential.

As each goal is achieved, the next is sought. Thus, at different stages of career development, each individual has different values, depending on their progress through this 'hierarchy of needs'. In 1959, Frederick Herzberg (see Herzberg, Mausner and Snydeman, 1959) added to Taylor's and Maslow's work by introducing the idea of 'hygiene factors'. If these factors are absent this will lead to dissatisfaction and demotivation. The four hygiene factors are:

1. the organisational policy and rules
2. the management styles and controls
3. retirement and sickness policies
4. pay and recognition of status.

Hygiene factors, although considered important, do not have lasting effects on motivation; other positive motivating factors must be present.

Money obviously plays an important role in motivation. There are also non-financial motivators, and these are highly important in achieving organisational goals.

Most people want to achieve – those in charge of teams must recognise this and provide opportunities for others to attain new levels of achievement. People also want recognition: praise and feedback spur them on to achieve even more.

People generally want to move on to more challenging situations. The team should aim to challenge its members. Certain workers (e.g. chefs) want to practise their skill and use their intelligence to maintain interest. Most workers want to accept responsibility and authority.

McClelland's N-Achievement theory contends that people have one of three needs: achievement, power and affiliation.

- **The need for achievement:** this person is achievement motivated and therefore seeks achievement, attainment of realistic but challenging goals, and advancement in the job. There is a strong need for feedback as to achievement and progress, and a need for a sense of accomplishment.
- **The need for authority or power:** this person is authority motivated; therefore this driver produces a need to be influential effective and to make an impact. There is a strong need to lead and for their ideas to prevail. There is also motivation towards increasing personal status.
- **The need for affiliation:** this person is affiliation motivated, has a need for friendly relationships and is motivated towards interaction with others. This motivates people to be liked and held in popular regard. These people are team players.

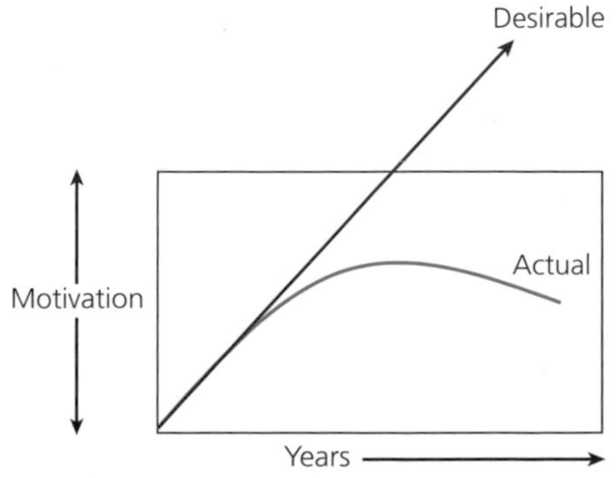

Figure 15.9 Employee motivation over time

Evaluation and assessment

Appraising the employee's performance can be a combination of informal feedback (weekly) and an annual review (appraisal), which is more formal. Tools for employee performance evaluation could include:

- job chats
- performance review or appraisal
- observation by supervisors
- end-of-shift debriefings
- completed customer questionnaires
- mystery guest reports.

The benefits of feedback for the employee are that they can work towards improving immediately. For example, at the end of the shift the supervisor may point out a few areas for improvement based on that day's performance; these could include attitude, speed, quality of work, etc. The feedback is measured against the job description and the set standards of the department.

Appraisal and evaluation

One of the most important and thorough methods of evaluation and assessment is the annual appraisal evaluation (or performance review). This is a formal process to evaluate the quality of the employee's performance within the organisation. It should be carried out by the employee's immediate supervisor once a year.

The first step is for the supervisor to sit down with the employee and define their responsibilities and what is expected of them. Once this has been agreed, the supervisor monitors the employee throughout the year based on these responsibilities. The performance appraisal is then used to measure the extent to which the employee has achieved her or his day-to-day responsibilities (see Figure 15.10).

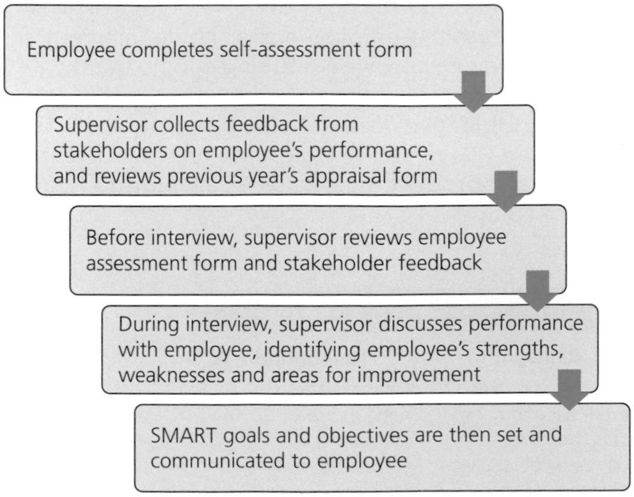

Figure 15.10 Steps involved in an employee appraisal

The appraisal process has a number of benefits:

- structured event to discuss performance
- focuses on outcomes
- recognition for employees
- identifies performance gaps
- feedback for the employee on their performance
- creates accountability in the workplace
- progressive – a clear link between performance and goal setting
- goal setting results in employees being more motivated and therefore in departmental improvements
- employee goals provide scope to develop new skills in addition to their day-to-day responsibilities
- a management tool to measure, develop, coach and monitor employees
- employee feedback can result in recognition and motivation, which can reduce absenteeism and turnover
- feeds in to training plans
- measures recruiting effectiveness.

A self-assessment/reflection form will be given to the employee in advance for them to reflect on and evaluate their own performance against a set of criteria (e.g. they may need to rate themselves on attendance, teamwork, presentation and problem solving).

As employees work with many stakeholders, individuals may be subject to a more robust evaluation, known as 360-degree appraisal (see Figure 15.11). This provides richer, more informative feedback for the individual to reflect on. For example, if a sous chef were being evaluated in this way, their immediate manager, peers, subordinates and suppliers would be asked for feedback. The process may identify, for example, that an individual is good at managing subordinates but poor at reporting information promptly to his/her boss.

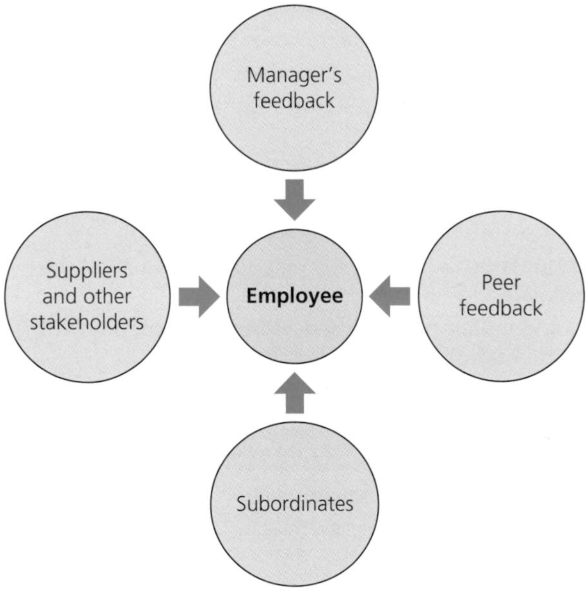

Figure 15.11 360-degree appraisal

During the appraisal an evaluation of the employee's performance on different tasks will be discussed. For example, the employee might feel that she/he scores 8 out of 10 for working in a team, but the supervisor may feel the employee scores only 5 out of 10 and that this needs to be improved. As shown in Table 15.10, errors can occur when this rating scale is used.

Table 15.10 Common errors and issues in evaluation

Interviewer error type	Explanation	Issue/problem
Leniency	When the interviewer is lenient in their evaluation; for example, the candidate in the interviewer's opinion is a 5/10, but is given a 6 or 7/10	This sometimes occurs when the interviewer is afraid to rate too low and upset the individual
Severity	The opposite to leniency; the interviewer is too hard in their rating, e.g. giving a 3 or 4 when the actual performance is a 5/10	This can sometimes be done in an effort to motivate the individual, but often has the opposite effect
Central tendency	This is when the supervisor rates all elements as a 5/10	This could be due to laziness or because they do not have the time to rate accurately
Past anchoring	The individual has been working for the organisation for one year; during the first 10 months they performed their duties very well, however, in the 11th month, the individual made a big mistake in work, which upset the supervisor; as a result of this the individual has scored low	The problem here is that the individual has performed well most of the time, but has been scored low due to one incident, which is not a fair and accurate reflection of the whole year's performance

Some guidelines for conducting performance evaluation reviews are as follows.

- Interview in a setting that is informal, private and free of distractions.
- Provide a courteous, supportive atmosphere.
- Encourage the employee to participate actively.
- Clearly explain the purpose of the interview.
- Explain problem areas thoroughly but tactfully.
- Listen when the employee talks; do not interrupt.
- Criticise job performance, not the employee.
- Criticise while you are calm; never become angry.
- Avoid confrontation and argument.
- Emphasise the employee's strengths, then discuss areas that need improvement.
- To set goals for improvement, focus on the future, not past performance.
- Assume nothing; instead ask for clarification.
- Ask questions to gather information, not to 'test' the employee.
- Assume the employee will disagree; be prepared with documentation and/or examples.
- Try to resolve differences; do not expect total agreement.
- Avoid exaggerations (such as 'always' or 'never').
- Help the employee to maintain self-esteem; do not threaten or belittle.
- Keep your own biases in check.
- Assure the employee that you will help him/her reach the goals.
- Maintain appropriate eye contact.
- End on a positive note.

Setting objectives

Following the appraisal, the supervisor will formulate objectives for the employee to work on over a period of 6–12 months. The purpose of these objectives is to develop both the employee and the department. The supervisor will provide ongoing support and monitor the progress of the employee for each objective. Objectives can be based on areas such as costs, standards or sales. They must be SMART to be effective and produce outcomes (see Figure 15.12 and Table 15.11).

S	M	A	R	T
Specific	**Measurable**	**Achievable**	**Relevant**	**Timebound**
Objectives must be very specific and clear. If too general, the employee will have difficulty knowing what is expected.	Objectives must be created in such a way that evidence is required to demonstrate the extent to which the employee has met the objective.	Objectives must be achievable for the employee: not too difficult and not too simple	Must have a clear rationale and basis. This can include company objectives, personal training needs or operational needs. If not relevant, objectives have no substance and will not be taken seriously.	Objectives must have a clear deadline for achievement, to facilitate monitoring and progress

Figure 15.12 SMART employee objectives

Table 15.11 Examples of SMART objectives for a restaurant waiter

Category	Rationale	Objective	Deadline
Standards	The restaurant has been receiving complaints that the lunch buffet is not ready for customers at midday	To ensure that the lunch buffet is fully set up by 11.45 am each day	Ongoing
Sales	During the appraisal the employee noted that he would like to develop his organisational skills	To create a one-week Spanish food promotion by June, achieving a profit of £3,000	By next June
Service	An initiative from head office is to collect more feedback from customers	To ensure that all customers complete a customer survey at the end of their meal; a minimum of 1,000 completed questionnaires to be achieved each month	Ongoing

Training and development

Nickson (2013) explains, 'It is increasingly recognized that HR development is crucial in ensuring effectiveness, quality and responsiveness in organizations to an ever-changing and complex environment.'

In large organisations, training is coordinated and delivered by a team of training professionals. However, managers, supervisors, consultants and suppliers also carry out training. Training can be delivered one to one, or in a group; on-site or off-site; daily, weekly or monthly.

Benefits of training include:

- fewer defects
- fewer discounts
- less waste
- fewer complaints
- increased employee motivation and retention
- increased customer satisfaction.

Increasingly the investment in learning and development is viewed as a strategic objective and, if planned and delivered well, provides multiple benefits for the organisation (see Table 15.12).

However, some challenges also exist, including cost, time interruption to the operation when training is conducted, and lack of enthusiasm among long-term employees. There is also the risk that, after time and money have been invested in an individual, they use this as leverage and leave, join competitors and earn more.

Situations when training takes place include:

- alignment with company goals
- new products
- new technology
- new standards and procedures
- promotion
- new employees
- team building
- repetition (fire, health and safety procedures)
- as a result of research.

The training manager's responsibility is to prepare the organisation's training plan for the year. The first step is to identify training needs by carrying out research. Tools to identify training needs include:

- mystery guest reports
- online reviews

Table 15.12 Benefits of training

Individuals	The team and organisation	Customers
Personal development	Greater professionalism	Customer satisfaction
Sense of belonging	Fewer customer complaints	Customer retention
Job satisfaction	Customer retention	Positive customer reviews
Opportunities for promotion	Greater efficiency and effectiveness	
More competitive	Attract employees	
Remuneration	Retain employees (less turnover)	
Recognition	Resource flexibility	
Retention	Competitive advantage	
Sense of achievement	Cost reduction	
Additional skill sets	Added value	
	Market share	
	Profits	

- quality audits
- observation by managers
- data from log books
- internal financial data on costs, profits and performance
- customer feedback (surveys, interviews and focus groups)
- employee feedback
- new standards, initiatives from HQ
- external trends.

Once the training has been identified, a plan is created, which includes the following considerations for organising a training session.

- What training is required?
- Why is it needed?
- What is the most effective method to deliver it?
- Who will attend?
- Who is the best person to deliver the training?
- Where will it be carried out?
- What benefit do you hope to achieve?
- What is the cost of the training, and the ROI?
- How will the effectiveness of the training be measured?

There are various methods that can be used for training. These could include workshop, video, role play, etc. A growing trend is in the use of online learning for employees. Organisations are investing in well-designed e-learning systems for employees, which allow them to complete courses online at their own pace. This provides greater flexibility for learners and reduces instructor costs for organisations. Online instructors can monitor progress and assist. On completion of the course HR is informed automatically. Many courses provide a certificate. Courses range from a few hours to weeks depending on the subject.

Training techniques include those described below.

1 **On-the-job training:** this can be very effective but is often conducted incorrectly. There are two types:
   (a) **job instruction training (JIT)** – a structured approach that requires trainees to proceed through a number of steps in a sequential pattern; it is good for task-oriented jobs such as operating equipment and preparing food
   (b) **job rotation** – moving a trainee from one job to another.

2 **Off-job training:** training in an environment other than the actual workplace. It can vary, as follows:
   (a) **vestibule training** – a simulation of the work environment in an off-site setting; it is expensive but is good to train employees on equipment such as cash registers or check-in systems
   (b) **programmed instruction** – enables trainees to learn at their own pace; for example, e-learning (see above)
   (c) **case studies** – these detail a series of events, and challenge participants to sort through the data to identify and solve problems
   (d) **business game** – another simulation through which participants learn to deal with issues in a mock business environment
   (e) **conference training** – a one-to-one discussion between a trainer and trainee
   (f) **coaching/mentoring** – a form of conference training/modelling; coaches and mentors often concentrate on improving the skills of subordinates.

8. Leaving employment

Individuals can leave employment for many different reasons, including:

- end of contract
- resignation
- retrenchment and redundancy
- termination
- redeployment
- sickness.

Following the notice period, on the final day it is good practice to carry out an exit interview with the employee, particularly if they have resigned. The objective is to gather constructive feedback on areas for improvement and things that the organisation does well. To encourage more open, honest feedback the employee's direct supervisor would not carry out this interview. An HR representative or another senior manager from another department would interview the employee. The information would then be channelled back to relevant employees for information and improvement.

Typical questions may include:

- What have you liked and disliked most about working in this organisation?
- Please tell me your reasons for leaving our organisation.
- How could we improve our working conditions for future employees?

➜ Managing diversity

Diversity recognises that people are different. It includes some of the more obvious and visible differences – such as gender, ethnicity, age and disability – and also the less visible differences – such as sexual orientation, background, personality and work style.

The world of work, especially the hospitality industry, has become more diverse in terms of age, gender and ethnicity. In the case of multinational organisations, domestic diversity is compounded by the diversity that is introduced through the movement of people around the globe. The mobility of labour is further encouraged by regional mechanisms such as arrangements for the free movement of people in the European Union. All these changes (and more) are also affecting the nature of customers and their needs.

Why is diversity management important?

Diversity management is about recognising, valuing and celebrating these differences. It is about harnessing difference to improve creativity and innovation, and is based on the belief that groups of people who bring different perspectives together will find better solutions to problems than groups of people who are the same.

The markets served are constantly changing (e.g. women and older people now have more spending power than previously, minority ethnic groups are an important market segment, people with disabilities and their carers want accessible holidays) and, in order to meet the needs of these diverse markets, the same groups need to be represented in the workforce. Taking a proactive approach to diversity management can achieve the following:

- access the best people from the widest labour pool available
- develop the creative talents of all employees
- motivate all employees
- reduce labour turnover
- improve quality and customer service.

Expatriate recruitment

Nickson (2013) explains that 'the continuing growth of world markets, increased availability of management and technological know-how in different countries, advances in telecommunications and greater regional political and economic integration are just some of the factors that are increasingly leading to the globalization of many tourism and hospitality multinational companies (MNCs)'.

The hospitality industry is a global one and provides many opportunities for individuals to work overseas. For example, a chef de partie in a large hotel chain in London may transfer to another hotel in Dubai. When individuals are transferred for a period of time within the same company, or through headhunting agencies, they are classified as expatriates. Many individuals will also find overseas employment independently and while travelling.

Opportunities to work in new environments with lots of excitement can be an attractive pull factor for many individuals. Table 15.13 outlines some of the challenges and benefits for both individual and organisation.

To meet the needs of a growing, mobile, international workforce and reduce a high turnover of expatriates many multinational organisations now provide pre-departure and acculturation training before the move to a new country. Some organisations also offer assistance during the relocation stage and immersion. This prepares the individual in areas such as those shown in Table 15.14.

Table 15.13 Overseas posting: evaluation

	Benefits	Challenges
For the individual	Exposure to new environments Learning of new cultures Opportunities to learn new languages Demonstrates an ability to work outside home country Independence Opportunities to travel and make new friends Can include good benefits and employment package (e.g. accommodation, relocation expenses) Develop self-sufficiency Recognition from peers back home Improve interpersonal skills	Failure to adapt to new environment Miss family and friends (homesickness) If accompanied by spouse and children they can find it difficult to adjust Loneliness In high-context cultures, culture shock can occur Cultural mistakes (faux pas) Discrimination from local employees can occur in certain situations Feeling of anxiety, helplessness
For the organisation	Presents a diverse workforce Individual brings new ideas, knowledge and working approaches Able to meet the needs of international travellers Marketing opportunities to promote diverse team and international image Increased operational diversity	Recruitment lead time can take longer High turnover in more challenging destinations High investment in package Working visa costs Local employees can feel resentful Delayed productivity

Table 15.14 Examples of pre-departure acculturation topics for expatriates

	Topics covered
General	Introduction to the country, history, culture, politics and religion
Geography	Location, accessibility, temperatures, recommended clothing
Business protocol	Meeting protocol, management approach, greetings, gifts
Communication and language	Key words and phrases, topics to avoid, non-verbals/hand gestures
Local etiquette	Dos and don'ts, food, entertaining, invitations
Practical	Useful contact numbers, shopping, places of interest
Festivals and holidays	List and description of major holidays

Case study

You have recently joined a hotel as operations manager. The general manager has asked you to look at employee productivity and motivation in the hotel because he believes it is significantly lower than in other local hotels. He has identified high employee turnover, absenteeism, employee theft and indiscipline as indicators of a problem, and has asked you to make a presentation to heads of departments in the hotel, offering a solution.

Your preliminary investigations reveal that the hotel has a very poor HR function, which is mainly concerned with wage administration and recruitment. Any training is done by the heads of department if they want to, and few employees have had a pay rise since they joined. The management teams have all been with the hotel for more than four years and were promoted internally.

Prepare your presentation; it should last for no more than ten minutes. An LCD projector, laptop and presentation software are available if you wish to use them.

Case study

Prepare a training plan for managers, giving them information about how to hold a performance review interview.

You should:

- explain the reasons why we should review performance
- recommend a format for successful interviewing (in any context, not just performance reviewing)
- deliver step-by-step instructions for a performance review using 'management by objectives' methodology
- cover the relevant legal framework.

Further reading

Birkinshaw, J., Luhabe, W., Nel, C. and Ungerer, M. (2011) Management and leadership. *Agenda*, 1, pp. 24–25. Available online at: www.usb.ac.za/ThoughtPrint/Thoughprint%20Publications%20%20Downloads/24_Leadership_Management.pdf.

Herzberg, G.F., Mausner, B. and Snydeman, B.B. (1959) *The Motivation to Work*. Wiley.

Leadergrow: www.leadergrow.com/articles/145-12-dos-and-donts-of-e-mail-communication-e-mail-communication-tip-sheet.

Maslow, A. (1954) *Motivation and Personality*. Harper & Row.

Nickson, D. (2013) *Human Resource Management for the Hospitality and Tourism Industries*, 2nd edn. Routledge.

Robbins, S.P. and Coutler, M. (2014) *Management*, 12th edn. Pearson Education Limited.

Taylor, F.W. (1911) *The Principles of Scientific Management*. Harper Bros.

www.instituteofhospitality.org/hospitality-assured/the_steps

www.youtube.com/results?search_query=hotel+careers

Topics for discussion

1 Consider what type of manager you would be and what style you would adopt.
2 Find the jobs section in a local newspaper and review the adverts for hospitality jobs. Identify three adverts and critically evaluate them identifying areas in which they could improve.
3 Time management is very important. Draft a personal schedule for the next week detailing what tasks you are doing and when. Once the week has been completed, refer back to the schedule and determine to what extent you followed it.
4 Carry out internet research and list ten tips that managers may use to organise their time.
5 You are the training manager of a large hotel. Consider five things you could do to ensure that new employees settle in better.
6 List three questions you might ask when attending a job interview.
7 What can organisations do to prevent their talent leaving to go to competitors?
8 Draft ten questions you would ask an employee who has resigned after working at a hotel for five years.
9 What local HR legislation exists within your country?
10 You are interviewing for the post of executive chef. List five questions you would ask.

INDEX